The Encyclopedia of
SAINTS

Rosemary Ellen Guiley

☑®
Facts On File, Inc.

The Encyclopedia of Saints

Facts On File, Inc.
132 West 31st Street
New York NY 10001

Library of Congress Cataloging-in-Publication Data

Guiley, Rosemary.
The encyclopedia of saints / Rosemary Ellen Guiley.
p. cm.
Includes bibliographical references and index.
ISBN 0-8160-4133-4 (alk. paper)—ISBN 0-8160-4134-2 (pbk.: alk. paper)
1. Christian saints—Biography—Dictionaries. I. Title.
BX4655.8 G85 2001
282'.092'2—dc21   00-069176

Facts On File books are available at special discounts when purchased in bulk quantities for businesses, associations, institutions, or sales promotions. Please call our Special Sales Department in New York at (212) 967-8800 or (800) 322–8755.

You can find Facts On File on the World Wide Web at http://www.factsonfile.com

Text design by Erika K. Arroyo
Cover design by Semadar Megged

Printed in the United States of America

VB FOF 10 9 8 7 6 5 4 3 2 1

This book is printed on acid-free paper.

CONTENTS

ACKNOWLEDGMENTS

I am especially grateful for the expertise and assistance of James G. Matlock and Joanne P. Austin in the research and compilation of this encyclopedia. I also would like to thank my editor, James Chambers, for his vision and support of this project.

INTRODUCTION

My long-standing interest in saints came to a turning point in 1997 after an unexpected, spontaneous and deeply moving experience.

In the spring of that year, I traveled to Montreal to speak at a conference. Montreal is home to St. Joseph's Oratory, a magnificent structure built on Mount Royal, a small mountain within the city environs. It is a healing shrine, the world's largest pilgrimage center dedicated to St. Joseph. Some 2 million people of all faiths from all over the world come here every year to pray for the intercession of a remarkable saint, Blessed Brother André, whose tomb lies within the oratory. One Sunday, I visited the oratory and joined a large throng of people lined up to pay their respects at the tomb. I came with no particular purpose other than to see the oratory and witness others. I didn't even know much about the life of Brother André. What happened to me there caused me to learn about his life and miraculous healing work.

Brother André was born Alfred Bessette in a village east of Montreal in 1845 to a poor and humble family. He was small and of delicate constitution, and suffered poor health all of his life. In 1870, he sought to enter the Congregation of the Holy Cross, a religious order dedicated to the teaching profession. The order accepted him despite his lack of education, and gave him the lowly job of doorkeeper at Notre Dame College in Mount Royal. He took the name André in honor of his sponsor, Pastor André Provençal.

Brother André spent much of his time in prayer. When he was off-duty, he visited the sick. Miraculous cures were attributed to him and he soon became renowned as the "Wonder Man of Mount Royal." People came from afar to see him. He always credited the cures to the intercession of his patron saint, Joseph.

Brother André's ability was not greeted with warmth within his own religious community. Some were skeptical and even opposed him. The quiet little man persevered, always within the requirements of authority, and finally realized his great dream to build an oratory in honor of St. Joseph. It began with a tiny chapel on Mount Royal in 1904. Over the years, donations in honor of Brother André have enabled expansions. The present basilica is the tallest point in Montreal, and holds 3,000 people.

Brother André died in 1937 and was beatified in 1987 by Pope John Paul II (r. 1978–   ). His death did not end his healing work. As millions of pilgrims attest, his intercession from beyond the grave enables continuing miracles of divine healing.

Brother André's heart is on view as a relic, encased in a clear glass container in the oratory. But the real attraction, the real power center, is his small black granite tomb, called the Black Coffin. Pilgrims come to touch the tomb and pray for healing.

So there I was this one Sunday morning, filing into the small alcove that contains the tomb. Outside the alcove, candlelight flickered over the high walls filled with the canes and crutches people had thrown away after miraculous healings there.

The tomb itself was small, plain and unadorned. The simplicity of its surroundings certainly gave no hint that therein lay the remains of a miracle healer revered around the world. Someone had placed a single red rose atop the tomb. People waited for a turn to touch the black granite while others crowded around them. At last I maneuvered to the front and placed both palms on top of the tomb.

When I touched the tomb, I felt a burning begin in the center of my chest. It astonished me. The feeling intensified, as though my heart center were on fire. This feeling of fiery heat radiated out to the rest of my body, growing stronger, until I felt as though I were enveloped in invisible flames. I felt strangely unable to move. As I stood riveted to the tomb, it came to me that I was touching the Heart of God, experiencing the burning fire of true unconditional love. It was flowing into me as a heat and fire that literally were burning away imperfections in me. Layer upon layer peeled away. The intensity and brilliance of this radiance were overwhelming.

Suddenly I understood that there is a difference between love and unconditional love. Love heals, nurtures, nourishes and sustains. Unconditional love purifies. This difference is at once subtle and profound; at once infinitesimal and vast. I was being purified in some way by unconditional love.

The burning sensation lasted as long as I held my hands on the tomb. I remained swept up in a rapture equal to that of any saint. I have never felt so much in the presence of God.

Afterward, the only thing I was capable of doing was walking into an adjoining chapel, where I wept and prayed, and tried to understand what I had just experienced.

On my last day in Montreal, I returned to the oratory. I was anxious to touch the Black Coffin again. I desired that incredible fire that had taken me into the presence of God. It was a weekday, with few people about, and so this time I had the entire alcove to myself. But when I touched the tomb again there was no burning. Instead I felt a deep and soft inner radiance. It was another extraordinary experience, but of a different sort.

In retrospect, I realized that of course I would not experience the same fire. A mystical experience is unique and not repeated. The expansion of consciousness that comes from it is needed only once.

What was the source of the power that facilitated such an experience? How can a holy person continue, from the other side of death, as a channel for divine grace? I do not know the answers, but only continue to explore the mystery. Was I changed? Yes. Like the experience itself, I was changed in both subtle and profound ways. I did not feel that I had become "holy" or anything of the sort. And though I felt "stuff" burned off of me, I still possessed the same flaws and shortcomings. But I have a much different awareness of love now, and of the importance of bringing love to its highest and purest expression, that of unconditional love.

This experience joins the records of countless other transformative experiences had by people the world over when they come into the presence of saints. As I mentioned at the beginning, I had already long been interested in saints as part of my study of mysticism. This experience with Brother André propelled me into a deeper study of both.

What exactly is sainthood? The Roman Catholic Church has a formal process of canonization for recognizing the holiest of the holy as saints—saints are not "made" but simply honored for their achievements. The Church thoroughly examines a candidate's life and works, and requires validation of at least two posthumous miracles. But fewer than 300 of the 10,000 or so documented saints throughout history have been canonized (Brother André has been beatified, a step that precedes canonization). The rest have achieved a saint status by popular acclaim. They are venerated locally. Some, popular once upon a time, have disappeared altogether from current devotion. And some belong more to legend than to history.

A saint's sanctity and purity, as well as writings and acts of charity and sacrifice, certainly are important considerations to formal sainthood. But what drives the popular interest and devotion is belief in the power of the saint to bring help and healing to the living. Some saints are important to the Church for their treatises and works on theology and philosophy. The people, however, look for miracles. We the public are drawn to saints because of the mystery around them: their rich inner lives of mystical and visionary experience, and their ability to work wonders and miracles.

There are too many saints to put them all in a single volume. In this book, I have made a selection of saints who have made important contributions to the Church and to society, especially in education, charity and health care. Among these are towering figures such as St. Thomas Aquinas, who shaped the development of Western philosophy. I have also included some of the early martyrs and legendary figures, as well as church fathers, church doctors and beatified and canonized popes. I have paid special attention to the inner, mystical lives of saints and to their miracles, for here is where we come closest to the Mystery.

I keep Brother André's picture at my desk, and carry some of the little medallions of him that the oratory sells, including one that contains a tiny piece of relic. They are links not so much to the man, but to what he and other saints represent: that miracles are made possible by a heart that loves.

—Rosemary Ellen Guiley

The Encyclopedia of
SAINTS

Adalbald of Ostrevant (d. ca. 650–652) *Martyr*
Also known as: Adalbald d'Ostrevant

Adalbald of Ostrevant was born in Flanders to a noble family. His mother or grandmother (sources differ) was St. Gertrude, founder of the monastery at Hamage. Adalbert served at the Merovingian court of King Dagobert I, great-great-grandson of Clovis I and St. Clotilde of the Franks, and Dagobert's successor, Clovis II. While in Dagobert's service against the rebellious Gascons, Adalbert fell in love with Rictrude (later sainted herself), the daughter of a Gascon noble family. Her relatives forbade the union, but Rictrude married Adalbert anyway. They had four children: St. Maurontius, St. Clotsindis, St. Eusebia and St. Adalsindis.

Rictrude's kin never accepted Adalbald, reportedly jealous of his reputation and political position. Members of her family assassinated Adalbald while he was traveling to Gascony. Devastated, Rictrude nevertheless retrieved the body and buried it. Almost immediately, rumors spread of miraculous healings at the tomb. Rictrude continued her work, reputedly founding the abbey at Marchiennes.

Feast: February 2
Patronage: parents of large families

Adalbert of Prague (b. ca. 939–956–d. 997) *Archbishop and missionary to Poland*
Also known as: Apostle of the Prussians; Adelbert; Voitech, Voytiekh, Voytech, Wojtech; Apostle of Bohemia

Christened Wojtech, Adalbert was born in Libice, Bohemia, to a princely family. The dates of his birth are placed anywhere from 939 to 956. He studied under archbishop St. Adalbert of Magdeburg and took his mentor's name when the archbishop died in 981. Adalbert became the second bishop of Prague in 983, but his righteous efforts to convert the Bohemian pagans made an enemy of Duke Boleslaus II of Bohemia, and Adalbert left for Rome in 990.

Released from his responsibilities by Pope John XV (r. 985–996), Adalbert joined the Benedictine monastery of SS. Boniface and Alexius. But two years later, Duke Boleslaus agreed to accept Adalbert's authority, and Pope John XV sent Adalbert back to Prague. The Bohemian people cheered his return, and he founded the monastery of Brevnov with Majolus of Cluny. Adalbert's relations with Duke Boleslaus and the nobility worsened, however, after an adulterous but penitent noblewoman seeking sanctuary in a convent was dragged out and killed. Adalbert excommunicated everyone involved and was forced to flee again to

Rome in 995. This time Boleslaus massacred some of Adalbert's family, and he did not return to Prague.

Adalbert's next mission was to Hungary, where he evangelized the Magyars and may have baptized Kings Geysa and Stephen. But at the invitation of Prince Boleslaus I of Poland, he traveled to Pomerania to evangelize the Prussians. The Prussian nobility and the pagan priests liked him no better than had the Bohemians, and Adalbert and his missionaries were assassinated as Polish spies in 997 near Danzig. One account says Prince Boleslaus I buried Adalbert's body at Gniezno, Poland; another says that the prince ransomed the body for its weight in gold.

Despite his disappointments, Adalbert exercised considerable influence. He was friends with Holy Roman Emperor Otto III and inspired St. Boniface of Querfurt. Adalbert composed Czech and Polish hymns in the vernacular and is credited with writing the Polish battle song, "Boga-Rodzica." His righteous zeal for religious compliance, which was not well appreciated, included extraction of the teeth of anyone found breaking fast on a holy day. His relics were taken to Prague in 1039.

Canonized: 999
Feast: April 23
Patronage: Bohemia (part of the Czech Republic); Poland; Prussia

FURTHER READING
Reston, James Jr. *The Last Apocalypse: Europe at the Year 1000 A.D.* New York: Doubleday, 1998.

Adelaide (931–999) *Princess, foundress of religious programs, regent*
Name meaning: noble person
Also known as: Adelheid

Adelaide was born in 931, the daughter of King Rudolph II of Burgundy. She became a political pawn at age two. Her father, embroiled in a war with Hugh of Provence for the crown of Lombardy (Italy), agreed to betroth her to Hugh's son Lothaire in order to end the fighting in 933. Her brother Conrad honored his father's agreement in 947, when Adelaide was 16; Rudolph had died years before, and his widow, Adelaide's mother, had since married Hugh. Meanwhile, Berengarius (or Berengar) II, Marquis of Ivrea, claimed Lombardy and forced Hugh to abdicate in favor of Lothaire. Lothaire and Adelaide were king and queen of Italy only a short while before Lothaire died, probably from poison at the instigation of Berengarius in 950.

Berengarius tried to force Adelaide to marry his son, but the young widow refused and was imprisoned in a castle in the middle of Lake Garda. Accounts differ about her escape from Castle Garda: One story says a priest named Martin dug a subterranean passage under the lake, rescued Adelaide and kept her in the passage, surviving on fish alone, until Alberto Uzzo, duke of Canossa, whisked the queen off to his castle. Nevertheless, the Italian nobles, tired of Berengarius and his wars, invited King Otto I of Germany, called the Great, to invade Italy and dispose of Berengarius. Otto entered Italy in 951, rescued Queen Adelaide (either from Castle Garda or from the eager duke) and married her on Christmas Day 951 at Pavia, thereby taking the title King of the Lombards. Berengarius fled to his castle at Montefeltro.

The couple did not linger long in Italy because Liudolf, Otto's son by his first wife Edith, was trying to start an uprising against the French influence of his stepmother. He failed, however, and the German people supposedly adored their new queen. She and Otto had five children, with the son and heir, Otto II, born in 955. Throughout the next 10 years, Otto I fought continuous wars over the control of Italy, which was not only plundered by soldiers but also allowed to decay under the debauched reign of Pope John XII. When Berengarius became a threat again in 961, the pope offered Otto I the crown of the empire in return for protection. The spectacular coronation of Otto I and Adelaide as Holy Roman Emperor and Empress of the German Nation on February 2, 962, not only assured Germany's dominance in Europe but also fulfilled Otto's ultimate goal of reestablishing a Christian empire with himself as the new Caesar.

In 969, Otto I designated his 14-year-old son Otto II as co-emperor, thereby securing the boy's right of succession. To further cement Otto II's authority, Otto I arranged his son's marriage to the Byzantine princess Theophano, daughter of the usurper John Tzimisces. Tzimisces, called Little Slippers, was the lover to the wife (also named Theophano) of the murdered Byzantine emperor Nicephorus II Phocas. Otto II and Theophano were married in Rome in 972 and ascended to the throne after Otto I died in 973. Theophano, a politically astute and strong-willed woman, exerted great influence on royal affairs and reputedly turned her husband against his mother. Relations with her mother-in-law Empress Adelaide were strained at best, and Adelaide left court to join her brother Conrad in Vienne, appealing to St. Majolus, abbot of Cluny, to intervene. The abbot arranged a reconciliation at Adelaide's court at Pavia.

Relations between the two women remained difficult until Otto II's death on December 7, 983. Theophano traveled to Pavia seeking refuge with Adelaide. The heir, three-year-old Otto III, was in the care of the bishop of Cologne, far too close to the domain of Prince Henry of Bavaria, called the Quarrelsome, who, along with Henry of Carinthia and Bishop Henry of Augsburg, was trying to take the crown. On Christmas Day, 983, Otto III was symbolically crowned Holy Roman Emperor in Aachen, Charlemagne's ancient seat. Almost immediately Henry of Bavaria kidnapped the child and took him to Quedlinburg, where Henry had himself proclaimed king.

Adelaide and Theophano appealed to Gerbert of Aurillac, a brilliant theologian, mathematician, counselor to Otto II and eventually Pope Sylvester II, to intercede, and he created a coalition of powerful kings and churchmen to put pressure on Henry. Conceding defeat, Henry returned young Otto III to his mother, Empress Theophano, on June 29, 984. Adelaide returned to Pavia, still unable to reconcile fully with Theophano, while the empress ably ruled as her son's regent until her sudden death in June 991.

But Otto III was still underage in 991, so his grandmother Adelaide assumed the regency until Otto III could be fully crowned at age 16 in 996. Writers of the period characterized Adelaide's regency as a wise and peaceful era in which the empress established monasteries and churches, supported the works of St. Adalbert of Magdeburg, St. Majolus of Cluny and St. Odilo, also of Cluny. She concentrated on converting the Slavs and other pagans on the empire's northern borders. After Otto III took the throne, Adelaide retired to a convent and continued her works of charity and conversion.

In 999 Adelaide traveled to Burgundy to arrange a reconciliation between her nephew Rudolph and his vassals. She died en route at her monastery at Seltz, near Strasbourg in Alsace, on December 16 at age 68. Her relics are enshrined at Hanover.

> *Canonized:* 1097 by Pope Urban II
> *Feast:* December 16
> *Patronage:* abuse victims; brides; empresses; exiles; in-law problems; parents of large families; princesses; prisoners; second parents; step-parents; widows

FURTHER READING
Reston, James, Jr. *The Last Apocalypse: Europe at the Year 1000 A.D.* New York: Doubleday, 1998.

Adeodatus I (d. 618) *Pope*
Also known as: Deusdedit

Adeodatus was born in Rome, the son of a subdeacon named Stephen. He had been a priest in Rome for 40 years when he was elected to the Chair of St. Peter to succeed St. Boniface IV. Consecrated on October 19, 615, he was the first priest who was not also a monastic to become pope since John II (r. 533–535).

His pontificate was conducted in a time of many troubles—war between the Lombards and Byzantines, a plague of leprosy, and a major earthquake. He gave generously to the victims and helped them in any way he could. He was equally supportive of his clergy, who were impoverished by the same events, leaving each a year's stipend in his will.

Adeodatus is thought to have been the first to use leaden bullae to seal his official pronouncements, thus the name "bulls," as papal documents are still known today.

He died in Rome on November 8, 618.

> *Feast:* November 8

Adrian III (d. 885) *Pope*
Also known as: Hadrian III

Little is known of the life or papacy of Adrian III, or why he is venerated as a saint. He was born in Rome and was elected to the Chair of St. Peter on May 17, 884.

During his reign, there was a great famine in Rome, which he mitigated as he could. He opposed an aristocratic faction led by Formosus, Bishop of Porto; had George of the Aventine, a member of the Formosan group and a notorious murderer, tried, condemned and blinded; and had a widow of another of the group whipped naked through the streets of the city.

Adrian died either in early September or on July 8, 885, near Modena, while on his way to a diet in Worms, Germany, at the invitation of Emperor Charles the Fat, probably to settle the question of Charles's succession and to seek help in defense against the Muslim Saracens. He was buried in the monastery of Nonantula, where his memory has ever since been held in veneration.

> *Cultus confirmed:* 1892 by Pope Leo XIII
> *Feast:* July 8 (formerly September 7)

Agapetus I (d. 536) *Pope and martyr*
Also known as: Agapitus

Agapetus was the son of a priest named Gordianus who was killed in riots during the reign of Pope St. Symmachus. He was archdeacon of the Roman clergy when he was elected to succeed Pope St. Felix IV in the Chair of St. Peter on May 13, 535.

Agapetus confirmed decrees barring converts from Arianism from becoming priests, and requiring those already ordained to serve in lay capacities only. However, he is remembered primarily for a trip he took to

Constantinople at the behest of Queen Amalasuntha of the Goths. The Byzantine Belisarius, having taken Sicily, was preparing to mount an offensive on Italy, and Amalasuntha hoped that a personal appeal from Agapetus would change the mind of Emperor Justinian.

He arrived in Constantinople to discover that the new patriarch, Anthinus, was an adherent of the Monophysite heresy, then very strong in Byzantium. Anthinus had been appointed by Justinian at the advice of Queen Theodora. When Agapetus ordered Anthinus to make a written profession of his faith, he refused. Justinian at first threatened to banish the pope, but then, convinced of Anthinus's heresy, he relented, and not only allowed Agapetus to dismiss Anthinus, but also permitted him (for the first time in the history of the Church) to consecrate his successor, Mennas.

Agapatus was not able to dissuade Justinian from his designs on Italy, however. While still in Constantinople, he fell ill and died on April 22, 536. His relics were translated to Rome in a leaden coffin on September 20 and interred in St. Peter's basilica in the Vatican. Like many other saints of the period, he owes his cultus to the devotion of Pope St. Gregory I (Gregory the Great, r. 590–604). He is venerated in both the Roman Catholic and Greek Orthodox churches. His name appears in the Roman Martyrology.

Feast: April 22 (formerly September 20; April 22 in Greek Orthodox Church)

Agatha (d. ca. 250) *Virgin and martyr*
Name meaning: good

Although Agatha has been venerated as a saint and martyr since ancient times, none of the legendary details of her life or death can be authenticated. The stories of her terrible persecutions appear in the *Martyrologium Hieronymianum* (Martyrology of St. Jerome) and the *Martyrologium Carthaginiense* (Carthaginian calendar of martyrs), the *Carmina* of Venantius Fortunatus, and the canon of the Mass, but many scholars now believe Agatha to have been an inspiring but fictional character.

Both Palermo and Catania in Sicily take credit as the site of Agatha's birth, supposedly to a wealthy and influential family. Her beauty attracted the attention of the Roman consul Quintinian, but Agatha refused his offer of marriage, having dedicated her life as a virgin to Christ. His ego bruised, Quintinian committed Agatha to a brothel, but she stood firm and retained her virginity. Enraged, Quintinian turned her over to a magistrate and accused her of being a Christian. The Acts of her martyrdom place her arrest during the reign of Emperor Decian, about 250—a period of horrific persecution.

First the magistrate ordered Agatha to be beaten and imprisoned, but when those tortures had no effect on her faith he condemned her to be stretched on the rack. Her cheerful confidence in Christ's love against such suffering so offended the magistrate that he had her breasts crushed and then cut off, ordering her to a dungeon without food, water or medicine. But St. Peter supposedly came to her in a vision of light, accompanied by a youth carrying a torch, and healed her wounds. Unimpressed by such a miracle, Quintinian ordered the magistrate to have Agatha rolled naked over live coals mixed with broken potsherds. Agatha prayed for release, and at that very moment an earthquake struck Catania. Asking Christ to receive her soul, Agatha died.

Her courage and spirit fostered a cult of worship all over Christendom. Pope Symmachus built a church in her honor on the Via Aurelia in Rome. Prayers by St. Lucy of Syracuse at St. Agatha's tomb reportedly cured the saint's mother, Eutychia, from hemorrhage. A letter from Pope Gelasius (r. 492–496) to a Bishop Victor in the fifth century referred to the basilica of St. Agatha. Pope St. Gregory I the Great (r. 590–604) mentioned a Roman church dedicated to St. Agatha given to the Arian Goths. Pope Gregory reconsecrated the church of Sant' Agata dei Goti for Catholic worship in the late sixth century.

Medieval church paintings of Agatha often showed her carrying her severed breasts on a platter—an image many mistook for loaves of bread. Consequently, the tradition arose of blessing "Agatha bread" on her feast day. The shape of her breasts also evoked bells, especially those used as fire alarms. The carrying of her veil, supposedly taken from her tomb, on a lance in procession reportedly has stopped or prevented eruptions of Mount Etna. Prayers for her intercession were credited with preventing the Turks from taking the island of Malta in 1551. Following the Peace of Constantine, Agatha's relics went to Constantinople, but they were translated to Catania about 1126.

Feast: February 5
Patronage: alpine guides; bell founders; breast disease; earthquakes; eruptions of Mount Etna; fire and fire prevention; girdlers; jewelers; martyrs; natural disasters; nurses; rape victims; shepherdesses; single laywomen; sterility; torture victims; volcanic eruptions; wet nurses; Catania, Sicily; Malta; Zamarramala, Spain

Agatho (d. 681) *Pope*
Also known as: Thaumaturgus

Agatho was born in Sicily, probably in Palermo. He had been married for 20 years and had become financially successful when he decided to join the Benedictine monastery of St. Hermes in Palermo. He is thought to be the Agatho whom Pope St. Gregory I (Gregory the Great, r. 590–604) authorized to join the monastery if his wife became a nun. In that case, he would have been more than 100 years old when he was elected bishop of Rome to succeed Pope Dounus (r. 676–678) on June 27, 678.

Agatho was renowned for his affability and charity. His life experience also made him an unusually good business man, and he maintained the Vatican's accounting books himself, contrary to custom.

Shortly after Agatho's election, Wilfrid, bishop of York, who had been dismissed from his see, appealed to Agatho, who ordered him reinstated. He also dispatched an envoy to teach the Britons about chanting and to report to him on the state of the English Church.

However, the signal event of Agatho's pontificate was the Sixth Ecumenical Council, held in Constantinople in 680. Although he was unable to attend, he sent emissaries who read a letter from him condemning Monothelitism, a heresy that held that Christ possessed a single, divine nature rather than a double, divine and human, nature. Monothelitism had at one time divided the Eastern and Western Church, but the council accepted Agatho's definitions, Patriarch George of Constantinople proclaiming: "Peter has spoken by Agatho." By the time the council's decrees reached Rome, however, Agatho had died.

He died during a plague on January 10, 681, and was buried in St. Peter's at the Vatican. The many miracles thereafter received through his intercession led to his being called Thaumaturgus (Wonderworker). He is venerated in the Greek Orthodox as well as the Roman Catholic Church. His memory is celebrated especially at York, England, and Palermo, Italy.

In art, Agatho is shown wearing a tiara and holding a long cross.

Feast: January 10

Agnes of Assisi (ca. 1197–1253) *Abbess and miracle worker; the younger sister of St. Clare of Assisi, founder of the Poor Clares*

Agnes of Assisi was born at Assisi, Italy, in 1197 or 1198 to a noble family. Her father was Count Favorino Scifi, and her mother, Bl. Hortulana, belonged to the noble family of the Fiumi. In addition, her cousin Rufino was one of the celebrated "Three Companions" of St. Francis of Assisi.

Agnes lived an idyllic childhood in luxurious surroundings in her father's palace in the city and in his castle of Sasso Rosso on Mount Subasio. On March 18, 1212, Clare, Agnes's sister, left home to follow the example set by St. Francis. Inspired, Agnes departed 16 days later and went to the Benedictine monastery of St. Angelo in Panso.

Furious, Count Favorino sent his brother Monaldo, with several relatives and some armed followers, to force Agnes to return home. According to an account in the *Chronicles of the Twenty-four Generals*, Monaldo drew his sword to strike Agnes, but his arm dropped, withered and useless, by his side. Others dragged Agnes out of the monastery by the hair, striking her and kicking her repeatedly until she was near death. Clare came to the rescue. Suddenly Agnes's body became so heavy that the soldiers dropped her in a field near the monastery.

Agnes stayed, and Francis rewarded her by cutting off her hair and giving her the habit of poverty. He installed Clare and Agnes at St. Damian's, along with their mother, their sister Beatrice and some noblewomen. The Order of the Poor Ladies of St. Damian's, or Poor Clares, was born.

Agnes became abbess and was well-loved. In 1219 Francis sent her to Monticelli, near Florence, to found and govern a community of the Poor Ladies. She also established communities at Mantua, Venice and Padua.

In 1253 Agnes attended Clare on her deathbed and assisted at her funeral. Clare had predicted that Agnes would soon follow her. Three months later, on November 16, Agnes died and was buried near her mother and sisters Clare and Beatrice in the church of St. Clare at Assisi. Miracles were reported at her tomb.

Benedict XIV (r. 1740–58) permitted the Order of St. Francis to celebrate her feast.

Feast: November 16

Agnes of Rome (d. ca. 304) *Virgin and martyr*
Name meaning: Pure one

Little is known about Agnes, and the circumstances of her martyrdom are not documented. According to St. Ambrose in *De virginitate*, she died by fire at age 12. Other versions of her martyrdom are given by Pope St. Damasus (r. 366–384) and Prudentius in *Peristephanon*.

Agnes is said to have been a beautiful, wealthy Roman maiden born during the reign of Emperor Diocletian (284–305) to Christian parents at a time when

St. Agnes of Rome (Library of Congress Prints and Photographs Division)

During the reign of Constantine (323–337), a basilica was built on the site of her grave near the Via Nomentana. It was remodeled by Pope Honorius I (r. 625–638) in 630.

Agnes's emblem in art is the lamb, a symbol of purity, and because of the similarity between her name and the Latin word for lamb, *agnus*. In art she is often depicted in flames and with a sword at her feet. On her feast day, two lambs are blessed, and their wool is then made into pallia and given to archbishops of the Church.

Feast: January 21
Patronage: young girls

Agostina Petrantoni (1864–1894) *Martyr of charity*
Also known as: Agostina Pietrantoni, Livia Pietranton

Little is known of Agostina Petrantoni's early life beyond her birthplace of Pozzaglia Sabina in Rieti, Italy. She was born on March 27, 1864, and was given the name Livia. She joined the Sisters of Charity and dedicated her life in service to the sick, working at the Holy Spirit Hospital in Rome. From 1886 on she worked with the most critically ill patients, succumbing to many of their diseases.

After contracting tuberculosis, Agostina asked to serve in the tuberculosis ward exclusively. She died in 1894 when a tuberculosis patient stabbed her to death after a rape attempt. Her last words were a prayer for her attacker's forgiveness.

In his speech at her canonization, Pope John Paul II said that Sister Agostina understood the gift of generous service, especially to the neediest, in whose faces is reflected the face of Christ.

Canonized: April 18, 1999, by Pope John Paul II
Patronage: abuse victims; martyrs; people ridiculed for piety; against poverty

Aidan of Lindisfarne (d. 651) *Bishop and monastic founder*

Most of what scholars know about Aidan comes from favorable accounts by the Venerable Bede in his *Ecclesiastical History of the English People*. In 635, Aidan, a monk at St. Columba's monastery on the island of Iona, traveled on foot to the city of Bamburgh in the old, Romanized part of Britain, now Northumbria, to serve as bishop at the request of St. King Oswald of Northumbria. Aidan followed the Celtic/Irish custom of establishing his see in a monastery, rather than in Northumbria's largest city of York, and founded Lindisfarne as a royal fortress protected by the king.

most of the nobility were pagan. Diocletian was an ardent persecutor of Christians.

One story holds that a rejected suitor betrayed her to the authorities.

According to an epitaph written by Damasus, preserved at her tomb and church, she announced her faith and was sentenced to die by fire. Before dying, she was stripped of all her clothing, and covered herself with her hair.

According to Prudentius, who composed a hymn in her honor, she was punished by being placed into a brothel. Miraculously, her virginity was preserved, for anyone who approached her was blinded and knocked down by a divine force. Her suitor tried and was thus punished, but Agnes prayed and asked Christ to restore his sight. She was then thrown into the flames.

Another version says that she remained unharmed in the flames, and so finally was decapitated. Yet another version says she was killed by a sword.

Aidan walked over all of Northumbria, gaining many converts and serving the poor, often with King Oswald translating the monk's Latin into common English.

The establishment of Lindisfarne monastery was Aidan's greatest achievement. The Lindisfarne Gospels, almost the only codex (a manuscript book rather than a scroll) that can be attributed to a single scribe, was written by Eadfrith, abbot of Lindisfarne after Aidan's death. However, Viking raiders, who pillaged the monasteries for their silver and precious objects, often destroyed the illuminated manuscripts for their gilded covers. Barbarians attacked Lindisfarne in 793, 801, 806 and 867; any survivors left the ruins for good in 875. The Lindisfarne Gospels were perhaps buried or sent to another monastery for safekeeping; one copy remains.

Aidan died in 651 after the murder of King Oswin, Oswald's successor. He was buried at the abbey.

Feast: August 31

FURTHER READING
Cahill, Thomas. *How the Irish Saved Civilization.* New York: Nan A. Talese/Doubleday, 1995.
Reston, James, Jr. *The Last Apocalypse: Europe at the Year 1000 A.D.* New York: Doubleday, 1998.

Alban (d. ca. 304) *Reportedly the first martyr in England during the persecutions by Emperor Diocletian (r. 284–305)*

The story of Alban, a pagan by birth, was recorded by the Venerable Bede in his *Ecclesiastical History of the English People.* A resident of Verulamium (now St. Alban's in Hertfordshire, between Birmingham and London), Alban gave shelter to a Christian priest who was trying to escape the persecutions. So impressed was Alban by the man's humble demeanor, prayer and wisdom that he converted and was baptized.

Authorities learned that the priest was hiding in Alban's house, and sent soldiers to arrest him. Alban donned the man's clothing, enabling him to escape, and was arrested in his stead. He was taken before the governor and repeatedly refused to renounce his new faith. He was severely scourged and tortured and condemned to die by beheading.

The route to the execution site required Alban and his guards to wade across a river. There were so many onlookers that progress was impeded. Tradition holds that Alban prayed, and the waters of the river divided to create a dry passage. The executioner was so moved by this miracle that he converted himself, and was martyred along with Alban.

When the party reached the hill where the executions were to take place, a fountain miraculously sprang up out of the ground.

The priest whom Alban had sheltered was captured several days later and stoned to death in Redbourn, near Verulamium.

Alban has been venerated in Britain since the fifth century, and was even known in France. Other accounts of his life have been written, some stating that he had been a soldier. A church was built on the site of the execution and became famous for miracles. A monastery was built there later.

Feast: June 20

FURTHER READING
St. Alphonsus Liguori. *Victories of the Martyrs.* Brooklyn: Redemptorist Fathers, 1954.

Albert the Great (ca. 1206–1280) *Doctor of the Church, theologian, bishop and philosopher*
Name meaning: noble; brilliant
Also known as: Albertus Magnus, Doctor Universalis, Doctor Expertus, Albert the German, Universal Doctor

The eldest son of Count Bollstadt, a military nobleman in the service of Emperor Frederick II, Albert was born ca. 1206 at the castle of Lauingen in Swabia, a southern German province along the Danube River. Nothing is known of his early childhood or education, but as a young man he studied at the University of Padua. At age 16 he became impressed with the Order of Preaching Friars, or Brothers, founded by St. Dominic, and became a postulant in 1222 under Blessed Jordan of Saxony, second master general of the Friars Preachers and immediate successor to Dominic. Rumors circulated that Albert's father, angry at his son's renunciation of title and wealth, would try to retrieve him by force, but they came to nothing when the Brothers, commonly called Dominicans, discreetly sent the young Albert to the friary in Cologne. There he completed his studies and taught others, as well as teaching at Hildesheim, Freiburg-im-Breisgau, Regensburg and Strasbourg.

Learning and thinking in 13th-century Europe were undergoing radical changes, and Albert's approach to these changes was intelligent, scientific and common-sensical. As a member of one of the new mendicant orders, Albert was not tied to a parish church or monastery, leaving him free to teach and preach anywhere, and, like the other friars, able to assume a key position in the new universities. Up until the 12th century, traditional education in the Latin-based world was based on the Scriptures and commentaries on them. Meanwhile, Islamic scholars had assimilated the logic and philosophy of Aristotle and other Greek works of mathematics and science. In the 12th century, Latin translations of these works became available, presenting Christian scholars with a challenge: how to use this valuable knowledge, reconcile it with earlier Christian thinking, and remove the heresy associated with Islam.

Albert's answer to this challenge was to learn all he could of the newly revealed information, try to understand it, examine it critically and accept what he could and adapt it to established Church dogma. He was interpreting Peter Lombard's *Book of the Sentences* in 1245 when he was sent to the university in Paris, generally acknowledged as the greatest school of theology. There he encountered the *Summa Theologiæ* of Alexander of Hales, the first book written after all the works of Aristotle had become known in Paris. He received his doctorate.

Among Albert's students accompanying him to Paris from Cologne was a young friar named Thomas Aquinas, who took his master's teachings and became the greatest philosopher of his day. Thomas returned to Cologne when Albert was selected regent of the new Studium Generale there in 1248 and became second professor under Albert and master of students. In 1250 Albert drew up the rules for direction of study and graduation from Dominican universities and institutions. Thomas remained with Albert until 1252. What Albert began, and Thomas perfected, became known as the Scholastic system or Scholasticism: the application of Aristotelian methods and principles to the study of revealed doctrine, or the reconciliation of reason and orthodoxy. Albert did not believe the works of Aristotle should be banned or totally subsumed to early Christian teaching, nor did he accept all of Aristotle's philosophy without question, but he showed that sense and experience were the basis of all human knowledge.

In 1254, Albert was named prior provincial of the Dominican Order in Germany. In 1256, he traveled to Rome to defend the mendicant orders against the attacks of William of St. Amour in the book *De Novissimis Temporum Periculis*, or "The Dangers of These Present Times." Pope Alexander IV (r. 1254–61) agreed with Albert and his peers, condemning William's book on October 5, 1256. While in Rome Albert served as master of the sacred palace, the position as the pope's personal theologian and canonist always filled by a Dominican. Albert returned to Cologne and resigned the office of prior provincial in 1257 to allow him more time for study and teaching. Three years later, in 1260, Alexander IV named the reluctant Albert bishop of Regensburg, a post that he resigned in 1262 to return to his beloved Studium in Cologne.

In 1270 Albert wrote a treatise against Siger de Brabant and the Muslim philosopher Averroës in defense of his former student Thomas. In 1274, Pope Gregory X called Albert to attend the 14th General Council at Lyons. While en route he learned that Thomas had died at Fossa Nuova, and Albert lamented that "the light of the Church" had been extinguished. Albert journeyed from Cologne once more, in 1277, again to defend himself and St. Thomas against Church conservatives—specifically, Stephen Tempier, bishop of Paris, who accused Albert and Thomas of being too favorable to the unbelieving philosophers. Albert hotly defended himself and Thomas, challenging his detractors to examine his theological record, but the so-called ape of Aristotle could not win on all points.

A prodigious writer, thinker and experimenter, Albert fearlessly tested previously accepted facts and made keen observations about science and nature. In one famous episode, Albert had himself lowered over a cliff edge so he could check firsthand whether eagles had one egg and offspring per season, as was thought at the time. For centuries, his works were the accepted authorities on physics, geography, astronomy, mineralogy, chemistry and biology. He was renowned as an alchemist and said to practice the magical arts; he reportedly carried a magic cup that cured the ill. He traced the chief mountain ranges of Europe, explained the influence of latitude on climate and proved the Earth was a sphere. He performed groundbreaking studies on insects. Albert also wrote works of theology and logic and composed the Mass for the Feast of Corpus Christi. All in all, Albert wrote 38 quarto volumes of scientific and theological literature.

By 1278, however, Albert was in poor health. His memory failed during a lecture that year, and his strength and mind continued to deteriorate. He died peacefully, sitting in a chair among his brethren at Cologne, on November 15, 1280, and is buried at St. Andrea's Church. His tomb became a pilgrimage site. Some of his remains were translated to Lauingen and Regensburg.

In art, Albert is shown in his Dominican habit.

Beatified: 1622 by Pope Gregory XV
Canonized: 1931 by Pope Pius XI
Declared Doctor of the Church: 1931 by Pope Pius XI
Feast: November 15
Patronage: all students and researchers of the natural sciences; medical technicians; miners; naturalists; schoolchildren; scientists; students; theology students; Cologne University

Alexander I (d. ca. 115) *Pope*

Alexander was a Roman and is said to have been a student of Pliny the Younger. He converted to Christianity and succeeded St. Evaristus as bishop of Rome, thus becoming the sixth pope. His reign lasted from ca. 105 to ca. 115.

Alexander is sometimes credited with having introduced the custom of blessing houses with salt water, but this was in fact an ancient Roman practice. He is also said to have introduced the commemoration of the Last Supper into the Mass, although this almost certainly came later.

According to tradition, Alexander was arrested by Emperor Hadrian and imprisoned along with two priests, SS. Eventulus and Theodulus. During his imprisonment, he managed to convert his jailer, St. Quirinus, and his daughter, St. Balbina. This, however, did not save him and his friends from being burned and then beheaded by Hadrian's soldiers on the Via Nomentana in Rome. In 1855, archaeologists discovered what are thought to be their bodies in a semisubterranean cemetery at the spot where they died. Their relics have since been moved to the church of St. Sabina, now under the charge of the Dominicans.

In art, Alexander wears a triple tiara and holds a triple cross and book.

Feast: October 18

Alexis (ca. 380–ca. 417–440) *Mystic and confessor known as "the Man of God"*
Name meaning: Defender, helper
Also known as: Alexis, Alexios, Alessio

There are no traces of Alexis in any early Western martyrology or liturgy. He apparently was an Eastern or Byzantine saint venerated in Rome during the 10th century.

Alexis was born in Rome to Euphemanius and Aglaia, a wealthy senator and his wife. The child devoted himself to God, but bowed to his parents' wishes that he marry. Apparently the ceremony took place, but Alexis—who had seen a vision of St. Paul calling him to service—could not live with his bride. She agreed to release him and he fled Rome for Edessa, in Syria, on his wedding night.

For 17 years Alexis lived in a shack next to the church of Bishop Rabula, begging for alms only in the evening, sharing his meager resources with the poor and keeping his identity a secret. At the end of that time, however, a statue of the Virgin apparently called on the people of Edessa to "seek the Man of God," and Alexis fled the city for Tarsus, following his early

vision of Paul. A storm stopped his voyage, and he was rescued and taken to Rome. Filled with desire to see his family, Alexis returned to his father's estate but was not recognized by his parents or bride, who lived with her in-laws. They allowed Alexis to minister to the peasants and children and to live beneath the stairs of the house, where he remained anonymous for another 17 years.

At the end of that 17-year period, another voice spoke to Pope Innocent I (r. 401–417), calling him to "seek the Man of God." The pope traced the voice to Euphemanius's house, to a cupboard under the stairs. There lay Alexis, dead, clutching a parchment letter explaining who he was and how much he loved his family.

Scholars now believe that the story of Alexis became confused over time with that of St. John Calybata, a Roman nobleman with a similar history. But accounts from the ninth century tell of a poor monk in Edessa, supposedly with patrician Roman parents, who lived as a beggar and died there, buried in a common pauper's grave.

Pope Benedict VII (r. 974–983) gave the exiled metropolitan of the Byzantine Church, Sergius of Damascus, the crumbling church of St. Boniface on the Aventine in Rome. Sergius erected a monastery and added Alexis's name as patron of the church and monastery. The church still stands, renovated many times, and reportedly contains the remains of the staircase under which Alexis lived, in his own father's house.

Feast: July 17 (in the West); March 17 (in the East)
Patronage: beggars; belt makers; against earthquakes; against lightning; nurses; pilgrims; against storms; travelers

Alfred the Great (849–899) *Anglo-Saxon king of Wessex*
Name meaning: Elf counsel; all peace

Alfred, the youngest of either four or five sons of the Anglo-Saxon king Aethelwulf of Wessex, was born in 849 in Wantage, Berkshire. King Aethelwulf may have considered a career in the Church for Alfred, as the boy visited Rome in 853. In 869, at age 20, Alfred married the Mercian princess Aetheswitha or Ealswyth to cement an alliance between Mercia and Wessex, and they had five or six children.

The greatest threat to Wessex in the ninth century were the invasions of Mercia, Northumbria and East Anglia by Danish Vikings. In 868, Alfred's older brother, St. King Aethelred, led his armies into Mercia to stop the Danes. Alfred, only 19, was Aethelred's deputy. By 871, the Danes were pushing the Anglo-Saxons farther south into Wessex. King Aethelred was killed at the battle of Merton, and the kingship passed to Alfred.

Although poorly supported, Alfred managed to hold back the Danes for seven years, mainly through alliances with the other Anglo-Saxon kingdoms: the beginnings of a united England. In 878, the Danes attacked Wessex for four months, and Alfred retreated into the marshes of Somerset to regroup. Reorganizing his army, Alfred defeated the Danes at Edington later that year. He signed the Treaty of Wedmore with the Danish king Guthrum and divided England along the road from London to Chester. Anything north of this line, including York and East Anglia, became the Danelaw—ruled according to Danish law—and lands south were English. Alfred forced the Danish leader to convert to Christianity. To prevent further invasions, Alfred built fortresses and strongholds throughout Mercia, rebuilt the army by requiring military service of all free men, and formed a navy with ships of his own design.

But Alfred's successes lay not just in conquest. He learned to read and write, eventually translating many Latin texts into Old English, including the treatise *Pastoral Care* by Pope Gregory the Great (Gregory I), the *Consolation of Philosophy* by Boethius and most probably the *Ecclesiastical History of the English People* by the Venerable Bede. Alfred also encouraged literacy among his nobles, founding a court school for the clergy and young people and inviting scholars from all over Europe to teach there. He introduced decent and fair laws throughout the kingdom, making no distinction between his English and Welsh subjects. But perhaps Alfred's greatest contribution was his patronage of the *Anglo-Saxon Chronicle*. The *Chronicle* tells the stories and events of Christianity from the time of Christ through 1154 and is often the only source of information about the Danish invasions. The book also includes accounts of the Norman Conquest. The *Chronicle* is one of the first books written in the vernacular, and its description of the reign of King Stephen shows the language moving from Old English to Middle English.

Alfred suffered from unspecified diseases, perhaps psychosomatic in nature, which caused him pain, illness and self-doubt all his life. He was never king of England, although his reign strengthened the rule of later English kings. Alfred's image did appear on coinage. Alfred died October 26, 899, and was deemed "the Great" in the 17th century.

Feast: October 26

FURTHER READING
Reston, James, Jr. *The Last Apocalypse: Europe at the Year 1000 A.D.* New York: Doubleday, 1998.

Aloysius Gonzaga (1568–1591) *Scholar and patron of youth*

Also known as: Luigi

The eldest son of Don Ferrante Gonzaga, marquis of Castiglione, and his wife, Marta Tana Santena, was born at castle Castiglione delle Stivieri in Lombardy on March 9, 1568. The Gonzagas (reputedly known for their brutality and immorality) were the ruling family of Mantua, and Don Ferrante also held a high position at the court of King Philip II of Spain. Marta Tana served as lady-in-waiting to Philip's queen. Don Ferrante desired his son to be a military commander, so at age four little Luigi, as the saint was called, was sent to military school. At seven Luigi felt drawn to a religious life, and at nine took a vow of chastity, never looking a woman—not even his mother—in the face again.

In 1579, when the boy was 11, Don Ferrante placed him and his younger brother Ridolfo at the court of the duke of Mantua, who had recently appointed Don Ferrante governor of Monferrat. But appalled by the vices of court, Aloysius decided to renounce his inheritance in favor of Ridolfo, even though Aloysius had already received investiture from the emperor. About this time Aloysius contracted kidney disease, which he welcomed as a way to stay in his room and pray. He also began practicing severe austerities: fasting every other day on bread and water, allowing no fire in his room no matter the temperature, and scourging himself. By age 12 Aloysius dreamed of being a Jesuit missionary, receiving his First Communion at Brescia from St. Charles Borromeo and filling his summer days at Castiglione by teaching the catechism to poor local boys.

In 1581, Philip II summoned Don Ferrante to accompany Empress Mary of Austria on a journey from Bohemia to Spain, and the family accompanied him. Upon arrival at court, Aloysius and Ridolfo became pages in the service of the Infante, Don Diego (James), prince of the Spanish Asturias. Although duty-bound to serve Don Diego, Aloysius continued his devotions and hardened his resolve to become a Jesuit. His mother approved his decision, but Don Ferrante adamantly opposed it by any means possible: threats of beatings, tempting the boy with the pleasures of the northern Italian courts, sending him on diplomatic missions all over Europe. When Don Diego died in 1584 and Aloysius and Ridolfo returned to Castiglione, Aloysius again pressed his case and his father relented, but only after an imperial commission officially transferred the succession to Ridolfo.

Aloysius joined the Jesuit novitiate house of Sant' Andrea in Rome on November 25, 1585. The Jesuits curbed his austerities, ordering him to eat and take recreation, and sent him to Milan. While praying one morning, Aloysius received a vision telling him he had not long to live, a revelation that filled him with joy. He returned to Rome and was professed in 1587. In 1591 plague struck the city, and Aloysius begged to serve in the Jesuit hospital, tending patients and performing menial tasks. He caught the plague but miraculously recovered.

But then Aloysius contracted a fever that severely weakened him for three months. Unable to work, he would nevertheless arise at night and worship before his crucifix and kiss his sacred pictures, then kneel in prayer propped between his bed and wall. He asked his confessor, St. Robert Bellarmine, whether it was possible to go straight to heaven without passing through purgatory, and St. Robert replied that he believed someone like Aloysius could hope for such grace. Aloysius immediately fell into an ecstatic state and revealed that he would die on the octave of Corpus Christi.

When the octave arrived on June 20, Aloysius seemed so much improved that the rector talked of sending him on a trip, but Aloysius maintained he was dying and requested the viaticum in the evening. After receiving the last rites, Aloysius lay very still, occasionally saying, "into Thy hands," and appeared to ebb away between 10:00 p.m. and 11:00 p.m. With Jesus' name on his lips, Aloysius died about midnight of June 20–21, 1589, at age 23. St. Robert Bellarmine testified that Aloysius had never committed a mortal sin and through his Jesuit service had developed total devotion to God and man. Aloysius is buried under the altar in the Lancellotti Chapel at the Church of St. Ignatius in Rome. Pope Benedict XIII (r. 1724–1730) named Aloysius the patron of young students in 1729, and Pius XI later designated him the patron of all Christian youth.

Beatified: 1621 by Pope Gregory XV
Canonized: 1726 by Pope Benedict XIII
Feast: June 21
Patronage: AIDS caregivers; AIDS sufferers; Catholic youth; against eye troubles and diseases; Jesuit students; against plague; relief from pestilence; teenagers; youth

FURTHER READING
Meschler, Maurice. *Life of St. Aloysius Gonzaga Patron of Christian Youth.* Rockford, Ill.: TAN Books and Publishers, 1985.

Alphonsa Hawthorne (1851–1926) *Dominican known for her work among cancer patients*
Name meaning: noble ready, battle ready
Also known as: Rose Hawthorne, Mother Alphonsa

Alphonsa was born Rose Hawthorne, the daughter of famous American author Nathaniel Hawthorne, and was a convert to Catholicism.

In the 1890s, cancer was considered a contagious disease, and destitute sufferers were usually warehoused in poor houses, shunned by friends and family and left to die without care or spiritual comfort. Believing she had found her life's work with these abandoned souls, Alphonsa first enrolled in a three-month nursing course at New York Cancer Hospital in order to provide the best care she could. Following the completion of her nursing training, and with hardly any money and relying on God to provide, Alphonsa moved into a three-room tenement apartment in New York's Lower East Side, one of the city's worst neighborhoods, and opened a home for incurable cancer patients.

The work was grueling and sad, but Alphonsa persevered. Charitable donations from private individuals allowed Alphonsa to move her charges to a larger apartment. Over time like-minded women joined Alphonsa in her mission, the first of them a young portrait painter named Alice Huber. Eventually the women became an American congregation of Dominican Sisters: the Servants of Relief for Incurable Cancer.

In 1899, public generosity allowed the women to purchase an entire building, which they christened St. Rose's Free Home for Incurable Cancer. Also that year the Servants of Relief became part of the Third Order of St. Dominic. A second home opened in 1901 in Sherman Park, now called Hawthorne, New York. Today the group, known as the Dominican Sisters of Hawthorne, has seven homes in six states.

Patronage: against death of children; difficult marriages; divorced people; loss of parents; sick children

FURTHER READING
Joseph, Sr. M., OP. "Out of Many Hearts." URL: http://www.hawthorne-dominicans.org/dsh/history_1.html. Downloaded June 26, 2000.

Alphonsus Marie Liguori (1696–1787) *Bishop, founder of the Redemptorist Congregation, moral theologian, mystic and Doctor of the Church*

The life of Alphonsus Marie Liguori was fraught with strife and illness, but the saint nonetheless made prodigious accomplishments. He was born Alphonsus Marie Anthony John Cosmas Damian Michael Gaspard de'

Liguori on September 27, 1696, at Marianella near Naples, to a somewhat impoverished noble family. His father, Don Joseph de Liguori, was a naval officer and captain of the galleys. His mother was of Spanish descent.

Alphonsus was a precocious child and learned quickly in his home tutoring. He was a skilled musician. At age 16, he took his doctor of laws degree even though the law required an age of 20. By age 19 he was practicing law in court and by age 27 was one of the leading lawyers in Naples. He enjoyed worldly pursuits, but retained his innocence.

In 1723, his legal career came to a crashing halt. He served as counsel in an important lawsuit involving the grand duke of Tuscany and prepared his case. After making his opening statement in court, the opposition informed him that he had overlooked a crucial document that undermined his entire case. Alphonsus was forced to agree. Devastated and humiliated, he refused to eat for three days and vowed never to return to court.

He spent days in prayer seeking God's will. On a charitable visit to a hospital, he had a mystical experience in which he found himself surrounded by light, and an interior voice said, "Leave the world and give thyself to Me." This occurred twice. Alphonsus went to the church of the Redemption of Captives, where he laid his sword before a statue of Mary and vowed to offer himself as a novice to the Fathers of the Oratory.

His father was not pleased, but consented, provided Alphonsus lived at home. On October 23, 1723, Alphonsus joined the Oratorians. He received his tonsure the following year, and joined the Neapolitan Propaganda, an association of missionary secular priests. For six years he traveled in and around Naples, preaching, and enrolled thousands in a sort of confraternity called the Association of the Chapels.

In 1729, Alphonsus left home and went to live with Matthew Ripa, the "Apostle of China," who had founded a missionary college in Naples. There he met Father Thomas Falcoia of the Congregation of the Pious Workers. The two became close friends despite a 33-year difference in their ages.

Falcoia had a vision to found a new order of men and women dedicated to the imitation of Christ's virtues. Meanwhile, Sister Maria Celeste, a nun at the convent of Scala, which Falcoia had helped to refound, was having visions of a new order, complete with a Rule. Thus in 1732 was born the new order, the Congregation of the Most Holy Savior (17 years later "Savior" was replaced with "Redeemer"). In accordance with another of Sister Maria's visions, Alphonsus became its director. In 1743 he was formally elected superior general. Pope Benedict XIV (r. 1740–58) approved the Rule and Institute of men in 1749, and the Rule and Institute of women in 1750. The new order suffered from dissension within the ranks, and political opposition from without. Alphonsus's health suffered, but he maintained his duties. He continued his missionary work until 1752. Even though the order had papal approval, it did not have state approval—there was a law forbidding new religious orders—and Alphonsus spent the rest of his life in a futile effort to gain state approval.

In 1762, King Charles of Naples forced Alphonsus to accept the bishopric of St. Agatha of Goths against his wishes. The tiny diocese near Naples had a lax clergy and largely uninstructed people. There Alphonsus labored until 1775. Not everyone was happy with his reforms, and he was repeatedly threatened with assassination. He often was seriously ill—eight times in his life he was given last rites. From May 1768 to June 1769, he suffered a terrible attack of rheumatic fever that left him partially paralyzed for the rest of his life. His neck was permanently bent, at first so badly that his head rested on his chest. He had to drink from a tube at meals and required assistance at mass to drink from the chalice. After he was permitted to resign in 1775, Alphonsus returned to his order's monastery at Nocera di Pagani, hoping for a speedy death. He would live 12 more years.

In 1780, a crisis arose that split the order. The Rule was drastically altered and presented to the deaf and nearly blind saint for signing to present for royal approval. Unsuspecting, Alphonsus did so. The order seemed destroyed. In 1781 the Papal States assumed control of the order and appointed a new superior general. Alphonsus was cut out of his own order. This state of affairs remained until after the saint's death. In 1793, the Neapolitan government recognized the original Rule, and the order was reunited under one head.

During the last three years of his life, Alphonsus weathered a dark night of the soul, in which he was besieged by temptations, dreadful apparitions and despair. Nonetheless, he died peacefully on August 1, 1787, at Nocera di Pagani near Naples, just as the midday Angelus was ringing. He was buried there and a shrine was erected. Another shrine was built at St. Agatha of the Goths.

Though gifted with words as a lawyer, Alphonsus did not become a writer until late in life. His first work was a small volume, *Visits to the Blessed Sacrament*, published at age 49. *Annotations to Busenbaum*, a work on moral theology, appeared in 1748. His great work, *Moral Theology*, appeared in two volumes in 1753 and 1755. He also published numerous treatises, and compiled stories of the early martyrs in *Victories of the Martyrs*. His writings and sermons remain popular today. Altogether, he wrote 110 books and pamphlets.

Alphonsus was a visionary and mystic, and miracles were attested to him. There are numerous cases of bilocation, in which he simultaneously heard confessions and in a distant location preached sermons. The most significant bilocation took place in 1774. After saying mass in Arienzo, he sank into a chair and remained unmoved until the next day. During that time, he had been at the bedside of the dying pope Clement XIV (r. 1769–74) in Rome.

Alphonsus also was seen to levitate on numerous occasions, even while preaching. In 1745 he was preaching in Foggia at a church where 14 years earlier he had beheld a vision of Mary. During his sermon a ray of light from a picture of Mary struck him, and he fell into an ecstasy and was raised several inches off the floor.

Alphonsus knew people's secret and hidden thoughts, and knew of events in distant locations. He controlled nature and the elements. In 1779 Mount Vesuvius was spewing flames and people feared an eruption. Alphonsus looked at the mountain, uttered the name "Jesus" and made the sign of the cross. According to witnesses, the flames disappeared.

He was buried wearing his scapular of Our Lady of Mount Carmel. Forty years later, he was exhumed. His body and clothing had turned to dust, but the scapular was incorrupt. In art he is shown as a young priest, or as an older man bent double with rheumatism.

Beatified: 1816 by Pope Pius VII
Canonized: 1839 by Pope Gregory XVI
Declared Doctor of the Church: by Pope Pius IX
Feast: August 1
Patronage: confessors; the lay apostolate; moral theologians; vocations

FURTHER READING
Jones, Frederick M. *Alphonsus De Liguori: Saint of Bourbon Naples, 1696–1787, Founder of the Redemptorists.* Liguori, Mo.: Liguori Publications, 1999.
Sermons of St. Alphonsus Liguori. Rockford, Ill.: TAN Books and Publishers, 1982.
The Way of Saint Alphonsus Liguori: Selected Writings on the Spiritual Life. Liguori, Mo.: Liguori Publications, 1999.

Alphonsus Rodriguez (1533–1617) *Widower, doorman and mystic*
Also known as: Alonso Rodríguez

Alphonsus Rodriguez was born in Segovia, Spain, on July 25, 1533, the third child in a large family of wool merchants. When he was about 10, Bl. Peter Faber arrived in Segovia to preach, stayed with Alphonsus's family, and took them up on their offer to spend some time in their country house. While there, he prepared Alphonsus for his first communion.

Peter was one of the group of seven who founded the Society of Jesus along with St. Ignatius of Loyola in 1540. In 1547, when he was 14, Alphonsus was sent along with an elder brother to study under the Jesuits at Alcalá. However, when their father died a short while later, Alphonsus was called home to help manage the family business. When his mother retired in 1556, he inherited the business. Four years later, he married Maria Suarez.

Alphonsus and Maria had three children, although two died young. Maria herself died shortly after giving birth to the last child, their only son. Two years later Alphonsus's mother died. Since the business wasn't prospering either, he sold it, and took his son to live with the boy's two maiden aunts, Antonia and Juliana. He had taken to praying and doing penance, and from Antonia and Juliana he learned to meditate daily. Finally, he decided to resume his studies with the intention of pursuing the religious life.

Alphonsus was then well into his 30s and barely literate. His health also was precarious. Not surprisingly, therefore, he was rejected by the Jesuits at Segovia. He turned to the novitiate of the Jesuits of Aragon at Valencia, where he was rejected as a candidate priest, but allowed to enroll in the school. He picked up his studies where he had broken them off in his youth; after two years, he applied to become a Jesuit brother, but was rejected again. At this point the provincial stepped in, declaring that if Alphonsus was not to be a Jesuit priest or brother, at least he could become a Jesuit saint. Thus, in 1571, Alphonsus joined the Jesuits and was sent to Montesión College on the island of Majorca. In 1585, at age 54, he professed his final vows as a brother.

At Montesión, Alphonsus held the position of doorkeeper. He was diligent in his duties, but he also spent much time in prayer. One day, tempted by impure thoughts, he passed in front of an icon of the Virgin Mary and cried in Latin: "Sacred Mary, Mother of God, remember me!" Immediately, he felt the temptations disappear. From then on dedicated himself to communicating with Mary, praying several rosaries each day and reciting psalms in her honor. He was rewarded with frequent visions, and in his most extreme illnesses felt as if he were living in Nazareth at the time she and her son were there.

Alphonsus was 72 in 1605 when he met St. Peter Claver, then a young man who wanted to serve God but didn't know how. Alphonsus had a vision in which he was told that Peter would do great things in South

America. He urged him to go as a missionary to Cartagena (Colombia), where he did indeed do great things, becoming apostle to the African slaves passing through the port.

In May 1617, when the rector of Montesión, Father Julian, was struck with rheumatic fever, he called Alphonsus to intercede with God and the Virgin Mary on his behalf. Alphonsus spent the night in prayer, and by morning Julian was completely recovered.

On October 29, 1617, Alphonsus entered his final ecstasy. This lasted until midnight on October 31, when the death pangs began for real. After half an hour, he briefly regained consciousness, looked lovingly at his brethren, kissed the crucifix, and expired. His last words were: "Jesus, Jesus, Jesus!" He was 84.

In art, Alphonsus is depicted as an old Jesuit with two hearts on his breast, connected by rays of light to Christ and the Virgin.

Beatified: 1825 by Pope Leo XII
Canonized: 1888 by Pope Leo XIII
Feast: October 30 (formerly October 31)

FURTHER READING
"San Alonso Rodríguez." Church Forum website. URL: http://www.churchforum.org/santoral/Octubre/3010.htm. Downloaded: February 13, 2000.
"St. Alphonsus Rodriguez, SJ." University of Detroit Mercy website. URL: http://www.udmercy.edu/htmls/Jesuits/saints/rodrigez.htm. Downloaded: February 13, 2000.

Ambrose (ca. 339–397) *Bishop of Milan, Latin Father and Doctor of the Church, known for his miracles and his writings*
Name meaning: divine immortal
Also known as: Ambrose of Milan; Ambrosio, Ambrogio; the Honey-Tongued Doctor

Ambrose was born about 339–340 in Trier (Treves), the youngest of three children. His father, Ambrosius, was the praetorian prefect of Gaul, an area that included the territories of present-day France, Britain, Spain and part of Africa—one of the four great prefectures of the Roman Empire and the highest office that could be held by a subject. Ambrosius died when his son was young, and the family moved to Rome. There Ambrose and his brother Satyrus studied law, literature, philosophy and Greek. They received religious instruction from their older sister Marcellina, who had already taken vows as a virgin nun in front of Liberius, the Roman pontiff, and who lived in her mother's house with another consecrated virgin. Like most Christians of his day, Ambrose was not baptized, because sins committed after baptism were regarded

with such horror that baptism was delayed. All three siblings eventually were canonized.

Upon completion of their studies, Ambrose and Satyrus began practicing law. Ambrose, in particular, came to the attention of Anicius Probus, the praetorian prefect of Italy. By his early thirties, Ambrose was the consular governor of Liguria and Aemilia with residence in Milan—a post obtained for him by Probus from Emperor Valentinian I. Ambrose became head of all civil administration, police and justice systems in Milan, the center of Western imperial government since the beginning of the fourth century.

Since 355, the see of Milan had been occupied by Auxentius, an Arian. (The Arian heresy taught that the Logos, or Word, is but a creature created by God and is not God incarnate. Many Christians were Arians in the third, fourth and fifth centuries, including the missionaries sent by Emperor Constantius, son of Constantine the Great, to evangelize the Gothic tribes.) When Auxentius died in 374, the provincial bishops begged Emperor Valentinian I to appoint a successor by edict, but Valentinian refused. Passions were high on both sides. As consular governor, Ambrose went to the cathedral and tried to maintain peace by giving a conciliatory speech. While he was talking, someone (Ambrose's biographer, St. Paulinus of Nola, said it was a child) called out, "Ambrose, bishop!" and the crowd roared its approval.

Ambrose, however, was still unbaptized and ignorant of theology. He immediately refused the position, even, according to Paulinus, inviting prostitutes into his home to make himself unworthy in the people's eyes. He appealed to Valentinian to excuse him, but the emperor, pleased that one of his governors could become bishop, promised severe penalties to anyone found hiding Ambrose. Ambrose reluctantly acquiesced, and in eight days he was baptized, ordained and passed through the orders to be consecrated bishop of Milan on December 7, 374.

The new bishop gave away all his wealth except a stipend for his sister St. Marcellina. His brother St. Satyrus left his legal work to handle Ambrose's secular affairs. He prayed often, fasted regularly, wrote, studied Scriptural texts and Greek philosophers—particularly Origen and St. Basil—and conducted Mass daily. His door was always open to speak to anyone, whether noble or peasant. St. Monica, mother of St. Augustine of Hippo, was one of Ambrose's followers, and the bishop managed to convince Augustine that the intellect could be reconciled with the spirit, bringing him back to the Church in 387. Ambrose took an early stand against capital punishment and was a vocal proponent of vows of virginity—so much so that some Italian mothers kept their marriageable daughters away from Ambrose's sermons. Ambrose retorted that virgins do not depopulate countries; wars do.

But much to the Arians' dismay, Ambrose was an unyielding Catholic. When Emperor Valentinian I died suddenly in 375, his brother Valens, an Arian, took control of the East and Valentinian's son Gratian assumed leadership of the West, except Italy. The army proclaimed the late emperor's four-year-old son by his second wife, Justina, as Emperor Valentinian II, and Gratian agreed to share power. This situation made the Arian Justina regent. In 377, the Goths invaded the eastern part of the empire and Gratian raised an army to aid his uncle Valens. Concerned that he might fall victim to Arian influence, Gratian appealed to Ambrose for guidance, and he responded with his famous treatise, *De Fide ad Gratianum Augustum,* or "To Gratian concerning the Faith."

After the usurper Maximus killed Gratian in 383, Justina begged Ambrose to act as ambassador on her son's behalf. In what is believed to be the first occasion that an ecclesiastic acted on behalf of secular politics, Ambrose managed to convince Maximus to confine himself to Gaul, Spain and Britain and not to invade the lands under the control of Valentinian II—and Justina. Justina had remained circumspect about her plans to further Arianism while her husband Valentinian and his son Gratian lived, but now that she was empress-regent and supported by a Gothic court, Justina began aggressively pursuing her agenda. In 385, Justina induced Valentinian II to demand that Ambrose relinquish the old Portian basilica to be used as a place for Arian worship. He refused, saying no bishop could surrender a temple of God. Valentinian sent messengers demanding the basilica, but Ambrose stood firm, calmly celebrating the Mass and rescuing an Arian priest seized by the crowd.

In January 386, Justina persuaded Valentinian II to pass a law authorizing Arian assemblies and proscribing Catholic ones. Ambrose disregarded the law. On Palm Sunday of that year he preached a sermon against relinquishing any church, and his followers, fearful of their lives, barricaded themselves and Ambrose in the basilica. Imperial guards surrounded the basilica, thinking to starve the congregants out, but by Easter they were still inside. To pass the time Ambrose had taught his people hymns and chants he had written, sung by two choirs singing alternate stanzas. (The Arian debate has long since faded from memory, but Ambrosian antiphonal singing remains a treasured legacy and still a popular form of worship.) Again, Valentinian conceded defeat to the bishop, with Ambrose remarking, "The emperor is in the Church, not over it."

Meanwhile, Valentinian's court learned that Emperor Maximus was planning to cross the Alps. Ambrose agreed to speak with Maximus a second time, rising above his battles with Justina. Ambrose publicly accused the tyrant of breaking faith and asked Maximus to send Gratian's remains as a sign of peace, but Maximus ordered the bishop to leave. The emperor was already displeased with Ambrose because the bishop had excommunicated him for the execution of the Spanish heretic Priscillian. The death of Priscillian and six followers was the first instance of capital punishment for heresy meted out by secular, rather than ecclesiastical, authorities.

Ambrose sent advance word to Valentinian of Maximus's intentions, and the emperor and his mother fled to the Eastern court of Theodosius I, leaving Milan defenseless. Theodosius engaged Maximus, killing him in Pannonia (Hungary), and restored Valentinian II to the throne and awarded him control of the usurper's territories. But although Valentinian II was the nominal ruler, Theodosius now controlled the entire empire. He stayed for a while in Milan and convinced the young emperor to denounce Arianism and accept Catholicism after Justina's death. At Ambrose's urging, Valentinian also thwarted efforts to reintroduce pagan worship of the goddess Victory in the Senate.

While Theodosius was still in Milan, a mob of Christians at Kallinikum, in Mesopotamia, destroyed a Jewish synagogue. Theodosius ordered the local bishop to rebuild the synagogue, and the bishop appealed to Ambrose. Ambrose responded that no Christian bishop could pay for a building used for false worship, but Theodosius ordered the reconstruction to proceed. Ambrose preached against Theodosius, they argued, and Ambrose threatened never to sing Mass at the altar unless Theodosius revoked the order. Rightly or wrongly, Ambrose won.

A more serious scandal occurred in 390. Word reached Milan that Butheric, the governor of Thessalonica, had imprisoned a popular charioteer for having seduced a servant girl in Butheric's family. Butheric refused to release the charioteer for the games, so enraging the crowd that they killed Butheric and stoned several guards to death. Theodosius ordered savage reprisals. When the people gathered in the circus for games, soldiers surrounded the building and massacred 7,000, with no regard to age, gender, guilt or innocence. Ambrose wrote Theodosius, exhorting him to perform public penance and warning the emperor that Ambrose neither would nor could accept the monarch's offering on the altar, nor would he ever celebrate the Divine Mysteries before him until he had offered penance. Theodosius did public penance like any commoner, thereafter ordering that henceforth no capital punishment should be carried out for 30 days after sentencing to allow time for calmer judgment to prevail.

Valentinian II was murdered by Arbogastes in 393 in Gaul. Ambrose mourned the emperor and left Milan before Arbogastes's emissary, the pagan Eugenius, arrived in Milan, threatening to overthrow all Christianity. Ambrose traveled throughout his diocese in 394, encouraging the people to resist, then returned to Milan to learn that his old friend Theodosius had defeated and killed Arbogastes at Aquileia, the final blow to paganism in the empire. A few months later, in 395, Theodosius died in Ambrose's arms, and the bishop who loved him conducted the emperor's funeral.

Ambrose died peacefully on Good Friday, April 4, 397. For several hours before his death he lay with his arms extended as if on a cross, then, after receiving the sacraments from St. Honoratus, bishop of Vercelli, he died. His followers buried him in his basilica near the relics of the holy martyrs Gervase and Protase. In 835 Bishop Angilbert II placed the relics of all three saints in a porphyry—the royal purple stone—sarcophagus under the altar, where they were discovered in 1864. Ambrose is one of the Four Great Doctors of the Latin (Western) Undivided Church, along with SS. Jerome, Augustine and Pope Gregory the Great.

Ambrose's writings include sermons and homilies; mystical writings, commentaries and hymns; of the latter, one is still sung in order to bring good weather.

Of his miracles, Ambrose healed by a laying on of hands, exorcized demons and is said to have raised the dead. When the son of Decentius, an important Christian in Florence, died, Ambrose spread himself over the corpse and brought the boy back to life.

Ambrose discovered the tombs of Gervase and Protase, and people were healed by touching the relics. The most famous incident involved a blind butcher, Severus, who touched the relics with his handkerchief and then applied the cloth to his eyes.

Feast: December 7

Patronage: bakers of honeybread; bees and beekeepers; bishops; candlemakers; chandlers; domestic animals; the French Army Commissariat; geese; gingerbread makers; learning; schoolchildren; stone masons; students; wax melters and refiners; Bologna, Italy; Milan, Italy

FURTHER READING

"Ambrose of Milan, Bishop and Doctor." URL: http://elvis.rowan.edu/~kilroy/JEK/12/07.html. Downloaded March 1, 2000.

Herbert, Albert J. *Raised from the Dead: True Stories of 400 Resurrection Miracles.* Rockford, Ill.: TAN Books and Publishers, 1986.

Nicene and Post-Nicene Fathers, Series 2: St. Ambrose. Philip Schaff and Henry Wace, eds. Grand Rapids, Mich.: William B. Eerdmans Publishing Co., 1984.

Ambrose Sansedoni, Blessed (1220–d. ca. 1286–1287) *Dominican, diplomat*

Also known as: Ambrose of Siena or Sienna; Ambrose Sassedoni

Although three brilliant stars heralded his arrival, Ambrose, born on April 16, 1220, was so ugly and deformed that his mother and father, a book illuminator, couldn't bear to look at him. They entrusted the baby to a nurse, who took the fretful child with her every day to Mass at the Dominican church of St. Mary Magdalene in Siena.

According to lore, Ambrose quieted down if near the altar of relics but cried loudly when removed. When Ambrose was about one year old the nurse took him as usual to church and covered his hideous face with a scarf. While she was praying, a pilgrim said to her, "Do not cover that child's face. He will one day be the glory of this city." A few days later the child stretched out his twisted arms and legs, distinctly said the name "Jesus," and became a normal and beautiful child.

With such a miraculous gift from God, Ambrose embraced piety from the beginning. When he was two or three years old, his father offered him one of two books—one secular, one on saints—and Ambrose chose the one about saints. The child naturally gravitated to the care of the sick, poor and abandoned. At age seven he rose at night to pray and meditate, reciting the "Little Office of the Blessed Virgin" daily.

Against the wishes of his friends and family, the handsome young Ambrose entered the Dominican order of preaching friars at age 17 in 1237. The friars sent him to Paris to study under St. Albert the Great, joining Albert's other famous pupil, St. Thomas Aquinas. In 1248 Thomas and Ambrose accompanied Albert to Cologne, where Ambrose taught in the Dominican schools. Supposedly Ambrose had desired to write, but recognizing his inability to compete with Thomas, he became a preacher instead.

Ambrose also served as a missionary and diplomat, traveling to Hungary in 1260 to evangelize the people. In 1266, he successfully represented Siena in its efforts to be released from an interdict, issued as the result of supporting Emperor Frederick II against the Holy See. Not only did the pope pardon Siena and restore her privileges, but he also forgave the city's misplaced allegiance a second time with Ambrose's intercession. Ambrose brokered peace between Emperor Conrad of Germany and Pope Clement IV (r. 1265–68) and preached the Crusade. Ambrose was named bishop of Siena but declined the office.

At the request of Pope Gregory X (r. 1271–76) Ambrose resumed teaching at the Dominican convent in Rome. Although Ambrose tried to retire after Gregory's death, Pope Innocent V sent him as papal legate to Tuscany. He restored peace between Venice and Genoa and between Florence and Pisa. For 30 years Ambrose's diplomatic skills gained him the regard of popes and kings.

Nevertheless, Ambrose never let his service stand in the way of his devotion. He prayed and meditated constantly, often in a state of ecstasy. Stories of his victories over carnal temptations were legendary, and he frequently levitated while preaching. Sometimes Ambrose was surrounded by a "circle of glory": a mystical light filled with birds of brilliant plumage. Shortly before his death in 1287 (brought on, according to some, by the vehemence of his preaching), Ambrose supposedly saw visions of great beauty. No collections of his sermons remain.

Beatified: 1622 (his cultus confirmed) by Pope Gregory XV
Feast: March 20
Patronage: betrothed couples; Siena, Italy

Anastasia (d. ca. 249) *Roman martyr*

Anastasia suffered particularly cruel tortures, according to the story of her martyrdom. After Valerian succeeded to the throne of the Roman Empire in 244, he showed benevolence toward the Christians, but near the end of 247 turned on them with vicious persecutions. Anastasia was a young Roman woman of both noble and Christian birth who decided to enroll in a Christian nunnery. Her holiness earned her a great reputation.

Valerian's inquisitors broke into the nunnery and arrested her. She was taken before the prefect general, Probus, who threatened her with torture if she did not renounce her faith. He promised her happiness if she would go with him to sacrifice at the temple of Jove. Anastasia chose torture. Her face was then beaten bloody and she was sent back to prison.

Her joy made Probus angrier. He had all of her limbs dislocated and her sides burned by torches. This did not break her, so he ordered her nails to be torn from her fingers, her teeth to be broken with a hammer, and her breasts to be torn from her body with hot iron pincers. Instead of dying in prison, her wounds were miraculously healed.

Probus then ordered her tongue to be pulled out by the roots. This was carried out before a crowd of spectators. Blood gushed from her mouth. She made signs to a Christian, Cyril, for water, and he gave her some.

Despite the loss of her tongue, Anastasia reportedly raised her hands to heaven and blessed the Lord and asked him to help her consummate her sacrifice. Probus had her hands and feet cut off, and then finally ordered her to be beheaded. Cyril also was beheaded for assisting her. The executions took place on the 27th or 28th of October, in about the year 249.

Anastasia's body was buried outside the city by Sophia, the head of the nunnery.

Feast: October 28

FURTHER READING
St. Alphonsus Liguori. *Victories of the Martyrs.* Brooklyn: Redemptorist Fathers, 1954.

Anastasius I (d. 401) *Pope and martyr*

Anastasius, son of Maximus, was a native of Rome. A priest in the Roman Church, he was elected the successor of Pope St. Siricius (r. 384–399) on November 27, 399.

Anastasius is known for his personal holiness and piety and for some important ecclesiastical pronouncements. He is responsible for the instruction to priests to read the Gospels standing and bowing their heads. In 400, he convened a synod to consider the writings of Origen, and upheld the council's condemnation of the work as heterodox. He also supported the Church in North Africa in its struggle against Donatism, a schism that lasted from about 311 to 411.

Anastasius died in 401 after a reign of only two years and was buried in the Pontian catacombs. Although his death was natural, he is honored in the Roman Martyrology.

Feast: December 19

Anastasius the Sinaite (d. 700) *Father of the Church, abbot and defender of the faith*

A Greek, Anastasius the Sinaite was born in Alexandria. He became the abbot of the monastery at Mount Sinai, where he earned the name of "the new Moses" for his vigorous attacks on groups seeking to influence the Church. He is best known for his work *The Guide,* a defense of the faith that remained popular for centuries.

Feast: April 21

Andrew the Apostle (d. 60) *One of Jesus' Twelve Disciples or Apostles*
Name meaning: Strong, manly, valorous
Also known as: Andreas; Endres

Jesus calling SS. Peter and Andrew. (Engraving, 19th century)

Andrew was born at Bethsaida on Lake Genesareth (the Sea of Galilee). He was the brother of St. Peter and in adulthood lived with him in a house at Capharnaum, on Lake Genesareth. The brothers were prosperous fishermen. They were also followers of St. John the Baptist, through whom they came into contact with Jesus. Andrew was the first to meet Jesus; immediately recognizing him as the Christ, he introduced him to Peter. They followed Jesus on an evangelizing tour and later were called by him to be among his twelve regular disciples or apostles.

Not much is known about Andrew's subsequent career. Together with St. Philip, he presented the Gentiles to Christ (as described in John 12:20–22). When as a result of the persecutions of Herod Agrippa I (r. 42–44) the apostles were forced to flee Galilee, Andrew is believed to have preached in many regions. By tradition, he spent some time in Byzantium, where he appointed St. Stachys as the first bishop. There is another unfounded tradition that he preached in Russia, reaching as far as Kiev in the Ukraine, whence the conversion of the Slavs spread in the 11th century.

The exact whereabouts and circumstances of Andrew's death are not known. According to an early account now known to be a forgery intended to counter Rome's claim to the relics of SS. Peter and Paul, Andrew was crucified on an X-shaped cross (today called a St. Andrew's Cross) at Patras (Patrae) in Achaia. This tradition has it that the Roman governor, Aegeas or Aegates, had him tied rather than nailed to the cross to extend his suffering, but that he used the opportunity to preach to all who came to view his execution. In any event, his martyrdom came during the reign of Nero, perhaps on November 30, A.D. 60.

Andrew's relics were translated to Constantinople, where they were deposited in the Church of the Apostles, about the year 357. Tradition has it that some were conveyed to Scotland in the fourth century, in response to a dream of St. Rule (Regulus) in which he was guided by an angel to a place called St. Andrew's, where he built a church to house the relics. Rule became the first bishop of St. Andrews and spent the next three decades evangelizing the Scots. When the French Lombards took Constantinople at the start of the 13th century, Cardinal Peter of Capua carried the remaining relics to Italy and placed them in the cathedral of Amalfi, where most are to be found today. Andrew's head, however, was returned to Constantinople by Pope Paul VI (r. 1963–78).

Andrew's feast has been universal in the West since the sixth century.

Andrew is represented as an old man with a book and an x-shaped cross; a man bound to a cross; a man preaching from a cross; a man sitting in a boat; a preacher holding some fish. His symbols include a fishing net, an x-shaped cross (saltire) and fish. In the oldest images, he is depicted with a normal Latin cross. The saltire became associated with Andrew beginning in the 10th century, becoming common only in the 14th.

Feast: November 30
Patronage: anglers; fishmongers; fishermen; against gout; maidens; old maids; singers; against sore throats; spinsters; against stiff-neck; unmarried women; women who wish to become mothers; Achaia; Amalfi, Italy; Avranches; Brabant; Brunswick; Burgundy; Greece; Holstein; Luxembourg; Minden; Patras, Greece; Pesaro; Russia; Scotland; University of Patras

Andrew Avellino (1521–1608) *Theologian, founder of monasteries, friend of St. Charles Borromeo*

Name meaning: strong, manly
Also known as: Lorenzo Avellino; Lancellotto

Andrew was born at Castronuovo, near Naples, in 1521. He was christened Lorenzo, but his mother called him Lancellotto. The young man dedicated his life to Christ quite early, embracing chastity. After finishing his elementary studies in Castronuovo, Lancellotto went to Venice to study the humanities and philosophy. His vow of chastity was so challenged by the lovely Venetian girls that he assumed tonsure and quickly left for Naples, where he studied canon and civil law. Lancellotto received the Doctor of Laws and was ordained a priest in 1547 at age 26.

For a while Lancellotto practiced canon law at the court in Naples. He was quite accomplished—so silver-tongued, in fact, that he feared his preoccupation with argument weakened his devotion to meditation and prayer. The situation came to a head when, in the heat of a friend's defense, he perjured himself. Filled with remorse, Lancellotto renounced the law and vowed to live as a penitent.

But the archbishop of Naples had other plans for him, sending him to reform the Sant' Arcangelo convent in Baiano. The nuns had become so lax in their vows that the convent was for all practical purposes a brothel. Through zeal and example Lancellotto brought the convent back to its rules, but he nearly died in the effort. Certain men of the area were so used to the services of the convent that in 1556 they captured Lancellotto and beat him severely. He was taken to the monastery of the Theatines to recover and there decided to join the order, only recently founded by St. Cajetan. At age 35 he was invested during the Vigil of the Assumption and took the name Andrew.

Following his novitiate he visited the tombs of apostles and martyrs in Rome, then returned to the monastery as master of novices. His success at improving the quality of priests gained him promotion to superior of the Naples house 10 years later. In 1570, at the request of St. Charles Borromeo, Andrew traveled to Lombardy to found Theatine houses in Milan and Piacenza and became a close friend of Charles Borromeo. Other houses were founded throughout Italy, and Andrew attracted many disciples, including Lorenzo Scupoli, author of the book *The Spiritual Combat*.

In 1582 Andrew returned to Naples, where he spent his last years teaching, preaching, writing, fighting heresy and converting Protestants. His many letters were published in two volumes in 1731, followed by five volumes of his other works in 1734.

On November 10, 1608, while preparing the Mass, Andrew suffered a massive stroke and died after receiving the Holy Viaticum. He was 88.

People who came to pay their respects clipped bits of his hair for relics. During this, his face was cut accidentally several times. When fresh-looking, red blood welled out of the cuts, some speculated that Andrew had not initially died but had been catatonic and actually buried alive. Physicians confirmed his death, and made more cuts in his skin and collected his blood for the next three days. Andrew was buried in the monastery church of St. Paul in Naples.

The blood reportedly bubbled in a vial. On the anniversary of his death, the hardened blood was said to liquefy and bubble (similar to the blood of St. Januarius) when brought out for veneration. The blood is said to bubble every year on the anniversary of his death.

Beatified: 1624 by Pope Urban VIII
Canonized: 1712 by Pope Clement XI
Feast: November 10
Patronage: against sudden death; apoplexy; for a holy death; strokes and stroke victims; Naples

Andrew of Crete (ca. 660–740) *Greek Father of the Church*

Andrew of Crete was born about 660 in Damascus. He became a monk at Mar Saba and served later at the Holy Sepulchre. Around 685, he was ordained a deacon at Hagia Sophia. He ran a refuge for orphans, the elderly and others. In 692 he became archbishop of Gortyna on Crete, where he remained for the rest of his life.

Andrew of Crete had substantial oratorical skills, as evidenced in his homilies and panegyrics to the saints. He is credited with authoring the "Great Canon" prayed by the Orthodox during Lent.

Feast: July 4

Andrew Kim Taegon (d. 1846) *One of the Korean Martyrs*
Also known as: Andrew Kim

Andrew Kim was born to the nobility. Both his parents converted to Christianity, and his father died a martyr. Christianity did not come to Korea until the 1600s and not to any extent until the late 1700s. Korea's rulers maintained a policy of total isolationism, keeping out any Western influence and making entry into Korea practically impossible. In 1784, Pietro Yi was the first Korean to be baptized at Pechino, but he denied his faith in the persecutions of 1791, started when a Korean Christian noble refused to burn incense to honor the memory of his mother.

By 1801, sporadic and localized persecutions had been extended to the entire country. One Chinese priest who had managed to enter Korea offered himself as a sacrifice, hoping that his death might stop the sufferings of other Christians. Authorities beheaded him on May 31, 1801, but did not end the persecutions. Martyrdom inspired the faithful, and Korea's tiny Catholic community petitioned other countries to send priests. France answered the Koreans' prayers, secretly slipping several bishops and priests, all members of the Foreign Mission Society of Paris, into the country.

In 1839, the return of the conservative faction to Korean government resulted in widespread persecution, lasting until 1846. Three French clerics—two priests and the bishop Msgr. Laurence Imbert—all died by beheading on September 21, 1839.

Andrew Kim had been baptized at 15. He then traveled 1,300 miles from Korea to the nearest seminary in China. He also studied Latin in Macao. Slipping back into Korea in 1845, he became the first native-born Korean ordained a priest, working tirelessly to bring the Sacraments to the people until Korean tribesmen captured, tortured, then beheaded him at the edge of a river at sunset on September 16, 1846. Terrified followers retrieved his body late that night, taking it into the mountains for a proper and safe burial.

Only two letters remain from Andrew Kim: one to the vicar apostolic bishop who ordained him, and one to his followers, exhorting them to keep the faith. One of those faithful was Paul Chong Hasang, who was killed less than a week later on September 22.

Persecutions rose again in 1861. Two more French bishops and a number of missionaries were martyred, as well as many ordinary Koreans. Estimates run as high as 10,000 over the two periods. Official persecutions ended in 1886; up until 1881, Christianity was referred to in government documents as "the perverse doctrine." Today Christianity flourishes in South Korea and struggles on as the Church of Silence in communist North Korea.

On May 6, 1984, Pope John Paul II held services in Seoul to canonize 103 saints, including Andrew Kim and Paul Chong Hasang, as representatives of the Korean martyrs. The saints' feast day was inserted into the Calendar of the Universal Church.

> *Beatified:* July 1925, martyrs of the 1839–46 persecutions by Pope Pius XI; October 1968, martyrs of the 1861–66 persecutions by Pope Paul VI
> *Canonized:* May 6, 1984, by Pope John Paul II
> *Feast:* September 20
> *Patronage:* Korean clergy

FURTHER READING
"Saints Andrew Kim Taegon, Paul Chong Hasang and Companion Martyrs in Korea." *Daily Catholic.* Section Two, vol. 10, no. 178, September 20, 1999. URL: http://www.DailyCatholic.org. Downloaded July 11, 2000.

Anencletus (d. ca. 91) *Pope and martyr*
Name meaning: Blameless
Also known as: Anacletus, Cletus

Almost nothing is known for sure about Anencletus, even his name. Some early Church documents identify him with Anicletus and Cletus, whereas others suggest these were different people. He is thought to have succeeded St. Linus as bishop of Rome when Linus died around the year 79. He was thus the third pope. During his 12-year reign he divided Rome into 25 parishes and ordained an unknown number of priests.

Anencletus was martyred by the Roman emperor Domitian around the year 91. He was buried near Linus at the foot of Vatican Hill, where his relics may be found today.

Feast: April 26

Angela Merici (1470 or 1474–1540) *Founder of the Order of Ursulines*
Name meaning: Angel, messenger
Also known as: Angela de Marici, Angela of Brescia

Angela Merici was born March 21, 1470, or 1474, at Desenzano, a small town on the southwestern shore of Lake Garda in Lombardy. Orphaned at 10, Angela and her brother and older sister went to live with a wealthy uncle at Salo. Angela's sister died suddenly, when Angela was 13, without benefit of the last rites. Angela prayed and suffered on her sister's behalf until receiving a vision of the Blessed Mother accompanied by the sister—confirmation to Angela that her sister was in heaven. In gratitude Angela consecrated herself to God, becoming a Franciscan tertiary at 15. She lived very austerely, shunning any possessions, even a bed, and living on bread and water and a few vegetables.

Angela's uncle died when she was 20, and she returned to Desenzano. Shocked at how little the poorest neighborhood girls knew of religion, she discussed her plans to begin teaching them with a few of her friends, mostly tertiaries like herself. A natural, charming leader, Angela had no difficulty enlisting other young women to her cause. Her plans were confirmed when a vision revealed virgins ascending a ladder of light, accompanied by angels playing golden harps, until the Savior called her by name to start a society of teaching women. Converting her home to a school, Angela and her friends began teaching the rudiments of religion to the local little girls—so successfully that

Angela was invited to open a similar school in nearby Brescia.

In Brescia, Angela came in contact with many influential people who supported her efforts and whom she inspired in their devotion. Her photographic memory of the Bible and knowledge of Latin placed her in a position as counsel and speaker as well. In 1524, Angela made a pilgrimage to the Holy Land, where reputedly she was struck blind in Crete. Resisting entreaties to return home, Angela completed her pilgrimage with enthusiasm. While praying before a crucifix upon the very spot in Crete where she had gone blind, her eyesight was miraculously restored.

The next year, 1525, Angela traveled to Rome to receive jubilee year indulgences from Pope Clement VII (r. 1523–34). His Holiness tried to persuade Angela to remain in Rome as head of a community of nursing sisters, but she declined. After hearing of her vision of the virgins on the ladder, the pope gave Angela permission to establish a community of teaching women. In another vision, St. Ursula—patroness of medieval universities and a leader of women—appeared to Angela, who was so transported by her ecstasy that she apparently levitated.

Years would pass before Angela could accomplish her goal, however. Shortly after returning to Brescia from her papal visit, war broke out in Lombardy. As Charles V neared Brescia, civilians fled the city, and Angela and some of her friends went to Cremona. After peace was declared, the citizens of Brescia welcomed Angela as a prophetess and saint. Finally, in 1533, Angela began training some young women to form a community. Angela and 28 companions consecrated themselves to God, under the protection of St. Ursula, on November 25, 1535, at St. Afra's Church in Brescia, with Angela as their first superior.

The Company of St. Ursula was the first teaching order of women, which was a radical concept for many years. The women took no formal vows and did not live communally or in a cloister. Although some lived with Angela in her home near St. Afra's, most lived in their own homes with their families. The women did not adopt a habit but were encouraged to wear a simple black dress. They met, worshiped and taught classes together or in their students' homes. Pope Paul III (r. 1534–49) formally recognized the Ursulines in 1544; they did not become a Congregation until 1565. In 1568, St. Charles Borromeo called the Ursulines to Milan and persuaded the women to assume a cloistered, communal life as a means of reform of the dioceses in which they worked. Unable to accept Angela's mission of a flexible society, rules of strict enclosure were enacted in France.

Angela directed her community for only four years, falling ill in January 1540 and dying January 27 in Brescia. Her sisters, surrounding her at the end, reported that a ray of light shone upon her at death, and that the Lord's name was on her lips. Her body later was found to be incorruptible.

Beatified: 1768 by Pope Clement XIII
Canonized: 1807 by Pope Pius VII
Feast: January 27
Patronage: bodily ills; disabled or handicapped people; loss of parents; sickness

Anicetus (d. ca. 166) *Pope and martyr*

Anicetus was born in Emesa, Syria. Around 155 he succeeded St. Pius I as bishop of Rome, making him the 11th pope. Anicetus ruled only until about 166, but his short reign was full of controversy.

Anicetus forbade priests to wear long hair, perhaps because the Gnostics did so. Gnostics and Marcionites, each preaching their own heresies, had not yet been stifled by the Church, and were very much in evidence in Rome at this time. There were also signs of a growing rift between Eastern and Western churches over the question of when Easter should be celebrated. Western churches followed Rome in celebrating Easter on Sunday, but Eastern churches celebrated the feast on the 14th day of the month of Nisan (that is, after the first moon of the vernal equinox), regardless of the day of the week on which it fell. St. Polycarp, bishop of Smyrna, an Eastern church, came to confer with Anicetus about the year 160, but left without resolving the conflict, which was to grow larger in the coming centuries.

Anicetus is said to have died a martyr, although his martyrdom may be only figurative, worn down as he was by the many problems he could not resolve. He died sometime between 160 and 166, on the 16th, 17th or 20th of April.

Feast: April 17

Anne, Matron (n.d.) *Believed to be the mother of the Virgin Mary and grandmother of Jesus Christ*
Name meaning: Grace, gracious one
Also known as: Ann or Anna

Anne receives no mention in the Bible, either by name or by any reference to Mary's parents. But by the second century, the apocryphal *Book of James* or *Protoevangelium Jacobi*, written about 170, fills in the legendary details of Anne's life and the birth and childhood of Mary. Anne's story also appears in *The Golden*

Legend, a book of the saints' lives written by Jacobus de Voragine.

Anne's story in the *Book of James* followed closely the Old Testament story of Hannah in I Samuel 1, 2:1–10; indeed, Anne or Anna is the Latin form of the Greek name Hannah, and both mean "grace." Hannah is one of the two wives of Elkanah. The other wife, Peninnah, bore Elkanah sons and daughters and taunted Hannah for her barrenness, so much so that Hannah prayed to the Lord to give her a son, and she would consecrate him to the Lord's service. Even though Hannah was old, her prayer was granted, and when her son Samuel was weaned she left him in the care of the priests.

Anne's husband, Joachim of Nazareth, endured embarrassments for his childlessness. Joachim was so despondent that he left Anne in Jerusalem and went to live for 40 days and nights in a rude shepherd's hut, praying ceaselessly for a child.

James wrote that Anne's sorrow was doubled, as a widow and as a barren woman. Praying in the garden, Anne despaired of ever finding favor in God's sight, until an angel appeared assuring her of a child. Anne promised that whether she had a son or daughter the child would be consecrated to the Lord. The angel told her that Joachim was returning, as he had received a visit from the angel as well, and Anne hurried to meet her husband. They embraced at the Golden Gate of Jerusalem and went home. Nine months later Anne delivered a daughter called Mary.

Medieval ecclesiastics believed that Mary was conceived merely through Anne and Joachim's embrace (James had delicately omitted the details of their return to the house), leading to the doctrine of Mary's Immaculate Conception.

The *Book of James* detailed Mary's childhood as well, giving a loving picture of Anne as a tender and godly mother. At six months, Mary took her first baby steps, and Anne quickly moved the child to an undefiled area of the bedroom so that Mary wouldn't walk on unclean ground before her consecration. On Mary's third birthday, Joachim and Anne took her to the Temple, where the child rejoiced in her new surroundings and lived until her 14th birthday. A major flaw in this story is that Judaic law forbade women in the Temple.

Anne's devotion as a mother and grandmother to Jesus Christ made her a popular figure in the early Church. By the eighth century, Pope Constantine introduced Anne worship into Rome, and the saint received her own feast day on July 26. Crusaders brought Anne to Western Europe, where she was venerated in England as early as 1030.

The popularity of Anne's story helped medieval ecclesiastics solve a thorny New Testament issue. Matthew 12:46 refers to Jesus' "brothers," yet the Church had decided that Mary remained a virgin throughout her life, as had Joseph. If that were true, who were these "brothers"?—not Joseph's children from a previous marriage, and not Mary's children. St. Jerome suggested that they were sons of Mary's sisters, or Jesus' cousins. This doctrine, called the Holy Kinship and popularized in medieval literature, art and prayer, pulled together all the Marys of the New Testament, except for Mary Magdalen, into one family and gave Anne two husbands after the death of Joachim. The Holy Kinship not only solved the problem of Jesus' brothers but also established a matriarchal lineage for Jesus, a factor in the extraordinary popularity of Anne's cult.

By the 16th century, Martin Luther attacked the worship of Anne as spurious, especially the so-called *selbdritt* paintings, which portrayed Mary and Jesus always accompanied by Anne. Despite Luther's efforts, veneration of Anne, concentrated in England, was extended to full canonical worship Churchwide in 1584.

In 1650, Breton sailors, caught in a storm at sea off the coast of Quebec, promised Anne a sanctuary if they safely reached shore. The sailors built a shrine at Beaupré, which was rebuilt in 1658, and attracts over one million pilgrims a year. Several of her relics are there, including a finger bone. St. Anne de Beaupré is especially famous for the crutches left behind by healed cripples.

In art, Anne often appears at her betrothal to Joachim or embracing him at Jerusalem's Golden Gate.

Canonized: 1584 by Pope Gregory XIII
Feast: July 26
Patronage: broommakers; cabinetmakers; carpenters; childless people; homemakers and housewives; infertility; grandparents, especially grandmothers; lace makers and workers; lost articles; miners; mothers; old-clothes dealers; against poverty; pregnant women; seamstresses; stablemen; turners; women in labor; Brittany; Canada; Quebec; Santa Ana Indian pueblo; Taos, New Mexico

FURTHER READING
Streep, Peg. *Mary, Queen of Heaven.* New York: Book of the Month Club, 1997.

Anne Line (ca. 1574–1601) *One of the Forty Martyrs of England and Wales*
Name meaning: Gracious one
Also known as: Anne Higham

Anne Line was born to the wealthy and strongly Calvinist family of William Heigham of Dunmow, in Essex. When she and her brother converted to Catholicism—an illegal religion from 1570 to 1791—they were disowned and disinherited. At 19, Anne married Roger Line of Ringwood, also a convert, but he was arrested for recusancy (failure to obey the law requiring Catholics to attend Church of England services) and exiled to Flanders in 1594, where he died within months.

Alone and in ill health, Anne devoted all her efforts to assisting fellow Catholics. She first moved to the home of Mrs. Wiseman in Braddox, but Mrs. Wiseman was executed for helping priests. Her next job was managing a house of refuge for priests in London organized by the Jesuit, Father John Gerard. Father Gerard was arrested and imprisoned in the Tower of London but escaped in 1597. His return to the safe house caused Anne to come under suspicion, so she moved again.

On Candlemas Day (February 2), 1601, Anne invited a large number of Catholics to celebrate Mass in her apartment. Noticing the large assembly, Anne's neighbors alerted the authorities. The priest-catchers broke into her home just as another Jesuit, Father Francis Page, was about to conduct the Mass. The heavily barred door gave Father Francis just enough time to remove his vestments and mingle with the crowd, but the discovery of an altar and communion vessels was enough to indict Anne.

Anne awaited trial at Newgate prison. She was so ill that she had to be carried in on a chair. But when questioned by Lord Chief Justice Popham at the Old Bailey on February 26 if she were guilty of the charge of harboring a priest from overseas (Act of 27 Elizabeth), Anne bravely replied that her only regret was that she had not received a thousand more. Even though the prosecution had very little evidence—only the altar and one witness who said Anne had been in her house with a man dressed in white—the jury found her guilty at the judge's direction, and she was sentenced to death.

The next day, February 27, Anne rode to Tyburn for execution. Composed to the end, she kissed the gallows and knelt in prayer. Hanged along with Anne were a Jesuit, Father Bl. Roger Filcock, her friend and confessor, and a Benedictine, Father Bl. Mark Barkworth, the first Benedictine to be martyred since the suppression of the monasteries.

Beatified: 1929 by Pope Pius XI
Canonized: October 25, 1970, by Paul VI as one of the Forty Martyrs of England and Wales
Feast: February 27
Patronage: childless people; converts; widows

Anselm (ca. 1033–1109) *Archbishop of Canterbury, Doctor of the Church*
Also known as: the Father of Scholasticism

Anselm was born about 1033 to a noble family from the Aosta region of the Piedmont in Italy. He was sent to a monastery school before he was five and suffered under the strict and sometimes cruel education practices of the day, leading him to champion more liberal teaching methods all his life. As a child he dreamed that he sought Heaven in the mountains and there received bread from the Lord. He tried to enter a monastery at about age 15, but the abbot, fearing that Anselm's father Gundulf would object, refused him admission. Anselm prayed for illness, hoping that the monks would relent if he were ill; he did become sick but to no avail. He soon fell in with less-religious friends and began enjoying the pursuits of a young nobleman, restrained only by his mother Ermenberga's love. Once she died, Gundulf's unremitting hatred and harshness drove Anselm away, and he crossed the Alps into France in 1056.

After nearly three years of study and wandering in France and Burgundy, Anselm traveled to Normandy, where the Blessed Abbot Lanfranc of Lombardy lived with a group of fellow scholars at Bec Abbey. Lanfranc, who was prior, welcomed the young man into the Benedictine order in 1060. In 1063 William, duke of Normandy, later King William I the Conqueror, named Lanfranc abbot of St. Stephen's Abbey at Caen, and young Anselm succeeded him as prior of Bec. Anselm served as prior for 15 years, during which time he wrote two of his major treatises: the *Monologium* and the *Proslogium*. The greater of the two, the *Proslogium*, attempts to present an ontological argument of the existence of God by showing that the mere fact that even nonbelievers understand the uniqueness of God as a perfect being validates His presence. Anselm's was heavily influenced by the writings of St. Augustine, and his arguments in turn influenced great thinkers of his day, such as St. Thomas Aquinas (who disagreed) and later philosophers such as Hegel, Kant and Descartes.

In 1078, the abbot of Bec, Blessed Herluin, died, and Anselm succeeded him—but not without great reluctance. As abbot, Anselm traveled to England, where the abbey owned property. He met often with his old mentor Lanfranc, whom King William I had named archbishop of Canterbury in 1070. Lanfranc served as regent on behalf of the king in his absence and helped ensure the smooth transition of power to William's son, William II Rufus (meaning "red-haired"), when the king died in 1087.

But when Lanfranc died in 1089, William Rufus did not replace him, seizing the see's revenues and leaving the Church of England in anarchy. The English bishops clearly wanted Anselm to succeed Lanfranc, but Anselm did not want the office. He even refused to travel to England for fear of appearing to seek the archbishopric. But in 1092, at the urging of Hugh, earl of Chester, Anselm came to England and was hailed as the new archbishop by the clergy, nobles and people. Anselm stayed for several months, often meeting with the king. But when he tried to return to Bec, the king denied him permission. The people prayed all over England that the king would choose Anselm to fill the Chair of Augustine. By early 1093, William Rufus fell ill and, fearing for his mortal soul, repented of his sins and named Anselm archbishop of Canterbury. Anselm tried to refuse the honor—he had to be dragged to the king's bedside and forced to receive the pastoral staff—but finally agreed to accept the office.

Once William Rufus regained health, he returned to his old ways. First he kept Anselm from calling the synods necessary to handle church business. Next the king and Anselm argued over the king's gift of Church property to his friends. Always looking for revenue, William Rufus demanded a gift of 500 pounds from Anselm to seal his election as archbishop. But when Anselm accumulated the money from his impoverished see, the king scornfully refused the levy as insufficient. Anselm angrily retorted that as long as the king treated him as a free man Anselm would serve him, but if he treated him like a slave the king would have nothing of him or his office. Anselm then gave the 500 pounds to the poor. He finally was consecrated archbishop on December 4, 1093.

To be fully invested, however, Anselm needed to receive the pallium from Rome. Complicating the situation was the dispute over papal authority between the rightful pope, Urban II (r. 1088–99), and the antipope Clement. William Rufus saw the schism as a means for him to assert his own power, so when Anselm asked to go to Rome to receive the pallium, William commanded that no one could communicate with either pope until he, William, had established his position on the matter. Anselm supported Urban II, and the question went to a council at Rockingham in March 1095. William finally assented to Anselm's trip to Rome to get the pallium from Urban II, and Walter, bishop of Albano, accompanied Anselm back to Canterbury as papal legate with the pallium. William demanded that he place the pallium on Anselm—thereby asserting royal authority over the Church—but Anselm would not acquiesce. In a compromise, the papal legate, Walter, placed the pallium on the altar on June 10, 1095, and Anselm invested himself.

In 1097, after the king's ineffectual campaign to Wales, William accused Anselm of providing poor support and formally charged him. Anselm demanded to plead his case in Rome, which William first denied then hurriedly granted. Anselm blessed the king, set sail for Rome, and did not return to England during the rest of William Rufus's reign.

Pope Urban II welcomed Anselm to Rome and allowed him to enjoy his exile at an Italian monastery. During this period Anselm wrote his most famous work, *Cur Deus Homo,* or "Why God Became Man." In his book, Anselm put forward the "satisfaction theory" of the Incarnation to explain the Atonement: that man's rebellion against God demanded satisfaction, but fallen man was incapable of making adequate satisfaction. God assumed human nature upon Himself, so that a God-made man could make perfect satisfaction and thereby save the human race.

Believing that he had failed as archbishop, Anselm begged Urban II to release him from office, but the pope refused. In 1098, Urban II asked Anselm to represent him at the Council of Bari, where Anselm helped the Italo-Greek bishops understand the papacy's position on the controversial doctrine of *filioque,* or the procession of the Holy Spirit. The clergy in attendance also discussed Anselm's persecution by William Rufus. They denounced William for simony, oppression and depravity, and only agreed to threaten excommunication rather than assess a solemn anathema at Anselm's urging.

William II Rufus died in an accident while hunting with his younger brother Henry in 1100. One of the party, Walter Tirel, shot William with an arrow (some believe on Henry's orders). Henry immediately went to Winchester and seized the treasury, then had himself crowned King Henry I before his oldest brother, Robert, duke of Normandy, could act. Henry also married Matilda of Scotland, daughter of St. Margaret, further cementing his claim. Anselm returned to England amid great rejoicing, but soon argued with Henry I about the king's demands to reinvest Anselm as archbishop. Anselm said that a Roman synod at Easter in 1099 expressly forbade lay investiture; offenders would be punished by excommunication.

Robert of Normandy invaded England in 1101. In order to have the Church on his side, Henry I promised to obey the Holy See, and Anselm helped persuade the barons of Henry's legitimacy, preventing a rebellion. The brothers agreed to a peaceful end to hostilities if Henry relinquished all claims to Normandy. As soon as the war was over, Henry resumed his demands of investiture and sent an emissary to Rome asking Pope Paschal II (r. 1099–1118) for an exemption from the Easter decrees. The pope refused the exemption, and Henry I sent another emissary to try again. The answer was the same, but the envoys claimed that the pope had orally agreed to the exemption, but not in writing. During this period the king continued to invest bishops and abbots, but Anselm was not required to consecrate them.

In 1102, Anselm held a council at Westminster to reinstate some English saints removed earlier from the calendar, to encourage the ordination of English priests, enforce celibacy and protest Henry's latest demands that the archbishop consecrate the bishops invested by the king. Also during that council, Anselm condemned slavery and prohibited the sale of men "like cattle." Anselm continued to resist Henry's demands for investiture, returning to Rome in 1103 to plead his case before Pope Paschal II, who again denied Henry's request for exemption. Returning to England, Anselm stopped in Lyons, where he learned that although the king's counselors had been excommunicated, the king had not. Anselm traveled on to visit with Henry's sister, Adela of Blois, who was ill. He informed her that he intended to excommunicate her brother, and she arranged a brief reconciliation in 1105. The agreement soon fell apart, with Henry again demanding the right of investiture while reneging on his promise to his brother Robert, invading Normandy and defeating Robert in battle. Henry's victory united England and Normandy, and the king imprisoned Robert in an English castle for 28 years.

Anselm again went to Rome to plead his case and secured a letter allowing him to absolve Henry of censures enacted for past offenses but not settling the question. At long last, at a royal council in London in 1107, the king agreed to relinquish his claim to invest bishops and abbots, and the Church allowed clergy to pay homage—fees of entitlement—on their possessions and properties. The Church emerged victorious over the Crown. Amazingly, this pact was kept by Henry I. He even designated Anselm his regent while the king was in Normandy in 1108.

By 1109 Anselm was 76 years old. He had spent the two years since the 1107 council peacefully, writing and tending to pastoral duties. He died at Canterbury on April 21, 1109, and is believed to be interred in the cathedral church. Dante Alighieri immortalized Anselm by placing the archbishop among the spirits of light and power, next to St. John Chrysostom, in the Sphere of the Sun (*Paradiso,* canto XII).

Anselm is especially venerated in Canterbury; Bec and Rouen, France; and Aosta and Turin, Italy. He is shown in his episcopal vestments in art. He was never formally canonized.

Declared Doctor of the Church: 1720 by Pope Clement XI
Feast: April 21

FURTHER READING
"Anselm of Canterbury, Monk, Archbishop, Theologian." URL: http://elvis.rowan.edu/~kilroy/JEK/04/21.html. Downloaded March 1, 2000.
Cantor, Norman F., gen. ed. *The Encyclopedia of the Middle Ages.* New York: Reference Works/Viking, 1999.
St. Anselm's Proslogion. M.J. Charlesworth. London: University of Notre Dame Press, 1979.

Anterus (d. 236) *Pope and martyr*
Also known as: Antheros, Antherus

The Greek Anterus was elected pope upon the resignation of St. Pontian. He reigned for 43 days, from November 21, 235, until January 3, 236. He caused the acts of the Christian martyrs to be collected and placed in the Vatican archives, and for this he himself was martyred. He was the first pope to be buried in the papal crypt of the Roman cemetery of San Callistus.

Feast: January 3

Anthelm (ca. 1105–07–1178) *Carthusian monk and bishop*

Little is known of this saint's early life. Anthelm was born ca. 1105–07 at Chignin Castle, six miles from the town of Chambéry, to nobility. Although he had chosen a life in the Church from an early age, he was more attracted to the things of this world, rather than the next, and pursued ecclesiastical positions to enhance his prestige. A visit to relatives at the Carthusian monastery at Portes changed his life, however, and he entered the strict order of St. Bruno in 1137.

Not long into his novitiate, Anthelm was sent to help rebuild the monastery at Grande Chartreuse, which had been nearly destroyed in an avalanche. His gifts for organization and business soon restored the life and prosperity of the monastery. He supervised rebuilding the ruins and then built a security wall. He brought water to the monastery with an aqueduct and renewed the farmlands and sheepfolds. When Hugh I resigned as prior of the monastery in 1139, Anthelm succeeded him. Throughout these activities Anthelm enforced the Carthusian rule and organized the various monasteries—previously answerable only to the bishop—into a unified order, calling the first general chapter about 1140. Grande Chartreuse became the mother house and Anthelm the first minister general. Anthelm's skills and reputation brought many new monks into the order, including his father, a brother, and William, count of Nivernais.

Anthelm resigned his post in 1152, hoping to retire in solitude, but succeeded Bernard, prior of Portes monastery, as abbot instead. The monks at Portes had become very prosperous—too prosperous, Anthelm believed, for an order with rules of poverty. He gave away most of the grain stores and even sold church ornaments for alms.

Two years later Anthelm returned to Grande Chartreuse, longing for the contemplative life, but was again called to service. In 1159 two popes vied for legitimacy: Alexander III (r. 1159–81), supported by King Louis VII of France and most of the bishops, and Victor IV, the favorite of Emperor Frederick Barbarossa. Anthelm threw himself into the argument and, along with Geoffrey, the Cistercian abbot of Hautecombe, recruited both clergy and nobility from France, Spain and England in support of Alexander. In gratitude, Alexander III appointed Anthelm as bishop of Belley, much against Anthelm's wishes, in September 1163.

Bishop Anthelm energetically promoted reform of his diocese. In his first synod he encouraged the priests and clergy to return to celibacy; many priests had married. When after two years he still found lapsed celibates he deprived them of their benefices. He tolerated no oppression or disorder from the laity, either, standing firm against the intrusion of secular kings into ecclesiastical affairs. Alexander III even sent him to England to try to mediate a truce between King Henry II and Archbishop Thomas Becket but with no success. Anthelm's flock so loved him that for a time the town of Belley was renamed Anthelmopolis.

Anthelm died at age 72 on June 26, 1178. He had devoted his last years to the Carthusian order and two other institutions: a women's community at Bons and a leper house. His tomb at Grande Chartreuse quickly became known for its miraculous powers; St. Hugh of Lincoln visited the shrine before he died in 1200.

Anthelm is depicted in art with a lamp lit by a divine hand.

Feast: June 26

Anthony (251–356) *Credited as a founder of monasticism*

Name meaning: Inestimable
Also known as: Anthony, Anthony or Antony of Egypt, Anthony of the Desert, Anthony the Abbott

Anthony was born in 251 to Christian parents in a little village (reported as Coma or Koman) south of

St. Anthony (Engraving by Albrecht Dürer, 1519)

Memphis in Upper Egypt. Perhaps fearing the persecutions ordered by Emperor Decius in 250, his parents kept him at home, unread and ignorant of any language except his own. Anthony was about 20 years old when his parents died, leaving him a large estate and the care of his younger sister. About six months after his parents' deaths Anthony heard the Gospel text, "Go, sell what thou hast, give it to the poor and thou shalt have treasure in heaven" (Matthew 19:21), and he resolved to sell and distribute all of the estate except what he and his sister needed to live on. Not long thereafter, Anthony again heard the Gospel, "Be not solicitous for tomorrow" (Matthew 6:34), and he gave away the rest. He placed his sister in a house of maidens or pious women, the first recorded description of a nunnery, and began a life of solitude about the year 272.

Anthony's first retreat was in the Libyan desert, not far from his home, where he lived in an abandoned tomb. He usually ate only after sunset, his meal consisting of bread with a little salt, and water to drink. Sometimes he would not eat for three or four days. He slept on a rush mat or the bare floor, and spent his days in prayer, reading and manual labor.

But the devil's temptations, particularly visions of sexual seduction, invaded the young man's solitude. One time, the devil beat Anthony so severely that he was left for dead, saved only by a friend who had come to bring bread to the tomb. The temptations of Anthony were a popular subject for medieval artists.

After emerging triumphant from the temptations, about 285, Anthony crossed the Nile River to live in the abandoned ruins of a mountain fort, where he stayed in almost total isolation for 20 years. He rarely had human contact except for the man who brought bread every six months, but nevertheless attracted the faithful and the curious. Anthony finally came down from the mountain in 305, at age 54, to respond to the entreaties of his followers, founding the first monastery at Fayum.

In the year 311, after the resumption of persecutions under Maximinus, Anthony traveled to Alexandria to comfort Christians awaiting martyrdom. He made no secret of his presence or intentions, but amazingly was not arrested. Once the persecutions abated, he returned to the desert, where he founded another monastery called Pispir. But Anthony still chose solitude, living in a cell on Mount Kolzim with his disciple Macarius and tending a desert garden. Unable to fully escape the world, eventually Anthony lived with a company of followers, instructing them in monastic life. In 337, Emperor Constantine and his two sons Constantius and Constans wrote Anthony, begging that the holy man remember them in his prayers.

Anthony returned to Alexandria in 355 to combat the Arian heresy, which taught that God the Son is a creature and not at the same level as God the Father. Anthony's friend and biographer, St. Athanasius, patriarch of the Church at Alexandria, reported that Anthony attracted crowds of both the faithful and pagans alike. St. Jerome wrote that while Anthony visited Alexandria, he met the famous holy man Didymus, the head of the catechetical school and completely blind. Anthony reportedly told Didymus that he "should not regret his loss of eyes, which were common even to insects, but to rejoice in the treasure of the inner light which the apostles enjoyed, by which we see God and kindle the fire of His love in our souls."

Shortly before his death, Anthony visited a community of his followers, but hurried back to his refuge at Mount Kolzim. Upon becoming ill, he directed his disciples to bury him secretly at Kolzim next to his followers Macarius and Amathas, and send his cloak to Athanasius. Anthony then lay down, assured his disciples that his body would rise incorruptible in the resurrection, and stopped breathing. The year was 356, and Anthony was 105 years old and apparently in good health until the end. In 561, his remains supposedly were discovered and moved first to Alexandria, then to Constantinople, then finally to Vienne, France, during the Crusades.

The Order of Hospital Brothers of St. Anthony, founded in 1096, tended the sufferers of "St. Anthony's Fire" or ergot—a horrible medieval disease with painful skin eruptions that blackened and turned gangrenous, often requiring amputation, caused by a fungus in rye bread flour. Nervous spasms and convulsions accompanied the eruptions. The Brothers, ignorant of the fungus, treated the afflicted with an herbal balm and prayers to St. Anthony, believed to have miraculous healing powers and who, with Christ, had suffered terrible torments. The most famous depiction of this role is by the 16th-century German artist Matthias Grunewald in the Isenheim Altarpiece in Colmar, in which Anthony, surrounded by the plants used in the balm, is tormented by demons trying to destroy his faith.

Feast: January 17

Patronage: amputees; basket makers and weavers; brushmakers; butchers; domestic animals; epileptics; gravediggers; hermits; monks; sufferers from ergotism; pestilence, eczema and other skin diseases and rashes

FURTHER READING

Athanasius, St. *Vita S. Antoni* (Life of St. Anthony). Internet Medieval Sourcebook. URL:http://www.fordham.edu. halsall/basis/vita-anthony/html. Downloaded on January 31, 2000.

Rubenson, Samuel. *The Letters of St. Anthony: Monasticism and the Making of a Saint.* Minneapolis: Fortress Press, 1995.

Anthony Mary Claret (1807–1870) *Archbishop and founder of the Claretians*

Anthony Mary Claret was born December 24, 1807, in Sallent, Catalonia, in northeastern Spain. His father was a weaver who kept his small factory in the family home. As a boy, he experienced his first miracle when he went swimming one day at the beach at Carceloneta, and was swept out to sea by a huge wave. His friends thought him drowned. Anthony had the presence of mind to pray to the Blessed Virgin Mary for help, and another wave deposited him back ashore.

Anthony intended to follow in his father's footsteps, and when he was 18 his father sent him to a designer's school in Barcelona. There he became attracted to the religious life and announced his intent to study for the priesthood and become a Jesuit. His health prevented him from being accepted. Instead, he became a secular priest in the diocese of Vich at age 28. He was assigned to Sallent. Soon he felt a calling to become a missionary, which he did with Rome's approval. He traveled through Catalonia, the Canary Islands and parts of Spain, working in the style of the apostles.

In 1849, Anthony founded the Missionary Sons of the Immaculate Heart of Mary, which became known as the Claretians. The same year, he was named archbishop of Santiago, Cuba, where he spent the next six years. He was popular and effective, but his success

St. Anthony Mary Claret

with his face transfigured, and surrounded by an aura of brilliant light.

Anthony also had the gifts of prophecy and discernment, knowing the sins and faults of those with whom he came into contact. He said he could "read their consciences."

He had the gift of miraculous transport. While a seminarian, he lived at Vich in the rectory of Don Fortunato Bres, his friend and adviser. Many years later, Bres, on his way to mass one winter day, slipped on ice and broke his leg. He asked for Anthony, who was many miles away, to be notified. Ten minutes later, Anthony arrived. The route was snow-covered, and it was snowing at the time, but Anthony was not wet. He said that "an irresistible impulse" had caused him to come to Don Fortunato.

While in Cuba, Anthony seemed to be able to prevent earthquakes during a time of frequent earthquakes. Once while preaching in a public square, the earth trembled, but the saint assured people that all would be well. There were no earthquakes. He also calmed storms.

Beatified: 1935 by Pope Pius XI
Canonized: 1950 by Pope Pius XII
Feast: October 24

FURTHER READING
"Saint Anthony Mary Claret: Tireless Apostle." Available on the Claretians website. URL: http://www.claret.org/anthonyclaret/E_Life.html. Downloaded Sept. 3, 2000.

attracted enemies, and Anthony was subjected to many trials.

In 1857 he returned to the court of Queen Isabella as her confessor. He endured political persecution and accompanied the queen into exile in France in 1868 for a year. He then participated in the First Vatican Council in 1869 and 1870, still enduring persecution.

Anthony returned to France and died on October 24, 1870, in the Cistercian monastery of Fontfroide in southern France. He had preached 25,000 sermons, written 144 works and performed many miracles.

So many miracles happened in the Church of Montserrat through the prayers of the saint that it became known as the Church of Miracles.

He was seen to levitate while deep in prayer, rising slowly into the air in a kneeling position until he was more than two feet off the ground. One witness attested to the "heat of great devotion" that emanated from his body during one such episode. People liked to touch his clothing or kiss his hand because of the sweet odor of sanctity that he carried. He also was seen

Anthony Mary Zaccaria (1502–1539) *Cofounder of the Barnabites, the regular Order of St. Paul*
Also known as: Antonio Maria Zaccaria

Anthony Mary was born in 1502 in Cremona, in Lombardy (Italy), to wealthy patrician parents. His father Lazzaro died when the boy was two, widowing his mother, Antonia Pescaroli, at 18. She devoted the rest of her life to her son and his education, sending him to school in Cremona and Padua. She also taught Anthony Mary compassion for the suffering and destitute. In 1520, Anthony Mary began studying medicine at Padua and received his doctor of medicine degree at 22. He returned to Cremona to practice, but instead began studying theology and ministering to the poor and sick.

Still a layman, Anthony Mary nevertheless began teaching the catechism to both children and adults from the small church of St. Vitalis next to his mother's home. He served in prisons and hospitals, especially during the plague of 1528, and the citizens of Cremona began calling him an apostle. Anthony Mary received ordination in January 1529 and preached his first sermon from St. Vitalis, surrounded by only family and friends. Legend holds that angels were seen at the altar.

Anthony Mary's work was so successful that he wanted to expand his ministry. But first the Dominican, Fra Battista, a friend of Girolamo Savonarola, named him chaplain to the wealthy Ludovica Torelli, countess of Guastalla. In 1531 the countess, Fra Battista and Anthony Mary traveled to Milan, where they joined the Confraternity of Eternal Wisdom. Along with two Milanese priests he met at the confraternity—Giacomo Morigia and Bartolomeo Ferrari—Anthony Mary organized a congregation of secular clergy to combat the effects of years of famine, war and plague that had scourged Milan and all of northern Italy. Their idea was to establish three religious families within the community—priests, sisters and lay people—and Pope Clement VII (r. 1523–34) agreed, approving the Sons of St. Paul in 1533. In 1535, the congregation became the Clerics Regular of St. Paul with the approval of Pope Paul III (r. 1534–49) and under the superiorship of Anthony Mary.

In 1536, Anthony Mary named Father Morigia as superior and went to Vicenza to reform the clergy and bring two communities of sisters to stricter observance of their rules. The countess, meanwhile, had been gathering young women in her home in Milan who yearned for a spiritual life. Pope Paul III recognized these women, known as the Angelicals of St. Paul, under the Rule of Augustine in 1535, formalizing the second part of Anthony Mary's vision. The third part, the lay followers, was the Marrieds of St. Paul. All three families shared the same zealous mission for reform and preaching, encouraging daily Communion, penitence and service to the sick and poor. They established the ringing of church bells at 3:00 P.M. every Friday to commemorate the death of the Lord on Good Friday, and the Forty Hours Prayers: exposition of the Sacrament by turns in the various city churches.

The zeal of Anthony Mary's congregation did not inspire all Milanese citizens, however. Anthony Mary and his followers were accused of Pelagianism and the heresies of the Beguines and the Poor Men of Lyons. Their association with Fra Battista made them suspect as well. Church and civil authorities tried the Sons of St. Paul on October 5, 1534; the trial ended in dismissal. Then both the Sons of St. Paul and the Angelicals were tried from June through August 1537; that trial ended in full acquittal. The trials only stiffened Anthony Mary's resolve, leading to more reform missions and the acceptance of the rule of poverty for the congregation. Anthony Mary had already relinquished his considerable inheritance many years before. By 1539, Anthony Mary sought a church to house his growing congregation. He was offered the Church of

St. Barnabas in Milan, which eventually gave the congregation their more common name: the Barnabites. Anthony Mary did not live to see his followers in the church, however. While back in Guastalla in May 1539 he fell ill with fever. Believing his end was near he asked to be taken home to his mother in Cremona, where he died peacefully on July 5 at age 37. He was supposedly granted a vision of St. Paul just before death.

After the funeral in Cremona, Anthony Mary's body was returned to Milan and buried at St. Paul's Convent of the Angelics. The faithful immediately venerated him as Blessed, but he missed automatic canonization after 100 years of veneration by only five years when Pope Urban VIII (r. 1623–44) issued new rules for sainthood in 1634. His body reportedly was still incorrupt 27 years after death. Anthony Mary's cause was reintroduced in 1802, with three miracles approved for full canonization in 1897.

Beatified: 1849 by Pope Pius IX
Canonized: May 27, 1897, by Pope Leo XIII
Feast: July 5

Anthony of Padua (1195–1231) *Franciscan; Doctor of the Church*
Name meaning: Inestimable
Also known as: Hammer of the Heretics, Ark of The Covenant, the Wonder-Worker

Anthony of Padua, one of the most beloved and revered saints of the Church, was born in Lisbon, Portugal, in 1195 to wealthy, noble parents. He was christened Ferdinand. Some have given his family name as de Bulhoes; writers of the 15th century linked him to Godfrey de Bouillon, commander of the First Crusade. But all that is known of his childhood is that he was educated at the cathedral school in Lisbon.

In 1210, at age 15, Ferdinand joined the Canons Regular of St. Augustine in the convent of São Vicente outside the city walls. To avoid the distractions of friends and visitors, Ferdinand asked to be reassigned to the convent of Santa Croce in Coimbra two years later. There he worked and studied for eight years, where his intelligence and amazing memory enabled Ferdinand to accumulate a wealth of knowledge of theology and Scripture.

Ferdinand's life changed in 1220, when Don Pedro brought from Morocco to Coimbra the relics of the first Franciscan martyrs. Fired with missionary zeal and seeking martyrdom, Ferdinand knew he had no chance to convert the Saracens merely as a canon regular. After pouring out his emotions to a group of Franciscan brothers who had come to the convent to beg, Ferdi-

St. Anthony of Padua (Library of Congress Prints and Photographs Division)

nand left his order and joined the Franciscan Order of Friars Minor at Olivares, taking the name Anthony after Antony Abbot, patriarch of monks and monasteries.

Anthony left for Morocco late in 1220, but became so ill on his arrival that he tried to return to Portugal. Shipwrecked during a storm at Messina, Sicily, Anthony remained there for several months to recuperate. While in Sicily, the brothers told Anthony that a general chapter of the Franciscans was to be held in Assisi, the last chapter open to all brethren. Anthony traveled to Assisi in May 1221 for the chapter, presided over by Vicar General Elias, with St. Francis sitting at Elias's feet. Once the chapter concluded, Anthony was assigned to the hermitage at Montepaolo near Forli, outside Bologna. There he lived quietly, celebrating Mass for the lay brethren and working in the kitchen. No one knew of his education.

But Anthony's talents were soon recognized. Due to a misunderstanding, there was no speaker for an ordination ceremony held at Forli for both Dominicans and Franciscans. Neither order had anyone prepared to give the homily. In desperation, the superior asked Anthony to speak whatever the Holy Spirit should put into his mouth. Anthony protested but obeyed, deliv-

ering a moving and eloquent sermon to the astonishment of his listeners. Brother Gratian, minister provincial, sent Anthony to preach throughout Lombardy, and St. Francis himself appointed Anthony as lector, or teacher, of theology to the Franciscans—the first member of the order to fill that position. Anthony taught at Bologna and the universities of Montpellier and Toulouse. He attended the general chapter at Arles, France, in 1226, and, following St. Francis's death in October of that year, served as envoy from the chapter to Pope Gregory IX (r. 1227–41) to present Francis's rule to the papacy. He was elected minister provincial of Emilia in May 1227, a demanding job that required travel to all the priories under his jurisdiction. He also wrote sermons for feast days, for saints' days and for regular Sunday worship.

Anthony's true gift, however, was preaching. His eloquence, powers of persuasion, messianic zeal and sonorous voice inspired thousands, and he never hesitated to use his pulpit to fight for the poor, the prisoners, debtors and disenfranchised. He was as likely to reprove a bishop for his ways as to cherish a child. Needless to say, Anthony attracted huge crowds to hear him speak, and the stories of his miracles soon followed. One legend says that while he was walking on a seacoast, reflecting about the frequent appearance of fish in the Gospels, the fish rose out of the water and gathered around him to listen. Another says he restored a field ready to be harvested after followers had trampled it. He miraculously protected his listeners from the rain, and he prophesied the destruction of his pulpit by the Devil during another sermon. In one village, a wife forbidden to go hear Anthony speak threw open the window to catch what words she could. Anthony's voice so inspired the husband that he repented.

One of Anthony's frequent sermon topics was heresy. Different heresies by the Cathars (or Albigensians) and the Waldensians wracked Germany, northern Italy and southern France. Known as the "hammer of heretics," or *malleus hereticorum,* Anthony zealously spoke out against their efforts to demean the role of the clergy (whom the heretics believed corrupt) and to question the Presence in the sacraments. One miraculous story tells that an Albigensian named Bonvillo challenged Anthony regarding the Eucharist. If a mule who hadn't eaten in three days bowed before the Eucharist before eating anything, then the Albigensian would believe. The mule was offered hay but he refused to eat before acknowledging the Holy Presence.

In May 1230, Anthony asked Pope Gregory IX (r. 1227–41) to release him from his duties as minister provincial in order that he might spend more time on preaching and prayer. Anthony retired to the convent of Padua, which he had founded, but continued his efforts for the people. Hating usury, he lobbied and persuaded the municipality of Padua in March 1231 to pass a law allowing debtors to remain out of debtors' prison if they had any other sources of recompense. The year before he had traveled to Verona to beg liberty for Guelph political prisoners from the Ghibelline tyrant Ezzelino.

His last major sermon was during Lent in 1231. Right after Easter, Anthony became ill with dropsy and left Padua with two other friars for a woodland retreat at Camposanpiero. The brothers built him a small house in a walnut tree, where he lived for a short while. Realizing he was dying, Anthony asked to return to Padua. He made it as far as the convent of Poor Clares in Arcella, where he died on June 13, 1231, in the chaplain's apartment. Anthony was 36.

Immediately after his death, Anthony supposedly appeared to the abbot at Vercelli, Thomas Gallo, who announced the holy man's passing to the grieving citizens of Padua. Reportedly a group of Paduan children also received the message and announced Anthony's death. Although the Poor Clares at Arcella tried to claim Anthony's body, it was taken to Padua for burial at the Church of Our Lady. Shortly after his canonization in 1232, a Moroccan-style basilica was begun in his honor, and his relics were transferred there in 1263. When St. Bonaventure, Minister General, opened Anthony's tomb for the transferral, he found the saint's tongue uncorrupted and still red in color. Bonaventure kissed the tongue and praised its former abilities of speech as a gift from God. References to Anthony's "honeyed tongue" are revealed in the appearance of bees in icons and paintings.

Artists since the 17th century have depicted Anthony holding the Infant Jesus—a legend says that once, while staying with friends, Anthony's host spied on him and found him enraptured, holding the Christ Child. Anthony also appears with a book for wisdom, with a lily for purity, and with his devout mule. On Tuesdays, Franciscans customarily give bread or alms to the poor called "St. Anthony's bread."

Canonized: 1232 by Pope Gregory IX

Declared Doctor of the Church: January 16, 1946, by Pope Pius XII

Feast: June 13

Patronage: amputees; animals; barrenness; boatmen; donkeys; elderly people; expectant mothers; fishermen; harvests; horses; lost articles; mariners; Native Americans; the oppressed; the poor; Portugal; against shipwrecks; against starvation; sterility; the Tigua Indian tribe; travelers

FURTHER READING

Stoddard, Charles. *St. Anthony, the Wonder-Worker of Padua.* Rockford, Ill.: TAN Books and Publishers, 1992.

Antoninus (1389–1459) *Archbishop of Florence*
Also known as: Antonius, Antonino

Antoninus was born in Florence on March 1, 1389, the only child of Niccolo Pierozzi, a lawyer, and his wife Thomassina. He was baptized Antonius or Antonio, but because of his small size and gentle nature he was called by the diminutive "Antoninus" or "Antonino" all his life.

Supposedly a pious child, at age 15 Antoninus applied to Blessed John Dominic for admission to the Dominican Order. In 1404 Bl. John was at the Convent of Santa Maria Novella in Florence, but he was reforming the Dominican priories in the area and organizing a new house at Fiesole. Afraid that the frail Antoninus could not tolerate the vigorous austerities of the new monastery, Bl. John did not turn the boy down directly but told him to go home and memorize the *Decretum Gratiani,* or *Decrees of Gratian,* an enormous compilation of Church law. Determined, Antoninus returned in a year, the book entirely committed to memory, and was accepted. Along with Fra Angelico and Fra Benedetto (natural brothers: one the famous painter, the other a miniaturist), Antoninus spent his novitiate in Cortona, then returned to Fiesole, where he stayed until 1409.

A zealous reformer like Bl. John, Antoninus was named vicar of the convent at Foligno in 1414, then subprior and prior of the convent at Cortona. From 1418 to 1428 he served as prior of convents in Naples, Gaeta, Siena and Fiesole, and then was named prior of the convent at Minerva in Rome in 1430. From 1433 to 1446 he was superior of the reformed Tuscan and Neapolitan congregations, in which post he restored the primitive rules of the Dominican order. In 1439 Pope Eugenius IV summoned Antoninus to attend all sessions of the General Council of Florence.

Antoninus's greatest achievement was the foundation of the convent of St. Mark, or San Marco, in Florence, in buildings formerly owned by the Silvestrines. The monastery and adjoining church—generously supported by Cosimo de' Medici—became a center for Christian art and scholarship, housing a large library and gracefully redesigned by Michelozzo. The chapel frescoes were painted by Antoninus's old friend Fra Angelico, and his brother Benedetto decorated the choir books. Scenes from Antoninus's life adorn the cloisters.

Reportedly to Antoninus's dismay, his great talents for preaching, Church reform, scholarship and diplomacy led Pope Eugene IV (r. 1431–47) to name him archbishop of Florence in 1446. He tried to hide on the island of Sardinia to escape the post, but was consecrated at the pope's command on March 13, 1446. Less than a year later, Eugene asked Antoninus to administer the final sacraments to him before he died on February 23, 1447, in the archbishop's arms. Antoninus pursued his new duties with enthusiasm, visiting all the parishes of his diocese on foot each year, reforming clerical abuses, putting a stop to gambling, opposing usury and magic, and preaching, praying and writing. He was especially active in helping the poor, often emptying the church's pantries and storerooms and even selling furniture when there was nothing else to give. He nursed and comforted victims of the plague of 1448 and attempted to rebuild shelters for those made homeless in the earthquakes of 1453–55. Pope Nicholas V (r. 1447–55) frequently consulted him on both civil and ecclesiastical issues, valuing the archbishop's opinion so highly that he forbade any appeal to Rome of Antoninus's decisions. Nicholas V even went so far as to declare that Antoninus, in his lifetime, deserved sainthood as much as the dead Bernardine of Siena, whom the pope was about to canonize. Antoninus often served as a papal ambassador, and Pope Pius II named him to a commission charged with reforming the Roman curia. A distinguished theologian, Antoninus was one of the first Christian writers to acknowledge the changes in economics and society brought on by the Renaissance, teaching that money invested in commerce and industry was true capital, and that receiving interest on such investment was not usury and therefore morally lawful.

Antoninus died on May 2, 1459, at San Marco, and Pope Pius II (r. 1458–64) himself presided over the funeral. Cosimo de' Medici, not particularly fond of the Dominicans, frankly admitted that Florence would not have survived the dangers, natural catastrophes and seditious plots against it without the intercession of the archbishop. Antoninus's incorrupt body was moved to a new chapel at San Marco in 1559.

Canonized: May 31, 1523, by Pope Adrian VI
Feast: May 10
Patronage: fever sufferers

Apollonia (d. 249) *Deaconess and martyr*

Apollonia lived in Alexandria, Egypt, as a deaconess. Under Emperor Philip the Arabian and his successor Trajanus Decius, mobs roamed about Alexandria persecuting Christians. Apollonia, who was elderly, was snared by a mob. She refused to deny Christ. The mob tortured her, tearing out her teeth with pincers. They took her to a pyre and threatened to throw her on the fire. Apollonia answered by throwing herself into the flame.

The account of the life of Apollonia was written by St. Dionysius to Fabian, bishop of Antioch. In art she is depicted with a golden tooth at the end of her necklace, or with pincers holding a tooth.

Feast: February 9
Patronage: dentists, toothache sufferers

Arnulf of Metz (ca. 580–ca. 640) *Bishop and member of the Frankish court*
Also known as: Arnold, Arnulph

Arnulf was born to a distinguished Frankish family in Austrasia, the eastern section of the original kingdom established by the Merovingian king Clovis I. He studied under Gundulf, mayor of the palace under Austrasian king Theodebert II, and was so skilled that he became a trusted minister of the king and eventual head of six provinces. These palace mayors (*major domus*) actually ran the civil and military affairs of the kingdom; later Merovingian kings were mere figureheads. Arnulf married Lady Doda, and they had two sons: Anseghisel and Clodulf.

In 610, Arnulf planned to join the abbey of Lerins as a monk along with his friend Romaricus; Doda had already become a nun at Treves. But the episcopal see of Metz was vacant, and Arnulf was consecrated bishop in 611. He remained an officer and adviser at court, handling both civil and ecclesiastical business. In 613, following the death of Theodebert II, he and other nobles—principally Blessed Pepin of Landen—negotiated the installation of Clothaire II, king of Neustria, as king of Austrasia. Upon Clothaire II's death in 623, Arnulf served as the new king Dagobert I's tutor as well as chief minister. Arnulf wielded so much power that succeeding ministers were known as "Arnulfings."

By 626, Arnulf yearned for the monastic life and resigned his see. His son Clodulf eventually became the third bishop of Metz. Arnulf and his friend Romaricus, later St. Romaric, withdrew to a hermitage in the mountains at Vosges, where he lived until his death in 640. The hermitage later became the Remiremont monastery.

Arnulf's other son, Anseghisel, married St. Begga, daughter of the nobleman Pepin of Landen. Their son Pepin II of Heristal was the father of Charles Martel—Pippinid mayor of the palace under kings Chilperic II and Theuderic IV, sole ruler but not king of Austrasia from 737 to 741, grandfather of Charlemagne and founder of the Carolingian dynasty.

Feast: July 18
Patronage: brewers; millers; music; finding lost objects

Athanasius (d. 373) *Bishop; Father of the Church and Doctor of the Church*
Also known as: "Pillar of the Church," "Father of Orthodoxy" and "Champion of Christ's Divinity"

Athanasius was one of the greatest opponents of the heresy of Arianism, a movement under the popular priest, Arius, which denied the divinity of Christ and the eternal nature of the Word of God. He was born around 296–298 in Alexandria, Egypt, to prominent Christian parents. He was well educated under the eye of Alexander—who became bishop of the city—studying Greek philosophy and rhetoric and Christian doctrine. He learned theology from teachers who had been confessors under Maximian I. In 313, Alexander succeeded Achillas in the patriarchal see. In 315, Athanasius went to the desert to spend some time in retreat with St. Anthony.

In 318, Athanasius was ordained a deacon and became archdeacon and secretary to Alexander. He is thought to have written his first work at around this time: *De Incarnatione Verbi Dei,* which concerns the redemptive work of Christ. From 323 on, he spent much of his life combatting the Arian heresy. In 325, he attended the Council of Nicaea with Alexander, where his influence began to be felt. This important council set forth the true doctrine of the Church and the confession known as the Nicene Creed, and confirmed the excommunication of Arius.

Five months after the council, Alexander died. On his death bed he recommended Athanasius—still in his twenties—as his successor as bishop. In consequence of this, Athanasius was unanimously elected patriarch in 326.

His refusal to tolerate the Arian heresy was the cause of many trials and persecutions for Athanasius. In 330, Eusebius of Nicomedia, the Arian bishop, returned from exile and persuaded Emperor Constantine to allow Arians to take Communion. Athanasius refused to follow the order and was accused of crimes by the Arians, including treason and misuse of Church funds and property. He was tried and found innocent. He was then accused of killing a bishop. This was proved groundless, for the bishop was alive and in hiding. Athanasius refused to attend an Arian synod to discuss the charges. Summoned by Constantine to the Council of Tyre in Lebanon in 335, Athanasius had to face angry Arians who assembled there and again charged him with crimes.

The Arians succeeded in having Athanasius exiled to Trier, Germany, where he remained two and a half years. Meanwhile, Arius and Constantine died, and Athanasius returned to Alexandria in 338.

Eusebius of Nicomedia had him deposed again, and a usurper took his place (the people refused to acknowledge the usurper). Athanasius went to Rome to defend himself to Pope Julian I (r. 337–352). His opponents failed to appear and he was vindicated. After the usurper died in 345, Athanasius was restored to Alexandria. But he was condemned again by the Arians in the councils of Arles, France, in 353 and Milan, Italy, in 355. Even his church was attacked and members of his congregation were wounded.

Athanasius retreated to the desert in Egypt, spending six years as a hermit. There he wrote *Apology to Constantius; Apology for His Flight; Letter to the Monks;* and *History of the Arians.*

He returned to Alexandria on February 22, 362. Though welcomed by an enthusiastic crowd, he was exiled back to the desert by Emperor Julian the Apostate as "a disturber of the peace and an enemy of the gods." There he remained until the emperor died in 363. Athanasius enjoyed another eight months in Alexandria under Emperor Jovian, but was thrown out once again by Jovian's successor, Valens. He hid in his father's tomb for four months. Finally, Athanasius was restored permanently to his see. He had been banished five times and had spent 17 years in exile.

During his last years, he consolidated the doctrines of the Council of Nicaea and wrote the *Life of St. Anthony.* He died in Alexandria on May 2, 373. Later his remains were translated to Constantinople and then Venice.

The Athanasian Creed was not written by him but is drawn from his work. His other important writings are *Contra Gentes* and *De Incarnatione Verbi Dei.*

Feast: May 2

FURTHER READING
Early Christian Fathers: A Selection from the Writings of the Fathers from St. Clement of Rome to St. Athanasius. Tr. Henry Bettenson. London: Oxford University Press, 1969.
Gregory of Nazianzus, "Oration 21: On Athanasius of Alexandria." URL: http://www.fordham.edu/halsall/basis/gregnaz-athan/html. Downloaded September 24, 2000.

Augustine of Canterbury (d. 604 or 605) *Benedictine and first bishop of Canterbury, Apostle to England, Apostle to the Anglo-Saxons*
Also known as: Austin

Augustine was by all accounts a timid man, a librarian and monk. In 596, Pope St. Gregory the Great (r. 590–604) chose about 30 monks from St. Andrew Monastery on the Coelian Hill in Rome, led by their prior, Augustine, to serve in the first papal mission to

St. Augustine of Hippo (Library of Congress Prints and Photographs Division)

convert the pagans. The band traveled as far as Provence, in Gaul; but, terrified by tales of the Anglo-Saxons and the dangers of crossing the English Channel, the monks persuaded Augustine to return to Rome and beg His Holiness to end their mission. Gregory knew, however, that the Saxon king Aethelbert was married to a Christian princess, Bertha. He told Augustine that he had no choice but to go on to England. They landed on the Isle of Thanet off the coast of Kent in late 596 and were warmly welcomed by the king and queen, who gave Augustine a house in Canterbury and permission to preach. On Pentecost in 597, Augustine baptized King Aethelbert.

Augustine traveled back to France almost immediately to receive consecration as bishop of the English by St. Virgilius, metropolitan of Arles. Instead of establishing his see in London, Augustine chose Canterbury, the royal capital of Kent. He rebuilt an ancient church that served as the center of the cathedral and erected a monastery to SS. Peter and Paul outside the walls. The

present cathedral, begun in 1070, stands on the original site. Augustine also established episcopal sees at London and Rochester and dedicated the first church in England to St. Pancras.

Gregory I gave Augustine very specific instructions regarding the conversion of the English. Pagan temples were not to be destroyed but instead cleansed and consecrated for Christian worship. Local customs and festivals were to be retained, with substitutions of feast days for saints and martyrs whenever possible. Consequently, by 601 Augustine had converted many of the English people.

Converting the clergy to a unified liturgy proved a more difficult task. Unable to communicate effectively with the Church in Rome, the British Church had established its own patterns of worship and practice. Many also were unwilling to evangelize the Anglo-Saxons, whom they considered their enemies. A meeting failed miserably when Augustine supposedly failed to rise at the arrival of the British bishops. Deeming Augustine arrogant, the bishops would not accept him as metropolitan.

Discouraged and exhausted, Augustine died on May 26, 604 or 605. He was buried at the abbey of SS. Peter and Paul outside the Canterbury Cathedral. From then on, the monastery became known as St. Augustine's, and succeeding archbishops of the English Church were buried there. The archbishop of Canterbury remains the head of the Church of England and is described as occupying the "Chair of Augustine."

Feast: May 27 (May 28 on some calendars; May 26 in England and Wales)
Patronage: England

FURTHER READING
Cahill, Thomas. *How the Irish Saved Civilization.* New York: Nan A. Talese/Doubleday, 1995.

Augustine of Hippo (354–430) *Father of the Church, Doctor of the Church*
Also known as: Aurelius Augustinus, Doctor of Grace

Augustine of Hippo was one of the greatest figures in the Church. His philosophical and theological thought influenced Christianity and philosophy for at least 1,000 years. His early years were spent in sin, which he later chronicled with great frankness in his remarkable work, *Confessions.*

Augustine was born November 13, 354, in Tagaste, North Africa. His mother, St. Monica, was Christian, and his father Patricius was a pagan, whom Monica eventually converted by her patience and good example. He was not baptized as an infant, but his mother enrolled him as a catechumen in the Catholic

Church. He studied Latin and Greek grammar and literature in his boyhood, complaining about rough treatment by his schoolmasters.

After his father died in 370, Augustine went to Carthage to study rhetoric as the first step to prepare for a public life. There he met a young woman at a church service, began to live with her and fathered a son named Adeodatus ("God's gift"). With adolescence, he confides to God in *Confessions*, "both love and lust boiled within me, and swept my youthful immaturity over the precipice of evil desires to leave me half drowned in a whirlpool of abominable sins. . . . my soul was sick, and broke out in sores, whose itch I agonized to scratch with the rub of carnal things," including stage plays, "with the mirror they held up to my own miseries and the fuel they poured on my flame."

Augustine was still making those judgments 20 years later. But, during the years in Carthage, he was probably embroiled in tensions set in motion by conflicting explanations of the human condition by his mother and his father's behavior (his father being guilty of marital infidelities) and religions. This tension was also at the base of the Manichaean religion, which Augustine joined in 373. The Manichees taught that there are two supreme gods, one good and one evil, and similarly two competing souls within the human person. For nine years he maintained interest in this cult. After his move to Rome in 383 to teach a better class of rhetoric students, he was the guest of a Manichee and socialized with many prominent members of the sect.

The next year, 384, he won an appointment as a professor of rhetoric in Milan. Within two years he abandoned Manichaeanism and gradually came under the influence of his Christian mentors: Ambrose, the influential local bishop, and Simplicianus, a wise elderly former bishop. At the same time, he wanted to advance himself in position and possessions, so marriage seemed the next step. His mother had joined him and helped him to arrange a marriage to a girl who was not yet 12, so he agreed to wait two years. Augustine's mistress of many years had to leave him as part of this marriage plan, which threw Augustine into emotional turmoil. "My heart which had held her very dear was broken and wounded and shed blood," he wrote. "She went back to Africa, swearing that she would never know another man, and left with me the natural son I had of her. . . . I was simply a slave of lust. So I took another woman, not of course as a wife; and thus my soul's disease was kept alive as vigorously as ever." He was tormented both by the loss of his former lover and the hopelessness for him of a life of continence, which

ran in circles alongside his growing seriousness in reexamining Christianity.

In *Confessions,* he tells how he experienced a striking conversion while in a garden, in which his self-doubt was expelled and "the light of utter confidence shone in all my heart." His mother was exultant. Augustine decided to give up his teaching position and was baptized along with his son Adeodatus and another close friend on Easter of 387. About a year later the group was at the port of Ostia on their way home to Africa when Monica died. She and Augustine had shared an ecstatic experience five days previously, after which she had told him that all her prayers had been answered in superabundance and she no longer hoped for anything in this world.

When Augustine finally returned in 388 to Tagaste in North Africa, he set up a sort of monastery on his family land with his close friends. His son Adeodatus died within a year, aged 16. (In *Confessions*, Augustine reveals his love for his son, crediting God entirely for the boy's many virtues and intelligence. He notes that his book *De Magistro* is a dialogue between the two, and "that all the ideas . . . put into his mouth were truly his, though he was but sixteen.") Augustine soon gave away his possessions, and for the rest of his life lived simply as a monk in community with men.

In 391 he was ordained a priest in Hippo by Bishop Valerius, who permitted Augustine to preach almost immediately. Upon Valerius's death in 396, Augustine became bishop of Hippo, and was to serve there for 35 years. He composed the Rule that the Augustinian Order follows to this day. In the 390s he started a convent for women following the Rule. He preached almost daily, and wrote incessantly: theological treatises, letters, polemics against heresies, the *Confessions* (finished in 400), and *The City of God,* written in installments between 413 and 426. He died on August 28, 430, while the city of Hippo was under siege by the Vandals. In 700, his remains were taken to the church of St. Pietro in Ciel d'Oro, Italy.

When Augustine was about 72, he sat down to review his writings and put them in chronological order, and was astounded at the quantity. His complete works, written in Latin, are about the size of an encyclopedia. Generations of scholars have consulted Augustine. The *Confessions* is not only his intimate spiritual autobiography, but it is also a presentation of the writer's mystical experiences during his spiritual struggle to accept Christianity. However, it is not a mystical work in the sense of a contemplative introspection or poetic reflection; rather it is an expression of what has been called Augustine's "mysticism of action."

The City of God is, in the words of Thomas Merton, "the autobiography of the Catholic Church." When Rome was sacked by the Goths under Alaric in 410, many intellectuals made accusations that Christianity had debilitated the empire, exhausted and made it vulnerable to attack. *The City of God* is Augustine's response. His defense of Christian doctrine was informed by politics and history, full of direct references to pagan philosophers from Plato to his contemporaries.

Augustine said that the fall of the earthly city of Rome was the inevitable result of the sinful wills of its rulers and citizens; at the same time the rise of the City of God (the Catholic Church) was a process that had begun before time and was infused with grace, personified by Jesus Christ. This concept of the two cities is eloquently summarized in a famous passage from Book XIV: "Two loves have built two cities: the love of self, which reaches even to contempt for God, the earthly City; and the love of God, which reaches even to contempt for self, the heavenly City. One glories in itself, the other in the Lord. One seeks its own glory amongst men; the greatest glory of the other is God, witness of its conscience. One, swollen with pride, uplifts its haughty head; the other cries out to God with the Psalmist: 'Thou art my glory, it is Thou who dost lift up my head.'" Augustine shows in Books XI and XII how the good and bad angels had inaugurated the two cities on the basis of the two loves.

Augustine believed that the soul by its nature is the equal of an angel's, and any inferiority is due to sin. By emulating the ways of angels, humans have the capacity to change into angelic form and join the City of God. These and other views about the soul and the restoration of its original status are discussed in other works.

Augustine vigorously defended Catholicism against various heresies, stating that pagan religion and magic were inventions of the devil to tempt people away from Christianity. He said that error had no rights; therefore, heretics had no rights.

The tension in the will that characterized Augustine's early life became the base of his theology, which, because of his great influence, became the core of Christian doctrine. It is in his later works that Augustine becomes more philosophically theological. His references to mystical experience appear in *Confessions* and in *The City of God*. In the latter, he said of experiences of the supernatural: "When . . . we hear with the inner ear some part of the speech of God, we approximate to the angels. But in this work I need not labor to give an account of the ways in which God speaks. For either the unchangeable Truth speaks directly to the mind of the rational creature in some indescribable way, or speaks through the changeable creature, either presenting spiritual images to our spirit, or bodily voices to our bodily sense."

Augustine usually is acknowledged to be second only to St. Paul in influence on Christianity. His writings established the theological foundation for medieval Christianity, and much later influenced the dualistic philosophy of René Descartes.

Roman Catholic religious orders and congregations called Augustinians trace a spiritual lineage to Augustine, but date their actual origins only from the 10th and later centuries. The young Martin Luther (1483–1546) was an Augustinian.

Feast: August 28
Patronage: Augustinians; brewers, printers, theologians, Carthage

FURTHER READING
Augustine. *The City of God.* Tr. Marcus Dods, George Wilson and J. J. Smith; intro. Thomas Merton. New York: Modern Library, 1950.
Augustine. *Confessions.* Tr. F. J. Sheed. New York: Sheed and Ward, 1943, 1970.
Battenhouse, Roy W., ed. *A Companion to the Study of St. Augustine.* New York: Oxford University Press, 1955.
Bourke, Vernon J. *Wisdom from St. Augustine.* St. Thomas, Texas: Center for Thomistic Studies, 1984.
Brown, Peter. *Augustine of Hippo.* Berkeley: University of California Press, 1967.

Balbina (d. ca. 130) *Martyr; Roman nun and daughter of the Blessed Quirinus, martyr*

According to the legendary *Acts of Sts. Peter and Balbina*, Balbina was baptized by Pope St. Alexander I (r. 105–115). She was martyred and was buried near her father in the Praetextus catacomb on the Via Appia of Rome. Her relics were later enshrined in St. Balbina's Church on the Aventine.

Feast: March 31
Patronage: Scrofulous diseases, struma

Barbara (d. fourth century) *Legendary martyr of enduring popularity, despite the suppression of her cult in 1969*
Name meaning: Stranger

William Caxton's version of *The Golden Legend* tells Barbara's story, which is probably entirely fictitious. She was not known prior to the seventh century. Her story spread in the ninth century, and by the Middle Ages she was one of the most popular of all saints.

According to lore, Barbara was the daughter of a rich Greek man, Dioscorus. Because of her great beauty, he kept her imprisoned in a high tower. Princes still sought her hand in marriage, but she refused, saying she did not want to marry anyone. She spent her time in prayer and study.

While Dioscorus was away on a long trip, Barbara descended from the tower to look at a bathhouse her father had under construction. She was dismayed that it had only two windows, and persuaded workmen to make a third window to honor the Trinity. Barbara lived in the bathhouse and was secretly baptized by a priest. She ate only honeysuckles and locusts, following the example set by St. John the Baptist.

She returned to the tower, where she received the Holy Ghost and other graces. She disfigured all the pagan idols in the tower.

Upon his return, her father was enraged. He tried to kill her with a sword, but she prayed (and perhaps became entranced) and was taken to a mountain, where two shepherds saw her fly. Dioscorus then seized her by the hair, drew her down from the mountain and had her thrown in prison. He denounced her before the civil tribunal. She refused to recant and was severely scourged and beaten. She endured the torture with the help of comforting visions of the Lord. The judge ordered her killed by the sword.

Dioscorus took her to a mountain and killed her; she received her martyrdom along with St. Juliana (perhaps Juliana of Cumae). Her father immediately was slain by fire from heaven (probably a lightning bolt), and his body was reduced to ashes.

St. Barbara (Library of Congress Prints and Photographs Division)

A nobleman named Valentine buried the bodies of Barbara and Juliana in a little town where many miracles were then reported.

Different versions of the legend of Barbara give various places and times of her martyrdom: Tuscany, Rome, Antioch, Heliopolis and Nicomedia, where Juliana of Cumae reportedly was martyred.

Barbara is invoked against fire, lightning, sudden death and impenitence. In art she is depicted holding a tower or the palm of martyrdom. She is one of the Fourteen Holy Helpers.

Feast: formerly December 4
Patronage: ammunition workers; architects; builders; dying; fire prevention; founders; gunners; miners; prisoners; stonemasons

Barnabas (d. ca. 61) *Apostle, martyr and patron of St. Paul*

Barnabas was not one of the original apostles of Jesus, but was named so by the apostles after he converted from Judaism (he was a Levite) to Christianity in Jerusalem.

He was born Joses Justus on Cyprus. Upon his conversion, he sold his property and gave the money to the Apostles. He persuaded the Christians in Jerusalem to accept Paul as a disciple. He went to Antioch, Syria, and brought Paul there from Tarsus. Barnabas, his cousin, John Mark, and Paul went on missions in Cyprus and Perga. John Mark left them, and Barnabas and Paul went on to Antioch in Pisidia and to Iconium, Lystria and Lycaonia (present-day Turkey). They were severely persecuted in Pisidion Antioch; and in Lycaonia they were welcomed as gods but then literally stoned out of the city. They returned to Antioch in Syria. Barnabas and Paul went to a council in Jerusalem, but fell out with each other upon their return to Syrian Antioch. Barnabas wished to have John Mark travel with them again, but Paul objected because John Mark had not stayed with them on their previous journey.

Barnabas returned to Cyprus with John Mark. Little is known about the rest of his life. He is said to have preached in Rome and Alexandria. Legend holds that he was stoned to death in Salamis, Greece, in A.D. 61.

His grave was discovered in 485 or 486, and his remains were taken to Constantinople (now Istanbul) by Emperor Zeno. Some of his remains were distributed to Milan, Edenna, Pavia, Genoa, Cremona, Naples, Cologne, Bologna, Florence, Prague, Namur, Tournai and Toulouse.

Barnabas is invoked against hailstorms, arguments and grief. His name is first in Eucharistic prayers. He is described in the Acts of the Apostles. Historians have established that he is not the author of the apocryphal epistle of Barnabas or the gospel of Barnabas. The Acts of Barnabas, supposedly written by John Mark, actually were composed much later, in the fifth century.

SS. Paul, center, *and Barnabas,* right

Feast: June 11
Patronage: missionary labors; weavers; Florence; Milan

Bartholomew the Apostle (first century) *One of the Twelve Disciples of Jesus; martyr*
Also known as: Nathanael bar Tolomai, Nathaniel

Bartholomew was a native of Cana who was introduced to Jesus by St. Philip and was called to the Apostolate, but beyond that nothing certain is known about him. He is described in various traditions as having preached in Mesopotamia, Persia, Egypt, Lycaonia, Phrygia, Armenia, and on the shores of the Black Sea.

Bartholomew is believed to have died at Albanopolis, Armenia, martyred on the order of Astyges for having converted his brother, Polymius, King of Armenia. According to the Roman Martyrology, he was flayed alive and beheaded, though other accounts say he was flayed and then crucified head-down. His relics are thought to have been interred on the island of Lipara, whence they were translated to Benevento, Italy, and later to Rome. They rest today in the Church of St. Bartholomew-on-the-Tiber. In the 11th century, King Canute's wife, Queen Emma, is said to have presented one of his arms to the cathedral at Canterbury in England.

Bartholomew's symbol is a tanner's knife. In art, he is represented as a bearded man holding a book or a tanner's knife and a human skin. Sometimes the skin he holds is his own.

Feast: August 24 (in Rome); August 25 (in Echternach and Cambrai); June 11 (in the East); June 13 (in Persia)
Patronage: bookbinders; butchers; cobblers; cornchandlers; dyers; glovers; Florentine salt and cheese merchants; furriers; leather workers; against nervous diseases; plasterers; shoemakers; tailors, tanners; trappers; against twitching; vinegrowers; whiteners; Armenia

Basil the Great (ca. 329–379) *One of the greatest Doctors of the Church, Father of the Church, Bishop of Caesarea*

Basil the Great was born in Caesarea, Cappadocia (now in Turkey), around 329 to a Christian family. His grandparents had suffered under Christian persecutions and spent several years in exile living in the harsh and wild mountains of Pontus. St. Basil the Elder, Basil the Great's father, was a teacher. He married a martyr, Emmelia; the couple had 10 children. Besides Basil, his sister Macrina and brothers Gregory of Nyssa and Peter of Sebaste became saints. Basil, Gregory, and Basil's friend St. Gregory of Nazianzus the Younger became known as the "Three Cappadocians," of whom Basil earned the highest esteem.

Basil received religious instruction in the tradition of St. Gregory Thaumaturgus from his grandmother, St. Macrina the Elder. The family moved to Macrina's estate on the River Iris after Basil the Elder died, when young Basil was still but a boy. After school in Caesarea, where Basil was instructed by Bishop Dianius, he was sent to Constantinople and Athens to study. He met Gregory of Nazianzus, and the two became close friends.

When he had completed his studies, Basil returned to Caesarea and was baptized and ordained Reader by Dianius. He was furthered influenced toward a spiritual life by his sister, Macrina, who had founded a religious community on the family estate with their mother. Basil visited monasteries in Egypt, Palestine,

St. Bartholomew (Engraving by Albrecht Dürer, 1523)

St. Basil the Great (Library of Congress Prints and Photographs Division)

Coele-Syria and Mesopotamia, gaining the inspiration for his own monastery, which he founded in 356 in Pontus, near Macrina's community. He composed a rule and thus became known as the father of Eastern monasticism, much the same as St. Benedict is regarded as the father of Western monasticism.

When Dianius died in 362, Eusebius was named his successor as bishop with the help of the elder Gregory of Nazianzus. Eusebius persuaded Basil to be ordained priest and gave him administrative duties. Basil was far more competent than Eusebius and their relationship deteriorated. Basil returned to Pontus, but was summoned back to Caesarea by Gregory of Nazianzus in 365 to combat the Arian heresy. Basil essentially ran the diocese without interference from Eusebius. He demonstrated superb administrative ability and was not afraid of powerful people. He also devoted much time and attention to the poor.

With the help of the elder Gregory, Basil became the bishop of Caesarea in 370, a position that enabled him to wield great power. He laid down the law, required spiritual discipline, settled disputes and vigorously opposed heresy. He was a formidable statesman and opponent, and incurred the wrath of Emperor Valens (r. 364–378), who favored Arianism and persecuted Basil.

In 373, a series of setbacks and sufferings began for Basil: In that year, his key friend and supporter, St. Athanasius, died, followed by Gregory of Nazianzus the Elder in 374. Basil also became estranged from his good friend, Gregory of Nazianzus the Younger. He had known enemies and lost ground to the Arians. A schism was erupting in the Church. His health was failing, and invading Goths threatened the empire. Pope Damasus (r. 366–384) suspected him of heresy, and St. Jerome accused him of pride.

Basil died on January 1, 379. His death was mourned by Christians, Jews and pagans alike. The honorific "the Great" was appended to his name posthumously. His relics were not mentioned until the 12th century, when parts of his body and other relics allegedly were brought to Bruges by a Crusader. In the 16th century, the Naples Oratory was given a relic sent from Constantinople to the pope.

Despite the setbacks in the latter part of his life, Basil left a lasting imprint on the Church. He was responsible for the victory of Nicene orthodoxy over Arianism in the East. Arianism was denounced at the Council of Constantinople in 381–382, thanks largely to his influence.

Basil wrote important works on dogma, especially defending the Divinity of the Three Persons of the Trinity; commentaries on the Scriptures; treatises on morals and monastic rules; and sermons. Some of his works have been lost. Three hundred and sixty-six of his letters survive. He either composed a liturgy or reformed an existing one; several Eastern liturgies have been attributed to him.

Feast: January 2
Patronage: hospital administrators; Order of St. Basil

FURTHER READING
The Fathers Speak: St. Basil the Great, St. Gregory of Nazianzus, St. Gregory of Nyssa. Georges Barrois, trans. and ed. Crestwood, N.Y.: St. Vladimir's Seminary Press, 1986.
Nicene and Post-Nicene Fathers, Series 2: St. Basil. Philip Schaff and Henry Wace, eds. Grand Rapids, Mich.: William B. Eerdmans Publishing Co., 1988.

Beatrix da Silva (1424–1490) *Cistercian abbess*
Also known as: Brites, Beatrice da Silva

Beatrix da Silva was born in Portugal in 1424 to a noble family with ties to royalty. She accompanied Isabel of Portugal to the court of Spain. She joined the Cistercian convent of Santo Domingo de Silos in

Toledo, and founded the Congregational of the Immaculate Conception.

Beatified: 1926 by Pius XI
Canonized: 1976 by Paul VI
Feast: August 16
Patronage: prisoners

Bede the Venerable (b. 672 or 673–d. 735) *Doctor of the Church and historian*

A scholarly man and one of the most learned of his time, Bede compiled meticulous historical records recounting the development of Christianity in his native England from Roman times to his own lifetime. Though he wrote extensively on many famous church figures, he had little to say about himself. Few details of his life are known. At the end of his great work, the five-volume *Ecclesiastical History of the English People,* he added only a paragraph about himself.

Bede was born in 672 or 673 in the area of Wearmouth-Jarrow, Northumberland, England. At the age of seven, he was taken by his relatives to the nearby monastery of SS. Peter and Paul and given over to the care of the abbot St. Benedict Biscop, and later to Abbot Ceolfrid. Bede spent the rest of his life at the monastery, occasionally traveling to visit friends. He devoted himself to the study of the Scriptures, observed monastic discipline and took part in the daily singing.

Bede was ordained deacon at age 19 and priest at age 30. Both ordinations were performed by Bishop John (later St. John of Beverly). From the time of his priesthood, Bede spent most of his time in study and writing. He seems to have enjoyed a peaceful and productive life. He was well regarded and loved by his peers.

He studied and wrote right up to the day of his death. During his final illness, his disciples—who included St. Cuthbert—read aloud by his bedside. On the day of Bede's death, the vigil of the Ascension in 735, he dictated a translation of the Gospel of St. John. He died sitting on the floor of his cell singing, "Glory be to the Father and to the Son and to the Holy Ghost."

Within two generations of his death, the honorific *Venerabilis* (the Venerable) was used in conjunction with his name. The title was officially bestowed in 835 by the Council of Aachen. Throughout the Middle Ages, a cult of Bede was maintained in northern England. In 1899 Bede was declared a Doctor of the Church, the only English person to hold that title.

His most important work, *Ecclesiastical History of the English People,* completed in 729, has remained through the centuries one of the most authoritative sources for historians of that time period. In his preface, addressed to King Ceolwulph, Bede said he was encouraged to undertake the writing by Abbot Albinus, who had been educated at the Church of Canterbury and who gave him considerable help. *Ecclesiastical History* was translated into Anglo-Saxon upon the orders of King Alfred, and was translated and published in Europe.

Bede wrote other chronological treatises, biographies, a description of Jerusalem and other holy places, a martyrology, works on science and numerous commentaries on books of the Bible. He also wrote verse and composed chant music. He is credited with initiating the custom of marking dates from the Incarnation with the term Anno Domini, or A.D.

Declared Doctor of the Church: November 13, 1899, by Pope Leo XIII
Feast: May 27
Patronage: scholars

FURTHER READING
Bede. *Ecclesiastical History of the English Nation.* URL: http://www.fordham.edu/halsall/basis/bede-book1.html. Downloaded: February 10, 2000.

Benedict (ca. 480–ca. 547) *Father of Western monasticism and founder of the Benedictines*
Name meaning: "Blessed"
Also known as: Benedict of Nursia

Benedict was born ca. 480 in the Sabine town of Nursia. As a youth he was attracted to the art of rhetoric, and was sent to Rome to be educated. He was so revolted by the licentiousness of the city that he and his nurse fled to Enfide, a village about 30 miles away. After a time Benedict then went to a remote place now called Subiaco, where he encountered a monk, Romanus, who led him to a cave. Here Benedict became a hermit, at about age 14, and spent three years living in the cave. Romanus brought him bread every day, which Benedict raised by rope to his cave.

While at Subiaco, Benedict was violently attacked one day by a black bird, which he sent off by making a sign of the cross. He knew he was under attack by Satan and was seized with a temptation against holy purity. To conquer it, he undressed and rolled himself several times in thorn bushes. His remedy worked, and he said throughout his life that he never again experienced such an attack on his purity. The thorn bushes became celebrated and were regarded as relics. His act inspired many later saints to mortify themselves whenever they felt themselves tempted or demonically assailed.

In about 525, Benedict went to Monte Cassino and destroyed the temple to Apollo at its top. In its place, he established ca. 530 the first structures of a monastery that would become the most famous in the world, the birthplace of Western monasticism. The monastery attracted a large following of disciples, as well as Church officials from Rome and Capua, who came to consult Benedict for his wisdom and prophetic powers.

At about this time, he probably wrote his famous *Regula Monachorum,* called the Rule (also Benedict's Rule or the Benedictine Rule), a monastic rule that became the standard for monastic living throughout the Western world. The Rule calls for a year of probation, a vow of obedience to a single abbot or abbess, moderate asceticism, and work and prayer (*ora et labora* became a motto of the Benedictines). Benedict's rule was influenced by, and passages were accommodated from, the *Rule of the Master,* a monastic document also dating from the sixth century but not as spiritual, personal and broad as Benedict's Rule.

Benedict expanded his activities beyond the monastery to the surrounding population, curing the sick, distributing alms and food, and providing aid and counseling. It is alleged that he raised the dead on at least several occasions. Benedict's tunic, of which he had just one, was reported to give off a fragrance sweeter than all the perfumes of India, as did Benedict himself.

His twin sister, St. Scholastica, settled nearby and pursued a religious life.

Benedict foretold his own death six days in advance, and instructed his monks to dig a grave in secret. As soon as the task was accomplished, he fell ill with fever and deteriorated. On the sixth day, he instructed his monks to carry him into the oratory, where he took Communion. In his final moments, he stood, supported by monks, and died with his hands raised in prayer.

The remains of Benedict and Scholastica—who had died some months earlier—were buried on Monte Cassino. One story holds that they were removed to Fleury, France, in 703. Another holds that they were unearthed at Monte Cassino during the World War II bombing.

Benedict was named a patron of Europe by Pope Paul VI in 1964.

The only source for documenting Benedict's life is *The Dialogues* by Pope St. Gregory the Great (r. 590–604). Gregory offers the following description of one of Benedict's mystical experiences:

> . . . . In the dead of night he [Benedict] suddenly beheld a flood of light shining down from above more brilliant

St. Benedict (copyright © Robert Michael Place. Used with permission)

Centuries later, in 1223, St. Francis of Assisi visited the cave. According to one story, he grafted rose bushes onto the thorn bushes. Another story says he blessed the thorn bushes, converting them into roses, which had healing properties to the pilgrims who visited the site.

Benedict's solitude eventually came to an end. His sanctity and alleged miraculous powers began to attract followers. Benedict organized them into 12 monasteries of 12 monks each, and each under a prior. He exercised supreme rule over all. The Subiaco monastic community became a permanent settlement, but Benedict at some point left abruptly, allegedly because another priest, Florentius, attempted to undermine him.

than the sun, and with it every trace of darkness cleared away. Another remarkable sight followed. According to his own description, the whole world was gathered up before his eyes in what appeared to be a single ray of light. As he gazed at all this dazzling display, he saw the soul of Germanus, the bishop of Capua, being carried by angels up to heaven in a ball of fire.

Many marvels and miracles were attributed to Benedict. He could move stones too heavy for others to lift. According to Gregory, his sanctity enabled a pupil, Maurus, to walk on water in order to rescue a drowning child. Benedict manifested money for a man in debt. Peregrinus, a Catholic layman, appealed to Benedict for help in relieving his great debt. Benedict told him to return in three days. Meanwhile, he prayed. When Peregrinus returned, they went to inspect a store of grain, where they found 13 gold coins. Benedict told him to take 12 for his debt and spend the 13th however he chose.

Benedict also is said to have multiplied flour and oil to feed his monks, thus demonstrating the power of faith. When the monks had difficulty finding water, Benedict prayed and water was found at that spot.

The saint had powers of prophecy, and foresaw the downfall of his own monastery. In 590, the Lombards invaded and destroyed it, forcing the monks to flee. The monastery was rebuilt, but was damaged by Saracen invaders in 883 and by an earthquake in 1349. The monastery was bombed to ruins during World War II, but was lavishly reconstructed.

The Order of Saint Benedict (O.S.B.) is the oldest order of monks in the West; for over five centuries it was the only monastic order in the West and greatly influenced the spread of civilization in the Middle Ages. During the Middle Ages, Benedictines were called the Black Monks, referring to the color of their habit. There are Benedictine monasteries worldwide today in Roman Catholic and Anglican churches, housing not only Benedictines but also Carthusians, Cistercians, Trappists and other related orders.

The Benedictine Rule continues to be one of the most important documents of Christian religious practice, and has been interpreted for, and applied to, the lay life as well as the monastic life. The Rule reflects what Benedict learned and understood about the power of words—and thus the power of the Word of God.

Central to Benedict's structure was daily prayer. His prayer of the Divine Office, chanted several times daily from the breviary, required all work to stop. If monks were out in the fields, they had to stop whatever they were doing, kneel and pray at the specified times. The Divine Office is considered the prayer of the Catholic Church.

Benedict also required the study of Scriptures (*lectio divinia*) as another way to pray the Word of God, and one that would especially harmonize the mind and heart. Four to six hours were set aside in the monastery for monks to read, memorize and repeat passages that seized the monks with inspiration. The idea was to allow the meaning of the words to penetrate the heart and become part of the person, finally losing all meaning except the power of the Word of God. At this point the monks surrendered to contemplation in the presence of God that was beyond intellectual understanding.

Feast: July 11 (Western Church), March 14 (Eastern Church)

Patronage: against poisoning; against witchcraft; speleologists; Europe

FURTHER READING

Chittister, Joan. *Wisdom Distilled from the Daily: Living the Rule of St. Benedict Today.* San Francisco: HarperSan Francisco, 1991.

Gregory the Great. *The Dialogues,* Book Two. Indianapolis: Bobbs-Merrill, 1967.

Happold, F. C. *Mysticism: A Study and an Anthology,* rev. ed. Harmondsworth, Middlesex, England: Penguin Books, 1970.

Benedict II (d. 685) *Pope*

The date of Benedict's birth is not known. He was a native of Rome, the son of John. As a youth, he was active in Church affairs. He was ordained a priest and became a respected scholar of the Scriptures and an expert in sacred chants. He was distinguished further by his humility, his generosity, and his love for the poor.

Benedict was elected to the Chair of St. Peter to succeed Pope St. Leo II (r. 682–683) upon the latter's death in June 683, though he was not consecrated until June 26 of the following year.

The delay in Benedict's consecration was due to the wait for the traditional approval of the emperor. The consecrations of Leo II and several other of his predecessors had been delayed for the same reason. In order to prevent this from happening again, Benedict sought and obtained a decree from Emperor Constantine Pogonatus (Constantine the Bearded) that abolished the practice of imperial confirmation.

During his brief reign, Benedict was an active head of the Church throughout Europe. He opposed the Monothelitism heresy and worked to bring several Spanish bishops in line with his views. He was also one of several popes to support the Englishman, St. Wilfred of York, who was trying to return to his see after having been forced out by St. Theodore. Benedict was also energetic in his support of the Church of Rome, restoring several churches and supporting the clergy and lay sacristans.

Benedict died on May 8, 685, and was laid to rest in St. Peter's.

Feast: May 8

Benedict XI (1240–1304) *Dominican monk and pope*
Also known as: Nicholas Boccasini

There is much uncertainty concerning the childhood of the man who came to be known as Pope Benedict XI. He was born in Treviso, Italy, in 1240, as Nicholas Baccasini. His father was either a poor shepherd or an impoverished nobleman; he died while Nicholas was young, and the boy was put in the charge of an uncle who was a priest in Treviso.

Since Nicholas proved to be highly intelligent, his uncle had him trained in Latin and other clerical subjects. When he was 10, he began acting as a tutor to noble children, a vocation he followed for four years, then entered the Dominican monastery at Venice. As a monk, he continued his teaching career, primarily in Venice and Bologna. In 1295, he received a master's degree in theology. He also became involved in administrative affairs, for a while serving as the Dominican prior general for Lombardy; in 1296 he was elected the order's ninth master general.

Nicholas was a strong supporter of Pope Boniface VIII (r. 1294–1303), widely unpopular for his treatment of his predecessor, Pope St. Celestine V (r. 1294). Nicholas issued a general ordinance forbidding Dominicans to show any favor to Boniface's opponents and enjoined them to defend the legitimacy of Boniface's election in their sermons. Boniface rewarded this loyalty by sending Nicholas on papal missions and, in 1298, by appointing him bishop of Ostia and dean of the Sacred College of Cardinals. Dominicans hastened to Rome to protest these appointments, only to hear from the pope a prophecy that God had reserved an even greater burden for Nicholas.

Nicholas stood by Boniface even in 1303, when forces unfriendly to him captured the Lateran Palace. Troops under King Philip the Fair of France's counselor William of Nogaret then besieged the pope in the castle of Anagni, whence he had fled, and demanded that he abdicate the papal throne. The soldiers stormed the house, where they were met by the pope and Nicholas, along with one other supporter, the cardinal-bishop of Sabina. For a time it seemed that all would die, but Nicholas succeeded in rallying the pope's forces, and they were rescued. Nevertheless,

Boniface had suffered much, and he died a short while later.

The Sacred College met on October 22, 1303, and elected Nicholas as Boniface's successor, thus fulfilling the latter's prophecy concerning the former. Assuming the name Benedict XI, Nicholas immediately set about making peace with Philip the Fair. He absolved the king and his subjects of censures Boniface had placed on them. However, he excommunicated William and summoned him to appear before his tribunal.

Benedict died suddenly at Perugia on July 7, 1304, after a reign of only eight months. It was thought that he had been poisoned by William, though this was never proved. Miracles at his intercession were reported even before his burial, and continued thereafter at his tomb. He is venerated especially in Perugia, though his feast is celebrated in Rome and throughout the Dominican order.

In art, Benedict is depicted as wearing a Dominican habit and papal tiara, while holding the keys.

Beatified: 1733 by Pope Clement XII
Feast: July 7

Benedict Biscop (ca. 628–ca. 690) *Benedictine abbot*
Name meaning: Blessed

A monastic founder, Benedict Biscop was born John Biscop Baducing ca. 628 in England to a family of Anglo-Saxon nobility that had close ties to the court of King Oswy of Northumbria. He spent much of his youth at court, serving the king as a warrior.

In 653, at age 25, Biscop was inspired to make the first of five pilgrimages to Rome with St. Wilfrid. His trips inspired him to become a monk and bring Roman elements of worship, including rituals and chant, to England. After his return to Britain, Biscop traveled again to Rome with Alcfrith, the son of Oswy. After his return in 666, he took the habit and was tonsured at St.-Honorat at Lérins, where he took the monastic name Benedict.

He made a third trip to Rome where he quickly found favor with Pope Vitalian, who in 668 sent him to serve as adviser to Theodore of Tarsus, archbishop of Canterbury. Theodore appointed Benedict abbot of SS. Peter and Paul monastery in Canterbury (now St. Augustine's). In 671 he resigned the post in order to make another pilgrimage to Rome.

On a fourth trip to Rome in 679, he assured Pope Agatho of the orthodoxy of the English Church. On this and his last two pilgrimages, he collected numerous relics, books and paintings. Many of these were given to two Benedictine monasteries he founded in England: Wearmouth in 674 and Jarrow in 682. He also introduced the teaching of Gregorian chant and the Divine Rule in these monasteries, under the direction of Abbot John of Rome. He is credited with introducing stone churches and glass church windows to England.

Benedict was paralyzed for the last three years of his life. He became a mentor to St. Bede the Venerable, who wrote his biography. Benedict died on January 12, c. 690. Around 980, his relics were translated from Wearmouth to Thorney. Glastonbury also claims his relics.

Feast: January 12
Patronage: musicians, painters

Benedict Joseph Labre (1748–1783) *Pilgrim recluse known for his sanctity, austerity and miracles of intervention*
Also known as: the "Beggar of Rome"

Benedict Joseph Labre was born in Amettes, France, on March 25, 1748, the oldest of 18 children. At an early age he showed great interest in austerity and mortification. His uncle was a parish priest in Erin, France, and at age 12 Benedict went to study with him for six years. He earnestly desired a religious life, but his parents did not approve. After his uncle died in 1766, he renewed his efforts to join an order and his parents acquiesced. He was rejected by the Trappists. He spent a brief six weeks as postulant with the Carthusians. He received permission to enter the Cistercian abbey of Sept-Fonts, but after a short stay his health failed, and he left.

Benedict was inspired to live like St. Alexis and be neither in a cloister nor in the wilderness, but simply be a pilgrim to the famous shrines of Christendom. Thus, he set out through Europe in 1770. He had only the clothes on his back, a rosary, a crucifix, a Testament, breviary, a copy of the *Imitation of Christ* and a few other books. If he could not find food in the wild or was not given any, he rummaged through garbage heaps.

In 1774 he settled in Rome. He became known for his devotion to the Blessed Sacrament, his attendance of the Forty Hours devotion and his ecstasies. Once he was seen levitating in a kneeling position while he prayed at the Church of Gesu in Rome. According to his biography (written by his confessor, Marconi), witnesses were amazed but the sacristan, who had seen it before, was not, and calmly continued his sweeping.

His body finally gave out from his austerity and mortification. He collapsed on April 16, 1783, on the steps of the Church of Santa Maria dei Monti in Rome and was carried to a nearby house, where he died.

Immediately miracles were attributed to his intervention. Marconi documented 136 such cases.

Declared Venerable: 1859 by Pope Pius IX
Canonized: 1883 by Pope Leo XIII
Feast: April 16
Patronage: beggars; the homeless; religious orders; toy makers

Benevenuto Scotivoli of Osimo (d. 1282) *Franciscan bishop*

Benevenuto Scotivoli of Osimo was born in Ancona, Italy. He studied law at Bologna and became a student of St. Sylvester Gozzolini. He entered the Franciscan order and served as archdeacon of Ancona and bishop of Osimo.

Canonized: by Pope Martin IV (r. 1281–85)
Feast: March 22

Berard and Companions (d. 1220) *Martyrs*
Also known as: Berardus and Companions

Berard was born in Carbio, Italy, to a noble family, and grew up well-educated. He learned to speak Arabic, which served him in his missionary work.

Berard joined the Franciscan order and was accepted by St. Francis of Assisi himself. He served the order as a friar minor, priest and preacher. St. Francis sent him and a party of Franciscans to preach to Muslims in Morocco. Joining Berard were Peter, Otho, Accurcius and Adjutus. Their work was short-lived. After their arrival, the Franciscans began preaching in the marketplace. They were immediately arrested and ordered to cease. When they returned to preach again, they were beaten. The Muslims demanded that they renounce Christ, but they refused to do so. The sultan had them all beheaded on January 16, 1220. It is believed that Berard and his party were the first Franciscan martyrs. They were canonized as a group.

Years later, St. Anthony of Padua saw their relics, and was inspired to join the Franciscans and go to Morocco himself.

Canonized: 1481 by Pope Sixtus V
Feast: January 16

Bernadette Soubirous (1844–1879) *Nun and visionary of the famous apparitions of the Blessed Virgin Mary at Lourdes, France*
Also known as: Bernadette of Lourdes

Marie Bernarde ("Bernadette") Soubirous was born on January 7, 1844, in Lourdes, France. Her parents,

Francis, a miller, and Louise Soubirous, were very poor. They had nine children; five died in infancy, and Bernadette was the oldest of the survivors.

When Bernadette was 12, her father lost his mill. The family moved several times, finally taking a tiny room loaned to them by a cousin. The conditions were horrible. The building had been a jail and was converted to a stable. The family's room overlooked a dung heap and the stable yard; the room next to theirs contained livestock. It was damp and smelly, which aggravated Bernadette's asthma.

In 1857 Bernadette was sent to live with a foster mother, Marie Lagues, who promised to send the child to school and teach her the catechism. Instead, she sent Bernadette out to tend her sheep. She did try to give her instruction in the catechism at night, but

St. Bernadette Soubirous (Library of Congress Prints and Photographs Division)

Bernadette struggled with the French—she spoke only a dialect—and thus remained a poor student.

On February 11, 1858, when she was 14, Bernadette was out gathering firewood along the Gave du Pau River near Lourdes with two companions. They waded in the water near a natural grotto at a place called Massabielle. Her friends went on ahead and Bernadette paused, afraid that the cold water would bring on an asthma attack. Suddenly she heard the sound of rushing wind and saw a brilliant light near the grotto. A small woman appeared in the light and bowed her head in greeting. Bernadette got out her rosary, and the apparition prayed with her. Speaking Bernadette's dialect, the woman instructed her to come back to the grotto every day for 15 days. She said, "I do not promise to make you happy in this world but in the next."

Bernadette reported her experience. When more visions occurred, crowds of the curious and skeptical began to gather at the grotto. In all, Bernadette experienced 18 visions through March 4. Mary gave Bernadette personal messages and messages for the world. She urged people to pray and do penitence. During the visions, Bernadette experienced trances or ecstasies, some lasting an hour.

On February 25, Mary told Bernadette to drink from a spring, pointing to a spot on the ground. Bernadette dug into the earth, and appeared to spectators to be eating mud. A spring emerged and subsequently became credited with miraculous healing powers. The water was determined to have no known natural therapeutic properties; believers attributed its curative powers to the patronage of Mary.

In the last apparition on March 4, the woman identified herself as "the Immaculate Conception," thus confirming dogma established four years earlier by Pope Pius IX (r. 1846–78). Bernadette revealed this message on March 25, along with the lady's instructions that a church should be built on the spot where she appeared. Bernadette's experiences were highly controversial, and some Church officials tried to delay or obstruct the building of the chapel. But when Empress Eugénie of France, the wife of Napoleon III, became interested and supportive, the chapel was erected.

Bernadette made her First Communion in June 1858. After two years with her foster mother, she returned to her family home in Lourdes. She was allowed to attend school free of tuition with the Sisters of Charity and Christian Instruction at Nevers.

In 1862 the Catholic Church authenticated Bernadette's visions. In 1866, Bernadette retired to the Sisters of Notre Dame convent in Nevers, not far from Lourdes, where she experienced the extremes of harsh treatment from the mistress of novices and admiration as a saint by some of her sisters. She worked as infirmarian and sacristan. Chronically ill most of her life, she became fatally ill with tuberculosis of the bone in the right knee. She suffered many complications and died on April 16, 1879, asking forgiveness for her faults, especially pride. During her life, she never deviated from her account of the visions. She refused to go to Lourdes to try to heal herself, saying that the site was for others, not her; it was her duty to bear her illness. She never revealed the personal messages given her by Mary.

Bernadette was buried in the Chapel of St. Joseph on the convent grounds. On September 22, 1909, 30 years after her death, her body was exhumed for the cause of her beatification. Though her clothing was damp and the coffin contained sawdust and bits of charcoal, Bernadette's body was incorrupt, and her arms and face still retained their natural tone and coloring. Her rosary, held in her hands, was rusted, and the crucifix upon her chest was covered with verdigris. Further examination showed that the incorrupt body was nonetheless emaciated, especially the afflicted right knee. The body was washed, reclothed and reburied.

The remains were exhumed a second time on April 3, 1919. The body was still incorrupt, except the face had discolored—probably from the washing during the first exhumation. A wax coating was applied to the face. Bernadette's relics were placed in a gold and glass coffin for public display at the Chapel of Saint Bernadette in the motherhouse at Nevers.

Lourdes became one of the most important pilgrimage sites in the world, now drawing millions of visitors every year who hope to be cured by the waters. The spring generates 27,000 liters of water a week—approximately 13 liters per minute. The Church investigates reports of miraculous healings and publishes the most noteworthy of them.

Beatified: 1925 by Pope Pius XI
Canonized: December 8, 1933, by Pope Pius XI
Feast: April 16
Patronage: shepherdesses

FURTHER READING
Harris, Ruth. *Lourdes: Body and Spirit in the Secular Age.* New York: Viking, 1999.
Trocem, François, *Saint Bernadette Soubirous.* Rockford, Ill.: TAN Books and Publishers, 1993.

Bernard of Clairvaux (1090–1153) *Cistercian abbot and Doctor of the Church*
Also known as: Doctor Mellifluus, "The Honey-Mouthed Doctor," for the spiritual sweetness of his teachings

St. Bernard of Clairvaux (Library of Congress Prints and Photographs Division)

Bernard of Clairvaux was born in Fontaines, near Dijon, in France, to a leading family of the nobility. He excelled in his early studies, especially in literature, while at the same time giving evidence of great piety.

Bernard's lifelong devotion to Mary began in childhood in 1098. He dreamed he saw a young woman praying in a stable, who suddenly held a radiant baby in her arms. He recognized the baby as Jesus. Mary smiled and allowed Bernard to caress him. He prayed often to Mary and felt a close bond to her. Bernard found himself equally attracted to the reformed Benedictine community at Cîteaux, and to a career as a writer and scholar as his family wished. In 1111, he prayed to God for direction. He had a vision of his own departed mother, whom he understood to be sent by Mary. He knew instantly that he was to become a monk.

At about age 23 he entered the monastery at Cîteaux along with 30 companions; he was eventually followed by his father and five brothers. In 1115, the abbot, St. Stephen Harding, sent Bernard to found a new daughter house that was to become famous as the Cistercian abbey of Clairvaux.

Though Bernard sought quiet and solitude to contemplate, the needs of the Church, the orders of his superiors and the urgent pleas of rulers caused him to spend much time in travels and controversies. Early in his career, when denounced to Rome for "meddling" in high ecclesiastical affairs, he won over his accusers by explaining that he would like nothing better than to retire to his monastery, but had been ordered to assist at the Synod of Troyes. He likewise found himself called upon to judge the rival claims of Innocent II and Anacletus II to the papacy, and traveled widely to bring others over to the side of Innocent. His other activities included assisting at the Second Lateran Council (1139), preaching the Second Crusade (1146) and countering the theological errors of Peter Abelard (1139) and of Gilbert, bishop of Poitiers (1147–48). Bernard was a key figure in the condemnation of Abelard by the Council of Sens.

Bernard's health suffered throughout his life. He ate very little and endured acute abdominal pains. Once when he was quite ill, he prayed at the altars of Mary and SS. Lawrence and Benedict. Mary and the two saints appeared to him, placed their hands on his abdomen and instantly healed his pain.

Worn out by his labors, and distressed by the failure of the Crusade, he died at Clairvaux on August 20, 1153. According to lore, Mary appeared to him to welcome his soul to heaven.

Despite his many activities, the real center of Bernard's life was prayer and contemplation: From them he drew strength for his labors and journeys and inspiration for his writings. Bernard, like all Christians, believed that the vision of God and union with Him was the end for which man was created. This can be fully attained only in the afterlife, but Bernard and many others throughout the ages have claimed an experience, even in this life, of that vision and union. This mystical experience, like the Beatific Vision of which it is a foretaste, is, in the Christian view, a free gift of God; the most that man can do is desire it and strive to remove obstacles to it. The methods of removing obstacles are the subject of ascetic and mystical theology. Many Christians before Bernard had described this mystical experience, but he was one of the first to address himself to the theological understanding of it, though not in any systematic way. His work shows a profound and precise knowledge of doctrinal subtleties.

Ascetic theology deals with groundwork of the spiritual life: the eradication of vices, the cultivation of virtue, the attainment of detachment, by which one learns to give up one's own will and accept God's will for one. Bernard's works in this field include *De Gratia et Libero Arbitrio* (Of grace and free will) and *De*

Gradibus Humilitatus et Superbiae (Of the steps of humility and pride). Bernard's teaching is typical of the paradoxical Christian view of man, simultaneously affirming his dignity as made in the image and likeness of God (which image, for Bernard, consisted primarily in man's free will) and his need for humility as a creature—a fallen creature, in whom the likeness to God is obscured by sin.

But for Bernard, as for the author of the Johannine book (Fourth Gospel) of the New Testament, the beginning, end and driving force of the whole mystery of creation and redemption is love: God's love for man enabling man to love God in return. In *De Dilgendo Deo* (Of loving God), Bernard presents motives for loving God, both those that all men may acknowledge (the gifts of creation) and those that compel Christians, who believe that God became incarnate and died to save them (the goods of redemption). Here, as elsewhere in his writings, the humanity of Christ has the central role.

Love is nurtured by conversation, and so in the four books *De Consideratione* (Of meditation), written for his pupil who had become pope as Eugene III, Bernard discusses meditation, or mental prayer, by which one converses with God and may, perhaps, attain a vision of God and union with Him even in this life. It is in the 86 *Sermones super Cantica Canticorum* (Sermons on the song of songs) that Bernard eloquently expounds on this vision and union, and the desire for it. As many would do after him, he sees these ancient Hebrew poems as describing the union of God and the soul as a mystical marriage. Bernard stresses that the mystical experience is, precisely, an experience, and thus strictly incommunicable, to be known only by one who has experienced it.

In addition to these works, Bernard composed more than 300 sermons and 500 letters, which demonstrate his deep devotion to Mary and the infant Jesus. A story is told that one letter to his cousin, Robert, was dictated in a field during a heavy downpour. The paper never became wet. The episode was looked upon as miraculous, and an oratory was built on the spot.

Of other miracles and unusual events ascribed to the saint, an interesting one concerns the "flies of Foigny." Bernard attended the dedication of a church in Foigny, and the service was disturbed by a great multitude of buzzing flies. Bernard cried, *"Excommunicabo eas!"* (I shall excommunicate them!). The next day the excommunicated flies were found dead. There were so many they blackened the pavement and had to be shoveled out of the church.

Bernard's symbol is a white dog. In art he is often depicted in Cistercian habit with a vision of Our Lady.

Canonized: 1174 by Pope Alexander III
Declared Doctor of the Church: 1830 by Pope Pius
    VIII
Feast: August 20
Patronage: bees; cancer victims; chandlers; Cistercians; climbers; Burgundy; Gibraltar; Liguria, Italy; Speyer Cathedral, Germany

FURTHER READING
Bredero, Adrian H. *Bernard of Clairvaux: Between Cult and History.* Grand Rapids, Mich.: William B. Eerdmans, 1996.
Brown, Raphael. *Saints Who Saw Mary.* Rockford, Ill.: TAN Books, 1955.
Gilson, Etienne. *The Mystical Theology of Saint Bernard,* tr. A.H.C. Downes. New York: Sheed & Ward, 1940.
Liddy, Ailbe J., O.Cist. *Life and Teaching of Saint Bernard.* Dublin: M.H. Gill & Son, 1950.
St. Bernard's Sermon on the Canticle of Canticles, tr. by a priest of Mount Mellary. Dublin: Browne and Nolan, 1920.
Williams, Watkin. *The Mysticism of Saint Bernard of Clairvaux.* London: Burns Oates & Washbourne, 1931.

Bernadine of Siena (1380–1444) *Franciscan missionary and preacher*
Also known as: "the second Paul"

Bernadine of Siena was born on September 8, 1380, at Massa Marittima near Siena, Italy. His father was the governor. Bernadine was ophaned at age seven and then raised by an aunt. He is said to have been sensitive, and had an intense dislike for indecent language. He fasted and spent time in prayer. In 1397 he entered the Confraternity of Our Lady, and in 1400 organized the hospitals of Siena to cope with a plague outbreak. His work with the ill left him exhausted.

Bernadine joined the Franciscans in 1402 and was ordained a priest in 1404. He had a weak and hoarse voice, and did not give his first sermon until September 8, 1417. He did very little preaching, and for 12 years lived as a hermit.

He then went to Milan on a mission, and suddenly found he was a charismatic speaker with a strong and commanding voice. The story goes that he prayed earnestly to Mary about his voice, and one day a globe of fire came down from heaven and stopped at his throat, instantly healing him.

Bernadine crisscrossed central and northern Italy on foot, preaching against immorality for hours at a time, several times a day. He also stressed punishment for sin, reward for virtue, the mercy of Jesus and the love of Mary. His special devotion was to the Holy Name of Jesus. He became the foremost missionary in Italy, and also healed people, especially lepers.

Once, he told a crowd he would show them devils, and then stunned everyone by telling them to look at each other, for they were doing the work of Satan.

Perhaps because of his great popularity, he was slandered by enemies and was silenced for a short while. In 1427 he was defended by Pope Martin V (r. 1417–31). The pope offered him the see of Siena, but Bernadine turned down that and several other offers to be bishop in various cities. He was unable to avoid being named vicar general of his order, the Franciscan Friars of the Strict Observance, in 1430. Due to his efforts, the order increased in size from about 300 members to more than 4,000.

Bernadine was devoted to Mary and had visions of her. In one, she appeared to him and showed him a farm near Bergamo where a friary could be built. Three years later, when Bernadine returned to dedicate the friary, Mary with the infant Jesus appeared in a brilliant light and was witnessed by many.

Even when it was clear he was dying, he preached for consecutive days. He died at Aquila on May 20, 1444. His relics were enshrined there. Some relics also are in Siena, Rome and Massa Marittima.

In art he is often depicted holding a sign with the letters IHS, the first three Greek letters of the holy name of Jesus, which he always displayed as a monogram from the pulpit and distributed to crowds. Sometimes mitres are at his feet, symbolizing his refusals of the office of bishop.

Canonized: 1450 by Pope Nicholas V
Feast: May 20
Patronage: against bleeding; against chest problems; against hoarseness; lungs and chest; wool workers; Massa Marittima

FURTHER READING
Brown, Raphael. *Saints Who Saw Mary.* Rockford, Ill.: TAN Books, 1955.

Blaise (d. ca. 313–315) *Bishop of Sebaste, Turkey; martyr*
Also known as: Blase

Blaise, a philosopher and physician, was elected bishop of Sebaste and then was forced to flee during the persecutions of Emperor Diocletian (r. 284–305). Tradition holds that he retired to a cave on Mt. Argeus. Throngs of people came to see him for his miraculous cures; even wild animals sought him out.

After Diocletian, persecutions continued under Emperor Licinius Licinianus (r. 308–324). Governor Agricolaus of Cappadocia was ordered to arrest Christians and feed them to wild beasts. Hunters sent out to capture the animals found Blaise; he was arrested and taken to Agricolaus. En route weeping followers of Blaise gathered to ask his blessing as he passed by. One such person was a woman who thrust at him her child, dying of a small fish bone stuck in his throat. Blaise healed the boy with prayer.

Blaise refused to renounce his faith and was scourged and imprisoned. The saint remained placid and in good humor, and continued to work miracles from his cell. The infuriated governor ordered him to be lacerated with iron hooks.

Certain holy women were induced to collect his blood. They were rounded up with two of their children and ordered to perform sacrifices to the gods. They asked for the idols, but flung the statues into a lake. The women and their children were beheaded.

Blaise was then hideously tortured. He was stretched on a rack, had his flesh torn with iron combs, and endured a red-hot coat of mail laid upon him. Agricolaus ordered him tossed into the lake. Legend has it that Blaise walked on water to the middle of the lake, sat down, and urged the pagans to do the same if they believed in their gods. Some tried and were drowned.

A voice from heaven told Blaise to accept his martyrdom. He returned to land and was beheaded.

Blaise's relics are in numerous cities, including Brunswick, Mainz, Lübeck, Trier and Cologne in Germany; Taranto, Milan and Rome in Italy; Paray-le-Monial in France; and Dubrovnik in Croatia.

On the day of Blaise's feast, throats are blessed and candles lit, in commemoration of the healing of the boy. Blaise is invoked against throat and neck complaints.

Feast: February 3
Patronage: builders; cattle; doctors; hat makers; hosiery workers; against neck complaints; pets; plasterers; shoemakers; stone carvers; tanners; against throat disorders; veterinarians; weavers; wild animals; wind musicians; wool dealers

FURTHER READING
St. Alphonsus Liguori. *Victories of the Martyrs.* Brooklyn: Redemptorist Fathers, 1954.

Bonaventure (1217–1274) *Cardinal-Bishop, Minister General of the Friars Minor, Doctor of the Church*
Also known as: the Seraphic Doctor

Bonaventure is considered one of the great theologians of the Church along with his contemporary, St. Thomas Aquinas. He wrote extensively on theology and philosophy; some of his works are mystical in nature.

Little is known about the early life of Bonaventure. He was born in 1217 in Bagnoregio near Viterbo, Italy,

to Giovanni Fidanza and Maria Ritella. It is not know why or when his given name of John was changed to Bonaventure. According to the saint himself, he was saved from death in childhood by the intervention of St. Francis of Assisi; Bonventure later became the official biographer of Francis.

In 1217 he went to the University of Paris where he met Franciscans. In 1243 he joined the Order of the Friars Minor and studied under the Franciscan scholars Alexander of Hales and John of La Rochelle. From 1248 to 1256 he taught and lectured at the university, quitting under opposition from secular professors to the Dominican and Franciscan professors. Pope Alexander IV (r. 1254–61) restored the Mendicants, and in 1267 both Bonaventure and Thomas Aquinas received their doctorate degrees.

Bonaventure was elected minister general of the Friars Minor in 1257 and became involved in internal disputes. He visited much of the order and instituted reforms.

In 1263, he assisted at the translation of the remains of SS. Clare and Anthony. His life of St. Francis was declared the official biography to the exclusion of all others. In 1264, he took over direction of the Poor Clares and founded the Society of the Gonfalone in honor of the Blessed Virgin Mary in Rome. In 1265, he declined a request from Pope Clement IV (r. 1265–68) to become the archbishop of York.

In 1266 Bonaventure generated much controversy when he convened a general chapter in Paris that decreed all accounts of Francis written prior to his should be destroyed. In 1269 he instituted the practice of mass being sung every Saturday throughout the order in honor of Mary.

Bonaventure played a key role in the election of Clement's successor in 1271, advising the cardinals to choose Theobald Visconti of Piacenza, who became Pope Gregory X (r. 1271–76). The pope named Bonaventure cardinal-bishop of Albano in 1273, much to the saint's displeasure. The pope also instructed Bonaventure to prepare the questions for the Fourteenth Ecumenical Council opening in Lyons on May 7, 1274. During the discussions, the pope relied heavily upon the counsel of Bonaventure.

While the council was in session, Bonaventure died suddenly on July 15, 1274. The cause is not known, but his secretary, Peregrinus of Bologna, attributed it to poison. The saint was buried the next day in the church of the Friars Minor in Lyons. The pope, the king of Aragon, the cardinals and other members of the council attended the funeral.

During his life, Bonaventure was known for his mystical experiences and miracles. His ecstasies no doubt provided inspiration for his more mystical writings. Once Thomas Aquinas visited him while he was at work on the life of Francis, and found him in ecstasy. Thomas left, saying, "Let us leave a saint to work for a saint." His sanctity inspired Dante Alighieri to place him among the saints in his *Paradisio*.

In 1434 his remains were moved to a new church in Lyons in honor of St. Francis. His head was found to be perfectly preserved, and his tongue as red as it had been in life. The people of Lyons then named him their patron.

In 1562, his shrine was vandalized by the Huguenots, who burned the urn containing his body. The superior hid Bonaventure's head and forfeited his life in the process. During the French Revolution, the head disappeared and has never been found.

Bonaventure left a legacy of important theological and philosophical works esteemed throughout the Middle Ages and still studied today. His greatest is *Commentary on the Sentences,* a sweeping treatment of the entire Scholastic theology, which is summarized in another of his works, *Brevoliquium.* Like Thomas Aquinas, he defended Aristotle, though he did not hesitate to criticize his shortcomings. His most exemplary mystical work is *De Triplici Via,* which explores perfection. In addition, he wrote numerous treatises and exegeses. Nearly 500 of his sermons have survived.

Canonized: April 14, 1482, by Pope Sixtus IV
Patronage: Lyons

FURTHER READING
Bonaventure: The Soul's Journey into God, The Tree of Life, The Life of St. Francis. Tr. Ewert Cousins. Mahwah, N.J.: Paulist Press, 1978.

Boniface I (d. 422) *Pope*

Nothing is known about the early life of Boniface, son of the presbyter Jocandus. He was ordained a priest by Pope St. Damasus I (366–384) and served as Pope St. Innocent I's (r. 401–417) representative in Constantinople. On December 29, 418, he succeeded St. Zosimus in the Chair of St. Peter, but not without incident.

Immediately after the obsequies for Zosimus on December 27, a faction of the Roman clergy consisting mainly of deacons seized the Lateran basilica and elected Archdeacon Eulalius as pope. When the higher clergy—who were opposed to Eulalius—tried to enter the basilica, they were met with violence. The following day they convened in the Church of Theodora and elected the aged Boniface instead. Both Boniface and Eulalius were consecrated on December 29, Boniface in the basilica of St. Marcellus. Each then proceeded to

act as pope, throwing the Church into schism, and dividing the city of Rome. The trouble persisted for 15 weeks until Emperor Honorius at Ravenna finally pronounced in favor of Boniface, on April 3, 418.

When Boniface fell critically ill early in 420, Eulalius and his backers tried again. They failed to receive support, however, and upon his recovery in July, Boniface appealed to Honorius to make some provision against a renewal of the schism following his death. In response, Honorius enacted a law stipulating that, in contested papal elections, neither claimant should be recognized, and a new election should be held.

Boniface's pontificate was marked by great zeal and activity in upholding the jurisdiction of the universal Church. He continued the papal opposition to Pelagianism, a heresy that denied original sin, supporting St. Augustine in his pronouncements against it. He was able to persuade Emperor Theodosius II to return the ecclesiastical provinces of Illyricum to Western control, over the claims of the patriarch of Constantinople. He was successful also in settling the issue regarding appeals to Rome within the African church. Although African bishops persisted in their disagreements with the Holy See, they promised to obey the rulings, thus recognizing the pope's role as guardian of the Church's discipline.

Boniface renewed legislation of Pope St. Soter (r. 166–175) that prohibited women from touching the sacred linens or ministering at the burning incense. He enforced laws forbidding slaves to become clerics.

Boniface died in Rome on September 4, 422. He was buried in the Catacomb of St. Maximus on the Via Salaria, near the tomb of St. Felicitas (Felicity), whom he revered and in whose honor he had erected an oratory.

Feast: September 4 (formerly October 25)

Boniface IV (d. 615) *Pope and martyr*

Boniface was born at Valeria, Abruzzi (Italy), the son of a physician named John. He may have been a Benedictine monk and student of Pope St. Gregory I (Gregory the Great, r. 590–604). He served under Gregory as deacon and dispensator (official in charge of administering the patrimonies). He was elected to the Chair of St. Peter to succeed Pope Boniface III (r. 607) late in 607, although he was not consecrated until August 25, 608, after Emperor Phocos had confirmed his election.

Phocos presented him with the Pantheon in Rome, which Boniface converted into a Christian church, consecrated to the Virgin Mary and all the Martyrs (the Santa Maria Rotunda). He had some 28 cartloads of bones translated from the sacred catacombs and placed in a porphyry basin beneath the high altar of the church.

Boniface later received a visit from Mellitus, the first bishop of London. Mellitus was long supposed to have left Rome carrying letters from Boniface to Lawrence, archbishop of Canterbury, and Ethelbert, king of England, "concerning what was to be observed by the Church of England," though these are now thought to be spurious.

Boniface died in 615 in retirement in his own home, which, following the example of Gregory, he had converted into a monastery. He relics were interred in the portico of St. Peter's Basilica at the Vatican, but were subsequently moved three times: in the 10th or 11th century, at the close of the 13th century, and finally on October 21, 1603, when they were placed in the new St. Peter's. His cult began during the reign of Boniface VIII (r. 1294–1303).

Feast: May 8 (formerly May 25)

Boris and Gleb (d. 1010) *Martyrs of Russia, betrayed by one of their own brothers*
Also known as: Romanus and David, respectively

Boris and Gleb were sons of St. Vladimir, grand prince of Kiev, who was the first Christian ruler in Russia. They had two other brothers, Iaroslav (Yaroslav) and Sviatopolk (Yaropolk). When Vladimir died in 1015, Boris and Gleb were away. Boris, a military officer, was off with his troops fighting the Pechengs.

Sviatopolk took over his father's throne, but even though he gave money to the townsfolk, their loyalty lay with the more popular Boris. The advisers of Boris urged him to make his rightful claim to the throne, but he declined, saying he would not raise his hand against his brother. His troops left him and only his servants remained with him in Alta.

Sviatopolk obtained the loyalty of the boyars, the ruling class, and instructed them to murder Boris. The assassins hastened to Alta, where they found Boris in prayer. He evidently knew they would come for him, and when he was done with vespers, he lay down on his couch and let them attack him with lances. In vain his faithful personal servant, a Hungarian named George, tried to shield him with his body. George was slain and was decapitated so that the assassins could steal the large gold necklace—a gift from Boris—that was around his neck.

Boris survived. He was wrapped in canvas, loaded onto a wagon and taken back to Sviatopolk. His brother ordered him finished, and he was fatally stabbed in the heart with a sword.

Sviatopolk then plotted to kill Gleb. He sent his brother a false message, telling him to come at once to Kiev because their father was gravely ill. But another brother, Iaroslav, warned Gleb and told him the truth about their father's death and Boris's murder.

Gleb was unable to avoid murder. Sviatopolk's assassins arrived and ordered the terrified servants to kill their master. Gleb's cook seized a knife and stabbed him to death.

Later, Iaroslav was able to transport the bodies of his two brothers to the Church of St. Basil in Vyshegorod. Miracles were reported at their tomb, which became a popular pilgrimage site.

Feast: July 24
Patronage: Moscow (Boris)

FURTHER READING
Nestor, "The Martyrdom of Boris and Gleb." URL: http://www.dur.ac.uk/~dm10www/borigleb.html. Downloaded Oct. 1, 2000.

Botwid (d. 1100) *Swedish martyr*
Also known as: Botuid

Botwid was a Swedish layman who converted to Catholicism while on a trip to England. Back in Sweden, he began preaching. He bought a Finnish slave, baptized him, gave him religious instruction and set him free with the request to spread the Gospel in his native land.

Botwid and a friend, Asbjorn, arranged to take the slave by boat across the Baltic Sea. On shore at night, the treacherous slave murdered the sleeping men and stole the boat. A search party set out to find the missing men. According to lore, a bird perched on the prow of their boat and sang until the bodies were found.

Botwid was buried in Sweden and is revered as an apostle of Sweden.

Feast: July 28

Brendan of Clonfort (b. ca. 460–486, d. ca. 577–584) *One of the greatest of Irish saints*
Also known as: Brendan the Navigator, Brendan the Voyager, Brandan, Brandon

Brendan was born sometime around 484 near the seacoast town of Tralee in County Kerry. A descendant of Ireland's first-century high king Fergus MacRoy, or McRory, the boy seemed destined for greatness. The entire Irish countryside supposedly lit up the night he was born. Brendan was baptized by Bishop St. Erc and spent his first five years in the care and education of St. Ita at her monastery school in Killeedy. Later he traveled to many of the great Irish monasteries to receive

St. Brendan of Clonfort (Library of Congress Prints and Photographs Division)

religious instruction from the abbots there, including Jarlath of Tuam, Finian of Clonard and Enda of Aran. Returning to Bishop St. Erc, Brendan received ordination in 512 and continued his wanderings, establishing monastic communities at Ardfert and Shanakeel (or Baalynevinoorach).

Although revered for his saintly ways, Brendan's fame comes from the *Navigatio Santi Brendani Abatis,* or the *Navigations (or Travels) of Saint Brendan the Abbot.* Legend says that Brendan, unable to shake his wanderlust, left the monastery at Baalynevinoorach with between 17 and 60 monks (accounts vary) to discover and evangelize the people living on islands beyond the western horizon. Most specifically, Brendan sought the "Lands of Delight," the "Land of Promise" or the "Isles of the Blessed Saints." Old Irish calendars assigned the feast day of March 22 to celebrate the *"egressio familiae S. Brendani,"* or Saint Brendan's departure, and St. Aengus the Culdee invoked the 60 monks in his eighth-century Litany. The voyages took seven years and included detailed descriptions of the construction of the group's hide-covered boats, called currachs or coracles. Currachs—small boats that ride high in the water, unaffected by currents—are still built in County Kerry today much the same as they were in the sixth century. The monks' tales seemed

incredible, telling of large sea-monsters that raised the boats on their backs, of huge crystals that rose to the sky, and of being pelted with "flaming, foul-smelling rocks by the inhabitants of a large island." The monks even tried to light an Easter fire on one island only to discover they were on a whale.

Word of Brendan's magical voyages spread and attracted many pilgrims to the monastery at Ardfert. After his return, Brendan continued his mission to spread the Word of God, founding a monastery at Inis-da-druim, now Coney Island in County Clare, about 550. He traveled throughout Ireland, to Wales, to St. Columba's monastery at Iona, to the Canary Islands and to Europe. His greatest contribution was the monastery at Cluain Fearta, or Clonfert in County Galway, built about 557. The monastic community at Clonfert reportedly housed 3,000 men under rules dictated to Brendan by an angel. Although most of the monastery fell into ruins years ago, the cathedral remains, regarded as an Irish national treasure and one of the finest examples of Irish Romanesque architecture. The doorway contains six decorated arches topped by a huge triangle containing ornaments and heads.

Brendan established a monastic community for women at Enach Duin (Annaghdown) and placed his sister Briga in charge. He died there in 577 at about age

93 while visiting her. Fearing that some might want his relics, Brendan arranged for Briga to keep his death a secret and send his body back to Clonfert in his luggage. He is buried at Clonfert.

From medieval times into the 18th century, maps of the western Atlantic Ocean included an island called St. Brendan's Isle. Mapmakers were unsure of the island's exact position, but it often appeared south of the Antilles and west of the Cape Verde Islands. Scholars speculate that locating this magical place inspired Christopher Columbus's voyage to the New World. Six copies of the *Navigatio* manuscript remain, but few have believed the fantastic tales were anything more than stories for the faithful.

In 1976, British navigation scholar Tim Severin and a crew decided to reconstruct Brendan's journeys by following the accounts in the *Navigatio* to prove that the trip was possible. To begin with, Severin and his crew built the currachs following Brendan's directions. They tanned ox-hides with oak bark, stretched them across the wooden frame, sewed them with leather thread and smeared the boats with animal fat to provide water resistance. Skeptics didn't believe the lightweight currachs could handle ocean current, but Severin found them quite seaworthy. The crew embarked from Brandon Creek on the Dingle Peninsula, supposedly Brendan's point of departure. Severin's study of nautical charts indicated Brendan's route was governed by prevailing winds, taking the monks across the northernmost part of the Atlantic, close to Iceland, Greenland and maybe Newfoundland. This was the same route Viking Leif Eriksson traveled about 400 years later. Most of the stops chronicled in the *Navigatio* were islands where the Irish monks established primitive monasteries. Indeed, the accounts of Viking explorations remarked on meetings with "Papers" ("papas" or fathers—priests).

Severin and his crew were surprised at the playful, friendly encounters with North Atlantic whales, and they speculated that the creatures were even friendlier in the sixth century—before they had been hunted—causing them to bump and lift the tiny boats, as the monks recounted. Off the coast of Canada, an iceberg punctured Severin's currach, which he patched with a piece of leather. Such icebergs may well have been Brendan's "towering crystals." And the active volcanoes of Iceland may explain the "flaming, foul-smelling rocks."

Other stops included the Hebrides Islands and the Danish Faroe Islands. Brendan had described an island as "the Paradise of Birds," and Mykines in the Faroe chain is populated by thousands of seabirds. Brendan called the largest island the Island of Sheep, and the word "faroe" means sheep. There is also another Bran-

don Creek on the main island. Severin and his crew landed on Newfoundland on June 26, 1977, proving that the possibility of a sea voyage in a currach was not just an old sailor's tale.

But the *Navigatio* says Brendan's voyages took seven years. Tim Severin found the boats extremely hard to tack against winds and currents, leading him to think that the return voyage to Ireland took much longer than the journey west. Most intriguing is the discovery of markers covered with Old Irish Ogham runic language in what is now West Virginia. If the monks were the first Europeans to explore America—what Brendan called the "Promised Land of the Saints"—their overland expeditions would have lengthened their trip as well.

Feast: May 16
Patronage: boatmen; mariners; sailors; travelers; watermen; whales

FURTHER READING
Plummer, Charles. *Lives of Irish Saints,* Vol. 2. Oxford: Oxford University Press, 1922.

Bridget of Sweden (1303–1373) *Wife, mystic and founder of the Brigittines order; patron of Sweden*
Also known as: Brigid, Birgitta, Brigitta

Bridget of Sweden was born in 1303, the daughter of Birger, the governor of Upland, Sweden, and his second wife, Ingeborg, daughter of the governor of East Gothland. Her parents were pious and instilled in her a sense of religious devotion at an early age. Her father consecrated all Fridays to special acts of penance.

Bridget's mother died when she was 12, and she was raised by an aunt in Aspenas on Lake Sommen. Before she was 14, her father married her to Ulf Gudmarsson, the 18-year-old prince of Nericia in Sweden. The marriage was happy, and Bridget bore eight children. The last was a daughter, Catherine, who became St. Catherine of Sweden.

In 1335, Bridget was summoned to be the principal lady-in-waiting to the queen of Sweden, Blanche of Namur. She did not like the loose lifestyle in court and tried to influence the royals, to no avail. She became known for her prophetic dreams and visions, many of them concerning politics and affairs of state. At the time, the Church was in upheaval; the pope resided in Avignon, not Rome, and many people felt there was a need for reform. From her visions, Bridget believed herself charged with a mission to work for reform.

Sometime after 1340, she obtained a leave of absence, and she and Ulf made a pilgrimage to Compostela in Galicia, Spain. Ulf became ill and nearly died. The couple vowed to commit themselves to God in separate religious houses. Ulf died in 1344 at the

Cistercian monastery of Alvastra. Bridget remained there for four years as a penitent.

Meanwhile, her visions began troubling her and she feared she was being plagued by the Devil, or deluded by her own imagination. At the direction of a vision, she confided in Master Matthias, canon of Linköping, who pronounced the visions as from God. Thereafter, she dictated her visions to the prior at Alvastra, Peter, who recorded them in Latin. One vision instructed Bridget to warn the king about his sinful ways. This she did, and for a time he complied.

Another vision instructed her to found a monastery at Vadstena on Lake Vattern. The monastery housed 60 nuns and in a separate house for men, 13 priests, four deacons and eight choir boys. The monastery was run according to instructions given in Bridget's visions. The order, which became known as the Brigittines, was for women; the men were admitted to provide them spiritual instruction.

In 1349 Bridget made a pilgrimage to Rome; she never returned to the monastery. Guided by her visions, she stayed to campaign for the return of the papacy to that city. Many of her revelations were uncomplimentary toward the Church and the pope. At St. Paul's-outside-the Walls, the crucifix spoke to her while she prayed. At the Church of San Francesco a Ripa, a vision of St. Francis of Assisi invited her to eat and drink with him in his cell. She went to Assisi, and then spent two years touring shrines in Italy. She made herself unpopular with her predictions that the Romans would be punished for their sins.

In 1371, a vision directed her to make what would be her last pilgrimage, to the Holy Land with Catherine, two sons and several others. In Naples, son Charles became involved with Queen Joanna I, despite the fact that they were both married. Bridget prayed for a resolution. Charles soon became ill and died in her arms, sending her into deep mourning.

Bridget's last pilgrimage was marked by many visions, including one from Christ that predicted her death and gave instructions for her burial and for the eventual editing of her revelations. She returned to Rome in March 1373 in poor health. Her condition deteriorated, and she died on July 23 at age 71. Peter of Alvastra administered last rites. Catherine had her body transferred to Vadstena.

Canonized: 1391 by Pope Boniface IX
Feast: July 23
Patronage: against miscarriage; Sweden

FURTHER READING
St. Bridget's Revelations to the Popes. URL: http://www/fordham.edu/halsall/basis/bridget-tractatus.html. Downloaded: February 10, 2000.

St. Bridget of Sweden (Library of Congress Prints and Photographs Division)

Brigid of Ireland (ca. 450–453–ca. 523–525) *One of the three patron saints of Ireland, along with Patrick and Columba*

Name meaning: Fiery arrow (Breo-Saighit in Gaelic)
Also known as: Bride, Brigid of Kildare, Mary of the Gael, Bride of the Isles, Queen of the South, Bridget, Ffraid (Wales)

Brigid was born half-princess, half-slave, ca. 450–453, to the Irish chieftain Dubthach (pronounced "Duffack" or "Duffy") and a Pictish bondwoman named Brocessa or Brocca at Faughart, near Dundalk in County Louth—an area associated with the mythical Irish queen Medb (Maeve). Her father allowed her to live with her mother—who had been sold to a druid—until she was older. Brigid showed an interest in God at an early age, reportedly after hearing St. Patrick preach, and gave whatever she had to anyone in need.

Her determination to further Christian charity by giving away all her father's goods angered Dubthach so much that he decided to sell Brigid in marriage to the Christian king of Leinster. Dubthach threw Brigid in his chariot and drove furiously to the king's castle, whereupon he left his sword with Brigid so as not to appear belligerent and went inside to strike the bargain. No sooner had he left than a poor leper begged alms of Brigid, and she, having no money, gave him the sword. When Dubthach returned and found his sword missing, he began beating Brigid, but the king stopped him. He asked Brigid why she had given away her father's sword, and she replied that she would gladly give away all the king's wealth as well if it could serve her brothers and sisters in Christ. The king of Leinster diplomatically declined to marry Brigid, telling Dubthach that, "Her merit before God is greater than ours."

Brigid left Dubthach to care for her ailing mother and run the druid's dairy, where she resumed her habit of giving everything away. The druid—realizing he was making no money from his dairy products—asked Brigid to bring him a large basket of butter, thinking he could entrap her. But miraculously the hamper was full. Impressed with Brigid's powers, the druid granted her request to release her mother from bondage.

Upon her return to Dubthach's home, her father attempted to marry his daughter to a poet, but she had vowed to remain a virgin. After finding a wife for the groom, she took the veil as a nun from St. Macaille at Croghan Hill, where she and seven other girls lived together. About 468, Brigid followed St. Mel of Ardagh, a pupil of Patrick's, to Druin Criadh, in the plains of Magh Life (Meath). There, under a large oak tree (a tree sacred to the druids), Brigid founded Cill-Dara (Kildare): the "church of the oaks."

Kildare was a double monastery, meaning it housed communities of both men and women. Legend tells that Brigid was ordained a bishop "by mistake" as justification for her leadership role at the abbey, including even her supposed canonical selection of St. Conlaeth as bishop of the men's community. As opposed to the Roman diocesan system, in which women had minor roles, the Celtic Christians were organized and governed by the monasteries. Many abbeys were governed by abbesses, who served as spiritual leaders, preached, heard confession and may have even performed Mass. Kildare was a school as well, teaching reading, writing, illumination and the practical arts of carpentry and blacksmithing. Artisans and goldsmiths created beautiful objects for churches, such as bells, crosiers, chalices, patens and bookrests, and scribes copied books sent throughout Europe. The Book of Kildare, older than the Book of Kells, was considered one of the finest Irish illuminated manuscripts until it disappeared over 300 years ago.

Brigid, who never left Ireland, was revered as the prototype of all nuns. She reportedly was beautiful and vivacious and wore a red-purple cloak over her habit. She was joyful, pious, hospitable and generous—the kind of person who might wipe her hands simply on her apron as she greeted a stranger. She loved both animals and people. She traveled all over Ireland, converting souls and tending to the sick and hungry. In many ways, Brigid resembled her namesake, the Celtic pagan goddess Brighid, who presided over the arts of inspiration and poetry, the crafts of smithing, and medicine and healing. And in keeping with druidic influences, Brigid kept an eternal flame burning on the altar of Kildare, tended by 20 nuns, as a symbol of the shining light of the Gospel.

Names of places such as Brideswell (the birth parish of St. Thomas Becket), Tubberbride, Templebride, Kilbride and even Bride's Island off the coast of Japan honor the saint. Many little girls, especially in Ireland, are still named Brigid. As patroness of the medieval knights of chivalry, Brigid was invoked each time a knight called his new wife "bride" (pronounced "brida"), supposedly becoming the English word "bride."

One interesting story about Brigid says that once the Virgin Mary was trying to speak to Brigid and became rather annoyed at Brigid's ability to draw a crowd, interrupting their conversation. In order to placate the Virgin, Brigid brought out a rake whose tines flashed like candles, distracting the onlookers. As a reward for her thoughtfulness, Mary granted Brigid's request of having her feast day ahead of Mary's: Brigid's memorial is February 1, while Our Lady's Feast of the Purification is February 2. On February 1 the faithful put out reed crosses, reminding followers to share whatever they have. (Interestingly, these dates are the same as for Imbolc, a pagan winter purification festival that celebrates Brigid (also spelled Briguid), the Irish Celtic goddess of fire, fertility, crops, livestock, wisdom, poetry and household arts.

As Brigid lay dying (ca. 523–525), she was attended by St. Ninnidh, known thereafter as Ninnidh of the Clean Hand because he encased his right hand—the one that had administered the sacraments to Brigid—in a metal covering to keep it undefiled. Brigid was buried at Kildare in a jeweled casket, but her relics were transferred to Downpatrick in 878 to avoid the Vikings, where she was entombed with Patrick and Columba. The relics of all three saints supposedly were found in 1185 and enshrined in Downpatrick Cathedral. In 1283, three knights allegedly carried Brigid's head with them on pilgrimage to the Holy Land. They died in Lumier, Portugal, near Lisbon, where the head is kept in a Jesuit chapel. Brigid remains a popular saint and is frequently invoked in prayer, because it is written in the *Leabhar Breac,* or Book of Lismore, that the Lord granted whatever Brigid asked of Him, and at once.

Feast: February 1

Patronage: blacksmiths; boatmen; cattle; children whose parents are not married; dairy workers; fugitives; healers; Irish nuns; mariners; midwives; newborn babies; poets; the printing press; scholars; travelers; watermen; Ireland

FURTHER READING

Cahill, Thomas. *How the Irish Saved Civilization.* New York: Nan A. Talese/Doubleday, 1995.

Reynolds, Wendy M. "The Goddess Brighid." The Medieval Sourcebook. URL: http://www.millersv.edu/~english/ homepage/ duncan/medfem/bride.htm 1. Downloaded January 18, 2000.

Brother André, Blessed (1845–1937) *Beatified brother of the Holy Cross Brothers, renowned healer and founder of St. Joseph's Oratory in Montreal*

Also known as: Frère André; the Wonder Man of Mount Royal

Brother André was born Alfred Bessette on August 10, 1845, in a village east of Montreal. His father, Isaac, was a carpenter. André was frail from his first breath—in fact, he was baptized immediately after birth out of fear that he would not live. He grew up small, slight and of delicate constitution. Due to chronic stomach problems, he could not eat any solid foods. Throughout his life, his health was poor, yet the power of God flowed through him to heal others. He was influenced in childhood by the religious devotion of his mother, Clothilde. From an early age, he was drawn to St. Joseph.

In 1870, he dedicated himself to a life of religious service with the Congregation of the Holy Cross, a religious order dedicated to the teaching profession. He was given the name André in honor of his sponsor, Pastor André Provencal. Due to his poor health and lack of stamina for physical work, the Holy Cross Brothers asked him to leave. He appealed to a bishop, who promised him he could stay.

Unschooled and untrained, the only thing André could do was pray. He was given a lowly job as doorkeeper at Notre Dame College in Mount Royal, a district of Montreal. At night he would go out and visit the sick. He demonstrated remarkable healing powers. The crippled walked and the cancerous were cured. Sometimes he rubbed holy oil on them, sometimes he touched them, sometimes he told them, like Jesus, simply that they were healed. He became renowned as the "Wonder Man of Mount Royal." People traveled great distances to seek his healing. He credited his

work to his patron, St. Joseph. He could be brusque and gruff with people, sometimes bluntly informing them that they could not be healed because they lacked faith in the power of God.

It was André's dream to build an oratory in honor of his patron saint. The archbishop of Montreal would give permission to do so only if André raised the money to pay for it. To that end, he saved small change and enlisted the support of others. In 1904, a tiny chapel was erected on Mount Royal on grounds opposite the college. It was often filled to overflowing by those who wished to be close to André. Over the years, donations funded expansions. Today the oratory's huge basilica, set on the hilltop, rises taller than any building in Montreal. It holds 3,000 people.

In his later years, André traveled around Canada and even to the United States, visiting New England, New York and New Jersey. He inspired Americans to make pilgrimages to Mount Royal.

During his life, André endured the skepticism and downright opposition of some of his peers and superiors, who doubted that such a simple man could pos-

Brother André

sess such healing power and ability to attract the masses. He shrugged off the poor treatment. He always worked within his religious system, gaining permission for everything that he did. He prayed ceaselessly. Officially, he never was anything but a doorkeeper for his order. He was fond of saying, "When I entered the community they showed me the door, and I remained there for 40 years." Though he seldom had much physical strength and often was ill, he always had stamina for healing and counseling. He attributed this to the intercession of St. Joseph. He often used oil from the lamp in the oratory as part of his healing.

André died on January 6, 1937, after several days of severe pain from acute gastritis, a condition that had afflicted him his entire life. Approximately 30,000 people gathered for his beatification 50 years later.

St. Joseph's Oratory is the world's largest shrine to St. Joseph. Some two million pilgrims come each year, many ascending the steps to the basilica on their knees. Brother André is buried inside the oratory in a small, black granite tomb, called the Black Coffin. Pilgrims come to touch the tomb and pray for healing, and numerous miracles have been reported. An entire wall inside the oratory is covered with canes and crutches that were discarded on the spot by people whom André healed.

André's heart is on view as a relic, encased in a clear glass container. Humble to the end, he could not envision such veneration of himself. "We keep relics of saints, not of persons like me," he said.

Beatified: May 23, 1987, by John Paul II
Feast: January 6

FURTHER READING

Bergeron, H.-P. *Brother André: The Wonder Man of Mount Royal.* Montreal: St. Joseph's Oratory, 1997.
Cruz, Joan Carroll. *Mysteries, Marvels, Miracles in the Lives of the Saints.* Rockford, Ill.: TAN Books, 1997.

Cadoc (d. ca. 580) *Bishop, martyr and one of the chief saints of Wales*

Cadoc's life was recorded in the 12th century by Lifris, a Norman monk at Llancarfan, and Caradoc, a Breton-born hermit of Gower.

Cadoc was born the grandson of Gwynllyw, a chieftain of Glamorgan; his mother, Gwladys, was Gwynllyw's daughter. (Lifris gives the romantic fantasy of Cadoc as the descendant of a long line of Roman emperors, unbroken from Augustus.) He went to Ireland to study. Upon his return, he converted his parents, and they adopted an austere lifestyle.

At Llancarfan, near Cardiff, Wales, Cadoc founded a great monastery and is said to have fed "daily a hundred clergymen, and a hundred soldiers, and a hundred workmen, and a hundred poor persons, with the same number of widows, and many guests besides." Some of the most famous Celtic saints, such as Brendan of Clonfort and Malo, trained at the monastery.

Cadoc then became a hermit on the Bristol Channel island of Flat Holm, where he was joined by a pupil, Finian of Clonard. According to lore, the rocks in the channel (known as "the wolves") were wolves who had attempted to swim the channel to get Cadoc's sheep, and he had turned them into stone.

In the 560s, Cadoc went to Scotland and reportedly founded a monastery west of Stirling. Machan became one of his disciples. A church is dedicated to Cadoc at Cambusland in the Clyde Valley. Later Cadoc traveled from Glamorgan north to the River Usk. He also went to Rome (seven times) Jerusalem (three times) and Greece.

At Jerusalem he visited the River Jordan and filled a flask with its water. He took the water back to Cornwall where he poured it into a healing well, thereby increasing its healing powers many times. St. Cadoc's well remained famous for 300 years. Also, the well is said to have been created on a journey to visit St. Michael's Mount, where Cadoc struck his staff on the ground and out sprang a well of water.

Cadoc went to Brittany where he worked as a missionary. After his return to Britain, he was involved in the Saxon occupation. He was martyred by the Saxons near Weedon, England.

Cadoc is the patron of at least 25 churches and chapels in Wales.

Feast: September 25
Patronage: glandular disorders

FURTHER READING
Doble, Gilbert H. *The Saints of Cornwall,* Part Four. Felifach, Cornwall: Llanearch Publishers, 1998.

Caesarius of Arles (ca. 470–543) *Bishop of Arles, Father of the Church*

Caesarius of Arles was the first bishop in western Europe to receive the pallium from a pope. He was born at Châlons, Burgundy, France (then Gaul), in 470 or 471, of a French-Roman family. He entered the monastery of Lérins in his youth but ill health forced him to leave the community soon after. His uncle, Æonus, bishop of Arles, took him into his monastery and ordained him deacon and priest. When Æonus died in 502 or 503, Caesarius was unanimously chosen to succeed him.

In 505, King Alaric II of the Visigoths accused Caesarius of treason. He had come to believe that Caesarius intended to deliver Arles to the Burgundians, and without putting him on trial had him exiled to Bordeaux. He soon relented and allowed Caesarius to return to Arles. In 506, Caesarius called the Council of Agde and promulgated the famous adaptation of the Roman Law known as the *"Breviarium Alarici,"* which eventually became the civil code of Gaul.

Following a siege in 508, the Ostrogoths occupied Arles and King Theodoric, son of Alaric, suspecting Caesarius of having plotted with the besieging Franks and Burgundians, had him deported again. Caesarius was still in exile in 513 when Theodoric summoned him to Ravenna and pardoned him. Caesarius then went to Rome where Pope St. Symmachus (r. 498–514) gave him the pallium, confirmed him as metropolitan, and (in 514) personally renewed his appointment as vicar of the Apostolic See in Gaul.

Caesarius used his office to update and strengthen various aspects of church doctrine. In 529 he presided over the Second Council of Orange, the confirmation of whose decrees by Pope Boniface II (r. 530–532) in 531 made them authoritative in the Universal Church. Caesarius brought the Divine Office into local parishes and introduced monastic reforms, placing his sister St. Caesaria as abbess of a convent he founded. He was known as a great preacher, with a strong mystic bent. In the many sermons that have come down to us he inveighed at length against the main vices of his day—adultery and concubinage, drunkenness, neglect of the mass, love of landed wealth, and the numerous pagan practices still in vogue.

When the Franks captured Arles in 536, Caesarius was once more forced to flee. However, he was later able to return to his see, and died there on August 27, 543. His name was entered in the Roman Martyrology. Today, he is venerated especially in Arles.

In art, Caesarius is depicted as a bishop led by people with candles.

Feast: August 27

Caesarius of Nazianzus (ca. 330–369) *Father of the Church, physician, younger and only brother of St. Gregory of Nazianzus; son of Gregory the Elder*

Most of the details of the life of Caesarius of Nazianzus are known from his funeral oration delivered by his older brother Gregory. Caesarius was born ca. 330 in Arianzus near Nazianzus. His father, Gregory the Elder, was bishop of Nazianzus, and all the children received a careful religious upbringing. He studied medicine, geometry and astronomy at Caesarea in Cappadocia and in Alexandria. He established an excellent reputation as a physician, and went to Constantinople, where his older brother, St. Gregory of Nazianzus, came in 358. Caesarius served as physician to the court of Emperor Constantine and then was appointed to the court of Emperor Julian the Apostate, who unsuccessfully attempted to convert him to paganism. Caesarius left the court but returned to Constantinople after Julian's death. He became physician for Emperor Jovian and then treasurer for Emperor Valens.

In 368 Caesarius narrowly escaped death in a great earthquake that nearly destroyed Nicaea. Shaken, he was baptized and devoted himself to an ascetic life. Soon thereafter he fell fatally ill, dying in the spring of 369. He instructed that all of his goods should be given to the poor, but his servants kept many things.

Caesarius's remains were buried at Nazianzus.

Feast: February 25

FURTHER READING
Gregory Nazianzus, "Oration 7: Panegyric on His Brother S. Caesarius." URL: http://www.fordham.edu/halsall/basis/gregnaz-caesar.html. Downloaded September 23, 2000.

Caius (d. 296) *Pope and martyr*
Also known as: Gaius

Caius is said to have been a Dalmatian and a relative of Emperor Diocletian. He succeeded St. Eutychianus as pope on December 17, 283.

Caius decreed that only priests could be consecrated bishops; other than that, nothing has come down to us about his pontificate, which must have been unusually tranquil. He ruled for 12 years, four months and seven days, dying of natural causes on April 22, 296.

Caius is honored as a martyr, though on a mistaken basis. He is supposed to have fled the Vatican and lived for eight years in a cave or catacomb during the Diocletian persecution—which, however, did not begin until seven or eight years after his death. He was the last pontiff interred in the papal crypt of the Catacomb of St. Callistus on the Appian Way. He shares a feast day with Pope St. Soter (d. ca. 175) and is venerated especially in Dalmatia and Venice.

In art, Caius is shown with St. Nereus, wearing the papal tiara.

Feast: April 22

Callistus I (d. 222) *Pope and martyr*
Also known as: Callixtus

Callistus, the son of Domitius, was a Roman. As a young Christian slave, he was put in charge of a bank by his master, Carpophorus, but somehow lost the money that had been entrusted to him. He fled Rome but was discovered on a ship off Portus (Proto); he jumped overboard but was caught and carried back to Carpophorus. Later he was arrested for fighting in a synagogue when he tried to borrow (or collect debts) from some Jews. Denounced as a Christian, he was sentenced to work in the mines of Sardinia. He was released after the intercession of Emperor Commodus's mistress, Marcia, but was in such poor health that he was sent to Antium to recuperate.

Callistus lived in Antium with the help of a pension from Pope St. Victor I (r. 189–199). About the year 199 he was called back to Rome and made a deacon by Pope St. Zephyrinus (r. 199–217), who put him in charge of a cemetery (later named the San Callistus in his honor) on the Via Appia. He was well known for his kindness, and when Zephyrinus died about 217, was elected his successor by popular vote of the Roman people and clergy.

He was not without enemies, however. Critics denounced him for admitting to Communion people who had repented of fornication, adultery, and murder. They were upset also with his teachings that the commission of a mortal sin was not enough to depose a bishop; that men who had been married more than once could be admitted to the clergy; and that marriages between free women and Christian slaves were legitimate.

One of the biggest critics was St. Hippolytus, his rival for the papal seat. Hippolytus was an opponent also of the Monarchianists, who denied the Trinity and held that Jesus was no more than a man who had received supernatural abilities at his baptism. Callistus excommunicated Sabellius, then the leader of the Monarchianists, but this was not enough for Hippolytus, who withdrew from the Church of Rome and had himself consecrated bishop (and antipope), producing a schism that was to last for decades.

Callistus died about October 14, 222, perhaps during a popular uprising, although the legend that he was thrown down a well has no basis in fact. He was buried on the Via Aurelia rather than in the cemetery on the Via Appia, where most other popes of his time were interred.

In art, Callistus is shown wearing a red robe with a tiara (the sign of a pope); as being thrown into a well with a millstone around his neck; or simply with a millstone around his neck. Often there is a fountain near him.

Feast: October 14

Camillus de Lellis (1550–1614) *Founder of the Order of Ministers of the Sick, or the Camillians*
Also known as: The Father of a Good Death

Camillus de Lellis was born in 1550 in Bocchianico, Italy, the son of a military officer. His mother died when he was an infant, and he was neglected as a child. As a youth he became a soldier and fought against the Turks. His gambling left him penniless, and he was ill from abscesses in his feet. He subsisted by begging. He tried to join the Franciscan order but was rejected.

In Rome, Camillus went to the Hospital for Incurables seeking help for his feet, and took a job there caring for the sick, only to be dismissed on account of his gambling and unruly behavior. He returned to soldiering and fought the Turks again in 1569. After the war, the Capuchins in Manfredonia hired him for a construction project. They admitted him to the order as a lay brother, but then dismissed him because of his diseased legs. Camillus went back to the hospital in Rome, where he was temporarily cured. He became a nurse and then director of the hospital.

Camillus had an idea to found an order of lay infirmarians, but his confessor St. Philip Neri advised him to become a priest. He entered the Jesuit College in Rome and in 1584 founded the Order of the Ministers of the Sick, which became known also as the Camillians. They devoted themselves to caring for plague victims.

The congregation was confirmed by Pope Sixtus V (r. 1585–90) in 1586, and Camillus served as the first general superior. The order adopted a red cross to wear on the front of their habits. Tradition holds that the saint's mother had had a vision of a child with a red cross on his chest and holding a standard, leading other children who wore the same symbol. The red cross preceded by nearly 200 years the red cross adopted as the symbol for the Red Cross volunteer organization established by Swiss businessman Henri Dunant.

In 1588 Camillus's order expanded to Naples. At that time, Rome's harbor was full of quarantine ships with plague victims aboard. Two members of the community died caring for them. The congregation was made a religious order in 1591 by Pope Gregory XIV (r. 1590–91).

Camillus established more houses throughout Italy. Though often seriously ill and debilitated himself from chronic conditions, he devoted most of his time to visiting and caring for the sick and the poor. He resigned as general superior in 1607 to make more time available for his caregiving work.

Camillus died in Rome on July 14, 1614. In art he is often shown in the robes of his order. He shares his patronage with St. John of God.

Eleven years after his death, Camillus was exhumed and his body was found to be in excellent condition. Large crowds came to view it and witnessed the flow of a pure, fragrant liquid from an incision made by one of the examining doctors. The liquid was collected in cloths and claimed to have remarkable healing properties.

The Camillians still wear red crosses on the front of their habits.

Canonized: 1746 by Pope Benedict XIV
Feast: July 14
Patronage: hospitals; infirmarians; nurses; the sick

Casimir (1458–1484) *Prince and patron saint of Poland and Lithuania*

Casimir was born in 1458, the second son and third of 13 children to King Casimir IV and Elizabeth of Austria. In childhood he became devoted to God through the influence of his tutor, John Duglosz. He refused to play the royal role, instead wearing plain clothes and sleeping on the floor. He spent much time in prayer.

His father expected something more traditional from Casimir, and in 1471 sent him to head an army and seize control of the Hungarian throne. Casimir obeyed, but felt the expedition was morally wrong. When soldiers began deserting, he turned around and went home. His furious father confined him to the castle at Dzoki.

The exile strengthened Casimir's resolve to adhere to his spiritual calling. He refused his father's arranged marriage for him, as well as other plans.

From 1479 to 1483, King Casimir was out of Poland, and son Casimir served as regent. While visiting Grodno, Lithuania (now Belarus), Casimir became ill with tuberculosis and died on March 4, 1483 or 1484. He was buried at Vilnius with his favorite song, a Latin hymn favored by St. Bernard of Clairvaux, called "Daily, Daily Sing to Mary." It is sometimes called the "Hymn of St. Casimir," though he did not write it. His tomb became renowned for miracles.

Canonized: 1522 by Pope Adrian VI
Feast: March 4
Patronage: Knights of St. John; Lithuania; Poland

Catherine de' Ricci (1522–1590) *Dominican mystic and stigmatist*

Catherine de' Ricci was born April 23, 1522, in Florence, Italy, to a patrician family. Her father, Pier Francesco de' Ricci, came from a lineage of respected merchants and bankers. She was baptized Alexandrina.

Catherine lost her mother in infancy, and she was reared by a stepmother, Fiammetta da Diacceto. As a young child, she spoke to her guardian angel and learned how to pray the rosary from the angel. She was often in prayer. Fiammetta, a pious woman, encouraged the child in her devotion. At age six Catherine was sent to the convent school of Montecelli, where her aunt, Louisa de' Ricci, was a nun. There she developed a devotion to the Passion that played a prominent role in her mystical life to come.

Her father was opposed to her becoming a nun but relented after she became ill. In 1535, when she was 14, she entered the Dominican convent of San Vicenzo in Prato, Tuscany, under the direction of her uncle, F. Timothy de' Ricci. The order offered her a desired strict religious life. She took the name of Catherine, and was professed in 1536.

Despite a series of illnesses that permanently damaged her health, Catherine strove to die to her senses and practiced severe austerities and mortifications. She fasted two or three days a week on bread and sometimes went for a day with no food at all. She wore a sharp iron chain next to her skin. She practiced obedience, humility and meekness.

Catherine advanced quickly in the convent, serving as mistress of novices, subprioress, and then by age 25 (some accounts say age 30 or 38) perpetual prioress. Her reputation for sanctity and prudence, as well as her astonishing mystical life, attracted numerous bishops, cardinals and princes who paid visits to seek her counsel. Three of them went on to become popes: Clement VIII (r. 1523–34), Marcellus II (r. 1555) and Leo XI (r. 1605). Catherine corresponded with St. Charles Borromeo and Pope Pius V (r. 1566–72) and had mystical visits with SS. Philip Neri and Mary Magdalen de' Pazzi.

Catherine's remarkable mystical life had a dramatic opening in 1542, when she was about 20. During holy week she experienced the first of her ecstasies in which she saw the passion of Christ enacted in sequence in

17 scenes. The 28-hour-long ecstasies went on for 12 years, repeating every week from Thursday midday to Friday at 4 P.M. During these raptures, Catherine's body would move as though going through the passion herself. She exhibited all the wounds experienced by Jesus. She had bleeding stigmata in her hands, feet and side, as well as the wounds from Christ's crown of thorns and from His scourging. By the time the raptures were finished, her shoulder was indented as though from carrying the cross.

Throughout the raptures, Catherine issued a sweet perfume that lingered on everything she touched, sometimes for up to a day later.

In her first such experience in 1542, Catherine meditated so intensely on the crucifixion that she became ill, and was healed by a vision of the resurrected Christ talking with St. Mary Magdalene.

Catherine's raptures attracted spectators. Sometimes she would speak out to them. The crowds increased to the point that Catherine's sisters prayed for her wounds to become less visible (in 1554, they did).

Also in 1542, Catherine experienced the mystical marriage. On Easter Sunday, Jesus appeared to her and placed on her forefinger a gold ring with a large pointed diamond. Others glimpsed the ring. Some saw only a swelling and reddening of the flesh. The reddened appearance could not be duplicated, nor made to go away.

Spectators also saw her passion wounds differently as well. Some people saw the actual wounds, while others saw only redness and swelling. Still others saw her hands actually pierced and bleeding, or the saint surrounded in a brilliant light.

Catherine had a mystical relationship with St. Philip Neri in Rome, with whom she exchanged letters. The two never met in person, but did meet in mystical visits, some of which were witnessed by others. Catherine had the ability to bilocate.

After a lengthy illness, Catherine died on February 2, 1590, in an odor of sanctity. Her incorrupt body can be seen in a reliquary below the major altar of the basilica of Prato.

Beatified: 1732 by Pope Clement XII
Canonized: 1746 by Pope Benedict XIV
Feast: February 13

FURTHER READING
"St. Catherine de Ricci, V., O.S.D." URL: http://www.cin.org/saints/cricci.html. Downloaded September 21, 2000.

Catherine of Alexandria (d. ca. 310) *Virgin and martyr whose cult was suppressed in 1969*
Name meaning: Pure one

St. Catherine of Alexandria (copyright © Robert Michael Place. Used with permission)

Catherine of Alexandria is believed to have been born in Alexandria, Egypt, to a noble family. She converted to Christianity through a vision, and denounced Emperor Maxentius (r. 306–312) for persecuting Christians. Catherine was arrested. She debated 50 pagan philosophers, all of whom converted on the strength of her words. They were burned to death by Maxentius.

The emperor offered Catherine a royal marriage if she would deny her faith. She refused and was sent to jail. While in prison, and while Maxentius was away, Catherine is said to have converted Maxentius's wife and 200 of his soldiers. He had them all put to death.

Catherine was condemned to death and was strapped onto a spiked wheel. The wheel broke (legend has it that an angel destroyed it). She was then beheaded. According to lore, an angel carried her body to Mount Sinai and buried her there. St. Catherine's Monastery is still there. Her relics are in Cologne, Rouen, Nuremberg and Grevenrode.

Catherine has been venerated in the Eastern church since the 10th century. She is one of the Fourteen Holy Helpers whose voices guided St. Joan of Arc. She has been invoked against diseases of the head and tongue; for harvests; and for assistance in drowning. In art she is shown wearing a crown and with a spiked wheel.

Feast: formerly November 25
Patronage: bakers; barbers; hospitals; jurists; libraries; Paris haute couture; philosophers; preachers; pupils; single women; teachers; theologians; universities; virgins; wheelwrights; University of Paris; Valais, Switzerland

Catherine of Bologna (1413–1463) *Mystic, writer, artist and Poor Clare*

Catherine of Bologna was born Catherine de Vigri on March 9, 1413. She was the daughter of a diplomatic agent of the marquis of Ferrara. At the age of 11, she was appointed maid of honor to Margaret d'Este, the daughter of the marquis, and shared her training and education. Margaret married when Catherine was 14. Catherine turned down marriage proposals, and at age 17 left the court and became a Franciscan Tertiary in Ferrara. Eventually her community became part of the Poor Clares.

Catherine assumed the duties of the bakers, then of novice mistress. A story is told that once she baked bread and left the loaves in the oven for five hours while she attended a sermon. The loaves did not burn, but turned out beautifully. After her death, the oven was said to emit a sweet perfume for 10 days before each of her feast days and for several days thereafter.

Catherine began to experience visions of Christ and the Blessed Virgin Mary. One Christmas Eve, Mary appeared and placed the infant Jesus in Catherine's arms. On another occasion, she heard angelic choirs singing after the Elevation of the Mass.

After 24 years at the Ferrara convent, Catherine was sent back to Bologna with 15 sisters to establish a convent. She was abbess there for the rest of her life.

Catherine was a writer and artist. *The Seven Spiritual Weapons*, a mystical work on her spiritual life, is her most important text. She also composed books of sermons, devotions and verses. She painted miniatures and illustrated a breviary.

In Lent of 1463, Catherine became seriously ill. On March 9, her birthday, she pronounced the name of Jesus three times, and a heavenly perfume came around her, signaling her death. Though 50 years old, her face took on the radiance of youth.

Catherine was buried within hours without a coffin. Her body was exhumed 18 days later because of the sweet scent coming from her grave and the miraculous cures claimed by those who visited it. Her body was found to be incorrupt and bathed in sweat. While sisters cleaned it, a pleasant perfume wafted from it. One sister pulled off a piece of skin hanging from a foot, and the corpse bled copiously. The next morning, Catherine's face was radiant. Three months later, the corpse, exhumed, was found to bleed copiously through the nose twice.

Since 1475, Catherine's incorrupt body has remained seated in an upright position in the church of the Poor Clare convent in Bologna. In 1500, Catherine appeared in a vision to a nun and requested that her body be moved to a special chapel—the location and layout were specified—and that her body be kept in its upright position. This was done, and in 1688 the body was moved to a larger and more elaborate chapel.

Until 1953, the relic was not covered, and pilgrims kissed the feet. In 1953 a protective glass urn was constructed. The hands, which were chapping, were covered with a light coat of wax during World War II. Catherine's skin has darkened, perhaps due to exposure from oil lamps.

Catherine's biography was written by Sr. Illuminata; the original is still at the convent in Bologna.

Canonized: May 22, 1712, by Pope Clement XI
Feast: March 9
Patronage: art; artists; liberal arts

Catherine of Genoa (1447–1510) *Extraordinary mystic*

Catherine of Genoa was born in 1447 in Genoa, Italy, to Jacopo Fieschi and Francesca di Negro, both members of illustrious families. The Fieschi family boasted two popes, Innocent IV (r. 1243–54) and Adrian V (r. 1276). Jacopo became the viceroy of Naples.

A delicate child with a rich inner life, Catherine began to do penance at age eight by replacing her soft bed with straw and a wooden block for a pillow. She felt intense physical pain whenever she gazed upon her favorite image of Jesus, "La Pietà." At age 12 she began to pray earnestly, and at age 13 announced her desire to become a nun at the convent of Our Lady of Grace, along with her sister Limbania. The convent turned her away because of her age, however.

When Catherine was 16, her parents married her against her wishes to a young nobleman, Giuliano Adorno, who proved to be unfaithful, mean-tempered and a spendthrift. Catherine spent five years in depressed misery and another five years trying to amuse herself in various activities.

Around 1473 she had a life-changing mystical experience. Urged by her sister nun to go to confession on the day following the feast of St. Benedict, Catherine complied but without enthusiasm. When she knelt in the confessional, she felt herself pierced by a burning ray of divine love that swept her into an ecstasy. She felt united with God and purged of her miseries. The confessor was not witness to this, having been called out of the booth. When he returned, she could only murmur that she would leave her confession for another time. She went home, on fire and wounded with the love of God, and closed herself in her room to weep and sigh. Thereafter, she often beheld a vision of Jesus nailed to the cross.

Catherine made her general confession and felt cleansed of her sins. For nearly 14 months, she remained in an exalted state of consciousness. She experienced intense contrition, self-hatred and total absorption in Christ, who showed her his flaming Sacred Heart. In her contrition, she would lick the earth with her tongue, not knowing what she was doing. So complete was her mystical union that she felt her own heart die within her and proclaimed, "I live no longer, but Christ lives in me."

Catherine's interior state remained profoundly changed for the rest of her life; she was sustained by a burning inner fire. She had many encounters with Christ and was taken into heaven to see the realms of the angels.

For four years, she quit the world as much as possible. She imposed upon herself strict mortification and penance. She wore hair cloth and ate no meat or fruit. She slept on "sharply pointed things" and kept her eyes cast downward. She spoke to others as little possible and in as low a voice as possible. She spent six hours a day in prayer in such states of intensity that she seemed like one dead to others. She yearned for death.

For 23 Lents and Advents, she was unable to eat, and could consume only a glassful of water, vinegar and pounded salt. Because of these and other measures, Catherine was often seriously ill. She received the conventional medical treatments, which included bloodletting. This especially was believed to relieve her inner fire.

In spite of her self-inflicted sufferings, Catherine managed to do volunteer work in hospitals and among the poor. Reduced to poverty herself thanks to Giuliano, she was given funds to aid others by the Ladies of Mercy. In her volunteer work, Catherine sought suffering for herself as well. She cleaned houses of "the most disgusting filth," often putting it into her own mouth in order to overcome the disgust it produced. She took home clothing covered with filth and vermin and cleaned them, returning them to their owners. Remarkably, she was never affected by what she touched.

Catherine became manager and treasurer of the largest hospital in Genoa.

Somehow she managed to convert her wayward husband, who became a Third Order Franciscan and agreed to live with her in continence. Giuliano died in 1497.

Beginning around 1491, Catherine began to suffer from a mysterious malady that doctors did not know how to treat. It did not seem to be either physical or spiritual; it left her greatly debilitated. In 1493, Catherine nearly died of the plague. She recovered, but remained permanently weakened.

Catherine followed her own inner guidance and would not submit to the spiritual direction of anyone else. She often told others that she could not put into words what she experienced. In 1495 a Father Marabotti became her spiritual adviser, and helped her to compile her memoirs in her *Life and Doctrine*.

In 1509 her food intake, which had never been good, declined drastically; she ate in a week what most people would eat in a day. That soon dropped to nothing more than small quantities of broth.

Nonetheless, Catherine attracted many visitors, who saw perfection in her. She touched others with her "burning words of divine love." But as her strength ebbed, she was able to utter only phrases and words, such as "Love of God" and "charity, union and peace," and finally just "God." She suffered violent attacks in which she would seem to writhe as if in flames of fire, and would cease breathing. She felt her heart wounded with a new ray of divine love, which caused more severe bodily pain.

On January 10, 1510, she lost sight and speech, and made signs to be given last rites. She recovered her senses but continued to suffer in agony. By May doctors said they could do nothing for her and that her affliction was "supernatural." Her last months were spent in excruciating pain. She could not tolerate taking any food or liquid.

On September 12, black blood flowed from her mouth and her body was covered with black stripes. She bled violently again on September 14. That evening, she indicated she would take her Communion in heaven. She died uttering, "Into thy hands, O Lord, I commend my spirit." She was seen by several persons ascending to heaven clothed in white and on a white cloud.

Catherine's body was interred in the hospital of the Pammatone, the largest hospital in Genoa, where she had done much of her work. It was disinterred nearly a year later when it was discovered that a conduit of water ran behind the tomb. Though the wood coffin was decayed and filled with worms, the body was untouched and incorrupt, and appeared to have been dried out. Her body was put on public display for eight days, and pilgrims claimed to be cured. Prior to her death, Catherine had instructed that her heart be examined after death to see if it had been consumed by divine love, but this was not done.

The body was placed into a marble sepulcher in the hospital. It was moved to various locations in 1551, 1593 and 1642. In 1694 it was moved to a glass-sided reliquary placed high on an altar in a church built in her honor in the quarter of Portoria, Genoa.

Catherine's body was examined by physicians in 1834 and on May 10, 1960. Though brown, dry and rigid, her relic was determined to be free of embalming or any treatment for preservation.

Catherine wrote *Spiritual Dialogue between the Soul, the Body, Self-Love, the Spirit, Humanity and the Lord God* and *Treatise on Purgatory,* two mystical works that proved her sanctity for canonization and remain respected today.

In her writings, Catherine exhorts people to seek nothing less than complete union with God. Without the grace of God, she said, man is nothing more than the devil. She said the human intellect could not comprehend the true nature of pure love, which is incapable of suffering.

Beatified: 1675 by Pope Clement V
Canonized: 1737 by Pope Clement XII
Feast: September 14

FURTHER READING
"The Life and Doctrine of Saint Catherine of Genoa." URL: http://www.ccel.wheaton.edu/c/catherine_genoa/life. Downloaded: February 6, 2000.

Catherine of Siena (1347–1380) *Doctor of the Church and second woman to be so named; one of the Church's greatest mystics; Dominican tertiary; papal adviser*

Catherine of Siena was born on March 25, 1347, in Siena, Italy, the youngest of 25 children in the Benincasa family. Her father, Giacomo di Benincasa, was a dyer; her mother, Lapa, the daughter of a local poet. From her earliest childhood Catherine saw visions and practiced extreme austerities; she wore a hair shirt. When she was five, it was said that angels levitated her up and down stairs, so pleased were they with her "Hail Mary" prayers. At age six, she had a remarkable vision of Jesus giving her a benediction, which took place while she was traveling on a road with an older brother. At the age of seven she consecrated her virginity to Christ. At 16, she took the habit of the Dominican Tertiaries.

For three years she engaged in celestial visitations and familiar conversation with Christ.

In 1366 she had a profound mystical experience of spiritual marriage. For a long time preceding, she had been advised of this by Jesus speaking in her interior voice. On the last day of Carnival, the voice told her, "I will this day celebrate solemnly with thee the feast of the betrothal of thy soul, and even as I promised I will espouse thee to Myself in faith."

While Jesus spoke, there appeared a glorious vision of Jesus, the Blessed Virgin Mary, St. John the Evangelist, St. Paul and St. Dominic, along with the prophet David, who played the psaltery set to music. Mary took Catherine's right hand and held out its fingers to Jesus, asking him to espouse himself to Catherine in faith. Jesus drew out a gold ring set with an exquisite diamond encircled with four pearls and placed it on the ring finger of Catherine's right hand. He said, "Lo, I espouse thee to myself, thy Creator and Savior in the faith, which until thou dost celebrate thy eternal nuptials with me in Heaven thou will preserve ever without stain. Henceforth, my daughter, do manfully and without hesitation those things by which the ordering of My providence will be put into thy hands; for being now armed with the fortitude of the faith, now will happily overcome all thy adversaries."

The vision disappeared. For the rest of her life, Catherine could see the ring upon her finger, though it was invisible to others. (Similarly, St. Teresa of Avila was given by Jesus a rosary made of "stones more precious than diamonds." It, too, was visible only to her.)

Catherine experienced other mystical gifts, including levitation during prayer, multiplication of food and the ability to smell the stench of sin in others. She performed miraculous healings and relieved others of diabolical possession. Supernatural rays of light issued forth from her face. She endured mystical fasts. In 1370, she was said to raise her mother, Lapa, from the dead after her mother died suddenly.

Once she fell into an ecstasy in which Jesus approached her holding a red human heart. He opened her left side and placed the heart inside, saying, "Dearest daughter, as I took your heart away, now, you see, I am giving you Mine, so that you can go on living with it forever." The heart was said to make loud noises of joy whenever Catherine was happy.

Catherine's peers resented her supernatural gifts and brought charges against her. She was cleared of

The mystical marriage of St. Catherine of Siena (Library of Congress Prints and Photographs Division)

charges and given a spiritual director, Bl. Raymond of Capua, who became her first biographer.

Catherine returned to Siena, and began to tend the sick (especially lepers and plague victims), help the poor and convert sinners. She suffered terrible physical pain, but forced herself to live for long periods on little food save the Blessed Sacrament. Nonetheless, she charmed everyone with her happiness, wisdom and spiritual insight, and was sought as a counselor and peacemaker. She gathered disciples.

During the summer of 1370 she received a series of special manifestations of Divine mysteries, which culminated in a prolonged trance, a kind of mystical death. She had a vision of hell, purgatory and heaven, and heard a Divine command to leave her cell and enter the public life of the world. From this trance, Catherine produced her great mystical work, *The Dialogue of the Seraphic Virgin Catherine of Siena*.

She also began to dispatch hundreds of letters to men and women, including the princes and nobility of the republics of Italy, and papal legates. She was consulted about the affairs of the Church, and counseled Pope Gregory XI (r. 1370–78) on numerous matters, including his plans for a crusade against the Turks, and for reforming the clergy and the administration of the Papal States. On a visit to Pisa in 1375, Catherine received the stigmata on the fourth Sunday of Lent. Praying before a crucifix, Catherine saw five rays of blood come from the points of the wounds to her, changing into rays of light as they reached her body. She prayed that the marks would not be visible to others as long as she lived; they appeared after her death. She said the five wounds did not pain her but strengthened her.

Gregory sent her to Avignon as a peace ambassador of the Florentines when war broke out between Florence and the Holy See, but she was unsuccessful. However, she impressed Gregory so much that he took her advice to return the papacy to Rome in 1377. In 1378 Gregory dispatched her again to Florence, where an attempt was made to murder her. Gregory died and was succeeded by Urban VI (r. 1378–89). She remained in Florence until peace was declared, and then returned to Siena.

Urban's election resulted in the Great Schism and the election of an antipope, Clement VII. Catherine supported Urban VI, and was summoned to Rome by him in November 1378. She remained in Rome for the rest of her life, working for the reformation of the Church, serving the sick and poor, and dispatching eloquent letters in behalf of Urban (she had miraculously learned how to write herself in 1377 and no longer had to rely on dictation). Her last political work, accomplished practically from her deathbed, was the reconciliation of Pope Urban VI with the Roman Republic.

In 1380 her health began to fail and Catherine prayed to join Christ. She could scarcely swallow due to severe inflammation in her throat. On Sexagesima Sunday, she suffered a violent stroke, followed by another one the next evening. Nonetheless, she rose every day during most of Lent and walked a mile to St. Peter's, where she prayed all day. Finally, overcome, she lay in bed for eight weeks, covered with sores and unable to lift her head. Her body wasted away. In her final hours, she rallied to berate herself for her imperfections and sins, and to pray for the Church, the pope and others. She asked for, and received, plenary indulgence to be absolved of all her sins, saying it had been granted to her by Popes Gregory and Urban.

Catherine died at age 33 on April 29, the Sunday before the Ascension. Her body was displayed for three days and remained intact, flexible and fragrant. Huge crowds came to touch her corpse.

Catherine was buried in the cemetery of the Church of Santa Maria sopra Minerva, and soon was moved to the foot of a column facing the Rosary Chapel, where she remained until 1430. However, in 1385 her head was severed, placed in a gilded copper reliquary and secretly sent to Siena, where it eventually was placed in the Hospital of St. Lazarus, where she had ministered the sick. Other relics taken from the body at the same time were an arm for Siena and three fingers for Venice.

In 1430, what remained of the body was placed in a new stone sarcophagus. It was opened from time to time for the taking of more relics for Dominicans throughout Europe, including:

- a hand taken in 1487 for the Dominican Sisters of the Monastery of S. Domenico et Sisto in Rome;
- the left foot, bearing stigmata, taken in 1487 for the Church of SS. John and Paul in Venice;
- a rib taken in 1501 for the convent of St. Mark in Florence;
- a shoulder blade taken in 1575 for the Dominican Sisters of Magnanapoli in Rome;
- two reliquaries of bone and skin taken in 1855 for St. Dominic's in Stone, England, and the convent of St. Catherine in Bow, England.

The finger that bore the mystical ring of Christ was given to the Chartreuse of Pontiniano near Florence. Other small relics were distributed as well.

On August 4, 1855, the sarcophagus of Catherine was placed below the main altar of the Church of Santa Maria sopra Minerva. This event is known as the Translation of the Relics of St. Catherine, which feast is commemorated on the Thursday after Sexagesima Sunday.

The feast of her Espousals is kept on the Thursday of the carnival.

Besides her *Dialogue,* Catherine's body of work includes more than 400 letters and a collection of prayers. Her writings are considered to be among the classics of the Italian language. The *Dialogue* comprises four treatises, on divine providence, discretion, prayer and obedience. Its style "bears upon it all the marks of true automatic composition of the highest type," according to mysticism expert Evelyn Underhill. Central to Catherine's teaching is that man, whether in the cloister or in the world, must always abide by "the cell of self-knowledge," through which one comes into perfect knowledge of God: "In self-knowledge, then, thou wilt humble thyself; seeing that, in thyself, thou dost not even exist."

Catherine is invoked against headaches and the plague. In art she is depicted in her Dominican Tertiary clothing. Her emblems are the lily and book, the crown of thorns, or sometimes a heart, referring to the legend of her having changed hearts with Christ. She is the second woman after St. Teresa of Avila to be named a Doctor of the Church, and one of only three women to hold the honor.

Canonized: 1461 by Pope Pius II
Named Doctor of the Church: 1970 by Pope Paul VI
Feast: April 29
Patronage: the dying; fire prevention; nursing homes; spinsters; Italy (since 1939); Rome (since 1866)

FURTHER READING
The Dialogue of Saint Catherine of Siena. Tr. Algar Thorold. Rockford, Ill.: TAN Books, 1974.
The Letters of Catherine of Siena. Tr. Suzanne O.P. Noffke. Ithaca, N.Y.: Cornell University Press, 2001.
Underhill, Evelyn. *Mysticism.* New York: New American Library, 1974.

Catherine of Sweden (1330 or 1331–1381) *Daughter of St. Bridget of Sweden and cofounder of the Brigittines*
Also known as: Catherine of Vadstena

Catherine of Sweden was born in 1330 or 1331 in Ulfasa, Sweden, one of eight children of St. Bridget. Like her mother, she married young; her husband, Eggared von Kurnen (Lyderrson), was a lifelong invalid. They took a vow of continence.

When Bridget went to live in Rome in 1348, Catherine received her husband's permission to follow her. He died while she was away. Catherine accompanied her mother to the Holy Land and elsewhere. She declined offers to remarry and stayed with her mother for 25 years. When her mother died, she returned to Sweden with her body to bury it at Vadstena, a monastery Bridget had founded.

Catherine took on the task of directing her mother's Order of the Holy Savior, or Brigittines. After several years, she returned to Rome for five years to work for her mother's canonization. In 1380 Pope Urban VI ratified the Brigittine rule.

While in Italy, Catherine became friends with St. Catherine of Siena and almost accompanied her on a trip to the court of Joanna of Naples, a notoriously immoral queen. Joanna had brought about the moral disgrace of Bridget's son, Charles, and St. Catherine of Vadstena could not bring herself to face the woman who had endangered her brother's soul. She returned to Sweden at the outbreak of the Great Western Schism.

Catherine returned to Vadstena before her mother was canonized. Her health failed, and after a painful illness she died peacefully at Vadstena. She was never formally canonized, but Pope Innocent VIII (r. 1484–92) confirmed her cult. Her feast is observed in Sweden and in the Brigittine Order. A chapel in the Piazza Farnese in Rome is dedicated to her.

Catherine is credited with raising the dead on at least two occasions. One case concerned a man who fell from a coach and was run over; another was a man who fell from a roof and was badly mangled. Both were declared dead, and Catherine touched them and restored them to life and health.

Feast: March 24

FURTHER READING
Herbert, Father Albert J. *Raised from the Dead: True Stories of 400 Resurrection Miracles.* Rockford, Ill.: TAN Books, 1986.

Catherine Labouré (1806–1876) *Virgin and mystic who received a vision of the Miraculous Medal from the Blessed Virgin Mary*
Name meaning: Pure one

Catherine Labouré was born on May 2, 1806, in the Côte d'Or, France, to a farming family. Her given name at birth was Zoe. She was eight when her mother died, and she assumed responsibility for helping to raise her siblings.

At age 18 she had a dream that foretold her destiny in the church. In the dream, she attended mass said by a saintly old priest. She then met him again when she visited a sick person. The priest told her, "My daughter, it is good to nurse the sick. Now you avoid me, but

St. Catherine Labouré

one day you'll be very glad to come to me. The good Lord has plans for you—do not forget it!"

In 1830 she joined the Daughters of Charity, founded by St. Vincent de Paul, in Paris. When she saw a picture of him, she was astonished to recognize him as the saintly old priest in her dream.

Three times in 1830, while Catherine was still a novice, Mary appeared to her. The first apparition occurred on July 18, after Catherine had retired to her partitioned cubicle, silently repeating a prayer. She went to sleep with the thought that she would see Mary that night. At about 11:30 P.M., she was awakened by the sound of someone calling her name. She saw a child dressed in white who appeared to be about four or five years old. The child told her to come to the chapel where Mary was waiting for her. Catherine was surprised to see that the way to the chapel was lit. She was even more surprised when she entered the chapel and saw all the candles and lights lit, which reminded her of midnight mass. After a long wait, Mary made

her presence known with a noise like the rustling of a silk dress. Turning, Catherine saw Mary—a sight that she described as "the sweetest moment in my life."

Mary told Catherine that God wished to charge her with a mission. She would suffer many trials and be contradicted, but she should never have fear. She would be inspired in her prayers. Mary advised her how to act with her director and also told her several secrets that she was not to disclose. She predicted that bad times were coming for France and that the whole world would be in upheaval due to "all sorts of troubles." The streets would be filled with blood and the whole world would be in sorrow. Catherine was never to lose faith. Mary, who seemed to be in great grief, departed. The child—whom Catherine felt was her guardian angel—took her back to her bed. It was 2 A.M. A few days later Catherine told her vision to her confessor, Father Aladel, but he paid little attention to it.

The second vision occurred on November 27, 1830, at 5:30 in the afternoon. Catherine was participating in a community meditation in the chapel. She saw Mary, exquisitely beautiful, dressed in white and standing on a globe. She held a small globe, above which was a small golden cross. Mary was looking up toward heaven. She held the globe against her heart and offered it to Jesus as advocate and mother of all mankind. Suddenly her hands blazed with dazzling light. Her fingers were covered with jewels that fell onto the globe at her feet and she lowered her hands. Mary looked at Catherine and said, "This globe which you see represents the world as a whole and France in particular and each separate individual." The streams of light were "the symbol of the graces which I shed on those who ask me for them."

Catherine then saw a slightly oval frame form around Mary. Over it were the words "O Mary conceived without sin, pray for us who have recourse to thee" written in gold letters. She heard a voice say, "Have a medal made according to this model. Everybody who wears it will receive great graces by wearing it around the neck. The graces will be abundant for persons who wear it with confidence." Catherine saw the reverse side of the medal, which featured the cross, the letter M, the two hearts of Jesus and Mary, and the 12 stars of the apostles.

Catherine shared her second vision with Father Aladel, but he dismissed this one, too.

The last vision occurred in December 1830. Catherine saw Mary standing above and in the rear of the tabernacle on the altar. Under Mary's feet was a green serpent with yellow spots. When she noticed that some of the jewels on Mary's hands did not shine, Catherine was told, "Those stones which remain dark symbolize the graces that people have forgotten to request." Catherine was again shown the design for the medal and instructed to have it made. Mary told her she would not appear again but would speak to Catherine in her prayers.

Father Aladel still refused to act. Catherine prayed about this, and was told by Mary that a day would come when he would do Mary's bidding. In 1832, after securing permission from the archbishop of Paris, he had 1,500 medals made. They were approved in 1836. When distributed, they immediately were associated with miraculous healings and conversions, and quickly spread throughout Europe. By 1836, more than six million medals had been made in Paris and Lyons, and millions more in 12 other cities.

Mary also instructed that Father Aladel should found and direct the Sodality Children of Mary. This he did.

The troubles for France proved to be the anticlerical revolt in Paris in 1870.

Catherine and Father Aladel told no one who had received the vision for this medal. Father Aladel took the secret to his grave; Catherine remained silent about it for 46 years. She continued her work as a Daughter of Charity. On all feasts of Mary she was sick or suffering extreme pain.

Early in 1876 she announced that she would be dead within a year. With Mary's permission, she gave a full account of the apparitions to her mother superior. She died on December 31, 1876, and was buried in the chapel of the Daughters of Charity of Paris. Her body was exhumed on March 21, 1933, and found to be incorrupt. Her hands were amputated and her heart removed for relics, as were several ribs, clavicle and the kneecaps. Her incorrupt body, with wax hands, is on display behind glass.

Canonized: July 27, 1947, by Pope Pius XII
Feast: November 25

FURTHER READING
Brown, Raphael. *Saints Who Saw Mary.* Rockford, Ill.: TAN Books, 1955.
Waters, Alma Powers. *St. Catherine Labouré and the Miraculous Medal.* Fort Collins, Colo.: Ignatius Press, 2000.

Cecilia (second century?) *Roman virgin and martyr*

The story of Cecilia, a popular saint, is thought to be fiction built upon fact. Cecilia is said to have been born in Rome to a patrician family and was brought up Christian. Dates of her life vary; by some accounts, she is believed to have lived in the second century and died about 177, and by other accounts she lived in the third century.

St. Cecilia inspired by angels (Author's collection)

She decided at a young age that she would remain a virgin for the love of God. Her father, however, pledged her to marry a young patrician man named Valerian. On the day of her marriage, Cecilia wore sackcloth next to her skin, fasted, and invoked the saints and angels to help her guard her virginity. She told her husband, "I have a secret to tell you. You must know that I have an angel of God watching over me. If you touch me in the way of marriage he will be angry and you will suffer; but if you respect my maidenhood he'll love you as he loves me." Valerian said, "Show me this angel. If he be of God, I will refrain as you wish." Cecilia answered, "If you believe in the living and one true God and receive the water of baptism, then you shall see the angel." Valerian agreed.

Cecilia sent him to Urban (destined to be pope from 223 to 230), who baptized him. When he returned, he found Cecilia praying in her chamber. Standing beside her was an angel with flaming wings, holding two crowns of roses and lilies. The angel placed the crowns on their heads and vanished. Shortly after, Tibertius, the brother of Valerian, entered the chamber and marveled at the fragrance and beauty of the flowers at that season of the year. He also consented to be baptized.

Valerian and Tibertius devoted themselves to burying the martyrs slain daily by the prefect of the city, Turcius Almachius. [Note: There is no record of a prefect by that name.] They were arrested and brought before the prefect, and when they refused to sacrifice to the gods they were beheaded. Dying with them was a man named Maximus, who declared himself a Christian after witnessing their courage.

Cecilia was called upon to renounce her faith. Instead she began preaching and converting others. She summoned 400 persons to her home, where Urban baptized them all. Cecilia was arrested and was condemned to be suffocated in the bathroom of her own house. She was shut in for a night and a day. The furnace was stoked with seven times the amount of normal fuel, but Cecilia was not harmed. When Almachius heard this he sent a soldier to cut off her head in the bath. The man struck three times without being able to sever her head. He left her bleeding. Cecilia lived three days. Crowds came and collected her blood with napkins and sponges while she preached to them or prayed. After she died, she was buried by Urban and his deacons in the catacomb of St. Callistus.

Pope Paschal I (r. 817–824) wished to transfer the saint's body to a place of honor but could not locate it. In a dream, she told him where to find it. He translated the relics, along with the bones of Valerian, Tibertius and Maximus, to the Church of St. Cecilia, an old and decayed church dedicated to the saint, and believed to be built on the site of her family home. He founded a monastery in their honor.

In 1599 Cardinal Paul Emilius Sfondrati, nephew of Pope Gregory XIV (r. 1590–91), rebuilt the church of St. Cecilia. The sarcophagus of Cecilia was opened and her body and clothing were found intact. The cypress casket was put on display for a month until November 22, the feast of Cecilia. A sweet fragrance issued from it. The relic was then placed in a silver coffin and interred behind the main altar.

The story of Cecilia may have arisen along with other stories that glorified virginity and were popular at the time. A Greek religious romance on the "Loves of Cecilia and Valerian" appeared in the fourth century, apparently intended to replace more sensual romances. The Roman calendar of the fourth century and the Carthaginian calendar of the fifth century make no mention of Cecilia, which surely would have been the case had her story been true.

Additionally, Christians were not persecuted and condemned by Emperor Alexander Severus, who reigned when Urban was pope, though it is possible some may have suffered. As for the prefect, Urbanus served in that capacity during the time of Pope Urban. Other versions of the story of Cecilia say events took place under the reigns of the emperors Commodus or Marcus.

Reportedly a church was dedicated to Cecilia in Rome in the fifth century, in which Pope Symmachus (r. 498–514) held a council in 500. But Symmachus held no council in that year, and subsequent councils were held elsewhere. Cecilia does not appear to have been known or venerated in Rome until about the time when Pope St. Gelasius (r. 492–496) introduced her name into his Sacramentary. Her name was entered into the Eucharistic prayer.

Cecilia is regarded as the patron of music because on the day of her marriage she heard heavenly music and sang to God in her heart. In art she is represented with an organ or organ-pipes in her hand.

Feast: November 22
Patronage: composers; music; musicians; organ builders; singers

Celestine I (d. 432) *Pope*

Celestine was born in Rome, the son of Priscus. He is said to have lived for a while with St. Ambrose in Milan and was a good friend of St. Augustine of Hippo. He served as a deacon in the Roman Church and on September 10, 422, succeeded Pope St. Boniface I (r. 418–422).

Like his recent predecessors, Celestine acted decisively as head of the universal Church. Much of his pontificate was concerned with combating various heresies—Manichaeanism, Donatism, Noviatianism, Pelagianism, and Nestorianism—some of which the Church had been battling for centuries. He is perhaps best known, however, for one of his last official acts—dispatching St. Patrick as a missionary to Ireland around the year 430.

Celestine died in Rome on July 26, 432, having reigned nine years, 10 months, and 16 days. He was buried the following day in the Catacombs of St. Priscilla in a tomb that he had had decorated with paintings representing the Council of Ephesus, at which he had condemned Nestorianism. In 820, his relics were translated to the church of St. Prassede (Praxedes). He is honored as a saint, especially in the Greek Orthodox Church.

In art, Celestine is a pope with a dove, dragon and flame.

Feast: April 6 (formerly July 27 and/or August 1); April 8 (Eastern Church)

Celestine V (ca. 1210–1296) *Hermit, founder of the Celestines, pope*

Also known as: Peter Celestine V, Peter of Morone (or Morrone), Pietro di Murrone

Celestine was born to a peasant family in the Neapolitan province of Moline about 1211, the 11th of 12 children. When he was between 17 and 20, he became a hermit, though he later studied for the priesthood and was ordained in Rome. He joined the Benedictines at Faizola in 1246. Five years later, he retired to Mt. Morone (Morrone) in the Abruzzi (hence his surname), though he spent some time also on the even more remote Mt. Majella.

Taking St. John the Baptist as his model, he wore a haircloth roughened with knots, draped himself with an iron chain, and fasted every day except Sunday. Each year he kept four Lents, passing three of them on bread and water, devoting entire days and the better parts of nights to prayer, reading, copying books or even hard labor, busying himself so that he would not be found and tempted by the devil. His austerities and penances attracted many imitators, leading to the establishment of a Benedictine suborder, the Celestines, approved by Pope Urban IV (r. 1261–64) in 1264.

At first Peter led the Celestines, but in 1284, tired of governance, he appointed a vicar, and once again departed for the wilderness. His peace was not to last, however. After the death of Pope Nicholas IV (r. 1288–92) in April 1292, the Sacred College of Cardinals was unable to agree on a successor. They had wrestled with the problem for over two years when Cardinal Latino Orsini told the assembly that God had revealed to a saintly hermit (whom they understood to be Peter) that if they did not fill the see of Rome within four months, there would be severe repercussions. This was enough for the cardinals to elect Peter, which they did on July 5, 1294. A month later a large delegation arrived to notify him. Peter, who was then in his 80s, is said to have been in tears, but acquiesced in what he believed was God's plan for him.

The cardinals asked Peter to come to Perugia, where they had been meeting, for his coronation, but under the influence of King Charles of Naples, he summoned them to Aquila (a town within the kingdom of Naples) instead. Although only three of the cardinals had arrived by the time that Peter had arrived, Charles ordered him to be crowned, and the ceremony had to be repeated a few days later (on August 29, 1294),

when all were in attendance—the only instance of a double papal coronation in history. Upon his consecration, Peter assumed the name Celestine V.

Peter's elevation was welcomed by the extremist spiritual movement within the Church, which saw it as the fulfillment of prophecies that the Holy Spirit would soon reign on Earth through a monk. However, Cardinal Latino was—it is said—so grief-stricken by the way things were turning out that he fell ill and died. Indeed, Celestine soon showed himself to be entirely unprepared to lead the Church. He was easily swayed by persons wishing to take advantage of him, especially King Charles. It took only a few months before the cardinals' second thoughts reached the point of investigating the possibility of papal abdication, another unprecedented event. The possibility being decided in the affirmative, the choice was put to Peter, who issued his resignation to the Sacred College meeting in Naples on December 13, 1294.

The cardinals then elected one of their own, Cardinal Gaetani, who took the name Boniface VIII (r. 1294–1303). Fearing Celestine's popularity would cause a schism within the Church, Boniface had him arrested and imprisoned in the castle of Fumone, near Anagni, Italy. Celestine was reportedly pleased with this latest turn. He is quoted as saying: "I wanted nothing in the world but a cell, and a cell they have given me." He died in Fumone on May 19, 1296, and was buried at Anagni. A half-century later his relics were translated to the church of his order at Aquila, where they remain the object of great veneration.

In art, Celestine is depicted as a pope with a dove at his ear and the devil trying to disturb him.

Canonized: 1313 by Pope Clement V
Feast: May 19
Patronage: Bookbinders

Chad (d. 672) *Bishop and founder*
Also known as: Ceadda

Much of what is known about the life of Chad comes from the Venerable Bede, who was one of his monks and disciples.

Chad was probably born in Northumbria. He was one of four brothers, all of whom entered the religious life. Cynibill and Caelin became priests. Cedd (with whom Chad is sometimes confused) became abbot of Lastingham and bishop of the East Saxons.

Chad went to Lindisfarne and studied under St. Aidan. He then went to Ireland to the Monastery of Rathmelsige (Mefont), where he studied with St. Ecgberht (Egbert). He returned to England, and helped Cedd found the monastery of Laestingeau (Lastingham) in Yorkshire. When Cedd died, Chad became abbot.

King Oswy made Chad archbishop of York. St. Theodore, archbishop of Canterbury, disciplined him for impropriety, but in 669 appointed him bishop of Mercia. Chad built a church and monastery at Litchfield.

He received a vision foretelling his death, and died in 672. A shrine was built for him, and the miracles reported there attracted pilgrimages. In the 12th century, the shrine was removed to the cathedral at Litchfield. During the Reformation, his relics were taken to Birmingham to the cathedral dedicated to him.

In art Chad is shown dressed as a bishop and holding a small church in his hand.

Feast: March 2

Charles Borromeo (1538–1584) *Cardinal and principal figure in the Catholic Reformation*

Charles Borromeo was born on October 2, 1538, to a noble family, Count Gilbert Borromeo and Margaret de' Medici, sister of Pope Pius IV (r. 1559–1565). Charles, heir to a great fortune, had a wealthy and gracious upbringing in the family castle of Arona on Lake Maggiore. At age 12 he was sent to the Benedictine abbey of SS. Gratian and Felinus, and received his clerical tonsure.

His uncle, Angelo de' Medici, became Pope Pius V in 1558, and in 1559 named Charles his secretary of state and cardinal and administrator of the see of Milan—even though he was not yet a priest.

With his access to the pope, Charles became influential in church politics and reform efforts. He persuaded the pope to reconvene the Council of Trent, which had been suspended in 1552. Charles took an active role in the council and its deliberations, and directed the writing of its decrees in the third and last group of sessions. In 1556, Charles began a program of radical reforms to improve the morals of both clerics and laity. He established seminaries, founded a Confraternity of Christine Doctrine, increased aid to the poor, aided the English college at Douai, and held six provincial councils and six diocesan synods. His reform efforts made him many enemies, one of whom wounded him in an assassination attempt in 1559. After the deaths of his father and older brother, Charles declined to become the head of his family. He took ordination as a priest in 1563 and was made bishop of Milan. When famine and the plague struck in 1576, he worked to aid the starving and the ill, using his own resources and even going into debt. He had a vision that told him when the plague would end. In 1578 he

founded the Oblates of St. Ambrose, now called the Oblates of St. Charles.

Charles died in Milan on the night of November 3–4, 1584. He was buried in a double coffin beneath the pavement in the middle of the cathedral of Milan, of which he was archbishop. Throngs of pilgrims came to his tomb over the years. By 1610, pilgrims had left 10,891 silver votive offerings and 9,618 precious gifts, such as jewelry, gems and lamps of gold and silver.

In 1605, during the cause for his beatification, his body was exhumed. Moisture had corroded the cover of both lead and wood coffins, and had penetrated to the body. His remains, however, were found intact. An oratory was constructed, and in 1607 the remains, revested and placed in new wood and lead coffins, were buried there.

In 1880, the body was exhumed again and was found to have been embalmed. It was determined that the embalming could not account for the remarkable preservation of his body 300 years after his death.

Over the years, the oratory has been improved, and a jewel-like reliquary was made of rock crystal set in silver and adorned with miniature angels and religious figures.

When Pope Paul VI (r. 1963–78) was still archbishop of Milan, he had the face of Charles covered in silver. The body is clothed in pontifical garments studded with gems.

Canonization: 1610 by Pope Paul V
Feast: November 4
Patronage: Apple orchards; boarding schools; catechists; against colic; learning and the arts; public libraries; secular clergy; seminarians; spiritual directors; against stomach diseases; against ulcers; dioceses of Lugano and Basel, Switzerland; Salzburg University, Austria

Charles of Sezze (1613 –1670) *Franciscan mystic*

Charles of Sezze was born John Charles Marchioni in Sezze, Italy, on October 19, 1613, to humble parents. His family name may also have been Melchior. He was raised by his grandmother, who instilled in him a love of God.

As a boy Charles worked as a shepherd and dreamed of becoming a priest. At age 17 he made a vow of chastity. His priestly ambition was thwarted by his lack of education, so instead he became a Franciscan lay brother at Naziano. He was given various menial jobs, such as cook, porter and gardener at different monasteries near Rome.

Charles had numerous mystical experiences and was given the gift of mystical knowledge. His wisdom impressed learned theologians. Among those who sought his advice were cardinals and Pope Clement IX (r. 1667–69). Charles became renowned for his holiness, simplicity and charity, and for his severe mortifications. One day while meditating on the Eucharist, a ray of light shot like an arrow from the host and pierced his left side, leaving a wound that remained even after his death.

When plague struck in 1656, Charles worked tirelessly for the victims. He also wrote several mystical works.

Charles died in Rome on January 6, 1670.

Canonized: 1959 by Pope John XXIII
Feast: January 6

Christopher *Martyr and one of the Fourteen Holy Helpers*
Name meaning: Christ-bearer

According to lore, Christopher, called Kester, was a large, ugly man who earned his living by ferrying people across a river.

Christopher was popularized by William Caxton's version of the *Golden Legend.* According to Caxton, Christopher was of the lineage of the Canaanites. Prior to baptism, his name was Reprobus. As Christopher, he bore Christ in four ways: on his shoulders by leading and conveying; in his body by making it lean; in his mind by devotion; and in his mouth by confessing and preaching.

The legend tells that one day Christopher decided to seek out the greatest prince in the world. He learned about the devil, and searched until he found him. But the devil fled at the presence of a cross, and told Christopher about Christ. Christopher wandered, found a hermit, and made a home for himself by a river. One day as he slept he was awakened by a child asking to be carried across the river. Christopher put him on his shoulders. As he waded into the water, the child grew heavier and heavier until Christopher feared for his life. The child then revealed himself to be Christ. He told Christopher to place his staff in the earth and be rewarded with flowers and fruit. Christopher did so, and the next day found his staff like a palm tree.

Christopher went to Lycia in Asia Minor (modern Turkey), where God granted him the ability to understand the foreign tongue. There he preached and converted 8,000 men. The king sent knights to fetch him; he converted them. The king executed the knights and had Christopher thrown in prison. He was severely tortured with iron rods and burning pitch but remained unscathed and refused to renounce his faith. The king

St. Christopher (Engraving by Albrecht Dürer, 1251)

had him bound to a stake and shot with the arrows of 40 archers. The arrows stopped in the air and did not strike him; one returned and blinded the king in one eye. Christopher told him that upon his death on the morrow, the king should take some of his blood, mix it with clay and anoint the eye, and it would be healed. The next day, Christopher was beheaded. The king did as instructed, and his sight was restored. The king converted.

From this legend arose the belief that whoever looks upon an image of Christopher will not be harmed that day. In the Middle Ages, statues of him were placed near the entrances to churches.

The legend may be based on a martyr named Christopher and called Kester, who made his living by ferrying people across a river, and who died ca. 251 in Lycia in Asia Minor. His relics were taken to Paris and Rome.

As one of the Fourteen Holy Helper saints, Christopher was especially invoked against the plague in the Middle Ages. He appeared to St. Joan of Arc.

Feast: July 25
Patronage: against accidents; bachelors; bus drivers; against mortal dangers; motorists; against nightmares; against the plague; porters; sailors; against sudden death; travelers; truck drivers; America

Clare of Assisi (1194–1253)   *Founder of the Franciscan Poor Clares*

Clare was born on July 11, 1194, to a noble family. Her father was Faverone Offreducio Ortolanadi Fiumi. During Lent in 1212, she heard St. Francis of Assisi preach and decided to imitate him and live a poor, humble life for Jesus. She ran away from home and dedicated herself to God on Palm Sunday in a little chapel outside Assisi. Francis cut off her hair and gave her the rough brown Franciscan habit. She went to the Benedictine convent near Bastia.

Clare's distraught parents tried to no avail to make her return home. Soon her sister, St. Agnes of Assisi, joined her, as well as other young women. In 1215 Clare became the superior of the Poor Clares and moved into a house adjoining the church of St. Damiano. The sisters wore no shoes, ate no meat, kept no money and kept silent most of the time. Clare's mother and another sister, Beatrice, joined the community. The

St. Clare of Assisi with church fathers (Library of Congress Prints and Photographs Division)

Poor Clares were granted a rule of absolute poverty by Pope Innocent III (r. 1198–1216).

Clare established other convents, and the order spread throughout Italy and into France and Germany. Many people sought her out for her wisdom, including high-ranking clergy and secular officials.

Clare performed numerous miracles. After prayer, her face was often lit with an unusual, dazzling radiance. Once her prayer saved her convent from attack by Saracens. Despite being ill, Clare had herself carried to the wall and had the Blessed Sacrament placed where the enemies could see it. She got down on her knees and begged God to save the sisters. "O Lord, protect these Sisters whom I cannot protect now," she prayed. A voice answered, "I will keep them always in my care." Suddenly the attackers fled.

On another occasion she saved the city of Assisi from attack by the army of Emperor Frederick II.

Clare was sick throughout much of her life. Toward the end, she had a vision of the Mass in her bed—and for this later became the patroness of television. She died on August 11, 1253.

Canonized: 1255 by Pope Alexander IV
Feast: August 11
Patronage: against sore eyes; Assisi; the blind; embroiderers; gilders; glass painters; glaziers; laundry women; television

Clare of Montefalco (ca. 1268–1308) *Abbess and mystic*
Name meaning: Brilliant, bright
Also known as: Clare of the Cross

Clare was born at Montefalco, Italy, around 1268. As a young woman she joined a convent of Franciscan tertiaries. This group established Holy Cross Convent at Montefalco in 1290, adopting the Rule of St. Augustine. Clare's sister Joan was the abbess of this community, but when she died Clare succeeded her. Clare led an austere life, being particularly devoted to Christ's passion and His cross. She became known as a miracle worker.

Clare was given an apparition of the Lord in which He said to her, "I have sought a place in the world where I might plant my cross, and have found no better site than your heart." Later, Clare told her sisters, "If you seek the cross of Christ, take my heart; there you will find the suffering Lord."

When Clare was on her deathbed in 1308, she repeatedly said, "Know that in my very heart I have and hold Christ crucified." Soon after her death, her sisters were inspired to take out her heart. When they did so, a quantity of blood rushed out and was collected in a vial that had been washed and purified.

Her heart was larger than normal. They opened it and found clear symbols of the passion of Christ that were part of the cardiac tissue itself. The symbols were:

- A thumb-sized crucifix. The body of Christ was white and his lance wound red, and his loins were covered in white tissue.
- A scourge formed of a hard, white nerve
- The crown of thorns composed of tiny sharp nerves
- The three nails formed of a dark, sharp fibrous tissue
- The lance and sponge formed of nerve tissue

In addition, three mysterious pellets were found in the gall. The pellets were about the size of hazel nuts, and were judged by theologians to be symbols of the Trinity. Any one of them was as heavy as the other two, while at other times any one of them equaled the weight of all three together.

The sisters locked the heart and vial of blood in a box. The next day these items were examined by a group of officials who included the chief magistrate, the leading doctor in the town and a public notary, with a representative of the Franciscan house at Foligno in attendance. More examinations were conducted later by other Church officials and politicians.

Clare's body and heart remained incorrupt. At various times the blood was seen to liquefy and also to boil and bubble. These episodes seemed to presage political disturbances and turmoil. Liquefactions were recorded in 1495, 1500, 1508, 1560, 1570, 1601, 1608 and 1618. In the 17th century a commission was established to investigate the mystery of the blood, and concluded that no natural explanation could be found.

In 1608 the body was moved from its shrine. The blood in the vial had dried and coagulated. The vial was dropped and everything broke into pieces. All the pieces were collected and placed in a crystal vessel. Over time this vessel cracked and was placed in a third vessel.

The incorrupt body of Clare can be viewed at the Sanctuario S. Chiara da Montefalco. Her incorrupt heart is enclosed in a bust and can be viewed under a crystal. The pellets are in a jeweled cross kept in the Church of the Holy Cross in Montefalco.

In art Clare is portrayed holding a crucifix, the bottom of which penetrates her heart.

Canonized: 1881 by Pope Leo XIII
Feast: August 17

Clement I (d. ca. 99) *Pope and martyr*
Also known as: Clemens Romanus

The identity of Clement is uncertain, though probably he was a freedman or the son of a freedman of Emperor Nero's household. It is also possible that he was of Jewish descent. He is said to have been baptized—and ordained a priest—by St. Peter and is accepted by most authorities as the fourth pope, following SS. Peter, Linus and Anacletus.

Clement is best known from an apostolic letter he wrote to the Church of Corinth when it faced an internal crisis. The letter is important not only as a homily on Christian life, but also for the example it gives of the bishop of Rome intervening authoritatively in the affairs of another apostolic church. On the basis of this letter, Clement is considered the first of the Apostolic Fathers.

It appears that Clement may have been forced into exile from Rome, thus ending his reign. Tradition has it that he converted Theodora, wife of Sisinnius, a courtier of Nerva, and then—after miracles—Sisinnius himself, together with 423 other persons of rank. Emperor Trajan then banished him to the Crimea, where he was made to work in the quarries. The nearest drinking water was six miles away, but—assisted by a miracle—Clement discovered a spring close by. Soon he had brought in so many new converts that 75 churches were needed to serve them. His success so enraged Trajan that he ordered him thrown into the Black Sea with an iron anchor around his neck. Angels came and built him a tomb under the water, but every year, the tide receded far enough to reveal it.

This account is no older than the fourth century, and there is no way of knowing how much of the truth it represents. About 868, St. Cyril, in the Crimea, dug up some bones and an anchor from a burial mound said to be Clement's, and carried them to Rome. The relics were deposited by Pope Adrian II (r. 867–872) with those of St. Ignatius of Antioch in the high altar of the basilica of St. Clemens Church. However, they may or may not be Clement's in fact.

In art, Clement is represented as a pope with an anchor and fish. Sometimes he is shown lying in a temple in the sea. He may also be shown with a millstone; keys; a fountain that has sprung forth at his prayers; or a book.

Feast: November 23
Patronage: Guild, Fraternity, and Brotherhood of the Most Glorious and Undivided Trinity of London (responsible for lighthouses and lightships); marble workers

Clement of Alexandria (d. ca. 215) *Greek theologian and Father of the Church*

Clement of Alexandria's date of birth is unknown; his birthplace is likely to have been Athens. He was converted and traveled about in search of religious instruction and eventually settled in Alexandria, where he enjoyed the diversity of race, culture and religion. He became attracted to the teachings of Pantaenus, head of the catechetical school of Alexandria. He succeeded Pantaenus in about 190.

In 202, persecutions began in Egypt and Clement left Alexandria for Caesarea in Cappadocia, where he met his friend and former pupil, Bishop Alexander, who was converting people from prison.

Clement had a profound effect upon another church father, Origen, who succeeded him at Alexandria. He died around 215, probably in Cappadocia.

Clement left a large body of writings. Some of his doctrines were found to be erroneous or suspect. Nonetheless, his name was entered in the martyrologies and he was venerated as a saint into the 17th century. Pope Clement VIII (r. 1592–1605) revised the Roman Martyrology and dropped Clement's name from the list. This decision was upheld by Pope Benedict XIV (r. 1740–58) on the grounds that no cultus had ever established itself around him. Clement's works have found new favor in modern times.

Feast: Formerly December 4

Clement of Ireland   (ca. 750–818) *Teacher and scholar*
Also known as: Clement Duns Scotus, Clemens Scotus

Clement Duns Scotus (meaning from Irish or Scottish ancestry) and his companion Albinus, or Ailbe, traveled to Gaul in 772 to establish a school. Charlemagne reportedly learned of their knowledge and called them to court to teach at his palace school.

Albinus eventually directed a monastery near Pavia, but Clement stayed in France and became regent of the school in 775, serving in that post until his death. During his tenure, learning and the production of books flourished at the school, which eventually became the University of Paris. Legend holds that Clement actually founded the university, but he did not.

Clement died in Paris on March 20, 818.

Clotilde (b. ca. 474–545) *Queen of the Franks*
Also known as: Clothilde of France, Clotilda

Clotilde was born at Lyons, France, about 474, the daughter of King Chilperic of Burgundy. She married the Salian Frankish king Clovis I in 493, who used their alliance as a means of strengthening his position with the Romanized Celts. Clovis had already defeated several minor Frankish kings in Gaul and the Rhineland and established himself as the sole Frankish king and founder of the Merovingian Dynasty.

Although not a Christian himself, Clovis allowed his Catholic Christian wife to baptize their children. His tolerance of Catholic Christianity angered other Germanic tribes, who were either pagans or Arians. In 496, while fighting the Alemanni tribes, Clovis prayed to "Clotilde's God" and promised to convert if victorious in battle. On Christmas Day of 496, Bishop St. Remigius (St. Remy) of Reims baptized Clovis I, supposedly with about 3,000 of his followers. Clovis and Queen Clotilde chose Paris as their capital city, where the monarchs founded the Church of the Apostles, later known as St. Genevieve.

Upon Clovis's death in 511, Clotilde was extremely wealthy but powerless to control her rebellious children. Clovis I had divided his kingdom among his four sons—Theodoric I, Clodomir, Childebert I and Clothaire I—but each desired the others' kingdoms. Clodomir was murdered, and Clotilde took his three sons under her care. Nevertheless, her son Clothaire murdered two of the boys, his own nephews. Clotilde secreted the youngest, five-year-old Clodoaldus, to a monastery at Versailles, where he grew to become St. Cloud.

Her daughter, also named Clotilde, was forced to marry the Arian Visigoth king Amalaric, who treated her cruelly. Childebert murdered Amalaric to avenge his sister, but Clotilde II died on her way back to Paris. Mortified at her children's sins and unable to change their ways, Queen Clotilde went to Tours, where she lived the rest of her life near the tomb of St. Martin of Tours, spending her time in prayer, penance and service to the sick and the poor. Historians attribute the founding of churches at Laon, Andelys and Rouen to Clotilde. She died at Tours in 545.

Feast: June 3
Patronage: adopted children; brides; disappointing children; exiles; parents of large families; queens; those who have suffered the death of children; the lame; widows; women with iniquitous husbands

Colette (1381–1447) *Founder of the Colettine Poor Clares (Clarisses), mystic*

Colette was born on January 13, 1381, in Corbie, Picardy, France. Her father, Robert Boellet, was a carpenter at the Benedictine Abbey of Corbie. Colette was orphaned at age 13. She joined the Bequines, Benedictines and Urbanists Poor Clares, and lived for a time as a hermit.

In 1406, she had a vision in which St. Francis of Assisi and St. Clare of Assisi instructed her to reform the Poor Clares, who had fallen into lax ways. She was empowered to do so by Pope Benedict XIII (the antipope recognized by France), and followed through with reforms and the founding of 17 new convents in France and Europe. She reformed the Franciscan friars (the Coletani), a small order that eventually was suppressed in 1417 by Leo X (r. 1513–21). Colette's reforms included extreme poverty, going barefoot, and perpetual fasts and abstinence. Colette was a friend of St. Vincent Ferrar, and helped him in his work to heal the Great Western Schism.

At her convent in Ghent, Belgium, she foresaw her own death. In February 1447, she announced that she would die soon. She told her sisters not to wait for her to say anything at her death, for she would say nothing. One month later, she donned the veil given her by Benedict XIII (r. 1724–30) in 1406 when he named her abbess general of the Poor Clares. She wore it only for special occasions. She laid down on her bed and said "This is the last time I shall lie down." She died two days later on March 6 at age 66. About 12 hours after her death, her worn body began to transform and become a beautiful and fragrant white. It still looked that way when she was buried three days later.

Colette had numerous mystical experiences and ecstasies and is credited with many miracles. Early in her religious life, she experienced a mystical marriage with St. John the Apostle (also called St. John the Divine). John appeared in a vision and placed a beautiful gold ring upon her finger, saying as he did so, "by my own right and on behalf of the sovereign King and Prince of virginity and chastity." Colette kept her ring in a box and showed it to very few people. She shared her experience with few as well. She remained especially devoted to St. John.

Colette had the gift of prophecy, seeing not only her own death, but also that of St. Vincent Ferrar. She accurately told him that he would die in less than two years in France.

On Fridays, Colette had 12-hour visions of the Passion from which she suffered torments and great bruises upon her body, in sympathy with the suffering of Christ.

In her travels, Colette seems to have been guided by angels who held her up on her mules and enabled her to walk extremely fast as though her feet did not touch the ground. Once during her reforms, she was opposed by the head of a monastery who punished the Franciscan friars of Dole—who had accepted her reforms—by cutting off their food supply. For an entire year, Colette's convent supplied the friars with grain, despite the fact that they did not have enough in their granary

to do so. The grain was always taken to the monastery on a very small donkey.

Beatified: January 23, 1740, by Pope Clement XII
Canonized: May 24, 1807, by Pope Pius VII
Feast: March 6

Colombian Martyrs of the Spanish Civil War (d. 1936)
Also known as: Mártires Colombianos de la Comunidad de San Juan de Dios

Seven Colombian members of the Comunidad de San Juan de Dios were among the thousands of Catholics killed by communists and anarchists during the Spanish Civil War (1936–39) that brought Francisco Franco to power. The Colombians were studying and working in Spain, dedicated to helping the mentally ill, when they were arrested, tortured and killed on August 7, 1936.

The group includes: Juan Bautista Velásquez, of Jardín (Antioquía), age 27; Esteban Maya, of Pácora Caldas, age 29; Melquiades Ramírez of Sonsón (Antioquía), age 27; Eugenio Ramírez, of La Ceja (Antioquía), age 23; Rubén de Jesús López, of Concepción (Antioquía), age 28; Arturo Ayala, of Paipa (Boyacá), age 27; and Gaspar Páez Perdomo, of Tello (Huila), age 23.

Beatified: 1992 by Pope John Paul II

FURTHER READING
"Los Mártires Colombianos de la Comunidad de San Juan de Dios." URL: http://www.churchforum.org. Downloaded: December 6, 1999.

Columba (521–597) *Abbot and one of the three patron saints of Ireland, with Brigid and Patrick; also a patron saint of Scotland, with Andrew*
Also known as: Colmcille, Columcille, Columkill, Colum, Columbus, Combs

Most of what is known about and attributed to Columba comes from the *Vita Columbae* (Life of Columba), a three-volume work composed between 688 and 692 by Adamnan, an abbot of Iona who was regarded in his own time as "the High Scholar of the Western world."

Columba (the Latinized form of Colmcille) was born on December 7, 521—or 60 years after St. Patrick died—in Gartan, County Donegal, Ulster, to the royal clan of Ui Neill, also known as Clan Conaill or O'Donnell. His mother was Eithne and his father Fedhlimidh, a descendant of the great fourth-century king Niall of the Nine Hostages. Columba's birth name was Crimthann, "the fox," and the boy may have had red hair. He expressed an interest in the Church early on, taking the name Colmcille, or "dove of the church," after his baptism by the priest Cruithnechan.

After learning all Cruithnechan could teach him, Columba entered the monastic school of Moville under St. Finian. After completing his training and ordination as a deacon, Columba left Moville to study Irish poetry and history under the aged bard Gemman in Leinster. He then joined the monastery at Clonard, headed by another Finian, a student of St. David of Wales. Columba became one of 12 disciples at Clonard known as the Twelve Apostles of Ireland. He also received priestly orders from Bishop Etchen of Clonfad. Legend tells that the bishop meant to consecrate Columba as a bishop but mistakenly designated him only a priest. Leaving Clonard, Columba went to the monastery of St. Mobhi Clarainech at Glasnevin, where he stayed until an outbreak of disease caused the monastery's closing in 544. Columba returned to Ulster, where he founded monasteries at Derry in 546, Durrow in 556 and Kells not long after. Altogether, Columba reportedly established 27 monasteries and founded approximately 40 churches.

According to his biographer St. Adamnan, Columba's missionary zeal and love of Christ led him to leave Ireland in 563 with 12 companions and settle on the small island of Iona, off the coast of Scotland. They established a monastery there that flourished as a center of scholarship, art and Christianity until the Viking raids of the ninth century.

But Columba's desire to spread the Gospel was perhaps not the only impetus for his travels to Iona. At some point, Columba made an illicit copy of a psalter owned by St. Finian (supposedly the one at Moville) and attributed to St. Jerome. Writing surreptitiously in the dark, with the fingers of his left hand allegedly burning like candles so he could see, Columba made the copy. He was found out, and Finian demanded that the young monk return the copy. Columba refused, and Finian referred the case to High King Diarmait (Dermott). Diarmait, a member of a clan unfriendly to Columba's clan, ruled in what amounts to the first copyright case: *Le gach buin a laogh* ("to every cow her calf"), or to every book its copy, and Columba was forced to relinquish the psalter.

Resentment over King Diarmait's decision later turned to rage, when Columba was sheltering his kinsman, Prince Curnan, who had fatally injured an opponent in a hurling competition. King Diarmait ordered his men to ignore the right of sanctuary and to seize Curnan and kill him. Columba demanded revenge and gathered his clan's army against Diar-

mait's at Cuil Dremne (Cooldrevny) in 561. When the battle was over, King Diarmait's clan had lost 3,000 men; Columba's clan had lost one. Columba regained his psalter as a spoil of war, and ever after the book was known as the Cathach, or "warrior," and served as the sacred Battle Book of the Clan O'Donnell. The Cathach is preserved at the Irish Academy and is the oldest surviving example of Irish majuscule writing.

Convening a synod at Telltown in Meath, church fathers condemned Columba for the 3,000 deaths and excommunicated him for a time—the standard punishment for a monk who had taken up arms. But Columba's conscience supposedly pained him more than the group's judgment, and he turned to his confessor, St. Molaise of Devenish, for guidance. Molaise ordered Columba to leave Ireland and never return, and to bring as many new souls to Christ as had been lost at Cooldrevny. Columba and his 12 companions left Ireland in a wicker currach covered with hide and landed on Iona ("holy island") in May 563—a place just far enough north to have no view of Ireland.

Columba first ministered to the Irish in Scotland—emigrants from the Dalriada region of Ulster—but eventually began converting the Northern Pictish people of Scotland. One of his first converts was King Brude at Inverness. When Columba and his monks arrived at the castle, the doors were shut and barred. Columba raised his arm to make the sign of the cross, and the bolts reportedly flew out and the doors opened—a scene reminiscent of St. Patrick's entrance to King Laoghaire's castle at Tara. Columba also reputedly anointed King Aidan of Argyll on the famous Stone of Scone. Even the name Scotland comes from Columba, for in those days *Scoti* or *Scotus* meant Irish.

Although Columba never again lived in Ireland, he traveled there often. In 580, Columba returned to Ulster for the assembly at Druim-Cetta, a conference to determine the obligations of the Irish in Scotland to the mother country. Participants decided that the Scottish-Irish should furnish a fleet, but not an army, to the Irish high king. Perhaps more important, Columba convinced the assembly not to suppress the Bardic Order—the bards and poets who sang and wrote about Celtic history, legend and culture.

Columba retained leadership of the monasteries and churches he founded in Ireland as well as those he established from Iona. This situation led to the development of a governing system unique to Celtic Christian churches and at odds with the Roman model for over 70 years following Columba's death: The abbots—and abbesses—had jurisdiction over the monastery and environs, even superior to the bishops.

The Celtic churches finally bowed to Rome's authority in 664.

By spring of 597, Columba knew he was dying. On June 8, he was copying the line from Psalms that says, "They that love the Lord shall lack no good thing" (Ps. 34:10), when he put down his pen and said, "Here I must stop; let Baithin [Columba's cousin and successor] do the rest." When the monks returned to the chapel for Matins prayers after midnight, they found Columba on the floor before the altar. The saint blessed the brethren and died on June 9 at age 77. He was buried at Iona for 200 years, then his relics were moved to the abbey at Down in Ireland to rest near SS. Patrick and Brigid. According to lore, a Viking stole his coffin from Iona and carried it onto his longship, hoping to find treasure inside. Finding only the saint's remains, he threw the casket and its contents overboard. They washed ashore at Down. Thus was fulfilled a prophecy of both Patrick and Brigid that Columba would rest with them.

For centuries afterward, Iona enjoyed prestige as a great center of Celtic learning, and attracted numerous religious exiles.

Adamnan's *Vita Columbae* gives considerable attention to the prophecies and miracles of Columba. The saint is credited with prophetic visions of wars, battles, deaths of kings and others, weather calamities and so forth. His miracles included healing the sick, driving out "armies" of disease-causing demons, taming wild beasts, calming violent weather, causing rain to fall, raising the dead, and turning water into wine. Columba was often seen surrounded by a brilliant holy aura. He enjoyed frequent visionary visits from angels. He saw angels carry the souls of the righteous to heaven and demons carry souls of the condemned to hell.

Feast: June 9
Patronage: bookbinders; computer hackers; Knights of Columbus (Columba); plagiarists; poets; Ireland; Scotland

FURTHER READING
Cahill, Thomas. *How the Irish Saved Civilization.* New York: Nan A. Talese/Doubleday, 1995.
"Columcille: The Saint." URL: http://www.w3.ixs.nl/~jove/columba2.htm. Downloaded March 30, 2000.
Jones, Norm. "The Saint Columba Home Page." URL: http://www.usu,edu/~history/norm/columb~1.htm. Updated on January 14, 1998.
Marsden, John. *The Illustrated Life of Columba.* Edinburgh: Floris Books, 1995.
Seyfried, Seth. Introduction to "Adamnan: Life of St. Columba." *Medieval Source Book.* URL: http://www.fordham.edu/halsall/basis/columba-e.html. Downloaded January 18, 2000.

Columban (ca. 543–615) *Irish abbot in France*
Also known as: Columbanus, the Younger Columba

Columban was born around 543 in Leinster, Ireland, to a noble family. He received a good education, and decided at a young age to enter monastic life. He went to an island in Lough Erne, where he studied with St. Comgall.

After his ordination in 590, Columban took 12 companions, among them St. Gall, and went to England and France. In France they established monasteries at Annegray, Fontaine and Luxeuil. They were not well received and encountered many difficulties. Columban denounced King Thierry II of Burgundy for keeping concubines, and the king exiled him in 610.

Columban spent two years traveling, eventually reaching Austrasia, where he and Gall parted company. Columban and the rest of his party returned to Ireland. They were shipwrecked en route and were taken in by King Clotaire of Neustria and King Theodobert at Metz, France. They stayed and evangelized in the area around Lake Constance in parts of modern Germany and Switzerland.

Columban died in 615 at Bobbio, Italy.

Feast: November 23

Conrad (d. 975) *Bishop and companion of Emperor Otto I*
Also known as: Conrad of Constance

Conrad was born into the famous Guelph family and was the son of Count Henry of Altdorf. He was educated at the cathedral school of Constance, Switzerland, and was ordained. In 934 he was made provost of the cathedral and was elected bishop of Constance, a post he held for 42 years. He avoided all secular matters.

Conrad gave all of his wealth to the Church and to the poor, built three grand churches and renovated many more in his see. In 862 he accompanied Emperor Otto I to Italy. He also is said to have taken three pilgrimages to Jerusalem.

According to lore, Conrad was saying mass one Easter when a large spider dropped into the chalice. It was commonly believed at the time that most spiders were poisonous, but the plucky saint swallowed the spider, anyway, and suffered no harm.

Conrad is best known for his grand vision, experienced in 948 when he was asked to dedicate the Chapel of Our Lady of the Hermits at Einsiedeln, Switzerland, the spot where the murdered St. Meinrad once had his hermit's hut and chapel. Conrad arrived in the Dark

Wood on September 13 with a party of knights, princes and the bishop of Augsburg. Near midnight, he and several others went into the chapel to pray. Conrad prayed to Mary to accept the shrine and help it to become a place of pilgrimage.

At midnight, Conrad and the others heard a beautiful chanting. The chapel was filled with dazzling light, and the altar was illuminated. A procession of angels came down from heaven, led by Michael the Archangel. Some of the angels sang and others swung censers. Then came St. Peter with a crozier, and the apostles SS. Mark, Luke, Matthew and John, followed by three of the greatest Doctors of the Church, SS. Ambrose, Augustine and Gregory the Great. Then came the martyred SS. Lawrence and Stephen, and finally Jesus Christ, clothed magnificently as high priest. Mary, attended by angels, installed herself over the altar. Jesus conducted Mass in minute detail and dedicated the chapel to his mother. The vision lasted for more than an hour. Conrad remained in ecstatic meditation for hours.

The next day, Conrad proclaimed to the crowd gathered that God had already dedicated the chapel, but he was pressed to continue with the service by others who did not believe his story. As he began, a booming voice heard by everyone said three times, "Stop! Stop, Brother. The chapel has been divinely consecrated."

In 964, Pope Leo VIII (r. 963–964) issued a bull confirming the miraculous dedication.

The Chapel of Our Lady of the Hermits is one of the most popular pilgrimage sites in Europe, attracting up to 200,000 people a year; many miracles are reported there. A basilica and monastery were built in the first part of the 18th century.

In art Conrad usually is represented with a chalice and a spider.

Canonized: 1123 by Pope Callistus II
Feast: November 26
Patronage: hernia sufferers

Constantine the Great (d. 337) *Roman emperor and champion of Christianity*
Also known as: Flavius Valerius Constantinus, the Thirteenth Apostle

Birth dates for Constantine range from 274 to 288. He was born at Naissus to Constantius Chlorus, a Roman officer who became junior emperor (r. 293–306), and St. Helena, a woman of inferior lineage. Constantine grew up in the court of Diocletian (r. 284–305) and served in the military. Upon the death of his father in battle in 306, his troops proclaimed him caesar.

Diocletian had attempted to establish a four-headed empire, but constant struggle ensued for the supremacy of one person as emperor. Constantine managed to stay out of the infighting until 311, when the emperor Galerius died. In 312 Constantine faced the army of his rival, Maxentius, in a decisive battle at the Milvian Bridge near Rome. He sought out pagan diviners who told him the battle would go badly for him. He then had first a waking vision and then a dream that convinced him that he would win if he invoked the name of Christ. He did and thus defeated Maxentius.

By 325 Constantine defeated the fourth rival, Licinius, and became sole emperor, a position he held until 337. He was preparing to march with his troops against a new enemy when he fell ill and died in March of that year.

Constantine was instrumental in stoping the persecutions of Christians, and as sole emperor made Christianity the religion of state. Tradition holds that he did so out of personal experience and conviction, but he also was influenced by the political and social forces of the times. Old ways were falling out of favor. The empire faced barbarian invasions from the north, which sapped resources that had been devoted to persecutions.

Constantine combined both paganism and Christianity into his personal life and political affairs. In 330 the dedication of Constantinople, the city he made the capital of the empire, was a mix of both pagan and Christian rites. As he got older, Constantine became increasingly Christian, but did not receive baptism until he was on his deathbed.

About 20 years after the death of Constantine, the historian Eusebius recorded an account of the visionnary experiences in 313, saying that Constantine had related them personally to him:

> Accordingly [Constantine] called on [God] with earnest prayer and supplications that he would reveal to him who he was, and stretch forth his right hand to help him in his present difficulties. And while he was thus praying with fervent entreaty, a most marvelous sign appeared to him from heaven . . . He said that about noon, when the day was already beginning to decline, he saw with his own eyes the trophy of a cross of light in the heavens, above the sun, and bearing the inscription, CONQUER BY THIS. At this sight he himself was struck with amazement, and his whole army also, which followed him on this expedition, and witnessed the miracle.
>
> He said, moreover, that he doubted within himself what the import of this apparition could be. And while he continued to ponder and reason on its meaning, night suddenly came on; then in his sleep the Christ of God appeared to him with the same sign which he had seen in the heavens, and commanded him to make a likeness

of that sign . . . and to use it as a safeguard in an engagements with his enemies.

At dawn of day he arose, and communicated the marvel to his friends: and then, calling together the workers in gold and precious stones, he sat in the midst of them, and described to them the figure of the sign he had seen, bidding them represent it in gold and precious stones.

The sign was the two Greek letters chi (X) and ro (P), the first two letters of Christ's name, combined one over the other as a monogram. Called the labarum, it became the symbol of the Roman emperors.

Feast: May 21

FURTHER READING

Eusebius of Caesaria. *The Life of the Blessed Emperor Constantine.* URL: http://www.fordham.edu/halsall/basis/vita-constantine.html. Downloaded Sept. 11, 2000.

Guiley, Rosemary Ellen. *Dreamwork for the Soul.* New York: Berkley Books, 1998.

Cornelius (d. 253) *Pope and martyr*

Cornelius was a priest in the Church of Rome at the time of his elevation to bishop to replace Pope St. Fabian, who had been killed at the beginning of persecutions under Emperor Decius. Fabian died on January 20, 250, but the persecutions delayed the election of a new pope for 14 months, until March 251.

The main issue facing Cornelius was the treatment of Christians who had denied their faith during the persecutions. He supported St. Cyprian, bishop of Carthage, whose council provided for the restoration of Communion after various forms of penance, against Novatian, a Roman priest who asserted that the apostates should not be pardoned. In the summer of 251, Novatian had himself consecrated bishop of Rome by some dissident deacons, establishing himself as antipope to Cornelius. This brought about a major schism in the Church, with many eastern bishops inclined to back Novatian. However, a synod of western bishops in Rome in October upheld Cornelius, condemned the teachings of Novatian and excommunicated him and his followers.

New persecutions suddenly broke out early in 252, and Cornelius was exiled to Centumcellæ (Civita Vecchia). He was beheaded there in June 253, having reigned two years, three months and 10 days. His relics were translated to Rome where they were interred, not in the Chapel of the Popes in the Catacomb of St. Callistus but rather in an adjoining catacomb, perhaps that of a branch of his noble family. The inscription on his tomb is in Latin, whereas those of his immediate predecessor and successor are in Greek.

Feast: September 16

Cosmas and Damian (d. ca. 303) *Arab twin brothers and physicians who became martyrs*

Cosmas and Damian were born in Arabia and studied science and medicine in Syria. It is not known how or when they became Christians. They lived at Aegeae on the bay of Alexandretta in Cilicia, where their generous practice of free medicine earned them the moniker "the moneyless ones."

During a persecution, they were arrested and brought before Lysius, the governor of Cilicia, in Cyrrhus (modern Turkey). They refused to renounce their faith, and were tortured and beheaded. Also executed were their brothers Anthimus, Euprepius and Leontius. They were buried at Cyrrhus and a cult grew up around them. Miracles of healing were claimed in which the saints came to the afflicted in their dreams and either cured them or told them how to be cured—much like the Greek tradition of inviting the healing god Aesculapius to appear in a similar fashion.

A basilica in Rome was dedicated to them about 530. They are named in the canon of the mass.

In the Middle Ages, romantic legends about their martyrdom appeared. According to lore, the saints defied death first by water, fire and crucifixion prior to their beheading. While on the crosses, they were pelted with stones and arrows, but the missiles recoiled back on the mob.

Feast: September 27
Patronage: barbers; chemical industries; druggists; physicians; surgeons

Crispin and Crispinian (third–fourth centuries) *Brothers and martyrs*

The story of Crispin and Crispinian probably is more legend than fact. Born to Roman nobility, the brothers, shoemakers by trade, traveled to France with St. Quintinus. They settled in Soissons and supported themselves by making shoes while they preached the Gospel and converted pagans.

Co-Emperor Maximian, a hater of Christians, ordered the brothers brought before an official named Rictiovarus (whose existence and position are not documented). Rictiovarus had Crispin and Crispinian tortured, but committed suicide when he was unable to cause their deaths. Maximian had them beheaded.

Crispin and Crispinian were especially popular during the Middle Ages. In art they are shown holding shoes and shoemaker's tools.

Feast: October 25
Patronage: cobblers; leatherworkers; saddlers; shoemakers; tanners

Crispina (d. ca. 304) *Noblewoman and martyr, acclaimed by St. Augustine*

Born in Thagara to a noble family, Crispina was raised as a Christian. During persecutions she was arrested and brought before the proconsul Anulinus. She refused to renounce her faith when threatened with punishment. Anulinus had her head shaved (a sign of degradation) and told her she would be executed if she did not deny her faith. Crispina replied that she cared not for this life. She was beheaded on December 5 in about 304.

In his sermons, Augustine held Crispina as a model for Christians: she could have lived a life of luxury and ease, but chose eternal glory.

Feast: December 5

FURTHER READING
St. Alphonsus Liguori. *Victories of the Martyrs.* Brooklyn: Redemptorist Fathers, 1954.

Curé d'Ars See JOHN BAPTISTE MARIE VIANNEY.

Cuthbert (ca. 634–687) *Monk, bishop and miracle-worker*
Also known as: Cuthbert of Lindisfarne

Most of what is known about Cuthbert, one of the most famous of Celtic saints, comes from the Venerable Bede's account of his life, written around 716 (in verse) and in 721 (in prose). Bede was moved to write about the saint upon hearing of the discovery of his incorrupt body.

Little is known about Cuthbert's early life. He was born probably around 634 to an Anglo-Saxon family near the River Tweed in southern Scotland. (An Irish hagiography claims him as one of their own, son of an Irish princess.)

In 651 Cuthbert entered the Celtic monastery at Melrose, where he served with his mentor, a priest named Boisil. In 661 he accompanied St. Eata, the abbot of Melrose, to Ripon to build a new abbey, where he served as guestmaster. Returning to Melrose, he became prior after the death of Boisil and held the position for many years. He had great skill as a preacher. He then took a group of monks to the Benedictine abbey at Lindisfarne, where he served as prior. Then desiring a solitary life, Cuthbert moved to Inner Farne Island and built his hermit's cell. However, others sought out the popular saint, wanting to confess and seeking his guidance. He helped all who came to him.

In 684 he was elected bishop against his own wishes. He refused to acknowledge all letters to the fact, and finally King Ecgfrith sailed to the island with a group of officials and begged him to do so. Cuthbert was consecrated bishop of Lindisfarne in 685. He resumed his active ministry, caring for the sick, prophesying and working miracles. In 687, Cuthbert knew his life was nearing its end. He resigned as bishop and went back to his beloved Inner Farne. Two months later he fell ill and died while praising God. He was buried on his island in accordance with his wishes. A year later, his body was moved to the monastery at Lindisfarne.

Nine years after his death, Cuthbert was exhumed for the taking of relics. The monks expected to find nothing but dry bones and decayed clothing, and were astonished to find his body incorrupt and fresh, as though he were sleeping. The body was placed in new clothing and reburied.

In 875, the Vikings raided Lindisfarne and destroyed Cuthbert's shrine. His incorrupt body was moved to Northumbria. It was given several resting places, and then finally was moved to Durham, where it was enshrined on September 4, 999. Numerous pilgrims visited, including St. Thomas of Canterbury, and in 1069 William the Conqueror.

The casket was opened in 1104 and the body was found still incorrupt and smelling sweet. In 1537, Henry VIII ordered the tomb destroyed as part of his dissolution of the monasteries. The jewels and ornaments were plundered. When the casket was opened, the body was found still intact, dressed in garments for the Mass, and with a fortnight's beard on the face. The monks were allowed to bury Cuthbert in the ground where the shrine had been. In 1827, the saint was exhumed. This time the remains were but a skeleton in decaying robes.

In art Cuthbert is shown in the dress of a bishop, holding the head of St. Oswald, whose skull is preserved in his coffin. Sometimes he is shown also with swans and otters.

Numerous miracles and extraordinary events are related about Cuthbert throughout his life. Bede relates several visits by angels early in life. One angel appeared as a man on horseback and told Cuthbert how to heal a painful and crippling tumor on his knee. One night while tending sheep, Cuthbert had a vision of choirs of angels descending from heaven, inspiring him to seek the spiritual life. When he was at Ripon, angels frequently appeared and conversed with him, and would bring him food.

According to Bede, he sowed a field with barley and reaped a harvest that the birds began to eat. He told them they had no right to the grain and to depart, and they did, never to return. In another instance involving birds, Cuthbert was annoyed by crows who stole pieces of thatched roof that Cuthbert had made for his brethren. He told the birds to depart and do no more harm. They did. Three days later, seemingly penitent crows returned bearing a gift of hog's lard, which Cuthbert gave to his brethren for the greasing of their shoes.

Bede recounts another episode involving Cuthbert's rapport with animals. One night he left his monastery and was followed by a curious brother. Cuthbert went down to the sea and waded into the water until he was up to his neck. He spent the night praising God. In the morning, he waded out and fell to his knees on the beach to continue praying. Two sea otters came out of the water and wiped him with their bodies and breathed upon his feet. Cuthbert blessed them and they returned to the sea.

Cuthbert banished the devils that reputedly haunted the island of Inner Farne, and produced a miraculous spring from the hard and stony ground where he built his cell. He was able to change the course of a fire threatening to destroy the house of a holy woman. He changed water so that it tasted like wine. He healed people with sprinklings of holy water, anointments with oil and consecrated bread. He healed others by a laying on of hands, and also at a distance with prayer. Miracles of healing continued to be reported after his death.

Feast: March 20

FURTHER READING

Bede. *Life and Miracles of St. Cuthbert.* URL: http://www.fordham.edu/halsall/basis/bede-cuthbert.html. Downloaded September 2, 2000.

Sellner, Edward C. *Wisdom of the Celtic Saints.* Notre Dame, Ind.: Ave Maria Press, 1993.

Cyprian of Carthage (ca. 200–258) *Bishop of Carthage, Father of the Church, martyr*

Cyprian's full Latin name was Thaschus Cæcilius Cyprianus. Nothing is known of his early life, apart from the fact that he was well-established and wealthy at the time of his conversion to Christianity. He was converted by a priest named Cæcilianus, with whom he lived for a while, and who on his deathbed asked him to care for his wife and family. His baptism took place around the year 246, apparently on April 18, Easter Eve.

Even as a catechumen Cyprian decided to observe chastity. He sold his property, including his gardens at Carthage, and gave most of his revenues to the poor. He was elected bishop of Carthage in 248 or 249, with the dissent of five priests who remained his lifelong enemies.

In its first centuries, the Christian Church was subjected to a series of persecutions from Rome. One, the Decian persecution, began in October 249 when Emperor Decius issued an edict sentencing all bishops to death and other believers to be punished and tortured until they recanted. Cyprian went into hiding, an action for which he was much criticized by his enemies. However, he continued to shepherd his see. He wrote panegyrics on Christians who were martyred and provided financial aid to the faithful. When the persecution let up early in 251, Cyprian made priests of some who had resisted, been tortured and banished.

Nevertheless, the majority of Christians—in Carthage as well as in Rome and elsewhere—had denied their faith. Their lives no longer threatened, many now clamored for forgiveness and restoration. Cyprian convened a council in April 251, which decided to accept the former apostates after they had done appropriate penance, a position endorsed by Pope St. Cornelius (r. 251–253). However, the five priests opposed to Cyprian accepted the lapsed without penance, while in Rome, a priest named Novatian held that none should be accepted again under any circumstances.

A related issue of rebaptism arose. Since heretics—and by extension apostates—did not follow the canonical teachings of the Church, were their baptisms invalid? Or were baptisms performed through the agency of God and therefore valid under any circumstance? Since the Church held that there could be only one baptism in a lifetime, this was not a trivial issue, but itself the basis for declaring heresy. Cyprian and the other Eastern bishops routinely rebaptized the lapsed, a practice condoned by Cornelius and Pope St. Lucius I (r. 253–254) although the Church of Rome believed it unnecessary. Pope St. Stephen I (r. 254–257) took a stronger stand on Church orthodoxy, declaring that the lapsed everywhere should be reconciled only with a laying-on of hands, thus alienating Cyprian and others.

A new round of persecutions (announced by numerous visions, according to Cyprian) began under Emperor Valerian, and this time Cyprian was not so fortunate. He was arrested on August 30, 257, and taken before the proconsul Peternus, but refused to renounce his faith. Early in September he had a dream foretelling his martyrdom. He awoke from the dream in terror, but once awake, calmly awaited its fulfillment. This came on the morning of September 14, when he was tried, sentenced and beheaded. Before dying, he ordered that 25 gold pieces be given to his executioner.

Members of his flock observing his execution held cloths and handkerchiefs before him to catch his blood. His dismembered body lay exposed for the rest of the day, but that night the brethren carried him in a funeral procession to the cemetery of Macrobius Candidianus in the suburb of Mapalia. He was the first bishop of Carthage to be martyred.

Feast: September 16 (in the West); August 31 (in the East)
Patronage: Algeria; North Africa

Cyril of Alexandria (ca. 376–444) *Patriarch of Alexandria, Father of the Church, Doctor of the Church*

Cyril was born in Alexandria ca. 376. He was the nephew of Theophilus, patriarch of Alexandria, and among those who deposed St. John Chrysostom. Cyril was raised, educated and ordained by his uncle, and went with him to Constantinople in 403 for the deposition of John. When Theophilus died in 412, Cyril succeeded him as patriarch of Alexandria, but only after a riot broke out between his supporters and those of his rival, Timotheus.

Cyril spent much of his career embroiled in the church politics of heresies. He closed the churches of one heretical sect, the Novatianists, and chased the Jews out of Alexandria. In 430 he began a battle against the heretic Nestorius, who was preaching that Mary was not the Mother of God, since Christ was Divine and not human, and consequently she should not have the word *Theotokos* ("God-bearer") applied to her.

Cyril persuaded Pope Celestine I (r. 422–432) to convene a synod condemning Nestorius, and Cyril convened his own synod in Alexandria to do the same. Cyril also presided over the Third General Council of Ephesus, at which he condemned Nestorius, but then was deposed himself. Both Cyril and Nestorius were arrested, but Cyril was released upon intervention of the pope. Eventually Nestorius was condemned and banished to the Great Oasis of Egypt.

A brilliant scholar, Cyril left a legacy of exegetical works, treatises, commentaries on the Gospels and the Pentateuch, sermons, letters and an apologia against Julian the Apostate. He is known especially for his writing on the Holy Trinity and the Incarnation. *On Adoration in Spirit and Truth* is a 17-book exposition on the spiritual nature of the Old Law.

Declared Doctor of the Church: 1882 by Pope Leo XIII
Feast: June 27

St. Cyril of Alexandria (Library of Congress Prints and Photographs Division)

Cyril of Jerusalem (ca. 315–ca. 386) *Bishop of Jerusalem, Father of the Church, Doctor of the Church*

Little is known of Cyril of Jerusalem's life. He was born in Jerusalem about 315 and probably was raised a Christian. He became a priest around 345–347, and was ordained by St. Maximus.

Cyril became the bishop or patriarch of Jerusalem, succeeding Maximus after the latter died; stories differ as to how he obtained the position. In one version, Cyril was promised the episcopate only if he repudiated his ordination. Cyril declined and agreed only to become deacon, but through fraud and manipulation got the position. In another version, Maximus was driven out and was succeeded by Cyril.

For the next 36 years, Cyril had to deal with the Arian heresy, and three times was exiled as a result of the politics involved. In 357–359 he went to Tarsus. In 360 he was driven out again, only to be restored in 361 by Emperor Julian the Apostate. In 367 Emperor Valens banished all bishops, and Cyril was exiled until Valens died in 378.

In 380, St. Gregory of Nyssa came to Jerusalem and approved of Cyril but found the city corrupt in morals.

Cyril and Gregory attended the Council of Constantinople in 381. At this council, Theodosius ordered the Nicene Creed to be promulgated.

The exact date of Cyril's death is unknown. He probably died on March 18, 386.

Cyril left a body of work highly valued by the Church. The most famous is his theological masterpiece *Catecheses*, a collection of 18 instructional addresses for baptismal candidates during Lent and five—known as the *Mystagogic*—for the recently baptized at Easter. Cyril composed numerous catechetical lectures and sermons (including his best-known on the pool at Bethesda). He wrote on the mystical origin of the Septuagint, the story of the phoenix and the mystical elements of the Mass.

> *Declared Doctor of the Church:* 1882 by Pope Leo XIII
>
> *Feast:* March 18 (in the East); March 18 or 20 (in the West)

Damasus I (ca. 304–384) *Pope*

Damasus was born in Rome, the son of Antonius, a priest of Spanish descent, and a woman named Laurentia. He became a deacon in the Spanish church of St. Laurence, where his father served.

In October 366, when Damasus was about 60, Pope Liberius died, and he was elected bishop of Rome. Though he received a substantial majority of votes, a dissident faction, adherents of Liberius (a controversial pontiff who became one of the few early popes to be revered neither as a martyr nor as a saint), rejected him and consecrated their own candidate, Ursinus. In promoting him, they were not beyond using violence, for which Emperor Valentinian had them exiled to Cologne. From Cologne and later Milan, Ursinus and his followers continued to harass Damasus. They charged him with incontinence in the imperial court in 378, but he was exonerated by Emperor Gratian. He was cleared also by a Church synod of 44 bishops, who then excommunicated his accusers.

In 380, Gratian and Theodosius I recognized Christianity as the religion of the Roman state. Damasus did much to clarify and promote its teachings. He argued that the supremacy of the Roman Church was based on the words of Jesus Christ (Matthew 16:18). He was a vigorous opponent of Arianism (supported by Liberius and Ursinus), Apollinarianism, Macedonianism and other heresies. At a synod in 374, he promulgated a canon of the Holy Scripture, specifying the authentic books of the Bible. Most important, he commissioned St. Jerome to revise the Latin text of the Bible, resulting in the Vulgate version of the Scriptures.

Like several of his immediate predecessors, Damasus promoted the construction of ecclesiastical properties in and around Rome. Among other projects, he provided for the proper housing of the Vatican archives, built a baptistery in honor of St. Peter at the Vatican, and drained and rehabilitated the sacred catacombs. He devoted much effort to gathering the relics of Roman martyrs and wrote new epitaphs for the tombs of many of them.

In the papal crypt of the Catacomb of St. Callistus he placed a general epitaph that ends, "I, Damasus, wished to be buried here, but I feared to offend the ashes of these holy ones." When he died on December 11, 384, he was buried with his mother and sister at a small church he had built on the Via Ardeatina.

In art, Damasus is a pope holding a ring. He may also be shown with Jerome; restoring sacred buildings; holding a screen with "Gloria Patri" on it; or in front of a church door.

Feast: December 11
Patronage: archaeologists

Damian   See COSMAS AND DAMIAN.

David (d. 601) *Confessor, bishop, monastic founder, patron saint of Wales*
Also known as: Degui; Dewi; the Waterman

Few facts are known about the life of David. According to tradition, he was born at Henvynyw (Vetus-Menevia) in Cardiganshire; some sources place his birth at about 520. He played a prominent role at the Synod of Brevi and in 569 presided over a synod held at Lucus Victoriae. He was bishop of Menevia, Pembrokeshire, also known as the Roman port of Menapia, and later renamed St. David's.

A longstanding tradition exists in Wales of wearing a leek on St. David's Day, in remembrance of a battle against the Saxons in which David is said to have told the Welsh to wear leeks in their hats to distinguish themselves from the enemy.

Legends about David were recorded by medieval writers, including Geoffrey of Monmouth. According to lore, his birth was prophesied 30 years in advance by an angel appearing to St. Patrick. Another story tells how an angel appeared to his father, Sanctus, in a dream and prophesied David's birth.

David was born to a violated nun. He was educated by St. Illtyd at Caerworgorn in Glamorganshire and then studied under St. Paulinus, who was blind due to excessive weeping. David cured him of his blindness by making the sign of the cross. Paulinus was directed by an angel to dispatch David to evangelize the British. During his travels, David founded 12 monasteries (Glastonbury and Bath are among those credited to him), suffered the temptations of women and had fabulous adventures. His monks tried to poison his bread, but David was warned by St. Schuthyn who rode from Ireland one night on the back of a sea monster. David blessed the bread and ate it without injury. He was credited with raising the dead and having a hill rise up under him so that a multitude could hear him preach.

David is said to have made a pilgrimage to Jerusalem with two other saints to be consecrated archbishop, but the story probably is not accurate.

King Arthur allowed him to move his see from Caerleon to Menevia, where David ruled for many years, dying at the unlikely age of 147 on a day he predicted. His soul was witnessed as it was borne to heaven. He was buried at the monastery, then moved to St. David's Cathedral. Supposedly his remains were moved to Glastonbury in 966, but they apparently were still at St. David's in 1346. That tomb is now empty.

In art David is shown standing on a small hill with a dove on his shoulder. He was nicknamed "the Waterman" because of his strict monastic rule prohibiting alcohol.

Canonized: 1120 by Pope Callistus II
Feast: March 1
Patronage: doves; poets; Wales

FURTHER READING
Doble, G.H. *Lives of the Welsh Saints,* ed. D. Simon Evans. Cardiff: University of Wales Press, 1971.
Sellner, Edward C. *Wisdom of the Celtic Saints.* Notre Dame, Ind.: Ave Maria Press, 1993.

Dionysius (d. 268) *Pope*

For a year after the murder of Pope St. Sixtus II in August 258, there was a vacancy in the Holy See of Rome as the persecutions under Emperor Valerian continued. Finally Gallienus came to power, and Dionysius, a priest in the Roman Church, was elected bishop on July 22, 259.

The signal event of his pontificate was the effort to discipline Sabellius, an Asian priest who, like Marcion, denied the Trinity and held that Jesus was but a man who had received supernatural powers at baptism. Dionysius called a synod in Rome about 260 to discuss the matter, then issued an important doctrinal letter explaining the Church's position.

Dionysius is also known for sending support to help the Christians of Cappadocia when faced with invasion by the Goths. Along with a letter he sent a large sum of money for the ransom of enslaved believers.

Dionysius died in 268 of natural causes and was interred in the papal crypt of the Catacomb of St. Callistus.

In art he is portrayed wearing papal vestments and holding a book.

Feast: December 26

Dionysius of Alexandria (ca. 190–265) *Bishop of Alexandria, Father of the Church*
Also known as: Dionysius the Great

Dionysius of Alexandria was one of the greatest bishops of the third century. He lived during a time of turmoil and persecution.

Dionysius was born in Alexandria to a distinguished pagan family. As a youth he had a vision that prompted him to convert to Christianity. He entered catechetical school and studied under Origen. Origen was banished by Demetrius in 231. After the death of Demetrius, Dionysius took over as head of the school, and may have retained the position even after becoming bishop of Alexandria in 247 and serving through 248.

In 249, an anti-Christian riot broke out in Alexandria, and scores of Christians, including the virgin Apollonia, were tortured and killed. The riot was stopped, but an official persecution was launched in January 250 by the newly crowned emperor Decius. Dionysius was arrested, but was rescued and taken into the Libyan desert, where he remained until the persecutions stopped in 251. The same year, a dispute arose between Pope Cornelius (r. 251–253) and Novatian, and Dionysius sided with Cornelius.

Famine and plague then descended on Alexandria and the city remained in turmoil. Throughout these tensions and difficulties, Dionysius sought to keep the Eastern and Western Churches in communication, and advocated indulgences for lapsed Christians who wished to return to the fold. He wrote books correcting errors in theology and went out into the villages to preach.

In 253 Valerian became emperor and began persecutions in 257. Dionysius was banished to Kephro in the Libyan desert. There he remained until tolerance was declared in 260 by Gallienus. Returning to Alexandria, Dionysius once again found the city in the grip of famine and plague. So difficult was travel that he had to communicate with his churches by letter. In 264 he regained the bishopric, which he held until his death in 265.

Dionysius wrote numerous letters, only one of which survives. He is cited in the works of Eusebius, who, along with St. Basil and others, referred to Dionysius as "the Great."

Feast: November 17

Dismas (d. first century) *The "Good Thief," crucified with Jesus on Calvary*

The *Gospel of Infancy,* an Arabic text of dubious reliability, tells how Dismas and the other crucified thief, Gestas, actually encountered the Holy Family when they fled to Egypt, and robbed them. Dismas supposedly saved the family from Gestas.

The Gospels do not name the thieves, but Matthew and Mark tell of one of them reviling Jesus on the cross. Luke 23: 39–43 tells of one reviling Jesus and being rebuked by the second thief, who said, "Do you not fear God, since you are under the same sentence of condemnation? And we indeed justly; for we are receiving the due reward of our deeds; but this man has done nothing wrong." The robber asked Jesus to remember him when Jesus came into his kingdom, and

Jesus said, "Truly I say to you, today you will be with me in paradise."

Feast: March 25
Patronage: death row inmates; funeral directors; prisoners; therapists; undertakers

Dominic (ca. 1170–1221) *Founder of the Order of Preachers, known as the Dominicans*

Dominic was born around 1170 in Calaroga, Old Castile, Spain, to a noble family. His mother, Joanna of Aza, was a devout woman who was beatified in 1828 by Leo XII (r. 1823–29). Brother Antonio became a priest, and brother Manes became a friar preacher and was beatified by Pope Gregory XVI (r. 1831–46).

From birth Dominic seemed destined for sainthood and greatness. Tradition holds that his mother had a vision prior to his birth of a dog with a lighted torch in its mouth. This was a sign that she would have a son who would set the world on fire with his ministry.

Dominic studied at the University of Valencia from 1184 to 1194, excelling in his subjects and garnering the admiration of others for his austerity and charity. He especially abhorred heresy. He sold his books to give money to the poor, and twice attempted to sell himself into slavery in order to buy captives held by the Moors.

In 1199 Dominic was called to the cathedral of Osma to assist in reforms of the Franciscan chapter there. He became a Franciscan canon regular and was appointed subprior. In 1201 he became superior and prior. Dominic spent nine years there, spending most of his time within the confines of the chapter.

In 1203, Don Diego, the bishop of Osma, was dispatched by Alfonso IX, king of Castile, to negotiate the hand of a Danish princess for his son in marriage. Diego chose Dominic to accompany him. En route, they were dismayed at the influence of the Albigensian heresy in Toulouse. Dominic was inspired with the idea of founding an order of preachers to evangelize and combat heresy. After the marriage was arranged, Diego and Dominic were sent to escort the princess to Spain. She died suddenly en route. Dominic and Diego set out to preach against the Albigenses in southern France and went on to Rome, arriving near the end of 1204.

Pope Innocent III (r. 1198–1216) refused to approve a new order, however, and sent the men to Languedoc to aid the Cistercians in their fight against heresy and to reform the monasteries. They found the Cistercians to be too lax. Their preaching won many converts, as well as threats from the Cistercians.

St. Dominic (Library of Congress Prints and Photographs Division)

approval of the bishop of Toulouse, forming a small group known as the Order of the Preachers, charged with the mission of spreading religious truth and stamping out heresy. The order received papal approval on December 22, 1216, from Pope Honorius III (r. 1216–27). In 1218, Honorius III gave the order the church of St. Sixtus in Rome.

Dominic spent the remainder of his life organizing and expanding the order. Dominic himself preached tirelessly; it is said that his words and miracles converted thousands. He established a third order, the Militia of Christ, as an organization of men and women living in the world and protecting the rights and property of the Church.

In June 1221 Dominic was in Bologna preparing for a missionary journey to Venice. He foresaw his own death, and told others that he would die before the next feast of the Assumption (August 15). Upon his return to Bologna, he spent several hours in prayer, and then was stricken with a fatal illness. He died three weeks later.

As the Inquisition gathered force in Europe, Dominicans played a major role in the prosecution of heretics. In 1233, Pope Gregory IX (r. 1227–41) issued a bull declaring that all inquisitors would be Dominicans and would be answerable only to the pope. In 1484, Pope Innocent VIII (r. 1484–92) was persuaded by two Dominican inquisitors, Heinrich Kramer and Jacob Sprenger, to issue a bull removing all impediments against inquisitors. The bull opened the way for the most extreme prosecutions of the Inquisition in the 15th and 16th centuries.

In art Dominic is shown in the black and white robes of his order, sometimes holding a lily or accompanied by a dog or globe of fire. A star is placed in his halo.

Numerous miracles were attributed to Dominic. With the help of holy water and prayer, he is said to have raised from the dead a cardinal's nephew who was killed when he was thrown from a horse and mangled. He had the gift of miraculous transport, not only of himself but of others as well. On one occasion, he and a Cistercian monk were traveling and stopped at a church to spend the night in prayer. It was locked, so they decided to spend the night on the church steps. Suddenly they found themselves inside at the altar. On numerous occasions he multiplied food. Once when the friary of St. Sixtus had no food, Dominic summoned all the brothers to the refectory and had the tables set for a meal. He prayed, and suddenly two angels in the guise of beautiful young men appeared carrying a large load of bread. They gave every brother an entire loaf, and then disappeared. It was recorded in 1528 that every year on the anniversary of this occa-

Dominic also founded a convent for women in Prouille in 1206.

In 1208, Pierre de Castelnau, one of the Cistercian papal legates, was murdered by the Albigenses. Innocent III responded with a crusade to stamp them out and appointed Simon de Montfort to head the effort. Dominic formed a close friendship with him and assisted him. During this seven-year crusade, Dominic played a role in the Inquisition. Simon attributed a critical victory at Muret to the prayers of Dominic, and erected a chapel there devoted to Our Lady of the Rosary. De Montfort also gave Dominic a castle at Casseneuil.

In 1214 Dominic returned to Toulouse. He turned down several offers of bishoprics and pursued his dream of establishing a new order. He did so with the

sion, a sweet perfume manifested for 40 hours at the spot where the rectory had been.

In his preaching, Dominic was known for his accurate prophecy. He also foretold deaths. He had the gift of tongues; on one occasion he enabled himself and some of his monks to converse with German monks in their own language. He could control the elements and tame storms.

Dominic seemed to have an immunity to fire. Once the Albigenses challenged him to a debate in writing, to be judged by a panel sympathetic to the heretics. After hearing the arguments, the judges declined to make a decision. The heretics then requested trial by fire. The works of both sides were tossed into the flames. The writings of the heretics burned immediately, but Dominic's work was not consumed, and even rose into the air. Three times his work was cast into the fire, with the same results each time.

On another occasion, Dominic traveled to Segovia and stayed at the home of a poor woman. He exchanged his hair shirt for a coarser one. The woman secretly kept the hair shirt. Later, after Dominic was gone, the house caught fire. The only thing left unburned was the hair shirt and the box containing it. The relic was taken to the monastery at Valladolid.

On May 24, 1233, Dominic's body was exhumed due to repairs at the Bologna monastery where he was buried. As soon as the flagstones were moved, a sweet perfume filled the air. When the casket was raised, the scent filled the entire church. Dominic's body was incorrupt and his countenance looked the same as in life. His head turned spontaneously. The perfume adhered to anyone who came near or touched the body. Three hundred years later, his relics were still fragrant.

Canonized: July 13, 1234, by Pope Gregory IX
Feast: August 8
Patronage: astronomers

FURTHER READING
Doray, Mary J. *Saint Dominic.* Rockford, Ill.: TAN Books and Publishers, 1993.
Drane, Augustus T. *The Life of Saint Dominic.* Rockford, Ill.: TAN Books and Publishers, 1988.

Dominic Savio (1842–1857) *Student of St. John Bosco; mystic; patron of youth*

Dominic Savio was spiritually advanced at a young age. He was born in Italy in 1842. By age five, he was an altar boy. When he was seven, he received his First Holy Communion. On that day, he chose a motto: "Death, but not sin!"

At age 12, he went with John Bosco to John's oratory in Turin. There Dominic created the Company of the Immaculate Conception, in order to help John with his work. He stood out from among the other boys, who looked up to him. John Bosco was impressed with his piety and purity. He had many gifts, including prophecy and visions. One of his visions influenced Pope Pius IX in 1850 to reestablish the Catholic hierarchy in England.

One day Dominic began to feel sick and was sent home. While at home he grew worse, and knew himself that he was dying. He was only 15. He is said to have faced death bravely, looking forward to going to heaven. He received the last sacraments. Just before he died, he tried to sit up. He said to his father, "Goodbye." He smiled and added, "I am seeing such wonderful things!" With that, he died.

Dominic became the patron saint of the falsely accused, due to an incident that happened while he was alive. One time, two boys filled the school stove with snow and garbage during the cold winter months. When the teacher came back into the room, they falsely accused Dominic of doing the deed. Although disciplined in front of the entire class, Dominic refused to tell on the two mischievous boys. When the truth was later revealed, Dominic was asked why he didn't confess to his innocence. He remarked that he was imitating Our Lord, who remained silent during His persecutions and crucifixion.

"A teenager such as Dominic, who bravely struggled to keep his innocence from baptism to the end of his life, is really a saint," said Pope St. Pius X (r. 1903–14).

On December 6, 1876, 20 years after Dominic's death, John Bosco—renowned for his lucid dreams—met him in a dream. The setting was a beautiful place of gardens, long avenues and magnificent buildings. John was given to understand that it was not technically "heaven." In a brilliant light, Dominic walked forward to greet him. Bosco described:

> Dominic now walked forward on his own until he stood close beside me. He stood there silently for a moment, smiling and looking at me. How wonderful he looked, how exquisitely he was clothed! The white tunic which reached to his feet was interwoven with golden threads and sparkling jewels. Around his waist he had a broad red sash, also interwoven with precious stones of every color, which sparkled and glittered in a thousand lights. Around his neck there was a necklace of wild flowers, but the flowers were made of precious stones and the light they reflected lit up further still the beauty and dignity of Dominic's face. His hair, which was crowned with roses, hung down to his shoulders and completed the quite indescribable effect of his total appearance.

Dominic told John that they were in "a place of happiness where all that is beautiful can be enjoyed." It was not heaven, for "no living person can ever see or imagine the wonders of eternity."

Dominic told John that he had done well with the boys under his care at his oratory, but that the Salesian order would be many more in number if he had "greater faith and confidence in God" and nurtured virtues in the boys. "What helped me most and gave me greatest joy when I was dying," replied Dominic, *"was the loving care and help of the great Mother of God. Tell your sons not to fail to keep close to her while they are alive."*

Dominic then accurately predicted that John would have many trials ahead of him. He predicted the death of Pope Pius IX (r. 1846–78) two years hence in 1878, and the coming deaths of some of John's charges.

His final gift was to give John three pieces of folded paper. The first paper bore a list of boys who had never been overcome by evil. The second had a list of boys who had "seriously offended God," but were trying to redeem themselves. The third paper bore the names of boys who had been conquered by evil. It was folded. Dominic warned Bosco that when he opened the third paper it would give off a terrible, unbearable stench of evil.

John did so and was overcome by the stench. He was saddened to see the names of some of his "best" boys. When he awakened, the stench filled his chamber. Dominic's words were borne out.

Canonized: 1954 by Pope Pius XII
Feast: March 9
Patronage: choir boys; the falsely accused; youth

FURTHER READING
Forty Dreams of St. John Bosco. Rockford, Ill.: TAN Books and Publishers, 1996.

Dunstan (d. 988) *Confessor, archbishop of Canterbury, abbot of Glastonbury and one of the greatest saints of the Anglo-Saxon Church*

Dunstan was born to a noble family in Glastonbury, England, probably around 910; some sources place his birth date as late as 925–26. According to lore, his mother, Cynethryth, received a sign of his sanctity while he was still in the womb. While in the church of St. Mary on Candleday (Candlemas), all of the candles suddenly went out. The candle she held relit, and everyone relit their candles from hers. This was taken as a sign that her child would be a "minister of eternal light" to the Church of England.

Dunstan was educated by Irish scholars who frequented the monastery at Glastonbury. He received a tonsure and minor orders, and served in the church of St. Mary. He devoted himself to prayer, study, the copying of illuminated manuscripts and the making of bells and other things for the church. So great was his devotion that his uncle Athelm, archbishop of Canterbury, summoned him into service.

At court, Dunstan was favored by King Aethelstan, which earned him enemies who accused him of pagan interests. Dunstan left court and went to Winchester, where St. Alphege the Bald, his uncle and also the bishop of Winchester, tried to convince him to become a monk. Dunstan demurred, but changed his mind after a near-fatal illness he believed to be leprosy (but may have been blood poisoning). He returned to Glastonbury and built himself a cell against the outside of the church that measured five feet long by two-and-a-half feet wide. Here he took up the life of a hermit, played his harp and endured temptation by the devil. According to lore, he seized the devil's nose with a pair of blacksmith's tongs.

In 940 King Aethelstan's successor, King Eadmund, summoned him to court at Cheddar, but Dunstan once again was tarnished by jealous lies, and Eadmund threw him out. One day, while the king was out hunting a stag, his prey rushed over a cliff and Eadmund saw he was powerless to stop his galloping horse from doing the same. He prayed that he would make amends to Dunstan if his life was spared. Miraculously, the horse stopped at the edge of the cliff. Eadmund took Dunstan to Glastonbury and made him abbot.

Thus began a revival of monastic life in England. Dunstan established Benedictine monasticism and worked to rebuild the Glastonbury abbey. He founded a school for youth. Two years later, Eadmund's successor, Eadred, invested Dunstan with more power, and for the next nine years the saint wielded tremendous influence in court and in monasteries throughout England.

After Eadred died in 955, Dunstan was once more the victim of court politics, and he was exiled to Flanders. He was recalled in 957 and appointed to the see of Worcester, and then to the see of London in 958. He became archbishop of Canterbury in 960, a position that restored his influence. In 975, he was instrumental in the selection of King Eadward. Civil war erupted, and Eadward was assassinated in 978. Under the next king, Aethelred the Redeless, Dunstan lost his influence. He retired to Canterbury and emerged only three times, in 980, 984 and 986.

On the vigil of Ascension Day in 988, he had a vision of angels warning him that he had three days to live. On the feast day, he said mass and preached three times, telling people of his impending death. He chose the location for his tomb and went to bed to die. On

May 19 Mass was celebrated in his presence, he was given the last rites and he died.

Dunstan was buried in Canterbury Cathedral. It burnt down in 1074, and his relics were translated to a tomb in the new church on the south side of the high altar. The tomb was opened in 1508. The shrine was destroyed during the Reformation.

Dunstan's notable work is *Regularis Concordia,* about the monastic life. In art he often is shown with a dove near him, with a band of angels, or holding a pair of blacksmith's tongs.

Feast: May 19
Patronage: armorers; blacksmiths; goldsmiths; jewelers; lighthouse keepers; locksmiths; musicians; silversmiths; swordsmiths

Dymphna *Virgin and martyr*
Also known as: Dympna, Dimpna

The story of Dymphna is told in legend and has no historical foundation. An oral tradition existed for centuries and was set down in writing in the mid-13th century. At that time Dymphna had been venerated for many years in Gheel, in the province of Antwerp, Belgium, and a church there was devoted to her. She was invoked against insanity.

According to the legend, Dymphna was the daughter of a pagan king in Ireland. She converted to Christianity and was baptized in secret. After her mother died, her father desired to marry her. With the priest Gerebernus, she escaped to Gheel. They became hermits. Her father found them. When he failed to persuade Dymphna to marry him, he had the priest slain and cut off his daughter's head. The bodies were placed in sarcophagi and entombed in a cave. The remains were found, probably in the 13th century. Dymphna was transferred to Gheel and Gerebernus to Xanten. Fragments of the sarcophagi are in Gheel, along with a

St. Dymphna (Library of Congress Prints and Photographs Division)

brick alleged to have been found in one of them, bearing the word DYMPNA.

In art Dymphna is shown with a sword in her hand and a fettered devil at her feet.

Feast: May 15
Patronage: against epilepsy; family harmony; against insanity; nerves; against mental disorders; against possession; runaways; against sleep disorders

E

Eleutherius (d. ca. 189) *Pope*
Also known as: Eleutheros

Eleutherius was from Nicopolis in Epirus (Greece). He became a deacon in Rome under Pope St. Anicetus (r. ca. 154–164), a position he held also under the pope's successor, Pope St. Soter. Upon Soter's death around the year 174, Eleutherius himself was elected pope.

Eleutherius decreed that any food fit for humans was suitable for Christians, a response to the teachings of the Gnostics and the Montanists (Phrygians). The latter was a prophetic sect with origins in the east. It was especially influential in Lyons, which sent a letter to Eleutherius on the matter. At first Eleutherius was inclined to be tolerant of its teachings, but after some reflection, he came out strongly against them. Nevertheless, Montanists continued to have followings in Rome and other Christian cities.

There is a legend that Eleutherius sent a mission to the British Isles (then a part of the Roman Empire) in response to an invitation from an English king named Lucius. However, this is now known to be due to a misreading of *Britio* for *Britanio*. Britio (short for Birtha-Britium) was the name of the fortress at Edessa in Syria, under the Christian king Lucius Ælius Septimus Megas Abgar IX, and it was he who wrote to Eleutherius. The misinterpretation may have been a deliberate attempt to lay a foundation for the subjugation of Britain under the Roman Church.

The persecutions of Christians during his pontificate were relatively light, and Eleutherius died a natural death on May 24 about the year 189. He was buried on Vatican Hill along with his predecessor popes.

Feast: May 26

Elizabeth (first century) *Mother of St. John the Baptist and kinswoman of the Blessed Virgin Mary*
Name meaning: Worshiper of God

Elizabeth is mentioned in Luke 1. She was a descendant of Aaron and lived with her husband Zachary, a priest of the temple in Jerusalem. She and Zachary prayed for a son, but she was barren.

When the couple was advanced in years, Gabriel the Archangel appeared to Zachary and told him Elizabeth would bear a son who was to be named John. When Elizabeth was six months pregnant, Gabriel informed Mary that she was to bear a son who was to be named Jesus. Mary, wishing to share her news, visited Elizabeth, who greeted her by saying, "Blessed are you among women, and blessed is the fruit of your womb!" Elizabeth said that her infant "leaped for joy" in her womb at the sound of Mary's voice. Mary then delivered the Magnificat ("My soul magnifies the Lord . . .").

The last information about Elizabeth in Luke tells of the infant John's circumcision and naming in the temple of Jerusalem.

Feast: November 5 (with Zachary)

Elizabeth Ann Seton (1774–1821) *Founder of the Daughters of Charity of St. Joseph and the American parochial school system; first native-born American saint Also known as:* Elizabeth Ann Bayley Seton; Mother Seton

Elizabeth Ann Bayley was born August 28, 1774, to a wealthy and influential Episcopalian family in New York City. Her father, Dr. Richard Bayley, was born in Connecticut and educated in England. He was the first professor of anatomy at King's College, now Columbia University, and although he remained a Loyalist during the American Revolution was appointed the new nation's inspector general in the New York Department of Health for the Port of New York. Elizabeth's mother, Catherine Charlton, was the daughter of the Anglican rector of St. Andrew's Church on Staten Island. She died when Elizabeth was three years old, leaving a younger daughter, Mary, as well. Dr. Bayley remarried, having seven children by his second wife, but took

St. Elizabeth Ann Seton (Library of Congress Prints and Photographs Division)

responsibility for the education of his first two daughters. Elizabeth was well read, industrious and pious.

On January 25, 1794, Elizabeth married William Magee Seton in St. Paul's Church, New York. William Seton was a first-generation American and heir to a wealthy shipping firm. Elizabeth became an active philanthropist, and she and William's sister Rebecca were known in New York as the "Protestant Sisters of Charity." By 1797 she had helped found the Society for the Relief of Poor Widows with Small Children. The couple had five children: Anna Maria, William Jr., Richard, Catherine and Rebecca.

Then disaster struck. The Napoleonic Wars between France and England resulted in the seizure of many of the Setons' ships, and the business failed. The elder Seton died in 1798, leaving William responsible not only for the mounting bills but also for his orphaned siblings. In 1802, Elizabeth's beloved father contracted yellow fever and died. And by 1803 William himself was seriously ill with tuberculosis.

Doctors recommended a sea voyage to sunny Italy, so William, Elizabeth and their eldest daughter Anna Maria left for Leghorn in late 1803 to winter with the Filicchi family, with whom William had done business before his marriage. After seven weeks at sea, Italian authorities kept the ship in quarantine for another four weeks due to a yellow fever epidemic in New York. William's health worsened, and he died on December 27, just nine days after being released from quarantine.

Poor health caused Elizabeth and Anna to remain with the Filicchis throughout the winter and spring of 1803–04. During this sad period Elizabeth often accompanied the Filicchis to Catholic services, where she was touched by the beauty of the Mass and especially impressed with the idea of the Presence in Communion. When Elizabeth and Anna returned to New York in June 1804, she began Catholic instruction, even in the face of fierce campaigning against such a step by her rector, Mr. Hobart, and all of her relatives. Then her dear sister-in-law Rebecca Seton died in July, throwing Elizabeth into total despair. Finally accepting the call, Elizabeth was received into the faith at St. Peter's Church by Father Matthew O'Brien on March 14, 1805. Family financial support would have been immediately forthcoming had Elizabeth remained Protestant, but now she was ostracized. She endeavored to run a boardinghouse for boys, then tried to teach at a girls' school, but fears that Elizabeth would teach Catholic dogma forced the school to close. When Elizabeth's 15-year-old sister-in-law, Cecilia, announced she was converting as well, threats were made to have the New York legislature expel Elizabeth from the state. Her sons William and Richard were in Georgetown College, courtesy of the Filicchis, and

Elizabeth unsuccessfully sought refuge for herself and the girls in a Canadian convent.

Desperate, Elizabeth went to hear Mass in August 1807 from Father William Valentine du Bourg, a Sulpician father and president of the Sulpician College of St. Mary's, a seminary in Baltimore. Father du Bourg suggested that Elizabeth found and head a girls' school near the seminary. After much prayer and consultation, Elizabeth traveled to Baltimore in June 1808 and opened St. Joseph's School for Girls next to the chapel at St. Mary's, an event that marked the beginning of the Catholic parochial school system in America. Other young women seeking quiet service joined the school, including Cecilia Conway of Philadelphia. They wore whatever clothes they owned for everyday, and for formal dress Elizabeth chose an outfit based on a nun's habit she had seen in Italy: a plain black dress with a shoulder cape and a bonnet. In 1809, a man named Cooper died and left the women $10,000 to found a school for poor children. Elizabeth bought a farm located a half-mile from Emmitsburg, Maryland, and two miles from the school at St. Mary's. Before establishing her new community, Elizabeth took vows in front of Archbishop Carroll, formally founding the Sisters of St. Joseph and henceforth becoming Mother Seton, and moved to Emmitsburg. Her sisters-in-law Harriet and Cecilia joined her, but Harriet died that December, followed by Cecilia in April 1810. That same year, Bishop Flaget petitioned the Sisters of Charity of St. Vincent de Paul in Paris to receive the rules of the Sisters of St. Joseph. Three sisters were to come to America to train the community, but Napoleon forbade the women to leave France. Bishop Flaget modified the rule somewhat, with Archbishop Carroll's approval, and in January 1812 the order officially became the Daughters of Charity of St. Joseph, with Mother Seton as superior. Elizabeth's daughter Anna Maria died March 12, 1812, during her novitiate but was allowed to profess her vows before she died. On July 19, 1813, Mother Seton and 18 women established the first American religious society.

The order quickly grew, establishing free schools, orphanages and hospitals in addition to the parochial schools. Mother Seton divided her time between the sisters and writing discourses, translations and hymns. Her triumphs continued, tempered by sadness, however, as her daughter Rebecca died in 1816. When the community reelected Mother Seton as their superior in 1819 she was suffering from a pulmonary disease, probably tuberculosis, which finally took her life on January 4, 1821. The Daughters of Charity were incorporated into the full Sisters of Charity of St. Vincent de Paul in 1850. Mother Seton's body is enshrined in the basilica at Emmitsburg. Only two of Elizabeth's children survived their mother very long (Richard died in Italy in 1821 as well), and both became important to the Church. William Jr. died in 1868 after joining the navy, but his son Robert became the Most Reverend Robert Seton, archbishop of Heliopolis. Her daughter Catherine (whom Elizabeth had once offered to God in despair over her father's illness) became the first postulant of the New York Sisters of Mercy and their mother superior, dying at age 91. And one of Elizabeth's half-nephews, James (the son of her stepbrother Guy Charlton Bayley), also converted and became the Most Reverend James Roosevelt Bayley, archbishop of Baltimore.

> *Beatified:* March 17, 1963, by Pope John XXIII
> *Canonized:* September 14, 1975, by Pope Paul VI
> *Feast:* January 4
> *Patronage:* death of children; loss of parents; people opposed to Church authorities; people ridiculed for their piety; people with in-law problems; widows

FURTHER READING

"Saint Elizabeth Ann Seton." *Christianity-Catholicism.* URL: http://www.suite101.com. Published July 31, 1998. Downloaded May 13, 2000.

Dirvin, Joseph I. *The Soul of Elizabeth Seton: A Spiritual Portrait.* Fort Collins, Colo.: Ignatius Press, 1990.

Elizabeth of Portugal (1271–1336) *Queen of Portugal, Franciscan tertiary*
Also known as: Isabella; Angel of Peace; the Peacemaker

Given the contentious nature of her royal ancestors, no one would have predicted that Elizabeth would assume the role of peacemaker almost from birth. Her great-grandfather was Holy Roman Emperor Frederick II, leader of Germany, Italy, Sicily and Jerusalem, and cousin to St. Thomas Aquinas. Her maternal grandfather, King Manfred of Sicily, was one of Frederick II's illegitimate sons. He met an untimely end when Charles of Anjou, son of King St. Louis IX of France, had him murdered and his body paraded through the streets on a donkey.

On her father's side, her grandfather, King James I of Aragon, banished his family from court because they criticized his incestuous affairs. But Elizabeth's birth at Aragon in 1271 stopped all the squabbling, at least temporarily; James reconciled with his son Peter in order to see Peter's child, named for her great-aunt St. Elizabeth of Hungary. The king fell in love with Elizabeth and took her to live with him.

By the time King James I died in 1276, the six-year-old child had learned the intrigues of her grandfather's marriages and affairs and understood the geopolitical significance of her own wedding. Edward I of England wanted Elizabeth to marry his son, and Charles of Anjou desired her for his son. But her father, now Peter III of Aragon, betrothed the girl, barely 12, to King Denis of Portugal, supposedly to keep her sunny, pious presence nearby.

Passion and retribution scarred the groom's family as well. Denis's father was the illegitimate son of King Alfonso III of Portugal. The father repudiated his wife and married Beatrice Guzma, Denis's mother—herself illegitimate. Denis was excommunicated, and all of Portugal was under a papal interdict for the royal family's refusal to conform. By her 19th birthday, Elizabeth—an astute politician—had negotiated a peace between her husband and Pope Nicholas IV and the removal of the papal interdict. At 21, she called for arbitration to settle a property dispute between Denis and his brother. When that failed, Elizabeth avoided war by ceding her brother-in-law a piece of her own estates.

The Portuguese remember the reign of King Denis and Queen Elizabeth as a golden age. The royal couple organized agricultural villages, and Elizabeth founded the nation's first agricultural college, where orphan girls learned to be good farmers' wives. Whenever one of the girls married, Elizabeth gave the couple a plot of her own land. She established foundling refuges, a hospital, travelers' shelters and a home for penitent women at Torres Novas. Even during their honeymoon, Elizabeth gave parties for the poor and whatever she had to the needy. One account says that when she had no money for her workmen, she gave them roses, which turned into money.

Elizabeth and Denis had two children, Constance and Alfonso, but Denis's infidelities brought nine more into the royal household. Elizabeth refused to denounce Denis or repudiate the children. It pained her, however, that Denis preferred his illegitimate son Alfonso Sancho over their own son. Jealous and rebellious, Alfonso attempted to kill Alfonso Sancho, but his plot failed. To punish her for helping Alfonso escape, Denis banished Elizabeth from Lisbon, the royal capital, and persuaded Pope John XXII (r. 1316–34) to issue a bull granting Portugal the right to ignore Alfonso's birthright in favor of the illegitimate children.

When she was allowed to return to Lisbon, Elizabeth again brokered peace between Denis and Alfonso and persuaded the pope to lift the bull. In 1323, when nothing else worked to allay war between father and son, Elizabeth rode at full gallop on a donkey between the opposing armies standing on the field of battle, shaming them into reconciliation. She reportedly averted war between Ferdinand IV of Castile and his cousin, and between Ferdinand IV and her own brother, James II of Aragon.

In 1324 Denis fell ill, and Elizabeth devoted herself totally to him. Denis finally admitted his sins and died repentant January 6, 1325. Immediately after his death, Elizabeth gave away all her possessions and made pilgrimage to Compostela, then left for a convent of Poor Clares she had founded at Coimbra. Dissuaded from joining the convent, she became a tertiary to the order of St. Francis and lived the rest of her life as Queen Mother in a house near the convent.

Always the peacemaker, Elizabeth attempted one final mission to reconcile her son, now Alfonso IV, and her nephew, Alfonso XI of Castile. Traveling to Estremoz at age 66, in the summer heat, she died on July 4, 1336.

Elizabeth is invoked in time of war, for peace.

Canonized: 1626 by Pope Urban VIII
Feast: July 4
Patronage: brides; charitable societies and workers; difficult marriages and victims of unfaithfulness or adultery; falsely accused people; widows; queens; tertiaries; victims of jealousy

Emiliana and Tarsilla (d. ca. 580–581) *Aunts of Pope St. Gregory I and nieces of Pope St. Felix III (IV)*
Also known as: Aemilianus; Tharsilla

Emiliana, a mystic, and Tarsilla lived in Rome at the home of Gregory's wealthy father, Gordianus, and were revered for their severe austerities and prayer. Tarsilla died on January 5, around 580–581, and Emiliana died a few days later.

Feast: January 5

Ennodius of Pavia (474–521) *Bishop of Pavia, Father of the Church*

Magnus Felix Ennodius is believed to have been born at Arles, in southern Gaul, in 474. As a youth he went to Pavia, Italy, where he was trained in rhetoric and became engaged. Later he decided to join the priesthood, his fiancée at the same time becoming a nun; it does not appear that they were ever married.

In 496, his uncle Laurentius, Bishop of Milan, had him transferred to that city. Ennodius was ordained a deacon and began teaching in the schools. He also became embroiled in ecclesiastical controversies when he served as secretary to his uncle, who weighed in on the side of Pope St. Symmachus (r. 498–514) in 498.

About 514, Ennodius was made bishop of Pavia. In 515 and 517 he was sent by Pope St. Hormisdas (r. 514–523) to Constantinople as part of his ultimately successful campaign to bridge the long-standing schism between the Eastern and Western churches.

Nothing further is known about Ennodius's episcopate, though the texts of several hymns he composed have come down to us. He died at Pavia on July 17, 521.

Feast: July 17

Ephraem (ca. 306–373) *Doctor of the Church*
Also known as: Ephrem; Ephraim, Ephraem the Syrian, the Harp of the Holy Spirit

Ephraem was born under Roman rule in Nisibis in Mesopotamia; his father was a pagan priest. He was raised in the Christian mysteries by St. James, bishop of Nisibis, and was baptized either at age 18 or 28. He went with James to the Council of Nicea in 325. Ephraem aided James in giving religious instruction to the people of Nisibis and was especially influential during sieges of the city in 338, 346 and 350. According to lore, he cursed Persian troops from the city walls, causing a cloud of flies and mosquitoes to descend upon the troops and drive them away.

In 363 Rome gave control of Nisibis to the Persians and most of the Christians fled. Ephraem left and settled finally in Edessa, the capital of Osrhoene, where he spent the last 10 years of his life as a hermit. He condemned heretical sects, especially the Arians and Gnostics. According to St. Gregory of Nyssa, Ephraem visited St. Basil in Caesarea in 370.

Ephraem died in 373 and was buried in a cemetery for foreigners. His body is claimed to be at the Armenian monastery of St. Sergius in Edessa.

Most of Ephraem's prolific writings were done during his hermit years. He composed commentaries on the Scriptures, most of which have been lost or survive in fragments. He wrote sermons and exhortations, mostly in verse, and composed hymns. He is credited with introducing hymns to the public.

Declared Doctor of the Church: 1920 by Pope Benedict XV
Feast: June 9

Epiphanius of Salamis (ca. 310–403) *Bishop of Constantia (Salamis) and Father of the Church*
Also known as: the Oracle of Palestine

Epiphania of Salamis was born sometime after 310 in Besanduk, near Eleutheropolis in Judea. He became an expert in scriptural languages and lived as a monk and hermit in Egypt. He returned to Besanduk, founded a monastery and was ordained. He became bishop of Constantia on Cyprus in 367.

As bishop, Epiphanius earned a reputation for asceticism, scholarship and orthodoxy. His advice was often sought. He went to Antioch in 376 to intervene in the schism there, siding with Rome against Meletius. He also intervened in the alleged Origenism of Bishop John of Jerusalem and in the heresy accusations against St. John Chrysostom. He died in 403 on his return to Cyprus from Constantinople.

Epiphanius was a vigorous defender of the faith. *Ancoratus,* or "The Well-Anchored," is a substantial treatment of Christian doctrine and argues especially against Arianism and Origenism. *Panarion,* or "Medicine chest," gives the remedies against the poisons of 77 heresies. He was a primary authority of his day in the devotion to the Blessed Virgin Mary.

Feast: May 12

Eucherius of Lyons (d. ca. 450) *Bishop of Lyons, Father of the Church*
Also known as: Eucharius

Eucherius was born in the latter half of the fourth century. A Gallo-Roman of high rank, he was married to a woman named Galla; they had two sons, Veranius and Salonius, both of whom became bishops and today are numbered among the saints.

Around 422, Eucherius withdrew to the monastery of Lérins, where his sons were living. His decision was probably spurred by the death of his wife, although she may have taken the veil. In any event, he did not stay long in the monastery, but soon retired to the island of Lerona (now Sainte-Marguerite), where he devoted himself to study and mortification.

Wishing to join the anchorites of the eastern deserts, he wrote to St. John Cassian, who, in reply, sent him descriptions of the lives of these hermits. However, this turn was not to be vouchsafed him. His reputation for wisdom and virtue brought him to the attention of Church officials and in 434 or 435 he was compelled to accept the bishopric of Lyons.

Eucherius left a considerable correspondence with Cassian, St. Hilary of Arles, and other church luminaries of the day, and a few other writings, including an account of the martyrs of the Theban Legion. He died about 450.

Feast: November 16

Eugene I (d. 657) *Pope*
Also known as: Eugenius

Eugene, the son of Rufinianus, was a Roman from the first ecclesiastical region of the city. He was known for his holiness, gentleness and charity. He became a cleric in the Church of Rome in his youth and held various positions before his elevation to the Chair of St. Peter to replace St. Martin I on August 10, 654. Although it is not known whether Martin I had officially resigned, he was being held in exile in the Crimea at the time, and evidently approved of Eugene as his successor. Martin died less than a month after Eugene's consecration.

Martin had gotten into trouble by his vocal opposition to Monothelitism (a heresy that held that Christ had a single divine nature rather than a double human and divine nature), and had been banished to the Crimea by Emperor Constans II. Eugene continued to uphold the Church's position, and was threatened with being roasted alive. Fortunately for him, Constans just at this time became involved in a conflict with the advancing Moors. They captured Rhodes in 654 and in 655 defeated Constans in a naval battle at Phoenix.

During his pontificate, Eugene consecrated 21 bishops for different parts of the world. He died in Rome on June 2, 657, and was interred in St. Peter's at the Vatican.

Feast: June 2

Eugene III (d. 1153) *Cistercian monk, pope*
Also known as: Bernard of Pisa

There is much uncertainty about the parentage, place of birth, and original name of the pope known as Eugene III. Each of his biographers gives different information on these matters. The only thing certain is that he was born into a noble family named Pignatelli. He was educated at Pisa, Italy, and following his ordination as a priest, became a canon at that city's cathedral.

In 1135, after meeting St. Bernard, he joined the Cistercian order at Clairvaux, apparently taking the name Bernard (Bernardo) after his mentor. Later he was sent by his order along with other monks to the ancient abbey of Farfa, but Pope Innocent II (r. 1130–43) instead assigned them to St. Athanasius (then Tre Fontane) in Rome. Thus, he was living in Rome when he was unexpectedly elected pope on February 15, 1145, the day his predecessor, Lucius II (r. 1144–45), died.

Eugene was enthroned in St. John Lateran but then, because the city threatened to erupt in violence (Lucius may in fact have been stabbed to death), he and his cardinals fled to the Farfa monastery. After Eugene's consecration in secret on February 18, he and his entourage moved to Viterbo. His elevation was soon welcomed by the entire Christian world with the

exception of Rome. There, under the instigation of Arnold of Brescia, pilgrims who happened to be in the city were attacked, the palaces of the cardinals and nobles who supported Eugene were razed, monasteries were pillaged, St. Peter's was turned into an armory. The violence was so extreme that it soon met resistance from influential families of the region, and they forced a reconciliation between the parties.

At issue was the independence of an elected Senate from both the monarchy and the Roman Church. A democratic party, with whom Arnold was affiliated, wanted the Church to be beholden to the Senate. Nonetheless, a treaty was worked out whereby the Senate would pledge allegiance to the pope. The pope and the Senate would have separate courts, with the right of appeal from either court to the other. The treaty enabled Eugene to return to Rome a few days before Christmas, 1145. However, when the democrats demanded the destruction of Tivoli, a town that had been faithful to Eugene, and he refused to allow it, the agreement broke down. With Rome again growing restless, Eugene left the city for the Castel Saint' Angelo, then for Viterbo, and finally, early in 1146, crossed the Alps into France.

For the next three years Eugene remained in France, convening councils to take action in regard to heresies such as Manichaeanism and ecclesiastical discipline in matters such as the dress and conduct of the clergy. In the spring of 1148, he began making his way back to Rome. On July 7 of that year, he excommunicated Arnold, still a leader of the democratic movement there. Then in the winter of 1149, Eugene entered the city with the military assistance of Roger of Sicily, and celebrated Christmas in the Lateran. However, he and his court were soon forced to take to the road again. It was not until the spring of 1153 that the Treaty of Constance, made between the Church and the Holy Roman Empire, caused the democratic cause to lose support and collapse, and they were able to return to Rome for good.

As vexing as the situation in Rome must have been for the Catholic Church during this period, it faced a much larger crisis in the Moslem advances in the Holy Land. The fall of Edessa in 1144 was bad enough, but then Christian principalities in Palestine and Syria were threatened. A Second Crusade was in order, and Eugene commissioned St. Bernard to preach it. The Crusade ended unfavorably, however, with the defeat of armies under the command of the king of the Romans and the king of France.

In the summer of 1153, Eugene retired to Tivoli to escape the heat. He died there on July 8 and his body was carried back to Rome where it was interred in front of the high altar in St. Peter's Basilica.

Beatified: December 28, 1872, by Pope Pius IX
Feast: July 8

Eusebius (d. 309 or 310) *Pope and martyr*

Perhaps a physician of Greek descent, Eusebius was elected successor to Pope St. Marcellus on April 18, 309 or 310. He reigned for only four months, until August 17 of the same year. His brief rule was marked by the rigorist controversy, which concerned the return of apostates to the church.

During the four years of persecution under Emperor Diocletian (r. 284–305) many Christians had deserted their faith. They now wanted to return to the Church, which Eusebius, following Marcellus and longstanding Church policy, ruled they could do, so long as they performed proper penance. In this he charted a middle course between Anaclitus, who believed that the lapsed were outside the Church and could not be reconciled to it, and Heraclius, himself an apostate, who insisted that they be allowed to return without penance. The controversy caused such an uproar in Rome that Emperor Maxentius charged both Eusebius and Heraclius with disturbing the peace and exiled them to Sicily. Eusebius died there soon after.

The relics of Eusebius were translated back to Rome, probably in 310, and placed in their own cubiculum in the Catacomb of St. Callistus on the Appian Way. Although Eusebius did not die a violent death, he is venerated as a martyr.

Feast: September 26

Eustathius (ca. 270–ca. 360, or 336–337) *Bishop of Antioch and Father of the Church*
Also known as: Eustathius of Antioch

Eustathius was born in Side, Pamphylia. He was the first bishop of Beroea in Syria and was transferred to Antioch in 323. There he became embroiled in the Arian heresy controversy and was a fierce opponent of the sect. He incurred many powerful enemies, including Eusebius of Caesarea, who succeeded in calling a synod in Antioch in 331 and having him deposed. Emperor Constantine exiled him to Trajanopolis. Eusathius's followers were enraged and ready to defend him by force, but he calmed them down and went into exile. Many of his clergy went with him. His followers formed their own community in Antioch, calling themselves the Eustathians. They refused to recognize any of the Arian bishops.

Eustathius died probably in 360, though some sources give 336 or 337 as the date. St. Meletius became bishop of Antioch, but the Eustathians refused to recog-

St. Eustathius (Library of Congress Prints and Photographs Division)

nize him. This created the "Meletian Schism," which lasted into the second decade of the fifth century.

Most of Eustathius's writings have been lost. He was a harsh critic of Origen.

Feast: July 16

Eutychianus (d. 283) *Pope*

Little is known about the life or pontificate of Eutychianus, who was elected to succeed St. Felix I in January 275. Legend has it that he personally buried 242 martyrs, but this is unlikely, since he lived in a time of peace. He died of natural causes on December 7, 283, and was buried in the papal crypt of the Catacomb of St. Callistus on the Appian Way.

Feast: December 8

Evaristus (d. ca. 105) *Pope and martyr*
Also known as: Aristus

Evaristus was born in Bethlehem. A Hellenic Jew, he converted to Christianity and eventually reached

Rome. There he accepted the dangerous office of bishop after the exile and death of St. Clement, around the year 97, thus becoming the fifth pope. He ruled for eight years. Although there are no extant accounts of his death, he is listed in early martyrologies. He is buried in the Vatican, near the tombs of St. Peter and other early popes.

Feast: October 26

Ewe (sixth century) *Patron saint of the Cornwall parish of St. Ewe*

Little is known about Ewe, who is believed to have come from Wales to evangelize the area of mid-Cornwall, England. From the 12th century on, Ewe was said to have been a woman. It is also thought that Ewe may be the same as St. Theo of Brittany, as *Th* was often placed at the beginning of saints' names beginning in vowels. The latter possibility is unlikely.

A church probably built by the saint exists in the parish of St. Ewe and is dated to the sixth century.

Ezequial Moreno (1848–1906) *Augustine missionary renowned throughout the Americas*

Ezequial Moreno was born on April 9, 1848, in Alfaro, Rioja, Spain, the child of Félix Moreno and Josefa Díaz. He was drawn to the religious life as a child, and in September 1864, when he was 18, he entered the Augustine monastery in Montegudo, Navarra.

Ezequial spent much of the early part of his career as a missionary in the Philippines, where he was sent in 1870. He was ordained a priest the following year, and later was named to head the Montegudo monastery and so returned to Spain.

In 1888, Ezequial traveled once again, this time to Colombia in command of a group of Augustinian missionaries. His success as an administrator led to his being named bishop of Pinar in 1893 and bishop of Pasto in 1895.

In 1905, Ezequial was diagnosed with cancer. The following year he returned to Spain for an operation, which turned out unsuccessfully, and he died in the monastery at Montegudo on August 19, 1906.

After his death, his fame grew rapidly, especially in Colombia. He is considered to have been one of the greatest evangelists of the Americas.

Beatified: 1975 by Pope Paul VI
Canonized: October 11, 1992, by Pope John Paul II
Feast: August 19
Patronage: cancer victims

FURTHER READING
"San Ezequiel Moreno." *Santos y Biatos de America Latina: Colombia* website. URL: http://www/aciprensa.com/santcolo. htm. Downloaded: November 26, 1999.

F

Fabian (d. 250) *Pope and martyr*

Fabian was a farmer who happened to be in Rome when the election to replace Pope St. Anterus began. Several important persons were under consideration, when a dove suddenly appeared and alighted on his head. The dove recalled the settling of the Holy Spirit on Christ, as described in the Scriptures. It was taken as a sign, and although he was a complete unknown, Fabian received unanimous approval on the first ballot.

During his 14-year reign, Emperor Philip was in power, and there was a lull in the persecution of Christians. Fabian was responsible for several important actions. He divided Rome into seven districts, each supervised by a deacon, and appointed seven subdeacons to collect the acta of the martyrs (that is, the proceedings of their trials). (A similar order had brought about the death of his predecessor.) He also made considerable improvements to the Catacombs of St. Callistus and had the body of Pope St. Pontian (r. 230–235) brought from Sardinia and interred there. He may also have sent St. Dionysius (Denis) and other preachers to Gaul, but this is uncertain.

Fabian died a martyr on January 20, 250, when upon the death of Philip and the accession of Decius the persecutions began anew. Decius ordered all Christians to deny Christ by offering incense to idols or through some other pagan ritual; those who refused to obey were killed. Fabian's body was interred in the Crypt of the Popes in the Catacomb of St. Callistus. Later some of his relics were translated to the Basilica of Saint Sebastian.

In art, Fabian is shown with a dove by his side; with a tiara and a dove; with a sword or club; or kneeling at a block (about to be beheaded). Sometimes he is shown with St. Sebastian, who was martyred on his feast day, or with a palm and cross. Fabian's image is included in a painting attributed to Diamante (ca. 1430–98) in the Vatican's Sistine Chapel.

Feast: January 20
Patronage: lead-founders; potters

Faith (d. third century) *Virgin martyr*

Faith was born in Agen, Aquitania (southwestern France), to a prominent Christian family. Tradition held that at a young age she dedicated herself to Christ and longed to become a martyr. Her wish was granted during the persecutions.

Many of the Christians of Agen took to the forests and hills to escape, but Faith remained in the city to face the arrival of Dacian, the prefect of Rome. She was arrested and brought before Dacian. He ordered her to sacrifice to the goddess Diana, upon which she would be rewarded. She refused, and was sentenced to be roasted alive on a gridiron. The spectators were so horrified at her suffering that they protested, and so Faith and several other martyrs were beheaded. Christians buried their bodies in secret.

After the persecutions ended, the bishop of Agen, Dulcitius, built a church in honor of Faith and placed the relics of the martyrs in it. The relics of Faith later were translated to the abbey of Conques, which was a popular pilgrimage site in the Middle Ages. Some of her relics also reportedly were taken to Glastonbury, and churches in England were dedicated to her.

Feast: October 6

FURTHER READING
St. Alphonsus Liguori. *Victories of the Martyrs*. Brooklyn: Redemptorist Fathers, 1954.

Faustina Kowalska (1905–1938) *Nun and mystic, originator of the Divine Mercy movement*
Also known as: Maria Faustina of the Most Blessed Sacrament

Faustina Kowalska was born Elena Kowalska in Glogowiec, a small village west of Lodz, Poland, on August 25, 1905. She was the third of 10 children.

When she was seven, during the celebration of Vespers, at the time of the exposition of the Blessed Sacrament, God called her to the religious life. After her First Communion, she went to confession every week and never missed Sunday Mass with her family. Her extraordinary holiness was manifest in the miraculous obedience the family cattle paid to her.

From the ages of 12 to 14, Elena attended public school. At 16, she began to work as a housemaid in Lodz. Then a few weeks before her 20th birthday, in the summer of 1924, she had a vision of Jesus in his Passion. He chastised her for her spiritual sloth and ordered her to join a convent. After being rejected by several religious orders, she entered the Congregation of the Sisters of Our Lady of Mercy in Warsaw on August 1, 1925.

In her year as postulant, Elena's guardian angel showed her purgatory in order to excite her devotion to the poor souls waiting there. On April 30, 1926, she entered her novitiate; she took the veil and was given the religious name Maria Faustina, to which she added, "of the Most Blessed Sacrament," as was her congregation's custom. On that occasion, Jesus revealed to her all that she would suffer for his name. The following year, he gave her a vision of potatoes changed into roses to teach her how pleasing was a lowly work done for His love. During the last six months of the novi-

tiate, Faustina passed through a dark night of the soul. At the end of that mystical experience, St. Thérèse of the Child Jesus appeared to her in a dream and foretold her final perseverance, her future heroic sanctity, and her canonization. On April 30, 1928, she took her first vows of poverty, chastity, and obedience.

Faustina spent the next 10 years in various houses of her order, working as cook, gardener and porter. She had a special devotion to Mary Immaculate and to the Eucharist and reconciliation, which gave her the strength to bear all her sufferings. She suffered in secret, with only her confessors and some of her superiors aware of what she was going through. Fortunately, she kept a diary in which she recorded the details of the visions and stigmata that began to visit her with increasing frequency. Since she was barely literate, she wrote phonetically, without punctuation, filling almost 700 pages. A poor translation reached Rome in 1958 and the work was judged heretical. However, when Karol Wojtyla (the future Pope John Paul II) became archbishop of Krakow, he ordered a better translation made, and the Vatican reversed itself, declaring that the diary proclaimed God's love. The diary was published as *Divine Mercy in My Soul*.

Despite her profession, the darkness that had come upon Faustina during her novitiate did not leave her. So challenging were some of her experiences that her confessors and superiors could not at first believe God was treating her in such a manner. On one occasion, Jesus commanded her to adore him in the Blessed Sacrament for one hour on nine successive days, praying in union with Mary and all the while attempting to make the Stations of the Cross. On the seventh day, she had a vision of Mary, standing between heaven and earth, dressed in a bright garment. Fiery rays issued from her heart, some ascending heavenward, others falling upon Poland.

Faustina received several striking communications from Jesus in the 1930s. In the most important of these, He sent her a message of Divine Mercy and asked her to spread it throughout the world. She was to be an instrument for emphasizing God's plan of mercy for all of humankind and a model of how to be merciful to others, living her entire life in imitation of Jesus, as a sacrifice. To assist in this project, Jesus asked that a picture be painted of Himself with an inscription reading, "Jesus, I Trust in You." Faustina commissioned this painting in 1935. It shows a red and white light shining from Christ's Sacred Heart.

Faustina died October 5, 1938, in Krakow, Poland, of tuberculosis, but her work was picked up by others, thanks especially to *Divine Mercy in My Soul*. A movement of priests, religious and lay people inspired by her experiences was organized under the name, Apostles of Divine Mercy. The movement was approved in 1996 by the archdiocese of Krakow, and has since spread to 29 other countries.

Faustina's congregation, the Sisters of Our Lady of Mercy, operates the Shrine of the Divine Mercy in Lagiewniki, Poland. The order opened its first house outside Poland—in Boston, Massachusetts—in 1988. In Eden Hill, Massachusetts, there is a National Shrine of the Divine Mercy, run by the Marians of the Immaculate Conception.

Faustina is credited with interceding in two miraculous cures that led to her beatification in 1993 and canonization in 2000. In the former, she caused a cure of a woman who suffered Milroy's disease, a hereditary form of lymphedema; in the latter, she caused the cure of a priest's heart condition.

Beatified: 1993 by Pope John Paul II
Canonized: April 30, 2000, by Pope John Paul II
Feast: October 5
Patronage: Warsaw, Plock, and Krakow, Poland; Vilnius, Lithuania

FURTHER READING
"Bl. Maria Faustina Kowalska, Apostle of the Divine Mercy." Apostolate Alliance of the Two Hearts website. URL: http://home.ici.net/~aath/alliance/apostles/faustina/life1.html. Downloaded: September 10, 2000.
Kreitzberg, Paul. "St. Faustina Kowalska, Nun." URL: http://www.smart.net/~tak/Patrons/faustina.html. Downloaded: September 10, 2000.
Pope John Paul II. "Canonization of Sister Faustina, Angelus Message." Catholic Information Network website. URL: http://www.cin.org/jp2/jp000430a.html. Downloaded: May 21, 2000.

Felicity   See PERPETUA AND FELICITY.

Felix I (d. 274) *Pope*

Nothing is known about the early life of Felix, the son of Constantius. He was presumably a presbyter or priest in the Church of Rome when he was elected to succeed St. Dionysius as bishop on January 5, 269.

Felix is remembered for his condemnation of the heresy of Paul of Samosata, for a time bishop of Antioch. Paul had already been deposed by the Synod of Antioch when Felix became aware of the matter, but as pope he dispatched a letter supporting the synod's views. Like other second- and third-century heretics, Paul maintained that there was no unity to the Holy Trinity and that Jesus had been a man who received supernatural powers at his baptism.

Felix died a natural death on December 30, 274, and was interred in the papal crypt of the Catacomb of St. Callistus.

In art, he is shown as a pope with an anchor.

Feast: May 30

Felix III (d. 492) *Pope*

Felix was born to a Roman senatorial family and is said to have been an ancestor of Pope St. Gregory I (Gregory the Great, r. 590–604). He was a widower with two children when he was elected bishop of Rome to succeed St. Simplicius upon his death in 483.

The year before, at the suggestion of Acacius, the patriarch of Constantinople, Emperor Zeno had issued an edict known as the Hereticon, or Act of Union. This edict was intended to bring about a reconciliation between the Catholics in the West and the Eutychians (or Monophysites) in the East on the issue of the nature of Jesus, but it backfired and resulted in splitting the Eastern Church into three or four branches. Felix's pontificate was largely concerned with this schism, which was to last for 35 years. He died on March 1, 492, having reigned eight years, 11 months and 23 days.

Feast: March 1

Felix IV (d. 530) *Pope*

Felix was a cardinal in Samnium when Pope St. John I (r. 523–526) died in prison in May 526. John I had been arrested by Theodoric, king of the Ostrogoths and of Italy, who was threatened by John's appeal to members of the Eastern as well as Western Church. Theodoric put forward Felix as a candidate for the Chair of St. Peter, and the Roman clergy and laity acquiesced to his wishes. Felix was consecrated on July 12.

On August 30, Theodoric died. The throne passed to his grandson, Athalaric, but because he was then a minor, the government was put in the hands of his mother, Theodoric's daughter, Amalasuntha. Fortunately, she was well disposed toward the Catholics. She allowed Felix the traditional privilege of judging clergy who were accused of misconduct and she gave him as gifts a pagan temple, which he had reconstructed as the church of SS. Cosmas and Damian. This church still exists; in its apse there is a large and magnificent mosaic executed on Felix's order.

In 529, Felix sent 25 pronouncements on grace and free will to Cæsarius of Arles, who presented them before the Synod of Orange. The synod accepted them as a confirmation of the teachings of St. Augustine and a condemnation of semi-Pelagianism.

Felix grew increasingly concerned about the Roman Church. On the one hand, many believers supported the Goths, while on the other, many leaned toward Byzantium. When he fell fatally ill in September 530, in the hopes of keeping peace Felix gave his pallium to his archdeacon Boniface and let it be known that Boniface was to be his successor. However, in the papal elections that followed his death, his wishes were disregarded. Felix's relics rest in the portico of St. Peter's Basilica in the Vatican.

Feast: January 30

Fiacre (d. 670) *Irish miracle-worker and healer who established a cult in France*
Also known as: Fiachra, Fiaker, Fiacrius, Fevre

Fiacre is not mentioned in the earlier Irish calendars. He was born in Ireland and became a hermit at Kilfiachra. In 630, desiring greater solitude, he went to France and settled at Meaux. St. Faro, bishop of that city, gave him land in a forest that was his own patrimony—called Breuil, in the province of Brie.

According to legend, Faro offered him as much land as he could turn up in a day. Instead of driving his furrow with a plough, Fiacre turned the top of the soil with the point of his staff. He cleared the ground of trees and briers, made himself a cell, cultivated a garden, built an oratory in honor of the Blessed Virgin Mary, and made a hospice for travelers, which developed into the village of Saint-Fiacre in Seine-et-Marne. He is said to have built the first hostel for Irish pilgrims on the Continent, and used the produce of his vegetable garden to feed them.

Fiacre's generosity and cheerful disposition attracted many people, who sought him out for advice, alms and especially healing, for he had the miraculous touch. However, his goodwill did not extend fully to women: He never allowed any woman to enter the enclosure of his hermitage or his chapel. Those who dared defy this prohibition, even centuries later, met with punishments. According to one story, a woman from Paris entered the oratory in 1620. She instantly became distracted and never recovered her senses. Anne of Austria, Queen of France, mindful of the prohibition, offered her prayers outside the doors.

Fiacre died in 670 and was buried at Meaux.

The fame of Fiacre's miracles of healing continued after his death and crowds visited his shrine for centuries. In the 17th and 18th centuries, Meaux was a major site for pilgrimages. High-ranking people and royalty testified to the healing power of Fiacre's relics and shrine. Mgr. Seguier, Bishop of Meaux in 1649, and John de Chatillon, count of Blois, gave testimony of their own relief. Anne of Austria credited the intercession of Fiacre with the recovery of Louis XIII at Lyons, where he had been dangerously ill. She expressed her thanks by making a pilgrimage on foot to the shrine in 1641. She also sent to his shrine a token in acknowledgment of his intervention in the birth of her son, Louis XIV. Before Louis XIV underwent a severe operation, Bossuet, bishop of Meaux, began a novena of prayers at Saint-Fiacre to ask a divine blessing.

Fiacre is invoked against all sorts of physical ills, including venereal disease. Many miracles have been claimed through his working the land and interceding for others. He is especially the patron saint of the cab drivers of Paris. French cabs are called *fiacres* because the first establishment to let hackney carriages for hire in the mid-17th century was in the Rue Saint-Martin, near the hotel Saint-Fiacre in Paris.

In art Fiacre is often shown with a spade in his role as patron of gardeners.

Feast: September 1
Patronage: cab and taxi drivers; all drivers; gardeners; against hemorrhoids; against syphilis

Finbar (ca. 560–ca. 633) *Founder and miracle-worker*
Name meaning: Fair crest
Also known as: Findbarr, Bairre, Barr

Finbar was born in Connaught, Ireland, around 560, the illegitimate son of a master smith or craftsman and a slave girl in the royal court (by some accounts a lady). His parents moved to the region of Macroom, where he was baptized Lochan (or Loan) by Bishop MacCuirb. At age seven he was given to three clerics of Munster to be educated. When they had his fair hair cut, they named him Finbar, meaning "fair crest."

Finbar went on pilgrimage to Rome with some of the monks, visiting St. David in Wales on the way back. David became a mentor. Legend tells that on another visit to Rome Pope Gregory I (r. 590–604) wanted to consecrate him a bishop but a vision told him that God had reserved that honor to Himself. Finbar returned home and was consecrated from heaven. Oil flowed up from the earth to cover the feet of him and the elders present; it had healing properties. Finbar preached throughout southern Ireland. He also may have preached in Scotland.

Finbar retired to live on the small island at Lough Eiroe, and started a school there. According to lore, an angel guided him to the place where he built a church. Nearby is a cave called Cuas Barrai (Finbar's Cave), and near that is a pool where Finbar caught a salmon in his net every night. The angel told Finbar that the spot would not be the place of his resurrection, however, and he went across the river to Cell na Cluaine (Gougane Barra) where he built a church and stayed for a long time. He built 12 churches and then founded a monastery that developed into the city of Cork, of which he was the first bishop. His monastery became famous in southern Ireland and attracted numerous disciples.

Finbar died at Cloyne about the year 633, although various accounts give his date of death as 610, 623 and 630. According to legend, the sun did not set for 12 days after he died. His body was taken to his church in Cork for burial. The church became a cathedral. His island retreat at Gougane Barra became a pilgrimage site, his hermitage and chapel marked with a wooden cross.

Many miracles are attributed to Finbar. He healed many people, had visions, prophesied and foresaw the time of his own death.

Feast: September 25

FURTHER READING
Sellner, Edward C. *Wisdom of the Celtic Saints.* Notre Dame, Ind.: Ave Maria Press, 1993.

Finian (d. 579) *Abbot and miracle worker*
Also known as: Finnio; Winin

Finian was born in Strangford Lough, Ulster, Ireland, to a royal family. Attracted to the religious life, he became a disciple of SS. Colman and Mochae, then became a monk in Strathclyde and was ordained in Rome. He returned to Ulster where he founded several monasteries and became the abbot of Moville in County Down. He also founded monasteries at Holywood and Dumfries in Scotland.

Finian was a teacher to St. Columba. Once when Columba came to see him, he saw the young man accompanied by an angel. He had a disagreement with Columba over possession of a copy of St. Jerome's psalter, and won the disagreement.

Finian also is credited with numerous miracles, including moving a river.

Feast: September 10

Finian of Clonard (ca. 470–549) *Founder and teacher of "the Twelve Apostles of Ireland" and other Irish saints*

Finian of Clonard was born about 470 in Myshall, County Carlow, Ireland. He studied under SS. Cadoc and Gildas in Wales, then returned to Ireland where he founded schools, monasteries and churches. His school at Clonard was the most famous, and attracted some of the most famous saints of Ireland, including Columba and Brendan of Clonfort. Finian was abbot, or by some accounts, bishop, though he may never have been officially consecrated in that position. He died during a plague epidemic.

Feast: December 12

Foillan (630–655) *Benedictine abbot and founder, brother of SS. Fursey and Ulan*
Also known as: Fullan

Born in Ireland, Foillan went to England in 630 with his family and friends. There he participated in the founding of Burghcastle, near Yarmouth. Foillan went to France and Belgium. In Belgium he was given land by Blessed Ita of Nivelles, and founded a monastery and worked as a missionary abbot. In 655, he was killed by outlaws after celebrating Mass in the Sneffe forest.

Feast: October 31

Fourteen Holy Helpers *Group of martyrs considered especially helpful against adversity*

The Fourteen Holy Helpers were especially invoked during the Black Plague in Europe from 1346 to 1349, when people took ill suddenly and often died violently, within hours and without last sacraments. Symptoms included a black tongue, parched throat, violent headache, fever and abdominal boils.

In 1445 and 1446 a shepherd boy named Herman Leicht, of Bamberg, Bavaria, saw apparitions first of one child and then of 14 while he was out with his flock. The children said they were the Fourteen Helpers and asked for a chapel to be built in their honor, and for Herman to serve them. The monks did not believe the boy, but people began praying at the spot where the apparitions appeared. When remarkable favors happened to them, the monks constructed a chapel in 1447–48. The site attracted pilgrims. In 1743, work was begun on a grand cathedral to replace the little chapel; work was completed in 1772. Churches and altars to the Fourteen Holy Helpers have been built elsewhere in Europe and around the world.

The 14 martyrs and their special patronages are:

Achatius	against death agony
Barbara	against fever and sudden death
Blase	against throat problems
Catherine	against tongue problems and sudden death

Christopher	against plague and sudden death
Cyriacus	against temptations, especially at death
Dionysius	against headache
Erasmus	against abdominal problems; protection of domestic animals
Eustachius	against family troubles
George	protection of domestic animals
Giles	making a good confession
Pantaleon	physicians; protection of domestic animals
Vitus	against epilepsy; protection of domestic animals
Giles	plague

FURTHER READING

Hammer, Fr. Bonaventure. *The Fourteen Holy Helpers*. Rockford, Ill.: TAN Books, 1995.

Frances of Rome (1384–1440) *Mystic, founder of the Oblates of Mary (Oblates of Tor de Specchi)*

Name meaning: Free one

Frances was born in 1384 at Trastevere in Rome to noble parents, Paul Bosco and Jacobella dei Roffredeschi. At the age of seven she began to mortify her body and express interest in being a nun, a decision she declared at age 11. Her father opposed it as he wished to marry her to another wealthy family. At 13 she was married to Lorenzo de Ponziani, a union that lasted 40 years.

Early in the marriage, however, Frances collapsed from strain. During her illness, she had a vision of St. Alexis, patron saint of beggars and the sick, who asked her if she wanted to live. She replied that she wanted only what God willed; the saint healed her, saying the Lord wished her to remain in the world to glorify Him.

Frances discovered that her sister-in-law, Vannozza, also would have preferred the religious life. The two became close friends, and went out into Rome together to minister to the poor and sick. They especially sought out those whom others refused or were reluctant to treat.

In 1400 her first child was born: John Baptist (Battista), followed by a second son, Evangelista, and a daughter, Agnes.

In 1408 Rome was seized by the troops of Ladislaus of Naples, an ally of the antipope. Frances's family home was looted and burned. Lorenzo was stabbed; Frances nursed him back to health. In 1410, Lorenzo's home and lands were seized and pillaged, and Battista was taken hostage. He was later released. The story goes that Frances refused to surrender her boy and fled. Her confessor told her to give him over. She did

so and went to the Ara Coeli Shrine of the Sorrowful Mother to pray. There Mary appeared to her and comforted her, and told her not to despair. The boy was returned to her when the soldier carrying him could not get his horse to budge.

Lorenzo was separated from the rest of his family. Frances lived in the ruined house with her children and Vannozza. Three years later, nine-year-old Evangelista died during a plague. According to lore, Frances was rewarded by God with the gift of healing, and she turned her home into a hospital. Agnes died two years after Evangelista.

In 1414 the Ponziani family regained their property, but Lorenzo's health was broken. At about this time, Frances brought to fruition a plan she had been developing for some time: the establishment of a lay order of women who would serve God and the poor. She had been inspired by a heavenly voice that told her Mary wished her to do so. She received permission for this order to be affiliated with the Benedictines of Mount Oliveto. The order first was called the Oblates of Mary and then the Oblates of Tor de Specchi. After seven or eight years, the order acquired its own facility. Frances spent as much time as possible with the order, but refused to be acknowledged as foundress. She dictated to her confessor the words of their Rule, which she said had been given to her by St. Paul, in the presence of Mary, St. Benedict and St. Mary Magdalen, who were the patrons of her community.

Lorenzo died in 1436, and Frances retired to the order. The superioress, Agnes de Lillis, resigned and Frances assumed the post.

In the spring of 1440, she went to visit Battista and his wife, and became ill on the way home. Her director met her en route and ordered her back to her son's home. She spent seven days on her deathbed and died on March 9. Her last act was to read her Little Office of the Virgin Mary. She was buried in Santa Maria Nuova, in the chapel of the church of her oblates. The church is now known as the church of Santa Francesca Romana. Her relics are on display there.

Frances had numerous mystical experiences of Mary, who invited her to attend various feasts in heaven. There she contemplated Mary in all her mysteries, and also was with the infant Jesus. At Christmas in 1432, she spent 48 hours in ecstasy after Mary gave her baby Jesus to hold. Thereafter, she proclaimed herself servant, subject and slave of Mary.

Frances also had numerous experiences involving angels. According to lore, she was given two guardian angels at birth. Frequent angelic visits began with the death of Evangelista. Just before dying, he exclaimed that angels had arrived to take him to heaven. On the one-year anniversary of his death, Frances had an extraordinary hour-long vision. Her oratory was filled with a brilliant light at dawn, and she beheld her son accompanied by a beautiful boy. Evangelista said he now resided in the second choir of the first hierarchy of angels, and introduced his companion as an archangel who had a place above his. He told his mother that God was sending her this archangel, who would not leave her day or night, and whom she would be blessed with seeing with her "bodily eyes." Evangelista then said he had to return to heaven, but the sight of the angel would always remind his mother of him.

Evangelista disappeared, never to manifest to Frances again. The angel remained, standing with arms folded across his chest. Frances fell to her knees and begged for his help in guiding her spiritual growth, and in defending against the devil. When she finally left the oratory, the angel followed her, enveloping her in a halo of light. The angel, and this halo around Frances, could not be perceived by other people.

Frances could not look upon the angel's brightness without hurting her eyes; so, she looked upon the glow around him. Over time, she was able to more directly see his features while she was at prayer; it seemed that the angel purposefully dimmed his own light to help her. He looked like a boy of nine, with sparkling eyes and an ever-present sweet expression upon his face and his eyes turned constantly toward heaven. He wore a white robe covered by a tunic that reached his feet, was clear as light and had an ethereal color like sky-blue and flaming red. His hair, like spun gold, fell across his shoulders. The light coming from his hair was so bright that Frances frequently did not need a candle, even at night.

She wrote that the angel was never soiled by dirt or mud when he walked beside her. If she committed even the slightest fault, however, he disappeared from her sight, and would reappear only after she had confessed her faults. If she was plagued by doubts, he gave her a kind look that immediately made her feel better. When he talked, she could see his lips move; his voice was incredibly sweet.

Much of the angel's guidance centered around Frances's worries as head of a family. The angel assured her that she was not lost in God's sight. He also enabled her to supernaturally discern the thoughts of others. Thus she reportedly was able to short-circuit evil intent, reconcile enemies, and help wandering souls return to the fold.

Frances also was engaged in a constant struggle against evil spirits. Whenever the devil would particularly plague her, she would appeal to the archangel for help. In the fashion of Samson, the angel's power was in his hair, for when Frances asked him for protection, the angel shook his hair and frightened the evil spirits away.

The archangel—who never announced a name—stayed with Frances for 24 years. In 1436, she joined her own community, and was granted a vision in which she saw God seated on a high throne and surrounded by myriad angels. God appointed one of the high-ranking powers to replace the archangel. In his human form, the power was even more beautiful than the archangel, and exhibited greater power and courage. He did not have to shake his hair to scare away evil spirits; his mere presence accomplished that. He carried in his left hand three golden palm branches, which symbolized three virtues that he helped Frances to cultivate: charity, firmness and prudence.

The power stayed with Frances for four years until she died. At the moment of her death, her face shone with a bright light and she uttered, "The angel has finished his task: he beckons me to follow him."

Miraculous events attributed to Frances include the multiplication of food: She increased corn and wine for the sick, needy and prisoners. She experienced frequent ecstasies and shone with a supernatural radiance. When Frances died, her face lit with youth and beauty, and her body exuded a sweet perfume. A sister who had a withered arm washed her body; her arm was restored to health. The perfume was still present when the saint's remains were moved to a larger tomb.

Canonized: 1608 by Pope Paul V
Feast: March 9

FURTHER READING
O'Sullivan, Fr. Paul. *All about the Angels.* Rockford, Ill.: TAN Books, 1990; first published, 1945.
Parente, Fr. Pascal P. *The Angels: The Catholic Teaching on the Angels.* Rockford, Ill.: TAN Books, 1973; first published, 1961.

Frances Xavier Cabrini (1850–1917) *First U.S. citizen to be canonized*
Also known as: Francesca Saverio Cabrini

Frances Xavier Cabrini was born on July 15, 1850, in the village of Sant'Angelo Lodigiano, in the diocese of Lodi, in the Lombardy region of Italy. She was the 13th child of Augustine Cabrini, a farmer, and his wife, Stella Oldini. Stella was then 52, and Frances seemed so fragile that she was carried to the church and baptized at once. She was given the name Maria Francesca Saverio, after the missionary St. Francis Xavier.

On the day of Frances's birth, a flock of white doves flew by her father's farm and circled the house,

St. Frances Xavier Cabrini (Library of Congress Prints and Photographs Division)

one of them dropping down to alight in the vines that covered the walls. Flocks of white birds were to appear several more times in her life. She compared them to angels or souls she would help save, or to new sisters who would join the religious community she founded.

In 1863, at the age of 13, Frances entered the convent of the Daughters of the Sacred Heart at Arluna, where she made a vow of virginity, and took courses that led to a teacher's certificate. When she graduated with honors in 1868, she was fully qualified as a teacher. She applied for admission to the convent, hoping that she might be sent as a missionary teacher to China. Her health was not good, however, and she was turned down.

Two years later, she lost both parents and 10 of her siblings to smallpox. She herself was stricken the following year, but an older sister nursed her back to health, and in 1872 she began to teach in a public

school. After reapplying and once more being rejected by the Daughters of the Sacred Heart, she was offered the job of managing a small orphanage at Codogno in the Lodi diocese, then encouraged to turn it into a religious community. She took her first vows there in 1877 and was made the superior by the bishop of Lodi. When he closed the institution three years later, the bishop counseled her to found a congregation of missionary nuns, since he knew of none. Frances then moved to an abandoned Franciscan friary in Codogno and drew up the rules for the Missionary Sisters of the Sacred Heart, whose object was to be the education of girls in Catholic schismatic or pagan countries. The Missionary Sisters received episcopal approval at the end of 1880 and the decree of papal approbation in 1888.

Bishop Scalabrini of Piacenza, who had established the Society of Saint Charles to work among Italian immigrants in the United States, suggested that Frances go there to support his priests. Archbishop Corrigan of New York sent her a formal invitation; Pope Leo XIII (r. 1878–1903) gave his blessing to the enterprise, and she arrived in New York on March 31, 1889, with six of her nuns. Although Frances was to return to Italy annually in search of new missionary sisters, she was to make the United States her home from then on, eventually, in 1909, taking U.S. citizenship.

Besides schools and charitable institutions, she founded four great hospitals, with nurses' homes attached, one each in New York and Seattle, and two in Chicago. Her Columbus Hospital in New York was opened in 1892, the 400th anniversary of Christopher Columbus's arrival in the New World. The work of the Missionary Sisters was by no means confined to the United States, however. Frances traveled to, and established orphanages, schools and hospitals, in Nicaragua, Costa Rica, Brazil, Argentina, Chile, Italy, Spain, France and England as well. By the time of her death, her order had grown to include 67 houses with over 4,000 nuns.

Frances's health, which had always been precarious, began to decline in 1911. She was visiting one of her schools in Chicago when, on December 21, 1918, she died of a heart attack, at age 67. At first her relics were placed at the Sacred Heart Orphanage in West Park, New York, her official home, but they have since been moved to a chapel in the Mother Cabrini High School in the Bronx.

Beatified: August 6, 1938, by Pope Pius XI
Canonized: July 7, 1946, by Pope Pius XII
Feast: November 13 (formerly December 22)
Patronage: displaced persons, emigrants and immigrants

FURTHER READING

"Francis Xavier Cabrini." Catholic Information Network website. URL: http://www.cin.org/kc87-2.html. Downloaded: November 12, 1999.

"Frances Xavier Cabrini 1850–1917." Catholic Information Network website. URL: http://www.cin.org/cabrinsd. html. Downloaded: November 12, 1999.

"Santa Francisca Javier Cabrini." Church Forum website. URL: http://www.churchforum.org.mx/santoral/Febrero/2002.htm. Downloaded: November 12, 1999.

Francis de Sales (1567–1622) *Bishop of Geneva, Doctor of the Church, founder and popular preacher*
Also known as: the Gentle Christ of Geneva

Frances de Sales was born on August 21, 1567, to a noble Savoy family in Thorens in the duchy of Savoy. His parents were François de Sales de Boisy and Françoise de Sionnaz, and he was the oldest of five boys. He was brought up a strict Catholic and followed his father's ambition for him to become a magistrate.

Francis was well schooled at the colleges of La Roche and Annecy. From 1583 to 1588 he studied under the Jesuits at the college of Clermont, Paris. While there, he studied theology, which had a profound effect on him. He made a vow of chastity and consecrated himself to the Blessed Virgin Mary. He then went to law school at the University of Padua, Italy. He excelled in studies, was eloquent and gentlemanly and was well liked.

In 1592 Francis received his doctorate of law and was appointed a lawyer before the senate of Chambéry, France. His father arranged for him to be appointed senator and to marry a noble heiress. But Francis refused, creating a serious rift with his father. Claude de Granier, bishop of Geneva, arranged for Francis to be appointed provost of the Chapter of Geneva, a position under the patronage of the pope. Francis's father relented, and Francis received his holy orders in 1593.

In Geneva, Francis threw himself with great energy into preaching and evangelizing. In 1594 he began work in Le Chablais, a district just restored to the duchy of Savoy. He traveled extensively, sometimes at risk to his life, and converted many from Calvinism. Francis had several conferences with Theodore Beza, the "Patriarch of the Reformation," but nothing came of them.

In 1599, Claude de Granier appointed him coadjutor and sent him—despite his refusal—to Rome. There Pope Clement VIII (r. 1592–1605) approved of him, and prophesied that he would have a great impact upon the world.

Francis returned to France and became friends with King Henry IV, who wished him to stay and preach in France. In 1602, de Granier died, and Francis was appointed bishop of Geneva. The next 20 years were the most productive of his life. He devoted himself to visiting the parishes, instituting reforms and religious instruction, and performing his ministerial duties. He did not care for the Calvinist influences in Geneva, and so worked primarily from Annecy, where he lived like a poor priest. His sermons were eloquent, and people loved to hear him preach. On at least one occasion he was witnessed illuminated by supernatural light as he preached.

During this period, Francis found the time to write innumerable letters and treatises, many of which are still popular. In 1607, he founded the Institute of the Visitation of the Blessed Virgin Mary for young girls and widows.

In 1622, Francis accompanied the court of Savoy to France. In Lyons, he suffered a sudden apoplexy on December 27. He was given last rites and constantly repeated, "God's will be done! Jesus, my God and my all!" He died the following day.

Huge crowds came to see his body. Lyons wished to keep his remains, but kept only his heart, with everything else going back to Annecy. He was entombed at the Visitation Convent, and miracles were claimed there. During the French Revolution, nuns carried his heart to Venice for safety, where it still remains.

His beatification in 1661 was the first beatification held at St. Peter's Basilica.

Francis's heart was placed in a silver coffer. At intervals over the years, it exuded a clear oil, or manna. The coffer was not hermetically sealed, and in 1948 the dry heart was wrapped in a new piece of linen and a layer of tissue paper the same color as the heart. In 1952 white salt-like spots appeared between the heart and the container. The heart was unwrapped for examination, and the linen cloth had bloodstains. The heart was rewrapped in fresh linen and placed in a hermetically sealed container, which was then placed inside the original reliquary. In 1953 the heart was again examined, by doctors and Church officials. No satisfactory explanation could be given for the bloodstains. One rather mystical explanation proposed that the heart had bled to express the saint's unhappiness with a decision following World War II to reorganize the independent Visitation into a confederation under the jurisdiction of Rome. The confederation was eventually dissolved.

In his sermons and writings, Francis showed a deep insight into human nature and psychology. He did not address himself to peers, as did many other great writers of the Church, but to the people. He was gifted in inspiring and motivating others to a higher spiritual life. Probably his best-known and loved work is

Philothea, better known as *An Introduction to the Devout Life,* published in 1608. In a warm and personal fashion, the book lays out the requirements for a devout life of prayer, practicing virtues, resisting temptation, maintaining a good marriage, and worshiping God. Francis's style translates easily for modern times, and *Philothea* remains a widely read and followed work.

Another of Francis's principal works is *Controversies,* which addresses the fundamentals of Catholic faith. It originally appeared in separate handbills and leaflets passed out to those whom Francis sought to evangelize in Le Chablais.

Other important works are: *Treatise on the Love of God,* a 12-book examination of the history and theory of Divine love; *Spiritual Conferences,* conversations on religious virtues, which Francis wrote for the Sisters of the Visitation; and *Defense of the Standard of the Cross,* a discussion of Catholic doctrine on the veneration of the cross. Francis wrote numerous sermons, especially for Lent—also still popular reading—and other treatises.

Various religious congregations have been formed under his patronage, among them the Missionaries of St. Francis de Sales, of Annecy; the Salesians, founded by St. John Bosco in Turin for underprivileged boys; and the Oblates of St. Francis de Sales, of Troyes, France.

Beatified: 1661 by Pope Alexander VII
Canonized: 1665 by Pope Alexander VII
Declared Doctor of the Church: 1877 by Pope Pius IX
Feast: January 24
Patronage: attorneys; authors; Catholic press; confessors; the deaf; journalists; teachers; writers

FURTHER READING
Francis de Sales. *Philothea, or An Introduction to the Devout Life.* Rockford, Ill.: TAN Books and Publishers, 1994.
Francis de Sales, Jane de Chantal: Letters of Spiritual Direction. Tr. Peronne Marie Thiebert. Mahwah, N.J.: Paulist Press, 1988.

Francis of Assisi (1181?–1226) *Stigmatist, considered to be the founder of all Franciscan orders*
Name meaning: Free one
Also known as: Little Poor Man, Il Poverello

Francis of Assisi was born in either 1181 or 1182 in the town of Assisi in Umbria, Italy, at a time when his wealthy father, Pietro Bernardone, was away. His mother, Pica, baptized him as Giovanni after John the Baptist. His father had the name changed to Francesco, "the Frenchman," in honor of the time he spent in France conducting his successful silk cloth trade.

Francis spent his early years in song, drink and extravagance, going through his father's money but showing no interest in his father's business. His companions were youths who loved the wild life. In 1201, war broke out between Assisi and neighboring Perugia, and Francis was captured. He languished for a year in prison, was ransomed and then suffered a long illness after his release. During his convalescence he kept receiving signs that he should change his ways.

After his recovery, a call was issued for knights for the Fourth Crusade. Francis outfitted himself in the finest of armor and garments with the intention of joining the forces of Walter de Brienne, who was fighting in southern Italy. Francis bragged that he would return a prince. But a day's journey out of Assisi, he met a poor gentleman or former knight and traded his fine clothes and armor for the man's rags. At Spoleto, he became ill, and either had a dream or an audition (direct voice experience) in which God told him that what he was doing was wrong, and that he should "serve the master and not the man" and go home. He did so.

At home, he began visiting the sick and poor, giving them whatever he had. He spent more time in prayer, even removing himself to a cave, where he wept and prayed about his sins. One day in prayer in the church of San Damiano (St. Damian), a voice emanated from the crucifix and told him three times, "Francis, go and repair my house, which you see is falling down." Francis took one of his father's horses and a large amount of cloth, both of which he sold to rebuild the ruined church.

His enraged father came to the church, but Francis hid. Several days later, Francis emerged in public after fasting and praying; crowds pelted him. His father took him home and tried everything to dissuade Francis from his "mad" ideas, including beatings and shackles, but Francis was immovable. He returned to the church, whereupon his father demanded that he either come home or renounce his inheritance and repay the cost of the horse and cloth. Francis responded by stripping off all his clothing and giving them to his father. He renounced his patrimony and took a vow of absolute poverty. He was given the dress of a laborer, marked it with a cross in chalk, and wore it. The white cross on an undyed woolen tunic was to become the trademark of Franciscan monks.

Francis soon attracted a band of 12 followers, all of whom wore long, rough tunics of undyed wool, shaved the tops of their heads and preached as itinerants among the poor and sick, depending solely on the generosity of strangers. He composed a rule based on the gospel's words about perfection, and in 1210 sought approval from Pope Innocent III (r. 1198–1216).

St. Francis of Assisi receiving the stigmata (Library of Congress Prints and Photographs Division)

According to lore, the pope had two dreams that prompted him to grant approval. In one, a palm tree grew at his feet. In another, Francis propped up the Lateran church, which seemed about to fall. Innocent gave Francis approval for spreading his rule only by word of mouth.

Francis made two attempts to preach among the Moslems. In 1212 his journey was ended by shipwreck, and a later journey was ended by his own illness. He did, however, travel to Egypt and Syria beginning in 1219.

A revision of his rule was approved in 1223 by Pope Honorius III (r.1216–27). The same year, Francis introduced a crèche at a Nativity Mass in Greccio in 1223 as a memorial of Jesus' humble birth—a practice that has become a central part of Christmas celebrations.

Perhaps his most unusual achievement was the acquisition of stigmata after an ecstatic vision in 1224. During the summer of that year, close to the Feast of the Assumption (August 15), Francis retired in seclusion to a tiny hut on Monte La Verna, part of the property of Orlando, count of Chiusi. He intended to suffer a long fast in honor of the archangel Michael, requesting that he be left alone until the angel's feast day on September 29. Francis was then 42 years old, racked with disease and fevers, and quite thin from self-mortification.

On September 14, the Feast of the Exaltation of the Holy Cross, Francis continued his fasting and prayer by concentrating on Christ's sufferings on the cross. As described in the *Little Flowers of St. Francis of Assisi*, he was contemplating the Passion so fervently that he believed himself transformed into Jesus. While in such an ecstatic state, his vision continued with the appearance of a seraph. The angel's six fiery wings descended from heaven, drawing closer to Francis, and revealed the crucified Jesus within their folds. Francis was filled with fear, joy and sorrow. When the vision ended, the saint found to his amazement that his hands and feet were marked with black excrescences in the form of nail heads and bent nails, and that a wound on his side—like the sword wounds suffered by Jesus—oozed blood frequently.

Francis was embarrassed and frightened by these stigmata, and for the remaining two years of his life kept his hands within his habit and wore shoes and stockings. He told none of his followers about the miracle, but they deduced the situation after finding blood on his clothing and noting Francis's inability to walk without hobbling. Sweet smells issued from cloths stained by the blood of the stigmata.

Several surviving accounts from various of Francis's followers refer to his bleeding wounds, the saint's inability to walk and the blackness of the marks. St. Francis's biographer, Thomas of Celano, reported that black marks resembling nails appeared on Francis's flesh even after death. And two paintings of Francis, painted within 10 years of his death, both show the stigmata. There were no verified reports of stigmata before Francis's designation in 1224, and very few since.

In 1225, suffering greatly from ill health, Francis composed his famous "Canticle of Brother Sun" poem and set it to music.

When doctors could do no more for him, he went to Assisi to die. On his last day, Saturday, October 3, 1226, he asked for the singing of that part of his Canticle that honors death. He broke bread with his brothers and was laid on the ground. He preached to them and blessed them, and died that evening.

Familiar with court poetry and the songs of the troubadours, Francis introduced a love of nature and creation, of song and praise, and of higher chivalric love into medieval worship.

There are many stories about his rapport with birds and animals, who tamely gathered around him to listen to him preach. Birds especially seemed fond of him. Francis would preach to them the same as he did to people. In one village, he subdued a ferocious wolf that was attacking humans and animals. He ordered the wolf to desist, and told the townspeople that the wolf would do them no more harm if they fed him every day. For the next two years until the wolf died, the townspeople fed the docile wolf as it went from door to door.

Francis multiplied food on more than one occasion. Once, when a priest complained that followers of Francis were eating too many of the church's grapes, Francis said that they should be allowed to do so, and the vineyard would produce more wine than normal. He also multiplied food when his ship was wrecked.

He is said to have influenced the weather, once ending frequent hailstorms that were destroying crops. Francis told the people to confess their sins and repent. The hailstorms ended. The people, however, eventually went back to their old ways, and were struck by pestilence and a fire that destroyed their town.

Francis was never ordained because he believed himself to be unworthy of the priesthood, yet he had a profound and lasting impact on the Church and on charity; there are Franciscans the world over carrying on his work. The "Canticle of Brother Sun" is still sung in Christian churches all over the world. Francis's simple appeal and total devotion —as well as the stories of his prophecies and miracle healings—continue to attract followers today.

Canonized: 1228 by Pope Gregory IX
Feast: October 4
Patronage: animals; birds; Catholic action; ecologists; merchants; zoos

FURTHER READING

Chambers, R., ed. *The Book of Days: A Miscellany of Popular Antiquities in Connection with the Calenda.*, Vol. 2. Detroit: Gale Research Co., 1967.

The Little Flowers of St. Francis. Tr. Raphael Brown. Garden City, N.Y.: Doubleday/Image Books, 1985.

Wilson, Ian. *Stigmata: An Investigation into the Mysterious Appearance of Christ's Wounds in Hundreds of People from Medieval Italy to Modern America.* San Francisco: Harper and Row, 1989.

Francis of Paola (ca. 1416–1507) *Founder of the Minim Friars*

Known as "The Miracle Worker" *and* "God's Miracle-Worker Supreme"

St. Francis of Paola was born around 1416 in Paola, Italy, to a humble family. Childless for years, the parents had prayed earnestly to St. Francis of Assisi for a son. When Francis was conceived, tongues of fire were seen dancing harmlessly over the family roof. At birth the boy was named after the saint. When he was 13, they sent him to the Franciscan friary at San Marco to be educated. The austere lifestyle appealed to Francis.

After a year, he took a pilgrimage with his parents to Assisi, Rome and other places. When they returned, Francis went into seclusion, first slightly outside Paola and then in a remote location in a cave by the sea. By 1436 he was joined by two companions. Neighbors built them cells and a chapel. A story is told that one day a goat rushed into Francis's cave, seeking refuge from hunters. Francis took it as a sign from God that he was to leave his hermitage and work for the Church.

Thus began Francis's order. The date of foundation is considered to be 1452. Seventeen years later a church and monastery were built, and Francis established a discipline for the order based on penance, charity and humility, and also on a perpetual Lent that required a strict vegetarian diet.

Pope Sixtus IV (r. 1471–84) approved the new order in 1474. Initially, they were called the Hermits of St. Francis of Assisi. Francis had this changed in 1492 to the Minim Friars, as he desired that they be recognized as the least (*minimi*) in the household of God.

In 1481 the dying King Louis XI of France sent for Francis and asked him to heal him in exchange for assistance to his order. Francis replied that the lives of kings are in the hands of God. The two men shared numerous meetings, and Louis died in Francis's arms. His successor, Charles VIII, relied upon Francis for much advice. He built for Francis three monasteries: two in France at Plessias and Amboise, and one at Rome.

Francis remained in France for the last 25 years of his life. He became ill on Palm Sunday, 1507, and died the following Good Friday, at age 91.

Francis was renowned as a miracle-worker. He was reported to bilocate, and was seen simultaneously in prayer in the chapel and out on the street talking to people, or working in the kitchens while he also attended the altar. He had the gift of miraculous transport, and took companions across water using his cloak for a boat. In 1483 he was observed by the king of Naples to levitate in an ecstasy and to be bathed in supernatural light in the middle of the night. The saint also levitated objects. During the building of his first church and monastery, he raised a large boulder that was in the way.

On numerous occasions, Francis multiplied food and wine, sometimes for large crowds of several hundred. Though portions were small, each person felt fully satisfied.

Throughout his life, Francis was very popular and was often mobbed by enthusiastic crowds when he ventured out in public. He was said to make himself invisible whenever he wished to travel undetected, or to have quiet moments for prayer and meditation. He also had the gifts of prophesy, clairvoyance, supernatural knowledge and control of the elements.

Once Francis had a confrontation with the Neapolitan king Ferrantes, a corrupt man who sought to curry favor with the saint by giving a large quantity of gold coins for the building of a monastery. Francis lectured the king on his corruption. He took a gold coin and broke it in two; blood dripped from the halves. Francis told him it was the blood that had been squeezed out of his subjects. He refused the money. Reportedly, the shocked king reformed.

Francis reportedly could produce sweet, often healing water by striking the ground with his staff. One such spring, called the Fountain of Seven Canals, is near the Church of the Holy Rosary in Paola. Its waters are given to the sick.

When the wall of a furnace in his monastery was near collapse, Francis entered the fire several times to repair the damage, and was unharmed by the flames, according to eight witnesses. The saint was unharmed by fire on other occasions. When he was on his deathbed and about to give his brothers his final instructions and blessings, a brazier in his room suddenly burst into flames. Francis got up, walked to it and picked it up, saying, "Be assured, my brothers, that it is not difficult for one who truly loves God to carry out what He wishes, which for me is holding in my hands this fire." He was unharmed.

Canonization: 1519 by Pope Leo X
Feast: April 2
Patronage: naval officers; seafarers

CHARITAS.

5

S. F. de Paule, agé de douze ans, recoit l'habit de l'Ordre de S. Francois, qu'il porta vn an pour accomplir le vœu de ses parens.

6

S. Francois de Paule, accompagné de ses parens, visite les S.ts lieux de Rome, et l'Eglise de S.te Marie des Anges a Assise.

7

S. F. de Paule, agé de quatorze ans se retire au Desert, ou jl demeure seul jusqu'au 19.me de son age, qu'il commence son Ordre.

8

S. F. de Paule, construisant l'Eglise de son pre.er Convent, est Diuinement aduerty par S. Fran. D'Assise, de la faire plus grande.

IIII.

Lommelin fecit

Scenes from the life of St. Francis of Paola (Library of Congress Prints and Photographs Division)

FURTHER READING
Simi, Gino J., and Mario M. Segreti. *St. Francis of Paola.* Rockford, Ill.: TAN Books, 1977.

Francis Solanus (Francisco Solano) (1549–1610)
Franciscan missionary in Peru
Also known as: the Miracle-Worker of the New World

Francis Solanus was born in Montilla in the Andalusia region of Spain on March 10, 1549. From an early age he demonstrated spiritual inclinations and talents, such as his ability to make peace between those who were fighting. It was enough for Francis merely to run to the combatants and ask them to desist in order to get them to stop.

After studying with the Jesuits, in 1569, at the age of 20, Francis entered a Franciscan monastery, drawn to the poverty and the life of sanctity of St Francis of Assisi. He was ordained a priest in 1576, and a few years later, when an epidemic of black typhus arrived in Andalusia, dedicated himself to attending the sickest. He himself contracted the disease and believed himself about to die, but then, unexpectedly, recovered. From this he understood that God was saving him for still greater challenges. He asked his superiors to send him as a missionary to Africa, but they denied his request. However, in 1589 King Philip II asked the Franciscans to send missionaries to South America, and they assigned him there.

Francis arrived in Lima, Peru, in May 1589, having survived a shipwreck off Panama. From Lima he was sent to Argentina, where the Franciscans had several missions. He had a great facility in learning the native languages, considered by his peers to be a divine gift. Even the most warlike tribes attended his sermons. One Good Thursday while Francis was preaching in La Rioja, the sound of thousands of Indians attacking the village was heard. Francis went out to meet them with crucifix in hand and placed himself in front of the attackers, who not only desisted, but soon thereafter also allowed themselves to be evangelized and baptized in the Catholic religion.

Like his namesake and patron, St. Francis of Assisi, Francis felt great compassion for animals. Birds frequently surrounded him and then rose in the air, singing happily. One day during a bullfight in the town of San Miguel a bull escaped the corral and took to the streets. Francis was called and he calmly approached the animal. People watched in admiration as the bull allowed Francis to take hold of him and lead him back to the corral.

In 1601, Francis was ordered back to Lima, where he spent his last years preaching to and converting sinners. He went to gambling houses and to theaters, where he interrupted plays he deemed immoral, delivering spirited sermons from the stage. In the town square he preached that God would bring terrible punishments if people did not desist from their sinful ways. Inevitably, these acts brought in many converts.

One day Francis announced in a sermon that thanks to the sins of the people, everything around him would be destroyed, leaving nothing but the site from which he was preaching. The following year an earthquake destroyed the church and its surroundings, sparing only the site where Francis had made his prediction.

In May 1610, the Miracle-worker of the New World (as he had come to be called) began to feel very weak. On July 14 a flock of birds flew into his room in the San Francisco Monastery, singing; Francis exclaimed, "Glory be to God," and died. His room was lit all that night by an unusual illumination visible from far away.

Beatified: 1675 by Pope Clement X
Canonized: 1726 by Pope Benedict XIII
Feast: July 14

FURTHER READING
"San Francisco Solano, Misionero." Church Forum Santoral website. URL: http://www.churchforum.org.mx/santoral. Downloaded: November 17, 1999.
"San Francisco Solano." Santos Peruanos website. URL: http://ekeko.rcp.net.pe/IAL/cep/santpapa/santoslos.htm. Downloaded: November 17, 1999.
"San Francisco Solano." Santos y Beatos de America Latina: Perú website. URL: http://www.aciprensa.com/sant-peru.htm. Downloaded: November 17, 1999.

Francis Xavier (Francisco Javier) (1506–1552) *First Jesuit missionary, considered the greatest missionary since St. Paul*

Francis was born in the castle of Javier (Xavier) near Sanguesa, in the Spanish kingdom of Navarre, on April 7, 1506. His father, Juan de Jasso, was the king's counselor, and his mother was heiress to the houses of Azupilqueta and Javier. They were Basques, like St. Ignatius of Loyola, who was born not far away. Also like Ignatius, Francis was the youngest of a large family, though unlike him, he early showed an aptitude for study, and at 19 was sent to Paris for his higher education.

Francis enrolled in the Collège de Sainte-Barbe (College of St. Barbara) of the University of Paris. He received his M.A. degree in 1530 and began teaching Aristotelian philosophy in the university. It was there that he first met Ignatius, who in 1529 resided in the college for a time as a guest. Together with five other

St. Francis Xavier

students, Francis and Ignatius formed a group to practice Ignatius's spiritual exercises. The group of seven took vows of chastity together at Montmartre on August 15, 1534.

Francis was ordained to the priesthood in Venice on June 24, 1537, and went to teach in Bologna. However, when Ignatius called his Paris companions together during Lent in 1539, he went to Rome to join them. The group decided to form a new religious order, the Society of Jesus, placing themselves at the disposal of the pope to be sent wherever he wished and for whatever duties. Pope Paul III gave verbal approval to the order on September 3, the written approbation coming a year later, on September 27, 1540.

By the time written approbation was promulgated, Francis had left Rome. When King John III of Portugal asked the Vatican to send two Jesuits to Goa, India, where a colony had been established 30 years earlier, Francis was assigned the mission. He reached Lisbon about June and quickly became busy assisting in hospi-

tals and schools. The following year he received four briefs from Pope Paul III, constituting him papal nuncio and recommending him to the princes of the East. He sailed for Goa on April 7, 1541, his 35th birthday, and landed there on May 6, 1542.

Francis spent five months in Goa, preaching and ministering to the sick in the hospitals, and teaching the catechism to children. He would walk through the streets ringing a bell to call the children to their studies. Then in October he moved to Travancore on the Pearl Fishery Coast to minister to the Paravas, a low-caste people who had been introduced to Christianity by the Portuguese. Twice while in Travancore he was credited with the miracle of bringing the dead to life. Word of the miracles spread, and he soon received invitations to minister elsewhere in southern India.

Leaving India in 1545, Francis took his ministry to areas of the western Pacific, though it is improbable that he ever reached the Philippines, as is sometimes claimed. He did, however, reach Japan and the Chinese coast.

In Malacca in July 1547, Francis met a Japanese called Anger (Han-Sir), whom he baptized with the name Pablo de Santa Fe. From Anger he learned about Japan, and the two left for the islands toward the end of June 1549, arriving at the city of Kagoshima on August 15. Francis spent a year learning the language and translating the principal church documents, then, about August 1550, he left Kagoshima and went inland, preaching the Gospel in some of the cities of southern Japan. At the beginning of 1551 he returned briefly to Goa, intent on converting China, about which he had heard much while in Japan.

Francis left Goa for the last time in April 1552, and arrived at the small island of Sancian off the coast of China that fall. He was planning how best to reach the mainland when he fell ill. Since the movement of his ship seemed to be aggravating his condition, he was taken ashore to a crude hut that was built for him. He died there on December 3, 1552, without the last sacraments or a Christian burial. His corpse was covered in lime so that the flesh would be quickly consumed in the grave. However, when his body was dug up on February 17, 1553, it was found to be incorrupt and in a remarkable state of preservation. His body was taken to Goa, where it was met with much devotion, displayed for four days and entombed in the former Jesuit church. Prior to entombment, it was examined by doctors to verify that no embalming had been done on it. The corpse gave off a sweet fragrance.

In 1614, by order of the general of the Society of Jesus, Claudius Acquaviva, the right arm was severed at the elbow and conveyed to Rome, where an altar was erected to receive it in the Church of the Gesu. The body was exhumed and examined again in 1694 and found to be remarkably lifelike, as though the saint were merely sleeping. The body since has dried and shrunk, but remains incorrupt. Numerous parts of it have been removed for relics.

In 1949 the severed arm was toured throughout Japan and the United States to commemorate the 400th anniversary of Francis's arrival in Japan. The body was placed on exhibition in Goa from November 1974 to January 5, 1975.

During his life Francis was credited with many miracles, besides raising the dead, among whom was a man whose entombed body had started to putrefy. Francis's bilocations were recorded so frequently that one biographer termed them "of quite an ordinary occurrence." He is said to have possessed the gift of prophecy and of tongues, to have healed the sick and wounded, and to have calmed storms. In one such storm near the Molucca Islands, the winds snatched his crucifix, which he was holding high above his head, and tossed it into the sea. When the saint's ship arrived safely at its destination, a great crab came out of the sea carrying the crucifix in its claws in an upright position. The grateful saint prostrated himself on the beach in prayer for half an hour.

No doubt this reputation aided in his ministry. It is estimated that in India alone he baptized 30,000 people.

Francis was canonized in 1622 along with SS. Ignatius of Loyola, Teresa of Avila and Isidore the Farmer.

In art, he is represented by a bell, crucifix, vessel or globe. He is also depicted as a young bearded Jesuit with a torch, flame, cross and lily; as a young bearded Jesuit in the company of Ignatius of Loyola; and as a preacher carrying a flaming heart.

Beatified: 1619 by Pope Paul V
Canonized: March 12, 1622, by Pope Gregory XV
Feast: December 3
Patronage: apostleship of prayer; Borneo; East Indies; foreign missions; Goa, India; immigrants; Japan; wineries and winegrowers

FURTHER READING
"San Francisco Javier." Church Forum website. URL: http://www.churchforum.org/santoral/Diciembre/0312.ht m. Downloaded: January 12, 2000.
Schurhammer, Georg. *Francis Xavier His Life, His Times: Europe, 1506–1541.* Vol. 1. Tr. M. Joseph Costelloe. Chicago: Loyola Press, 1977.
———. *Francis Xavier His Life, His Times: India, 1541–1545.* Vol. 2. Tr. M. Joseph Costelloe. Chicago: Loyola Press, 1977.

Fulgentius of Ruspe (468–533) *Bishop of Ruspe, Father of the Church*

Fabius Claudius Gordianus Fulgentius was born at Telepte (Thelepte), in the North African province of Byzacena, in 468. His grandfather, Gordianus, had been a senator in Carthage who had been exiled to Italy by the Vandals; but the family still owned property and had status in the region. Fulgentius's father, Claudius, died soon after his birth, and he was brought up by his mother, Mariana. He was well educated and when he came of age helped Mariana manage the family estate. Proving himself in his abilities, he was appointed procurator of Telepte and tax receiver of Byzacena.

However, he was drawn to the religious life. After practicing austerities privately for a time, he entered a local monastery when he was 22. There he became ill from excessive abstinence, but recovered. When renewed persecutions forced the abbot to flee, Fulgentius also left, going to another monastery, this run by a friend of his named Felix. Felix tried to abdicate in favor of Fulgentius, but the two finally agreed on a co-rule, Felix caring for the house while Fulgentius instructed the brethren.

Felix and Fulgentius ruled together for six years until in 499 they were forced to flee invading Numidians. They went to Sicca Veneria, where they were arrested on the demand of an Arian priest, scourged, and tortured, but finally released when they refused to deny their faith. The two monks then split up, Fulgentius intending to visit the anchorites in the Egyptian desert, though he instead went to Rome where in 500 he visited the tombs of the Apostles. When he returned to Byzacena, he built his own monastery, though he chose to live apart as a hermit.

During this period, the Vandals did not allow orthodox Catholic bishops to be elected in Africa, and several sees fell vacant. Finally, in 508, the remaining North African bishops decided to get new bishops in place before the Vandals could stop them. Fearing he would be elected, Fulgentius went into hiding. He returned when he thought all of the vacancies had been filled, but unfortunately for him landed at the seaport of Ruspe (now Kudiat Rosfa, Tunisia), where the election had been delayed. He was promptly elected and consecrated bishop of a town he had never before seen.

He quickly erected a new monastery, placing Felix in charge. However, it was not long before he and the 60 other new bishops were exiled to Sardinia. Fulgentius quickly emerged as spokesman of this community, and in Cagliari founded yet another monastery. There he began writing an important series of theological works addressing the Arian heresy, some of which came to the attention of the Vandal king Thrasimund. In 515, Thrasimund had Fulgentius taken to Carthage for discussions with the Arian clergy.

In Carthage, Fulgentius found a receptive audience among the city folk. His presence became a threat to the Arians, who insisted that he be deported. He was put aboard ship one night but contrary winds kept it in port for the next several days and many were able to take his leave and to receive Holy Communion from his hands. To one weeping religious man, he prophesied his speedy return and the liberty of the African Church. This came with the death of Thrasimund in 523. Fulgentius returned to his monastery outside Ruspe, where he continued to rule for the remaining years of his life, insisting on austerity for himself and his priests.

Perhaps sensing his end was near, in 532 Fulgentius suddenly left Ruspe and retired to a small monastery he had caused to be built on the island of Circinia (Circe). His flock did not permit him to remain there long, however, and shortly after his return to Ruspe, he fell ill. He was sick for 70 days before expiring on January 1, 533. He was 65, and in the 25th year of his episcopate. So beloved was he for his gifts of oratory that he was buried within his church, contrary to the law and custom of his age.

Feast: January 1 (formerly January 3)

Fursey (d. 648) *Irish abbot, monastery founder, visionary and miracle-worker*

Fursey was born to a noble family on the island of Inisguia en Lough Carrie, Ireland, and was the brother of SS. Foillan and Ulan. He founded a monastery at Lagny-en-Brie, France, and became its abbot. Desiring a good source of water, he prayed to God and then struck the ground with his staff. A fountain of water issued forth that served not only the monastery but also the entire town. The water was said to have healing properties, and it attracted many pilgrims, especially on Ascension Day.

In 630 he went to England with family and friends. According to the Venerable Bede, Fursey experienced intense ecstasies, many of which occurred during illnesses. After arriving in England, he fell ill and had a vision in which God urged him to proceed with his ministry and continue his prayers. With great speed, he built a monastery near Ugremouth on land donated by King Sigebert.

During a subsequent illness, Fursey fell into a trance one evening and left his body until dawn. He saw and heard choirs of angels and was told, "The saints shall advance from one virtue to another." Three days later, another trance journey took him to visions of the joys of the blessed and the extraordinary efforts of evil spirits who attempted to obstruct his journey to heaven but were restrained by angels.

The angels had him look down upon the Earth, where he saw four fires that would consume the world: falsehood, covetousness, discord and iniquity. The flames increased in intensity and joined into one, and devils flew through the fire. The angels told Fursey he would not be burned by anything he did not kindle. There followed accusations hurled by the devils at Fursey, and defenses provided by the angels. Fursey also was shown more of heaven, and the holy men of his nation.

Upon the departure of Fursey and the angels, the flames opened and a devil tossed out a man, striking Fursey on the shoulder and jaw and burning him. An angel tossed the man back into the fire. Fursey had known the man and had accepted his garment after he died. A devil said that since he accepted the clothing of a damned man, he had to share in the man's punishment. The angel told the devil that Fursey had not accepted the garment in avarice, but to save his soul. The fire ceased. The angel said, "that which you kindled burned in you; for had you not received the money of this person that died in his sins, his punishment would not burn in you." The angel then gave him advice for salvation.

For the rest of his life, Fursey bore burn marks on his shoulder and jaw. He also was perpetually hot, and even in winter sweated in the thinnest of garments.

Fursey preached the practice of virtues, but talked about his visions with only a select few. After a time, he could no longer bear the crowds who came to the monastery. He resolved to end his life as a hermit, and went off to live with his brother, Ulan, also a hermit. But after a year he reentered the world, traveling to France where he was welcomed by King Clovis and the patrician Erconwald. He built another monastery near Paris.

In 648 Fursey fell ill again and died. Erconwald took his body to a church under construction in Perrone. Fursey's body remained on the porch incorrupt for 27 days until the church was dedicated. His remains were buried near the altar; four years later the still-incorrupt body was translated to a chapel. Many miracles were claimed at his burial site. For many years some of his relics, sent back to Ireland, were paraded to the fountain he had found every Ascension Day for a special ceremony. Thanks to Bede, he is one of the best known early Irish saints.

Feast: January 16

FURTHER READING

Bede. *Ecclesiastical History of the English Nation.* URL: http://www.fordham.edu/halsall/basis/bede-book1.html. Downloaded: February 10, 2000.

G

Gabriel the Archangel

Name meaning: "Hero of God," "the mighty one" or "God has shown himself mighty" in Hebrew

The angel Gabriel—given the rank of archangel in post-biblical lore—is one of the three principal angels of Christianity, and figures prominently in Judaic, Christian and Islamic angelology. In Christianity, the cult of Gabriel began early in Rome.

Gabriel is the angel of revelation, wisdom, mercy, redemption and promise. He sits at the left hand of God. Gabriel is mentioned four times in the Bible, and always in connection with important news. In the Old Testament, he first appears as Daniel's frequent visitor, bringing prophetic visions of apocalyptic proportion (Daniel 8:16, 9:21). In the New Testament, Gabriel gives his name to Zechariah—"I am Gabriel who stand in God's presence" —when he announces the coming birth of John the Baptist (Luke 1:19). He is cited in the Annunciation to Mary of the coming birth of Jesus (Luke 1:26).

It is in his role as annunciator of the coming of the birth of Christ to Mary that Gabriel is best known and best depicted in art. He is the most painted of angels, for the Incarnation is the most common subject in Western art. He is often shown holding one or more lilies, the symbol of purity, or holding a scroll inscribed with the Ave Maria.

Luke 1:26–38 describes the encounter between Gabriel and Mary. He appears to her, tells her she has found favor with God, and she will become pregnant with a son who is to be named Jesus. When Mary wonders how this can happen, since she is a virgin, Gabriel tells her the Holy Spirit will come upon her, and the child will be holy. When she consents ("Behold, I am the handmaid of the Lord; let it be done unto me according to your word") the angel departs. Though the angel who announces the birth of Jesus to the shepherds (Luke 2:8–14) is called only an "angel of the Lord," Catholic tradition credits this to Gabriel.

In Catholic devotion to angels, Gabriel has a prominent place because of his role in the Annunciation. Gabriel's salutation, "Hail, full of grace, the Lord is with thee, blessed art thou among women" is reiterated in the Hail Mary. Because of his role in the Annunciation, other lore about Gabriel holds that he guides the soul from paradise to the womb and there instructs it for the nine months prior to birth.

Gabriel also is credited with other major acts of unnamed angels concerning Jesus: as the angel who appears in a dream to Joseph, warning him to take his family and flee to Egypt to avoid Herod's hunt for the baby Jesus (Matthew 2:13); as the angel who appears in the Garden of Gethsemane to provide strength and support to Jesus in his agony (Luke 22:43); and as the

Archangel Gabriel announcing the birth of Jesus to Mary (Library of Congress Prints and Photographs Division)

"angel of the Lord" who has a countenance as lightning and a raiment as snow, who rolls back the stone from the tomb of Jesus and sits upon it (Matthew 28:2). In addition, Gabriel is said to be the unnamed archangel in 1 Thessalonians 4:15 who sounds the trumpet of judgment and resurrection. Thus, he is shown in art blowing a trumpet. Gabriel's symbols are a spear and a shield emblazoned with a lily.

Devotion to Gabriel and other angels is fostered as a way of becoming closer to God.

Feast: September 29
Patronage: clerics; diplomats; messengers; postal workers; radio broadcasters; stamp collectors; telecommunication workers

FURTHER READING
Guiley, Rosemary Ellen. *The Encyclopedia of Angels.* New York: Facts On File, 1996.
O'Sullivan, Fr. Paul. *All about the Angels.* Rockford, Ill.: TAN Books, 1990; first published, 1945.
St. Michael and the Angels. Rockford, Ill.: TAN Books, 1983; first published, 1977.

Gabriel Francis of Our Lady of Sorrows (1838–1862) *Passionist monk who advised St. Gemma Galgani*

Gabriel Francis of Our Lady of Sorrows was born Francis Possenti in Assisi, Italy, in 1838. He joined the Passionist monks in Morovalle in 1856. He died of consumption in 1862 in Isola.

Gabriel Francis's cult was confined to local calendars in 1969.

Canonized: 1920 by Pope Benedict XV
Feast: February 27

Gall (ca. 550–630) *Irish missionary, companion of St. Columban, patron saint of Sweden and Switzerland*

Gall was born ca. 550 in Ireland and studied under SS. Columban and Comgall. He was a priest and biblical scholar, and one of the 12 companions who accompanied Columban to France, where they founded the abbeys of Annegray, Fontaine and Luxeuil; Gall lived at the latter for 20 years. When Columban was forced into exile in 610, Gall went with him, and they eventually went to Austrasia. There they preached for two years amidst opposition from the pagans.

In 612 Columban decided to retire to Italy, but Gall said he could not go along due to illness. Columban did not think him that ill, but merely unwilling, and so sentenced him to a penance of never celebrating the mass for the rest of his life. Gall obeyed, and went off to Arbon, where he stayed with a priest, Willimar, who

had given them shelter during Columban's exile. The deacon Hiltibod instructed him to live as a hermit, and so he chose a spot by the river Steinach to live. Disciples gathered around him, and they followed the rule of Columban.

Gall learned of Columban's death at Bobbio in 615 in a vision. St. Eustace, whom Columban had left in charge of the abbey at Luxeuil, died in 625. The monks asked Gall to succeed him as abbot, but Gall preferred to remain a hermit, leaving his cell only to teach and preach. He undertook missionary activities in Switzerland.

King Sigebert twice offered Gall a bishopric, but he declined these as well. He died around 630 in Bregenz, Austria.

The Saint Gall monastery grew up on the site of his hermitage, as did the town of Saint Gall. During the Middle Ages, it was a prominent center of arts and learning. The library was secularized and is now part of the cathedral of Saint Gall.

According to legend, Gall had miraculous gifts, including the ability to communicate with animals. Once he is said to have dispatched a bear to fetch firewood for the monks.

Feast: October 16
Patronage: birds; geese; poultry; Sweden; Switzerland

Gelasius I (d. 496) *Pope*

Gelasius, the son of an African named Valerius, was born in Rome. He served as secretary to Pope St. Simplicius (r. 468–483) and Pope St. Felix III (r. 483–492), holding the position of archdeacon under the latter. He was elected Felix's successor in the Chair of St. Peter on March 1, 492.

During his pontificate, Gelasius made little attempt to breach the schism between the Western and Eastern Churches that had arisen at the end of Simplicius's reign. His more modest aim was to assert papal authority over the Church of Constantinople, which had emerged as a see second only to Rome and as leader of the Eastern Church. Although he meet with little success in this regard, he did exercise a deep influence on the development of Catholic ecclesiastical discipline and liturgy. A considerable number of his decrees were incorporated into canon law. He also composed many hymns, prefaces and collects, and arranged a standard missal, although the *Sacramentarium Gelasianum* actually belongs to the next century and it is not known how much of Gelasius's work it contains.

In his private life, Gelasius was much devoted to prayer, penance and study. He delighted in the company of monks and gave freely to the poor, dying penniless as a result of his lavish charity.

Gelasius died in Rome on November 19, 496, and was buried in St. Peter's on November 21.

Feast: November 21

Gemma Galgani (1878–1903) *Mystic, stigmatist*
Also known as: the Passion Flower of Lucca

Gemma Galgani was born on March 12, 1878, in Camigliano, a small town near Lucca in Tuscany, Italy. She was the oldest daughter of eight children. Her mother died when she was seven, and her childhood was fraught with hardships. She was chronically ill. Her relatives, burdened with caring for her, treated her poorly.

From an early age, she exhibited supernatural gifts: visitations, visits by Christ, assaults by the devil, and stigmata.

Gemma took her First Communion on June 17, 1887. She had an intense desire to become a Passionist nun, but was turned away because of her ill health.

At age 19, Gemma turned down two marriage proposals and then fell seriously ill with meningitis. She felt herself tempted by the devil, and prayed for help to the Venerable Francis Possenti (a Passionist later canonized as St. Gabriel Francis of Our Lady of Sorrows). She was miraculously cured, and credited the intercession of Possenti.

The stigmata appeared on her wrists, feet and side from 1899 to 1901. The first episode occurred on June 8, 1899. Gemma felt an intense sorrow for her sins and a willingness to suffer. She had a vision of her guardian angel and the Blessed Virgin Mary. Mary opened her mantle and covered her, and told her she was much loved by Jesus, who was giving her a special grace. Then Jesus appeared with his wounds open; flames, not blood, issued forth. The flames touched Gemma's hand, feet and heart, and she felt as though she were dying. Mary supported her for several hours. The vision ended, and Gemma found herself on her knees, a sharp pain in her hands, feet and heart. Her guardian angel helped her into bed, and blood began to flow from her wounds.

Thereafter, every Thursday evening to Friday afternoon, Gemma would fall into a rapture and the five wounds would open and issue a bright red blood. She would utter the words of Jesus and Mary. The wounds would abruptly stop bleeding, close and leave only white marks. Sometimes the obliteration took until Saturday or Sunday to complete. When the ecstasies ended, Gemma would serenely go about her normal business. However, she suffered great inner torments

and trials from the devil. Throughout these difficult experiences, she maintained a great serenity and peace.

A Passionist, Father Germano, took an interest in Gemma and became her spiritual director and confessor. An expert on fraudulent mystical phenomena, he had Gemma thoroughly tested and was convinced her experiences were genuine. He recorded her utterances and later became her biographer. With Germano's help, Gemma went to live with a family as a mother's helper, where she was shielded from unfriendly attention and had the freedom to experience her ecstasies.

In 1901, Germano forbade her to accept the stigmata. She prayed and the phenomenon ceased, though the white marks remained.

Gemma sought to help the poor, and especially prayed for the conversion of souls.

In 1903, she was diagnosed with tuberculosis of the spine. She died peacefully with a smile on her lips in the company of her parish priest on Holy Saturday, April 11, 1903.

Gemma's rich visionary life was recorded in detail in her diaries and letters, as well as in Germano's writings. She was especially known for her angelic visions. She saw her guardian angel and heard his voice. Her conversations with her angel were observed and recorded by others who could hear only one side of the conversation—hers. Germano commented that whenever she saw or listened to her angel, she entered into an ecstatic state of consciousness, lost in another world; as soon as she turned her eyes away, she resumed her usual personality.

Gemma's angel was her constant companion, so familiar that she often treated him like a brother. She was once admonished by Germano—who overheard one of her one-way conversations—that she should treat him with more respect. She agreed, and vowed to remain 100 steps behind the angel whenever she saw him coming.

Whenever Gemma was plagued by evil spirits, she called upon her angel. In 1900 she recorded an episode in which she was harassed for hours by the devil in the form of a horrible "little fellow." She was assaulted by blows upon her shoulders while she prayed. Her angel appeared and, curiously, attempted to beg off her request to stay with her all night. He told her he had to sleep. When she replied that the "Angels of Jesus do not need to sleep," he said he still needed to rest. Nonetheless, he remained, and spread his wings over her while she slept.

Sometimes the angel was severe with her, in word or expression, as a way of trying to keep her on the straight and narrow spiritual path. He would find fault with her, and tell her he was ashamed of her. If she strayed from the path, he would depart from her presence for awhile.

Perhaps the most remarkable trademark of Gemma's angel was his couriership. She would send him off on errands to deliver verbal messages to people in distant places, and return with their replies. Gemma considered this angelic postal service to be a natural thing, and did not like asking for stamps. Others reportedly received the messages. Sometimes replies were delivered back to her by the guardian angel of Father Germano. When some suggested this was the work of the devil, Germano subjected Gemma to various spiritual tests, asking for irrefutable signs, and got them.

For one test, Germano told Gemma to give her aunt Cecilia a letter addressed to him; she was to lock it in a place unknown to Gemma. Cecilia gave the letter to a priest who locked it in a chest in his room and pocketed the key. The next day Gemma sensed the angel passing with her letter. She notified the surprised priest, who found the letter missing from the chest. The letter was received by Germano—apparently by angelic post. This test was successfully repeated a second time under different circumstances.

Gemma was visited by other angels, and often by Germano's guardian angel, who, she said, had a brilliant star over his head. No thought or deed of hers ever escaped angelic attention. If she was distracted in prayer, her angel would punish her. If she did not feel well, or if she would not eat enough, the angel exhibited a tender side, inquiring after her welfare and urging her to eat.

Many other marvels were ascribed to her. Like St. Martin de Porres, she was seen levitating and kissing a crucifix on a wall in her home. She also could "smell" the purity of a person's soul. If she was in the company of a wicked person, she found they gave off such a stench that she became physically ill. She reportedly undertook a mystical fast of extraordinary length at the end of her life, from Whitsunday on June 1, 1902, until the day she died. She would eat only the Blessed Sacrament.

Though she never officially was a Passionist, Gemma's remains are interred at the Passionist monastery at Lucca. She had accurately predicted it would be built two years after her death.

Beatified: 1933 by Pope Pius XI
Canonized: May 2, 1940, by Pope Pius XII
Feast: April 11
Patronage: pharmacists; tuberculosis sufferers

FURTHER READING
O'Sullivan, Fr. Paul. *All about the Angels.* Rockford, Ill.: Tan Books and Publishers, 1990; first published, 1945.

St. Gemma Galgani

George (d. ca. 303) *Martyr, one of the Fourteen Holy Helpers, patron saint of many countries*

St. George is considered to be one of the most illustrious martyrs in the Church, though most of what is known about him in various "Acts of St. George" is probably more legend than fact.

However, George was an historical figure. According to an account by Metaphrastes, he was born in Cappadocia (in modern Turkey) to a noble Christian family; his mother was Palestinian. After his father died, he went to live in Palestine with his mother. George became a soldier and was promoted to high rank by Emperor Diocletian. But when Diocletian began persecuting Christians, George went to him and protested. He was jailed and tortured at or near Lydda, also known as Diospolis. On the following day (April 23, probably the year 303), he was paraded through the streets and then beheaded. He was buried at Lydda.

George immediately became an important martyr in the churches of both East and West, and altars and

St. George with slain dragon (Engraving by Albrecht Dürer, n.d.)

The Golden Legend, translated into English by William Caxton, tells of St. George and the dragon, a story that probably dates to the 12th century. A monstrous dragon lived in the swamp near Silena, Lybia, and terrorized the countryside by bringing pestilence with its breath. To placate it, the townsfolk fed it two sheep every day. The dragon grew weary of sheep and started demanding human victims. Lots were drawn and no substitutes were allowed. One day the king's little daughter was marked as the next sacrifice. She was taken to the swamp. George came by, and when the dragon appeared he made the sign of the cross and stabbed it with his lance. He asked the maiden for her girdle and put it around the beast's neck. They led the dragon back to town. George exhorted the people to be baptized and have no fear; then he cut off the dragon's head. All the people were converted. George declined the king's offer of half his kingdom, saying he must ride on. He told the king to take care of the churches, honor the clergy and have pity on the poor.

Numerous religious and secular orders of St. George have existed throughout Europe and in Russia and England (despite the fact that the saint's cult was suppressed in Protestant England). As a Holy Helper, he was invoked for the protection of domestic animals during the plague.

In art, George is most often depicted as a knight on a horse lancing a dragon, the medieval symbol of evil.

Feast: April 23
Patronage: Boy Scouts; cavalry; farmers; soldiers; Aragón; England; Genoa; Germany; Portugal; Spain; Venice

FURTHER READING
Hammer, Fr. Bonaventure. *The Fourteen Holy Helpers.* Rockford, Ill.: TAN Books, 1995.

churches were built in his honor. The early pilgrims of the sixth to eighth centuries knew of Lydda as the seat of his veneration. Some Acts of St. George were in existence by the end of the fifth century.

During the Middle Ages, George became a patron of arms and chivalry in England, and the best-known image of George, as a dragon-slaying knight, was born. By the 11th century, his Acts had been translated into Anglo-Saxon, and churches were dedicated to him. He was invoked as a champion of the Crusades. The arms of St. George, a red cross on a white background, were carried into battle, and by the 14th century were used as an insignia on the uniforms of English soldiers and sailors. The red cross was incorporated into the Union Jack. In 1347, King Edward III founded the chivalric Order of the Garter, of which George was the principal patron. Edmund Spenser wrote of George in his *Faerie Queen* as the "Red Cross Knight."

Gerard Majella (1726–1755) *Disciple of St. Alphonsus Liguori and Redemptorist lay brother*
Also known as: the Wonder-Worker

Gerard Majella was born in April 1726 in Muro, south of Naples. His father, Dominic Majella, was a tailor, and died while Gerard was a child. Gerard's mother was forced to apprentice the child to a tailor, who treated him cruelly.

Gerard was attracted both to the priesthood and to suffering. He became the servant of a bishop. When the bishop died, he resumed work as a tailor. In 1745 he opened his own shop, and divided his earnings between his mother and the poor, and offerings for the souls in purgatory.

Gerard unsuccessfully tried to become a Franciscan, and then a hermit. In 1749 he became a Redemptorist and was professed by Alphonsus Liguori in 1752. In his vows, he promised to always do that which seemed to him to be more perfect. Though sickly, he obeyed all orders, performed his duties and was a model of virtue, much to the appreciation of Alphonsus. He also seemed to know the needs of others even when absent. Alphonsus declared him a saint.

Gerard accompanied the fathers on missions, and converted many to the faith. He desired to spend so much time in church that he had to do violence to himself to keep himself away. When a woman falsely accused him, he was defended by Alphonsus, and was sent to Naples and then Caposele. The woman then admitted she had lied. Gerard remained in Caposele raising funds. He died there of tuberculosis on October 15, 1755, at age 29. After his death, Gerard became a powerful intercessor, especially for expectant mothers.

During his short life, Gerard experienced many miracles and mystical experiences. He bilocated, and used his gift to spend more time in prayer, sometimes in ecstatic prayer. He fell into raptures and levitated before witnesses. On one occasion, he was seen to fly rapidly about one-quarter of a mile. He also could make himself invisible. He was often attacked and annoyed by demons, who left him bruised; he used holy water to heal the bruises.

Sometimes when he fell into ecstasy, rays of light shot from him, so bright that the very room he was in seemed to be on fire. His face and body glowed until he became like a sun.

He was often permeated with a heavenly odor. When he was dying, even his vomit smelled sweet.

One day while traveling along the Neapolitan seashore, he saw a ship in danger of capsizing in a sudden squall. While onlookers screamed, he made the sign of the cross and ordered the boat to pause in the name of the Most Holy. He took off his mantle, laid it on the water, walked to the ship and took hold of it and pulled it to safety. Gerard's explanation was that when God wills, all things are possible. He also controlled the elements and stopped torrential rain.

He had an amazing rapport with animals, and birds were attracted to him. On one occasion he slew mice. He met a poor farmer whose field was being ravaged by mice. Gerard asked him if he would like the mice to move or to die. The farmer said he wanted them to die. Gerard made the sign of the cross, and in moments the field was covered with dead and dying mice.

On numerous occasions, Gerard manifested money—after intense periods of prayer—for the poor and for church projects. He also multiplied food for the poor and for his brethren. He healed people, some-

St. Gerard Majella

times using dust from the tomb of St. Teresa of Avila to cure illness and prevent accidents.

He had the gift of prophecy, and knew when others would die. He predicted his own death six months in advance. He said he had prayed to die of tuberculosis, knowing that few would want to attend him, and he would die virtually abandoned. He predicted the day and hour of his death.

Gerard had the gift of mystical knowledge, and spontaneously said profound things at the right time. He knew the sins of others and could read souls and hearts. He knew when people had not confessed all they should, and sent them back to the confessional.

Posthumous miracles are recorded as well. In 1855, during his cause of beatification, Gerard's remains were exhumed. The head and bones oozed a perfumed oil or manna in such abundance that a basin overran with it. The manna was collected on handkerchiefs and linens and given to the sick, many of whom were healed. In 1892, the remains were exhumed again. The bones, found to be humid, were dried and placed in a casket.

Four hours later, they were found to be oozing a sweet, white oil. The oil never appeared again.

In 1895, two years after Gerard's beatification, people gathered at Caposele to celebrate his feast day. After delivery of a panegyric and prayer, three flashes like lightning illuminated the chapel containing the saint's tomb, the basilica of Materdomini.

Beatified: January 29, 1893, by Pope Leo XIII
Canonized: December 1904 by Pope Pius X
Feast: October 16
Patronage: childbirth; expectant mothers; the falsely accused

FURTHER READING
Gerard Majella: The Mother's Saint. League of Saint Gerard Staff. Liguori, Mo.: Liguori Publications.
Saint-Omer, Edward. *St. Gerard Majella.* Rockford, Ill.: TAN Books and Publishers, 1999.

Germanus I (d. 733 or 740) *Patriarch of Constantinople, Father of the Church*

Germanus was born to a patrician family; his father, Justinianus, held various high-level positions in the government. Germanus became a cleric at the cathedral, and some time after the death of his father was made bishop of Cyzicus.

Germanus opposed Monothelitism, which rejected the two wills of Christ, but was forced to accept it by Emperor Philippicus. Philippicus was dethroned in 713, and his successor, Anastasius, restored orthodoxy. In 715, Germanus was recognized as patriach by Pope Constantine (r. 708–715).

Germanus opposed Emperor Leo III the Isaurian in his support of Iconoclasm, and Leo sought to depose him. Germanus appealed to Pope Gregory II (r. 715–731). In 730 the pope summoned Germanus to a council and he was instructed to support the prohibition of the use of images in worship. Germanus refused and was forced to resign. He returned to the home of his family, where he died either in 733 or 740. In 787 the Council of Nicaea praised Germanus.

Feast: May 12

Gertrude the Great (ca. 1256–1302) *Benedictine mystic*
Name meaning: Spear-strength

Gertrude was born on January 6, 1256, near Eisleben in Saxony, Germany. Nothing is known of her parents, except that they were well-to-do. Gertrude was orphaned and at age five was placed in the Benedictine convent at Rodalsdorf, where she became a student of St. Mechtilde. She became a nun in the same monastery, and was elected abbess in 1251. The following year she took charge of the monastery at Helfta, to which she moved with her nuns.

Gertrude was such a devoted student that later she repented for neglecting her prayers in order to study more. She wrote and composed in Latin. She was especially devoted to the Sacred Heart, and wrote prayers with Mechtilde.

On January 27, 1281, Gertrude had her first vision of Christ, who appeared to her as a 16-year-old youth. The vision appeared as she raised her head from prayer at twilight. Christ told her that her salvation was near at hand, and he would welcome her tenderly. Thereafter for 20 years, Gertrude had at least one vision of Christ a day. He often urged her to come to him through his mother, the Blessed Virgin Mary, who would be her protector. Only once did the visions cease—during an 11-day period when he punished Gertrude for a "worldly" conversation.

Gertrude was so humble that she wished no outward manifestation of these visions, as she did not want to appear special.

After Mechtilde's death in 1298, one of the nuns received this revelation from Jesus: "I have done great things in Mechtilde, but I will accomplish still greater things in Gertrude."

Jesus bestowed seven graces upon her, and confirmed his promises by revealing his heart and telling her to extend her hands. When she withdrew them, she saw on one hand seven gold ringlets, one on each finger and three on the signet finger.

In visions, Gertrude saw Jesus also give his mother his Sacred Heart, and also kneel down before her. She also had numerous visions of Mary. Once Gertrude prayed to Mary, asking her to fill her heart with virtues. In a vision, Mary came and planted in Gertrude's heart symbolic flowers: the rose of chastity, the lily of purity, the violet of humility, the sunflower of obedience, and others.

Gertrude also saw Mary appear in the presence of the Holy Trinity. In another vision on the Feast of the Assumption, she saw Mary invite her to take her place on the heavenly throne, explaining that she could offer Gertrude's merits to God for the privilege. Mary ascended to heaven, conducted by Jesus and amidst rejoicing saints and angels.

Gertrude died in Hefta on November 17, 1302. According to lore, Mary came and supported her during her dying, and helped her soul to heaven. She was buried alongside Mechtilde. In 1342, the monastery was transferred to New Helfta inside the city walls of Eisleben, but there is no record of any translation of the relics and remains of the two saints.

The death of Gertrude the Great (Library of Congress Prints and Photographs Division)

Many of Gertrude's writings are lost. Extant are *Legatus Divinae Pietatis* (Herald of divine love), *Exercises of St. Gertrude,* and the *Liber Specialis Gratiae* (Book of special grace) of *St. Mechtilde,* all written in Latin. Her mysticism is that of all the great contemplative workers of the Benedictine Order.

Legatus Divinae Pietatis comprises five books containing her life story and accounts of many of the favors granted her by God. Only book two of the five is her work, with the remainder being compiled by members of the Helfta community. The seven "Exercises" range from the work of the reception of baptismal grace to the preparation for death. Gertrude exhibits a profound knowledge and understanding of liturgy and Scripture, and uses rich symbolism and allegory to convey her message. Central to her work is her devotion to the Sacred Heart.

The superiors of Helfta appointed renowned Dominican and Franciscan theologians to examine the works of Gertrude. Her writings were approved and propagated. St. Teresa of Avila chose Gertrude as her mentor and guide, and Gertrude's works were favorably viewed and recommended by SS. John of the Cross and Francis de Sales.

Gertrude never was canonized, but in 1677 her name was inscribed in the Roman Martyrology, and Pope Clement XII (r. 1730–40) decreed that her feast should be observed by the entire Church. In art she is depicted as an abbess, sometimes with a mouse and sometimes holding a flaming heart. She is considered to be the forerunner of St. Margaret Mary Alacoque in devotion to the Sacred Heart and is the only woman saint to be called "Great."

The seven mystical rings are commemorated by the Church in St. Gertrude's Office, in the third antiphon at Lauds: "My Lord Jesus has espoused me to Him with seven rings, and crowned me as a bride."

Gertrude is especially invoked for living sinners and souls in purgatory. In a vision, Jesus had told her that a certain prayer would release 1,000 souls from purgatory each time it is said. The prayer was extended to include living sinners as well:

"Eternal Father, I offer Thee the Most Precious Blood of Thy Divine Son, Jesus, in union with the Masses said throughout the world today, for all the Holy Souls in Purgatory, for sinners everywhere, for sinners in the universal church, those in my own home and within my family. Amen."

Feast: November 16
Patronage: against rats; West Indies

FURTHER READING
Brown, Raphael. *Saints Who Saw Mary.* Rockford, Ill.: TAN Books, 1955.
Gertrude of Helfta: The Herald of Divine Love. Margaret Winkworth, ed. Mahwah, N.J.: Paulist Press, 1993.

Gleb   See BORIS AND GLEB.

Gorgonia (d. ca. 370–373) *Daughter of SS. Gregory of Nazianzus and Nonna, sister of SS. Gregory of Nazianzus the Younger and Caesarius*

Most of what is known about Gorgonia comes from the eloquent funeral oration for her delivered by Gregory of Nazianzus the Younger. Gregory described her as a model of piety and morals who was generous to the poor. She was married and had children, and the sole wealth she left them was "the imitation of her example, and emulation of her merits."

Gregory described how on more than one occasion she was remarkably healed by her intense faith. Once her mules went wild with her carriage and overturned it. She was dragged and so badly injured that others thought she would die. She refused all medical help and relied upon the will of God. On another occasion, she fell seriously ill with "an extraordinary and malignant disease" that left her fevered, paralyzed and even comatose. From this she seemingly miraculously recovered.

Gorgonia was told by God when she would die. She made her preparations, went to bed, and passed away, surrounded by her family and friends. Her last words were, "I will lay me down in peace, and take my rest."

Feast: December 9

FURTHER READING
"Gregory Nazianzus: On His Sister Gorgonia." URL: http://www.fordham.edu/halsall/basis/gregnaz-gornogia.html. Downloaded: September 24, 2000.

Gregory I (540–604) *Pope, Father of the Church, Doctor of the Church*
Also known as: Gregory the Great

Gregory I is one of only two popes called "the Great"; the other is Pope Leo I (r. 440–461). Gregory was the first monk to become pope. His reign is distinguished by his statesmanship, his writings, and his encouragement of the monasteries, as well as his miracles. He is considered one of the four great Latin fathers of the Church.

Gregory was born in 540 in Rome to a patrician family. His father, Gordianus, owned large estates in Sicily. His mother, Silvia, is recognized as a saint, and two of his aunts, Tarsilla and Aemilians (Emiliana), were canonized.

Little is known of his early years. He was drawn to the religious life and spent long hours meditating on the Scriptures. In 573 he became the prefect of Rome, but a year later abandoned the job to become a monk. He turned his home into a monastery under the patronage of St. Andrew, and turned his six Sicilian estates into monasteries. For about three years, Gregory lived in happy retirement from the world, probably following the Rule of Benedict, and practicing severe austerities that weakened his health for the rest of his life. He suffered chronic gastrointestinal problems and a "slow fever."

In 579, with the Lombards threatening Rome, Pope Pelagius II (r. 579–590) sent Gregory to Constantinople to be permanent ambassador to the court of Byzantium. Several of Gregory's brothers from St. Andrew's went with him. Gregory disliked court life and, with his fellow monks, adhered to monastic life as much as possible. During the six years he was in Constantinople, Gregory played the key role in suppressing a heresy by Eutychius, the patriarch of Constantinople, that held that Christ's risen body had no substance, but would be "more light than air." Gregory and Eutychius engaged in such a battle that the health of both was impaired. The emperor supported Gregory and ordered Eutychius's book to be burned. Crushed and in failing health, Eutychius took to his deathbed, recanting his error just before he expired.

Gregory was recalled to Rome in 585 or 586. He returned to St. Andrew's and became abbot. He wrote and preached, and his reputation grew. After meeting some pagan Englishmen (or boys), Gregory was inspired to evangelize in Britain. The English were either men visiting Rome, or, according to the Venerable Bede, young boys being sold in Rome as slaves.

Pope Pelagius II granted Gregory permission to go to Britain, but the Roman people, with whom he was supremely popular, demanded his return. Gregory was stopped in mid-journey and recalled. Back in Rome, he served as the pope's chief adviser and assistant.

In 590, Pelagius II died on the heels of two years of flood, famine and disease. Gregory was immediately

St. Gregory the Great (Library of Congress Prints and Photographs Division)

elected his successor. He attempted to demur, but Emperor Maurice confirmed the election. Gregory thought about fleeing, but he was seized and brought to St. Peter's Basilica and was confirmed on September 3, 590.

For the next 14 years, Gregory kept an exhausting schedule of administrative duties and writing. He preached to huge crowds. He expanded the power and authority of his office and established it on an equal footing with the imperial government. He expanded the Church's missionary efforts throughout the world, including Britain; he is recorded in the Venerable Bede's *Ecclesiastical History of the English People.* He supported the monasteries, enforced discipline, and encouraged the wealthy to establish more monasteries. Personally, he lived as simply as possible.

During his last years, Gregory suffered deteriorating health and depression. He died on March 12, 604, and was buried the same day in St. Peter's Basilica. He was canonized by popular acclaim immediately. His relics were moved several times, the last occurring in 1606 when Pope Paul V (r. 1605–21) moved them to the chapel of Pope Clement V (r. 1305–14).

In art he is shown dressed as a pope with tiara, carrying the double-barred cross. Sometimes he is shown seated at a desk or at an altar; a dove also is sometimes shown with him.

Among Gregory's most important works are the *Liber Regulae Pastoralis* (Book of pastoral rules), guidelines of religious practice; four *Dialogues,* collections of saints' lives and their miracles; the *Magna Moralis,* a mystical commentary on the Book of Job; and homilies. Of his letters, 850 are extant.

Gregory is credited with creating Gregorian chant, a form of musical worship with Jewish, Palestinian and Syrian roots. Gregory ordered this music to be collected and preserved. Gregorian chant grew over the centuries and now numbers about 3,000 chants.

Numerous miracles are attributed to Gregory. Best known is the story of his writing of his homilies on Ezekiel, around 593. He dictated to a secretary, who was seated on the other side of a veil. He would remain silent for long periods of time. Once during one of these silences, the curious secretary made a hole in the veil and peeked through. He saw a white dove seated upon the pope's head with its beak between his lips. When the dove withdrew its beak, the pope began to speak. During another silence, the secretary again saw the dove with its beak between the pope's lips.

Another story from tradition involves a woman at Communion who did not believe in the host as the true body of Christ, for she had made the bread herself. Gregory placed the bread upon the altar, and it began to bleed.

Feast: September 3
Patronage: musicians; popes; singers; teachers

FURTHER READING
Bede. "Gregory the Great" in *Ecclesiastical History of the English Nation.* URL: http://www.fordham.edu/halsall/source/bede-greggrea.html. Downloaded: September 23, 2000.
"The Earliest Life of St. Gregory the Great by a Monk or Nun at Whitby, A.D. 713." URL: http://www.umilta.net/gregory.html. Downloaded: September 23, 2000.

Gregory II (ca. 669–731) *Pope*
Also known as: Dialogus, Gregory the Lesser, Gregory Junior

Gregory was born about 669 to Marcellus and Honesta, Roman nobles. While very young he showed an interest in the Church and was placed by the pope in the *schola cantorum,* the choir school. He became a Benedictine monk. Pope St. Sergius I (r. 687–701) made him a subdeacon and appointed him *sacellarius* (almoner and treasurer) of the Roman Church. Later he also became its librarian, and has the distinction of being the first known papal almoner or librarian.

In 710, Gregory, now a deacon, accompanied Pope Constantine (r. 708–715) to Constantinople to protest the anti-Western canons of the Second Quintisext (Trullan) Council. He distinguished himself in his replies to Emperor Justinian II and helped to secure Justinian's acceptance of papal supremacy. The two returned to Rome in 711.

Constantine died in 715, and on May 19 of that year, Gregory was elected his successor. One of his first official actions was to repair the walls of Rome as a defense against the Muslims, who were then in control of much of the Mediterranean. In 716, Gregory peacefully regained papal territory from the Lombards, and when their king Liutprand threatened to invade Rome in 729, Gregory dissuaded him.

Although Gregory acknowledged allegiance to the Greek emperor Leo III the Isaurian (Leo the Iconoclast), he opposed Leo's illegal taxation of the Italians, and demanded that Leo stop interfering in Church matters. He rebuked Leo severely at a synod in Rome in 727, proclaiming the true doctrine on the matter of the worship of images. In return, Leo plotted (unsuccessfully) to have him killed.

During his pontificate, Gregory received several distinguished pilgrims—including the Anglo-Saxons, Abbot Ceolfrid and King Ina, the latter of whom became a monk in Rome in 726—and in 719 sent SS. Corbibian and Winfrid (or Boniface) as missionaries to Germany. In 722, he consecrated St. Winfrid bishop and interested the great Frankish chief Charles Martel in his work. Gregory also assisted St. Nothelm in his researches in the papal archives to provide material for St. Bede's *Ecclesiastical History.*

Gregory was a great supporter of the monastic order. On his mother's death, he followed his papal namesake, Gregory I (Gregory the Great, r. 590–604), in converting his family mansion into a monastery. He also founded or restored many others monasteries, including the abbey of Monte Cassino, which had been destroyed by Lombards 150 years before.

Gregory is regarded as the greatest of the great eighth-century popes. His Western contemporaries called him Gregory the Younger or Gregory Junior, while those in the East, who confused him with Gregory I, author of the "Dialogues," knew him as "Dialogus."

Gregory died of natural causes on February 11, 731, and was buried in St. Peter's. He is honored as a saint in the Roman and other martyrologies.

Feast: February 11 (sometimes February 13)

Gregory III (d. 741) *Pope*

Gregory's date of birth is not known. The son of a Syrian named John, he became a priest in Rome, earning a reputation for holiness and learning. So great was his following that he was elected pope by acclamation, as he was accompanying the funeral procession of his predecessor, St. Gregory II (r. 715–731), on February 11, 731. He was not consecrated for another month, however, as he awaited confirmation from the exarch at Ravenna.

Gregory continued his predecessor's opposition to Iconoclasm and in 731 convened two councils in Rome, both of which condemned the image-breaking heresy. He paid particular attention to images and relics, especially those of St. Peter the Apostle, and built a special oratory in the Vatican basilica of St. Peter's to honor them. In response, Emperor Leo the Iconoclast seized papal properties in Calabria and Sicily and transferred ecclesiastical jurisdiction over those two provinces (and Illyrium) to the patriarch of Constantinople, long a rival to the pope in Rome.

Gregory also followed his predecessor in supporting the missionary activities of St. Boniface in Germany, sending St. Willibald to assist him.

The end of Gregory's pontificate was largely concerned with preventing the Lombards from once again sacking Rome. He completed the rebuilding of the city walls, a task begun by Gregory II, and took other precautions, including enlisting the assistance of the Frankish king Charles Martel. This last decision was to have far-reaching consequences for the meddling of the state in church affairs.

Gregory died in November or December 741, in the midst of the Lombard campaign. He was buried in the oratory of Our Lady which he had had built in St. Peter's.

Feast: December 10 (formerly November 28)

Gregory VII (ca. 1021–1085) *Pope*
Also known as: Hildebrand, Holy Satan

Gregory was highly influential in the Roman Church even before his elevation to the papacy. He was largely responsible for changing the rules for selecting popes from election by all the Christians of Rome to election by the College of Cardinals. The widespread reforms he instituted during his own reign won him the perverse epithet, "Holy Satan." However, he is recognized today as one of the greatest popes of the Middle Ages.

Gregory was born in Ravaco, near Saona, in Tuscany, Italy, around 1021. His father was a poor peasant, perhaps a carpenter, named Bonizo. He was baptized Hildebrand (Hellebrand). While still a youth, he was placed in the care of his uncle Laurentius, superior of the monastery of Santa Maria in Rome. He joined the Benedictine order and was educated at the Lateran Palace school, where one of his teachers was John Gratian, the future pope (or antipope) Gregory VI (r. 1045–46).

When Gratian was elected pope in May 1045, he made Hildebrand his secretary, and when he was deposed the following December, Hildebrand followed him into exile in Cologne, Germany. After Gratian died in 1047, Hildebrand moved to Cluny, where he resumed the monastic life. It was there, in January 1049, that he met Bruno, Bishop of Toul, then recently elected Pope St. Leo IX (r. 1049–54), who took him back to Rome.

Leo created Hildebrand a cardinal-subdeacon and made him administrator of the Patrimony of St. Peter's. Under Hildebrand's leadership, much Church property was recovered and the revenues of the Holy See increased. Leo then appointed him propositus of the monastery of St. Paul-Outside-the-Walls, which had lost much of its monastic discipline. Women attended the monks in its refectory, and sheep and cattle roamed freely through the broken doors of its sacred buildings. Under Hildebrand's direction, the monastery's austerity was restored.

In 1054, Leo sent Hildebrand as his legate to the Council of Sens. He was still in France when news came of Leo's death, and he hurried back to Rome. There was talk of electing him pope, but he worked to secure the election of Victor II (r. 1055–57) instead. Under Victor, Hildebrand continued to work behind the scenes. After Victor, he was instrumental in the elevation of Popes Stephen (r. 1057–58) and Nicholas II (r. 1058–61). During Nicholas's reign, he engineered the papal decree overturning the traditional manner of electing popes and mandating the College of Cardinals as the electoral body. He was also responsible for negotiating the 1059 Treaty of Melfi, which allied the Roman Church with the Normans. Alexander made him archdeacon and appointed him chancellor of the Apostolic See.

When Alexander died in June 1073, Hildebrand himself was elected pope by an overwhelming majority. He was consecrated on June 30, took the name Gregory VII, and immediately set about his widest reforms to date. He convened councils in Rome in 1074 and 1075 at which he enacted decrees against married clergy, simony and the royal investiture of bishops and abbeys. A council convened in Paris in response declared the decrees to be intolerable, but Gregory enforced them through depositions and excommunications.

Gregory's reforms made him many enemies and found a varied response in Europe. The most intractable region turned out to be Germany, then under the rule of Henry IV. Henry had Gregory kidnapped by Roman nobles while he was celebrating a Christmas Eve midnight Mass in St. Mary Major's, and he was held for several hours before being rescued by parishioners.

This was only the beginning, however, for Henry tried to have Gregory deposed, whereupon Gregory excommunicated Henry. Gregory lifted the excommunication when Henry repented, but reinstated it in 1080 when Henry reneged on his promises. Henry then invaded Italy and attacked Rome, taking it in 1084 and forcing Gregory to take refuge in the Castle Sant' Angelo. Henry demanded that Gregory crown him emperor, but when the pope refused, Henry thew his support behind Guibert, archbishop of Ravenna. Guibert was duly consecrated as antipope Clement III, and in turn crowned Henry.

Gregory remained at Sant' Angelo until he was rescued by Robert Guiscard, the Norman duke of Calabria, whom he had summoned to his aid. Unfortunately, in retaking Rome from Henry, the Normans sacked the city, which added to Gregory's growing unpopularity, since he was seen as responsible for the pillaging. He fled to Monte Cassino and then to Salerno, having been abandoned by 13 of his cardinals.

Gregory's health began to decline and he died in Salerno on May 25, 1085. On his deathbed, he forgave his enemies and withdrew all his censures and excommunications except those against Henry and Guibert. His body was interred in the church of St. Matthew at Salerno.

In art, Gregory is shown as a pope holding a book and ring or with the Virgin and Child, from whom a ray of light shines and pierces his heart, while a dove rests on his shoulder. He has also been depicted being driven from Rome by soldiers.

Canonized: 1606 by Pope Paul V
Feast: May 25

Gregory X (1201–1276) *Pope*

Gregory was born in 1201 in Piacenza, Italy, as Theobald Visconti. He was archdeacon of Liège, though not yet ordained a priest, when he was elected to succeed Pope Clement IV (r. 1265–68) on September 1, 1271. The Holy See had then been vacant three years due to disagreements among French and Italian cardinals, and Theobald was a compromise candidate who did not even know that he was in the running. He was on a pilgrimage to the Holy Land when news came of his election, and he hurried to Viterbo, where the cardinals were meeting, arriving there in February 1271. He made his entrance into Rome on March 13. On March 19 he was ordained a priest and on March 27 he was consecrated in the Chair of St. Peter, assuming the name Gregory X.

Gregory is best remembered for convoking the 14th General Council at Lyons in 1274, which approved a new crusade to retake possession of Christian sites in the Holy Land from the Muslims, a decision that prepared the way for reconciliation between the Roman Catholic and Eastern Churches. However, although money was raised for the crusade, it proved impossible to bring it off, and the schism between East and West in the end went unbridged.

Gregory died in Arezzo (Rezzo) on January 10, 1276, on his way back from Lyons. He is honored as a saint in Rome and in several dioceses. Pope Benedict XIV (r. 1740–58) added his name to the Roman Martyrology.

Beatified: 1713 by Pope Clement XI
Feast: January 10 (formerly February 16)

Gregory of Elvira (d. ca. 392) *Bishop of Elvira; Father of the Church*

Gregory Bæticus was born in the Spanish province of Baetica (hence his surname). He supported the Nicene Creed at the Council of Rimini in 359, and was then and later a strong supporter of Roman Catholic Christianity in its battle with the Arian heresy. He was considered the head of the anti-Arian movement in Spain. By 375, he ruled as bishop of Elvira (Illibrius), now in the diocese of Granada.

Feast: April 24

Gregory the Illuminator (257?–337?) *National saint and patron of Armenia, the first Christian state*
Also known as: the Apostle of Armenia

Gregory was brought up in a Christian family in Caesarea, Cappadocia (in modern Turkey). He married and had two sons. According to tradition, Christianity had been brought to Armenia by the apostles Bartholomew and Thaddeus. The Persians overtook the country and destroyed the churches, but eventually were driven out by King Trdat.

Trdat, a defender of the old Armenian religion, persecuted Gregory but was converted by him. The two evangelized the country and Trdat made Christianity the national religion. Gregory returned to Caesarea to be ordained, and was made bishop of the Armenians. He went to Ashishat to live, and there preached to the masses. Toward the end of his life, he retired and was succeeded by his son, Aristakes. The date of his death is uncertain, but probably was around 337. His relics were deposed in Thortan.

An embellished legend of his life and trials tells of Gregory being thrown into a poisonous pit by Trdat, and coming out alive thanks to prayer. He fasted 70 days, and had many adventures defeating the pagans throughout the land.

Feast: October 1

Gregory of Nazianzus (ca. 325–389 or 390) *Father of the Church; Doctor of the Church*
Also known as: Gregory the Theologian, Gregory the Divine

Gregory Nazianzus was born ca. 325 in Arianzus, Asia Minor, to a wealthy family. His father, St. Gregory of Nazianzus the Elder, and his mother, St. Nonna, were converts to Christianity; his father was bishop of Nazianzus and his sister was St. Gorgonia. Gregory and his brother Caesarius were sent to a school in Caesarea in Cappadocia (in modern Turkey) headed by Carterius, later a tutor to St. John Chrysostom. At school Gregory met Basil and formed a lasting and influential friendship with him. Gregory continued his studies in Palestine, where he learned rhetoric under Thespesius, and in Alexandria, where St. Athanasius was bishop in exile. Going on to Athens, Gregory reunited with Basil, and the two studied rhetoric under Himerius and Proaeresius, two famous teachers. Gregory remained in Athens for about 10 years, and left at age 30 to return home via Constantinople.

In Nazianzus, Gregory was undecided whether to pursue a career in law or rhetoric, or to enter a monastic life. He consulted Basil, and for two or three years joined his friend in a monastic community that Basil established at Neocaesarea in Pontus. He helped Basil to compile his rule.

In 361 Gregory returned home to find a heretical father. He steered him back to orthodoxy, but was ordained a priest only at the behest of his father and against his own wishes. During the next several years, Basil was embroiled in political maneuverings with Emperor Valens, and established a new see at Sasima. He asked Gregory to become his first bishop there. Gregory agreed, but disliked the job and soon left it to return to Nazianzus and become coadjutor to his father. As a result, a permanent rift was created in his friendship with Basil.

Gregory's parents died in 374. He gave away most of his inheritance to the poor, keeping for himself only a small plot of land. He declined to succeed his father as bishop, and in 375 withdrew to a monastery in Seleuci to live in solitude for three years. Basil died in 379, but Gregory's poor health prevented him from going to his friend or attending the funeral. He wrote poems commemorating the saint.

The same year, Gregory found his monastic peace shattered by politics. Theodosius was named the Eastern emperor, and he prevailed upon Gregory to come to Constantinople and campaign against the heretics there. Gregory established the Anatasia, a chapel in a private home, where he developed and delivered some of his greatest oratorical works in the face of hostile persecution.

In 380, Theodosius banished the Arian bishop of Constantinople and placed Gregory in his stead. But a few months later in 381, Gregory was opposed by a general council of bishops. He resigned in June 381 and returned to Nazianzus. There he found the Church in poor condition, and reluctantly took over its administration. Poor health forced him to leave, and he went to Arianzus to spend the rest of his life in retirement at the tiny piece of land he had retained from his inheritance.

During his last years, Gregory produced most of his poetical works. The date of his death is not known, but probably falls in 389 or 390. He was buried in his family vault; his body is said to have given off a sweet odor.

St. Jerome, who was influenced by Gregory, said that the saint wrote 30,000 verses of poetry. If the figure is accurate, only about one-third have survived. Gregory also composed numerous epistles, sermons and orations. Of his orations, best-known are his five "Theological Discourses" written while in Constantinople. He is called one of the three "Cappadocian Fathers," with SS. Basil the Great and Gregory of Nyssa.

FURTHER READING
The Fathers Speak: St. Basil the Great, St. Gregory Nazianzus, St. Gregory of Nyssa. Tr. Georges Barrois. Crestwood, N.Y.: St. Vladimir's Seminary Press, 1986.

Gregory of Nazianzus the Elder (276–374) *Bishop of Nazianzus and father of St. Gregory of Nazianzus*

Gregory the Elder was born in 276 in Nazianzus, Cappadocia (in modern Turkey), and was a contemporary of SS. Basil the Great and Gregory of Nyssa. He was a member of the Hypsistarri (or Hypsistiani) heretical sect. His wife, St. Nonna, converted him to Christianity. All three of the couple's children—sons Gregory and Caesarius and daughter Gorgonia—became saints. The family was wealthy and owned much land.

Gregory was consecrated bishop in 328. He fell under the influence of the heretical creed of Rimini, and was brought back into orthodoxy by son Gregory in 361. He died in 374.

Feast: January 1

Gregory of Nyssa (d. after 385 or 386) *Bishop of Nyssa; Father of the Church; brother of SS. Basil the Great, Macrina the Younger and Peter of Sebaste*

Gregory was born in Caesaria, Cappadocia (in modern Turkey); some sources place his birth ca. 335. He was influenced by his older brother Basil, who steered him toward the religious life. As a youth Gregory served as rector. He met with Basil's strong disapproval when he began studying for a career in rhetoric. At some point he married a woman named Theosebia. After his appointment as bishop, Gregory continued to live with her but as a sister; at an unknown time she died.

Basil at last prevailed with Gregory and consecrated him bishop of Nyssa, near Caesarea, around 371. But he was disappointed in his younger brother's administrative ability, which was not as good as his own.

Gregory had enemies in Nyssa, and was accused of wasting church property and other crimes. He was arrested, and in 376 a synod of Nyssa deposed him. In 378, the new emperor, Gratian, restored him to his bishopric and issued an edict of tolerance for the Christians.

Gregory's reputation as one of the greatest theologians in the Eastern Church was earned for his opposition to the Arian heresy, and for his orthodoxy. He was named bishop of Sebaste in 380 (against his wishes) and in 381 he was among the orthodox leaders at the Council of Constantinople. He also distinguished himself as an orator.

Gregory died sometime after 385 or 386; some sources place his death at 395.

Gregory wrote numerous treatises on the Scriptures, and produced works on theology and the ascetic life. His *Catechesis* defends Catholic teaching. He defended Basil against the heretic Eunomius, and defended the Nicene Creed against Arianism. His *De anima et ressurectione* (Life and resurrection) is a dialogue between Gregory and his dead sister Macrina about death and resurrection. He is called one of the three "Cappodocian Fathers," with Basil and St. Gregory of Nazianzus.

Among Gregory's ascetic works on Christian life are *On Perfection, On Virginity* and *On the Meaning of the Christian Name or Profession.* Many of his sermons and homilies, and 22 of his letters, are extant.

Feast: May 9

FURTHER READING
The Fathers Speak: St. Basil the Great, St. Gregory Nazianzus, St. Gregory of Nyssa. Tr. Georges Barrois. Crestwood, N.Y.: St. Vladimir's Seminary Press, 1986.
Nicene and Post-Nicene Fathers, Series 2: Gregory of Nyssa. Vol. 5. Philip Schaff and Henry Wace, eds. Grand Rapids, Mich.: William B. Eerdmans Publishing Co., 1994.

Gregory Palamas (ca. 1296–1359) *Athonite monk and archbishop of Thessalonica*

Gregory of Palamas was born ca. 1296 to a noble Anatolian family, probably in Constantinople. After his father died, he and two of his brothers became monks, and his mother, two of his sisters and several servants became nuns. Gregory entered a monastery on Mt. Athos and followed the Rule of St. Basil, living in solitude for most of the next 20 years.

In the 1330s, he began to defend the *hesychast* practice, centered on a method of prayer used by monks in Byzantine monasticism—possibly linked to Buddhist techniques—that involved controlled breathing and posture to induce a vision of light, often compared to the light seen at Jesus' transfiguration on Mt. Tabor. Hesychast comes from *hesychia,* which means "stillness" or "light." Opponents of hesychasm denied that the light of Tabor, which hesychasts experienced, was the uncreated light of the Godhead.

The breathing techniques to experience this uncreated light were dangerous, and if done improperly or done to excess, could cause physical and mental damage.

Gregory's defense of the reality of the monk's prayer experience was called Palamism. He maintained that though God had an unknowable essence, the energies of God's grace—a part of God—were knowable. Thus God could be experienced through sacraments and mystical experience. This was made possible by the incarnation of Christ. Palamism contrasted with Catholic theology, which maintains that God is ineffable and cannot truly be experienced.

Hesychast, prayer, or Palamism, created controversy and conflict that drew in lay people and became quite political. A hesychasm party formed. The 1341 Council of Constantinople upheld Gregory's teachings, and Palamism was officially adopted by the Orthodox Church.

Gregory, however, was excommunicated in 1344. In 1347, he was consecrated bishop of Thessalonica, an appointment that required the aid of the Byzantine emperor, due to the controversy over Palamism. Gregory worked diligently to reconcile deep social and political divisions.

In 1354, invading Turks captured Gregory and held him prisoner for a year. He died in 1359.

Gregory left behind a large body of works, several of which are included in *The Philokalia* compilation. He is considered one of the great spiritual masters of Orthodox Christianity.

FURTHER READING
"Hesychasm: Selected Readings." Introduction by Paul Halsall. URL: http://www.fordham.edu/halsall/source/hesychasm1.html. Downloaded: September 24, 2000.

St. Gregory Palamas, "A Homily on the Dormition of Our Supremely Pure Lady Theotokos and Ever-Virgin Mary." URL: http://www.ocf.org/OrthodoxPage/reading/dormition.html. Downloaded: September 24, 2000.
The Philokalia: The Complete Text Compiled by St. Nikodimos of the Holy Mountain and St. Makarios of Corinth. Vol. 4. Tr. G.E.H. Palmer, Philip Sherrard and Kallistos Ware. London: Faber and Faber Ltd., 1995.

Gregory Thaumaturgus (213–270 or 275) *Bishop of Neocaesarea renowned for his miracles, Father of the Church*
Also known as: Gregory Thaumaturgos; Gregory the Wonder-Worker; Gregory of Neocaesarea

Much of what is known about Gregory Thaumaturgus comes from a *Life* written by St. Gregory of Nyssa and delivered on the saint's feast day, November 17, in 380. Gregory of Nyssa obtained much of the information from his grandmother, St. Macrina the Elder, who was schooled in the tradition of Gregory Thaumaturgus.

Gregory was born at Neocaesarea, Pontus (also Pontos), now in modern Turkey, to a distinguished pagan family in 213. He was named Theodore ("the gift of God"). His father died when he was about 14. About 233, he and his brother Athenodorus set out for Beirut to study law there. They were accompanied by their sister, who was joining her husband in Caesarea, Palestine.

In Caesarea they met Origen, head of a famous catechetical school there, and decided to enter it to pursue the study of theology instead of law. Origen converted them, and they became his disciples. Gregory received his Christian name at his baptism by Origen.

Origen encouraged his pupils to study all the great philosophical works, including pagan, but not atheist. The broad teachings created the foundation of Gregory's religious and philosophical life.

The brothers returned to Neocaesarea in 238 or 239. According to Gregory of Nyssa, Gregory spent some time in solitude. He was elected bishop by the 17 Christians of the city (interestingly, by the time of Gregory's death there were but 17 pagans remaining in Neocaesarea).

After his election, Gregory had the first recorded dream or vision of St. John, who appeared in the form of an old man accompanied by the Blessed Virgin Mary. Gregory was told that Mary had requested John to reveal the mystery of truth. The radiance around the figures was so brilliant that Gregory could not look upon them. He heard the voices of other learned men speaking to him about truth. Mary told him to immediately write down the revelation and proclaim it in the church. St. John then dictated a creed of Christian faith pertaining to the eternal existence of the Trinity.

Gregory took a great deal of inspiration and courage from this vision. He proved to be a charismatic and eloquent figure, and also gifted with miraculous powers. He became known as Gregory Thaumaturgus ("the wonderworker"). His words, wisdom and miracles won over many converts. He built a church and dispensed advice to many.

In 250, during the Decian persecution, Gregory and his flock fled to the desert. Upon their return, they had to deal with plague and attacks by the Goths in 252–254. In 264–265 Gregory participated in the synod of Antioch, Turkey. He argued against Sabellianism and Tritheism.

Among Gregory's important writings are *Oratio Panegyrica,* an enthusiastic and admiring homage to Origen; *Exposition of the Faith,* in which he asserts his orthodox views about the Trinity; *Epostola Canonica;* and a dissertation addressed to Theopompus concerning the passibility and impassibility of God.

Gregory died in Neocaesarea in 270 or 275. He is invoked against floods and earthquakes. In 1969 his feast was confined to specific calendars.

In his *Life of Gregory Thaumaturgus,* Gregory of Nyssa gives accounts of some of the saint's miracles. Some undoubtedly are of a legendary nature, intended to enhance the saint's reputation. Nonetheless, Gregory did possess remarkable abilities. He healed the sick and vanquished demons. He converted a pagan temple keeper by moving, through the power of faith, a huge stone. When flood waters threatened Neocaesarea, he struck his staff into the river banks; it turned into a tree and checked the flow of flood waters. When a heckler accused him of being under demonic influence, Gregory blew upon him and caused the heckler to become temporarily possessed. He then healed the young man.

Gregory's miracles continued after death. According to Gregory of Nyssa, an earthquake damaged most of the city but left Gregory Thaumaturgus's church untouched. It is likely that the saint was buried there.

Feast: November 17
Patronage: against earthquakes; against floods

FURTHER READING

Gregory of Nyssa. *Life of Gregory Thaumaturgus.* URL: http://www.sp.uconn.edu/~salomon/nyssa/thaum.html. Downloaded: September 26, 2000.

Origen, "On Classical Learning." Letter to Gregory Thaumaturgus. URL: http://www.fordham.edu/halsall/source/origen1.html. Downloaded: September 24, 2000.

Gregory of Tours (538 or 539–593 or 594) *Bishop and historian*

Gregory was born in Tours in 538 or 539 to an illustrious family with ties to the great houses of Gaul. He was named Georgius Florentius, but later took the name Gregory in memory of his maternal great-grandfather, who was the bishop of Langres.

Gregory's father died when he was young, and he was sent to be educated by his uncle Gallus, bishop of Clermont. A serious illness convinced him to serve the Church. After Gallus died in 554, he was turned over to Avitus, a priest who later became the bishop of Clermont.

In 573 Gregory was named bishop of Tours by King Sigebert I, and he went to Rome to be consecrated. In his role as bishop, Gregory was faced with almost constant civil war. He increased the number of churches and attended to the suffering of the people, all the while managing to stay out of politics.

Gregory began his career as an historian during his episcopate. He was fascinated by the lives and miracles and intercession of the fathers, saints and martyrs, subjects on which he wrote numerous books. He is perhaps best-known for his 10-volume *Historia Francorum,* an early Frankish history beginning with Adam, and for his three books on the life and miracles of St. Martin of Tours. A fourth book was never completed. Other notable works are *De Vitae Patribus* (Lives of the fathers) and *Gloriam Martyrum* (Book of the glories of the martyrs), about the miracles of the martyrs in Gaul during Roman persecutions. Gregory put his theology into the introductions of his books, and wrote only one purely theological work, *De cursu stellarum ratio* (On the courses of the stars), which discusses using the stars to set the proper time for the singing of the night office.

Gregory died in Tours on November 17, 593, or 594.

Feast: November 17

Helena (d. ca. 326–328) *Empress, mother of Constantine the Great*
Also known as: Helen of the Cross

Helena, a native of Turkey, married Constantius I Chlorus, a Roman general who reigned as junior emperor from 293 to 306. The marriage took place in 270, and a son, Constantine, was born soon thereafter. After his elevation to caesar, Constantius was required to divorce Helena, a woman of a lower class than he, and marry Theodora, the stepdaughter of co-emperor Maximian (r. 286–305).

Son Constantine became a junior emperor upon the death of his father in 306. In 312, he won a major military victory over Maximian and became emperor. Helena was named empress.

Helena converted to Christianity and was renowned for her charity and building of churches. She went on a pilgrimage to the Holy Land—by some accounts when she was nearly 80 years old—in search of the holy cross. In excavations, three crosses were discovered, including one that seemed to be the "true cross." Hence in art she is often shown holding a cross.

Helena died probably in Nicomedia (in modern Turkey). Her sarcophagus is in the Vatican Museum.

Feast: August 18
Patronage: converts; against divorce; empresses

Henry Suso, Blessed (ca. 1295–1366) *Dominican mystic, preacher, poet and author*
Also known as: Amandus

Henry Suso was born Heinrich von Berg in Constance, Swabia, to a noble family on March 21, about 1295. He took his name from his mother's family, Sus or Süs. He was creative, quick, highly imaginative and restless. He was of frail health and often ill. Perhaps because of this, his parents took him at age 13 to the Dominican convent at Constance, where he would spend a large part of his life. He was professed at age 14.

At age 18, he had a mystical experience that propelled him to become "the Servant of the Eternal Wisdom." He was flooded with divine light and joy and felt transported out of the world. This experience changed his thinking and opened the way for frequent visions and ecstasies throughout his life. He initiated a practice of severe austerities.

Henry excelled in his studies, and in 1324 he was sent to Cologne to the Dominican house of advanced studies. There he had the privilege of studying with the great and controversial German mystic, Johann Eckhart, or Meister Eckhart, for three years, becoming his ardent supporter. He also studied the works of SS. Thomas Aquinas, Peter Lombard and Dionysius.

After his return to Constance, he was named lector and pursued his writing. In 1329, Pope John XXII (r.

St. Helena (Library of Congress Prints and Photographs Division)

crushed by this defamation. At the height of the scandal, another woman came to him in secret and offered to destroy the child. She argued that unless the child were eliminated, he would be forced to accept it. Henry, of course, could do no such thing. He accepted the child as his and gave it to the care of the woman. This damaged his reputation even further. Friends deserted him and he was nearly expelled from the religious life.

Henry was devoted to the Blessed Virgin Mary and venerated the holy name of Jesus. He took a stiletto and carved the name into his chest above his heart, so that the name moved with every beat of his heart. He never revealed the carving to anyone, but once while in ecstasy, a brilliant radiance streamed from his heart.

Henry died on January 25, 1366, in Ulm.

Henry began writing while he was a student in Cologne. His early works, heavily influenced by Eckhart, were The *Little Book of Truth* and *The Little Book of Eternal Wisdom.* The latter is considered a classic, and was the most widely read meditation book in German until Thomas à Kempis produced *Imitation of Christ.* Kempis was influenced by Suso.

Henry also wrote his autobiography, *The Life of the Servant,* which discusses his inner life. Extant are 28 letters and five sermons.

Beatified: 1831 by Pope Gregory XVI
Feast: March 2 (in the Dominican Order)

FURTHER READING
Underhill, Evelyn. *Mysticism.* New York: New American Library, 1974.
Henry Suso: The Exemplar, with Two German Sermons. Tr. Frank Tobin. Mahwah, N.J.: Paulist Press, 1989.

Hilarion (ca. 291–ca. 371) *Ascetic and hermit, founder of the anchorite life in Palestine, miracle-worker*

Most of what is known about Hilarion comes from a biography written by St. Jerome in 390 and containing much legend. Hilarion desired the life of a hermit, but his fame and public adoration kept him moving from one place to another.

Hilarion was born in Palestine, in Tabatha, south of Gaza, to pagan parents. He was sent to Alexandria to be educated. He was a quick student and an excellent speaker. While in Alexandria he sought out St. Anthony and desired to follow his example and retire to the desert. He stayed with Anthony for two months, greatly admiring the anchorite's discipline and mortifications.

Thus inspired, the 16-year-old Hilarion returned home, gave away his money and possessions to the poor, and built a tiny hut of reeds and sedge for himself in the desert of Majuma near Gaza. It was a dan-

1316–34) condemned Meister Eckhart. Henry defended him, earning censure from his superiors and suffering the loss of his teaching job.

In 1334 Henry began his apostolic career, earning an outstanding reputation for his preaching throughout Europe. In particular he worked with the Friends of God, whom he called the Brotherhood of Eternal Wisdom, helping to restore religious practices. He especially influenced Dominican convents of women, including the famous Katherinenthal, a home to mystics in the 13th and 14th centuries, and Toss, where Elsbeth Stagel preserved some of his writings and most of his letters.

Throughout his life, Henry suffered the persecutions and ill will of others, despite his brilliance as a preacher. A woman accused him of fathering her child, and the gossip destroyed his reputation for a time. Henry was

gerous area, full of robbers, but Hilarion was unconcerned. He spent most of his time in prayer and meditation, and wove baskets to support himself. He wore a hair shirt that he never washed, and wore it to rags before he acquired a new one. He restricted himself to one meal a day, 15 dried figs eaten after sunset. He slept on a bed of rushes and shaved his hair once a year on Easter Day. He endured all the temptations of devils. After two years, he built himself a cell—Jerome described it as more like a tomb—that was five feet in height and about five feet long.

Hilarion was 18 when he was assaulted by robbers, according to Jerome. He showed no fear, and they went away pledging to reform themselves to a better life.

Jerome described in detail Hilarion's eating habits, which imitated those of Anthony. At age 20, Hilarion began to alter his strict diet somewhat. For three years he ate a half-pint of moistened lentils each day, and for the next three years he ate dry bread with salt and water. From age 27 to 30 he ate wild herbs and raw roots, and from 31 to 35 ate six ounces of barley bread and vegetables cooked without oil. By then he was suffering severely from malnutrition. His body shriveled, his eyesight grew dim, and his skin erupted in scabs and mange. He added only oil to his diet. At age 64, he thought he was going to die, so he cut bread out of his diet. But at age 80, he modified his diet once again, making a daily six-ounce broth from meal and bruised herbs.

During his early desert life, Hilarion became famous for his miracles. He was known for curing the sick and the dying, and for expelling demons. He brought needed rain. By 329 he had attracted a band of disciples, and people sought out his counsel, and converted because of him.

Desiring solitude, Hilarion left and journeyed to Egypt, visiting the places where Anthony had lived and died. He then went to Bruchium near Alexandria. When news reached him that Emperor Julian the Apostate had ordered his arrest, he withdrew to an oasis in the Libyan desert. After a time he went to Sicily, and took up the hermit's life near the promontory of Pachinum. But his devoted disciple, Hesychius, who had been searching around the ancient world for him, discovered him there, and soon Hilarion once again was surrounded by disciples and admirers.

He left Sicily and went to Epidaurus to seek solitude, but his fame went before him, and he was besieged by people. He was there when the great earthquake of 366 struck. Fearful of a tidal wave, the people begged him for help. He knelt in the sand and made three crosses, and the turbulent sea calmed itself. He also aided the injured and destitute.

Hilarion left Epidaurus and went to Cyprus. He found the most remote place possible—a cave 12 miles inland amidst rugged mountains—and there he remained for the rest of his life. While there, he met St. Epiphanius, the archbishop of Salamis.

Hilarion died at age 80. He bequeathed to Hesychius his sole possessions of his hair shirt, cowl and cloak, and a copy of the Gospels; he was buried immediately in the same clothes near the town of Paphos. Hesychius arrived, ostensibly to take up residence there, but after a few month's stay secretly stole the body. He found Hilarion's corpse incorrupt and sweet-smelling, and his clothing intact. Hesychius took the body back to Majuma.

Feast: October 21

FURTHER READING

St. Jerome. *The Life of St. Hilarion.* URL: http://www.newadvent.org/fathers/3003.htm. Downloaded: September 21, 2000.

Hilarus (d. 468) *Pope*
Also known as: Hilary

A native of Sardinia, Hilarus became archdeacon of the Church of Rome under Pope St. Leo I (r. 440–461), who in 449 sent him as representative to the so-called Robber Council of Ephesus. The Robber Council considered statements made by Eutyches to the effect that Jesus was possessed of but a single nature, his human nature being subsumed by his divine nature. The orthodox view of the Church was that Jesus possessed a dual nature; the outcome of the Robber Council, however, favored Eutyches. It was followed with much violence, and Hilarus escaped with his life only by hiding out in a crypt dedicated to St. John the Apostle.

Hilarus succeeded Leo as bishop of Rome on November 19, 461. His pontificate was typical for his era, being concerned with fighting heresies, upholding Church discipline, and otherwise conducting Rome's leadership role in the universal church. In 465, he convened a synod to condemn the practice of bishops naming their own successors. When in 476 a favorite of Emperor Anthemius embraced the Macedonian heresy, Hilarus exhorted the emperor from the grave of St. Peter to come out against the false views.

Hilarus erected several churches and other ecclesiastical buildings in Rome, and added two oratories—one to St. John the Apostle and one to the Lateran baptistry. The following inscription can still be seen above the baptistry doors: "To St. John the Evangelist, the liberator of Bishop Hilarus, a Servant of Christ."

Hilarus died on February 28, 468, and was buried in the Church of St. Laurence-Outside-the-Walls, one of the churches he had built.

Feast: November 17

Hilary of Poitiers (ca. 315–368) *Bishop of Poitiers, Father of the Church and Doctor of the Church*
Also known as: Athanasius of the West, the Doctor of Divinity of Christ

One of the most esteemed theologians of his day, Hilary was born in Poitiers, Aquitaine, in what is now southwestern France. His family was noble and wealthy, though pagan. After studying rhetoric and philosophy, he married and had a daughter. He was already in middle life when he was converted to Christianity through his reading of the Bible. His daughter Abra (Abram, Afra, Apra) also is counted among the saints.

Hilary was elected bishop of Poitiers around 350 (when he was 35) and thereafter he and his wife lived apart in perpetual continence. Soon after his consecration, he wrote a commentary on the Gospel of Saint Matthew, which, together with his commentaries on the Psalms, St. Jerome recommended for reading especially by virgins and the devout.

Hilary quickly became embroiled in the controversy over Arianism, a heresy that denied the divinity of Jesus. Arianism had been embraced by Emperor Constantine (Constantius) II, who had compelled the Eastern churches to embrace the creed. In 355, Constantine II called a synod in Milan to further its spread in the West as well. In response, Hilary wrote his *First Book to Constantius*, begging Constantine II to restore peace to the Church. However, the following year, he was condemned by a synod at Béziers (Bitterae), and Constantine II banished him to Phrygia.

Hilary used his exile for study and writing. To this period belongs his most celebrated work, *De Trinitate*, 12 books arguing the consubstantiality of the Father, Son and Holy Spirit, intended to refute Arianism. He proved to be such an effective apologist for orthodox Christianity that Arian bishops, fearing his influence in the East, pressured Constantine to return him to his see in 360.

On his way back to Gaul, Hilary traveled through Illyricum and Italy, preaching against Arianism. He was received enthusiastically by the people of Poitiers, and once returned to his see set about more formal condemnation of the heresy, both in the senate and in a synod he convened. With Constantine II's death in 361, the Arian persecutions came to an end, though the heresy was still strong. In 364, therefore, Hilary traveled to Milan to engage in public debate with one of its exponents. His oratorical skills proved so strong that the man, Bishop Auxentius, lost his imperial support and was sent into exile.

In his battle against Arianism, Hilary turned against the heresy one of its own innovations and strengths—hymns. During his exile, he had realized that Arian hymns were used to spread the false views, and he wrote some of his own. Three have survived—one about Jesus' temptations in the wilderness; a second about Easter; and a third, 70 verses long, about the Trinity.

Hilary died in Poitiers in 368, on either November 1 or January 13. His remains were initially laid to rest there, though some were burned by Huguenots. Others were translated to the abbey of St. Denys, near Paris, while yet others appear to have been taken to Limousin. Miracles reported at his tomb were recorded by St. Gregory of Tours, among others.

So renowned was Hilary that the spring term at English courts of law and at Oxford University is named the "Hilary term" in his honor.

In art, Hilary is portrayed as a bishop holding an open book of the Gospel; with three books; with a pen or stick; or with a child (sometimes in a cradle at his feet, raised to life by him). Sometimes he is shown with his friend St. Martin of Tours, or with a snake and dragon.

Declared Doctor of the Divinity of Christ: 1851 by Pope Pius IX
Feast: January 13 (formerly January 14)
Patronage: retarded children; against snakebite

Hilda (614–680) *Benedictine abbess*

Most of what is known about Hilda comes from the Venerable Bede's *Ecclesiastical History of the English People*.

Hilda was nobly born in 614, the daughter of Hereric, nephew of King Edwin of Northumbria. Bede tells the story that Hilda's mother, Bregusuit, had a dream during the child's infancy. Bregusuit's husband was in exile. In the dream, she looked everywhere for him, but could not find him. Instead, she found a precious jewel under her garment, which cast a light that spread throughout all Britain. The jewel would prove to be Hilda.

At age 13 Hilda became a Christian after hearing the preaching of St. Paulinus, the first bishop of the Northumbrians. When her sister, Hereswith, became a nun in Gaul, Hilda decided to follow in her footsteps. After a year she was recalled by St. Aidan, who gave her land on the River Wear, where she led a monastic life with a small group of companions.

Hilda then was made abbess at Hartlepool, a double monastery of men and women. Hilda set the place in order, and received extensive religious instruction from Aidan and others. After a few years, she undertook to build or improve a monastery at Streaneshalch (later renamed Whitby). Hilda became famous for her wisdom, and kings and princes were among those who came to seek her advice. Whitby was known especially for the study of the Scriptures. Under her administration, Whitby produced five distinguished bishops: Bosa, Hedda, Oftfor, John (Bishop of Haexham) and Wilfrid (Bishop of York).

In 664 an important synod was held at Whitby at which King Oswy set the observance of Easter. Hilda's work was instrumental in the spread of Christianity during a crucial period of struggle against paganism.

In 663, Hilda was stricken with a serious fever that lasted until her death seven years later. During that time, she neglected none of her duties. According to Bede, she died at dawn after receiving Communion and admonishing her disciples to preserve evangelical peace. When the bell was tolled to announce her passing, it was miraculously heard by a nun, Begu, in a monastery 13 miles away. Begu had a vision in which she saw the soul of Hilda borne up to heaven by angels in a radiance of light. She reported the vision to her abbess, Frigyth, who assembled all the nuns to pray and sing psalms for Hilda's soul. When monks came the next day to announce the news of Hilda's death, the sisters said they already knew.

Legend has it that Hilda's body was translated to Glastonbury or Gloucester by King Edmund, but these stories are doubtful.

Feast: November 17

FURTHER READING
St. Bede, "Of the Life and Death of the Abbess Hilda," in *Ecclesiastical History of the English Nation.* URL: http://www.fordham.edu/halsall/basis/bede-book4.html. Downloaded: September 27, 2000.

Hildegard of Bingen (1098–1179) *Benedictine abbess and acclaimed prophet, mystic, theologian, writer, poet, composer and early feminist*
Also known as: Hildegarde

The first major German mystic, Hildegard of Bingen is best known for a series of mystical illuminations, or visions, which she experienced and chronicled in midlife and which were far in advance of the religious outlooks of her day. Her power and influence made her one of the most important women of her time. Her work has enjoyed renewed and serious interest in contemporary times.

Hildegard was born to parents of high nobility in the summer of 1098 in the German village of Bickelheim (also given as Bockelheim), located on the Nahe River, a tributary of the Rhine. The village was near Bingen, an important river town about 50 miles southwest of Frankfurt. Hildegard's father, Hildebert, was a knight of the Castle Bickelheim. The area had been heavily settled by Celts, and Celtic mystical beliefs strongly influenced her religious development.

The youngest of 10 children, Hildegard was sickly as a child and was sent to an aunt, Blessed Jutta, a recluse, to be raised in a hermitage near Spanheim. She had religious visions from the earliest times she could remember. Because of this and her upbringing, she was drawn to the Church. When she was eight, her parents took her to the Benedictine cloister in Disabodenberg, where she began her religious studies under Jutta von Spanheim. She became a nun at 18 and advanced to prioress at age 38.

Hildegard believed in the equality of men and women, but sometimes doubted herself because of criticism from men and their oppression of women. She was often ill, and she blamed it on her frustrated passivity.

Though she had had visions since the age of five, Hildegard's great spiritual awakening came in 1141 when she was 42. She began to experience particularly intense illuminations and clairaudient messages about the nature of God, the human soul and all being, and the interconnectivity among all things in the universe. She also experienced visions on sin, redemption and the nature of the cosmos.

At the onset of these visions, Hildegard said that "a burning light coming from heaven poured into my mind. Like a flame which does not burn but rather enkindles, it inflamed my heart and my breast, just as the sun warms something with its rays. And I was able to understand books suddenly, the psaltery clearly, the evangelists and the volumes of the Old and New Testament, but I did not have the interpretation of the words of their texts nor the division of their syllables nor the knowledge of their grammar."

Though a voice instructed her to write and speak of her supernormal insights and tell others "how to enter the kingdom of salvation," Hildegard initially refused to do so, out of humility. She became ill, "pressed down by the scourge of God," and remained ill for a long time, until she relented and started recording her visions. She then returned to strength. It took her at least 10 years to write down and explain her "hidden mysteries of God."

The visions galvanized Hildegard to shake off her doubts about her "proper place" as a woman. Still, she had to work within the system. She consulted her confessor, who in turn consulted the archbishop of Mainz. A committee of theologians validated her visions.

Hildegard's first book, written in collaboration with a monk, was *Scivias* (Know the ways), a record of 26 illuminations. Composed in Latin, *Scivias* concerns prophecy, denunciation of vice and the universe as egg or sphere. Central to the work is the idea of God as the Living Light: "All living creatures are, so to speak, sparks from the radiance of God's brilliance, and these sparks emerge from God like rays of the sun." Hildegard worked on *Scivias* for a decade, finishing it sometime between 1152 and 1158. St. Bernard of Clairvaux recommended it to the archbishop of Mainz and Pope Eugenius III (r. 1145–53), who both approved of it.

With *Scivias*, Hildegard's fame spread, and she became known as "the Sybil of the Rhine." Pope Eugenius III encouraged her to keep writing. She appreciated his approval, but that didn't stop her from scolding the pope to work harder for reform in the Church.

Around 1147, while Hildegard was still at work on *Scivias*, she and her sister nuns left Mount St. Disabodenberg for another monastery in Rupertsberg, Germany, where they could have more room to live and work. She was consecrated an abbess.

From 1158 to 1163, Hildegard composed her second visionary work, *The Book of Life's Merits*, or *The Book of the Rewards of Life*, which juxtaposes virtues and sins. In 1163 she began work on her third book, *Book of Divine Works*, completing it in 1173. This third work presents a complex cosmology on the origin of life, the nature of heaven and the history of salvation.

In 1165, Hildegard founded another monastery in Eibingen, across the river from Bingen, and commuted between there and Rupertsberg every week.

Hildegard kept up an active, work-filled schedule to the end of her life. She traveled widely throughout Europe, preaching to clergy, nobility, scholars and the lay public. Her views influenced many of her powerful contemporaries, such as Frederick I Barbarossa. She drew much opposition as well as support.

She denounced corruption in the Church, and criticized the Christian, Jewish and Muslim faiths for being "dried up" and lacking care and compassion.

Hildegard challenged the Church time and time again. She downplayed the role of Eve in the fall of Adam, saying Eve was not at fault. Instead, she said the devil had used Eve as an instrument to influence Adam. She celebrated human sexuality as the beautiful, spiritual union of two human beings, not just the means for procreation.

Hildegard had a tremendous interest in science and medicine, and between 1150 and 1157 wrote two medical books far advanced for her time. *Physical Things*, about nature, and *Causes and Cures*, about medicine. Her approach to medicine was holistic, integrating the four-element, four-humor natural healing system of the ancient Greeks with spiritual wisdom. She prescribed numerous herbal and dietary remedies, all inspired by her spiritual visions.

She considered music to be the ultimate celebration of God. She composed 77 songs, perhaps divinely inspired, that were more complex than most 12th-century songs. She considered music to be a better medium than words for the expression of wisdom; wisdom, she said, dwells in the heart of God, is part of all creative effort and is the "elusive treasure" sought by the strong and virtuous soul.

Her other books include two works on the lives of SS. Rupert and Disibod, an explanation of the Rule of St. Benedict, an explanation of the Athanasian Creed, and a commentary on theology and Scriptures called *Answers to Thirty-eight Questions*.

She also wrote a morality play set to music, *Ordo Vitutum*, which is included in *Scivias*; more than 70 poems; 50 allegorical homilies; and 300 letters. She even invented her own language, composed of an alphabet of 23 letters and with 900 words, which she used to describe scientific terms. She said all of her writings were dictated by the Holy Ghost.

During the last year of her life, Hildegard opposed the vicar general of Mainz in a dispute over the body of a young man buried at the cemetery of St. Rupert's. He had been excommunicated at one time, but Hildegard had provided for him to have last sacraments. The vicar general ordered the body removed, but Hildegard refused, saying she had been told in a vision that her actions were appropriate. The vicar general placed the church under interdict. Hildegard appealed to the archbishop, succeeding in getting the interdict removed. This sort of dispute was typical of the pluck she demonstrated throughout life. She was never afraid to challenge authority.

In her last days, Hildegard was quite infirm, due to a long history of illnesses and to her mortifications. She could not stand upright and had to be carried about. Nonetheless, she continued her duties with as much vigor as possible. She died peacefully on September 17, 1179. Two beams of light were witnessed crossing in the skies over the room in which she lay.

Miracles were reported after her death, and people declared her a saint.

Hildegard is included in the Roman Martyrology, though she never was formally canonized as a saint. Three attempts were made to canonize her, under Pope Gregory IX, Pope Innocent IV and Pope John XXII. After 1317, she gradually slipped into obscurity, though Benedictine sisters carefully preserved and copied her texts. Since World War II, her works have been rediscovered, published and analyzed. In 1979, on the 800th anniversary of her death, Pope John Paul II called her an "outstanding saint."

Feast: September 17

FURTHER READING

Flanagan, Sabina. *Hildegard of Bingen: A Visionary Life.* London: Routledge, 1998.

Hildegard of Bingen. *Book of the Rewards of Life.* Tr. Bruce Hozeski. Oxford, Eng.: Oxford University Press, 1997.

Hildegard of Bingen's Scivias. Tr. Bruce Hozeski. Santa Fe: Bear and Co., 1986.

Hildegard of Bingen's Book of Divine Works with Letters and Songs. Matthew Fox, ed. Santa Fe: Bear and Co., 1987.

Hippolytus (d. ca. 236) *Martyr, priest, antipope, Father of the Church*

Little was known about Hippolytus until the 19th century, when *Philosophumena,* a manuscript apparently written by the saint, was discovered. Hippolytus was a Christian priest in Rome at the beginning of the third century. (SS. Eusebius and Jerome referred to him as a bishop, but his name was not on any of the lists of bishops.) He may have been a disciple of St. Irenaeus.

During the reign of Pope Zephyrinus (198–217), Hippolytus became embroiled in controversies over heresies. When the pope declined to rule on whether or not the Modalists were heretics, the incensed Hippolytus castigated him as unfit for his office. Pope Zephyrinus died in 217 and was succeeded by Callistus (r. 217–222), of whom Hippolytus disapproved and called a heretic. Hippolytus left the Church and had himself elected antipope by a small group of followers. He remained antipope during the reigns of two more popes, Urban (r. 222–230) and Pontian (r. 230–235). It may have been during this period that he wrote *Philosophumena.*

Pontian resigned in 235 in the face of persecutions from Emperor Maximus the Thracian. Both he and Hippolytus were banished to the island of Sardinia. Both of them died there, probably in 236. Prior to death, Hippolytus reconciled with the Church and ended the schism. Their remains were returned together to Rome during the reign of Pope Fabian (236–250). Pontian was buried in the papal vault in the Catacomb of Callistus, and Hippolytus was interred on the Via Tiburtina.

Hippolytus was considered an important theologian of his day, and he was a prolific writer. Sadly, most of his work has been lost. He wrote in Greek rather than Latin and thus became better known in the Eastern Church. He wrote numerous commentaries on books of the Bible, some of which survive in fragments, and numerous treatises against heresies.

According to legend, Hippolytus did not die in exile but had himself secretly consecrated bishop after leaving the Church. He was arrested and executed by being dragged to death by wild horses. His relics were returned to Rome.

Feast: August 13

Hormisdas (d. 523) *Pope*

Hormisdas was born at Frosinone (Frusino) in the Campagna di Roma (Italy). He married and had at least one son, but after his wife died he entered the Roman clergy. He served as archdeacon under Pope St. Symmachus, succeeding him in the Chair of St. Peter on July 21, 514.

The signal event of his pontificate was the healing of the schism that had existed between the Eastern Church and Western Church since 484. This was accomplished on March 28, 519, with the signing of the Formula of Hormisdas in Constantinople. Hormisdas's formula condemned the heretical beliefs that had brought about the schism and affirmed unequivocally the primacy and infallibility of the Roman see. The document was signed by Patriarch John of Constantinople along with some 250 Eastern bishops.

The healing of the schism with the East was not the only important event of Hormisdas's pontificate. Shortly before his death he received word that Thrasamund, king of the Vandals, had died, ending the persecution of Christians in northern Africa.

Hormisdas died in Rome on August 6, 523, and was buried at St. Peter's.

In art, he is portrayed as a young man with a camel.

Feast: August 6
Patronage: grooms; stable-boys

Hugh of Lincoln (1140–1200) *Missionary to England, Carthusian bishop*

Hugh was born in a castle at Avalon in Burgundy, France. His father, William, was a knight and lord of Burgundy. Hugh was eight when his mother died. His father joined the Canons Regular of St. Augustine and took Hugh with him.

Hugh, however, was more attracted to the contemplative Carthusian order, and joined them at age 23. At age 33 he was ordained a priest and made procurator of the Grand Chartreuse. In 1179, King Henry II made him prior of Witham, a Carthusian monastery the king had built as penance for his role in the murder of St. Thomas Becket. The monastery was in decline, and Hugh worked to improve it and attract new recruits. His work impressed the king, and in 1181 Henry named him bishop of Lincoln, the largest diocese in England. Hugh expanded and restored the grand cathedral there, which was the highest structure in Europe until the building of the Eiffel Tower in Paris. Hugh was able to maintain the respect of Henry, his son Richard I (the Lion-Heart) and Richard's brother, John Lackland, though he often disagreed with them. Hugh also defended the Jews against angry mobs, visited lepers and gave funerals for the abandoned dead.

In 1200 Hugh visited his home castle at Avalon and the Grand Chartreuse while traveling in France as ambassador of King John. He returned to England seriously ill, and died in London on November 16, 1200. He was embalmed and his body was taken to Lincoln where he was given a grand burial attended by many officials of church and state. His coffin was carried by three kings and three archbishops.

His relics were translated to a shrine on October 6, 1280. His body was found to be incorrupt, and his Carthusian habit, in which he had died, was in excellent condition. When the archbishop of Canterbury laid his hand on the saint's head, it separated from the shoulder, leaving the neck fresh and red as if death had been recent. This was taken as a miracle, for the new reliquary was not long enough for both body and head. When the body was taken out, observers saw that a pure, clear oil, or manna, had collected at the bottom of the tomb.

The body and head were washed and dried. The next day, the head exuded a flow of fresh oil when handled. The flow ceased when the head was placed on a silver dish to be carried through the crowd in a procession to the new shrine.

Hugh's relics were encased in a coffer of gold, silver and gems, and the shrine itself was embellished with the same. The coffer was placed beside the altar of St. John the Baptist in the church not far from John's shrine.

In 1364 vandals stole the head and other treasures from the shrine and abandoned the head in a field. According to lore, a raven watched over it until it was found and returned to the church. The vandals gave themselves up and were hanged.

In 1540 King Henry VIII, in his closure of churches and monasteries, ordered the shrine dismantled and the valuables—some 2,621 ounces of gold and 4,215 ounces of silver, plus jewels—transported to the Tower of London. Hugh's relics were destroyed. A legend holds that somehow the relics were saved and hidden away, but no evidence exists to support the story. The only relic remaining is a fragment of bone kept at the Grande Chartreuse.

Feast: November 16

Hyacinth (1185–1257) *Dominican missionary and wonder-worker*

Also known as: the Apostle of Poland; the Apostle of the North; the Polish St. Dominic

Hyacinth was born in Oppeln, Silesia, which belonged to Poland. He studied at Cracow, Prague and Bologna, earning the degrees of doctor of laws and divinity. Returning home, he went to work as an administrative assistant to the bishop of Cracow.

In 1218 he went to Rome with his uncle, Yvo, who had been appointed bishop, and his brother, Ceslas. In Rome they met St. Dominic, and Yvo asked the saint to send friars to Poland. None of the Dominicans knew Polish, however. Hyacinth and Ceslas were inspired to join Dominic's order, and received the habit from Dominic himself. Hyacinth was appointed superior of the Dominican mission in Poland. They preached along their way home and attracted new members.

Hyacinth was an effective preacher and was devoted especially to Mary. He was hugely popular in Cracow. He traveled throughout northern Europe, the Baltic, Scandinavia, Lithuania, Russia, China and Tibet. He was known as a wonder-worker and his sermons and miracles attracted many converts.

On three occasions he reportedly was witnessed walking on water. Once in Moravia, Hyacinth was traveling with three companions to Wisgrade. They reached the Vistula River; on the other side were about 400 persons waiting for them. Hyacinth made the sign of the cross and walked across the water. Another such incident took place in Russia.

On another occasion Hyacinth was at a convent that was being threatened by invading Tartars, who set the building on fire. Hyacinth hurried to hide the Blessed Sacrament, when he heard the Blessed Virgin Mary telling him not to leave her statue behind to be desecrated. The statue was quite heavy and Hyacinth doubted he could move it himself. Mary told him she would lighten the load. He then picked up the statue with one hand, held the Blessed Sacrament in the other, and fled the convent. He walked across the Dnieper River to safety.

Hyacinth died in Cracow on August 15, 1257.

Canonized: 1594 by Pope Clement VIII
Feast: August 17

St. Hyacinth

Hyginus (d. ca. 140) *Pope*

Hyginus was Greek. He may have been a philosopher before his conversion to Christianity. He was the ninth bishop of Rome, thus the ninth pope, following St. Telesphorus in about 136. His rule lasted only four years, until ca. 140.

Gnostics began to preach their heresy during Hyginus's rule, and two (Valentinus and Cerdo) are thought to have been resident in Rome for at least part of that time. However, it is not known what action, if any, he took against them.

Hyginus does not appear in the ancient lists of martyrs, such as the Roman Martyrology, and nothing is known about how he died. He was buried on Vatican Hill, near the tomb of St. Peter.

Feast: January 11

Ignatius of Antioch (ca. 50–ca. 107) *Martyr*
Also known as: Theophoros, or God-Bearer

Little is known for certain about the early life of Ignatius, who probably was born in Syria around the year 50. Legend identifies him as the child Jesus set down among his disciples, as described in the Bible (Matthew 18:1–6; Mark 9:36–37). Some sources say that he was a persecutor of Christians who became a convert and a disciple of St. John the Evangelist or of St. Peter or St. Paul. He called himself both a disciple and a "bearer of God" (*theophoros*). At about age 17, he became the second or third bishop of Antioch, Syria. He is said to have been appointed and consecrated by St. Peter after he left the deathbed of St. Evodius, the previous bishop.

Ignatius longed to give his life in martyrdom during the persecution of Christians under the Roman emperor Domitian, but did not have the opportunity. However, he received his wish when a later emperor, Trajan, visited Antioch about 107. Trajan had decreed that Christians should unite with their pagan neighbors in the worship of the gods, under penalty of death. Ignatius went out of his way to disobey, with the predicable effect that he was taken before Trajan and sentenced to die in the Roman Coliseum.

The last months of Ignatius's life are relatively well known, thanks to a series of pastoral letters he wrote, and to contemporary accounts of those who traveled with him on his last voyage to Rome. Their ship stopped at various ports around the Mediterranean, and at each stop Ignatius was greeted by crowds of Christians. They docked for an extended stay at Smyrna, where Ignatius met St. Polycarp of Smyrna, then a young man, and received delegations from Magnesia and Tralles. Two of his first four letters were written to the faithful in these places, a third was addressed to the Ephesians and the fourth to the Christians of Rome, whom he asked not to interfere with his martyrdom. In these letters, Ignatius became the first to use the term "the Catholic Church."

Ignatius's ship arrived in Rome on December 20, the final day of the public games in the Coliseum, and he was rushed to the amphitheater. Of his imminent fate, he wrote, "I pray that they will be prompt with me. I shall entice them to eat me speedily." Legend has it that as he was offered to the lions, he called himself "the wheat of Christ," exclaiming: "May I become agreeable bread to the Lord."

After his death, the image of Jesus is said to have been found engraved on Ignatius's heart. His relics were carried back to Antioch and buried outside the gates. Later, Emperor Theodosius II had them moved to the Tychaeum (Temple of Fortune), which was converted into a Christian church under Ignatius's patronage. In 637, his relics were again translated, this time to St. Clement's in Rome, where they now rest.

Ignatius is highly venerated in the Eastern Orthodox as well as Roman Catholic Church. A Greek icon with his likeness can be seen at the Saint Isaac of Syria Skete site.

In art, Ignatius is shown looking at a crucifix, a lion at his side; standing between two lions; in chains; holding a heart with "IHS" on it; or holding a heart with "IHS" torn out by lions. He may also be depicted with the image of Jesus on his breast; holding a fiery globe; or in an arena with lions.

Feast: October 17 (formerly February 1)
Patronage: Church in the eastern Mediterranean; throat diseases

Ignatius of Loyola (Ignacio de Loyola) (1491–1556)
Founder of the Society of Jesus
Also known as: Ignatius Loyola, Ignatius de Loyola

Ignatius was born in Loyola Castle near Azpeitia, in the Basque province of Guipúzcoa, Spain, on Christmas Eve, 1491. The youngest child of Beltrán Yañez de Oñez y Loyola and Marina Saenz de Lieona y Balda, he was baptized Iñigo, after St. Enecus (Innicus), Abbot of Oña. He assumed the name Ignacio (Ignatius) in middle life, when he was living in Rome.

At the age of 16, Ignatius was sent by his father to live and work with Juan Velásquez de Cuellar, treasurer to the king of Castile, in Arevalo. As a member of the Velásquez household, he had easy access to the court, and developed a taste for the decadent life. He dressed in a coat of mail with a breastplate and carried a sword and other arms. He was enamored of the ladies, was much addicted to gambling, and on occasion engaged in swordplay. However, he also learned to be an accomplished horseman and courtier and practiced the soldierly virtues of discipline, obedience and prudence.

When Velásquez died in 1517, Ignatius joined the army under the duke of Najera, a kinsman. Four years later (on May 20, 1521), he was leading the defense of the fortress of Pamplona, the capital of Navarre, under bombardment by the French. A cannon ball passed between his legs, tearing open his left calf and breaking his right shin. With his wounding, the Spanish troops surrendered. Out of respect for his courage, the French set the bones and sent him in a litter to his father's castle, 50 miles away. The leg did not heal, so it was necessary to break it again and to reset it. This second operation involved sawing off part of a bone, leaving one of his legs shorter than the other. In perpetual fever, Ignatius was told to prepare for death, but on the

feast day of SS. Peter and Paul (June 29), he took an unexpected turn for the better; he eventually recovered fully, although he walked with a pronounced limp.

His recuperation at Loyola was a turning point for Ignatius. The only books at hand were a life of Jesus and a biography of St. George. He began reading these with little interest but gradually became so immersed in them that he spent entire days reading and rereading. This was the beginning of his conversion and also of his discernment of disembodied spirits and of the practices and insights he later described in his classic work, *Spiritual Exercises.* By the time he left the castle in March 1522, he had decided to devote himself to the religious life.

His first action was a pilgrimage to the shrine of Our Lady of Montserrat, in the mountains above Barcelona. After three days of self-examination, he confessed, gave his rich man's clothes to the poor, and donned a sackcloth that reached to his feet. He hung his sword and dagger by Our Lady's altar, then spent the night watching over them. The next morning, after Communion, he left the shrine.

Continuing toward Barcelona he stopped along the River Cardoner at a town called Manresa, where a woman named Iñes Pascual showed him a cave where he could retire for prayer and penitence. Ignatius intended to stay in the cave only a short while, but ended up living there for 10 months. During this time he began making notes on what would become his *Spiritual Exercises.* He also experienced several visions, including one he regarded as the most significant of his life. He never described this vision, but it appears to have been more of an enlightenment, in which God was revealed to be inherent in all things—a grace that was to become one of the central characteristics of Jesuit spirituality.

Ignatius left the cave in February 1523 and journeyed to the Holy Land, where he planned to labor and preach. He visited the scenes of Jesus' life with such obvious zeal that the Franciscan Guardian of the Holy Places ordered him to leave, lest he antagonize the fanatical Muslim Turks then in control of the area and be kidnapped and held for ransom. Raising ransoms for Christian prisoners had become such a problem that the pope had granted the Franciscans oversight in the region. Reluctantly, Ignatius returned to Europe, arriving back in Barcelona about March 1524.

Now determined to prepare for the priesthood, he began studying Latin in a boys' school. After two years he was proficient enough to enroll in the University of Alcalá, near Madrid, newly founded by Grand Inquisitor Jimenes (Ximenes) de Cisneros. There his evangelizing zeal again got him into trouble. Living at a hospice for poor students, he wore a coarse gray habit and begged his food. He also taught children the catechism and led adults through his spiritual exercises. Since he had no training or authority for these things, the vicar-general, Figueroa, accused him of presumption and had him imprisoned for six weeks. When he was released, Ignatius was forbidden to give religious instruction for three years or to wear any distinguishing dress.

Leaving Barcelona at the end of 1527, Ignatius entered the University of Salamanca. Within two weeks, he was back in prison. Although the Dominican inquisitors could find no heresy in what he taught, they told him that he could teach only children and then only simple religious truths.

Once more he took to the road, this time heading for Paris. He arrived there in February 1528 and entered the Sorbonne, attending lectures in Latin grammar and literature, philosophy and philology. He continued promoting his spiritual exercises, gathering the group—including St. Francis Xavier—who were to join with him in founding the Jesuit order. The six of them took vows of chastity and poverty in a chapel on Montmartre on the feast of the Assumption in August 1534. They agreed to travel together to the Holy Land, or if that proved impossible, to go to Rome and place themselves at the disposal of the pope.

Ignatius was ordained a priest in 1534, and received his M.A. degree in March 1535. Ill health then forced him to leave Paris rather than staying to complete his doctorate. He returned to his native Guipúzcoa, but instead of staying in his family's castle, he took up quarters in a nearby hospital, where he continued teaching his special brand of Christianity. He remained there until the winter of 1537, when he and two of his Paris companions decided it was time to go to Rome.

At a chapel in La Storta, a few miles outside the city, Ignatius had the second most significant of his mystical experiences. He seemed to see Father and Son together, the latter speaking the words: *Ego vobis Romae propitius ero,* "I will be favorable to you in Rome." Ignatius was unsure what this meant, since Jesus had experienced persecution as well as success. However, in Rome, Pope Paul III received the men graciously and put them to work teaching Scripture and theology and preaching. Also in Rome, on Christmas morning of 1538, Ignatius celebrated his first Mass, in the Chapel of the Manger in the church of Santa Maria Maggiore (St. Mary Major). It was believed that this chapel had the actual manger of Bethlehem, so since Ignatius was not able to say his first Mass in Jerusalem as he had hoped, this was thought to be the best substitute.

The group disbanded again, but during Lent in 1539, Ignatius asked all to join him in Rome to discuss

St. Ignatius of Loyola (Library of Congress Prints and Photographs Division)

their future. Going to the Holy Land was still out of the question. They had not previously thought of founding a religious order, though they had for some time been calling themselves the "Company of Jesus"—company to be understood in its military sense. Now they agreed to take the next step, and found a new religious community. Following the military model, they would vow obedience to a superior general who would hold office for life. They would place themselves at the disposal of the pope to travel wherever he should wish to send them for whatever duties. A vow to this effect was added to the ordinary vows of poverty, chastity and obedience. Pope Paul III issued a bull approving of the new order—which came to be known in English as the Society of Jesus—on September 27, 1540.

On April 7, 1541, Ignatius was unanimously elected superior general, and on April 22, at the church of St. Paul Outside-the-Walls, the friends pronounced their vows in the new order. Some headed overseas immediately, in time to become superiors of provincial branches. Meanwhile, Ignatius remained in

Rome, where he directed all the overseas missions, and worked on the rules of the order. In 1547, he was joined by a secretary, Father Palaneo, who helped him with his correspondence and in drafting the constitution, which was completed, approved and published in 1552. *Spiritual Exercises* was published in 1548, with papal approval.

Besides the Society of Jesus, Ignatius established several foundations, including one for Jewish converts to Catholicism and another for loose women who were anxious to reform but felt no call to the religious life. However, it is with the Jesuits that he will forever be associated.

Ever since his student days in Paris, Ignatius had suffered from gallstones, and must often have been in considerable pain. His condition became increasingly troublesome in Rome. Then, in the summer of 1556, he contracted Roman fever. On July 30 he asked for the last sacraments and the papal blessing, but because his doctors believed him to be in no imminent danger, his staff did nothing. The next morning he was found near death. The last blessing was given but he died without the pope's blessing and before the holy oils could be brought. His relics lie beneath an altar designed by Pozzi in the Gesù.

Miraculous phenomena were recorded about Ignatius. Once after severe illness he was witnessed in a rapture, levitating in a kneeling position while he prayed aloud. On other occasions in prayer, he was seen surrounded by a brilliant supernatural light. During an ecstasy, a flame of fire was seen hovering over his head.

His emblems are a book, a chasuble, the Holy Communion, and the apparition of the Lord. In art, Ignatius is a bearded Jesuit, often with a book of the Jesuit Rule, kneeling before Christ. He may also be shown: with Christ bringing him a Cross; with Christ as the Good Shepherd; with Christ and Saint Peter before him; holding the Rule, with Saint Francis Xavier or other Jesuit saints (IHS on his breast); in Mass vestments, his hand resting upon his Rule, light in the heavens; with a dragon under his feet; holding the Rule, IHS, and Heart pierced by three nails.

Beatified: July 27, 1609, by Pope Paul V
Canonized: March 12, 1622, by Pope Gregory XV
Feast: July 31
Patronage: Jesuit Order; soldiers; spiritual retreats and exercises

FURTHER READING
Ignatius of Loyola: The Spiritual Exercises and Selected Works. George E. Gauss, Paramanda Divalcar and Edward J. Malatesta, eds. Mahwah, N.J.: Paulist Press, 1991.

Meissner, William W. *Ignatius of Loyola: The Psychology of a Saint.* New Haven, Conn.: Yale University Press, 1994.
O'Neal, Norman. "The Life of St. Ignatius of Loyola." Le Moyne University website. URL: http://maple.lemoyne.edu/~bucko/V_ignat.html. Downloaded: October 27, 1999.

Innocent I (d. 417) *Pope*

Innocent, son of Innocentius, was born in Albano, a town near Rome. He grew up among Roman clergy and in the service of the Roman Church, succeeding Pope St. Anastasius I as bishop on December 22, 401.

In 410, the Goths began a siege of Rome. Their leader, Alaric, declared that he would withdraw if a peace favorable to him could be negotiated, and Innocent was one of the delegation that went to meet with him. The negotiations failed, however, and the Goths resumed their siege. They had entered and sacked the city before Innocent and the rest of the Roman party were able to return to it.

Innocent was zealous about the purity of Church doctrine and discipline, took actions against heretical sects, and was a strong proponent of clerical celibacy. Moreover, he believed strongly in Rome as the leader of the universal Church. He intervened in the affairs of churches outside Rome and advised all to send decisions to him for confirmation. When the Church of Constantinople removed St. John Chrysostom, Innocent stepped in and reinstated him. He commended the bishops of Carthage and Mileve for sending their condemnations of Pelagianism to him in a letter that caused St. Augustine to remark: "*Roma locuta, causa finita est*" ("Rome has spoken, the matter is closed").

Innocent died in Rome on March 12, 417, and was buried in the basilica above the Catacomb of Pontianus. Afterward he was venerated as a saint.

Feast: July 28

Innocent V (ca. 1225–1276) *Dominican monk and pope*
Also known as: Peter of Tarentaise

Innocent was born around 1225 in the Tarentaise region of Burgundy, France, probably in the town of Champagny. He was barely 10 when he was admitted to the Dominican order, took the religious name Peter and was sent to Paris to study. In 1259 he graduated from the University of Paris with a master's degree in sacred theology and began teaching at the university, where he became known as *Doctor famosissimus,* "the most famous doctor." He wrote a number of commentaries on Scripture and a *Commentary on the Sentences of Peter Lombard* and worked with Thomas Aquinas on a plan of study that is still the basis of Dominican teaching.

Peter was made provincial of the Dominicans in France and traveled on foot to visit all the houses under his care. In 1272 he became archbishop of Lyons and in 1273 was created cardinal-bishop of Ostia (Italy) as well. In these capacities, he played a prominent role in the Second Ecumenical Council of Lyons in 1274, where he and Franciscan friar St. Bonaventure devoted much attention to ongoing clerical reforms and to healing the schism with the Greek Church. Bonaventure died before the council was over, and Peter pronounced his funeral oration.

Peter became an adviser to Bl. Pope Gregory X (r. 1271–76) and was with him in Arezzo (Rezzo) when he died in January 1276. The College of Cardinals subsequently met in Arezzo to decide on a successor, and on January 21 elected Peter, who received every vote save his own. The first Dominican pope, he assumed the name Innocent V.

Peter restored the custom of personally assisting at choral functions with the canons of the Lateran and initiated other reforms in the matter of religious observance. He also instigated a new crusade against the Muslim Saracens—as mandated by the Council of Lyons—and succeeded in settling many of the issues involved with the schism between the Greek and Roman churches and actually brought about a temporary truce. However, his unexpected death on July 22, 1276—after a reign of only six months—cut short his efforts.

Cultus approved: 1898 by Pope Leo XIII
Feast: June 22

Irenaeus of Lyons (ca. 130–202) *Bishop of Lyons, Father of the Church*
Name meaning: Lover of peace

The writings of Irenaeus rank him among the greatest of the fathers of the church; he is considered the first great Christian theologian. His work—much of it still extant—helped to lay the Gnostic heresy to rest and laid the foundations of Christian theology. Although he wrote in Greek, he was quickly translated into Latin, and was highly influential in his day.

Irenaeus was born in Asia Minor, probably around the year 130 (between 125 and 142), although some scholars believe earlier, between 115 and 125. This area had been heavily worked by the Apostles, and their memory would have been strong. While still very young, he heard St. Polycarp preach at Smyrna.

Irenaeus joined the Christian priesthood and was sent as a missionary to the Church of Lyons in Gaul during the time of Emperor Marcus Aurelius's bloody persecution of Christians. In 177 or 178 he was sent to Rome to deliver a letter asking for mercy on Montanism, a heretical sect, to Pope St. Eleutherius (r. 175–189), and thus escaped the persecutions in Lyons that resulted in the martyrdom of Bishop St. Pothinus. When he returned to Lyons, he was elected to the vacant bishopric, and remained in that capacity for the rest of his life. He spent his time preaching and traveling in missionary work, especially targeting pockets of Gnosticism in Gaul.

The persecutions having subsided, Irenaeus found the greatest challenge to the Christian Church in Gnosticism, and set about clarifying the errors of the various sects in relation to the true teachings of the Apostles. He also took a stand on the Quartodeciman controversy concerning the celebration of Easter, interceding with Pope St. Victor (r. 189–199) in 190 or 191 to lift the sentence of excommunication upon the Christian communities of Asia Minor.

Irenaeus is believed to have died in 202, although this is not certain. Probably he died a natural death. His remains were interred in a crypt under the altar of what was then known as the Church of St. John, but later called after him. The tomb became a shrine and was destroyed by Calvinists in 1562; all trace of his relics has been lost.

Irenaeus wrote numerous treatises and letters and has been quoted by numerous church theologians since. He was vigorous in his defense of orthodoxy and in his opposition to heresy. Composed in Greek, none have survived in their original editions, but are extant in Latin or Armenian translations. His best known work is *Adversus haereses,* considered an excellent exposition of the Gnostic heresy as well as other heretical philosophies. A second treatise, *Proof of the Apostolic Preaching,* expounds on the Gospels as interpreted through Old Testament prophecies. Only fragments exist of Irenaeus's other works.

Feast: June 28 (West); August 23 (East)

Isidore the Farmer (1082?–1130) *Confessor*
Also known as: Isadore the Farmer, Isidro Labrador, Isidoro Labrador

Isidore Merlo Quintana was born in or about 1082 in Madrid, Castile (now part of Spain), to a poor peasant family. He was named after St. Isidore, Archbishop of Seville (560–638). Since he was an obscure person in his day, the details of his life are not well known, and accounts vary.

Isidore married Maria Toribia (or Torriba, the future St. Maria de la Cabeza). The couple had a child who died as a baby, which they took as a sign that God wanted them to remain childless. Although they continued to live together, they took vows of chastity and remained celibate for the rest of their lives.

Isidore was orphaned at the age of 10 and was employed as a day laborer by a wealthy landowner, Juan (or perhaps Ivan) de Vargas, on his estate at Torrelaguna, outside Madrid. He and Maria were very pious. Although he worked hard and diligently, Isidore went to Mass each morning, before going to work in the fields, and took time out during the day for prayers.

These habits caused some resentment from his fellow peasants, who complained to Vargas. He went and spoke to Isidore, who defended himself. Still, Vargas followed him to the fields one morning. As he approached Isidore and his plow, he fancied he saw a second plow at work, but as he gained on it, this second plow disappeared. Isidore denied there was anybody there but himself. "Sir, I work alone and know of none save God to whom I look for strength," he told his master. The incident gave rise to the story that Isidore's sanctity was so great that angels even helped with his plowing.

Another story has it that one snowy day, on his way to the mill with corn to be ground, Isidore passed a flock of hungry pigeons, vainly scratching for food on the frosty earth. As people watched and mocked him, he poured half of his sack out for the birds. By the time he reached the mill, however, the bag was once again full, and when ground, the corn produced twice the usual amount of flour.

Isidore always made sure that the oxen and other animals he worked with were treated well, and although he and Maria were themselves poor, they gave freely to the needy. Isidore divided his earnings into thirds, giving one to the church, a second to the poor and keeping only one portion for himself and Maria. One day he was invited to a luncheon, but when he arrived with a group of beggars, his host protested in disgust that only he was invited; Isidore nevertheless divided his meal with those whom he had brought.

According to another story, Isidore pricked the ground with his staff and a spring issued forth. The spring, near Madrid, is considered to have healing powers and its waters are bottled as a remedy against sudden illness.

Some accounts say that Isidore had to leave Madrid for a time when it was attacked by Moors, but this is dubious because Madrid had been captured from the Moors in 1083, about the time of his birth.

Isidore died on May 15, 1130, and was buried in the cemetery. Miracles and cures were reported at his grave, and when his body was transferred to a shrine in the church 43 years later, it was found to be incorrupt, as if he only recently had died.

Isidore has enjoyed the support of Spanish royalty. He is said to have appeared as an apparition to King Alfonso VIII of Castile in 1211, and to have shown the king a previously unknown path that he used to surprise and defeat the Moors, who were still holding onto much of what later became a unified Spain. In the 1500s, Charles, king of Spain and Holy Roman Emperor, built the Hermitage of the Patron of Madrid after his son Philip was healed by water from a fountain that by tradition had been opened by Isidore to slake the thirst of his master, Juan de Vargas. Isidore's canonization came at the insistence of King Philip III of Spain (r. 1598–1621), who attributed his recovery from a serious illness (perhaps that which had so impressed his father) to Isidore's intercession.

Isidore's cult quickly spread beyond Spain, although it is still in Spain that he is most revered. His feast is celebrated in Madrid with ringing church bells, street fairs and a parade.

In Spanish art, his emblems are a spade or a plough. He has also been depicted as a peasant holding a sickle and a sheaf of corn; with a sickle and staff; with an angel who ploughs for him; giving a rosary to children by a well; striking water from dry earth with an angel plowing in the background; before a cross; and with an angel and white oxen near him.

Beatified: ca. 1460 by Pope Pius XII
Canonized: March 12, 1622, by Pope Gregory XV
Feast: May 15 (formerly March 22 in United States, and May 10 and October 25 elsewhere)
Patronage: death of children; farmers and farm laborers; for rain; husbandmen; livestock; Madrid, Spain; U.S. National Rural Life Conference

FURTHER READING

"San Isidro, labrador: Patrón de la villa de Madrid." http://www.fplanet.es/castizos/Agrup004.htm. Downloaded: January 30, 2000.

"St. Isidore the Farmer, Confessor." Mater Dei website. URL: http://web2.airmail.net/~carlsch/MaterDei/Saints/isidoref.htm. Downloaded: January 30, 2000.

Isidore of Pelusium (d. ca. 449–450) *Monk and perhaps abbot of Pelusium, Egypt; Father of the Church*

Isidore of Pelusium was born in Alexandria in the last half of the fourth century. At some point he was inspired to leave his family and belongings and become a monk at the monastery of Lychnos on a mountain near Pelusium. He may have become abbot there. He was renowned for his strict observance of the rule and his austerities. He wore only skins and subsisted on herbs. He said that monks should eat nothing more unless a superior ordered it on account of physical weakness, and they should always obey their superiors. He believed strongly in practicing what one taught and preached.

Isidore was devoted to the teachings of St. John Chrysostom and was a contemporary of St. Cyril of Alexandria. He argued against heresy, especially that of the Nestorians.

Isidore wrote two treatises, *Adversus Gentiles* and *De Fato*, but they are lost. The only surviving writings of the saint are 2,182 of his estimated 10,000 letters. Some of the extant letters deal with dogma, Scripture, heresy, and ecclesiastical and monastic discipline.

Feast: February 4

Isidore of Seville (ca. 560–636) *Archbishop of Seville, Doctor of the Church, Father of the Church*
Also known as: Isidore the Bishop; Schoolmaster of the Middle Ages

The last of the great Latin Fathers, Isidore was born at Cartagena, Spain, about 560, into a noble Hispano-Roman family. His elder brother Leander, younger brother Fulgentius and sister Florentina also came to hold senior positions within the Christian Church.

Isidore received his elementary education in the cathedral school of Seville, the first of its kind in Spain. His brother Leander, then archbishop of Seville, was one of his teachers. As he matured, Isidore most likely assisted Leander in governing the archdiocese, because he succeeded him as archbishop in 601.

As archbishop, Isidore devoted himself to strengthening the Spanish Church. He worked hard to turn the Visigoths away from the Arian heresy, rewriting liturgies and breviaries for their use. He convened councils at Seville in 613 and Toledo in 633. At the latter, attended by all the bishops of Spain, he was given precedence over the local archbishop on the basis of his exceptional merit as the greatest teacher in the country. Indeed, it was in the area of education that Isidore made his greatest mark, earning him his sobriquet, "Schoolmaster of the Middle Ages." At the Toledo council, he introduced and saw passed a decree commanding all dioceses to establish cathedral schools along the lines of that school he himself had attended in Seville. He compiled a 20-volume encyclopedia of knowledge (containing information on everything that was known in seventh-century Europe), a chronicle of events from the Creation to his own time, and a history of the Goths and Vandals. He completed and updated St. Jerome's biographies of the great men and women of the Bible. He also wrote books on theology, astronomy and geography, as well as new rules for monasteries.

As he felt his death approaching, he invited two bishops to visit him. On April 4, 636, they accompanied him to the church, where one covered him with a sackcloth while the other put ashes on his head. Thus dressed in the habit of a penitent, Isidore raised his hands to heaven and prayed for forgiveness. After receiving the viaticum, he asked for the prayers of those present, forgave those who had sinned against him, exhorted all to charity, bequeathed his earthly possessions to the poor and gave up his soul to God.

In art, Isidore is depicted as an elderly bishop with a pen and a book, or with his encyclopedia. Sometimes he is shown with his brothers and sisters, SS. Leander, Fulgentius and Florentina. More rarely, he is a bishop standing near a beehive, or surrounded by bees—bees symbolizing oratorical eloquence.

Canonized: 1598 by Pope Clement VIII
Declared Doctor of the Divinity of Christ: 1722 by Pope Innocent XIII
Feast: April 4
Patronage: computer technicians; computer users; computers; the Internet; savants; students

Jacinta and Francisco Marto (1910–1920 and 1908–1919) *Sister and brother, the youngest of the three visionaries who saw the Virgin Mary in Fatima, Portugal, in 1917*

Jacinta and Francisco were the sixth and seventh children of Manuel Pedro Marto and Olimpia dos Santos, humble farmers and pious Christians. They were born in the village of Aljustrel, near Fatima, not far from Leiria, Portugal—Francisco on June 11, 1908, and Jacinta on March 11, 1910. Since there was no school in their village, they were educated at home and took catechism lessons from the parish priest and a maternal aunt.

From a young age, Jacinta and Francisco worked as shepherds together with their cousin Lucia. The three children thus developed a close bond. All were of a religious bent. In 1916, they announced that they had thrice seen an angel who had urged them to pray and do penance for the remission of sins and to obtain the conversion of sinners. They followed these instructions to the best of their ability.

Then on May 13, 1917, Jacinta, Francisco and Lucia dos Santos, their elder cousin, were granted the privilege of seeing the Virgin Mary. She appeared to them thereafter on the 13th of each month until October 13, when a crowd (estimated at 70,000) witnessed a "miraculous solar phenomenon" immediately afterward. On June 13 she communicated to the children a premonitory vision in three parts, which she ordered them not to divulge. This vision became known as the Secret of Fatima. Its substance was not revealed for many years.

Municipal and Church authorities were initially skeptical of the apparitions and visions. The children were prevented from entering the parish church, were beaten and briefly jailed, but refused to recant. They refused also to divulge the secrets entrusted to them by Our Lady, even under the threat of death. "If they kill us we'll soon be in heaven! Nothing else matters!" Francisco exclaimed. After the spectacle on October 13, the bishop finally accepted the truth of the visions, and the harassment changed to adulation.

The children were even more affected by the visions of Mary than they had been by the earlier apparitions of angels. Francisco developed a special devotion to the Eucharist and spent much time in church, adoring the Sacrament of the Altar, which he called the "Hidden Jesus." He assisted at Mass on feasts and whenever possible on weekends. He recited the 15 mysteries of the Rosary at least once daily. Jacinta began to seek silence and solitude, and at night would get out of bed to pray. She loved to contemplate Christ Crucified and was moved to tears by the Passion. She also venerated Mary, honoring her with recitation of the Rosary and with pious exclamations.

More than Francisco, she was also given to penance. She wore a rope around her waist, deprived herself of food, in order to give it to the poor, and refused water, especially in the summer heat.

During her June 13 visit, Our Lady told the children that she would soon be taking Jacinta and Francisco to heaven. Indeed, in October 1918, they caught influenza during an epidemic. Once confined to bed, Francisco was never able to leave it again, and died on April 4, 1919. Realizing she had only a short time to live, Jacinta stepped up her sacrifices, penances and privations. She was sent to a hospital in Lisbon, where she died alone and in the midst of great suffering on February 20, 1920.

Jacinta's body was buried first in Vila Nova de Ourem in Lisbon but subsequently was translated to the cemetery of Fatima, where Francisco's body was interred. After the basilica was built in Fatima, the relics of both were moved there. Near to their tombs is a third, reserved for the mortal remains of their cousin Lucia dos Santos, now Sister Lucia of the Immaculate Heart of Mary. Born on March 30, 1907, Lucia, a Carmelite nun at a convent in Portugal, was 93 years old in 2000.

Pilgrims began to visit Fatima even before the deaths of Jacinta and Francisco. The first national pilgrimage took place in 1927. The basilica was begun in 1928 and consecrated in 1953. It faces a large square in which stands the little Chapel of the Apparitions. Many cures have been reported at this shrine, one of the greatest Marian shrines in the world. On May 13, 1967, the 50th anniversary of the first vision, an estimated 1,000,000 pilgrims gathered at Fatima to hear Pope Paul VI (r. 1963–78) say Mass and pray for peace.

Lucia was induced by the bishop of Leiria (but with Our Lady's permission) to write down the Secret of Fatima in 1941, although the third part was not recorded until 1944. The first two parts were revealed in 1942. The first part was a brief vision of hell, while the second was interpreted as a prediction of World War II, later as World War II and the fall of communism. The third part was widely rumored to foretell the Apocalypse, but during the beatification ceremony for Jacinta and Francisco in 2000 it was revealed to be a prediction of the attempt to assassinate Pope John Paul II (r. 1978–) on May 13, 1981 (the 64th anniversary of the children's first visit from Our Lady).

When the full text of the third part was published on June 26, 2000, however, the vision turned out to have only vague reference to the assassination attempt. It depicted a bishop (said to be the bishop of Rome) and all those around him being shot by army troops, whereas only John Paul II was shot, by a lone gunman, the Turk Mehmet Ali Agca. Yet John Paul II had no doubts. He credited Our Lady with saving his life, by deflecting Mehmet Ali Agca's bullets away from his vital organs, and has donated one of the bullets to the Shrine at Fatima, where it has been set into the crown of the statue of Our Lady.

The process of beatifying Jacinta and Francisco began in 1946. The Vatican committee on canonization decided that the children had lived lives of intense holiness, especially after the appearance of Our Lady, when they had become models of prayer and penance, notwithstanding the young age at which they died. The beatification was clinched in 1999 with the acceptance of a healing miracle. A woman paralyzed from the waist down by a spinal injury had been treated by doctors for 22 years without success when she made a novena to Jacinta and Francisco. Soon thereafter she heard a voice telling her, "Now you can sit up." She discovered that not only could she do this, but moreover she could stand and walk around unaided. Jacinta and Francisco are the youngest persons ever beatified without dying as martyrs.

Beatified: May 13, 2000, by Pope John Paul II in Fatima, Portugal
Feast: February 25
Patronage: bodily ills; captives; people ridiculed for their piety; prisoners; sick people

FURTHER READING
"Blessed Jacinta and Francisco Marto." Shrine of the Immaculate Heart of Mary website. URL: http://www.immaculate.force9.co.uk/children.htm. Downloaded: September 10, 2000.

James the Greater, Apostle (d. 44) *One of Jesus' Twelve Disciples; martyr*

Also known as: Giacomo; Iago; Iakob; Jacobo; Jacques; Jacobus Major; James Boanerges; Santiago; Yakob

James was the son of Zebedee and Salomone and the elder brother of St. John the Divine. Zebedee and his family were prosperous fishermen, and James and John were followers of St. John the Baptist before they met Jesus. When Jesus called them to become "fishers of men," they left their occupation to become his full-time disciples. James is referred to as James the Greater because he was taller than another of the apostles, St. James the Lesser. James and his brother were given the surname "Boanerges," meaning "Sons of Thunder," by Jesus, in recognition of their fiery personalities and evangelizing zeal.

Little is known for certain about James's apostolate. There is a tradition that he preached the Gospel in

Spain, but this is suspect both because St. Paul, who definitely did evangelize Spain, wrote in his Epistle to the Romans that he was not building "upon another man's foundation," and because contemporary Spanish writers do not mention him. According to this tradition, which was current by the year 700, James returned to Jerusalem, where he was killed by King Herod Agrippa I (r. 42–44), grandson of Herod the Great. Of greater credence is another tradition, which holds that James had not left Jerusalem by the time of his martyrdom.

Herod Agrippa, a great defender of the Jewish faith, was concerned with the rapid spread of Christianity. He chose Passover of the year 44 to launch a persecution against the Christian community in Jerusalem, and James became his first victim. Agrippa is said to have beheaded James together with his accuser, who had been so moved by James's confession that he had converted to Christianity. James's martyrdom fulfilled a prophecy of Jesus that those who shared his chalice would share in his sufferings.

The tradition that has James evangelizing Spain holds also that his relics were miraculously translated to Iria Flavia in the northwest of that country, whence they were transported to Compostela. During the Middle Ages, the latter town was one of the most famous pilgrimage places in the world, inspiring the creation of the Order of Knights of St. James of Compostela in the 12th century. The authenticity of the sacred relics of Compostela is vouched for in a Bull of Pope Leo XIII (r. 1878–1903). However, they are also claimed by the Church of St.-Saturnin at Toulouse, France, so they may have been divided.

In art, James is represented by a cockleshell; a key; a pilgrim's staff; and a sword. He is depicted as an elderly, bearded man wearing a hat with a scallop shell; as a man with shells around him; and as a pilgrim with wallet and staff.

Feast: July 25

Patronage: apothecaries; arthritis; blacksmiths; druggists; funeral directors; furriers; knights; laborers; pharmacists; pilgrims; rheumatism; rheumatoid sufferers; Chile; Guatemala; Nicaragua; Spain; Spanish conquistadores

James the Less, Apostle (d. ca. 62) *One of the Twelve Disciples of Jesus; first bishop of Jerusalem; martyr*

Also known as: Giacomo; Jacobo; Jacques; Jacobus Minor; James the Younger; James the Just; James the Lesser

James should not be confused with another of Jesus' disciples, James the Greater, who evidently was of greater physical stature than he. The son of Alpheus and Mary, he was a brother of St. Jude and most likely a first cousin of Jesus. The biblical reference to James as "the brother of our Lord" seems best understood in an extended sense, although some scholars interpret it to mean that James was Jesus' actual brother. Another interpretation is that there were two men named James, one of them Jesus' disciple, the other his brother.

Jesus called James to the apostolate together with Jude, though we know little about his membership in the group of 12 until after the Crucifixion. In I Corinthians (15:5–7), St. Paul tells us that Jesus appeared to James before the Ascension. James was among those who later met in the Upper Room.

St. Peter was treated by Jesus as head of the apostles, and he was the recognized leader of the early Christian community. He was imprisoned under King Herod Agrippa I sometime between 42 and 44, and though he escaped miraculously, was forced to flee Jerusalem, leaving the Church there in James's care. As bishop of Jerusalem before the Church of Rome gained ascendancy, James was consulted by evangelists such as Paul, who sought his approval on several occasions. He also presided over a meeting of the apostles around the year 51, in which he supported Peter in his attempt to define Christian customs in contrast to Jewish law, as in the controversy over circumcision. This was a Jewish practice, unknown to Gentiles, and James ruled with Peter that Christians should not be held to it.

James was called the "Just" because he abstained from wine and animal flesh, refused to shave, anoint himself or bathe in a tub. He died in Jerusalem around the year 62 after being thrown from a pinnacle of the Temple by the Pharisees. He died on the ground below, while praying for his attackers. According to some accounts, he was stoned to death, whereas *The Golden Legend* says he was killed by the blow of a fuller's club. Catastrophes that subsequently struck Jerusalem were believed by the Greek historian Eusebius to be a divine punishment for this act.

In art, James often bears a close resemblance to Jesus. He is shown with a club or large mallet; holding his epistle, either as a book or scroll; as a child with a toy mill; or as flung from the pulpit or pinnacle of the Temple in Jerusalem. He especially is known as the patron of the dying because of his deathbed forgiveness of his murderers.

Feast (celebrated with St. Philip): May 3 (formerly May 1 and May 11; in the East, November 14)

Patronage: apothecaries; dying people; fullers; hatters; milliners; pharmacists; Uruguay

Januarius (d. ca. 304–305) *Martyred bishop*
Also known as: Gennaro

Few facts are known about Januarius, who is famous for the miraculous liquefaction of his dried blood several times a year. The bishop of Benevento, Italy, he was caught up in the persecutions of Emperor Diocletian. According to one account, Januarius was denounced under torture by Socias, deacon of the church of Miseno, Proculus, deacon of Pozzuoli, and laymen Eutychetes and Acutius, who had been imprisoned in Nola by Timothy, governor of the province of Campania. Timothy had Januarius arrested and brought to him. When Januarius would not deny his faith, Timothy had a fire stoked in a furnace for three days and threw the saint into it. The flames would not touch him. He was sent back to prison.

Hearing of his travail, his deacon, Festus, and lector, Desiderius, traveled to Nola and were arrested. They were bound in chains and dragged by chariot to Pozzuoli, where Timothy had decreed that all seven men would be thrown to the lions. The beasts, however, ran to Januarius and laid down at his feet.

Enraged, Timothy declared this to be magic and ordered them beheaded. Januarius prayed for God to punish him with blindness, and Timothy was struck blind. He suffered such great pain that he summoned Januarius and begged for his vision back. Januarius prayed and the man's vision was restored. So amazed was the crowd of 5,000 that they converted. The execution was still carried out, and Januarius and his companions were beheaded on September 19. Three days beforehand, Januarius's mother had a dream of him flying to heaven. Upon hearing of his imprisonment, she became so distraught that she died. After the executions, Timothy suffered great torments and pain and died.

The relics of Januarius were buried near the town of Marciano between Pozzuoli and Naples. In 402, the bishop of Naples had the body taken to Naples, where it was interred in the catacombs. Ceremonies were observed in April and September.

In 831 a Benevento nobleman managed to take possession of all the relics save for the skull. For several hundred years, the saint's bones toured Italy, finally returning to Naples at the end of the 13th century. Charles II, king of Naples, had a cathedral built for the enshrinement of the skull.

Two vials of dried blood also appeared. According to legend, the blood had been collected by a serving woman from the stone upon which Januarius had been beheaded. The vials had been buried with his body in Naples. It is not known whether the vials of blood toured with the rest of the relics, or if they were added after their return to Naples. Most likely, they were added. The two feasts in honor of Januarius were formalized in 1337, and records make no mention of the vials of blood.

The first miracle of the liquefying blood was recorded in 1389, while a priest was holding the vials in a procession. On the Mass of St. Januarius, a vial of dried blood was set upon the altar and shortly seen to soften and change color, as though taken from a living man.

From 1608 to 1646, a special chapel was constructed next to the cathedral solely for the skull. Beginning in 1659, the Church has documented the ritual liquefaction of the blood. More than 1,000 books, articles and studies, in Italian alone, have been written on this miracle. Some limited scientific tests have been done. No natural explanation has ever been found.

The hermetically sealed vials are enclosed in a cylindrical silver and glass case, which is attached to a large silver monstrance that has a handle. One vial is larger than the other, and is about two-thirds filled with dried blood. The second, smaller vial has only a few drops. Only the blood in the larger vial undergoes the liquefaction.

The vials are kept in a vault in Naples Cathedral and brought out for certain occasions: the first Sunday in May, which commemorates the translation of the relics to Naples; September 19, the feast day of the saint; and December 16, the commemoration of the eruption of Mt. Vesuvius in 1631, when the blood liquefied for 30 days.

In the ceremonies, the blood is brought out by procession to the altar, where rests a silver bust containing the skull of Januarius. A key part of the ceremony is the presence of the "relatives of Januarius" or "aunts of Januarius," a group of elderly women who have inherited their status down through the generations. As soon as the blood is taken out of the vault, they begin to scream and beg Januarius to liquefy his blood. The entire event becomes one of increasing hysteria as onlookers join the shouting and screaming.

Sometimes the blood liquefies quickly, within minutes, and sometimes takes several hours to change. A red cloth is waved at the first sign of liquefaction, which adds to the hysteria. The dignitaries are allowed to kiss the container. The blood is then paraded through the cathedral while a Te Deum is sung.

On rare occasions, the blood does not liquefy. This is considered an ill omen for the city. In May 1976, the blood did not change, and an earthquake soon struck Naples. Other failures have been associated with famine, disease and political upheaval.

The blood does not simply change from solid to liquid, but goes through several stages. It first changes color from dark brown to yellow-red to scarlet. The dried substance becomes pasty and finally more viscous than normal blood. Usually a small lump remains unchanged and floats in the liquid. Sometimes the liquid bubbles and froths. The volume of the dried blood changes dramatically, as does its weight. During the May ceremonies, the larger vial often fills with liquid, but during the September ceremonies, the volume of the vial decreases. Strangely, the volume increases when liquefaction occurs slowly and decreases when it occurs quickly—the opposite of what might be expected. Furthermore, the weight of the vials increases when the volume decreases, and vice versa.

The liquefaction does not seem to be the result of temperature, for it happens regardless of the temperature inside the cathedral. The container is held only by the handle and the crystal sides are not touched. It is not shaken, though it is turned upside down by officials to check for the beginning of liquefaction.

In 1902, a spectroscopic analysis determined that the vials did contain real blood. Unfortunately, the vials are permanently sealed by hardened putty and cannot be opened for further testing of the contents. Opening them would break them and some or much of their contents would be lost. And even if the vials could be safely opened, tests would still require the sacrifice of some of the contents.

As early as the beginning of the 20th century, it was hypothesized that the psychic hysteria of the onlookers and the "aunts" created the conditions that made the liquefaction possible. However, the blood has been known to liquefy spontaneously when it has been moved for cleaning.

Another mysterious phenomenon involving Januarius has occurred when his ceremonies are observed. In Pozzuoli, a Capuchin monastery has the marble block upon which Januarius was beheaded. When the ceremonies are held in Naples, the stone has turned deep red. On rare occasions it also has dripped blood. Samples of the blood have been laboratory tested and determined to be genuine human blood. Besides some feast ceremonies, the stone bled on February 22, 1860, when a church in Naples dedicated to the saint caught fire.

Feast: September 19
Patronage: blood banks

FURTHER READING
"The Life of St. Januarius." Tr. Edward P. Graham. URL: http://www.fordham.edu/halsall/basis/januarius.html. Downloaded February 13, 2000.
Rogo, D. Scott. *Miracles: A Scientific Exploration of Wondrous Phenomena.* London: Aquarian Press, 1991.

Jerome (347–419) *Scholar, Doctor of the Church, translator of the Latin Vulgate Bible*
Name meaning: "Sacred name"

Jerome was one of the greatest thinkers of the early Church, and also one of the most controversial. He was born Eusebius Hieronymous Sophronius at Stridonium near Aquileia, Italy, to an affluent Christian family. He was baptized at age 18 by Pope Liberius. His father sent him to Rome to be schooled, and he was tutored by a well-known pagan scholar, Donatus. He learned Greek and Latin and oratorical skills.

Despite his Christian upbringing—and perhaps because of his education—Jerome devoted himself to an intense study of the pagan classics. After three years in Rome, he went traveling with a friend. During this time, he experienced a conversion back to his religious roots. On his return to Aquileia, he was on good terms with the clergy.

In 374, he was inspired to travel to Antioch. There, he suffered a great illness that killed some of his friends and traveling companions. While delirious, he had either a dream or a vision in which he was rebuked for his pagan interests. In his own account, he said:

Suddenly I was caught up in the spirit and dragged before the judgment seat of the Judge; and here the light was so bright, and those who stood around were so radiant, that I cast myself upon the ground and did not dare to look up. Asked who and what I was I replied: "I am a Christian." But he who presided said: "Thou liest, thou art a follower of Cicero and not of Christ. For 'where thy treasure is, there will thy heart be also.'" Instantly I became dumb, and amid the strokes of the lash—for He had ordered me to be scourged—I was tortured more severely still by the fire of conscience, considering with myself that verse, "In the grave who shall give thee thanks?" Yet for all that I began to cry and to bewail myself, saying: "Have mercy upon me, O Lord: have mercy upon me." Amid the sound of the scourges this cry still made itself heard. At last the bystanders, falling down before the knees of Him who presided, prayed that He would have pity on my youth, and that He would give me space to repent of my error. He might still, they urged, inflict torture on me, should I ever again read the works of the Gentiles. . . .

Accordingly I made an oath and called upon His name, saying "Lord, if ever again I possess worldly books, or if ever again I read such, I have denied Thee." Dismissed, then, on taking this oath, I returned to the upper world, and, to the surprise of all, I opened upon them eyes so drenched with tears that my distress served to convince even the credulous. And that this was no sleep nor idle dream, such as those by which we are often mocked, I call to witness the tribunal before which I lay, and the terrible judgment which I feared. . . . I profess that my shoulders were black and blue, that I felt

St. Jerome dying alone (Library of Congress Prints and Photographs Division)

the bruises long after I awoke from my sleep, and that thenceforth I read the books of God with a zeal greater than I had previously given to the books of men.

This event proved to be life-changing, and Jerome retired to the desert at Chalcis, southwest of Antioch, to live as a hermit for four years. He learned Hebrew. It was a time of suffering for him, both of health and from temptations.

He then resumed his career as scholar and biblical consultant. He consented to ordination only if he could remain a monk or a recluse. Jerome went to Constantinople to study under St. Gregory Nazianzus. In 382, he went to Rome, where he won the favorable attention of Pope Damasus (r. 366–383), who named him papal secretary. When Damasus died, Jerome found himself out of favor. He had alienated many people, not only pagans, but also those whom he had attacked with his sarcasm and barbed wit. Rumors began to circulate that his relationship with St. Paula was not appropriate.

Jerome, St. Paula and Eustochium (Paula's third daughter), and others exiled themselves to Jerusalem and then toured Egypt and Palestine. At Bethlehem, they established monastic communities for men and women, a free school and a hospice.

Jerome vigorously fought anything he considered a heresy. From 405 until his death, he attacked the Pelagian heresy. He defended attacks on the perpetual virginity of Mary, nonsecular celibacy and the veneration of relics. He opposed the teachings of Origen and argued with St. Augustine.

In 404 Paula died. Several years later, Rome was sacked by barbarians, who pursued refugees east. Jerome's life and work were interrupted with violence, beatings, killings and arson. Eustochium's convent was destroyed; she never recovered, and died in 419.

Jerome died in 420, his health, voice and eyesight failing from work and penance. He was buried beside Paula and Eustochium at the church of the Nativity in Bethlehem. Later his remains were moved to St. Major's in Rome.

Jerome's ecclesiastical writings include a continuation of the *Historia Ecclesiastica* of Eusebius of Caesarea, to 378, and *De Viris Illustribus* (392), about leading ecclesiastical writers. He also translated Origen and wrote controversial treatises. A large number of his letters survive.

Jerome's greatest accomplishment was his translation of the Bible, including the Apocrypha, from Greek and Hebrew into Latin. The Latin Vulgate Bible was the primary authority until about the mid-20th century. Jerome spent years working on the translation.

He believed that a guardian angel is assigned to each soul at birth. Even the souls of sinners receive a guardian angel, he said, though mortal sin will put them "into flight." He organized angels into ranks of seven, eliminating the principalities and virtues in the rankings of other Church theologians. He questioned the distinctions between ranks of angels.

Despite his own dream experience, Jerome sided with the Old Testament prophet Jeremiah in skepticism about dreams. He agreed that dreams can be a vehicle of revelation to a soul, but also held that the impure and unrighteous could twist dreams for their own self-serving ends. He declared that the word of God could not be sought through pagan practices of dream incubation, such as offered in the Aesculapian temples.

According to the Christian scholar Morton Kelsey, Jerome may have deliberately mistranslated a Hebrew word so as to condemn dreams as witchcraft or soothsaying. According to Kelsey, Jerome's mistranslation was of the Hebrew term *anan*, which means witchcraft or soothsaying. *Anan* appears 10 times in the Old Testament. Seven times Jerome correctly translated it as "witchcraft." Three times he translated it as "observing dreams." For example, Leviticus 19:26 was changed from "You shall not practice augury or witchcraft" (soothsaying) into "You shall not practice augury nor observe dreams." Another reference against soothsaying that he changed is found in Deuteronomy 18:10–11: "There shall not be found among you . . . any one who practices divination, a soothsayer, or an augur, or a sorcerer, or a charmer, or a medium, or a wizard, or a necromancer." These passages are part of the body of rules, regulations and laws laid down to govern Hebrew society. The mistranslation is curious, says Kelsey, in light of the fact that Jerome was an excellent scholar and correctly translated the term seven other times. Kelsey concludes that the mistranslation may have been deliberate, perhaps because of Jerome's frightening dream. The New Oxford, New Jerusalem and other modern editions of the Bible have restored the original meaning of *anan*.

Feast: September 30
Patronage: libraries and librarians

FURTHER READING
Kelsey, Morton. *God, Dreams and Revelation: A Christian Interpretation of Dreams.* Minneapolis: Augsburg Publishing House, 1968, 1974, 1991.
St. Jerome: Selected Letters. Tr. F. A. Wright. Cambridge, Mass.: Harvard University Press, 1992.

Joachim (d. first century) *By tradition, the father of the Blessed Virgin Mary*
Also known as: Cleophas, Eliacim, Heli, Jonachir, Sadoc

St. Joachim and the Angel (Library of Congress Prints and Photographs Division)

No historical information about the names or lives of the parents of Mary exists. What is known comes from *The Golden Legend* and the aprochryphal *Book of James*, or *Protoevangelicum Jacobi*. Joachim is said to have been born in Nazareth, and wed Anne when both were very young. Their childlessness was the cause of much humiliation. Joachim withdrew to the desert, where he fasted and prayed for 40 days. An angel appeared to him and told him that Anne would bear a child. (Legend also tells that an angel appeared to Anne with the same news.)

Joachim was said to have died some time after witnessing the presentation of Jesus in the Temple at Jerusalem. He is venerated in both the Western and Eastern churches.

Feast: July 26

Joan of Arc (1412–1431)

Name meaning: God is gracious
Also known as: Jeanne d'Arc, Jean D'arc, Jehanne d'Arc, the Maid of Orleans, la Pucelle (the Flea)

Joan was born in January 1412 to Jacques and Isabelle Darc (allegedly, a French poet changed the surname to d'Arc) in the village of Greux-Domremy in the Lorraine region of France, near the province of Champagne. Although peasants, the family was not poor, and young Joan spent her childhood tending the animals, learning domestic skills and in pious devotion and prayer. She never learned to read or write.

But she and her neighbors were affected by politics. Since 1337, France and England had been at war, with some periods of peace, over the disputed ownership of several large provinces, including Aquitaine, Gascony, Poitiers, Normandy and Brittany. These regions had been fiefdoms of English kings for over 300 years, especially after the marriage of Henry II and Eleanor of Aquitaine, but did not accept English rule graciously. Nor did these regions desire absorption into France. Fiercely independent, the provinces continually fought with their English overlords, first allying themselves with one king, then another, to further their own agenda.

By the time Joan was three, the French had suffered defeat after defeat, first at the hands of England's King Edward III and his son Edward, the Black Prince, then through the loss of Aquitaine and the port city of Calais in the Treaty of Bretigny in 1360, and most recently at the disastrous battle of Agincourt in 1415, in which the heavily outnumbered English (skilled at longbow) under Henry V routed the French: 6,000 French soldiers killed in battle as against English losses of 300. Even more horrible was Henry V's order to massacre the French prisoners to prevent their rebellion—an act contrary to all accepted conventions of warfare and chivalry. Charles VI of France sued for peace, signing the Treaty of Troyes in 1420, in which Henry V won the right to rule his conquered French territories; was recognized as the heir to the French throne, disinheriting the dauphin, Charles VII; and received Charles VI's daughter in marriage.

The loss at Agincourt hardened French resolve, but men and supplies were few. And many French nobles, most important, those of the House of Burgundy, allied themselves with the English. Further complicating the situation was that both Henry V and Charles VI died within two years after signing the Treaty of Troyes, leaving the infant Henry VI the legal heir but unable to rule, providing an opportunity for the dauphin's supporters to reinstate him as king. In Joan's little village of Domremy, sympathies were with the Armagnacs, or the French party supporting the cause of the dauphin. And the villagers believed stories of a prophecy—perhaps spoken by King Arthur's wizard, the great Merlin—that a virgin maiden would come from the oak forests of Lorraine to lead the king to victory and restore all of France to the French.

When she was 13, Joan began hearing voices accompanied by great blazes of light. At first the unidentified voices exhorted her to go to church and be good, but gradually Joan understood that the speakers were St. Michael the Archangel and the virgin martyrs SS. Catherine of Alexandria and Margaret of Antioch (extremely popular in the Middle Ages, these two saints have been dropped from the calendar and their cults suppressed). They spoke to Joan often, eventually becoming visible to her as well. Soon they began to give Joan commands: She was to lead an army against the English and raise the siege at Orleans, then see the dauphin, Charles VII, crowned king of France at Reims. Joan protested that she was merely a young girl, unschooled in warfare and unable to lead an army. But her voices insisted the mission was God's will, so in 1428 Joan persuaded an uncle to take her to Vaucouleurs, where Robert Baudricourt, commander of the dauphin's forces, was headquartered. She explained her mission and asked to be taken to the dauphin, but Baudricourt rudely dismissed her, suggesting to her uncle that he have Joan's father whip the girl for such impudence.

Joan returned to Domremy, but her voices gave her no rest, insisting she return to Vaucouleurs. She arrived in Vaucouleurs in January 1429 and demanded to see the dauphin. Although again dismissed by Baudricourt she remained in the village, where in February she told Baudricourt of a terrible French defeat at the battle of the Herrings outside Orleans. When Baudricourt learned confirmation of the loss days later, he finally conceded. With an escort of three armed men and dressed as a man, Joan traveled to the village of Chinon in March to meet the dauphin. Charles kept the little party waiting for two days, fearing a trick, but finally agreed to an audience. He disguised himself so that Joan would not recognize him. But with the help of her voices Joan knew Charles immediately and gave him a secret sign known only to him, assuring him of the authenticity and supernatural power of her mission. Historians have speculated on this secret sign, believing it to be a confirmation of Charles's questionable legitimate birth.

Charles still dithered about Joan's motives, and finally decided to have her examined by a committee of bishops and doctors in Poitiers—the churchmen to assess her strength of faith, and the doctors (at Charles's mother's instigation) to verify her gender and the state of her virginity. All found Joan to be sincere, ardent and pure, so she returned to Chinon to lead an expedition. She wore white armor and carried a special standard bearing the words "Jesus: Maria" with a representation of God receiving the French fleur-de-lis from two kneeling angels. But instead of using the sword Charles presented her, Joan's voices told her to look for an ancient sword buried behind the altar in the chapel of Ste. Catherine-de-Fierbois. It lay right where they described.

Joan audaciously called upon England to withdraw from France, and when the English refused she and her troops entered Orleans on April 29–30, 1429. The city had been under siege since the previous October. Such a bold maneuver and Joan's inspiring presence invigorated the French soldiers, who captured all the surrounding English forts by May 8, liberating Orleans. Joan was wounded by an arrow, an act that she had foretold. Joan begged to continue her successful campaign, but Charles's advisers cautioned against proceeding. They did allow Joan a sortie on the Loire River in June, joined by troops of her friend the Duc d'Alençon, which resulted in a crushing defeat of the English forces led by Sir John Fastolf at Patay. Joan

Joan of Arc (Library of Congress Prints and Photographs Division)

pressed for the dauphin's coronation. On June 17, 1429, Charles VII was crowned king of France at Reims Cathedral. Joan stood next to the king, in full armor, holding her standard aloft.

The mission from the voices complete, Joan may have wished to return to Domremy, or, taking heed of the voices' warning that she had only a short time left, to press her military advantage. An abortive attempt to take Paris in late August failed, damaging Joan's prestige, and when Charles signed a truce with the duke of Burgundy for the winter, Joan was left inactive and miserable at court. Perhaps to cheer her, Charles ennobled Joan and her family in late December 1429, allowing them to add the name Du Lis (of the lily). When hostilities resumed in April, her voices told Joan that she would be taken prisoner before midsummer. This prophecy was soon fulfilled. While fighting to defend Compiègne from the Burgundians on May 24, she and some of her soldiers were unfortunately left on the other side of the river when the drawbridge was raised, and Joan, pulled from her horse, became the prisoner of John of Luxembourg. No attempt was made by Charles to rescue Joan or bargain for her ransom, even though the French had the earl of Suffolk prisoner, and the two could have been exchanged. Instead, John of Luxembourg sold Joan to the duke of Burgundy in November for 10,000 francs, and he turned her over to his English allies, an event foretold by the voices.

The English, enraged and terrified over Joan's military success and her supernatural powers, couldn't execute her for her fighting abilities but instead sought to prove her a witch and a heretic. They had a willing prosecutor in Peter Cauchon, bishop of Beauvais (Compiègne was in his diocese), who hoped the English would install him as archbishop of Rouen. He set up a tribunal composed mainly of theologians and doctors from the University of Paris, most of whom were English supporters, and began interrogating Joan on February 21, 1431, not long after her 19th birthday. Joan complained bitterly about her incarceration in the secular Rouen prison, and she declared that since she had been judged orthodox in Poitiers in 1429, the trial should take place in an ecclesiastical council. All her pleas were ignored; she was harassed by the guards and even kept in chains in an iron cage after she attempted to escape.

The 37-member tribunal questioned her mercilessly about her visions, her voices and her choice to wear men's clothing. With no advocate to defend her, Joan spoke honestly and forthrightly about the truth of her visions and her mission from God. She was charged with 70 counts of sorcery, heresy, prophesying, conjuring and divining, but that number was reduced to 12. The tribunal denounced Joan and threatened torture if she did not recant her heresy, but Joan stood fast. In March she even told her English accusers that within seven years they would suffer a defeat much worse than Orleans, and this also came true when Henry VI lost the battle for Paris in November 1437.

On May 22 Joan was again urged to recant, and when she did not, the authorities erected a stake in St. Ouen cemetery. Admonished and sentenced before a large crowd, Joan's courage failed, and she signed a retraction agreeing that her voices were lies and that she would wear only women's clothing. She was led back to prison, ostensibly with female guards. But whether the jailers took her clothes, leaving her only men's apparel, or whether she despaired of her voices' rejection, Joan resumed wearing men's clothes, a clear violation of her retraction, and declared the truth of her voices. She was condemned as a relapsed heretic on May 29 and sentenced to burn at the stake.

The next morning at 8:00 A.M. Joan was led out to the stake in the marketplace of Rouen dressed in a long white garment and wearing a mitre cap that bore the words "Heretic, Relapsed, Apostate, Idolator." She asked for a cross to hold, standing on a pyre so high that the executioner could not administer the coup de grace to save her from pain. She called out "Jesus" until the end, and legend says her heart did not burn but was found whole in the ashes. An English soldier swore he saw a white bird rise out of the pyre. Afterward the authorities threw her ashes into the River Seine. Joan was 19 years old.

In 1454, Joan's mother and two brothers appealed to the Vatican to reopen the case, and Pope Callistus III appointed a commission to reexamine the episode. Popular opinion in France had swung back to veneration of Joan, and the pope's appellate panel reversed and annulled the sentence on July 7, 1456—only 25 years too late.

The question of whether Joan's voices were divinely inspired or manifestations of modern schizophrenia was examined by the English psychical researcher Frederic W. H. Myers. Myers believed that the visions and voices came from Joan's own subconscious, her "subliminal self." Anthropologist Margaret A. Murray even speculated that Joan was indeed a witch. But author Andrew Lang asserted that Joan's lack of hysteria, her steadfast belief in the truth of the voices and the absence of other miraculous events connected to the voices and visions proved their veracity. As C. S. Lewis once said, "If anything extraordinary seems to have happened, we can always say we have been the victims of an illusion."

Beatified: 1909 by Pope Saint Pius X
Canonized: 1920 by Pope Benedict XV

Feast: May 30

Patronage: captives; martyrs; people opposed to Church authorities; people ridiculed for piety; prisoners; rape victims; service women; soldiers; virgins; women in the air and naval services; women in Women Appointed for Voluntary Emergency Service (WAVES); women in the Women's Army Corps (WACs); France

FURTHER READING

Gordon, Mary. *Joan of Arc: A Penguin Life.* New York: Viking Penguin, 2000.

Guiley, Rosemary Ellen. *The Encyclopedia of Witches and Witchcraft,* 2nd ed. New York: Facts On File, 1999.

Lang, Andrew, "The Voices of Jeanne d'Arc," *Proceedings of the Society for Psychical Research,* Part XXVIII, Vol. XI (July 1895), pp. 198–212.

Nash-Marshall, Siobhan. *Joan of Arc: A Spiritual Biography,* New York: Crossroad Publishing Co., 1999.

Joaquina de Vedruna (1783–1854) *Founder*

Name meaning: God will order
Also known as: Joaquina Vedruna de Mas

Joaquina de Vedruna was born on April 16, 1783, in Barcelona, Spain, the daughter of Lorenzo de Vedruna, a government functionary, and Teresa Vidal. Her family was very religious and, even as a child, so was Joaquina. She paid particular devotion to the infant Jesus. She was also obsessively clean, not letting even a speck of dirt mar her clothes. At 12, she wished fervently to become a Carmelite nun, but the order wouldn't accept her because they considered her too young to make such an important decision.

In 1799, at the age of 16, Joaquina married Teodoro de Mas, a friend of her father and like him an employee of the government. Undecided about which of Lorenzo's three daughters to wed, Teodoro had given them a box of candy. The older girls had rejected it as a childish gift, but Joaquina had accepted it with joy, exclaiming: "I love almonds."

Joaquina bore Teodoro nine children before Spain came under French domination in 1808 and Teodoro went to fight in the wars of liberation. Joaquina fled Barcelona with her children, and on their way out of town met an old woman who conducted them to Vich, where she took them into her home. Joaquina always believed that the Virgin Mary had had a hand in helping them. Then one day she heard a voice that told her that she would soon be a widow. Indeed, news soon came that Teodoro had been killed.

Leaving all her clothes with the woman who had befriended her, Joaquina dedicated herself to helping the poor and attending the sick and injured in the hospitals. At first people thought she had gone mad from grief at her husband's death. For the next 10 years she dedicated herself to penitence, prayer and works of charity, asking God to let her know what he planned for her future. When four of her daughters entered convents and her four sons married, she was at last free of the responsibilities of the home and able to realize her childhood dream of becoming a nun.

Joaquina chanced to meet a Capuchin friar, Esteban de Olut, who advised her on founding her own order, the Congregation of Carmelite Sisters of Charity, in 1826. With the support of the bishop of Vich, Jesús Corcuera y Corcuera, the order began with eight sisters, but soon spread throughout Catalonia, establishing hospitals and schools, especially for the poor. The Carmelite Sisters of Charity received papal approval in 1850 and has since spread worldwide.

In 1850, Joaquina began to feel the first symptoms of a paralysis that eventually was to make her completely immobile. She gave up all of her charges and devoted herself to a life of prayer, dying of cholera during an epidemic in Vich, August 28, 1854.

Beatified: May 19, 1940, by Pope Pius XII
Canonized: April 12, 1959, by Pope John XXIII
Feast: May 22
Patronage: abuse victims; death of children; exiles; widows

FURTHER READING

López-Melús, Rafael María. "Santa Joaquina de Vedruna." Carmelnet website. URL: http://www.carmelnet.org/chas/santos/joaquina.htm. Downloaded: November 17, 1999.

"Joaquina de Vedruna." Carmelnet website. URL: http://www.carmelnet.org/galleries/Saints/Saints_3/Joachina/joach ina.htm. Downloaded: November 17, 1999.

John I (d. 526) *Pope and martyr*

John was a native of Tuscany. He became archdeacon in the Church of Rome and, after an interregnum of seven days, succeeded Pope St. Hormisdas on August 13, 523.

John was by this time very old and frail, and protested when Theodoric, king of the Ostrogoths and of Italy, asked him to lead a delegation of Roman senators to Constantinople. Earlier in 523, Emperor Justin had issued a decree against the Arians in the Eastern Empire, requiring them to return to the Catholics churches they had seized. Although he was himself Arian, Theodoric was concerned about the larger political implications of this move, and wanted the delegation to get the edict repealed. He threatened reprisals against Western Catholics, should John fail in the mission.

He was unexpectedly well received in Constantinople. The common people of the city came out in throngs to greet him, and on meeting the pope, Justin prostrated himself at his feet. Some time later, he had John crown him. Most of the patriarchs of the Eastern churches came to see him and see John officiate in the Church of Santa Sofia in the Latin Rite on Easter Day of 526, in the place of Epiphanius, patriarch of Constantinople.

This grand reception clearly showed the respect given John as the leader of the universal Church. Unfortunately, it also threatened Theodoric, who feared that it might presage a revival of ancient sentiment for imperial unity. Upon landing in Italy on his return trip, therefore, John was arrested and incarcerated at Ravenna. He died there soon thereafter, on May 18 or 19, 526. His relics now lie in St. Peter's Basilica in Rome.

In art, he is shown looking through the bars of a prison or imprisoned with a deacon and a subdeacon. He is venerated especially at Ravenna and in Tuscany.

Feast: May 18 (formerly May 27)

John XXIII (1881–1963) *Much-beloved pope who promoted social reforms and interfaith communication and convened the liberalizing Second Vatican Council*
Also known as: Il Papa Buono (The Good Pope)

The man who as pope would take the name John XXIII was born on November 25, 1881, at Sotto il Monte, near Bergamo, in the foothills of the Alps of northern Italy. He was baptized Angelo Giuseppe Roncalli. His parents were farmers. As a youth, after helping out in the fields, he went to a seminary in Bergamo to study for the priesthood. He won a scholarship to the Pontifical Seminary Seminario Romano (called the Apollinare) in Rome, where he completed his studies. He was ordained in Rome in 1904 and said his first Mass at St. Peter's.

Now Father Roncalli, he returned to his home diocese with the positions of professor of Church history and apologetics at the Bergamo seminary and secretary to Bishop Radini-Tedeschi. Radini-Tedeschi was a socially involved bishop with liberal views who ran afoul of Pope St. Pius X (r. 1903–14) and his campaign to suppress modernism. Roncalli himself came under suspicion for a time, but survived. During this period, he wrote scholarly works, beginning a five-volume life of St. Charles Borromeo (published between 1936 and 1952). He also worked for a diocesan organization of Catholic women and a residence hall for students.

During World War I, Roncalli was drafted into the Italian army, serving first as sergeant in the medical corps and later as lieutenant in the chaplains' corps. After the war ended in 1918, he returned to Bergamo and worked there until Pope Benedict XV (r. 1914–22) called him to Rome to reorganize the Congregation for the Propagation of the Faith.

In 1925, Pope Pius XI (r. 1922–39) made Roncalli an archbishop and appointed him apostolic visitor to Bulgaria. Ten years later, Pius XI made him apostolic delegate to Greece and Turkey, and he moved to Istanbul, where he remained throughout World War II. He did what he could to help the Greeks suffering from famine and made contact with members of the Eastern Orthodox churches, long separated from Rome by schism. During the war, Hitler's ambassador to Turkey, Franz von Papen, gave him money that had been sent to bribe the Turks to side with Germany, which he then used to support Jewish refugees fleeing the Nazis.

At the conclusion of World War II in 1945, Pope Pius XII (r. 1939–58) sent Roncalli as nuncio to France, where he mediated both between conservative and liberal clergy and between church and the state. He dissuaded Charles de Gaulle from forcing the Holy See to remove 25 French bishops who had cooperated with the Nazi-collaborating Vichy regime during the war. As an unofficial observer at UNESCO, he showed that he understood the need for international understanding. Thanks to his ministry and diplomatic skills, he continued to advance in the Church, Pius XII creating him a cardinal and patriarch of Venice in 1953.

When Pius XII died in 1958, Roncalli was put forward as a compromise candidate for the papacy. He was elected on October 28, 1958, and took the name John XXIII. Although he was then 77, he soon showed himself to be an energetic man with a vision. In a 1961 encyclical, he advocated social reforms and assistance to underdeveloped countries. He broke the tradition of the pope as "prisoner of the Vatican," travelling outside Rome, and advanced cooperation with other religions and even atheistic communist states. Among his visitors were many Protestant leaders, the head of the Greek Orthodox Church, and a Shinto high priest. During the 1962 Cuban missile crisis, he helped ease tensions between President Kennedy and the Khrushchev regime. At the same time, he did not neglect his pastoral duties, and his humble personality had an effect on Catholics and non-Catholics alike.

In 1959, John announced his intention of calling an ecumenical council to consider the renewal of the Church in the modern world, embracing reforms that were being promoted by ecumenical and liturgical movements within the Church. This council, known as the Second Vatican Council or Vatican II, was convened on October 11, 1962. The council introduced many important reforms, such as the Mass said in the vernacular rather than in Latin, but John was not to live to see its work completed. He died of cancer on June 3, 1963.

Devotion to John began almost immediately. His tomb in St. Peter's Basilica has become a favorite pilgrimage site, and letters beseeching his intercession arrive from all over the world. He is credited with several miraculous cures, including one in Naples in 1966, in which a nun was healed of multiple stomach ulcers and serious intestinal disorders, and another in Sicily in 1967, in which another woman was healed of tubercular peritonitis and a heart condition.

Some at the Second Vatican Council wanted to canonize John by acclamation, as had been the practice in the early centuries of the Church. However, others believed that this would unfairly elevate him above his more conservative predecessor, Pius XII. In the end, Pope Paul VI (r. 1963–78) ruled that the process would begin for both popes simultaneously. The cause of Pius XII has since been dropped, but John was finally beatified in 2000 along with another conservative pope, the controversial Pius IX.

Beatified: September 3, 2000, by John Paul II
Feast: June 3

FURTHER READING
Bursher, Joseph. "Pope John XXIII." In *Popes through the Ages*. New Advent website. URL: http://www.newadvent.org/Popes/ppjo23.htm. Downloaded: September 10, 2000.
O'Grady, Desmond. "Almost a Saint: Pope John XXIII." American Catholic website. URL: http://www.americancatholic.org/Messenger/Nov1996/feature1.asp#F1 Downloaded: February 1, 2000.
Woodward, Kenneth L., "When Saints Go Marching In," *Newsweek*, September 4, 2000, pp. 50–51.

John the Baptist (first century) *Prophet, martyr, Precursor or Forerunner of the Lord*
Also known as: "the man sent from God"

John's story is told in the Gospels. He was born to Zachary, a priest of the temple at Jerusalem, and his wife Elizabeth, a kinswoman of the Blessed Virgin Mary. Both Zachary and Elizabeth were advanced in years—and Elizabeth was barren—when Gabriel the Archangel announced that a son, John, was to be born to them. John was born about six months before Jesus.

Nothing of John's early years is known. He probably was about 32 when he began his spiritual mission by withdrawing into the desert near Jordan to fast and pray. He wore only a garment made of camel's hair tied with a leather girdle, and he survived on locusts and wild honey. He then started preaching, and his intensity appealed to many, despite his disheveled appear-

St. John the Baptist (Library of Congress Prints and Photographs Division)

ance. He baptized people in the River Jordan as they confessed their sins.

Many thought him to be the Messiah who was prophesied to come, but he said he was not: "After me comes he who is mightier than I, the thong of whose sandals I am not worthy to stoop down and untie. I have baptized you with water; but he will baptize you with the Holy Spirit" (Mark 1:7–8).

When Jesus came to be baptized, the heavens split, the Holy Spirit descended upon Jesus like a dove, and a voice said, "Thou art my beloved Son, with thee I am well pleased" (Mark 1:11). Jesus later said there was no greater prophet than John.

John ran afoul of King Herod Antipas (r. 4 B.C.–A.D. 39), the provincial governor under Emperor Tiberius Caesar of Rome. John criticized Herod's private affairs, including his marriage to his niece, Herodias, who had been married to Herod's half-brother, Philip. Herod imprisoned John in the fortress of Machaerus on the Dead Sea.

John continued to preach from prison. Herodias despised him and plotted against him. On Herod's birthday, Herodias's 14-year-old daughter by Philip, Salome, pleased the king with her dancing. He swore an oath promising her anything in return. Coached by her mother, Salome answered that she wanted the head of John the Baptist brought to her on a platter. Herod had no choice but to comply, and John was beheaded. Salome accepted it and presented it to her mother.

Jesus' disciples removed the body to a tomb, and Jesus and his followers went into the desert to mourn John's death.

According to Patristic tradition, John was freed from original sin and sanctified in his mother's womb. In art, John is depicted as an ascetic hermit, sometimes holding a lamb. He carries a staff that ends in a cross. His baptism of Jesus has been painted often.

Feast: June 24 (birth) and August 29 (martyrdom)
Patronage: baptism; conversion; farriers; monastic life; tailors

John Baptist de la Salle (1651–1719) *Founder of the Institute of the Brothers of the Christian Schools; educational pioneer and reformer; the father of modern pedagogy, or the profession of teaching*
Also known as: Jean-Baptiste de la Salle

John Baptist de la Salle was born on April 30, 1651, in Reims, France, to a distinguished family. He was the oldest of 10 children. His parents, hoping he would continue the family tradition of a career in law, sent him to the College des Bons Enfants, where he earned a master of arts degree in 1669. John, however, had been attracted to the Church from age 11. On March 11, 1662, he received his tonsure, and he became a canon of the See of Reims on January 7, 1667.

In 1670 he was sent to the seminary of Saint-Sulpice. He also attended theology lectures at the Sorbonne. As a student he was noted for his brilliance and his piety. In 1671 his mother died, followed by his father in 1672. John was required to leave and return home to become the head of his family. He was ordained subdeacon on June 2, 1672, and was ordained deacon in Paris on March 21, 1676. He attempted to resign his canonry in favor of work in the parish, but was refused. He was ordained a priest in 1678, and received his doctorate in theology in 1680.

John's pioneering work in education began with his administering of the last will and testament of Nicholas Roland, canon and theologian of Reims. The dying Roland had asked him to take over administration of the newly formed Congregation of the Sisters of the Child Jesus. He assisted in the opening of free elementary schools.

John soon found that the teachers were disheartened and lacked the proper training. He took them in, first helping them in class, subsidizing their living expenses and even feeding them at his own table. In 1681, he created a community of teachers. It failed, but a second effort was successful. He resigned his canonry in July 1683 and gave his money to the poor the following winter. From then on he dedicated himself to training young men for teaching, and the Institute of the Brothers of the Christian Schools was born. The teachers were prohibited from becoming priests, and priests were prohibited from entering the institute.

John revolutionized how subjects were taught. One of the first reforms he instituted was the teaching of reading in the vernacular instead of in the traditional Latin, which enabled students to learn more quickly. He also used the "Simultaneous Method" in which students were grouped accorded to ability so that they could all learn the same lessons at the same pace. The Simultaneous Method was employed in all subjects in all levels of education.

In 1684, he opened a seminary for lay teachers for instruction in the new methods of teaching, and an academy for youths who were preparing to enter the brotherhood. In 1699, he founded the Christian Academy, a Sunday school for adults in the parish of Saint-Sulpice. Its curriculum included geometry, architecture and drawing, in addition to religious studies.

John endured many trials, criticisms and opposition in his work. He was deposed in 1702 for a time. From 1702 to 1713, he was engaged in a constant struggle for the recognition and survival of his institute. He was strongly motivated to improve the wretched condition of the masses under Louis XIV by providing them education. In addition to the elementary free schools, John established technical schools and colleges. In 1705, John established a boarding college at Saint-Yon, the first of its kind and a model for subsequent colleges. He later created a technical school.

John desired to see his institute gain papal approval, but it did not happen during his lifetime. He spent his last years in retirement at Saint-Yon. He died on Good Friday, April 7, 1719. Nearly six years later, on February 26, 1725, Pope Benedict XIII (r. 1724–30) gave his approval to the institute.

John is remembered as one of the greatest educational pioneers both of his day and of all time.

Canonized: May 24, 1900, by Pope Leo XIII
Feast: May 15
Patronage: teachers

FURTHER READING
Blain, John B. *The Life of St. John Baptist de la Salle.* Winona, Minn.: Lasallian Publications, 1998.

John Baptist Marie Vianney (1786–1869) *Renowned fiery preacher and patron saint of priests*

Also known as: Jean-Baptiste-Marie Vianney; St. John Vianney; the Curé d'Ars; the Servant of God

John Baptist Marie Vianney was born on May 8, 1786, in Dardilly, France, to modest circumstances. His father, Matthieu Vianney, was a shepherd. As a child he did farm work and received only two years of schooling. At age 20, in 1806, John enrolled in a new ecclesiastical school in Ecully. Handicapped by his lack of education, he was an average student. When France went to war against Spain, Emperor Napoleon rescinded the military exemption for ecclesiastical students, and John was drafted into the army. A reluctant soldier, he soon fell in with some deserters and remained in hiding for 14 months. His arrest was prevented when his younger brother took his place in the army.

John returned to Ecully in 1810 and resumed his studies. In 1812 he was sent to a seminary in Verrières. He struggled and did poorly in his courses, but succeeded in being ordained a priest on August 13, 1815. He was sent to Ecully, where Abbé Balley encouraged him to persevere, and interceded on his behalf when he failed his exams.

Balley died in 1818, and John was named curé, or parish priest, of Ars, a village about 20 miles north of Lyons. This remote area was lax in religious observances, and John devoted himself to instilling a stricter discipline. He spent from 16 to 20 hours a day in the confessional listening to his parishioners.

John composed strong, fiery sermons intended to wake people up from their sinful slumber. He labored away every week, writing out his sermons in his own hand—a necessity, since he had a poor memory. He spent hours in prayer to receive inspiration. He sometimes used the sermons of others as models, and also consulted sources of the day, including sermon manuals and the anonymous *Catachiste des Peuples*. His intensity appealed to people, and they flocked to hear him. As his reputation grew, people came even from foreign countries to hear him preach. As many as 300 people a day arrived in Ars.

Several years after arriving at Ars, John founded the Providence, an orphanage for girls that became popular for the catechism teachings that he gave there. The Providence served as a model for similar institutions that followed throughout France.

John also became interested in the story of St. Philomena, and built a shrine to her, which became a popular pilgrimage site.

John endured the criticisms of his peers that he was too uneducated to serve as parish priest. For 30 years, he suffered diabolical attacks that encouraged more criticism.

St. John Baptist Marie Vianney ((Library of Congress Prints and Photographs Division)

For more than 40 years, John practiced severe mortification of food and sleep that probably would have proved fatal to many others. But he kept going with constant energy and drive, reclaiming lapsed Catholics and converting others.

John died at Ars on August 4, 1869. He refused all honors due him.

Numerous miracles were recorded of John. He was witnessed levitating while deep in prayer, his face transfigured and surrounded by a brilliant aura. He manifested money. Once, when in need of funds for the foundation of a mission, he prayed to Our Lady of Salette, to whom he was devoted, and subsequently found the sum he needed. When food ran short at the Providence orphanage, John took a relic of St. Francis Regis and placed it in a small pile of corn and prayed with the children. The attic was then found to be full of corn heaped into a pyramid shape, and of a different color than the other corn. John also healed people, especially children.

John had numerous mystical experiences, including the mystical marriage, in which he received a gold ring of extraordinary brilliance, which he wore on the fourth finger of his left hand. Many who came to confession reported that an unearthly radiance emanated from his side of the booth, and that fiery rays shot from his face. He also spoke in tongues and entered a rapturous state in the confessional. He possessed mystical knowledge; he could read the thoughts of others and could discern the future.

During his beatification process, John's body was exhumed and found to be dried and darkened, but perfectly intact. His heart was removed and placed in a reliquary in a separate building called the Shrine of the Curé's Heart. His face was covered with a wax mask, and his body was placed in a golden reliquary open to view.

Unfortunately, some of John's sermons are lost. In 1845, Canon Perrodin, the superior of the seminary at Brou, borrowed 20 copies of sermons to use in the preparation of a spiritual book. He returned them to the Abbé Raymond, John's assistant. Raymond respected John but considered him no great speaker, and so he put the sermons in a drawer. After he was appointed pastor at Jayat in 1853, he tossed the sermons and other papers away.

Other sermons were given away or even sold by John in order to raise money for the poor. Some he sent to the Abbé Colomb, forbidding them to be published without examination by Rome. The sermons were forgotten. After John's death, interest in his work, believed to be saved only in letters, caused the sermons, about 85 in number, to be sent to Rome. They were soon published. All but three of the originals remain in Rome in the motherhouse of the Canons of the Immaculate Conception. Two were made into reliquaries and presented to Pope Pius X in 1905 and to Cardinal Coullie, archbishop of Lyons. The third was sent to Ars, where it was framed in gilded bronze and double crystal.

Proclaimed Venerable: October 3, 1874, by Pope Pius IX
Beatified: January 8, 1905, by Pope Pius X
Canonized: 1925 by Pope Pius XI
Patronage: parish priests

FURTHER READING

Trochu, Abbe Francis. *The Curé D'Ars: St. Jean-Marie-Baptiste Vianney.* Rockford, Ill.: TAN Books and Publishers, 1977.
Vianney, John. *Sermons of the Curé d'Ars.* Rockford, Ill.: TAN Books and Publishers, 1995.

John Berchmans (1599–1621) *Jesuit confessor renowned for his intense piety*

John Berchmans was born on March 13, 1599, in Diest, Brabant. His father was a shoemaker. Even as a child he displayed great piety, attending Mass and Sunday sermons and making pilgrimages to the sanctuary of Montaigu near Diest. He also spent much time caring for his sick mother.

John decided to become a Jesuit after reading the life of St. Aloysius Gonzaga. Against the wishes of his family, he entered the Society of Jesus in September 1616 and studied for two years at their college in Malines. He was sent to Antwerp to study philosophy, but after only a few weeks set out for Rome. He continued his philosophy studies at the Roman College. Early in his third year, he was selected to participate in a philosophical disputation at the Dominicans' Greek College. Upon his return, he was suddenly taken with a severe fever and died on August 13, 1621, clutching his rosary, crucifix and rules. He had not yet been ordained.

Numerous miracles were reported after his death. His relics are in the Church of St. Ignatius.

John was a model of piety for many and strove for perfection. He was noted for his fidelity, kindness, courtesy and obedience. He told others that if he did not become a saint when he was young he would never become one.

In art he is shown standing with his hands clasped, holding his rosary, crucifix and rules book.

Beatified: 1865 by Pope Pius IX
Canonized: 1888 by Pope Leo XIII
Feast: August 13
Patronage: altar boys and girls; altar servers; youths

John Bosco (1815–1888) *Founder of the Society of St. Francis de Sales, known as the Salesians*
Name meaning: "God is gracious"

John Bosco, mentor to St. Dominic Savio, was renowned for his work with boys. He could well be called the "Dreaming Saint," for he used his frequent and vivid, lucid dreams not only for his own guidance but also as teaching tools to his young charges. At the request of Pope Pius IX (r. 1846–78), he kept detailed records of his dreams.

John Melchior Bosco was born in Becchi, Piedmont, to a peasant family. His father died when he was two, and he was raised by his mother. He had his first lucid dream when he was about nine years old, which left an impression on him for the rest of his life. In it he learned of his spiritual mission, which he undertook with great seriousness and from which he never wavered.

In the dream, John was in a field with a crowd of children. They began cursing and misbehaving. Shocked, John jumped into their midst and shouted at them to stop. John wrote of his dream:

At that moment a Man appeared, nobly attired, with a manly and imposing bearing. He was clad with a white flowing mantle, and His face radiated such light that I could not look directly at Him. He called me by name and told me to place myself as leader of those boys, adding these words:

"You will have to win these friends of yours not with blows but with gentleness and kindness. So begin right now to *show them that sin is ugly and virtue beautiful.*"

Confused and afraid, I replied that I was only a boy and unable to talk to these youngsters about religion. At that moment the fighting, shouting and cursing stopped, and the crowd of boys gathered around the Man who was talking. Almost unconsciously, I asked:

"But how can you order me to do something that looks so impossible?"

"What seems so impossible you must achieve by being *obedient* and by *acquiring knowledge.*"

The Man (perhaps Jesus), said he would give John a teacher. Then appeared a Lady (perhaps Mary) of majestic appearance, wearing a beautiful mantle, glowing as if bedecked with stars. The children all vanished and were replaced by wild animals. The Lady told John this was his field where he must work, and to make himself humble, steadfast and strong. The animals then turned into gentle lambs. The Lady said to the confused John, "In due time everything will be clear to you."

John shared his dream with his family the next morning. His brothers laughed, and predicted that he would become a shepherd of animals or the leader of a gang of robbers. His mother said, "Who knows? Maybe you will become a priest." And his grandmother said, "You mustn't pay attention to dreams."

John was inclined to agree with his grandmother, but his lucid dreams only increased as he got older.

At age 16 he began studying for the priesthood and was ordained on June 5, 1841, at age 26. He was so poor that all of his clothes came from charity. He went to Turin and enrolled at the Convitto Ecclesiastico, a theological college that trained young priests for the pastoral life. There he began a Sunday catechism for poor boys, a sort of wandering oratory that changed locations several times in Turin. This proved to be quite successful, and soon John was taking in and housing destitute boys. In 1853 he opened workshops for tailors and shoemakers. He succeeded in constructing a church, placing it under the patronage of his favorite saint, Francis de Sales. By 1856 he had 150 resident boys, plus four workshops and some 500 chil-

St. John Bosco

dren in the oratories. This effort became the Society of St. Francis de Sales in 1859, when John received permission to establish a religious congregation from Pope Pius IX.

In 1872 John established an order of women called Daughters of Our Lady, Help of Christians, which also grew rapidly.

John was adept at building churches, and raised funds for a large basilica in Turin, dedicated to St. John the Evangelist. In Rome he undertook a project to build a church in honor of the Sacred Heart. But funds were not forthcoming, so he went to France, where he was hailed as a miracle worker. The church was built and consecrated in 1887.

By then, John's health was failing due to overwork. He deteriorated and died on January 31, 1888. Forty thousand people came to see his body prior to burial.

Today the Salesians extend around the world.

John's unusual dream life attracted the interest of Pope Piux IX who instructed him to write his dreams down for the pope. More than 150 of John's unusual dreams were collected and recorded by his followers. Many of the dreams were prophetic and concerned his boys and the Salesian Order. Other dreams were pedagogical and still others were parables. These dreams were in harmony with his religious training and beliefs, couched in symbols of his religious life, and concerned the need to follow Catholic doctrine in order to attain salvation.

John's lucid dreams were quite long and involved much specific detail. Unlike most ordinary dreams, they were logical and followed a complete story line from beginning to end. He was usually accompanied by a guide figure, variously an angel, St. Francis de Sales, St. Dominic Savio, or a man he referred to as "the man with the cap." He would carry on long conversations with others in his dreams, which he was able to remember. The dreams seemed more like real experiences than dreams. His sensory impressions were so strong that sometimes he would clap his hands or touch himself in the dream to try to ascertain whether he was dreaming or was awake. This is a technique used today by lucid dreamers to verify that their experience is real.

Sometimes physical phenomena followed him out of the dream and into waking consciousness. He would awaken exhausted. In one dramatic dream where he was shown the horrors of hell, the putrid smell of evil remained after he awakened. This bleed-through between worlds is characteristic of shamanistic journeys, and belongs to Jung's "psychoid unconscious," a level in the unconscious that is not accessible to consciousness, but has properties in common with the physical world. Similarly, St. Jerome was beaten in a dream and awakened bruised and sore.

John derived a great deal of guidance from his lucid dreams. He was intensely devoted to his young charges, and his prophetic dreams seem to have had the purpose of learning about certain boys' spiritual misconduct so that he could try to set them on the right course again. His dreams were uncannily accurate in revealing the secrets of others, and also in matters concerning impending deaths.

John would recount his dreams in lectures to his young audience. He would sometimes say that "it was a dream in which one can know what one does; can hear what is said, can ask and answer questions." He cautioned his boys not to speak of his dreams in the outside community, for others would consider them fables. When peers and superiors questioned his dreams, he would gravely reply, "It was a great deal more than a dream." If he did not wish to answer probing questions, he said that he could remember so much detail "by means of Otis Botis Pia Tutis." This was a meaningless phrase that served to deflect further questioning.

If not for the papal interest, John's dreams may have been lost to history. They remain interesting to researchers who study dreams and prophecy.

In addition to his unusual dreams and powers of prophecy and clairvoyance, John is credited with multiplying food—some nuts—for his boys, levitating during Mass, and influencing the weather. In 1864, John was invited to preach at the feast of the Assumption in Montemagno, which was suffering a severe drought. He promised rain if the people would make good confessions, attend three nights of prayer and receive Communion, and if farmers would invoke the intercession of Mary when in a state of grace. On the night of the feast, a great storm broke and pelted the town with rain.

John was protected by a mysterious dog who suddenly appeared whenever he was in danger. The dog looked like a large and ferocious Alsatian. John named it Grigio because it was gray in color. In the 1850s, religious factions were opposed to his teachings and threatened him. Once someone even shot at him; the bullet passed under his arm, making a hole in the cassock but leaving his flesh untouched. John also was accosted as he walked about, especially in lonely places. Grigio would suddenly appear and attack anyone who assaulted him or seemed threatening. The dog would mysteriously disappear when he returned safely to his oratory. Grigio refused offers of food; however, others could see him and touch him. Grigio's vigilance lasted far longer than the typical lifespan of a dog. Some people suggested he was an angel in animal form.

John's scapular was found in perfect condition when the saint's body was exhumed the first time. All other fabric in the coffin had deteriorated.

Canonized: 1934 by Pope Pius XI
Feast: January 31
Patronage: apprentices; editors

FURTHER READING
Forty Dreams of St. John Bosco. Rockford, Ill.: TAN Books and Publishers, 1996.

John Cassian (ca. 360–433) *Abbot, Father of the Church*

There is general agreement among authorities that John was born around the year 360—but not about where. Among the possibilities suggested are Gaul, Syria, Palestine and Scythia. Nothing is known about his childhood and youth. He is first met in history in 380, when he and his friend Germanus became monks at Bethlehem, in a monastery near the place of the Nativity.

They stayed there until about 385, when John was 25, then left for Egypt. For the next several years (until about 400) they traveled throughout Lower Egypt and the Nile delta, staying with the most famous monks and anchorites of the region and absorbing their Origenist ideas. John kept a journal, recording everything he saw with a vivid style and minute accuracy, a sense of humor and an eye for the picturesque.

John and Germanus left Egypt to go to Constantinople, where Bishop St. John Chrysostom ordained Germanus a priest and John a deacon. In 405, after John Chrysostom was deposed, they went to Rome, carrying a letter to Pope St. Innocent I (r. 401–417) from the clergy of Constantinople protesting this act. In Rome, John was ordained a priest. Ten years later he was in Marseilles (Germanus having disappeared in the interim), where he founded (and served as abbot of) the monastery of St. Victor for men and the convent of St. Savior for women.

Asked by a neighboring bishop, Castor of Apt, to compile a summary of all he had observed and learned during his travels, John set about writing his 12-volume work, *Remedies for the Eight Deadly Sins*, that describes the rules and organization of communities in Egypt and Palestine, and of the means used by the monks in their spiritual combat with the eight chief hindrances to a monk's perfection. It appears that John was not unduly impressed by their extreme asceticism, because he did not recommend it for the monasteries of the West. Instead, he held that perfection was to be achieved through the charity and love that makes man most like God.

John's next work was *Conferences on the Egyptian Monks*, in which he relates discussions he and Germanus had with the monks. John emphasized continual prayer as the purpose of the monk. He found great results in a prayer technique, which became part of the *hesychast* practices of the Eastern Orthodox Church, of the continual repetition of a prayer, especially the "Jesus Prayer": "Lord Jesus Christ, Son of God, have mercy on me." John found that the constant repetition infused the prayer with intense energy. Many others, however, found it only monotonous. The idea of repetition of a prayer became established in Western practice about 800 years later with the development of the rosary. Unfortunately, the doctrine he expressed was unorthodox, giving too much importance to free will and not enough to divine grace. His position was in line with the heresy of "semi-Pelagianism" and was publicly criticized. The criticism did not keep the work from being highly popular and influential, however, and no less than St. Benedict prescribed it as one of the

books to be read aloud by his monks after their evening meal.

About 430, John was commissioned by the future pope St. Leo to write a seven-volume critique of the Nestorian heresy, *On the Incarnation of the Lord*. This hastily written book assisted in the condemnation of Nestorius by the Council of Ephesus in 431. Ironically, after his death, John's *Conferences* was declared apocryphal, by a decree attributed to Pope St. Gelasius I (r. 492–496), and in 529 he too was condemned by a church council.

John died at Marseilles on July 23, about the year 433.

Feast: July 23

FURTHER READING

Funk, Mary Margaret. *Thoughts Matter: The Practice of the Spiritual Life.* New York: Continuum International Publishing Group, 1999.

John Cassian: Conferences. Tr. Colm huib heid. Mahwah, N.J.: Paulist Press, 1985.

John Chrysostom (ca. 347–407) *Doctor of the Church, Greek Father of the Church, bishop of Constantinople, esteemed theologian*
Also known as: "the golden-mouthed" for his eloquence as a speaker

John Chrysostom is considered to be the greatest of the Greek fathers of the church and one of the greatest of all preachers of the faith. More writings of his are extant than of any other Doctor of the Church. His exact surname is not known. Chrysostom, which comes from the Greek *chrysostomos* ("golden-mouthed") was first used in 553 in the Constitution of Pope Vigilius (r. 537–555). The chronology of John's life is incomplete. He lived during a time of great political and religious unrest and intrigue.

John was born ca. 347 in Antioch. His father, Secundus, was a high-ranking officer in the Syrian army. Secundus died shortly after John's birth, leaving his young wife, Anthusa, to raise John and his older sister. Anthusa sent John to the best schools in Antioch, where he attained considerable Greek scholarship and classical learning.

Around 367 John met Bishop Meletius, patriarch of Antioch and a key figure in a schism between bishops. Under Meletius's influence, John was drawn into an ascetic and religious life. After three years, he was baptized and ordained lector. He entered one of the ascetic societies near Antioch—under the spiritual direction of Carterius—and devoted himself to prayer, study of the Scriptures and manual labor. He began to write on ascetic and monastic subjects.

After four years, John went off to live in a cave near Antioch. He spent two years there, but his fasts and exposure to harsh elements nearly ruined his health. He returned to Antioch and his post as lector.

Around 381 Meletius made John deacon and left for Constantinople. The new bishop, Flavian, ordained John a priest in 386. During this period and until 397, John enjoyed the golden age of his life. He was a prolific writer and a popular, charismatic preacher. His fame spread throughout the Byzantine Empire.

In 397 or 398 he was abruptly sent to Constantinople to replace Bishop Nectarius, who had died. John found himself thrust into a difficult role. Constant intrigue and a lavish lifestyle prevailed at court, and intrigue and a lax lifestyle abounded in secular quarters as well. John was scandalized by the dress of women. He set about asserting discipline and reform. Initially, Empress Eudoxia was a supporter.

John achieved great popularity with the people but was not able to establish order for long. Disputes and intrigues earned Eudoxia's alienation. She took many of his sermons—such as the one against the vanity of women—as personal affronts. Rivals and malcontents, under the leadership of Theophilus, patriarch of Alexandria, also made trouble for John. When Theophilus was ordered in 402 to apologize for his actions to a synod presided over by John, he managed to twist his situation around. In 403 he assembled a synod of 36 bishops and archbishops, called the Oak, and made charges against John, including one that he had called Eudoxia a "Jezebel." John was ordered to appear before the synod, comprised chiefly of his enemies, and apologize.

John refused and was exiled by Emperor Arcadius. This agitated the people, and after three days of public uproar Eudoxia recalled him to Constantinople. Theophilus and his supporters were obliged to flee the city.

The victory for John did not last long. In 404 a silver statue of Eudoxia went up before the great church of the Holy Wisdom. The public celebrations were loud and scandalous, and John spoke out against them. Eudoxia, affronted, recalled Theophilus and had John exiled for a second time.

Soon after John left the city, a huge fire broke out and destroyed the cathedral, senate house and other buildings. John's followers were accused and prosecuted. John was sent to Caucasus, a rugged area on the eastern frontier of Armenia continually under invasion by Isaurians. It took him 70 days to walk there. In 405 John was forced to flee in order to escape the barbarians. Meanwhile, he continued to write to his supporters and to maintain hope for his restoration to Constantinople.

John appealed to Rome for help. Emperor Honorius and Pope Innocent I (r. 401–417) attempted to intercede on his behalf, but their legates were jailed and then sent home. The pope broke off contact with the patriarchs of Alexandria and Antioch.

In the summer of 407 John was marched toward Pithyus, located near the Caucasus Mountains at the extreme edge of the empire. As his enemies hoped, he did not survive the journey. His health already was impaired by previous illnesses, and the soldiers who accompanied him made the conditions as cruel as possible. He was made to walk for long periods regardless of scorching heat, freezing cold and downpours of rain. On September 14, he asked to rest at Comana in Cappadocia but was forced to continue his march. When he was too weak to continue, the party returned to the chapel of St. Basiliscus near Comana, where John died within hours. His final words were *"Doxa to theo panton eneken"* ("Glory be to God for all things").

John was buried at Comana, and his remains were translated to Constantinople on January 27, 438, with great pomp and fanfare. He was entombed in the Church of the Apostles, where Eudoxia, who had died in 404, also was buried.

John Chrysostom's most famous work is his book *On the Priesthood*, written as a dialogue between himself and St. Basil. His 21 sermons (he may not have written the 19th) from his Antioch days are full of moral, dogmatic and historical knowledge. He wrote hundreds of homilies on the Scriptures. Some 238 of his letters survive; most are from his days in exile. He was quoted as an authority as early as 415 by Pelagius and 421 by St. Jerome, one of the great Doctors of the Church himself. John also was invoked at the Council of Ephesus in 431. During the Reformation, debate arose as to whether John had been a Catholic or a Protestant, in part because he did not clearly advocate confession and the primacy of the pope. However, his writings do assert the authoritative teaching of the Church as the one Bride of Christ.

John is called the Doctor of the Eucharist for his witness to the Real Presence. In art he is portrayed as a cardinal attended by a lion, or as a hermit.

Declared Doctor of the Church: 451 by Pope Leo I
Feast: September 13 (in the West); November 13 (in the East)
Patronage: orators; preachers

FURTHER READING
Kelly, J. N. D. *Golden Month: The Story of John Chrysostom-Ascetic, Preacher, Bishop.* Ithaca, N.Y.: Cornell University Press, 1998.
Mayer, Wendy, and Pauline Allen. *John Chrysostom.* London: Routledge, 2000.

John Climacus (ca. 570–ca. 649) *Abbot of Sinai, mystic, Father of the Church*
Also known as: John the Scholastic, the Sinaita

Little is known about the details of John Climacus's life, and the estimated dates of his life vary considerably. The prevailing view is that he was born in or shortly before 579 and died around 649. Some scholars have placed his life at ca. 525–600 or 605. Others have fixed his date of death as late as 670–680.

John was born in Syria sometime around 525, and had at least one brother, named George. At the time, Mount Sinai was famous for its hermits, and at age 16 John decided to withdraw from the world and study under Abba Martyrius. He joined the Mount Sinai monastery built on the site of the burning bush where Moses had spoken to God. He received his tonsure at age 19 or 20.

Soon thereafter Martyrius died, and John withdrew to a hermitage called Tholas at the foot of the mountain. There he lived in near isolation in a cave for about 20 years, studying the lives of the saints. He practiced stringent mortifications and austerities, reducing sleep to an absolute minimum. He received the grace of continual prayer and the gift of tears, a sign of the presence of God and the purification of body and soul. His spiritual depth gained him recognition as a spiritual father among his fellow monks.

At some point during his stay at Tholas, John visited monks in Egypt, staying at a large monastery outside of Alexandria. He was impressed by the unity he witnessed there. He even spent time in "the Prison," a place about a mile from the monastery where erring monks were sent to do penance.

In 600 he was persuaded to become abbot of the central monastery at Sinai. On the day of his installation, a large group of 600 pilgrims arrived and had to be fed. During the meal, John saw what he described as "a man with short hair, dressed like a Jew in a white tunic, going round with an air of authority and giving orders to the cooks, cellarers, stewards and other servants." As soon as the meal was finished, the man mysteriously disappeared. John said the stranger was Moses, and his monks took this as a sign that they had found in him another Moses.

John attracted many disciples. Pope St. Gregory the Great (r. 590–604) wrote to him asking for his recommendation in prayers, and sent him money for the hospital at Sinai that took care of pilgrims. Toward the end of his years, he turned his responsibilities over to his brother, George, and retired again to solitude. He died at Mount Sinai, probably around 649.

John is best-known for his important work, *The Ladder of Divine Ascent*, from which he later earned his surname. *Klimakis* is "ladder," and John Climacus means "John of the Ladder." He composed the book during his years as abbot.

The Ladder of Divine Ascent is composed in 30 chapters, intended to correspond to the age of Jesus at the time of his baptism by St. John the Baptist. The 30 chapters are 30 steps, or *logoi*, of the spiritual life. Each step describes a certain virtue or passion, and the path that can lead from it. The book offers no formulae, but instructs that "the life you have is hidden with Christ in God." The stages of the spiritual life set forth in the book are the break with the world; the practice of asceticism; the struggle against the passions; the practice of simplicity, humility and discernment; and union with God.

The union with God is achieved through *heyschia*, an Eastern Orthodox method of mystical prayer in which one arrives at a deep interior peace and stillness "at the very center of the mysteries" through the constant remembrance of God. *Hesychast* prayer featured breathing techniques and constant repetition of a prayer, especially the "Jesus Prayer": "Lord Jesus Christ, Son of God, have mercy on me."

Other ways to achieve union with God are *apatheia* or detachment, in which the soul stretches out toward God; and charity.

Ladder became one of the most important texts in the Eastern Orthodox Church. Through his years of intense study, John was able to synthesize the traditional teachings of the Fathers of the Church, including the Desert Fathers. It was written at a significant time of transition. Arab invaders were destroying the monasteries of Egypt and Palestine, and monasticism withdrew to Mount Athos. John's work served as a significant bridge.

Because of his stature, John is celebrated in feasts twice a year in the Eastern Church. His book continues to inspire monastics and people interested in the spiritual life. The Trappist monk Thomas Merton was inspired by it and wrote a review of it.

The monastery where John lived, first dedicated to Our Lord's Holy Transfiguration, is now dedicated to St. Catherine.

Feasts: March 30 and the fourth Sunday of the Great Lent

FURTHER READING
Climacus, John. *The Ladder of Divine Ascent*. Mahwah, N.J.: Paulist Press, 1982.

John of the Cross (1542–1591) *Spanish mystic, Renaissance poet, a founder of the Discalced Carmelite Order, and Doctor of the Church*
Name meaning: "God is gracious"
Also known as: San Juan de la Cruz

At five-feet-two, John of the Cross was small in stature but "great in the eyes of God," as his friend St. Teresa of Avila described him. He was especially devoted to the Blessed Virgin Mary, and had numerous experiences of her during his life.

John was born Juan de Yepes y Alvarez in Fontiveros, Old Castile, Spain. He was the youngest of three children. His father had been disinherited for marrying beneath his station, and died when he was an infant. John was raised by his mother, Catalina Alvarez. He studied at the Jesuit school of Medina, but was attracted to the Carmelites, a Roman Catholic order founded in the 12th century by a group of hermits on Mount Carmel, Israel, and devoted to the ancient prophets Elijah and Elisha, who once lived on the mount. At 21, John entered the Carmelite monastery of Medina del Campo, where he was given the name of John of St. Matthias. After profession, he wanted to be a lay brother, but instead was sent to the Carmelite monastery near the University of Salamanca. He was ordained a priest at age 25.

He became unhappy with the laxity he saw in the order, and worked toward reform with his confidante and friend, Teresa of Avila, who was in her fifties when they met and formed their friendship. Together they founded Carmelite monasteries and advocated disciplinary reforms. They enjoyed a deep and mystical correspondence.

Teresa had been given permission to establish a stricter order of Carmelites, and to found two reformed houses of men. She told John he should be the first to carry this out. He founded the first Discalced Carmelite monastery at Duruelo and adopted the name John of the Cross. (The term "discalced" literally refers to being barefoot; however, discalced monks in modern times may wear sandals, rather than shoes, as symbolic of their stricter observance.) The Discalced Carmelites were strongly opposed by the original Carmelites.

From 1571 to 1572 John served as rector of a new Carmelite college at Baeza. He then became confessor at the convent of the Incarnation at Avila, serving until 1577. He was ordered by the provincial of Castile to return to Medina but refused. He was kidnapped by unreformed Carmelites, who imprisoned him in a nearly lightless cell in Toledo when he refused to abandon his reforms. He spent nine months in his cell, which had a tiny, high window. John stood on a stool in order to be able to read his offices. He was severely beaten. The beatings at first took place every evening, then three times a week, then on Fridays only. John would be led to the refectory and forced to sit on the floor to eat his meager meal of bread and water. Then he would be made to bare his shoulders. The monks would file by and scourge him with whips. The scars

remained for years. The story goes that on two occasions his jailers saw brilliant light shining from his cell, which vanished when they entered. It was believed that Jesus and Mary visited him.

According to lore, Mary helped him to escape. She appeared in a radiant vision on the night of her feast and told him his trials would soon be at an end. Several days later, she showed him a window by which he would make his escape. John unscrewed the lock of his door (said to be loosened by Mary) and quietly walked past the guard. He took only the mystical poetry he had written. He tore a blanket into strips and made a rope, which he used to climb down out of the window shown to him by Mary. John hid in a convent infirmary, entertaining the nuns by reading his poetry.

One of John's fervent prayers was to be granted three things: not to die as a superior; to die where he was not known; and to die after having suffered a great deal. His prayer was realized.

In 1579 John became head of the college at Baeza. In 1581, he became prior of Los Martires, near Granada. In 1582, Teresa died and dissension broke out among the Discalced Carmelites. John, who favored a moderate policy, became vicar provincial of Andalusia. He did not get along with the vicar general, who removed him from authority and had him disgraced. He was sent to the remote friary of La Peñuela, where he spent his time in prayer and meditation. Meanwhile, efforts were under way by his opponents to have him expelled from the order. John became ill and was sent to Ubeda in 1591. He suffered dreadful treatment for three months, and died on December 14.

John wrote his famous mystical work *The Spiritual Canticle*, while in prison. Shortly after his escape, he wrote *The Ascent of Mount Carmel, The Living Flame of Love* and his most famous work, *The Dark Night of the Soul*, a continuation of *The Ascent of Mount Carmel*. These works describe the soul's mystical journey toward God, and detail three stages of mystical union: purgation, illumination and union. Detachment and suffering are presented as requirements for the purification and illumination of the soul. John describes the "dark night of the soul" as "an inflowing of God into the soul, which purges it from its ignorances and imperfections, habitual, natural and spiritual, and which is called by contemplatives "infused contemplation, or mystical theology." The phrase "dark night of the soul" has become a reference to the state of intense personal spiritual struggle, including the experience of utter hopelessness and isolation.

Trained by Jesuits and thoroughly familiar with the teaching of St. Thomas Aquinas, John brought Scholastic theology and philosophy to his poetic genius. He is critically acclaimed as one of the greatest poets of the

Spanish Renaissance, as well as one of the greatest Western authorities on mysticism.

Numerous miracles and marvels are recorded concerning John, whom Teresa of Avila called "one of the purest souls in the Church of God." When John was on his deathbed, he predicted he would be with God by midnight—and he died at that hour, holding his crucifix and saying, "Into Thy hands, Lord, I commend my spirit." The room was filled with a sweet perfume, and a sparkling sphere of light "like that of the sun, moon and stars together" shone above the bed. A triple crown of light seemed to encircle the dead saint's head.

John once reportedly was found levitating in the chapel with his head touching the ceiling, having been lifted up during prayer.

Two stories are told of his miraculous rescues from drowning. Both incidents occurred in boyhood. When he was five, he fell into a lagoon while playing and sank to the bottom. There he saw a beautiful lady who stretched out her hand, but he was afraid to grasp it because his own hand was muddy. He floated to the surface and was rescued by a peasant with a pole. In the second incident, he fell into a well but did not sink. He remained calm and held onto a rope, and was pulled to safety. Throughout his life, he credited both rescues to the Blessed Virgin Mary.

Mary rescued him on another occasion in his monk's cell. Construction work caused a wall of the monastery to fall on his cell. John was assumed to be crushed to death, but he was found standing in a corner unharmed. He said Mary had covered him with her white mantle to protect him from the falling debris.

After his death, he was entombed beneath the floor of the church at Ubeda. Several nights later, a bright light was seen radiating from the spot. Nine months later, his tomb was opened upon a legal order obtained by Dona Ana de Pensacola, who wished to remove his bones to a house she had established for John in Segovia. The saint's body was found incorrupt and smelling of a sweet fragrance. The body was covered with lime and reburied. The tomb was opened again nine months later, but the body was still incorrupt. Three fingers of the right hand were cut off, and blood issued forth as though from a living person. The body was taken to Segovia, and en route smelled so strongly of perfume that it drew the attention of passersby. In Segovia, thousands flocked to see it for eight days, before its enshrinement in a reliquary of marble and bronze. The incorrupt body was examined in 1859, 1909, 1926 and 1955.

Beatified: 1675 by Pope Clement X
Canonized: 1726 by Pope Benedict XIII
Named Doctor of the Church: 1926 by Pope Pius XI

St. John of the Cross levitating

Feast: December 14
Patronage: mystics

FURTHER READING
Brown, Raphael. *Saints Who Saw Mary.* Rockford, Ill.: TAN Books, 1955.
The Collected Works of St. John of the Cross. Tr. Kieran Kavanaugh and Otilio Rodriguez. Washington, D.C.: ICS Publications, 1991.
Frost, Bede. *Saint John of the Cross: Doctor of Divine Love, an Introduction to His Philosophy, Theology and Spirituality.* New York: Vantage, 1980.
John of the Cross. *Dark Night of the Soul,* 3rd rev. ed. Tr. E. Allison Peers from the critical ed. of P. Silverio de Santa Teresa, C.D. Garden City, N.Y.: Doubleday Image Books, 1959.

John Damascene (ca. 676–754 to 787) *Patriarch of Jerusalem, last Eastern Father of the Church, Doctor of the Church, poet*
Also known as: John of Damascus; the Doctor of Christian Art

Only one account of the life of John Damascene exists. It was written by John of Jerusalem about 200 years after the death of the saint, and contains both fact and legend.

John was born about 676 in Damascus to a wealthy family. His father, a Christian, enjoyed high rank in judicial offices serving the Muslim caliph. When John was 22, his father searched for a suitable tutor for him. He happened upon a learned monk named Cosmas, who had been captured by Saracen pirates and was being sold as a slave. The father either bought Cosmas or begged his life, and gave him his freedom and set him up as tutor. When the schooling was finished, Cosmas retired to the monastery of St. Sabas and then became the bishop of Majuma.

When John's father died, he reluctantly took his position. He resigned in 719 and became a monk at the monastery of St. Sabas near Jerusalem.

John became involved in the Iconoclast heresy over the veneration of religious images, a well-established practice in the Eastern Church. In 726 Emperor Leo III prohibited the veneration of religious images. Around 730, John wrote his famous defense of the use of icons, *On Holy Images*. The fact that he lived in Muslim territory gave him a freedom of expression that he might not have had otherwise. Legend has it that the irate emperor forged a letter, purportedly from John to him, offering to betray the city of Damascus, and had it sent to the caliph. The caliph ordered John's hand to be cut off in punishment. John prayed to the Blessed Virgin Mary that his hand might be restored. He fell asleep by her image, and when he awoke his hand had been miraculously restored. The caliph sought to reinstate him, but John went to the monastery of St. Sabas instead. The story, however, is indeed legend, for John was already at the monastery, and not in the service of the caliph, at the time he wrote the treatise.

At the monastery, John spent his time writing and in prayer. He wrote more than 150 works on philosophy, religious education, theology and hagiographies. His friends called him *Chrysoorhoas* ("golden stream") for his oratorical gifts. His legacy is noted not so much for original theology as for his ability to compile the works of others in encyclopedic fashion.

His most famous work is *The Fountain of Wisdom*, which is divided into three parts: "Philosophical Chapters," "Concerning Heresy" and "An Exact Exposition of the Orthodox Faith." The book was the first summary of connected theological opinions and basic truths of the faith, drawing on such eminent theologians as SS. Gregory of Nazianzus, Gregory of Nyssa, Basil the Great, Cyril of Alexandria, Leo the Great, Athanasius, John Chrysostom and Epiphanius. It became a standard work for the Scholastics, among them the great St. Thomas Aquinas.

John also wrote numerous sermons and treatises, including a defense of the Blessed Virgin Mary's title as *Theotokos* ("God-bearer"), and three great hymns or canons on Easter, the Ascension and St. Thomas's Sunday.

John's defense of icons earned him the undying hatred of the Iconoclasts, who anathematized him posthumously at a pseudo-synod of Constantinople in 754. This was rectified in 787 by the Seventh General Council of Nicaea. The Iconoclastic controversy finally ended in 843 when Empress Theodora restored the use of icons.

An Arabic romance, *Barlaam and Josaphat*, popular in the Middle Ages, is sometimes attributed to John, but it is doubtful that he authored it.

Declared Doctor of the Church: 1890 by Pope Leo XIII
Feast: December 4

FURTHER READING
"Saint John of Damascus." URL: http://www.balamand.edu.lb/theology/WritingsSJD.htm. Downloaded: October 1, 2000.

John the Divine (ca. 6–ca. 100) *Youngest of Jesus' Twelve Disciples; author of the fourth gospel and the book of Revelation of the New Testament*
Name meaning: God is gracious
Also known as: Apostle of Charity; Beloved Apostle; Beloved Disciple; Fourth Apostle; John Boanerges; John the Evangelist

John was born in Galilee about the year 6 to Zebedee and Salome. He was the younger brother of St. James the Greater. The brothers earned their livelihood as fishermen on Lake Genesareth and, like many of those who became disciples of Jesus, were first followers of St. John the Baptist. Jesus gave them the surname "Boanerges," meaning "Sons of Thunder," apparently in recognition of their passionate natures.

John held a prominent position among the disciples, and was present for several important events. Only John and Peter were sent into the city to prepare for the Last Supper, at which John was seated next to Jesus. After Jesus' arrest, John and Peter followed Christ into the palace of the high priest, and of the apostles only John remained near Christ on the cross, and took Mary into his care. After the Resurrection, John and Peter were the first apostles to go to his tomb, and John was the first to accept that Christ had risen. Later, when Jesus appeared at Lake Genesareth,

John was the first to recognize him standing on the shore. There Jesus apparently prophesied that John would outlive the other apostles, and it was believed by many that he was immune to death.

After Christ's Ascension and the Descent of the Holy Spirit, John took a leading role in the founding of the Christian Church. He often acted together with Peter, whom he accompanied on an evangelizing expedition to Samaria, and with whom he was briefly imprisoned by Herod Agrippa I sometime between 42 and 44. After their miraculous escape, he and Peter were forced to flee Jerusalem. By tradition, John began his apostolic work among the Jews in the provinces of Parthia. He may also have gone to Ephaseus (Ephesus) in what is now Turkey, where he founded the Christian community. In any event, he was back in Jerusalem about the year 51 to join the other disciples for the first Apostolic Council. He also attended the Council of 62, after which he definitely went to Ephesus, where he established churches and governed the congregation.

In the year 95, during the second general persecution under Emperor Domitian (r. 81–96), John was arrested and carried to Rome as a prisoner. He was thrown into a cauldron of boiling oil before the Porta Latina, but emerged unharmed. His persecutors attributed this miracle to sorcery and exiled him to the island of Patmos.

According to legend, John also escaped death when he drank from a chalice of wine poisoned by the high priest of Diana. At his blessing, the poison is said to have risen from the chalice in the form of a serpent. This event is taken by some as fulfillment of Jesus' prophecy as given in Mark 16 that his apostles who drank poisoned drinks would not be harmed by them.

On Patmos, John reputedly experienced the vision that inspired his Book of Revelation, written at that time. After Domitian's death in 96, he was released and returned to Ephesus, where he is believed to have written his gospel. The book of Revelation and the Gospel of John are so different in tone that some scholars have questioned whether John could have authored both, but the present consensus is that he did.

John died at Ephesus around 100, when he was well into his 90s. He is the only apostle who did not die a martyr. A church, later converted into a mosque, was built over his tomb.

John originally shared his December 27 feast day with St. James the Greater, though at an early date it became his alone. He was venerated also at the Feast of St. John Before the Latin Gate, supposed to honor his experience in the cauldron, and marking the dedication of the church near the Porta Latina, first mentioned in the Sacramentary of Pope Adrian I (r. 772–785).

St. John the Divine (Library of Congress Prints and Photographs Division)

John's symbols are an eagle; a book; a chalice, sometimes in association with a serpent. Generally he is portrayed as a young and handsome man in various scenes from his life. When he is portrayed in later life, he is usually reading, writing or holding his epistle.

Feast: December 27 (September 26 in Eastern Church; May 8 in Greek Orthodox)

Patronage: art dealers; bookbinders; booksellers; against burns; compositors; engravers; lithographers; painters; against poison; printers; publishers; papermakers; sculptors; tanners; theologians; writers; Asiatic Turkey; Taos, New Mexico

John Eudes (1601–1670) *Initiator (with St. Margaret Mary Alacoque) of the devotion to the Sacred Heart*

John Eudes was born at Ri in Normandy, France, on November 14, 1601, to a farming family. At age 14 he attended the Jesuit college at Caen. Although his parents wanted him to marry, he joined the Congregation of the Oratory of France in 1623. He studied at Paris and at Aubervilliers and was ordained in 1625.

John helped victims of the plagues that struck Normandy in 1625 and 1631, and spent the next decade giving missions. He earned a reputation as an outstanding preacher and confessor, and was esteemed for his opposition to the heresy of Jansenism. He became interested in helping fallen women. In 1641, with Madeleine Lamy, he founded a refuge for them in Caen under the direction of the Visitandines.

He resigned from the Oratorians in 1643 and founded the Congregation of Jesus and Mary (the Eudists) at Caen, composed of secular priests not bound by vows but dedicated to upgrading the clergy by establishing effective seminaries and to preaching missions. His foundation was opposed by the Oratorians and the Jansenists, and he was unable to obtain papal approval for it. But in 1650 the bishop of Coutances invited him to establish a seminary in that diocese. The same year the sisters at his refuge in Caen left the Visitandines and were recognized by the bishop of Bayeux as a new congregation, the Sisters of Our Lady of Charity of the Refuge.

John founded seminaries at Lisieux in 1653 and Rouen in 1659 and was unsuccessful in another attempt to secure papal approval of his congregation. In 1666 the Refuge sisters received Pope Alexander III's approval as an institute to reclaim and care for penitent wayward women. John continued giving missions and established new seminaries at Evreux in 1666 and Rennes in 1670.

He shared with Margaret Mary Alacoque the honor of initiating devotion to the Sacred Heart of Jesus (he composed the Mass for the Sacred Heart in 1668) and the Holy Heart of Mary, popularizing the devotions with his "The Devotion to the Adorable Heart of Jesus" (1670) and "The Admirable Heart of the Most Holy Mother of God," which he finished a month before his death at Caen on August 19, 1670.

Canonized: 1925 by Pius XI
Feast: August 19

John of God (1495–1550) *Founder of the Brothers Hospitallers (Brothers of St. John of God)*

John of God was born March 8, 1495, in Montemor o Novo, Portugal, to devout Christian parents. Tradition holds that at the time of his birth, the church bells in town rang of their own accord, heralding the arrival of a saint.

His early life was checkered, however. He ran away from home at age eight or nine, following a Spanish priest to Spain, and never saw his parents again. He and the priest subsisted by begging. John fell ill, and was taken in by the manager of a large estate. After he regained his health, John worked for the man as a shepherd tending cattle and sheep. He was obedient, pious and good-natured. When he grew up, his boss tried to press him into marrying his daughter. At age

27 John escaped by joining the Spanish army, and then a regiment that went to Austria to fight the Turks. As a soldier, John fell into immoral and dissolute ways. One day he was thrown from a stolen horse near the French lines, and feared capture. The experience shook him up, and he resolved to mend his ways.

He returned to his birthplace and sought to atone for his sins. He went to Africa to aid Moorish captives, and fully expected to be martyred. A confessor told him that martyrdom was not God's plan for him. John went to Gibraltar, selling religious books and pictures at barely above cost.

John had a vision of the infant Jesus, who gave him his name of John of God and told him to go to Granada. There he continued his activities of selling religious books and pictures, making scant profit. He became impressed with the preaching of Blessed John of Avila, but also was plunged into deep remorse over his sinful past. John went about the streets beating his breast and crying out to God for mercy. His behavior was so extreme that he was placed in an insane asylum for a time, and was subjected to the standard treatment of daily whippings and being tied down to a bed. John of Avila counseled him to stop the lamentations and find a more productive way to atone for his past.

John made a pilgrimage to the shrine of Our Lady of Guadeloupe, where he had a vision of what he was to do with himself. Returning to Granada, he rented a house and began to nurse the sick and care for the poor. If the sick did not come to him, he searched them out, even carrying them to the house. He was aided in this work not only by charitable people but also by angels, including the archangel Raphael.

It was John's custom to impulsively help people, including giving his cloak to any beggar he met. Don Sebastian Ramirez, bishop of Tuy, wisely ensured that the saint would retain his own clothing by designing for him a habit. This habit was adopted by those who became followers of John.

John did not intend to found an order, but one grew up around his work. It became known as the Brothers Hospitallers, and also the Brothers of St. John of God. After John's death, the order was given approval by Pope Pius V (r. 1566–72) in 1572.

John's death resulted from his impulsiveness to help others. He was ill in bed when he heard that a flood was bringing driftwood near town. Impulsively, he got up and gathered friends and went to the swollen river to gather pieces for firewood. One of the companions fell in, and John immediately dove into the water in an effort to save him. He was unable to do so, and caught fatal pneumonia. He died on Saturday March 8, 1550, in Granada in an unusual manner, kneeling before the

St. John of God (Library of Congress Prints and Photographs Division)

altar in the sickroom in his rented house. His body remained in that position for some time and exuded a sweet perfume that filled the entire house. When the archbishop called to pay his respects, church bells tolled once again of their own accord. For a short time, the kneeling body was placed on a platform in front of the house so that others could pay their respects as well.

John was buried in the vault in the church of Minims, Our Lady of Victory, in a ceremony befitting a prince. A large procession followed him to his resting place—the homeless and poor whom he had helped, and the rich who had aided him. His body was left exposed for veneration for nine days, and it exuded the perfume throughout the entire time.

The room where John had died was converted into a chapel. Every anniversary of his death for at least 50 years, the same perfume filled the house from Friday through Saturday evening.

In 1570 John was exhumed and his body was found to be incorrupt, save for the tip of his nose. At a later date, only bones remained. These were distributed as relics to churches around the world, and especially to churches and hospitals of the order. The skull and major bones were sent to the Basilica of St. John of God in Granada, where they are housed in a wooden chest inside a silver urn, atop a golden altar.

It is interesting that John died in the same year that St. Camillus de Lellis was born in Italy. Camillus also was devoted to caring for the sick, and founded an order, the Ministers of the Sick, which became known as the Camillians.

Beatified: September 21, 1638, by Pope Urban VIII
Canonized: October 16, 1690, by Pope Alexander VIII
Feast: March 8
Patronage: alcoholics; booksellers; the dying; firefighters; heart patients; hospitals; nurses; printers; the sick

John Massias (1585–1645)

Name meaning: "God is gracious"
Also known as: Juan Masías, Juan Macías

John Massias was born in Rivera de Fresno, Badajoz, Spain, on March 2, 1585. His parents died when he was young, leaving him in the care of an uncle. He got to know a merchant from Seville who planned to go to America and enter a religious order, and with him left for the New World in 1619. They landed at Cartagena, in what is now Colombia, and John traveled to Quito, Ecuador, and then by mule and on foot to Lima, Peru, the country in which he was to spend the remainder of his life. He arrived in Lima in February 1620, just before his 35th birthday.

For two years John worked on a cattle ranch on the outskirts of Lima, then moved into the city. After distributing his earnings to the needy, he was admitted as a brother to the Dominican monastery of Santa María Magdalena (La Recoleta), taking the habit on January 23, 1622.

John was a man of elevated sensitivity, one of the purest mystics of his century. His life in the monastery was marked by profound prayer, penitence and charity. He acted as doorman, a position that placed him at the center of meetings with the poor, the sick and the disadvantaged of Lima. He also walked about the city in search of alms to share with the poor, never missing the opportunity to give advice and to speak about the Christian life and the love of God. His council was wise, and even the Spanish viceroy and Lima's nobility sought him out on occasion.

John Massias died on September 16, 1645, at 60 years of age. Many miracles have since been attributed to his intervention.

Beatified: October 22, 1837, by Pope Gregory XVI
Canonized: September 28, 1975, by Pope Paul VI
Feast: September 18

FURTHER READING

San Juan Macías. Santos Peruanos. URL: http://ekeko.rcp.net. pe/IAL/cep/santpapa/sanjuan.htm. Downloaded: November 20, 1999.

San Juan Macías. Santos y Biatos de America Latina: Peru. Available online: URL: http://www.aciprensa.com/sant-peru.htm. Downloaded: November 20, 1999.

John Nepomucene (ca. 1330–1383) *Martyr and patron saint of Bohemia*

John was born at Nepomuc, Bohemia, near Prague in what is now the Czech Republic (then a part of the Holy Roman Empire). His family name was Woelflein or Welflin, but he used and has come to be known by the name of his native town instead.

Soon after his birth John became very ill and his parents were afraid they would lose him, but they prayed to the Virgin Mary for his recovery, and she intervened on his behalf. His parents were so grateful for the miracle that they decided to consecrate John to the service of God. When he was still a child, they sent him to the local monastery, where he spent his mornings listening to Mass after Mass. He proved to be a fine student and after completing his early studies in Nepomuc was sent to Staaze to learn Latin. Later he attended the University of Prague (founded in 1356), where he studied philosophy, divinity and canon law, eventually taking a doctorate in the latter subjects. When he completed his studies, John, true to his parents' wishes, spent a month in fasting, prayer and penance, preparing himself to enter the priesthood.

Upon his ordination, he became vicar general of Archbishop John of Genzenstein at Prague and was sent to preach in the parish of Our Lady of Tein, where he was very popular. When Charles IV of the Holy Roman Empire died in 1377, the throne passed to his son, Wenceslas IV, then only 16. Wenceslas, like Charles, lived in Prague, and hearing about John, invited him to preach the Masses of Lent to his court. These were so successful that Wenceslas offered him the first vacant bishopric, that of Leitomeritz, but John declined. He declined also the provostship of Wischeradt, finally accepting the position of almoner of the court. As almoner, he could better minister to the needy, the job he loved, and many sought him out for advice and the settlement of disputes.

John became the confessor of Queen Sophie, the second wife of Wenceslas, who had turned out to be a mercurial and intemperate drunkard, given to fits of jealousy. When he noticed Sophie becoming more pious under John's influence, he demanded that John reveal Sophie's confessions, and when he refused, had him thrown in a dungeon. It is said that the pretense for the imprisonment was John's appeal on behalf of the king's cook, whom Wenceslas had ordered to be put on a spit and roasted when he prepared a meal not to his liking. Wenceslas sent the message that John would stay in the dungeon until he revealed Sophie's confessions, but after a few days, he relented, and John was let go. When he still refused to reveal the confessions, however, he was returned to the dungeon and tortured on the rack, over a slow fire. He was released finally only when Sophie intervened with Wenceslas.

John resumed his preaching with new fervor, not at all defeated but full of joy and courage. In one of his sermons, he is said to have predicted not only his own imminent death but also the political crisis that engulfed Bohemia soon thereafter.

In 1383 (or perhaps 1393) Wenceslas sentenced John to death, but accounts of the reason vary. One has it that Wenceslas demanded once again that John reveal Sophie's confessions, and when he again refused, had him killed. Another account states that John became involved in a dispute between Wenceslas and the archbishop when the king sought to convert a Benedictine abbey into a cathedral for a new diocese (to be given to a friend) when the abbot died. The archbishop thwarted him by approving the election of a new abbot immediately upon the death of the old abbot. In any event, on the night of May 16, John was cruelly tortured, then murdered and his body flung head-first into the Moldau River at Prague.

According to legend, a heavenly light appeared over John's body as it floated in the river, attracting many to the banks, and drawing the attention even of Sophie in the castle. She ran to Wenceslas to ask what he knew about the lights on the river, whereupon he fled to his estate in Zebrac, a few miles from Prague. In the morning, John's body was rescued from the river and carried to the nearby church of the Holy Cross of the Penitents. People rushed to kiss his hands and feet and to tear off pieces of his clothes or other possessions. Wenceslas had the relics secretly removed, but their hiding place was discovered, and they were translated to the Prague cathedral, where they were interred in a stone tomb.

Fearing an uprising in Prague, Wenceslas stayed in Zebrac until he felt it was safe to return. However, his empire soon came under immense strain, and in 1400 the princes of its various states banded together at

Mentz to depose him from the throne. He was imprisoned twice, but managed to escape both times, eventually dying of an apoplexy, without repentance. Sophie, meanwhile, had died a holy death in 1387.

Miraculous healings at John's intercession began to be received during the translation and interment of his relics and at his tomb. Indeed, the tomb itself was miraculously protected from destruction by Protestant Hussites, and in 1618 by Calvinists who had invaded Prague. Several officers and workmen attempting to demolish the tomb were deterred by various adverse events, some of them dropping dead on the spot. John also is credited with helping to save Prague (and Bavaria) in 1620, his apparition appearing to imperial troops on the eve of battle, in response to their pleas for his assistance. In 1680, his intercessions helped to preserve Nepomuc from the bubonic plague. When the count of Althan, later archbishop of Bari, fell from a balcony in Rome, he called aloud to John, who saved his life, and Cardinal Michael Frederic Althan, viceroy of Naples, was cured of a paralytic disorder, which had caused him to lose the use of one arm, the moment he began to address his prayer to John on his feast day in the Minims church.

On April 14, 1719, John's tomb was opened. The flesh was gone from his body but his bones were perfectly joined together, showing the marks of his fall into the river behind his head and on his shoulders. More astonishingly, his tongue was found to be fresh and incorrupt, as if he had only just died.

In art, John is portrayed as an Augustinian canon with a bridge nearby. Sometimes he is shown holding a finger to his lips, with seven stars around his head; in Bohemia and Austria, his lips may be padlocked.

Beatified: by Pope Innocent XIII (r. 1721–24)
Canonized: 1729, by Pope Benedict XIII
Feast: May 16
Patronage: bridges; confessors; against detraction

John Nepomucene Neumann (1811–1860) *First American bishop to be canonized*
Also known as: John Henry Cardinal Neumann

John Nepomucene Neumann was born in Prachititz, Bohemia (in what is now the Czech Republic), on March 28, 1811, the third of six children of a German father and Czech mother. He was named after the 14th-century Bohemian martyr St. John Nepomucene.

John began his studies at the diocesan seminary in Budweis in 1831, but two years later transferred to the Charles Ferdinand University in Prague. When he had completed his studies but found his ordination postponed due to an overabundance of clergy in his dio-

cese, he decided to go to America as a missionary. He arrived in New York City in June 1836, was ordained by Bishop James Dubois on June 28, then sent to work among German-speaking Catholics clearing forests in upstate New York. After four years of this work, he entered the novitiate of the newly established branch of the Redemptorists at Saint Philomena's in Pittsburgh, Pennsylvania. He made his vows in Baltimore, Maryland, in 1841, becoming the first Redemptorist to do so in the United States.

John continued his missionary activities as a preacher in Maryland, Ohio, Pennsylvania and Virginia, but he was destined for greater things. In 1844, he became rector of Saint Philomena's; in 1847, he was named vice regent and superior of the American Redemptorists; and then in 1852, Pope Pius IX (r. 1846–78) appointed him the fourth bishop of Philadelphia.

As bishop, John reorganized his diocese, establishing new parishes and inaugurating a widespread pro-

St. John Nepomucene Neumann

gram of new construction, including 100 new churches and 80 new parochial schools. He also began work on a cathedral. To staff the schools and an orphanage, he founded the School Sisters of Notre Dame, who observe the rule of the "active" Franciscan Third Order, and attracted a number of other teaching orders. John also introduced the devotion of 40 hours, wrote extensively and produced two catechisms that were endorsed by American bishops at their first plenary council in 1852 and were very popular in their day.

John died of a stroke while walking on Vine Street in Philadelphia on January 5, 1860. A little more than a century later, he became America's first male saint.

Beatified: 1963 by Pope Paul VI
Canonized: June 19, 1977, by Pope Paul VI
Feast: January 5 (United States); May 16 (elsewhere)

FURTHER READING
The Autobiography of St. John Neumann, C.SS.R. Tr. Alfred C. Rush, C.SS.R. Boston: St. Paul Media and Books, 1977.

Josemaria Escriva (José María Escrivá) (1902–1975)
Founder of Opus Dei and the Priestly Society of the Holy Cross

Josemaria was born in Barbastro, Aragón, Spain, on January 9, 1902. In 1915, his father's business failed, and the family moved to Logrono, where he found other work. It was in Logrono also that Josemaria first conceived of entering the priesthood. When he saw a monk's bare footprints in the snow, he felt God was calling him. He entered the Logrono seminary and continued at the seminary in Saragossa, where he was ordained on March 28, 1925.

In 1927, Josemaria moved to Madrid to study law. He still felt God wanted something particular from him, but did not know what. Then while on a retreat, on October 2, 1928, he realized that God wanted him to found Opus Dei, with the mission of encouraging all baptized Christians throughout the world, and in any station of life, to spread the word of God and to evangelize for the Catholic faith. Two years later, on February 14, 1930, he realized that Opus Dei was meant to develop its apostolate among women as well as men.

Josemaria was forced into hiding by the religious persecution during the Spanish Civil War; he continued to practice his ministry clandestinely and finally was able to leave Madrid. Escaping through the Pyrenees Mountains, he took up residence in Burgos. When the war ended in 1939, he returned to Madrid, where he finally received his law degree.

On February 14, 1943, Josemaria founded the Priestly Society of the Holy Cross as a complement to Opus Dei. This new society provided for the priestly ordination of lay members of Opus Dei and allowed priests from diverse dioceses to share in the spirituality and ascetic life of Opus Dei, while remaining dependent on their own bishops.

In 1946, Josemaria moved to Rome. There he obtained a doctorate in theology from the Lateran University and was named consultor to two Vatican Congregations, as well as an honorary member of the Pontifical Academy of Theology and Prelate of Honor, by Pope Pius XII (r. 1939–58).

Josemaria made frequent trips to various countries in Europe in order to develop the organization. In 1970, he traveled to Mexico, and in 1974 and 1975 he made long trips to Central and South America, where he held large gatherings. Everywhere he fostered vocations to the priesthood and to the religious life. At his death, Opus Dei had more than 60,000 members of 80 nationalities. On November 18, 1982, Opus Dei was erected by John Paul II as a personal prelature of international scope, and renamed the Prelature of the Holy Cross and Opus Dei.

Josemaria died in Rome on June 26, 1975. Many miracles have been attributed to his intercession since then. In one, Carmelite sister Concepcion Boullon Rubio was at the point of death in 1976 when she was suddenly and completely cured of a rare disease called lipomatosis after family members prayed to God for a cure through Josemaria. The miracle was unanimously approved by the Board of Physicians for the Congregation of the Causes of Saints, by a meeting of the Theological Consultors, by the Congregation of Cardinals and Bishops, and finally, by Pope John Paul II.

Beatified: May 17, 1992, by John Paul II

FURTHER READING
"About Opus Dei." Opus Dei website. URL: http://www. opusdei.org/about/home.html. Downloaded: January 27, 2000.
"Blessed Josemaria." Opus Dei website. URL: http://www. opusdei.org/blessed/home.html. Downloaded: November 12, 1999.
"Decree Cause of Canonization of the Servant of God Josemaria Escriva, Priest, Founder of the Priestly Society of the Holy Cross and Opus Dei (1902–1975)." Eternal Word Television website. URL: http://www.ewtn.com/ library/CURIA/CCSESCRI.HTM. Downloaded: November 12, 1999.

Joseph (d. first century) *Husband of the Blessed Virgin Mary and father of Jesus*

According to the Gospels, Joseph was a descendant of the royal house of David, and worked as a carpenter. After his betrothal to Mary, he learned she was pregnant, and planned to divorce her quietly after marriage so as not to bring shame and punishment down upon her. An angel then informed him in a dream that Mary was pregnant by the Holy Spirit. He married Mary. It is not certain whether the marriage took place before or after the Incarnation.

Jesus was born in Bethlehem. Joseph was warned by an angel in a dream to take Mary and Jesus to Egypt to avoid the deadly search by King Herod for the Messiah child. The family stayed in Egypt until Herod died and Joseph was told by an angel that it was safe to return to Nazareth. Joseph apparently raised Jesus as his own son. The last reference to him in the context of Jesus' life is the time when Jesus stayed in the Temple and Joseph and Mary searched for him with great anxiety for three days (Luke 2:48).

Joseph is not mentioned in scriptural descriptions of Jesus' ministry, or his Crucifixion, passion, Resurrection or Ascension. Many historians conclude that perhaps he died before these events took place.

Veneration of Joseph is widespread throughout the Eastern Church as well as the Western from about the 15th century. He was commemorated as early as the ninth century in the Eastern Church.

SS. Teresa of Avila and Francis of Assisi helped to spread devotion to him, and in the early 20th century Bl. André Bessette had built and dedicated St. Joseph's Oratory in Montreal, the world's largest shrine devoted to Joseph.

In 1870 Joseph was declared patron of the Universal Church by Pope Pius IX (r. 1846–78). In 1899, Pope Leo XIII (r. 1878–1903) gave him the same rank as Mary. Pope Benedict XV (r. 1914–22) named him protector of workers; Pope Pius XI (r. 1922–39) named him patron of social justice. Pope Pius XII (r. 1939–58) declared the Feast of Joseph the Worker on May 1.

In art Joseph is depicted as a man with a lily, or holding the baby Jesus. Sometimes he is shown with the symbol of the carpenter's trade.

Feast: March 19 (Joseph the Husband of Mary) and May 1 (Joseph the Worker)

Patronage: carpenters; against doubt; dying; engineers; families; fathers; happy death; against hesitation; married couples; social justice; social workers; working men; the Universal Church

St. Joseph with the child (Library of Congress Prints and Photographs Division)

Joseph of Arimathea (d. first century) *Figure in the story of Jesus and in Christian lore*

Joseph was a wealthy Israelite born in Arimathea. The Gospels of Mark and Luke refer to him as "senator"; he may have been a member of the Sanhedrin, or supreme council, of the Jews. He was a disciple of Jesus but did not declare himself out of fear. He opposed the Sanhedrin's condemnation of Jesus.

After the Crucifixion, Joseph boldly asked Pontius Pilate for Jesus' body and was granted it. He and Nicodemus treated the body with spices, wrapped it in linen and grave bands, and placed it in the tomb. Historians place little reliance on stories about what happened to Joseph after that. According to apocryphal texts, such as the Acts Pilati and Gospel of Nicodemus, he helped to establish the Christian community of Lydda.

In the Middle Ages, Joseph was a popular figure in legends of the Holy Grail. He appears in William of Malmesbury's 12th-century *De Antiquitate Glastoniensis Ecclesiae*, Thomas Malory's 15th-century *Morte d'Arthur*, and Robert de Barron's *Joseph d'Arimathea*, an early-13th-century romance. Joseph actually was added to William of Malmesbury's work in the 13th century.

According to medieval lore, Joseph held the cup that caught the blood of Jesus as it spurted from the spear wounds during the Crucifixion. Joseph was

St. Joseph of Arimathea taking the body of Jesus from the cross (Engraving by Gustave Doré, c. 1875)

arrested and accused of stealing Jesus' body. He languished in prison, and was nourished by a dove who visited him daily, depositing a wafer in the cup. After his release, he and his sister and a band of followers brought the cup to England, landing on the St.-Just-in-Roseland peninsula near St. Mawes in Cornwall. They journeyed to Glastonbury, where Joseph established the first Christian church in England, and hid the cup at the Chalice Well. The waters at the Chalice Well at the Glastonbury Tor are reddish from iron and have long been believed to have healing properties.

Feast: March 17

Joseph of Copertino (1603–1663) *Franciscan mystic*
Also known as: Joseph of Cupertino

Joseph of Copertino was born Joseph Desa in 1603 in Cupertino, Italy, the town that later gave him his surname. His father, a poor carpenter, died before his birth. Creditors drove his mother out of her home, and she was forced to give birth to Joseph in a stable. He had deformed feet.

As a child, Joseph exhibited mental dullness and an irascible temper. At age eight he had his first ecstatic vision. He was a poor student, and was nicknamed "Bocca Apertura" ("the Gaper") because of his incessant staring and going about with his mouth open—characteristics of his trance states.

At age 17 he applied for admission to the Friars Minor Conventuals, but was rejected because of his lack of education. The Capuchins at Martino near Tarento took him in as a lay brother, but then dismissed him because his continual ecstasies made him unable to work. Finally the Franciscans at La Grotella near Cupertino admitted him as an oblate, or lay brother, and assigned him to work in the stables. There his disposition improved and in 1628 he was ordained as a priest.

Joseph's life was comprised of visions and mystical experiences. Almost anything holy would trigger an ecstatic experience: the name of God, Mary or a saint; the tolling of a church bell; church music; sacred images; and even thoughts about sacred things would send Joseph into another state of consciousness. He was especially prone to mystical experience during Mass. During his trances, he did not respond to any stimuli, even the piercing of his flesh with needles or the dragging about of his body, except for the voice of his superior.

Joseph especially became famous for his spectacular levitations and aerial flights. He would rise several feet into the air, sometimes enraptured by the sound of heavenly music that only he could hear. He would fly about over the heads of others and remain suspended in the air for long periods of time. He flew up to holy statues and to altars. Whenever he rose into the air, he would give out a shriek of ecstasy. The total number of his levitations is not known; more than 70 were recorded during his early years at La Grotella alone.

His flights happened both indoors and outdoors. Once he saw a lamb in the garden of the Capuchins at Fossombrone, and went into a rapture over the Lamb of God, rising into the air with the lamb in his arms. After hearing a priest say, "Father Joseph, how beautiful God has made heaven," he flew up to a branch on an olive tree and knelt on the branch for half an hour, bending it no more than would a small bird.

In 1644 he amazed the Spanish ambassador to the Papal Court, his wife and attendants, by flying over their heads to a statue of Mary in church. The ambassador's wife fainted and had to be revived with smelling salts.

When he visited Pope Urban VIII (r. 1623–44) in Rome, he kissed the pontiff's feet and rose spontaneously into the air. The amazed pope said that if Joseph died before he, he would attest to the miracle himself.

Joseph's ecstasies and aerial flights—and the crowds who came to witness them—were so disruptive that for more than 35 years he was not allowed to say Mass, take part in any processions or choir exercise, or even eat meals with the other friars. He was ordered to remain in his room, where a private chapel was built for him.

In 1653 Joseph was brought before the Inquisition. Asked by the inquisitors to say Mass, he began doing so and suddenly rose in the air with a joyous shriek. He remained suspended in the air over flowers and lighted candles with his arms out like a cross, unaffected by the flames.

For the last 10 years of his life, he was shuttled from one remote Capuchin or Franciscan monastery to another, a virtual prisoner. Whenever people discovered him, crowds would gather to see him. Throughout this banishment, Joseph remained in remarkably good humor. He maintained his rigorous fasting and mortifications. He kept seven Lents of 40 days every year, eating nothing except on Thursday and Saturdays.

Joseph's last monastery was the conventual house in Osimo. There he flew eight feet into the air to kiss a statue of Jesus, and then carried it to his cell, where he floated about with it. He also carried another friar into the air. On one occasion he had a vision of angels ascending to and descending from heaven, and flew into an almond tree. The tree became known as "the almond tree of St. Joseph."

Other miraculous powers and abilities were attributed to Joseph. He could bilocate. He was prophetic and had numerous accurate visions of the future. He could read the minds and hearts of others, and knew their secret, unconfessed sins. He could control the elements and stop storms. He had command over animals, even greater than that of St. Francis of Assisi. Once he sent a bird to the nuns of St. Clare at Cupertino to accompany them in their singing. Another time he summoned sheep to gather around him and began recitation of the Litany of Loreto. The sheep bleated the responses.

He exuded a sweet perfume that clung to everything he used, and permeated the rooms he entered. He could detect the stench of sin. Once he was overcome with stench, and asked permission to go to town. There he went straight to a home wherein dwelt sorcerers. Furious, he broke all their vessels with his cane.

When Joseph had arrived at Osimo, he predicted he would die there, and his death would come on a day when he would not receive the Eucharist. On August 10, 1663, he was stricken with fever. For five days he was able to get up and say Mass in his private oratory.

St. Joseph of Copertino levitating

Then he was confined to bed and could receive only the Eucharist. Once, he heard the sound of the bell announcing the approach of the Eucharist, and went into a rapture, rising up from his bed and flying to the stairs above the chapel, his face suffused with radiance. He had numerous other levitations and ecstasies during this period. On September 17, he received his last Eucharist. As he lay dying the following day, Joseph asked God to burn and rive (tear) his heart. The embalmers were shocked to find his heart withered and dry, and the ventricles without blood. Joseph is entombed in the basilica at Osimo.

Pope Clement XIV (r. 1769–74) extended his office to the entire Church, but his cult now is confined to local calendars.

Beatified: 1753 by Pope Benedict XIV
Canonized: July 16, 1767, by Pope Clement XIII
Feast: September 18
Patronage: air travelers; astronauts; aviators; fliers; pilots

FURTHER READING

Charles, Rodney, and Anna Jordan. *Lighter Than Air: Miracles of Human Flight from Christian Saints to Native American Spirits.* Fairfield, Iowa: Sunstar Publishing, 1995.

Pastrovicchi, Angelo. *St. Joseph of Copertino.* Tr. Francis S. Laing. Rockford, Ill.: TAN Books and Publishers, 1994.

Juan Diego (1474–1548) *Aztec Indian who saw one of the few accepted apparitions of the Virgin Mary*

Juan Diego was born in 1474 in a Nahua village established in 1168 and conquered in 1467 by the Aztec chief Axayacatl. He was named Cuauhtlatoatzin, meaning "one who talks like an eagle." He belonged to the largest and lowest-ranking class of the Aztecs, but owned some land, which he farmed and on which he built a small house. He made a living weaving mats and selling produce from his farm. He was married, but had no children.

When Cortez conquered the Aztecs in 1521, he brought Catholic Christianity with him. The Aztecs at that time revered Tonantzin (meaning "mother") as the goddess of earth and corn. They prayed to her at an ancient hilltop shrine, imploring her blessings for themselves and their crops. Franciscan priests, however, told them that their practice had no religious value and was no longer acceptable.

Cuauhtlatoatzin converted to Christianity and in 1525 was baptized Juan Diego (a double name); his wife converted also and was baptized María Lucía. Juan Diego had a reserved and mystical character and was very religious. He enjoyed silence and was given to frequent penance. Every Saturday and Sunday he walked the 14 miles from his village to Tenochtitlán, now Mexico City, to attend Mass and receive religious instruction. When María Lucía died in 1529, he went to live with his uncle, Juan Bernardino, in Tolpetlac, which was nine miles from Tenochtitlán.

Before dawn on the morning of December 9, 1531, he set off as usual for Tenochtitlán. Day was breaking as he reached the bottom of a hill known as Tepeyacac, on whose summit had once stood the shrine to Tonantzin. Suddenly he heard a beautiful chorus of birdsong and a voice calling to him in Nahuatl. Filled with joy, he went toward the voice, and when he reached the hilltop saw a beautiful dark-skinned woman in Aztec dress, her face and garments radiant like the sun. He knew instantly who she was. He bowed before her, and she asked him where he was going. "My Lady and Child, I have to reach your church in Mexico," he replied. She then acknowledged herself as the Virgin Mary, and told him that she wished that a church be erected at the spot where she stood. He was to go to the bishop of Mexico, in Tenochtitlán, describe what he had seen and ask for the church to be built.

Juan Diego had to wait a long time to see the Franciscan bishop, Father Juan de Zumarraga, who politely heard him out, but said only that he would take the petition under advisement. Juan Diego left, disheartened, and returned to Tepeyacac Hill. There he again found the Virgin and related what had occurred. She told him to return to the bishop the next day and petition anew. Juan Diego agreed to do so, and went home. The next morning, Sunday, he went again to see Father de Zumarraga, who questioned him intently, but, still unbelieving, asked for a sign. Juan Diego returned to the hilltop and again saw the Virgin, who promised she would give him a sign to take to the bishop the next day.

He returned home, only to find his uncle gravely ill with the plague. Juan Bernardino asked that a priest be summoned to receive his last confession and confer his last rites. The next morning, therefore, Juan Diego tried to bypass Tepeyacac Hill and go directly to Tenochtitlán. He was in a hurry, and wanted to avoid another encounter with the Virgin, but she appeared before him anyway. He explained about his uncle, but the Virgin told him that he had been cured and not to worry further about him. Relieved, Juan Diego then asked for the sign to take to the bishop. The Virgin instructed him to climb to the top of the hill, where he would find flowers, which he was to cut, gather and bring to her. He ascended to the summit and was astonished to find there many types of Castilian roses blooming on the rocky outcrops. Not only were they of a species unknown in Mexico, they grew at a place where nothing should grow, especially considering that it was December. He placed the roses in his *tilma* (a type of cloak) and returned to the Virgin. She held the flowers briefly, then replaced them in the *tilma*, saying that they were the sign he would take to the bishop.

When he was again admitted into Father de Zumarraga's presence, Juan Diego opened his *tilma*, letting the roses fall to the floor, and was shocked when the bishop dropped to his knees before him. Looking down, Juan Diego himself saw the glowing image of the beautiful dark-skinned woman imprinted on the white cloth inside the *tilma*. Her hands were clasped, her eyes cast downward, her black hair held back in the Aztec style. The bishop begged his forgiveness, then untied the *tilma* and carried it to his chapel. He invited Juan Diego to spend the night with him so that in the morning he could show him where the church was to be erected.

The next day, after pointing out the spot, Juan Diego excused himself to go home to his uncle. He arrived to find him well and happy. Juan Bernardino then related that he himself had seen the Virgin, and that through her he had understood that Juan Diego had gone once more to Tenochtitlán to see the bishop. Moreover, she had given him his own mission, to instruct that she be called Holy Mary of Guadalupe. It is believed that Our Lady actually used the Nahuatl word *coatlexopeuh,* pronounced quatlasupe—meaning, "he who crushes the serpent," referring to the native religion—and that this was translated into Spanish as Guadalupe. In any event, she has come to be called Our Lady of Guadalupe, and is typically depicted with her foot on a snake.

At the time of his encounter with Our Lady, Juan Diego was 57, already elderly in a place and time where the life expectancy for men was about 40. The first of several churches on Tepeyacac Hill was completed in 1533 and Father Zumarraga moved Juan Diego's *tilma* with the image into it. Juan Diego gave his business and property to his uncle and went to live in a small room attached to the chapel that housed the sacred image. He spent the rest of his life spreading word of the apparitions among the people of the town and died on May 30, 1548, at the age of 74. What is known about Juan Diego and this miracle comes from a document called the *Nican Mopohua,* written in Nahuatl in the mid-16th century and first published in Spanish in 1649.

The image of the Virgin on the *tilma* remains visible to this day. Investigations were conducted in 1555 and 1723, then again in the early 20th century. No natural explanation for the image has ever been found. In 1921, at the start of the Mexican Civil War, a bomb placed beneath the image exploded, causing great damage to the chapel, but the *tilma* survived unaffected.

Beatified: May 1990 by Pope John Paul II in Mexico City
Feast: December 9

FURTHER READING
"Beato Juan Diego." Aci Digital website. Santos y Beatos de America Latina: Mexico. URL: http://www.aciprensa.com/Maria/juandiego.htm. Downloaded: March 1, 2000.
Elizondo, Virgil P. *Guadalupe: Mother of the New Creation.* Maryknoll, N.Y.: Orbis Books, 1997.
"The Story of Juan Diego." Mississippi State University website. URL: http://www.msstate.edu/fineart_online/Gallery/Trophies/story/diego.htm. Downloaded: September 10, 2000.
Our Lady of Guadalupe website. URL: http://ng.netgate.net/~norberto/materdei.html.

Jude (first century) *One of Jesus' Twelve Disciples, author of the Epistle of Jude, martyr*

Name meaning: sweetness or gentleness of character (Thaddeus)
Also known as: Judas Jaccobi; Jude Thaddeus; Judas Lebbeus; Lebbeus; Thaddeus

Jude was born in Galilee, the son of Alpheus and Mary, and was a fisherman by trade. He was a brother of St. James the Less and a first cousin of Jesus, who called him to be one of his disciples or apostles. Very little more is known about Jude apart from his brief epistle, which is concerned with the purity of the Christian faith and the good reputation and perseverance of the faithful. Although placed after the Second Epistle of Peter, it is believed to have been the major inspiration for that book. The Epistle of Jude probably was written around A.D. 80 for converts in an unknown location. Tradition affirms Jude as the actual author of the epistle. Some historians say that a pseudonymous author probably would have chosen a more prominent pen name.

St. Jude (Library of Congress Prints and Photographs Division)

Jude appears again in the apocryphal Passion of Simon and Jude, which serves as the basis for traditions about his later life. According to this source, Jude was a healer and an exorcist who could expel demons from pagan idols, leaving the statues crumbling. With St. Simon, he left Palestine to evangelize Persia. Since the sixth century, there have been legends about their martyrdom there, though the manner of death varies. Some accounts say they were killed with a saw or falchion (a short sickle-shaped sword). Others say they were beaten to death with a club, then beheaded.

By tradition, this occurred on July 1, the day the Feast of Simon and Jude is celebrated by the Eastern Church. The Western Church celebrates the feast on October 28, the day the saints' relics were translated to St. Peter's in Rome in the seventh or eighth century.

In art, Jude typically is represented as a young or middle-aged, bearded man holding a carpenter's rule or a club, saw, axe or halberd. He is sometimes confused with his fellow apostles St. Matthew (who may also hold an axe or halberd) and St. Thomas (who may also hold a carpenter's rule). He may also be shown with books or scrolls in commemoration of his epistle. When he is pictured with Simon, one holds a saw and the other a falchion. Fish, boats and oars that sometimes appear in his images symbolize his putative profession as a fisherman.

> *Feast (together with Simon):* October 28 (in the East, July 1; without Simon, in the East, June 19)
> *Patronage:* desperate situations; forgotten, hopeless, lost and impossible causes; hospital workers; hospitals

Juliana of Cumae (d. ca. 305) *Virgin and martyr of Cumae, Italy*

According to one story, Juliana was martyred when she refused to marry a Roman prefect. She was tortured and beheaded. In another story, she was martyred at Nicomedia and her relics were taken to Cumae. In art she is often shown surrounded by flames or binding the devil.

> *Feast:* February 16

Julian the Hospitaller (ca. 13th century) *Legendary saint popular in the Middle Ages*
Also known as: the Poor Man

The story of Julian the Hospitaller is told in William Caxton's version of *The Golden Legend*; a French manu-

script dated circa 1286 is the only surviving version in verse. The story was spread by troubadours.

Julian was the only child of Geoffrey, duke of Angers, France, and Duchess Emma. As a youth he loved to hunt. One day at age 16, he went off into the woods with a band of men and became separated from them and lost. He came upon a beast lying in rest and fatally shot it with an arrow. Before it died, the beast spoke to him, and foretold a terrible and unavoidable fate, that one day he would slay his mother and father with a single blow.

Julian vowed to run away to avoid the fate. He rode his horse into Brittany, where he sold it and his belongings. He set off wandering, praying intensely for God to deliver him from the cruel fate predicted by the beast. Eventually he found himself in Rome, where he had an audience with the pope. The pope ordered him to spend two years across the sea.

Julian obeyed, going to Syria. He joined the Order of the Knights Hospitallers and fought in the Crusades against the Turks. He distinguished himself in battle and was made a knight. One day he heard from pilgrims that his father was dead. Thinking himself free of the curse, he resolved to return home to his mother. He crossed the sea, but could not find his way home. He wandered again and eventually found himself in Spain.

There he found lodging in a castle that was fortified against attack by the Turks, but the king of the Turks was intent on capturing the countess there. The Turks attacked and Julian fought bravely, succeeding in taking the king hostage. He was made a count, and he and the countess married. For two years they lived in great happiness.

Meanwhile, Duke Geoffrey was still very much alive, and he and Emma had spent four years searching in vain for their son. At last they heard news about him and his whereabouts, and they journeyed to the castle disguised as pilgrims. They arrived on a day when Julian was out hunting. The countess welcomed them and bade them bathe and rest in the bed she shared with Julian. They did so, and everyone went to sleep, including the countess in another room.

Julian returned and thought it strange that his wife did not come to meet him as was her custom. The hall was empty. Going to their chamber, he perceived two sleeping forms in the bed in the dark. He immediately concluded that his wife was having an affair. Enraged, he cut them both in two, and the bed in half, with a single blow.

The countess awakened from the noise and rushed into the chamber. The horror of his crime—the unavoidable destiny—was too much for Julian. He attempted to kill himself with his own sword, but was stopped by his wife. He vowed to do penance in exile, and the countess pledged to join him.

After the burial of his parents, Julian and his wife dressed in the clothing of beggars and left the castle. They wandered and begged for food. They suffered hardships and insults. They went to Rome and confessed to the pope, and professed their desire to live in poverty. The pope's penance was that they should find themselves in a place of perilous passage and there establish a hostel for sheltering travelers and the poor.

After more wandering and many hardships and trials, they at last came to a place by a stream where many had died trying to cross the water. The area was full of thieves. There they constructed a humble hostel with beds made from grass, and devoted themselves to serving those who came for shelter. Julian was able to barter for a boat, and ferried people safely across the stream. For a long time they lived this way.

One night they were awakened by a man's voice from the opposite bank asking to be ferried over and given shelter. The traveler was an exhausted leper. Julian and his wife showed him every courtesy. When the stranger asked Julian to lend him his wife to sleep with him for the night, Julian protested but his wife did not, and agreed to comply. But when she went to the leper's bed, he had vanished. From outside came his voice, telling them that they had been tested, and were now expiated of their sins.

For seven more years, Julian and his wife lived at the hostel, serving others. One night thieves came and killed them the same way in which Julian had slain his parents. Afterward, miracles without end occurred there. The bodies of Julian and his wife were placed in a gold and silver reliquary.

Feast: February 12
Patronage: boatmen; circus people; ferrymen; hotel employees; innkeepers; travelers

FURTHER READING
The Life of Saint Julian Hospitaller. Tr. Tony Devaney Morinell. URL: http://www.fordham.edu/halsall/basis/julian.html. Downloaded: July 21, 2000.

Julian of Norwich (1342 or 1343–ca. 1423) *Mystic*
Also known as: Julian; Juliana of Norwich

Little is known about the life of this Benedictine recluse, whose mystical revelations on the love of God, redemption, prayer, the Incarnation and divine consolation made her one of the most important writers of her day in England. She was born in 1342 or 1343; no records exist to show location, family, upbringing or education. She probably entered a religious order at a young age. At the time of her mystical experience,

she was a solitary anchoress living in a cell adjoining the Church of St. Julian in Conisford, Norwich. The church was opposite an Augustinian friary that no longer exists. This church belonged to the Benedictines of Carrow, and so it is possible that she had spent some time as a Benedictine nun before embarking on the solitary life of an anchoress, but the evidence is insufficient. Evidence also is lacking of the date of her reclusion, whether before or after the revelations, and of the exact date of her death.

Julian evidently was well-educated, for her writing rivals that of Chaucer, and she demonstrated an extensive knowledge of the Latin Vulgate Bible. She also seemed to be familiar with other Latin manuscripts circulated among the monasteries.

Julian's 16 revelations occurred during an apparent near-death experience. She left a detailed record of these revelations and a small amount of information about her life in her only book, *Showings,* also called *Revelations of Divine Love.*

According to Julian, early in life she yearned to show her devotion to God through her own suffering. She desired three graces: to recollect the Passion, to have a bodily sickness, and to be given three wounds of contrition, compassion and "longing with my will for God." She prayed ardently to God that in her 30th year, she would be stricken with a bodily sickness so severe it would seem mortal to her and all around her. She would be given the last rites and experience every kind of physical and spiritual pain, and assault by devils (believed to happen during dying). However, she asked that God not let her actually die. Rather, she would be miraculously saved at the last moment, purified through her suffering and thus better able to serve God in the rest of her life.

On May 30, 1373, when she was halfway through her 30th year, Julian was stricken with a severe illness. She lay in bed suffering for three days and three nights. On the fourth night she was given last rites. She lingered on for another three days and nights. On the third night, she felt she truly was going to die, and was reluctant to do so. By daybreak, the lower portion of her body felt "dead."

She was propped up in bed with her mother, curate and parson present. The curate had brought a cross, which the parson placed so that Julian could gaze upon it in her last moments. By then her eyes were fixed in a stare and she could not speak. As she looked at the cross, her sight began to fail. The entire room became dark and full of devils—but a mysterious light shone upon the cross.

Julian then felt her upper body die away. She lost control of her arms and had great difficulty breathing. Just as she felt herself on the point of death, all pain left her, and her revelations began. She shouted out, "Blessed be the Lord!"

Julian was granted her desire to experience the Passion, which she did in vivid detail. She beheld the bleeding and dying Christ. She saw the crown of thorns upon the head of the crucified Jesus, and a shower of dark red pellets of blood running down from it like a summer rain, until the entire chamber was filled with blood. The 16 visions and their teachings sprang from Jesus crowned by thorns. They occurred as she followed the blood, which first rushed to hell, where she felt the devil clutching her throat, smelled his breath and saw his face and claws. The realm of the damned was dark with devils all around. Then the blood rushed upward to a high mountain cathedral (the heart), where Christ sat on a throne (coming to live in the heart). This cosmos was filled with light.

Her visions took three forms: "bodily," which probably meant perceived with the physical senses; "bodily and yet more spiritual," which probably meant a combination of sensory and inner perception; and "spiritual," which probably referred to an inner visioning seen with the spiritual eye only.

The visions dealt with God's creation of, and love for, humanity, how the relationship with God persists despite the shortcomings and sins of humanity, and how redemption is achieved through Christ. Julian perceived the feminine, nurturing side of God: "And so I saw that God rejoices that he is our Father, and God rejoices that he is our Mother, and God rejoices that he is our true spouse, and that our soul is his beloved wife."

Julian saw three properties of God, life, love and light: "in life is wonderful familiarity, in love is gentle courtesy, and in light is endless nature."

Some of her most penetrating insights deal with prayer. For Julian, the most sublime expression of the relationship between humanity and God is contemplative prayer, in which there is a complete surrender and trust. She said that prayer "one-eths," or unites, the soul with God. What we pray for in "rightful prayer" springs not from us but from God: first he makes us to wish it, then he makes us to beseech it. Thus, how could we not obtain that for which we pray? In other words, God motivates us to pray for that which he wishes to manifest in the world. The fruit and end of all prayer is to be "united and like to the Lord in all things." The prayer of thanksgiving enables the power of the Lord's word to enter the soul and enliven the heart.

Two versions of her book exist: a short text, usually called *Showings*, which sets forth the fundamentals of her experience, and a long text, usually called *Revela-tions of Divine Love,* which evidently was written much later, for it has more detail, allegories and insights. It is evident that Julian reached a full understanding of her experience by 1388. She continued to receive "inward instructions" about its meaning. She was led to move deeper into her religious life, from contemplation to solitude within her cell.

In her writings, she does not present her revelations systematically; images and ideas recur and lead to one another in a way that has its own inner order. She interprets all her images in terms of the Scriptures and Christian theology. Certain themes are typically hers: Though she acknowledges the insignificance of everything else compared to God ("all that is made" is shown to her like "a little thing, the size of a hazelnut"), yet she also maintains, with Genesis, the goodness of all He has made. His works "are wholly good," and all that is made "exists . . . because God loves it."

Julian's revelations are shamanic in nature, involving such hallmarks as the "initiatory" illness, descent to the underworld, exposure to horror and suffering, and spiritual rebirth. After her experience, people from all over were drawn to her, though she confined herself to a cell. She had a great reputation as a healer and counselor. Margery Kempe, who was born in 1373, the year of the revelations, recorded her visit to Julian in about 1403 for spiritual counsel. Julian, however, did not confide her revelations to Kempe.

Her handwritten manuscript received scant circulation prior to the mid-17th century. It was her own intent that this be so. She recognized her revelations as of "exalted divinity and wisdom," and prayed that they would come into the hands only of those who desired to be the faithful lovers of God, dedicated to the virtuous life and wholesome understanding of the depths of the mystery of God. The long text was rescued from obscurity by the Augustine Baker school of exiled English Benedictine monks in France and the Netherlands.

The lack of biographical data on Julian has prevented her beatification; nonetheless, she is called Blessed.

Feast: May 13

FURTHER READING

Chambers, P. Franklin. *Juliana of Norwich: An Introductory Appreciation and an Interpretive Anthology.* London: Victor Gollancz, 1955.

Julian of Norwich. *Showings.* New York: Paulist Press, 1978.

Julian of Norwich. *Revelations of Divine Love.* Tr. James Walsh. New York: Harper and Row, 1961.

Molinari, Paul, S.J. *Julian of Norwich: The Teaching of a 14th Century English Mystic.* New York: Longmans, Green, 1958.

Julitta (d. 304) *Noblewoman and martyr with her son, Quiricus*

Julitta was a noblewoman of Iconium, Lycaonia (Turkey), who converted to Christianity. At the time, under the reigns of the Roman emperors Diocletian and Maximian, severe persecutions were conducted. Julitta took her three-year-old son and several servants and fled to Seleucia, Tarsus, attempting to find safety. However, she was recognized and arrested and was taken with her son before the proconsul, Alexander.

Ordered to renounce her faith and sacrifice to the pagan gods, Julitta refused. Infuriated, Alexander took Quiricus away from her and ordered her scourged. Julitta did not relent. Quiricus, meanwhile, struggled in the grip of Alexander. Tradition holds that he declared, "I also am a Christian." Alexander either beat him to death or dashed his head against the stone steps of the throne, killing him.

Julitta thanked God for having taken her son before her. Alexander ordered her sides to be torn with iron hooks, and boiling pitch to be poured on her feet. She was then beheaded. The remains of her and her son were thrown out of the city.

Julitta's servants, who were in hiding, secretly recovered the remains and buried them in a field. They were rediscovered during the reign of Emperor Constantine. St. Amator, bishop of Auxerre from 388 to 418, is said to have carried the remains to France, where they were dispersed to Nevers, Toulouse, St. Amand in Flanders, and other locations. Churches and monasteries were dedicated to Julitta and Quiricus.

Some scholars believe that all or part of the story is fictitious.

Feast: June 16

FURTHER READING

St. Alphonsus Liguori. *Victories of the Martyrs.* Brooklyn: Redemptorist Fathers, 1954.

Julius I (d. 352) *Pope*

Julius was a native of Rome. For unknown reasons, the see of Rome was vacant for four months following the death of Pope St. Marcus in October 336. Julius was elected to the post on February 6, 337.

Much of his pontificate was concerned with the situation of St. Athanasius, the bishop of Alexandria who for a while was forced into exile and took up residence in Rome. Through Athanasius, the Egyptian monastic life became well known in Rome, and the example of the hermits of the Egyptian deserts became very influential there. Julius supported Athanasius against rivals and eventually helped to return him to Alexandria. His letter on the matter is considered one of the most important pronouncements of the Roman see, asserting as it did the Roman primate's role in the universal Church.

Under Julius, the Roman Christian community grew rapidly. He raised two new basilicas, the titular Church of Julius (now the Santa Maria in Trastevere) and the Basilica Julia (now Church of the Twelve Apostles). He built three churches over catacombs outside the walls of the city as well. During his time, also, catalogs of saints' feast days came into use.

Julius died on April 12, 352, and was buried in the Catacombs of Calepodius on the Aurelian Way. His cultus began to be celebrated soon after his death. Later his relics were translated to Santa Maria in Trastevere.

Feast: April 12

Justin Martyr (d. ca. 167 or 168) *Martyr, philosopher and defender of Christianity*

Justin Martyr was born about the beginning of the second century in Neopolis, the capital of Samaria, to heathen parents. As a young man, he was attracted to philosophy. The story is told that one day he was out in a solitary place to meditate when a mysterious old man appeared and told him that if he wished to have knowledge of the true God, he should cease studying philosophy and turn to the prophets of the Bible, who had announced the coming of Jesus, Son of God. In addition, the old man told him, pray to God to illuminate his mind. With that, the man disappeared.

Inspired, Justin followed the old man's guidance, and was baptized a Christian at about age 30. He was especially impressed with the sufferings and sacrifices of the martyrs. According to some accounts, Justin was ordained a priest; this is disputed by some historians. He preached extensively and worked to convert pagans.

Justin went to Rome where he continued his preaching. Around the year 150, he wrote and presented to Emperor Antoninus Pius and the Roman Senate his first apology in defense of the Christian faith. The apology favorably impressed the emperor, but did not stop the persecution of Christians. When Marcus Aurelius succeeded Pius, the persecutions intensified. Justin did not hesitate to engage in public debates and controversy.

Shortly after Justin issued a second apology to the emperor, he was arrested with several other Christians and brought before Rusticus, the prefect of Rome. Rusticus placed the six on trial and ordered them to obey the imperial edicts to recognize the pagan gods and

St. Justin Martyr (Library of Congress Prints and Photographs Division)

submit to the emperors. Justin and the others stood up in defense of Christianity. They were questioned at length about their beliefs and practices.

Rusticus asked them whether, if they were scourged and beheaded, they believed that they would ascend to heaven. Justin said, "I hope that, if I endure these things, I shall have His gifts. For I know that, to all who have thus lived, there abides the divine favor until the completion of the whole world." Rusticus ordered them to "offer sacrifice with one accord to the gods," which they declined.

The martyrs were sentenced to be scourged and beheaded. The bodies were carried away by other Christians for burial.

Besides his first and second apologies, Justin's other extant works include *Dialogue with Trypho, Hortatory Address to the Greeks, On the Sole Government of God* and *Discourse to the Greeks,* plus fragments of a work on the Resurrection, and other fragments.

Feast: June 1
Patronage: apologists; philosophers

FURTHER READING
St. Alphonsus Liguori. *Victories of the Martyrs.* Brooklyn: Redemptorist Fathers, 1954.
"The Martyrdom of the Holy Martyrs Justin, Chariton, Charites, Paeon and Liberianus, Who Suffered at Rome." URL: http://www.newadvent.org/fathers/0133.htm. Downloaded: February 11, 2000.

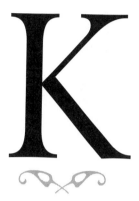

Kateri Tekakwitha, Blessed (1656–1680) *Indian mystic and convert*

Also known as: Catherine Tegakwitha, Catherine Takwita, Kateri Tekawitha, Lily of the Mohawks, Genevieve of New France

Kateri Tekakwitha was born in the Mohawk village of Gandahouhague (Ossernenon, now Auriesville, New York), in 1656, the daughter of a captive Christian Algonquin woman and a non-Christian Mohawk warrior. Her parents and brother died of smallpox when she was four; the disease permanently disfigured her face and impaired her eyesight. She was converted to Catholicism and baptized by a Jesuit missionary, Father Jacques de Lamberville, on Easter of 1676, when she was 20. In 1679, she took a vow of chastity. Shunned by her tribe because of her beliefs, she walked over 200 miles to the mission village of St. Francis Xavier de Sault, or Caughnawaga, near Montreal, Quebec. There she dedicated herself to prayer and penitence and care for the sick and aged; she was allowed to open a convent in 1679.

Kateri died at Caughnawaga, on April 7, 1680, at the age of 24. Her grave became a pilgrimage site for Christian Indians and French colonists, and the place of many miracles. In 1884, the Rev. Clarence Walworth raised a monument there.

Devotion to Kateri has been responsible for establishing Native American ministries in Catholic churches throughout the United States and Canada. The Tekakwitha Conference, an international association of Native American Catholics and those in ministry with them, was named for her.

Kateri was the first Native American proposed for canonization. Her cause was started in 1884–85 under Pope Leo XIII (r. 1878–1903), and she was declared venerable by Pope Pius XII (r. 1939–58) on January 3, 1943.

Beatified: June 22, 1980, by Pope John Paul II
Feast: July 14 (formerly April 17)
Patronage: environment and ecology

FURTHER READING

"Blessed Kateri Tekakwitha." http://www.pitt.edu/~eflst4/Kateri.html. Downloaded: January 25, 2000.
Blessed Saint Kateri Takakwitha Honoring Page. URL: http://pw1.netcom.com/~rnroybal/kateri.html. Downloaded: January 25, 2000.
The Cross in the Woods website. URL: http://www.rc.net/gaylord/crossinwoods/blessed.htm. Downloaded: January 25, 2000.
Kateri On-line. URL: http://home.earthlink.net/~paula74/Kateri/indexx.html. Downloaded: January 25, 2000.

Katharine Drexel (1858–1955) *Founder of the Sisters of the Blessed Sacrament, missionary*

St. Katharine Drexel (Archives of the Sisters of the Blessed Sacrament)

Katharine Drexel was born November 26, 1848, in Philadelphia, Pennsylvania, the second child of Francis and Hanna Drexel. Francis Drexel was a wealthy railroad tycoon and founder of a Philadelphia bank. A month after her birth, her mother died, and Katharine and her sister, Elizabeth, were cared for by their aunt and uncle. In 1860, their father married Emma Bouvier. A third daughter, Louise, was born in 1863.

The girls were well-educated and traveled throughout the United States and Europe. They assisted their stepmother in charitable service for the poor. Even at a young age, Katharine was drawn to the religious life, and at age 14 took a vow to remain chaste. By her late teens she was mortifying herself at Lent; she practiced self-flagellation throughout her life.

Katharine was 21 when Emma developed cancer, and she nursed her stepmother for three years of intense suffering until she died. During this time, Katharine was further inspired to become a religious.

Katharine's father died of pleurisy in 1885, and she and her sisters inherited large fortunes: $14 million in trust each, generating annual incomes of $400,000. Katharine used her money to build and support schools and missions for Native and African Americans.

When Katharine asked Pope Leo XIII (r. 1878–1903) to send more missionaries to Wyoming for her friend Bishop James O'Connor, the pope suggested that she herself become a missionary. In 1889, she made her novitiate with the Sisters of Mercy in Pittsburgh. She visited the Dakotas, met the chief, and in 1891, founded the Sisters of the Blessed Sacrament for Indians and Colored People, now known as the Sisters of the Blessed Sacrament. St. Frances Xavier Cabrini advised her on getting the order recognized by the Vatican.

Katharine pursued her ministry, receiving requests for sisters from throughout the South and Southwest. She built and maintained missions and schools and sent her nuns to staff them. In 1894, she helped to open the first mission school for Indians, in Santa Fe, New Mexico. In 1917, she founded a school to prepare teachers in New Orleans, which in 1925 became chartered as Xavier University. It is the only predominantly black Catholic university in the United States.

Katharine suffered a heart attack in 1935 but continued to travel to her missions, taking an active interest in the work of each one. By 1942 she had a system of 40 mission centers, 50 Indian missions, black Catholic schools in 13 states, and 23 rural schools, in addition to Xavier University. She kept up continual correspondence with all of them, usually including in her letters a generous check.

During the last years of her life, Katharine was an invalid, spending much time in prayer and meditation. By the time of her death in 1955, she had spent $20 million of her inheritance for the American Indian and black American missions. She died March 3, 1955, at the age of 96, of natural causes. She is interred in a crypt at the motherhouse in Bensalem, Pennsylvania.

More than 4,000 people have attributed miraculous cures and favors to her intercession. In 2000 Katharine became the second American-born person to be canonized; the first was St. Elizabeth Ann Seton, in 1975. The two miracles accepted by the Vatican that were attributed to her intercession were the curing of deafness in two persons, a 17-month-old boy who had been born with nerve deafness, and a seven-year-old deaf girl.

Beatified: November 20, 1988, by Pope John Paul II
Canonized: October 1, 2000, by Pope John Paul II
Feast: March 3

FURTHER READING
O'Reilly, David. "The Saving Mission of Katharine Drexel." URL: http://inq.philly.com/content/inquirer/2000/10/01/sunmag/ drexel01 htm. Downloaded: October 24, 2000.
"Saint Katharine Drexel." Sisters of the Blessed Sacrament website. URL: http://wwwkatharinedrexel.org. Downloaded: October 24, 2000.

Laura Vicuña, Blessed (1891–1904) *Popular saint*

Laura Vicuña was born April 5, 1891, in Santiago, Chile, the first child of José Domingo Vicuña and Mercedes del Pino. Her father was a well-connected member of the Chilean aristocracy, though her mother came from a poor family. Due to the difference in social class, Laura's mother was never accepted by the Vicuña family. The difficulties worsened when Laura's father found himself on the losing side in a civil war and was forced to flee the capital for the small town of Temulco. He died there in 1895, two days after the birth of his second child.

Laura's mother moved with Laura and her younger sister to the pampas of neighboring Argentina, where she was struggling to make ends meet when she met Manuel Mora, the owner of a ranch outside the town of Junin. Soon the family moved to the ranch, and Laura was well provided for with food and clothing. Mora even arranged to send the girls to a school run by the Salesian Sisters of María Auxiliadora in Junin. Laura started attending this school in 1900, when she was nine.

At the school, Laura heard how a couple are bound above all by love; she also heard one of the nuns inveighing against couples living in sin. The first time she heard this, she fainted. When the nun returned to the same theme in the following lecture, she blanched.

But the strength of her growing faith led her to conceive a plan. She would offer her life to God if he would release her mother from the sinful life she was leading with Mora. When she mentioned her plan to her confessor, he cautioned that if she made such an offer, God might accept and could take her life quickly. Nevertheless, on the occasion of her First Communion, Laura tendered her offer.

When Laura went to the ranch on vacations, Mora treated her badly, striking her and apparently even trying to take sexual advantage of her, but Laura is said to have held him off. She prayed regularly—although her mother told her not to let Mora know—and suffered her trials as penance.

Back at school, when the building flooded in winter, Laura braved frigid water for hours to bring younger children to safety. In the process, one of her kidneys became infected, and her health began to deteriorate.

As Laura grew steadily worse, her mother brought her back to the ranch and sought medical help for her, but she did not improve. Laura was sure that she was going to die, and believed that this stemmed from the pact that she had made with God. On her deathbed, she told her mother about this pact, and pleaded with her to leave Mora, which she promised to do. Laura died happy and smiling on January 22, 1904, at the age of 13. True to her word, her mother changed her name and moved away, never again choosing a life of sin.

Laura's remains were buried in a chapel of the Church of María Auxiliadora. She is held up as a model for young people.

Beatified: September 3, 1988, by Pope John Paul II
Feast: January 10 or 22
Patronage: young people; Argentina; Chile

FURTHER READING

"Beata Laura Vicuña." *Santos y Biatos de America Latina: Argentina.* URL: http://www.aciprensa.com/santarge.htm. Downloaded: November 15, 1999.

"Beata Laura Vicuña: Un regalo de Dios a la Juventud de América." *Santos y Biatos.* URL: http://www.geocities. com/~catolicos/santose.htm. Downloaded: November 15, 1999.

"¿Quién fue Laura Vicuña?" *Red Informática de la Iglesia Católica en Chile: Testigos de Christo.* URL: http:// www.iglesia.cl. Downloaded: November 15, 1999.

Lawrence (d. 258) *Deacon and martyr*

Lawrence was one of seven deacons of the Church in Rome under Pope Sixtus II (r. 257–258). He was martyred following the execution of Sixtus II. Little else is known about Lawrence, but tradition has built up a story around him.

In 257 Emperor Valerian issued an edict against Christians, forbidding them to assemble and requiring them to participate in pagan rites. In August 258, Valerian ordered all bishops, priests and deacons killed. On August 6, Sixtus II defied the order and assembled his followers in the Catacomb of Prætextatus (on the Appian Way across from the Catacomb of St. Callistus). He and several church officials were beheaded.

According to lore, Lawrence was told by Sixtus that he would follow in martyrdom in three days' time. Lawrence gladly awaited his fate. He gave away all his money to the poor. The prefect of Rome heard about

The roasting of St. Lawrence over the gridiron (Library of Congress Prints and Photographs Division)

this and ordered Lawrence to produce the Church's wealth. Lawrence said he would in three days' time. He gathered up the sick, beggars, the lame and the poor—all the cast-offs of society—and summoned the prefect. The prefect was not amused at the sight of this sorry lot and demanded to see the treasures. Lawrence is said to have replied, "What are you displeased at? These are the Church treasures!"

The enraged prefect ordered Lawrence to be executed by slow death over a gridiron. He was stripped and tied to an iron bed over a slow fire. His flesh roasted little by little and gave off a sweet smell. He was surrounded by a beautiful light. After a long time, he said to the judge, "Let my body be turned; one side is broiled enough." When his body was turned, he said, "It is cooked enough; you may eat." Lawrence then prayed for the conversion of Rome, and expired. Noblemen gave him an honorable burial in the cemetery of Cyriaca on the Via Tiburtina.

The martyrdom of Lawrence was cited by SS. Augustine, Maximus and Jerome, and by the poet Prudentius, who said his death marked the end of idolatry in Rome. Lawrence became one of the most venerated of the Roman martyrs, and miracles were ascribed to his intercession. At the spot where Lawrence was buried, Emperor Constantine the Great (Blessed) built the first chapel of what became St. Lawrence-Outside-the-Walls Church, the fifth patriarchal basilica of Rome.

For many years, a small quantity of Lawrence's blood, kept in a reliquary, would liquefy for eight days every August.

Feast: August 10
Patronage: cooks; cutlers; glaziers; against lumbago; the poor; Sri Lanka

Lawrence of Brindisi (1559–1619) *Capuchin Friar, Doctor of the Church*

Lawrence of Brindisi was born Julius Caesar de Rossi in Brindisi, Italy, in 1559. From an early age he was precocious in his studies, and exhibited a natural gift for oratory. His father died when he was 12, and he went to Venice to study with the clerics of St. Mark's. In 1575 he joined the Capuchin Friars Minor, a strict offshoot of the Franciscans, and took the name of Brother Lawrence. He studied at the University of Padua. He was a quick study in foreign languages and learned the principal ones of Europe as well as Semitic ones. He was reputed to know the entire original text of the Bible.

Lawrence preached and evangelized throughout Europe. His skill and gifts enabled him to hold all the offices of his order. From 1596 to 1602 he lived in Rome and evangelized the Jews at the behest of Pope Clement VIII (r. 1592–1605). He traveled about evangelizing Jews, and establishing houses of his order. He was popular because of his speaking ability and his miracles.

In 1601, while establishing a house in Prague, Lawrence was made chaplain of Emperor Rudolf II's army, which was fighting the Turks. Lawrence galvanized the troops with inspiring speeches and even led the army in spite of his feebleness, mounted on horseback and crucifix in hand. Miraculously he was never wounded.

In 1605 Lawrence was sent to evangelize Germany, where he served as papal nuncio to the court of Bavaria and became involved in the politics that preceded the Thirty Years' War.

In 1618 he retired to a monastery in Caserta, Italy, but was recalled and sent on a mission to Spain to advise King Philip III. The journey exhausted him, and he never returned home. He died in Lisbon on July 22, 1619.

Lawrence's writings include hundreds of sermons, commentaries on books of the Bible (he is especially noted for his commentary on Genesis), various treatises and religious polemics.

Beatified: 1783 by Pope Pius VI
Canonized: 1881 by Pope Leo XIII
Declared Doctor of the Church: 1959 by Pope John XXIII
Feast: July 21

Lawrence of Canterbury (d. 619) *Benedictine and second archbishop of Canterbury*

According to the Venerable St. Bede, Lawrence of Canterbury was one of the original missionaries who left Rome with St. Augustine in 595 and arrived in Thanet (Canterbury) in 597. After Augustine was consecrated, he sent Lawrence back to Rome to deliver to Pope St. Gregory I the Great (r. 590–604) the news of the conversion of King Ethelbert and his people, to announce his consecration and to ask for direction on certain questions. Lawrence returned with the pope's responses.

Augustine consecrated Lawrence as bishop, and Lawrence succeeded him as archbishop upon Augustine's death in 604. According to Bede, Lawrence worked diligently to strengthen the Church, and urged Celtic bishops to agree to peace and unity with Rome. But Lawrence's efforts were undone in the turmoil that followed the death of King Ethelbert in 616, and the reestablishment of pagan kings, including Edbald, son of Ethelbert.

SS. Mellitus and Justus, bishops of the newly founded sees of London and Rochester, took refuge with Lawrence at Canterbury and urged him to flee to Gaul with them. The two men left. The discouraged Lawrence was preparing to follow them when he had a dream in which St. Peter appeared to him and rebuked him for abandoning his flock and beat him. In the morning Lawrence found wounds on his back and showed them to King Edbald. Impressed by the dream, the king converted. Mellitus and Justus were recalled to England, and evangelized throughout Kent and the surrounding areas.

Shortly after these events, Lawrence died on February 2, 619, in Canterbury and was buried near Augustine in the north porch of St. Peter's Abbey church, afterward known as St. Augustine's. Lawrence is commemorated in the Irish Stowe Missal.

His dream of the beating by St. Peter resembles the dream of St. Jerome, in which that saint was beaten by God for his pagan interests.

Feast: February 2

Lazarus (d. first century) *Brother of Martha and Mary of Bethany, friend of Jesus who was raised from the dead*

The story of the resurrection of Lazarus is given in John 11:1–44. Lazarus fell ill and Jesus was notified.

St. Lazarus being raised from the dead by Jesus (Engraving, 19th century)

He said the illness was not unto death, and stayed two days longer in the place where he was at. He told his disciples, "Our friend Lazarus has fallen asleep, but I go to awaken him out of sleep." Then he explained more clearly, "Lazarus is dead; and for your sake I am glad that I was not there, so that you may believe. But let us go to him."

By the time Jesus arrived in Bethany, about two miles from Jerusalem, Lazarus had been dead four days and entombed. Jesus was met by Martha, who told him Lazarus would not have died had he come earlier, but she acknowledged that God would grant whatever Jesus asked. Jesus promised that Lazarus would rise again, and Martha thought he meant in the resurrection at the last day. Mary, weeping, also told Jesus that Lazarus would not have died had he come earlier.

Jesus went to the tomb and ordered the stone rolled away. Martha protested that there would be an odor, but the stone was taken away. Jesus called out, "Father, I thank thee and thou hast heard me. I knew that thou hearest me always, but I have said this on account of the people standing by, that they may believe that thou didst send me." Then he cried out in a loud voice, "Lazarus, come out." Lazarus, his hands and feet bound in bandages, came out of the tomb. Jesus commanded, "Unbind him and let him go."

Word of this feat reached the Pharisees, who began plotting how to put Jesus to death. After this, Jesus no longer went openly among the Jews. Soon thereafter, he was betrayed, arrested and crucified.

The Gospels do not relate what happened to Lazarus after his resurrection. Tradition holds that after the Crucifixion, Lazarus and his sisters went to the south of France, where Lazarus became the first bishop of Marseilles and then was martyred. Other legends purport that they went to Cyprus, where he became the bishop of Kition, or they went to Syria. Tradition also holds that the relics of Lazarus were translated to Constantinople. His cultus was popular in the early Church.

Feast: July 29

Leo I (d. 461) *Pope and Doctor of the Church*
Also known as: Leo the Great

Leo was born in Tuscany, or perhaps in Rome of Tuscan parents. He entered the Roman Church and became a deacon under Pope St. Celestine I (r. 422–432). During the pontificate of St. Sixtus III (r. 422–440), Emperor Valentinian III sent him to Gaul to settle a dispute between the chief military commander, Aëtius, and the chief magistrate, Albinus, whose quarrels were leaving the province open to attack. While he was with the two men, a deputation arrived to announce the death of Sixtus and his own election to the Chair of St. Peter. Leo returned to Rome and was consecrated on September 29, 440.

He began his pastoral duties with a series of 96 still-extant sermons on faith, encouraging various acts of charity, elaborating on Christian doctrine, defending papal primacy in the jurisdiction of the Church, and strenuously opposing the heresies of Manichaeanism, Pelagianism, Priscillianism and Nestorianism. Later in his papacy he argued against the teachings of Eutyches, who held that Jesus had but a single nature, his human nature being subsumed by his divine nature; the orthodox view was that Jesus had a dual nature. The Council of Chalcedon in 451 not only agreed with him but also recognized his ruling as "the voice of St. Peter," thus affirming Rome's leading role in the universal Church. However, the council also gave the Church of Constantinople a dignity second only to Rome and thus above those of Alexandria and Antioch (both of which had been founded by apostles of Jesus), something Leo refused to accept.

After Attila the Hun plundered Milan and destroyed Pavia in 452, the emperor sent Leo as part of a delegation to meet him and offer an annual tribute if he would withdraw from Italy; Attila accepted, and so Rome was saved. Unfortunately, Leo could not stop the North African Vandals from sacking the city in 455, though he did manage to get them to desist before they had burned it and killed its inhabitants. The Vandals took captives, however, and after their departure, Leo dispatched missionary priests with money to minister to the captives and to purchase their freedom.

Leo died in Rome on November 10, 461, and was buried in the vestibule of St. Peter's in the Vatican. In 688, Pope St. Sergius I (r. 687–701) had his relics translated to the basilica itself and a special altar erected over them.

In art, Leo is depicted as a pope with a dragon near him. He is also shown with SS. Peter and Paul; with St. Peter giving him the pallium; with angels surrounding him; meeting Attila the Hun at the gates of Rome; on horseback, with Attila and his soldiers kneeling before him; and praying at the tomb of St. Peter.

Declared Doctor of the Church: 1754 by Pope Benedict XIV
Feast: November 10 (formerly April 11); February 18 (Eastern Church)
Patronage: choristers; musicians

Leo II (d. 683) *Pope*

Leo was born in Sicily, the son of Paul. Although he was elected to the Chair of St. Peter to succeed Pope St. Agatho (r. 678–681) a few days after the latter's death in June 681, he was not consecrated until August 17 of the following year, after Emperor Constantine IV Pognatus confirmed his nomination. Leo was known as a fine preacher with an interest in music (he was trained in the papal choir school). He had a profound concern for the poor.

Leo's most important act as pope was to confirm the acts of the Sixth Ecumenical Council of 680–681, which condemned the heresy of Monothelitism and censured Pope Honorius I (r. 625–638) for his failure to do likewise.

Fearing that the Lombards, who had sacked Rome, might again ravage the catacombs, Leo had many of the relics of the martyrs removed and translated to a church he had built to receive them.

Leo died on June 28, 683, after a reign of only 10 months. He is commemorated as a saint in the Roman Martyrology.

Feast: June 28 (formerly July 3)

Leo III (d. 816) *Pope*

Leo was the son of Atyuppius and Elizabeth, Romans of the lower class. He joined the priesthood and served as cardinal-priest of the church of Santa Susanna as well as *vestiarius* (chief of the pontifical wardrobe and treasury).

Leo was elected to the Chair of St. Peter on the day that his predecessor, Hadrian (Adrian) I (r. 772–795), was buried, December 26, 795, and consecrated the next day. This unusual haste may have been due to the Romans' wish to forestall any influence from the Franks in the election. However, Leo was quick to inform the Frankish king, Charlemagne, sending along the keys to the confessional in St. Peter's basilica and the flag of Rome. Charlemagne in return sent Leo a considerable part of the treasure he had captured from the Avars. This unexpected wealth allowed Leo to be an especially generous benefactor of Roman churches and charitable institutions.

Leo was not without his enemies, however. Two of Pope Hadrian's nephews had hoped to succeed him, and on St. Mark's Day (April 25), 799, they hired a gang of young nobles to attack Leo as he was riding in a procession. The youths dragged the pope from his horse and attempted to blind him and cut out his tongue, defects that would have made him unable to rule. With the help of a supporter, Leo managed to escape to the monastery of St. Erasmus, where he recovered quickly, some believe miraculously.

Charlemagne was then in Paderborn, Germany, and Leo crossed the Alps to see him. He returned to Rome a few months later, accompanied by an armed escort assigned by the king, to be met by rejoicing crowds. Hadrian's nephews, however, were not through with him. They accused him of adultery and perjury. Charlemagne convened a council to consider the charges, but when the accusers could not prove them, they were arrested and carried as prisoners to Frankland (France). They were condemned to die, but at Leo's request, the sentence was commuted to life in exile.

Charlemagne visited Rome in 800, and in a special Christmas Day ceremony in St. Peter's, Leo crowned him Holy Roman Emperor. This was the beginning of the Holy Roman Empire, an attempt to realize St. Augustine's ideal of the City of God and an alliance intended to halt the spread of Islam in Europe. In effect, the Holy Roman Empire revived the ancient Western Roman Empire and pitted it against the Eastern Empire, with its capital in Constantinople. In 801, Leo attempted to bring about a marriage between Charlemagne and the Eastern empress Irene, hoping thereby to resurrect the original, unified Roman Empire and ensure the supremacy of Christianity throughout its domain, but the match did not come about.

In the ensuing years, Leo and Charlemagne worked closely together to combat the heresy of Adoptionism in Spain, to settle disputes in Germany and England, and to protect the northern Mediterranean against incursions from Islamic Saracens. In 804, Leo gave his blessing to Charlemagne's plan to divide his empire between his two sons.

When Charlemagne died in January 814, Leo lost his protector, and new conspiracies were launched against him. He managed to put these down, but his life was coming to an end. Leo died on June 12, 816, and was interred in St. Peter's, where his relics are to be found today alongside those of Popes SS. Leo I (Leo the Great, r. 440–461), Leo II (r. 682–683) and Leo IV (r. 847–855).

In art, Leo is generally shown crowning Charlemagne. A restored, near-contemporary mosaic depicting St. Peter giving the pallium to Leo and a standard to Charlemagne survives in the Lateran Palace. Another image from the *Grandes Chroniques de France* depicts the "Torture of Leo III."

Canonized: 1673 by Pope Clement X
Feast: June 12

Leo IV (d. 855) *Pope*

Leo was born into a Lombard family in Rome. He studied at Saint Martin's monastery in that city and became a Benedictine monk. He was made subdeacon of the Lateran Basilica by Pope Gregory IV (r. 827–844) and soon thereafter was named cardinal-priest of the church of the Quatuor Coronati by Pope Sergius II (r. 844–847). He was unanimously elected to the Chair of St. Peter to succeed Sergius and was consecrated on April 10, 847.

One of Leo's first official actions was to repair the walls of Rome, which had been destroyed in the Saracen attack of the previous year. He also solicited the help of the Holy Roman Emperor, and of all the cities and agricultural colonies of the duchy of Rome, to build a wall around the Vatican, a project that required four years to complete. The newly fortified area became known as the Leonine City in his honor.

In addition to these fortifications, Leo also restored many Roman churches, including parts of St. Peter's Basilica, which had suffered especially heavy damage. The list of his benefactions to churches takes up 28 pages in the *Liber pontificalis*.

In 849, Leo entered into an alliance with several Greek cities. Thanks to his prayers and exhortations to the soldiers and sailors, and to a fierce storm at sea, the alliance soundly defeated the Moslem Saracens at the Roman port of Ostia.

The latter part of Leo's reign was largely concerned with enforcing Church discipline. He died in the midst of these endeavors and was buried in St. Peter's on July 17, 855. He is credited with miracles and his name appears in the Roman Martyrology.

Feast: July 17

Leo IX (1002–1054) *Pope*
Also known as: Bruno of Toul, Peregrinus Apostolicus

A reputed miracle-worker whose travels earned him the nickname "Peregrinus Apostolicus," Leo was at home with the army as well as the court. Disagreements and possibly miscommunication during his reign led to the Great Schism between Constantinople and Rome in 1054.

Leo was born at Egisheim, near Colmar, in Alsace, on June 21, 1002, and christened Bruno. His father Hugh was a first cousin of the future emperor Conrad. It is said that once he refused to look at an exceptionally beautiful book that his mother, Heilewide, had bought and given to him. Eventually it was discovered that the book had been stolen from the Abbey of St. Hubert in the Ardennes. When Heilewide returned the book to the abbey, Bruno was once again able to study.

At the age of 5, Hugh and Heilewide sent Bruno to live with Berthold, bishop of Toul, who ran a school for the sons of the nobility. At home one summer vacation,

Bruno was attacked in his sleep by an animal. His wounds were so serious that for a time he was on the brink of death. He survived, however, and afterward said that he had had a vision of a visit by St. Benedict, who had cured him by touching his wounds with a cross.

In 1017, Bruno became a canon at St. Stephen's of Toul, and in 1024, when Conrad succeeded Emperor Henry I, he transferred to the chapel of the king's court. He quickly became known as "the good Bruno," in contrast to others of the same name.

When Conrad set out for Italy in 1026, he asked Bruno to lead his troops in place of the elderly Herimann, the then-bishop of Toul; when Herimann died shortly thereafter, Bruno was elected his successor. He was consecrated bishop in 1027, and served for the next two decades during a period of extreme stress, proving to be an exceptional political as well as spiritual leader.

When the German pope Damasus II (r. 1048) died in 1048, the Roman Church asked Henry III (Conrad's successor) to let them have either Bruno or Halinard, archbishop of Lyons, as the new pope. Henry decided on Bruno, who went to Rome barefoot and dressed as a pilgrim, and was elected by acclamation. Assuming the name Leo, he was enthroned in the Chair of St. Peter on February 12, 1049.

Leo quickly set about pushing through various needed ecclesiastical reforms. In April 1049, he convened a council in Rome that condemned clerical incontinence and simony. After that he spent several months traveling throughout Europe, convening councils and issuing excommunications as required.

He returned to Rome in January 1050, and for the next few years was concerned with the Normans in southern Italy. More than once he led troops into action, bringing criticism from St. Peter Damian, among others. The military campaigns, moreover, proved disastrous when Leo and his army were defeated at Civitella in June 1053, and the pope surrendered to his conquerors. He was imprisoned at Benevento for nine months before being released.

During this same period, relations between the Churches of Rome and Constantinople—strained for centuries—were reaching a breaking point. Michael Cærularius, patriarch of Constantinople, attacked the Roman Church because it used unfermented bread in the sacrifice of the Mass, struck the name of the pope from the sacred diptychs, and closed Roman churches in Constantinople. Leo protested and (evidently while in prison) began to study Greek to better understand the issues, but his efforts failed. The end came with Michael's excommunication by the cardinals Humbert

and Frederick on July 16, 1054, effectively separating the Greek and Roman churches.

By the time this occurred, however, Leo had died. Upon his return to Rome in March 1054, he ordered his bed carried to St. Peter's Basilica and placed next to a coffin. There he died on April 19. His name was entered in the Roman Martyrology.

Canonized: 1087 by Pope Victor III
Feast: April 19

Leontius Byzantinus (d. sixth century) *Monk, theologian, Father of the Church*

Little is known about the life of Leontius Byzantinus. He may have been born around 485 in Constantinople. He joined the heretical Nestorians, but converted and became one of their opponents. He was a monk in Jerusalem and at Constantinople, where he died, possibly around 543.

Despite the lack of information about his life, Leontius was an important theologian. He wrote books against heresies, notably those of the Nestorians, Monophysites and Appollinarists, as well as all the known heresies of the time, even the Jews and Samaritans. He defended the title of *Theotokos* ("God-bearer") for the Blessed Virgin Mary. He is considered one of the first of the Scholastics.

Linus (d. ca. 79) *Pope*

Very little is known about Linus. By tradition, he was the son of Herculanus, from Tuscany. Apparently he is the Linus mentioned by St. Paul in II Timothy 4:21. SS. Peter and Paul are said to have turned the governance of the Church of Rome over to him, and he is considered to have followed Peter in the office of bishop of Rome, making him the second in the roster of popes. His reign lasted 12 years, from A.D. 64–67 to 76–79. He was probably buried at the foot of Vatican Hill, possibly beside Peter.

Feast: September 23

Louis IX (1214–1270) *King of France, Crusader, confessor*
Name meaning: Famous warrior
Also known as: Louis Capet

Louis IX represented the ideal medieval monarch: a devout Christian, a Crusader, a willing warrior but an eager peacemaker, just, fair, chaste, intelligent, capable. He was born in Poissy on April 25, 1214, the eldest son of King Louis VIII and Queen Blanche of Castile.

St. King Louis IX in prayer (Library of Congress Prints and Photographs Division)

Blanche was the granddaughter of King Henry II of England and Queen Eleanor of Aquitaine, while Louis VIII was the grandson of King Louis VII of France, Eleanor of Aquitaine's first husband. Louis was only eight when his grandfather, Philip II, died, elevating his father, Louis VIII, to the throne, and 12 when his father died in November 1226, making the young boy king. His mother, Queen Blanche, pressed for an immediate coronation to forestall an uprising by the restless nobles, and Louis IX was crowned at Reims by the end of November.

Queen Blanche acted as regent for the next eight years during her son's minority and was an extremely capable ruler. In her son's name she quashed several revolts by the nobility, including a campaign in Languedoc by Raymond VII of Toulouse, an uprising by Pierre Mauclerc, known as Peter I of Brittany, another by Philip Hurepel in the Île de France (the only land really designated the nation of France, encompassing the city of Paris and environs) and various campaigns by King Henry III of England, who supported the activities of the warring French nobles. England still claimed huge territories of what is now France, based on the inheritances of Eleanor of Aquitaine. Blanche skillfully won the sympathies of

Pope Gregory IX, who had earlier supported Henry III, due to the efforts of her friend and papal legate Frangipani. Frangipani personally accepted the surrender of Raymond VII in front of Notre Dame Cathedral, paving the way for annexation of the southern provinces to France in the Treaty of Paris, 1229. When Louis IX began ruling on his own behalf in 1235, his nation was stronger and at peace.

In May 1234, Louis married Margaret, a noble woman of Provence, France. Margaret's younger sister, Eleanor, was the wife of King Henry III of England (making the two kings brothers-in-law), and the next sister, Sanchia, was the wife of Henry III's brother, Richard of Cornwall. Louis IX's brother Charles was married to another of Margaret's sisters, Beatrice. Louis and Margaret had 11 children: five sons and six daughters.

Louis's reign was marked by peace, diplomacy and Christian virtue. One of his first royal acts was building the Royaumont monastery with funds left by Louis VIII for that purpose. He gave great sums from the treasury and personal support to various religious orders, including the establishment of the Carthusians at Vauvert in Paris and the founding, along with Queen Blanche, of the convent of Maubuisson. The king promoted a codification of the laws and worked to eliminate trial by combat in favor of jury trials. Louis protected the weak from oppressive nobles, reformed taxation, outlawed usury and even ordered branding as punishment for blasphemy, an edict lessened to fines on the advice of Pope Clement IV.

The king also sent money to the Latin princes ruling the Crusader kingdoms in the Holy Land. In gratitude, in 1239 King Baldwin I of Jerusalem offered to sell Louis—an avid collector of sacred relics—a piece of what Baldwin claimed was Christ's Crown of Thorns from the Crucifixion. Unfortunately, Baldwin had pawned the relic to Venetian moneylenders, but Louis delightedly paid an exorbitant sum for the relic and sent two Dominican friars to Venice to retrieve it. He and his entire court met the Dominican delegation at Sens and accompanied the treasure to France. In 1241, Louis purchased pieces reported to be from the True Cross. To house these divine objects Louis demolished the chapel of St. Nicholas in Paris and built Sainte-Chapelle, one of the most beautiful examples of Gothic architecture still standing. The walls of the second floor, which was used for worship and veneration of the relics, are made almost entirely of stained glass panels illustrating Bible stories and events from Louis's reign. In one, Louis and Margaret are depicted holding the Crown of Thorns on a pillow. Interestingly, several of the windows illustrate stories of women from the Bible as an homage to the king's mother. The relics were lost during the French Revolution.

In 1242, Louis quelled a rebellion led by Hugh of Lusignan, count de la Marche. The count was married to Isabel, the widow of King John I of England and the mother of Henry III. Louis defeated Henry III at Taillebourg, establishing the Peace of Bordeaux and the annexation of a part of the province of Saintonge to France. In 1259, Louis settled with Henry III by signing the Treaty of Paris, in which Henry agreed to relinquish claims to the provinces of Normandy, Anjou, Maine, Touraine and Poitou, and Louis ceded the Limousin, Quercy and Perigord to Henry III along with compensation. Most historians believe that if Louis had pressed his advantage with Henry III the later Hundred Years' War between the two nations might have been averted. Nevertheless, peace lasted for 24 years.

After surviving a deadly fever in 1244, Louis declared his intention to lead a Crusade upon learning that the Turcoman Muslims had invaded Jerusalem. Before he could leave, however, affairs of state delayed his departure for three years; during that time all benefices were taxed a 20th of their income to finance the Crusade. Louis, Queen Margaret and three of the king's brothers finally left for Cyprus in June 1248, where they spent the winter accompanied by William Longsword, earl of Salisbury, and 200 English knights. The Crusaders' objective was Egypt, whose sultan, Melek Selah, had been attacking Palestine. Louis's troops easily took the port city of Damietta, in the Nile Delta, in early 1249, but could not continue their success. To the king's horror, the soldiers engaged in debauchery and looting, occasionally interrupted by desultory fighting, for about a year until, weak from dysentery, Louis himself was captured in April 1250.

Queen Blanche, again serving as regent for her son, began raising a huge ransom. Upon learning of the king's capture, peasants, called the "Pastoureaux" and led by someone called the Hungarian Master, banded together in the "crusade of the shepherds" to try to rescue Louis. But when the peasants took up arms against the clergy, Blanche engaged them in battle near Villeneuve in June 1251, routing the rebellion. By late 1250, the Mamluk emirs had overthrown Sultan Melek, and the emirs accepted the city of Damietta as ransom for Louis and a million bezants for the other prisoners. Louis and the remnant of his forces sailed for Palestine, where he remained, visiting holy places, until 1254, when he learned of Blanche's death two years before.

For the next 13 years, Louis pursued philanthropy and diplomacy. He arranged the above-mentioned Treaty of Paris with Henry III in 1259, and in 1263 arbitrated on behalf of Henry against the English barons who sought to limit Henry's authority. In 1258,

Louis imposed the Treaty of Corbeil upon the king of Aragon, who agreed to relinquish all claims to Provence and Languedoc, except Montpellier, in return for French concessions to claims for Roussillon and Barcelona. A patron of architecture and academics, he helped his friend and confessor, Robert de Sorbon, establish the College de la Sorbonne as the theological school of the University of Paris in 1257. In 1254, Louis established the House of the Felles-Dieu for reformed prostitutes and the Hospital Quinze-Vingt for 300 blind men ("quinze-vingt": 15 score, or 300). He personally tended the poor and sick. Eschewing royal raiment for plain clothing, he often met with churchmen, including St. Thomas Aquinas, and continued to wear the Crusader's cross as a pledge. He became a Franciscan tertiary. Consequently, no one was surprised—nor were they pleased—when Louis announced his second crusade in 1267.

Organizing the Crusade again took three years, during which time the pope granted Louis one-tenth of all Church revenues. In addition, the king levied a toll tax on his French subjects. After naming the abbot of St. Denis and Simon de Clermont as co-regents, Louis and his three eldest sons—Philip, John and Peter—sailed from Aigues-Mortes at the mouth of the Rhone in southern France on July 1, 1270. He landed at Tunis in North Africa, awaiting reinforcements from his brother Charles of Anjou, king of Sicily, and was crushed to learn that rumors of the Mamluk emir's conversion to Christianity were false. Shortly thereafter typhus and dysentery broke out; Louis's second son, John, died, and the king and his eldest son, Philip, came down with typhus.

Louis declined rapidly, and he gave detailed instructions to his children about ruling the kingdom and remaining faithful to God. On August 24, the king received the last rites and then called for the Greek ambassadors, whom he urged to reunite with the Roman Church. The next day Louis lay unable to speak until noon, then repeated Psalm 5:7. Speaking again at 3:00 in the afternoon, he commended his soul to God and died. Louis's bones and heart were returned to France and enshrined in the Abbey of St. Denis until they were vandalized and scattered during the Revolution.

Canonized: 1297 by Pope Boniface VIII
Feast: August 25
Patronage: barbers; builders; buttonmakers; construction workers; Crusaders; death of children; difficult marriages; distillers; embroiderers; French monarchs; grooms; haberdashers; hairdressers; kings; masons; needleworkers; parents of large families; prisoners; sculptors; the sick;

soldiers; stonemasons; tertiaries ; Archdiocese of St. Louis, Missouri

FURTHER READING

"Biography of Louis IX, King of France." URL: http://elvis.rowan.edu/~kilroy/JEK/08/25.html. Downloaded July 11, 2000.

Weir, Alison. *Eleanor of Aquitaine: A Life.* New York: Ballantine Books, 1999.

Wilding, Eloise. "Saint Louis, King of France 1214–1270." URL: http://stlouis.baltimore.md.us/html/king.htm. Updated April 27, 2000.

Lucius I (d. 254) *Pope*

Lucius was born in Rome, the son of Porphyrius. After Pope St. Cornelius died in exile in June 253, Lucius was elected to his place. He himself was exiled soon after his consecration, but when Emperor Valerian assumed the throne, was allowed to return to Rome.

St. Cyprian declared that the banishment and return were miraculous, God's plan to shame the heretics and bring Lucius greater authority against those "whom the Devil protects as his own"—the Novatians, whose schism had begun under Cornelius and continued under Lucius. The Novatians wanted no pardons for Christians who had forsaken their faith in the face of persecution. Lucius agreed with Cornelius and Cyprian, who held that with proper penance apostates could once again receive Communion.

Lucius died in Rome on March 4, 254, after only nine months in office. The cause of his death is not known, but it is unlikely that he died a martyr. He died during a period of relative calm, the inscription on his tomb in the Catacombs of St. Callistus does not indicate martyrdom, and his name does not appear in early martyrologies. His relics were moved either by Pope Paul I (r. 757–767) to the church of San Silvestro de Capite or by Pope Paschal I (r. 817–824) to the basilica of St. Praxedes, whence they were translated once again by Pope Clement VIII (r. 1592–1605) to the church of St. Cecelia, where they now lie.

Feast: March 4

Lucy of Syracuse (d. 304) *Virgin and martyr*
Name meaning: Light; bringer of light
Also known as: Lucia

Although venerated as one of the holy virgin martyrs, little truth is known about Lucy. The accepted story, as told by the English bishop St. Aldhelm of Sherborne in the seventh century, says that Lucy was born in Syracuse, on the island of Sicily, to wealthy parents, perhaps Christians. Her father died when she was an

St. Lucy of Syracuse (Library of Congress Prints and Photographs Division)

infant. Lucy consecrated herself to God and vowed to remain a virgin at a young age. Her mother Eutychia, however, pledged her in marriage to a young pagan named Paschasius. To convince her mother of the seriousness of her resolve, Lucy accompanied Eutychia to the tomb of St. Agatha at Catania, where Eutychia's long suffering from a hemorrhagic illness was cured. Eutychia agreed to let Lucy remain a virgin.

But the rejected bridegroom denounced Lucy as a Christian to the authorities under Emperor Diocletian. The judge first sentenced Lucy to serve as a prostitute, but supposedly her body became immobile, and neither guards nor even teams of oxen could move her. Next the judge tortured her, perhaps putting her eyes out, but her sight was restored. He then tried burning her, but the fires went out. Finally Lucy died from a sword thrust to her throat. Another story says Lucy put out her own eyes and carried them on a tray to dissuade a suitor from looking at her.

Whether any of the acts attributed to Lucy are true, she has a large following. In the Scandinavian countries, the feast day of Lucia is the Festival of Lights. In some Swedish farming communities, a young girl dressed in white with a red sash and a crown of lingonberry twigs and candles goes from house to house, carrying a torch and leaving baked goods. In most Norwegian and Swedish families, usually the youngest daughter dresses in white as the "Lussibrud" (Lucy bride) on Lucy's Day, December 13, and wakes the rest of the family with a song and a tray of coffee and saffron buns called "Lussikattor" (Lucy cats). Both celebrations can be traced to her role as "bringer of light." Under the old Julian calendar, the winter solstice occurred on December 13 rather than on the later Gregorian December 21, meaning the long northern nights of darkness would turn into the long days of light. Lucy's Day also ushered in the Yuletide, with Lucy candles in the house and Lucy fires in the fields to welcome the birth of the True Light of the World. All preparations for Christmas were completed by Lucy's Day.

The Church did not always venerate Lucy. Because of the meaning of her name in Latin, Lucy was originally associated with the fallen angel Lucifer. The saffron buns that the Lucy bride delivers represented the devil's cats. Indeed, the buns are made in a crossed shape where the front rolls, or arms, are turned inward, much as a cat often sits.

Lucy's remains supposedly went to Constantinople and then to Venice during the Crusades, where they are buried in the Church of Santa Lucia. Venetian gondoliers honor her by singing the famous song "Santa Lucia" as they row visitors through the canals.

Canonized: Added to the Canon of the Mass by Pope Gregory in the seventh century

Feast: December 13

Patronage: Authors, blind people and blindness, cutlers, sufferers of eye diseases, sufferers of hemorrhagic illnesses, glaziers and glass workers, laborers, peasants, salesmen, writers, sufferers of throat infections, Venetian gondoliers

Luis Beltrán (1526–1581) *Patron saint of Colombia who evangelized throughout the Americas*

Luis Beltrán was born in Valencia, Spain, in 1526. At 18 he joined the Order of St. Dominic and in 1547 was ordained a priest. Five years later he was put in charge of instructing the novitiates. As a teacher he was very strict and severe, concerned that his students sincerely renounce the world and unite perfectly with God.

In 1562, Luis was sent to Cartagena, Colombia, to evangelize the natives of the New World. He worked in missions throughout Colombia, Panama and the islands of the Caribbean. Although he spoke only Spanish, God gave him the gifts of tongues, prophecy and miracles.

Luis returned to Spain in 1569 and dedicated himself to training new missionaries to continue with the evangelization of the Americas. He died on October 9, 1581, after a debilitating illness.

Canonized: 1571 by Pope Pius V
Feast: October 9
Patronage: Colombia

FURTHER READING
"San Luis Beltrán, Patrono de Colombia." Santos y Biatos de America Latina: Colombia. URL: http://www/aciprensa.com/santcolo.htm. Downloaded: November 15, 1999.

Luke the Evangelist (first century) *Author of the third gospel and of the Acts of the Apostles*
Name meaning: Bringer of light
Also known as: Luca; Lucas; Lucanus; Luke the Apostle

Luke is mentioned often in the Holy Scriptures, and himself authored two of its longest books. He was from Antioch, of Greek descent, perhaps a slave. He was one of the earliest converts to Christianity following Jesus' death and Resurrection. Although he never met Jesus or heard him preach, he worked closely with St. Paul and would have known other of the apostles.

At the time of his conversion, Luke was a physician. He may have studied medicine at Tarsus, and there met St. Paul and been converted by him. In any event, following Paul's vision of the Macedonian, Luke was one of those who traveled with him on his second missionary journey to Macedonia. He stayed behind at Philippi to continue the evangelical work there (around A.D. 51–57). When Paul came back to Philippi on his third journey, Luke left with him and returned to Jerusalem. He was with Paul in Jerusalem when Paul was arrested, beaten and imprisoned, though he himself escaped, probably because he did not look Jewish. However, over the next two years (about 57–59), while Paul was in prison in Caesarea, Luke visited him frequently. After Paul was released, Luke again traveled with him, and he was in Rome when Paul was arrested for the second and then for the third and final time. He would have been present when Paul was martyred, about the year 67.

Luke may have written his Gospel between Paul's first and second imprisonment, although it is possible that he wrote it later, at the end of his life. His writing style is the most literary of any of the Gospels; he has been called "a painter in words." The Gospel is based largely on Paul's writings and teachings, together with Luke's own experiences. It was intended for Gentile Christian converts like himself and emphasizes Jesus' reaching out to Gentiles. It is the Gospel of the poor and of social justice, and gives special prominence to women, especially the Virgin Mary. Interestingly, Luke frequently juxtaposes accounts of miracles involving a man with another involving a woman. For example, the demoniac is cured (4:31–37), then Peter's mother-

St. Luke the Evangelist (Library of Congress Prints and Photographs Division)

Gospel was written. Acts is a history of the early Church, based in part on Luke's own experiences. It might been have better titled as Acts of the Holy Spirit, because of its emphasis on God working through the apostles.

Tradition has it that Luke was a painter as well as a physician and a fine writer. Without doubt he was "a painter in words," and his descriptions of events such as the Annunciation, the Visitation, the Nativity, the Presentation and the shepherd and lost sheep have inspired countless artists. He is said to have carried a painting of the Virgin Mary with him wherever he went, and this is said to have been the source of many conversions. However, all the extant paintings attributed to him have been shown to be the work of other, later artists. The legend that he was a painter arose first in Greece, but was confirmed in the popular mind by a rough drawing found in the catacombs and inscribed as "one of seven painted by Luca."

It is not known when and how Luke died. According to tradition, he died in Boeotia (in present-day Greece) at the age of 74 (possibly, 84). Although he is said to have been martyred, this is doubtful, given the place and time. The churches of Constantinople (now in Turkey) and Padua (now in Italy) claim to have translations of his relics.

Luke's emblem is the winged ox—the ox being the Jewish sacrificial animal—because his Gospel begins with the sacrifice in the temple by Zachary, the priest, father of St. John the Baptist. It may also allude to Luke's emphasis on the atonement made by Christ's suffering and death. In art, he appears as a physician or bishop with a book or scroll; painting the virgin; in a doctor's cap and gown, holding a book; giving his book to St. Theophilus.

Feast: October 18
Patronage: art guilds; art schools; artists; bookbinders; brewers; butchers; butlers; doctors; glass makers; goldsmiths; lacemakers; notaries; painters; physicians; sculptors; stained-glass workers; surgeons

in-law is cured (4:38–39); the centurion's slave is healed (7:1–10), then the widow of Nain's son is raised from the dead (7:11–17); the Gerasene demoniac is healed (8:26–39), then Jairus's daughter is raised and the woman with the hemorrhage is healed (8:40–56). Luke also recounts several of Jesus' parables not related elsewhere, including those of the lost sheep, the Good Samaritan, the prodigal son, the Pharisee and the publican, the barren fig tree, and Lazarus.

Luke's Acts of the Apostles is in a way a continuation of his Gospel, although it may have been written before it. The earliest Christian writers contradict themselves on this point, as they do on when his

M

Macrina the Elder (d. ca. 340–350) *Grandmother of SS. Basil the Great, Gregory of Nyssa, Macrina the Younger and Peter of Sebaste*

Macrina the Elder was born in Neocaesarea in Pontus, Cappadocia (in modern Turkey), probably before 270. She received her religious training from St. Gregory Thaumaturgus, the first bishop of her native town. She married a Christian man. During persecutions she and her husband were forced to live in the Pontus wilderness for several years. Macrina had a great deal of influence upon the religious upbringing of her famous grandchildren.

Feast: January 14

Macrina the Younger (ca. 330–379) *Granddaughter of Macrina the Elder and sister of SS. Basil the Great, Gregory of Nyssa and Peter Sebaste*

Macrina the Younger was named after her grandmother. Her parents were Basil the Elder and Emmelia, both Christians. At birth she was given another, secret name because of a dream or vision experienced by her mother. According to an account by Gregory of Nyssa, Emmelia fell asleep during her labor and beheld a man "in form and raiment more splendid than a human being" who addressed the child she was carrying by the name of Thecla, the virgin martyr in the apocryphal work, *Acts of Paul and Thecla*. The apparent angel did this three times and then gave her easy delivery. When Emmelia awakened, she saw that she had given birth to a girl. The child was called Thecla in private and Macrina in public.

Macrina received a strong religious upbringing and education from her Christian parents and her grandmother. She was engaged to be married at age 12, but her fiancé died, and she decided to pursue a religious life, and to never leave her mother.

When Basil returned home from his studies in Athens, she influenced him toward the life of Christian perfection. After the death of her father, Macrina persuaded her mother to help her form a contemplative religious community on the family estate in Pontus on the River Iris. Within the community everyone was equal and shared equally in food and housing. They were assisted by Macrina's brother, St. Peter of Sebaste, who presided over the men in the community. Basil established his own monastery across the river.

Macrina and Emmelina remained in the monastery for the rest of their lives. Macrina became head of the community when her mother died. In 379, after the death of Basil, brother Gregory of Nyssa visited Macrina and found her seriously ill. They had a discourse about life after death and meeting in heaven, which inspired Gregory to write his *Dialogue on the Soul and Resurrection.* Macrina died soon after their meeting.

Feast: July 19

FURTHER READING
Gregory of Nyssa. *Life of Macrina.* URL: http://www.fordham.edu/halsall/basis/macrina.html. Downloaded September 11, 2000.

Madeleine Sophie Barat (1779–1865) *Founder of the Society of the Sacred Heart*

Madeleine Sophie Barat was born on December 12, 1779, in Joigny, Burgundy, France. She was educated by her brother Louis, who took her to Paris. There Abbé Joseph Varin d'Ainville persuaded her to reorganize a group of women living under a religious rule; this group became her congregation in 1800.

Madeleine and the group went to Amiens and formed a school in 1802 with Madeleine as superior general and principal. In 1804 Madeleine founded the Society of the Sacred Heart in Grenoble. She admitted to the order Blessed Rose Philippine Duchesne, who took the society to America in 1818. In 1826, the order received formal approval from Pope Leo XII (r. 1823–29).

The society spread quickly through Europe and America—hundreds of institutions existed by the time of Madeleine's death—but the organization was fraught with internal dissension. Madeleine maintained control, and in 1830 moved the headquarters to Switzerland to escape the political instability in France.

Madeleine foretold her own death and died on Ascension Thursday, May 25, 1865, at the society's motherhouse in Paris.

In 1893 she was exhumed. Though the coffin was damp and her garments were mildewed, her body was incorrupt and even her tongue was flexible. She was reclothed and reinterred in a tomb in the chapel of Our Lady of Dolours above the crypt where she previously had been buried.

From 1901 to 1908, religious suppression was widespread in France, and 46 of the society's convents were closed. Madeleine's body was removed to Jette, Belgium, where it remains enshrined. The body was exhumed again in 1908, the year of her beatification, and was found still incorrupt. So well preserved was the body that no relics were taken; the face and hands were covered with silver.

A special shrine in the Sacred Heart Convent in Jette was built in 1934, and the body was placed in a reliquary beneath the altar. The shrine is popular with pilgrims, especially on the first Sunday of the month.

Beatified: 1908 by Pope St. Pius X
Canonized: May 24, 1925, by Pope Pius XI
Feast: May 25

Marcellinus (d. 304) *Pope*

Marcellinus, son of Projectus, was born in Rome. He was elected bishop of Rome to replace St. Caius on June 30, 296. Almost nothing has come down to us concerning his pontificate, which came at the beginning of the persecution of Emperor Diocletian.

For centuries, Marcellinus was believed to have apostatized when the persecution's first edict appeared, surrendered the Vatican's sacred books, and offered incense to the pagan gods of Rome, then repented, for which he was put to death. However, St. Augustine, among others, gave no credence to these rumors, which have since been largely discredited. Probably they constituted disinformation put forward by Diocletian or his henchman, Maximianus Herculeus.

There is little reason to believe that Marcellinus's death on October 25, 304, was not natural. His name does not appear in early martyrologies. The Catacomb of St. Callistus on the Via Appia (which for the last two centuries had served as the final resting place of the popes) having been confiscated, his body was interred in the Catacomb of Priscilla on the Via Salaria. His tomb was venerated from a very early date by Roman Christians, and the site appears on the itineraries of seventh-century pilgrimages.

Feast: April 26 or October 25

Marcellus I (d. 309) *Pope and martyr*

St. Marcellinus, the predecessor of Marcellus, died in October 304, but the continuing persecutions of Emperor Diocletian made it impossible to hold a new election to the papacy at that time. It was only after Diocletian's abdication to Maxentius in October 306 that it could be contemplated. However, Marcellus was not elected bishop of Rome until May or June of 308.

The Roman Church was then in considerable disarray, most of its meeting and burial places having been confiscated during the persecution, and Marcellus took immediate steps to return order. He reorganized the church into parishes, appointing at the head of each parish presbyters who were given responsibilities to prepare catechumens for baptism, direct the performance of penances, oversee burials of the dead, and perform celebrations commemorating the deaths of martyrs.

Marcellus also was faced with a large number of lapsed Christians, who had denied their faith in the face of the persecutions and now wanted to return to the Church. He ruled that they could do so, though only after having made appropriate penance. Although this decision followed longstanding Church practice, it did not sit well with many. Serious conflicts, some resulting even in bloodshed, arose, causing Emperor Maxentius to exile Marcellus from Rome.

Marcellus probably died in exile, although there is a tradition that he was made a slave by Maxentius and forced to work in his stables (or in the stables of a station on a public highway). Although celebrated as a martyr, it appears that his death was not violent. He was buried in the Catacombs of St. Priscilla on the Via Salaria on January 16, 309, but 300 years later his relics were translated to their present resting place under the high altar of the church of San Marcello al Corso.

In art, Marcellus is depicted as a pope with a donkey and a crib near him, sometimes in a stable.

Feast: January 16

Marcus (d. 336) *Pope*
Also known as: Mark

Nothing has come down to us concerning the early life of Marcus. He was a Roman priest and may have served as first deacon under Pope St. Sylvester, whom he succeeded in the Chair of St. Peter on January 18, 336.

Marcus is said to have invested the bishop of Ostia with the pallium and ordained that he consecrate the pope upon taking office, though this is historically uncertain. Marcus certainly enjoyed the continuing support of Emperor Constantine the Great, who provided land and liturgical furniture for two new churches—San Marco in Rome and another, which was constructed over the Catacombs of St. Balbina.

Marcus died on October 7, 336, after only 10 months in office, and was buried in the Catacomb of St. Balbina. His grave was on the itinerary of seventh-century pilgrimages.

Feast: October 7

Margaret of Antioch (d. ca. 304) *One of the Fourteen Holy Helpers*
Also known as: Margaritha, Margaretha, Marina, Marine

Margaret of Antioch was one of the most popular virgin martyrs in the canon of the Church during the Middle Ages, but later scholars believe that while she may have been martyred, anything else attributed to her was purely legend and attributable to a forgery written in the 10th century, allegedly by Theotimus, Margaret's servant. She is no longer a part of the Catholic calendar.

Her story is as follows: Margaret was the daughter of a pagan priest in Antioch, Pisidia, and was nursed by a Christian woman who became her guardian after Margaret's own conversion. One day, while tending her guardian's flocks, Margaret came to the unfortunate notice of the prefect Olybrius, who lusted for her. Margaret spurned his advances, and Olybrius vindictively turned her in to the tribunal as a Christian. She was imprisoned, where the devil appeared to her as a dragon and swallowed her. But brave Margaret, holding a cross, so irritated the devil-dragon that he either disgorged her or exploded. The next day the authorities tried to torture Margaret, first by fire then by immersion in a cauldron of boiling water. Neither worked, and the thousands who witnessed her ordeal were so moved that they converted to Christianity en masse, then were promptly executed. Finally, the prefect ordered her beheading, and she died. Her executioner fell dead at her feet so he could join the virgin in heaven, and a noble widow buried her body in Antioch.

Margaret was one of the voices heard by St. Joan of Arc, along with SS. Catherine of Alexandria and Michael the Archangel. Pregnant women often pray for Margaret's intercession, believing that her disgorgement from the dragon is a sign of safe delivery during childbirth. Her supposed relics were stolen from Antioch in 980 and brought to San Pietro della Valle, then translated to Montefiascone in 1145. Some relics were moved to Venice in 1213, and others are claimed in churches throughout Europe.

> *Feast:* July 20 in the West; July 13 in the Eastern Church
>
> *Patronage:* against death; against sterility; childbirth; escape from devils; exiles; kidney disease; loss of milk by nursing mothers; martyrs; nurses; peasants; people falsely accused; pregnant women; women; women in labor; Queen's College, Cambridge

Margaret of Castello, Blessed (1287–1320) *Dominican tertiary*
Also known as: Margaret of Citta-de-Castello; Margaret of Metola

Margaret of Castello was born in 1287 as a blind, lame, hunchbacked dwarf. Because of her deformities, her parents kept her hidden from sight. In 1293 they took her to a healing shrine in Citta-de-Castello, Italy, and when a miraculous cure was not forthcoming, they abandoned her. She was found in a parish church. Sympathy poured out to her, and she was cared for by a succession of families in the village. Nuns at a local convent gave her a home, but the arrangement was not mutually satisfying. Margaret found the convent too lax, and the nuns did not care for her religious fervor; nor did she bring them any profit.

Margaret then settled in a permanent foster home. At age 15 she became a Dominican tertiary. She cared for the sick and the dying, and also cared for the village children and gave them religious instruction. She helped prisoners.

Margaret also had miraculous gifts. She prophesied and healed. Though blind, she had many visions. During periods of intense prayer, she was known to levitate up to 20 inches off the floor and remain suspended for a long time.

Margaret often exclaimed, "Oh, if you only knew what I have in my heart!" When she died in 1320 at age 33, her heart was cut open. In it were three pearl-like pellets carved with images of Jesus, the Blessed Virgin Mary and St. Joseph. After her death, more than 200 miracles occurred that were attributed to her intercession.

In June 1558 Margaret's coffin was observed to be rotting, and it was opened in order to transfer her remains to a new one. Her clothing had turned to dust, but her body was incorrupt. It was determined to be free of embalming chemicals. Margaret's body was reclothed and buried in a new coffin. It now lies in a glass reliquary beneath the high altar of the Church of St. Domenico in Citta-de-Castello. The body still has its eyelashes and fingernails and toenails, and the arms are flexible. It is dressed in a Dominican habit.

One of Margaret's most notable miracles took place when she was living in a private home. One day fire swept through the area, and the house burned. Margaret was trapped upstairs. She calmly went to the top of the stairs, took off her mantle, rolled it up and threw it down to the firefighters, telling them to throw it on the fire. They did so, and the fire immediately went out.

Beatified: 1609 by Pope Paul V
Feast: April 13

FURTHER READING
Bonniwell, William. *The Story of Margaret of Metola.* New York: P.J. Kennedy and Sons, 1952.

Margaret of Cortona (1247–1297) *Franciscan tertiary and mystic*
Also known as: Magdalen of the Seraphic Order

Margaret of Cortona was born in Laviano, Tuscany, Italy, in 1247. Her mother died when she was seven. Her father remarried, but the stepmother mistreated the girl. Margaret grew to be a great beauty. At age 17, she ran off with a cavalier and lived with him as his mistress in his luxurious castle in Montepulciano for nine years, during which she bore a son. She desired to be married, but her lover always reneged on his promises to do so. Her arrangement scandalized people, but according to lore, Margaret asserted she would die a saint and pilgrims would visit her shrine.

One day her lover set out on a journey with his dog. The dog returned without him and led Margaret to his mangled body in a shallow grave—he had been brutally murdered. She gave up all her possessions to his family. Her family refused to accept her, and so she and her son set out for Cortona to seek entry with the Franciscan Friars there. They were taken in.

Margaret struggled to adjust to life as a religious. She publicly repented for her life of sin. She once tried to mutilate her beautiful face, but was prevented from doing so by Father Giunta. She earned her living nursing women. After three years she was admitted to the Third Order of St. Francis. She took a vow of strict poverty, and subsisted on alms and ministered to the sick and poor.

In 1277 she had the first of her mystical experiences. While praying in the church of the Franciscan Friars, she heard these words: "What is thy wish, *poverella?*" She responded, "I neither seek nor wish for aught but thee, my Lord Jesus." From then on she experienced a continuing and intense communion with Christ. Initially, He called her *"poverella"* ("poor one") and then "my child." In her frequent ecstasies she received many messages from Him, some for her and some for others, which she delivered. Father Giunta recorded some of the divine messages.

Margaret was instrumental in the establishment of a hospital in Cortona for the sick and poor. She established a congregation of Tertiary Sisters, called *le poverelle* ("poor ones"), to serve as nurses to the sick and poor, and she also established a confraternity of Our Lady of Mercy to support the hospital and the needy in the community.

She also did not hesitate to speak up, and twice criticized the bishop of Cortona for his lavish lifestyle.

Margaret lived in the hospital and then moved to the ruined church of St. Basil, which she had repaired. She lived the remainder of her life in the church, working miracles of healing. She knew the date of her death in advance, and died on February 22, 1729. She was buried at the church, which later was rebuilt in a grander style and dedicated to her.

The body of Margaret remains incorrupt, with all of the nails on her hands and feet intact. The body is exposed in a glass-sided reliquary decorated with precious gems and ornaments that have been donated by pilgrims.

Canonized: 1728 by Pope Benedict XIII
Feast: February 22
Patronage: homeless; midwives; single mothers; tertiaries

Margaret Mary Alacoque (1647–1690) *Mystic and leader of the devotion to the Sacred Heart of Jesus*
Also known as: Margaret Mary

Margaret Mary Alacoque was born at L' Hautecour, France, on July 22, 1647, to Claude Alacoque and Philiberte Lamyn. As a child she preferred to sit in silence and prayer. Her father died when she was eight, and she was sent to the Poor Clare school at Charolles. She took her First Communion at age nine, and secretly practiced such severe mortifications that she contracted rheumatic fever and spent four years paralyzed in bed. She is said to have healed instantly when she vowed to the Blessed Virgin Mary that she would consecrate herself to a religious life. She was 15.

Margaret Mary's family suffered great poverty, but recovered its property when she was 17. Her mother felt that Margaret Mary could serve God at home by penance and charity to the poor. Though she still bled from her mortifications, she engaged in worldly activities. But one night after returning home from a carnival ball, she had a vision of Christ as he was during the scourging, reproaching her for infidelity to him. She spent the rest of her life regretting two faults committed at this time: the wearing of some ornaments and a mask at the carnival to please her brothers.

On May 25, 1671, Margaret Mary entered the Visitation Convent at Paray, where she was subjected to many trials to prove herself. She was professed in November 1652.

On December 27, 1652, she had the first of a series of revelations that would last a year and a half. In these visions Christ told her that he had chosen her to spread devotion to his Sacred Heart. He told of his ardent desire to be loved by humanity and his design of manifesting his Heart with all its treasures of love, mercy, sanctification and salvation. He called Margaret Mary "the Beloved Disciple of the Sacred Heart" and the heiress of its treasures.

Christ instructed her in a devotion that became known as the Nine Fridays and the Holy Hour, and he asked her to establish the feast of the Sacred Heart on the Friday after the octave of the feast of Corpus Christi. Margaret Mary was inspired to pray lying prostrate with her face to the ground from 11 until midnight on the eve of the first Friday of each month, to share Jesus' sadness at being abandoned by his apostles. She also was inspired to receive Holy Communion on the first Friday of every month.

Margaret Mary later recorded in her *Autobiography* that during these visions she felt intense, burning and all-consuming heat from the Sacred Heart of Jesus:

> The Sacred Heart was represented to me as a resplendent sun, the burning rays of which fell vertically upon my heart, which was inflamed with a fire so fervid that it seemed as if it would reduce me to ashes . . . His Five Wounds shining [sic] like so many sounds. Flames issued from every part of his Sacred Humanity, especially from his Adorable Bosom, which resembled an open furnace and disclosed to me His most loving and most amiable Heart, which was the living source of these flames.

Margaret Mary's visions earned her scorn and criticism from her peers; her mother superior rebuffed her. Eventually Margaret Mary won over her superior, but she failed to convince members of her own community and a group of investigating theologians that her apparitions were real. Bl. Claude La Colombière, who served as the community's confessor for a time, supported her and declared that her visions were genuine.

A breakthrough came in 1683 when a new mother superior was elected and Margaret Mary was named her assistant. She later became novice mistress. The convent began to observe the feast of the Sacred Heart privately in 1686. In 1688 a chapel was built at Paray to honor the Sacred Heart, and the feast spread to other Visitation convents.

In her final illness she refused all treatment, repeating frequently: "What have I in heaven and what do I desire on earth, but Thee alone, O my God?" She died pronouncing the Holy Name of Jesus on October 17, 1690, at Paray-le-Monial.

Her body rests under the altar in the chapel at Paray, and attracts many pilgrims, who obtain favors through her intercession. When her tomb was canonically opened in July 1830, two instantaneous cures took place.

Margaret Mary's intense devotion to the Sacred Heart, and to the need to suffer, permeated all of her writings, including her autobiography and her letters. For her, the only glory was in complete annihilation of the self and surrender to God. There was no "middle course" for ensuring salvation for eternity. "Our falls are the continual revolt of our passions," she wrote. "But we need not be troubled, cast down or discouraged by them: we must do violence to ourselves and draw profit from them."

Margaret Mary, St. John Eudes and Bl. Claude La Colombière are called the "Saints of the Sacred Heart," a devotion officially recognized and approved by Pope Clement XIII (r. 1758–69) in 1765.

Declared Venerable: March 1824 by Pope Leo XII
Beatified: September 18, 1864, by Pope Pius IX
Canonized: 1920 by Pope Benedict XV
Feast: October 17
Patronage: against polio

FURTHER READING
Bougaud, Emile. *The Life of Saint Margaret Mary Alacoque.* Rockford, Ill.: TAN Books and Publishers, 1994.
Margaret Mary Alacoque. *The Autobiography of Saint Margaret Mary.* Rockford, Ill.: TAN Books and Publishers, 1995.

Margaret of Scotland (ca. 1045–1093) *Queen of Scotland*

Margaret of Scotland probably was born around 1045, though the date is not reliable. She was the grand-daughter of King Edmund Ironside of England and daughter of Edward the Aethling. Her mother, Agatha, was related to Gisela, the wife of St. Stephen of Hungary. According to tradition, Margaret and her family were exiled to Hungary when Canute and the Danes controlled England. Her father became known as "Edward the Exile." They returned to England in 1057, but when the Norman Conquest came, Agatha went back to Europe and Margaret and other members of her family went north to Scotland to the court of King Malcolm III. In 1069 Margaret married Malcolm, despite her original desire for a life of piety.

Margaret devoted herself to piety as much as possible. She was well educated and had a keen intellect. She convened a synod, at which various reforms were instituted. She persuaded Malcolm to romanize the Celtic Church, substitute Saxon for Gaelic as the court language, and replace the clan system with a feudal system. Such reforms earned her much criticism.

Margaret founded several churches, including the abbey of Dunfermline, where she placed a true relic of the Cross, as well as many objects made of gold. She built a chapel at Edinburgh Castle. She worked to improve the literacy at court and among the people.

Tradition holds that Margaret did not hesitate to help the poor, and even washed their feet and fed children from her own dish.

According to legend, Margaret and Malcolm enjoyed a true love relationship. Malcolm could not read or write, but bought for her a book of the Gospels and had it encrusted with jewels. One day the book fell into a river and was miraculously recovered. The book now is housed in the Bodleian Library in Oxford.

Margaret severely impaired her health by following strict austerities. By the time she was 40, her health was permanently damaged from fasting and abstinence, and also from the rigors of birthing seven children.

Malcolm tried to expand his kingdom into England, but was met with resistance by William the Conqueror. There was much fighting. Margaret foretold the day of her death, November 16, 1093. Prior to that she was severely ill and preparing for her death. She passed away upon hearing the news that her husband and oldest son had been killed several days earlier in England, where they had gone on a raid. Ambushed, they had surrendered, but the king was then murdered in treachery and his body dumped on the battlefield. Son Edward was killed soon thereafter.

Margaret died in Edinburgh Castle, which was under siege. A thick mist arose, enabling the transport of her body to the abbey of Dunfermline, where she was buried before the high altar. Her body exuded a sweet perfume. Malcolm's body, which had been buried at Tynemouth after his murder, was moved to the abbey 20 years later. In 1250 her remains were translated to the shrine of the Lady Chapel at the abbey. Legend has it that her coffin became too heavy to move, until the coffin of her husband was moved as well. Both repose beneath the high altar. Margaret became the only Scots monarch ever to be canonized. Three of her sons became kings of Scotland: Edgar, Alexander and David.

After 1560, during the Protestant Reformation, Margaret's relics were moved for safety. The torso of Margaret and body of Malcolm were sent to Madrid. Margaret's head went to Edinburgh Castle, where Mary Queen of Scots thought it would aid the birth of her child, James, the future king James VI of Scotland and king James I of England. In 1567 Mary fled to England, and the head was given to a Benedictine monk to keep in the castle of the laird of Durie. In 1597 the head was taken to Antwerp by a Jesuit. In 1627 it went to the Jesuits of the Scots College at Douai in northern France, where it was placed in a silver case. The college was destroyed in the French Revolution, and Margaret's head disappeared.

Meanwhile, the remains sent to Spain mysteriously disappeared by 1863, save for one six-inch piece of bone, now kept in the Ursuline Convent of St. Margaret in Edinburgh. Bone splinters were sent to two churches in Hungary. In 1991 a set of teeth identified as Margaret's were found in Spain.

Margaret's holy rood, which she requested as she lay dying, disappeared sometime during the Protestant

Reformation. It was a gold cross set in diamonds with a figure of Christ carved out of ivory. It was taken to England, then returned to Scotland. In 1346, King David II took it into battle with him and lost it to the English.

Canonized: 1250 by Pope Innocent IV
Feast: June 10
Patronage: learning

FURTHER READING
Wilson, Alan J. *St. Margaret Queen of Scotland.* Edinburgh: John Donald Publishers, 1993.

Marguerite Bourgeoys (1620–1700) *Founder of the Sisters of Notre Dame*

Also known as: Margaret Bourgeoys, Marguerite Bourgeous, Marguerite Bourjeoys

Marguerite Bourgeoys was born in Troyes, France, on April 17, 1620, the sixth of 12 children of devout Catholic parents. Her mother died when she was 19, her father when she was 27. Marguerite applied for admission to the Carmelites and Poor Clares, but was refused entry by both orders. She joined an uncloistered community, but was not happy with this decision. Then in 1652 when the governor of Ville-Marie, New France (now Montreal, Canada), came to Troyes to recruit teachers, she decided to go with him.

Marguerite arrived in Ville-Marie for the first time in 1653 and set about teaching children and caring for the sick. In 1658, she helped to organize the first school in the community, and was appointed headmistress. She went back to France in 1659 and returned the following year with four new assistants; in 1670 she went to France again.

Upon her return to Ville-Marie in 1672, Marguerite decided to found a religious congregation, called the Sisters of Notre Dame, and after some discussion, was given approval by her bishop in 1676. Before the new order was approved by the Vatican in 1688, it had established missions to the Indians and admitted 18 sisters, seven of them French Canadian and two Native American. Marguerite passed the role of superior on to her successor—Marie Barbier, the first Canadian to join the order—in 1693.

The Sisters of Notre Dame obtained the right from King Louis XIV of France to teach throughout Canada, and the apostolate increased in spite of the difficulties the sisters encountered, such as fires and massacres by the Iroquois to the south. Marguerite established schools for Indian children as well as schools for the French at Quebec and Trois Rivières. When the King sent untrained orphans to Canada as colonists, she set up a school for the

The only authentic portrait of St. Marguerite Bourgeoys, painted on January 2, 1700, by Pierre LeBer immediately after her death (Courtesy Chapelle Notre-Dame-de-Bon-Secours, Montreal)

women to teach them how to survive in the new, harsh environment.

In 1889, the congregation received papal approval to spread into the United States. Today Marguerite's congregation has 200 convents.

Marguerite spent her last years praying and writing her autobiography. On December 31, 1699, she asked the Lord to take her life in exchange for a young sister who was then near death. By the morning of January 1, the sister was completely well, but Marguerite had a raging fever. She suffered another 12 days, then died, on January 12, 1700, at the age of 79.

Beatified: 1950 by Pope Pius XII
Canonized: April 2, 1982, by Pope John Paul II
Feast: January 19
Patronage: against poverty; impoverishment; loss of parents; people rejected by religious orders

FURTHER READING
Simpson, Patricia. *Marguerite Bourgeoys and Montreal, 1640–1665.* Montreal: McGill-Queen's University Press, 1997.

Marguerite d'Youville (1701–1771) *Superior of the Sisters of Charity*

Also known as: Mary Margaret Dufrost de la Jemmarais d'Youville

Marguerite D'Youville was born at Varennes, Quebec, Canada, on October 15, 1701, the daughter of Christophe Dufrost de la Jemmerais and Renée de Varennes. Her father, a French soldier, died in her youth. After studying with the Ursulines, she married François D'Youville in 1722, when she was 21. The marriage was unhappy, but the couple produced three children, one of whom died young. When François died in 1730, Marguerite had to work to support herself and her two surviving children. However, she also devoted much time to charitable activities. Herself a battered wife, she opened a shelter for other battered women, prostitutes and Indian women.

In 1737, Marguerite and three companions took their initial vows in a new religious congregation, the Sisters of Charity (the Grey Nuns); a formal declaration of the new order followed in 1745. Two years later, Marguerite was appointed director of the General Hospital in Montreal, thenceforth under the management of the Grey Nuns. In 1755, the bishop of Pontbriand of Quebec gave his approval to the order, acknowledging Marguerite as superior.

From 1756 to 1763, Canadians fought the Seven Years' War, which brought Quebec under British rule. After the war, Marguerite was involved with the politics of society, church and government, as the predominantly French Quebecois struggled to find their place in a new reality. They were made to feel unwelcome in a land they had always called home, living under the ominous threat that England would not long tolerate the practice of Catholicism. The Grey Nuns, however, persevered and have survived. Since Marguerite's death in Montreal on December 23, 1771, the order has established schools, hospitals and orphanages throughout Canada, the United States, Africa and South America. They are known especially for their work among the Canadian Inuit (Eskimos).

> *Declared Venerable:* April 28, 1890, by Pope Leo XIII
> *Beatified:* 1959 by Pope John XXIII
> *Canonized:* December 9, 1990, by Pope John Paul II
> *Feast:* April 11
> *Patronage:* death of children; difficult marriages; in-law problems; loss of parents; opposition of Church authorities; people ridiculed for their piety; victims of adultery; victims of unfaithfulness; widows

FURTHER READING

Fitts, Mary Pauline. *Hands to the Needy: Marguerite d'Youville Apostle to the Poor.* Yardley, Pa.: Grey Nuns of the Sacred Heart, 2000.

McGuire, Rita. "St. Marguerite d'Youville." URL: http://www.renc.igs.net/~marguerite/D%27YOUVIL.htm. Downloaded: January 27, 2000.

Mariana of Quito (Mariana de Jesús de Quito) (1618–1645)

Also known as: Lily of Quito; Mariana de Paredes y Flores of Quito; Mariana of Jesus

Mariana of Quito was born Mariana Paredes y Flores in Quito, Ecuador, then part of Peru, in 1618. She led a life of sanctity remarkably similar to that of Rose of Lima, with whom she is often compared.

Her parents died when she was four and she went to live with her elder sister and her husband. From childhood she showed an extraordinary piety. She was much concerned with poverty and the plight of the poor. She spent hours on end counting her rosary and took her First Communion when she was seven or eight, an unusually young age for her time. When she was 12, she wanted to go and evangelize Japan.

From childhood, she mortified herself in food, drink and sleep. She hid a basket under the table, served herself the same amount as others, but secretly put most of the food in the basket and distributed it to the poor. On especially hot days she refused all liquid while she contemplated the thirst of Jesus on the cross. Her favorite meditation was on the Passion and the death of Jesus, and she often wore a crown of thorns while counting the rosary. She allowed herself only a few hours of sleep a night.

Mariana at first wanted to enter a convent, but twice things occurred that prevented her from doing so. She concluded that God wanted her to remain in the world and built a hut for herself in her sister's house in which she stayed, except to go out to the church or to help people in need. She is said to have acquired a coffin and slept in it several nights a week, during the day stuffing it with cushions to resemble a corpse, in order to remind herself of her mortality.

Mariana was quite musical and played the guitar and piano wonderfully. She also sang, preferring religious songs, which helped her to meditate. Like Rose of Lima, she also enjoyed sewing and embroidery, and spent much of her time alone on these activities. Also like Rose, she ministered to the needy and taught Indian children in her home.

Many pictures of Mariana show her holding a lily. She became known as the "Lily of Quito" following an illness during which she was bled. A nurse who assisted at her bedside drained her blood into a spittoon, from which a lily subsequently bloomed. This supernatural event was not the only one with which Mariana is credited. She had the gift of prophecy, predicting events that subsequently occurred as she had said they would. One of these prophecies was a foretelling of the date of her own death on a Friday the 26th.

In 1645, when Mariana was 27 years old, Quito was shaken by a series of earthquakes accompanied by an epidemic of disease that took the lives of many. Mariana heard a priest say in a sermon that he would willingly give his life to have the earthquakes stop and responded that the priest's life was too valuable and she would sacrifice hers instead. A short while later the earthquakes stopped and the epidemic ended, but Mariana herself became sick and died. The day was Friday the 26th of May.

Mariana's burial was met with an ovation from the entire city of Quito. In 1946, the Congress of Ecuador acknowledged her sacrifice by bestowing on her the title of "Heroína de la Patria" (Heroine of the Fatherland). She is credited with a continuous series of miracles after her death.

Beatified: by Pope Pius IX (r. 1846–78)
Canonized: 1950 by Pope Pius XII
Feast: May 26

FURTHER READING
"Santa Mariana de Jesús, Azucena de Quito." Church Forum Santoral. URL: http://www.churchforum.org.mx/santoral. Downloaded: November 30, 1999.
"Santa Mariana de Jesús de Quito." Santos y Biatos de America Latina: Ecuador. URL: http://www.aciprensa.com/santecua.htm. Downloaded: November 30, 1999.

Maria Soledad (1826–1887) *Founder of the Handmaids of Mary Serving the Sick*
Also known as: Emanuela Torres; Vibiana Torres; Maria-Desolata Torres Acosta; Maria Soledad Torres Acosta; Mary Soledad

Maria Soledad was born December 2, 1862, in Madrid, the daughter of Francis Torres and Antonia Acosta. She was baptized with the name Emanuela.

When Emanuela was old enough to leave home she applied to the Dominican convent in Madrid, but was refused entry due to poor health. She spent much time in prayer asking God for guidance. Then in 1848, when she was 22, a Servite tertiary priest named Michael Martinez y Sanz recruited her and six other women for a new religious community to serve the poor and sick of Madrid; the religious had become concerned that so many were dying without receiving the Last Sacraments. This community was formally established on August 15, 1851, as the Handmaids of Mary Serving the Sick. When she donned the habit, Emanuela took the name Maria-Desolata, or Maria Soledad.

In 1856, Father Martinez took half of the members of the order with him to found a new house overseas, leaving Maria-Desolata behind as superior of the motherhouse in Madrid. Maria was to devote the rest of her life to running the convent. The Handmaids of Mary received diocesan approval in 1861 and papal approval in 1876.

Maria contracted pneumonia on October 11, 1887, at age 60. She died quietly at the motherhouse after receiving the Last Sacraments. She was buried in the sisters' plot at the cemetery, but then on January 18, 1893, her remains were exhumed and transferred to the motherhouse. Her body was found to be intact, though it exuded a bloody liquid, and a sweet odor was noticed by everyone there. A few years later, however, nothing remained but her bones.

Beatified: 1950 by Pope Pius XII
Canonized: 1970 by Pope Paul VI

FURTHER READING
"Santa María Soledad Torres." Church Forum website. URL: http://www.churchforum.org/santoral/Octubre/1110.htm. Last modified: May 17, 1999. Downloaded: November 20, 1999.

Marie of the Incarnation, Blessed (1599–1672) *Missionary to Indians in Canada*
Also known as: Marie of the Ursulines

Marie was born in Tours, France, on October 28, 1599, the daughter of a baker named Guyard. In 1616, she married a silk manufacturer, Claude Martin, and they had one son. When Claude died in 1618, she became a bookkeeper for her brother-in-law. However, in 1629 she decided to become a nun, and joined the Ursulines at Tours, taking the name Marie of the Incarnation.

In 1639, Marie was sent as a missionary to Canada. She laid the cornerstone of the first Ursuline convent in Quebec in 1641, rebuilding it when it was destroyed by fire in 1650. She taught the Indians of the region and compiled dictionaries in the Algonquin and Iroquois languages. Although she suffered periods of spiritual aridity, she also experienced mystical visions. She died in Quebec on April 30, 1672.

Beatified: 1980 by Pope John Paul II

Mark the Evangelist (d. ca. 70) *Author of the second book of the New Testament; by tradition, founder and first bishop of the Church of Alexandria*
Also known as: John Mark; Marcos; Marcus; Markus

St. Mark the Evangelist (Library of Congress Prints and Photographs Division)

Mark is mentioned several times in the New Testament, sometimes with variations of his name, but most biblical authorities today consider them to refer to the same person. If so, then he was the son of Mary, a friend of the Apostle St. Peter, and a cousin of the evangelist St. Barnabas. Like Barnabas, he may have held a position in the Jewish clergy before his conversion to Christianity. His Jewish name was John, to which was added the Roman Marcus; thus he is sometimes known as John Marcus or John Mark. It is not certain that he ever met Jesus; his Gospel is based on the teachings of Peter.

Mark's mother was evidently a person of some wealth and position. She was a member of the early Christian community in Jerusalem. Her home was a gathering place for the Christians and it was there that St. Peter went after miraculously escaping from prison, about the year 44.

At the time of the famine of 45–46, Mark accompanied Barnabas and St. Paul from Jerusalem to Antioch. From there he started with them on Paul's first missionary journey, but soon left and returned to Jerusalem. Why he returned alone is not known, but he was in Salamis on Cyprus about 47 and at Antioch again about 49. When Paul refused to take Mark along on his second journey, around the year 50, Barnabas split with Paul and he and Mark sailed together to Cyprus.

Mark's activities for the next 10 years are unknown, but by the year 60 he was in Rome with Paul, with whom he had apparently mended his quarrel, and was about to make a trip to Asia Minor. It appears that he did go, but later, at Paul's request, returned to Rome and was there when Paul was martyred in about 67. After this, he began to work with Peter, who was then also in Rome.

According to tradition, Mark wrote his Gospel from Peter's teachings around this time, in response to requests from Roman Christians. Mark stresses Jesus' miracles rather than his prophecies, perhaps because he himself was most impressed by them, or perhaps because he thought they would most impress his audience. His was probably the first Gospel written, although it is positioned second in the New Testament.

Another tradition credits Mark with founding the Church of Alexandria. The date when he first arrived in Alexandria is uncertain, though it may have been about the year 50, after the trip to Cyprus. The Bible is silent on his activities of this period. Afterward, he went to Rome to assist Paul and Peter, and later returned to Alexandria. There he is also said to have founded a Christian school.

Mark died in Alexandria, although when is unclear. It may have been as late as the year 75, although an uncertain tradition dating from the fourth century says that he was martyred by strangulation on April 25, A.D. 68. His relics were interred first in Alexandria, but in the ninth century were translated to Venice, Italy, where a cult had arisen. The original Church of St. Mark in Venice was destroyed in 976, but the rebuilt basilica contains Mark's relics. The basilica is decorated by a magnificent series of mosaics on Mark's life, death and translation dating from the 12th and 13th centuries.

In the Eastern Orthodox Church, Mark the Evangelist and John Mark are believed to be different people.

Mark's emblem is a winged lion. The winged lion was originally a Jewish symbol for one of the four archangels, and later for one of the four major prophets. By the fourth century, Christians had transferred the emblem to the four evangelists. The traditional explanation for the winged lion as Mark's symbol is that his gospel speaks to the rural dignity of Christ and he begins his account of Saint John the Baptist with the "voice crying in the desert."

In art, Mark sometimes appears with a book or scroll along with the lion. He has also been depicted as a bishop with his throne decorated with lions; as aiding Venetian sailors; as a man with a halter around his neck; or as rescuing Christian slaves from the Saracens.

Feast: April 25 (in the West); September 23 (in the East). The translation of his relics to Venice is celebrated on January 31.

Patronage: attorneys; barristers; captives; glaziers; against impenitence; against insect bites; lions; notaries; against scrofulous diseases; secretaries; Spanish cattle breeders; stained glass workers; against struma; Egypt; Venice, Italy

Martha (d. first century) *Sister of SS. Lazarus and Mary of Bethany, Israel*

The Gospels mention Martha in connection with a visit by Jesus and also his resurrection of Lazarus from the dead. Luke 10:38–42 tells how Jesus and his disciples were received into Martha's home. While Martha waited on the men, her sister Mary sat at Jesus' feet to listen to his teaching. Martha complained and asked Jesus to instruct Mary to help her. He replied, "Martha, Martha, you are anxious and troubled about many things; one thing is needful. Mary has chosen the good portion, which shall not be taken away from her." John 11:2 identifies Mary as the one who anointed Jesus' feet with oil and wiped them with her long hair.

John 11 recounts the raising of Lazarus. Martha went out to meet Jesus, and told him she knew her dead brother will "rise in the resurrection on the last day." Jesus said, "I am the resurrection and the life; he who believes in me, though he die, yet shall he live,

St. Martha at the feet of Jesus with her sister, Mary (Engraving, 19th century)

and whoever lives and believes in me shall never die. Do you believe this?" Martha answered, "Yes, Lord; I believe that you are the Christ, the Son of God, he who is coming into the world." At the tomb, Jesus commanded the stone to be rolled away, but Martha protested, saying, "Lord, by this time there will be an odor, for he has been dead four days." The stone was taken away and Lazarus rose from the dead.

Feast: July 29
Patronage: cooks; dieticians; domestic help; housekeepers; servants; waitpersons

Martin I (d. 655) *Pope and martyr*

Martin was born at Todi on the Tiber River in Umbria (Italy), the son of Frabricius. He was of noble birth, of commanding intelligence and profound learning, and was noted for his charity to the poor. A member of the order of St. Basil, he became a deacon in the Roman Church, and on July 21, 649, was elected successor to Pope Theodore I (r. 642–649).

Martin had himself consecrated without waiting for the imperial confirmation, as was the custom, and almost immediately called a council to consider Monothelitism. This heresy asserted that Christ had only divine will and was lacking in human will. One hundred and five bishops from Europe and Africa met in five sessions; they issued several proclamations, excommunicated some Church leaders, and condemned the Typus, the edict of the reigning emperor Constans II, which favored Monothelitism. They then sent Constans a copy of the acts in Latin along with a Greek translation.

The response must have been predictable. Martin was sick when the emperor's soldiers arrived to arrest him, and he grew sicker aboard ship on his way to the island of Naxos. He was held on Naxos for as long as a year in abominable conditions, then taken to Constantinople. Arriving there on September 17, 653, he was left on the ship's deck for several hours, exposed to the insults of crowds of spectators, then carried to prison on a stretcher. After another 90 days of confinement, he was put on trial for treason and convicted. He was paraded through the city in chains, publicly flogged and again imprisoned. Three months later he was taken before the Senate, where the imperial treasurer acted as judge, and he was asked to sign the Typus. When he refused, he was condemned to death, but thanks to the intercession of the dying Paul, patriarch of Constantinople, was exiled to Cherson (Kherson) in the Crimea instead. He left for Cherson on March 26 and arrived there on May 15, 654.

Martin's letters from Cherson describe how he was deserted by his Church and his friends, though he nevertheless continued to pray that their faith would remain intact. He suffered for 18 months before dying on September 16, 655. It is likely that he died of starvation, as Cherson was suffering from famine at the time. He was buried in the church of Our Lady near Cherson, though the greater part of his relics were later translated to Rome, where they are now to be found in the church of San Martino ai Monti.

Many miracles were credited to Martin's intercession after his death. He was the last pope to die a martyr.

In art, he is portrayed as pope and with geese around him, or as seen through prison bars (the last, possibly a confusion with St. Martin of Tours).

Feast: April 13 (formerly November 12; November 10 in York; April 13 in Greek Orthodox Church; April 14 in Russian Orthodox Church; September 20 in Eastern Orthodox Church generally)

Martin de Porres (1579–1639) *Dominican known for his charitable works*
Also known as: Martin of Charity, Martin of Porres, the Saint of the Broom

The first black South American saint, Martin de Porres was born on November 9, 1579, in Lima, Peru, one of two illegitimate children of Juan de Porres, a Spanish knight, and Ana Velásquez, a freed slave of African descent from Panama. He was a contemporary of Rose of Lima and was baptized in the same basin and by the same priest as she.

Martin had a difficult childhood, partly because he was looked down upon for being a dark-skinned mulatto. Although Martin's father acknowledged his paternity later, his name does not appear on Martin's birth certificate, which states "father unknown." Juan de Porres took little interest in his children in their early years, leaving Martin and his sister to grow up in the care of their mother alone. However, he later took them to live with him in Guayaquil, Ecuador, and provided them with private tutors. Martin returned to Lima when his father was named governor of Panama, and at age 12 was apprenticed to become a barber, at that time a well-paying profession that included not only hairdressing but also surgery and herbal healing. He is said to have planted a lemon tree that bore fruit all year round and was still doing so for at least 50 years after his death.

From his youth, Martin was devoutly religious, continually praying to God for guidance. At 15, he decided to dedicate himself to the religious life, and joined the Third Order of Dominic, the same order

Rose of Lima joined a few years later. He entered the Dominican Friary of Rosario in Lima, though due to his color, he was admitted only as a lay servant of the community, and assigned the most menial of chores. These he performed well and without resentment, earning him the nickname "Saint of the Broom."

After nine years, the monastery bent its rules of admittance to allow Martin to become a brother. He was given the responsibilities of barber and healer, and was able to dedicate himself fully to charitable endeavors. Yet he continued to be humble, wearing the oldest, most patched garments he could find, and spending hours each night in prayer and penitence. He lived in great austerity, never eating meat and fasting continuously, and often had himself flogged until he bled.

Martin collected alms in astonishing numbers (some said that he caused them to be increased miraculously) and returned all to the poor and needy. He raised his sister's dowry in three days. He administered to everyone, rich and poor alike, including prisoners, plague victims and African slaves, healing and counseling people on a variety of personal problems. He went so far in tending the sick that the other friars complained that he wanted to make the monastery into a hospital. With the help of the Spanish viceroy, the archbishop and Lima's moneyed class, he established an orphanage and a foundling hospital. On the hills above the city, he planted fruit orchards for the disadvantaged.

Martin grew herbal plants in his cell, though he cured as much through prayer as through his knowledge of medicine. When the archbishop of Lima once became very sick he called for Martin to heal him. Placing his hands on the most painful spot, Martin prayed, and the archbishop was cured. Among the many other cures attributed to him are those of a priest dying from a badly infected leg and a young student whose fingers had been mangled in an accident.

Martin's ministrations extended to animals, with whom he seemed able to communicate in some way. Animals came to him for healing and he ran a hospital for cats and dogs in his sister's house. The story is told that when the prior ordered him to set out poison for mice that were devouring the cloth of the sacristy, Martin did as instructed, but then went out into the yard and called the mice. They came out and he reprimanded them for their bad manners, explained about the poison, and offered a deal—if they stayed out of the buildings, he would set food out for them in the yard. The mice agreed, and from that time on none were seen in the church.

Martin was widely known also for a variety of supernatural feats, including not only prophecy and clairvoyance, but also levitation and bilocation.

St. Martin de Porres

When he prayed devoutly he sometimes became entranced and rose in the air, where he would be seen by his fellow friars, suspended several feet above the church floor. Martin wanted deeply to go off on a foreign mission so he could give his life as a martyr. This was not possible for him, but traveling Peruvian merchants and missionaries reportedly saw him in Central America, Mexico, China, Japan and the Philippines, earning him the title of the "flying brother." Martin sometimes bilocated in Lima also; he is said to have been seen at deathbeds counseling people at the same time that he was in the monastery.

Martin often put his abilities to work in practical ways. He could enter and exit the closed monastery door without a key. Once when he was on a picnic with some novices, the group lost track of time and suddenly realized that they would be late for their prayers. Martin had all join hands and before they knew what had happened, they were standing again in the monastery yard. When enemies once arrived in his room to harm him, he turned invisible.

Three times he was visited by the devil who tried to deflect him from the path of his faith, but each time he managed to defeat him. The first time the devil took the form of a man who accosted him at the bottom of a flight of stairs. The second time the devil appeared in his cell one night while Martin was sharing it with a friend. The door came open on its own, but Martin recognized the devil and other demons. They hit and shook him and set the cell on fire, frightening Martin's friend immensely, but when it was all over, the cell appeared as if nothing had happened. The third time was shortly before Martin's death. The devil came not to strike him but with reverence, telling him how saintly he was, making Martin suffer by making him feel vain and superior. The Virgin Mary, St. Dominic and St. Vincent Ferrer joined him, and together they pushed the devil away again.

Martin contracted quatrain fever and accurately predicted the date and hour of his death. While waiting to die, he had visions of saints and Mary. He was visited by the viceroy, who came to ask his blessing. He died on November 3, 1639, while praying and kissing a crucifix.

While Martin's body lay on display, mourners tore so many pieces from his habit that it had to be changed three times. Miracles began almost immediately to be credited to his intervention. His cause was so strong that the long process of canonization began as early as 1660.

In 1664, his casket was opened so that his remains could be moved to a better tomb. A sweet smell of roses emanated from it. His body was found to be incorrupt, though the bones were easily disjointed. Permission had not yet been granted for the taking of relics; however, one friar secretly removed a rib and hid it under his habit. The bone immediately began to radiate intense heat. The friar removed the bone inside his cell, but during the night the heat increased to the point where the friar decided to confess and surrender the bone. He detached a small fragment for his own veneration. The fragment emanated intense heat as well, and the friar was once again forced to confess and surrender what he had taken.

Many accounts of his supernatural feats in life are well documented. Martin's companions called him the "Flying Brother." His bilocations were reported in Mexico, China, Japan, Africa, the Philippines and perhaps even France. Martin especially bilocated to help the sick. On one occasion, he persuaded a sick man to try a remedy that he said he had seen successfully used in a hospital in Bayonne, France—which he could have visited only through extraordinary means. In Africa, he appeared to help people imprisoned as captives in Barbary.

Martin was seen levitating three to four feet off the ground on numerous occasions; one such ecstasy was reported to have lasted an hour. On another occasion, he was seen to be level with a crucifix on a wall with his lips pressed against it. Oddly, his own body was somehow smaller in size so as to be similar to the body on the cross. No one ever seemed to witness him rising into the air, but rather witnesses would come upon him already floating as he prayed. When done, he would descend and walk calmly away.

Martin also helped others by cloaking them with invisibility. Once two escaped criminals took refuge in his monastery cell. He had them kneel and pray. When authorities came to search the monastery, including Martin's cell, the criminals could not be found. Martin told them they must mend their ways.

Martin was observed surrounded by, or even emanating, rays of supernatural light, especially during his ecstasies in which he levitated. He also had gifts of prophecy and clairvoyance, and knew instantly where he would be needed, and what were the specific needs of others. He healed people and animals by touch.

Martin has many devotees in the United States as well as Latin America and elsewhere around the world. The government of Peru declared him to be the patron of social justice.

Beatified: 1837 by Pope Gregory XVI
Canonized: May 5, 1962, by Pope John XXIII
Feast: November 3
Patronage: barbers; hairdressers; innkeepers; people of mixed race; public education; public health; racial harmony; social justice; state schools; television

FURTHER READING
Cavallini, Giuliana. *St. Martin de Porres-Apostle of Charity.* Tr. Caroline Holland. Rockford, Ill.: TAN Books and Publishers, 1999.
"Martín de Porres, religioso (1579–1639)." Archidiócis de Madrid. URL: http://www.archimadrid.es. Downloaded: November 4, 1999.
"San Martín de Porres." Santos Peruanos. URL: http://ekeko.rcp.net.pe/IAL/cep/santpapa/santoslos.htm. Downloaded: November 4, 1999.

Martin of Tours (ca. 316–ca. 397) *Bishop and pioneer of Western monasticism*

Martin of Tours was born around 316 in Sabaria, Pannonia (now Hungary), to pagan parents. His father was a military tribune. The family was transferred to Pavia,

Italy, when Martin was a child. At age 10, he went to church and begged to become a catechumen. At age 12, he would have retired to live as a hermit had he been old enough to do so. When he was 15, however, he was drafted into the Roman army. Though not formally a Christian, Martin was attracted to Christian ways and lived more as a monk than a soldier.

The most famous incident of his early life occurred in 337. Martin was in Amiens, Gaul, with his unit. One extremely cold day, he met a half-naked beggarman shivering and begging for alms at the city gates. Moved, Martin took off his cloak, cut it in half with his sword, and gave one piece to the man. That night he had a dream in which Jesus appeared with a multitude of angels and said, "Martin, yet a catechumen, clothed me with this robe." (Martin's half of the cloak became a relic after his death.) After this, Martin was inspired to be baptized. At the entreaties of his tribune, he remained in the army for nearly two more years.

When barbarians invaded Gaul and Julian Caesar needed an army, Martin declined the soldier's bounty and asked to be released to the service of Christ. Julian Caesar had him imprisoned, but soon released him.

Martin went to Poitiers, where he was taken in by the bishop, St. Hilary (later a Doctor of the Church), who ordained him an exorcist. Not long thereafter, Martin was urged in a dream to return home and attend to his parents. He converted his mother but failed with his father. His opposition to the Arians resulted in his public scourging and banishment. Hilary, meanwhile, was suffering his own problems and had been forced from Poitiers. Martin retired with a priest to the island of Gallinaria in the Gulf of Genoa until 360, when Hilary returned to Poitiers.

Hilary gave Martin some land about two miles outside the city, now called Liguge, where Martin became a hermit in a wooden hut. He soon attracted other hermits, thus creating the first monastic community in Gaul. He probably would have stayed there indefinitely had not the bishop of Tours died around 371–372. Asked to take the office, Martin declined. His supporters tricked him into coming to Tours, where he was persuaded to stay as bishop. The monastic community of Liguge grew to a great monastery that continued until 1607 and was revived in 1859 by the Solesmes Benedictines.

As bishop, Martin was loathe to give up his hermit ways. He lived first in a cell near the church and then moved to Marmoutier, in a desert-like location enclosed by a steep cliff and a tributary of the Loire. He founded an abbey and was joined by about 80 hermits. Many lived in caves carved out of the cliff. They wore camelhair shirts and spent their time in prayer.

St. Martin of Tours splitting his cloak for a beggar (Library of Congress Prints and Photographs Division)

Martin preached about the countryside, and many miracles were attributed to him. He is credited with converting many persons throughout a wide area surrounding the abbey, and even as far as Chartres and Paris.

One of his most difficult situations occurred around 384, when a Gnostic-Manichaean sect known as the Priscillianists, in Spain and Gaul, were condemned as heretics and excommunicated. Martin initially persuaded Emperor Maximus not to execute them, but the emperor reneged and had the heretics beheaded. Martin interceded on behalf of the Spanish Priscillianists, who were threatened with persecution.

Martin went to Rome and then to Candes, where he established a religious center. He fell ill and died there on November 9, 397 (some accounts give 400 as the year). His successor, St. Britius, built a chapel over his grave. A basilica was later built, and remains one of the most important pilgrimage sites in Europe.

Martin's chief biographer was his friend Sulpitius Severus, who wrote his biography about one year before Martin's death. Sulpitius compared Martin to the apostles and attributed numerous miraculous feats to him, including healing, exorcisms, visions of angels and temptations by devils. He is said to have raised the dead on three occasions: a monk who was about to be buried; a slave who had hanged himself; and a child brought to Martin by his mother. Most of these events are dismissed by many historians as fiction or greatly embroidered fact. However, it is likely that he performed healings and exorcisms, as these skills would have been expected from a religious of his repute. He likely had visionary experiences as well.

> Feast: November 11
> Patronage: horsemen; the impoverished; soldiers; tailors

FURTHER READING

Sulpitius Severus on the Life of St. Martin. URL: http://www. users.csbsju.edu/~eknuth/npnf2-11/sulpitiu/lifeofst.tx   t. Downloaded: February 9, 2000.

Martyrs of Japan (d. 1597) *A group of 26 priests and lay brethren who were killed in Nagasaki*

Christianity had been introduced into Japan by St. Francis Xavier, beginning in 1549. By 1587 there were some 200,000 Christians in Japan, greatly unsettling a feudal lord, Toyotomi Hideyoshi, who was ruling Japan in the name of the emperor; he ordered all missionaries to leave the country within six months. Some did so, but many donned disguises and stayed, setting the stage for confrontation. This came when a Spanish ship's pilot bragged to Hideyoshi that Japan would soon be a Christian country, thus easing the way for conquest by Spain and Portugal.

Hideyoshi had 24 of the martyrs rounded up beginning in December 1596. Their left ears were cut off and they were paraded from town to town for a month, until they reached the hill in Nagasaki where they were sentenced to die on February 5, 1597. The last two of the 26 were taken from the crowd that came to watch the executions. All were permitted to confess to two Jesuits, then tied to crosses with ropes or chains, iron collars around their necks. The crosses were raised and spaced about four feet apart in a long row, and each martyr was stabbed twice with a spear by his own executioner.

The martyrs are said to have died happily, with smiles on their faces, many crying out: "Jesus, Joseph and Mary, unto you I commend my heart and spirit." The crucifixion was watched by many Christian converts who later collected the martyrs' blood and garments. Miracles began to be attributed to the martyrs almost immediately.

The group included six first-order Franciscans and three Jesuits as well as 17 Japanese laymen, among them 12 Franciscan tertiaries and three young acolytes. The martyrs are:

> Philip de las Casas (b. 1571 or 1572). Also known as: Felipe de las Casas; Felipe de Jesus; Philip of Jesus. Philip was born in Mexico City, Mexico, a son of Spanish immigrants. He studied for a while at the Reformed Franciscan Convent of Santa Barbara at

Puebla, Mexico, but wasn't happy there, and left. His father sent him on a business trip to the Philippines, where in 1590 he joined the convent of Our Lady of the Angels in Manila, taking his vows in 1594. He was on his way back to Mexico with other Franciscans in 1596 when a storm caused his ship, the *Saint Philip,* to be wrecked off Japan. Amid the storm, Philip saw over the islands a white cross, which after a while became blood-red, an omen of his fate. The captain sent Philip and two others to the emperor to gain permission for them to continue their voyage, but they were denied an audience. They continued to the Franciscan house in Macao to see if their brethren could help. In the meantime, the pilot of the *Saint Philip* got in to see Hideyoshi, setting off the persecution. Philip was the first of the martyrs to die. He is the patron saint of Mexico City and its archbishopric.

> Diego Kisai (b. 1534). Also called: Diego Kizayemon, Santiago Kisai. A Japanese layman who was a temporal coadjutor of the Jesuits and a catechist in Osaka. He was admitted to the Society of Jesus while in prison, awaiting execution.

> Francis Blanco (Francisco Blanco). Born in Monterey, Galicia, Spain, Francis studied in Salamanca, then joined the Franciscan order at Vallalpando. He first worked as a missionary at Churubusco, Mexico, then in Manila, the Philippines, before going to Japan in 1594.

> Francis of Saint Michael (Francisco de San Miguel). Born at Parilla, near Valladolid, Spain, Francis joined the Franciscans as a lay brother, and was sent first to the Philippines and then to Japan as a missionary. He was arrested in Osaka along with Peter Baptist in 1596.

> Gundisalvus Garcia (b. 1556). Also known as: Gonsalo Garcia. Gundisalvus was born at Bassein near Bombay, India, of Portuguese parents, though they may have been Indian converts who had taken Portuguese names. He first served the Jesuits as a catechist, but joined the Franciscans in the Philippines in 1591. He worked in Japan as an interpreter to Peter Baptist.

> John Soan de Goto. A 19-year-old Japanese native, arrested for being a Jesuit temporal coadjutor and catechist at Osaka. Like Diego Kisai, he was admitted to the order in prison as he awaited execution.

> Martin Loynaz (de Aguirre). Born in Vergara, near Pamplona, Spain, Martin studied in Alcala, joining the Franciscan order in 1586. He first worked as a missionary in Mexico and the Philippines before Japan.

Paul Miki (b. 1562). Paul was born the son of a Japanese military leader at Tounucumada and educated at the Jesuit college at Anziquiama, Japan, joining the Jesuits in 1580. He became famous for his eloquent preaching, and in fact delivered one last sermon from the cross on which he died.

Peter Baptist (Pedro Bautista) (b. 1545). A native of Avila, Spain, Peter joined the Franciscans in 1567. Like other of his fellow martyrs, he served as a missionary in Mexico and the Philippines before arriving in Japan in 1593. He was credited as a miracle worker and considered the leader of the Franciscans in Japan. In 1596 he was arrested in Osaka, along with Francis of Saint Michael.

Antony Deynan, born at Nagasaki, was a 13-year-old altar boy and a Franciscan tertiary when he died. When he heard the names Jesus, Joseph and Mary, he began to sing psalms he had learned in his catechism classes.

Caius Francis was a Japanese soldier who had only just been baptized and received as a Franciscan tertiary. He insisted on being arrested along with the friars.

Cosmas Takeya, from Owari, Japan, was a Franciscan tertiary who preached in Osaka and also served as an interpreter.

Francis of Miyako, from Miyako, Nagasaki, was a physician who converted to Catholicism and became a Franciscan tertiary and lay catechist.

Gabriel de Duisco was the 19-year-old son of the Franciscans' native porter.

Joachim Sakakibara (or Saccachibara) was the Japanese-born cook for the Franciscans at Osaka. He also was a tertiary and catechist.

John Kisaka (or Kimoia), born at Miyako, was baptized and received as a Franciscan tertiary shortly before his death.

Leo Karasumaru (or Carasuma), a native of Korea living in Japan, was baptized by the Jesuits in 1589. He became the first Korean Franciscan tertiary and was the Franciscans' chief catechist.

Louis Ibaraki (or Ibarki) was the 12-year-old nephew of Leo Karasumaru and Paul Ibaraki. He served the Franciscans as acolyte.

Matthias of Miyako, a Japanese native, was a Franciscan tertiary.

Michael Cozaki, a Japanese native, was a hospital nurse to the Franciscans. He was killed along with his son, Thomas.

Paul Ibaraki (Yuanki or Yuaniqui) was Leo Karasumaru's brother and Louis Ibaraki's uncle. He was a Franciscan tertiary, catechist and interpreter.

Paul Suzuki, from Owari, Japan, was baptized by the Jesuits in 1584. He later became a Franciscan tertiary and was an outstanding catechist.

Peter Sukejiro (or Xukexico), a native of Japan, was a Franciscan tertiary who served as a catechist, house servant and sacristan. He was arrested when he was sent by a Jesuit priest to help the Franciscans.

Thomas Cozaki (or Kasaki), a Japanese native, served the Franciscans as an acolyte. He was 15 when he was executed along with his father, Michael.

Thomas Xico (Dauki) was a Japanese Franciscan tertiary, catechist and interpreter.

Ventura, from Miyako, had been baptized by the Jesuits, but gave up his Catholicism when his father died. He was brought back into the Church by the Franciscans, with whom he died.

From their canonization in 1862 until the revision of the Roman calendar in 1970, the feast day of the Martyrs of Japan was celebrated on February 5 in Japan and by the Franciscans and Jesuits. With the calendar revision, their feast was moved to February 6, and today they are remembered universally as the first martyrs of the Far East.

Beatified: September 14, 1627, by Pope Urban VIII
Canonized: June 8, 1862, by Pope Pius IX
Feast: February 6 (formerly February 5)

FURTHER READING
St. Alphonsus Liguori. *Victories of the Martyrs.* Brooklyn: Redemptorist Fathers, 1954.

Martyrs of Mexico (20th century) *A group of 25 priests and lay religious leaders murdered in Mexico in 20th-century religious persecutions*

The first martyr, killed in 1915, was caught up in the series of revolutions and counterrevolutions of the 1910s; the last died under a left-wing government in 1937. The rest were victims of the regime of Plutarco Calles, elected to the presidency in 1924. Strongly anticlerical, Calles closed Church institutions and began deporting priests. The Catholic clergy first protested these actions through nonviolent organizations such as the Acción Católica and the National League for the Defense of Religious Freedom. When these efforts failed, some supported the more militant Cristeros, who mounted a civil war against the government, attacking federal forces and destroying federal property such as schools. A settlement was not reached until

1929, by which time several priests had been killed. The martyrs are:

David Galván (1881–1915). Born in Guadalajara on January 29, 1881, David entered the Guadalajara seminary in 1895 and was ordained a priest in 1909. During uprisings in 1913–14 he was arrested for being a priest and taken to Guadalajara, where he was eventually set free. However, on January 30, 1915, an altercation erupted in the city between rival rebel forces, leaving many wounded and dead in the streets. When he set about taking the dead for burial, David was stopped by federal troops and was shot.

Luis Batis (1870–1926). Born in San Miguel del Mezquital on September 13, 1870, Luis entered the seminary in Durango in 1882. He was ordained a priest in January 1894, and from then until his death worked as spiritual director of the seminary and parish of Chalchihuites. He founded a workshop and a school for children, yet he yearned to do more with his life. He prayed before a statue of Jesus that he might spill his blood in his name. His prayers were answered when he became the first of the martyrs of the 1920s. He was arrested on August 14, 1926, and executed the following day along with three members of the Acción Católica who had come out on his behalf.

Manuel Morales (1898–1926). Manuel was born in Mesillas on February 8, 1898. He studied in the Durango seminary for a time but had to leave to help support his family. He remained active in religious affairs, was a member of the Acción Católica and president of the National League for the Defense of Religious Freedom. He died with Luis Batis on August 15, 1926.

David Roldán (1907–1926). David was born in Chalchihuites on March 2, 1907. He entered the Durango seminary, but later left to help support his family. He joined the Acción Católica and in 1925 was named its president. He also served as vice president of the National League for the Defense of Religious Freedom. He died with Luis Batis on August 15, 1926.

Salvador Lara (1905–1926). Born in Súchil on August 13, 1905, Salvador entered the Durango seminary, but his family's precarious economic situation forced him to drop out. Nevertheless, he continued to be active in religious affairs, helping out with pastoral work in his parish, and serving as secretary of the National League for the Defense of Religious Freedom and president of the Acción Católica. He too died with Luis Batis

on August 15, 1926. As he was going before the firing squad, he cried: "Long live Christ the King and the Virgin of Guadelupe!"

Jenaro Sánchez (1886–1927). Jenaro was born in Zapopán on September 19, 1886. He attended the Guadalajara seminary and was ordained a priest in 1911. He was shot by federal troops on January 17, 1927. His body remained where it was thrown until it was recognized, and townspeople buried him in the cemetery. In 1934 his relics were moved to the parish church in Cocula.

Julio Alvarez (1866–1927). Born in Guadalajara on December 20, 1866, Julio studied at the Guadalajara seminary and was ordained a priest in 1894. When the persecutions under Calles began, he left his parish and hid with the help of followers, but was discovered. He was shot at dawn on March 30, 1927. His relics were thrown in a dumpster close to the church, where a monument has since been raised in his honor.

David Uribe (1888–1927). David was born in Buenavista de Cuéllar on December 29, 1888. He studied at the Chilapa and Tabasco seminaries and was ordained in 1913. On the night of April 11, 1927, he was taken out of his cell and shot in the back. His relics are venerated today in the parish of his natal town.

Sabás Reyes (1879–1927). Born in Cocula on December 5, 1879, of a poor family, Sabás studied at seminaries in Guadalajara and Tamaulipas; he was ordained a priest in 1911. The persecutions of the 1920s found him working in Tototlán. On April 11, 1927, he was taken before a military assembly where he was thrown on the ground between two fires, one at his feet, the other before his face, and asked to reveal the hiding places of two other priests. He refused, and on the night of April 13 was taken to the local cemetery and shot against the wall. His relics reside today in the parish church of Tototlán.

Cristóbal Magallanes (1869–1927). Cristóbal was born in Totalice on July 30, 1869. He entered Guadalajara seminary in 1888 and was ordained a priest in September 1899. He was chaplain and subdirector of the school of arts and trades in Guadalajara and served as parish priest in Totalice for 17 years. On May 25, 1927, he was conducting a religious ceremony at a ranch when a shootout began between Cristeros members and federal troops. Cristóbal was arrested and taken to Colotitlán, where he was shot along with Agustín Caloca.

Agustín Caloca (1898–1927). Agustín was born in San Juan Bautista del Teúl on May 5, 1898. He enrolled in the Guadalajara seminary, but had to return home when it was closed in the early 1910s. When the seminary reopened in 1919, he resumed his studies, and was ordained a priest in August 1923. In May 1927, he was arrested and taken to the jail in Totalice where Cristóbal Magallanes was being held. The two priests were carried to Colotitlán, where they were shot in the burned-out city hall, their bodies subsequently being used in the reconstruction of the walls. When Agustín's relics were exhumed and moved back to the Totalice parish hall in 1933, his heart was found to be incorrupt.

José Isabel Flores (1866–1927). Born in San Juan Bautista del Teúl on November 20, 1866, José Isabel began his studies in the Guadalajara seminary in 1887. He was ordained a priest in 1896. When the 1920s persecutions began, he was denounced; he was arrested but offered his freedom if he agreed to support Calles. When he refused, he was taken to the cemetery in Zapotalnejo and shot, June 21, 1927.

José María Robles (1888–1927). José María was born in Mascotaon on May 3, 1888. In 1900, at the age of 12, he entered the Guadalajara seminary, and was ordained a priest there in 1913. In 1918 he founded a religious society, the Brothers of the Sacred Heart of Jesus. He was celebrating the Eucharist in a private home in June 1927, when federal troops arrived and took him prisoner. He was taken out of town and shot. His relics lie today in the novitiate of the Brothers of the Sacred Heart of Jesus.

Rodrigo Aguilar (1875–1927). Rodrigo was born in Sayula on March 13, 1875. He attended a seminary and was ordained a priest in 1905 and worked in various parishes. In October 1927, he was taken to the town square for execution where he pardoned everyone concerned and gave his rosary to one of the soldiers about to kill him, shouting out as he died, "Long live Christ the King and the Virgin of Guadelupe!"

Margarito Flores (1899–1927). Margarito was born in Taxco on February 22, 1899. He entered the seminary in 1913, when he was 14, and was ordained a priest in 1924. He was soon named a professor in the seminary, where he remained until forced to take refuge in Mexico City. He was captured there, but set free, and decided to return to Chilapa. Upon his arrival he was arrested and taken to Tulimán tied to a horse, semi-nude and barefoot. He was executed on November 12, 1927.

Pedro Esqueda (1887–1927). Born in San Juan de los Lagos on April 26, 1887, Pedro began his education in a private school at the age of four. At 15 he entered the seminary in Guadalajara, but in 1914 it was closed and confiscated. He later returned to the seminary and was ordained a priest in 1916. He was named vicar of his natal parish, the job he held for the 10 years of his ministry. In 1926 he went into hiding, but federal troops found him on November 18, 1927. They took him to the abbey where they held him incommunicado and tortured him daily. He was shot on November 22.

Mateo Correa (1866–1927). Mateo was born in Tepechitlán on July 22, 1866. He attended the Zacatecas seminary and was ordained in 1893, after which he served in various parishes. He was caught and arrested in 1927, taken to Durango and imprisoned in the military headquarters. The general in command ordered him to hear confessions from a group of persons who were to be shot and then demanded that he reveal the confessions. When the priest refused, he was killed. His relics now lie in the Durango cathedral.

Miguel de la Mora (1874–1927). Miguel was born in Tecalitlán on June 19, 1874. He was ordained a priest in 1906 and preached in the Colima diocese. In 1927 he was captured and imprisoned in the army headquarters, then taken to the stable where he was shot as he counted his rosary. Today his relics are venerated in the Colima cathedral.

Román Adame (1859–1927). Born in Teocaltiche on February 27, 1859, Román studied in the Guadalajara seminary and was ordained a priest in November 1890. He was characterized by a profound devotion to the Virgin Mary and founded a religious order, the Daughters of Mary and the Nocturnal Adoration. When religious practices were banned in the 1920s he was captured and taken to Yahualica, where he spent several days tied up, denied food and water. Later he was moved to the cemetery and shot by his open grave, together with a soldier who refused to execute him.

Toribio Romo (1900–1928). Born in Jalostotitlán on April 16, 1900, Toribio studied at the Guadalajara seminary and was ordained a priest in 1922. He joined the Acción Católica, in which he distinguished himself in social works. The persecution forced him into a nomadic life together with his parish priest, Justino Orona. At dawn on February 25, 1928, a detachment of soldiers burst into his house and room. They riddled him with bullets, pulled off his night dress, and carried his body to Tequila, where they threw it in front of the city hall. Twenty years later his relics were returned to his natal town and were interred in a chapel constructed for him.

Justino Orona (1877–1928). Born in Atoyac on April 14, 1877, Justino completed his early studies in Zapotlán, then in 1894 entered the seminary in Guadalajara. He was ordained in 1904 and assigned to various parishes. He founded a society to help poor orphaned girls in Cuquío. On June 28, 1928, he took refuge in a ranch with Atilano Cruz. Government troops learned of the hiding place, however, and stormed the building the following morning, shooting Justino when he answered the door.

Atilano Cruz (1901–1928). Atilano was born in Teocaltiche on October 5, 1901, to a Catholic Indian family. He entered a local seminary in 1918 and two years later transferred to Guadalajara where he was ordained in June 1927. A year later he was sent to Cuquío. He went immediately to the ranch where Justino Orona was hiding. The soldiers shot Atilano as he knelt on his bed, threw his body on the patio along with Orona's, then took them to Cuquío, where they were dumped in the town square. The faithful buried them that day in the cemetery, but their relics have since been moved to the parish church of San Felipe de Cuquío.

Tranquilino Ubiarco (1899–1928). Born in Zapotlán el Grande on July 8, 1899, Tranquilino entered a seminary in his youth, only to have it closed. Later he was able to resume his studies in the Guadalajara seminary and was ordained a priest in August 1923. In the midst of the persecution under Calles he was named vicar of the parish of Tepatitlán, where for 15 months he exercised his ministry in various homes and established a public dining hall. On October 5, 1928, he was finishing celebrating Mass in a house when several soldiers arrived and arrested him. He was executed a short while later.

Jesús Méndez (1880–1928). Born in Tarímbaro on June 10, 1880, Jesús entered the seminary in Michoacán in 1894, when he was 14. He was ordained in 1906 and conducted his ministry in various parishes. One day in 1928, Jesús had just finished celebrating Mass when federal troops arrived. He tried to escape carrying the pyx under his cloak. The soldiers stopped and searched him and on finding the pyx recognized him and took him prisoner. The first shots they fired were blanks; Jesús was searched again, his crucifix and medallions removed, and then shot to death. The soldiers placed his body on train tracks, but the officers' wives removed his relics and allowed them to be buried in Cortázar.

Pedro de Jesús (1892–1937). Born in Sacramento on June 8, 1892, Pedro entered the Chihuahua seminary in 1909 and was ordained a priest in El Paso, Texas, in 1918. He managed to avoid the persecutions of the 1920s, perhaps by fleeing to the United States, but when they resumed the following decade, he was not so fortunate. In Mexico in 1934, he was arrested and banished to El Paso, but he immediately returned to his native country and resumed his ministry. Three years later, on Ash Wednesday, a group of armed men appeared at his house. He was made to walk barefoot behind horses to Santa Isabel, where he was imprisoned in the courthouse and beaten unconscious. Later he was taken to the civil hospital of Chihuahua where he died on the morning of February 11, 1937.

Another martyr of this period, Bl. Miguel Pro, was beatified in a separate ceremony and given a different feast day.

Beatified: November 22, 1992, by Pope John Paul II
Feast: May 25

FURTHER READING

Mabry, Donald J., "Mexican Anticlerics, Bishops, Cristeros, and the Devout during the 1920's: A Scholarly Debate," *Journal of Church and State* 20 (1978): 81–92.

"Santos y Beatos de América Latina: México." Aciprensa website. URL: http://www.aciprensa.com/santmexi.htm. Downloaded on November 13, 1999.

Ratliff, Chris. "20th Century Mexico." Historical Text Archive. URL:http://www.msstate.edu/Archives/History/text/ratliff.html. Downloaded on January 19, 2000.

Martyrs of Paraguay *Three Jesuits who died seeking to convert native people to the Christian faith.*

Roque Gonzalez, Alphonsus Rodriguez and John of Castillo helped to found the system of Jesuit "reductions"—missions to which Indians of various tribes were brought—in the interior of South America. Besides serving as missions, the reductions were centers of education in construction techniques, architecture, crafts, farming, animal husbandry, printing and other skills. The reductions in greater Paraguay (encompassing territories that today form parts of Argentina, Uruguay, Brazil and Bolivia) provided a refuge for Tupi- and Guarani-speaking Indians fleeing the predations of slave traders as well. Unfortunately, they were also death camps for many natives, who did not carry immunities to the European diseases that swept easily through them. These challenges to the traditional way of life were not welcomed by all, and in the end the three Jesuits were killed, at the behest of a Guarani chief, in reductions they had built. More about the martyrs:

> *Roque Gonzalez (1576–1628). Also known as:* Roch Gonzalez; Rocco Ganzalez; Roque Gonzáles de Santa Cruz. Roque Gonzales was born in the city of Asunción, Paraguay, to a well-connected family. He was the son of Bartolomé Gonzáles Villaverde and María de Santa Cruz, Spaniards, but perhaps of mixed blood. He was raised in a religious atmosphere, and at the age of five, motivated by the numerous biographies of saints he had heard, decided to devote his life to prayer and penitence.

Roque was ordained a Roman Catholic priest in 1599, when he was 24. He preached at the cathedral in Asunción and soon found himself tapped for administrative roles—the bishop of Asunción named him assistant superior of the dioceses. In 1603, he participated in a local synod, during which he joined in condemning the enslavement of the Indians. Then in May 1609, his desire to be of service to the natives of the region led him to resign his posts and join the Jesuit order.

In 1611 Roque was sent to head the reduction of San Ignacio (St. Ignatius). After three years there, he left to found other reductions, a half-dozen in all in the Parana and Uruguay river regions.

In 1628, Roque, together with Alphonsus Rodriquez and John of Castillo, founded a reduction on the Ijuji (Yhui) River, named Asunción de Yhui (Our Lady's Assumption). Father Castillo was left in charge there, while Roque and Alphonsus pressed on to Caaro, in what is now Brazil, to build yet another reduction, this named Todos Santos (All Saints). The All Saints reduction was in an area controlled by a chief called Nezu, who opposed the Jesuit efforts, and instigated an attack on the new settlement. Roque had just said Mass on November 15, and was preparing to hang a small church bell, when he was struck on the head from behind and killed. Alphonsus was killed in a similar manner when he went to investigate the noise. The wooden chapel they had constructed was set on fire and their bodies thrown into the blaze.

Roque Gonzalez had devoted his life to helping the Guarani. It is said that the Indians who killed him did not know who he was, and when they learned who they had killed, bitterly regretted their involvement.

> *Alphonsus Rodriguez (Alonso Rodríguez) (1598–1628).* Alphonsus Rodríguez was born in Zamora, Spain, on March 10, 1598, the son of Gonzalo Rodríguez y Maria Obnel, both devout Christians. He entered the Jesuit order as a novitiate at Villagarcía and was ordained a priest in 1624. In 1626 he traveled to Paraguay to work in the reductions there.

In 1628 Alphonsus began to work with Roque Gonzalez, founding first the reduction of Our Lady's Assumption and then the reduction of All Saints. He died along with Roque at the latter, on November 15.

> *John of Castillo (Juan del Castillo) (1596–1628). Also known as: Juan de Castillo.* John of Castillo was born in Belmonte, Spain, on September 14, 1596. He entered the Jesuit novitiate at Madrid on March 21, 1614, at the age of 17. After being ordained as a priest, he went to the mission of San Nicolás where he dedicated himself to Catholic education.

In 1628 he helped Roque Gonzalez and Alphonsus Rodriquez found the reduction of Our Lady's Assumption, where he stayed in charge while they went on to found All Saints. On November 17, two days after Roque and Alphonsus were killed, he was working in the reduction when it was attacked and he was seized, bound and beaten, before being stoned to death.

The three Jesuit martyrs were beatified and canonized as a group. The first steps toward their beatification were made within six months of their deaths. However, the records were misplaced for over three centuries; the process was revived in 1934, when the originals unexpectedly turned up in Argentina.

> *Beatified:* January 28, 1934, by Pope Pius XI
> *Canonized:* May 16, 1988, by Pope John Paul II
> *Feast:* November 16
> *Patronage:* native traditions; Paraguay

FURTHER READING
"San Roque Gonzales de Santa Cruz." Santos y Beatos de America Latina: Paraguay. URL: http://www.aciprensa.com/santpara.htm. Downloaded: December 12, 1999.
"El Padre Alonso Rodríguez." Santos y Beatos de America Latina: Paraguay. URL: http://www.aciprensa.com/santpara.htm. Downloaded: December 12, 1999.
"El Padre Juan del Castillo." Santos y Beatos de America Latina: Paraguay. URL: http://www.aciprensa.com/santpara.htm. Downloaded: December 12, 1999.

Mary, Blessed Virgin (d. first century) *The mother of Jesus Christ*

Also known as: Mother of God, Our Lady of the Angels, Queen of the Angels, Queen of Martyrs, Our Lady and other titles

Little is known about Mary's life. According to tradition, she was born in Jerusalem to SS. Anne and Joachim. She was presented to the temple and took a vow of virginity. Her Immaculate Conception was announced by the Archangel Gabriel (Luke 1:26–38). Gabriel told her that the Holy Spirit would come upon her in order to conceive her son. Mary became betrothed to St. Joseph. Her cousin Elizabeth—whom Gabriel announced would bear St. John the Baptist—called her the Mother of God. Mary replied with the Magnificat, "My soul magnifies the Lord . . ." (Luke 1:46–55).

Mary and Joseph went to Bethlehem, seat of Joseph's family, to comply with a census. There Jesus was born and visited by the Three Kings, or Magi. The baby was presented to the temple. Warned that King Herod was searching for an infant boy destined to become King of the Jews, the family fled to Egypt, returning to Nazareth after Herod died.

Little is said in the Bible about the further activities of Mary. She visited the Temple of Jerusalem and was instrumental in Jesus' first recorded miracle of turning water into wine at a wedding feast in Cana (John 2:1–5). She was present at the Crucifixion and given into St. John's care (John 19:25–27). She was with the disciples before Pentecost (Acts 1:14). Tradition holds that she was present at the Resurrection and Ascension of Christ, though no records state so. The Bible does not tell of her last years. According to one tradition, she remained in Jerusalem; another holds that she went to Ephesus.

Tradition also has long held that Mary did not die a physical death, but was assumed into heaven. Her Assumption was made an article of faith in 1950 by Pope Pius XII (r. 1939–58).

According to Catholic doctrine, Mary's Immaculate Conception makes her the one exception to the state of Original Sin (the state in which all humankind is born, due to the fall of Adam and Eve). Because Mary was destined to be the mother of Christ, God infused her soul with grace at the moment of her conception in the womb of her mother, St. Anne, which freed her from lust, slavery to the devil, depraved nature, darkness of intellect and other consequences of Original Sin. The Immaculate Conception was proclaimed in 1854 by Pope Pius IX (r. 1848–78).

The idea of the Immaculate Conception was rejected by St. Thomas Aquinas in the 13th century. Many modern theologians, challenging doctrines, consider the Immaculate Conception to be symbolic and not literal. The Bible makes references to Jesus' brothers and sisters.

Mary and her place in Christian theology have been the subject of much controversy over the centuries. She absorbed characteristics of previous pagan goddesses, thus fulfilling the universal need for worship of a mother-figure. Some early Church fathers attempted to discourage worship of her by saying that God would never be born of a woman. For the first five centuries after Christ, she was depicted as lower in status than even the Magi, who were graced by haloes in sacred art. The Marianite sect, which considered her divine, was persecuted for heresy. In the early fourth century, Constantine I ordered all goddess temples destroyed and forbade the worship of Mary, so that she would not overshadow her Son. The people, however, refused to accept Christianity without worship of Mary. She was prayed to as a mother who intercedes for her children. In the fifth century, she was given the title *Theotokos* ("God-bearer") at the Church councils at Ephesus in 431 and at Chalcedon in 451. By the sixth century she was given a halo in art, and by the ninth century she was named Queen of Heaven. By the 11th century, great Gothic cathedrals were built for her.

Mary has a special role in salvation; Pope Benedict XV (r. 1914–22) wrote in 1918 that she "redeemed the human race together with Christ." She is seen as the Mediatrix of All Graces, ever present at the side of every person from baptism to death, ready to give support, hope, encouragement and strength.

She reigns in the splendor of heaven, where angels behold her glory and are ravished at the sight of her. She is second only to Jesus in suffering, and so commands the obedience of the angelic host. It may be the archangel Michael who leads the good angels in the celestial war against evil, but he is under the command of Mary. The Queen of Paradise may even be considered the mother of angels, since she loves them and treats them as her own children. The Precious Blood shed by Jesus is the song of angels, the light of Mary and the jubilee of her woes.

The theological, philosophical and other academic studies of Mary are collectively called "Mariology," a distinct discipline that includes biblical references to her, doctrines and devotions associated with her, and her role in religious history and thought. There is a Mariological Society of America and several centers of Mariological research, including the Marianum, the theological faculty directed in Rome by the Servite Fathers. There is also the Marian Library at the University of Dayton, Ohio, one of several schools owned and operated by the Society of Mary (Marianists), a Roman Catholic religious order devoted especially to "filial piety," a devotion to Mary similar to that which they believe is accorded Christ.

Countless visions of Mary have been reported worldwide; the numbers rose dramatically beginning in the latter part of the 20th century, spurred by the Catholic Church's acceptance of Mary's assumption into heaven as an article of faith in 1950, by a general increase in desire for spiritual experience, and by apocalyptic thinking concerning the change of millennia. The Catholic Church, which conducts rigorous investigations into such reports where it deems warranted, has authenticated eight of them. Some popular sites of Marian apparition pilgrimages, such as those in Zeitoun, Egypt, from 1968 to 1969, and those in Medjugorge, Bosnia-Herzegovina, beginning in 1981, have been neither investigated nor authenticated by the Church.

Numerous saints have seen visions of Mary, often accompanied by angels. Mary appears when she is needed in order to give comfort and important messages. Frequently, she exhorts people to pray to counter the evil at loose in the world.

In Catholic tradition, an unnamed Benedictine sister had a vision in which she saw the desolation wrought by evil. She heard Mary tell her that the time had come to pray to her as the Queen of the Angels, to ask her for the assistance of the angels in fighting the foes of God and men. The sister asked why could not Mary, who is so kind, send the angels without being asked. Mary responded that she could not, because prayer is one of the conditions God requires for the obtaining of favors. Mary then communicated the following prayer, which is part of the many devotions to Mary:

> "August Queen of Heaven! Sovereign Mistress of the angels! Thou who from the beginning hast received from God the power and mission to crush the head of Satan, we humbly beseech thee to send thy holy Legions, that, under thy command and by thy power, they may pursue the evil spirits, encounter them on every side, resist their bold attacks and drive them hence into the abyss of eternal woe. Amen."

The major events of Mary's life are observed as feast days throughout the year, among them the Immaculate Conception, the Nativity, Purification, Annunciation and Assumption. The most popular devotion to Mary is the rosary, which is the saying of 50 "Hail Marys," five "Our Fathers" and five doxologies ("Glory be to the Father. . . .") while meditating on specific traditional mysteries. This association with the rosary stems from apparitions of Mary seen at Fatima, Portugal, in 1917, in which she identified herself as the Lady of the Rosary, and asked that believers say the rosary every day. Devotion to Mary is a vital part of Catholic liturgical life.

Ex-canonical works such as the Book of John the Evangelist refer to Mary as an angel herself. The

The Blessed Virgin Mary with the infant Jesus (Library of Congress Prints and Photographs Division)

Apocryphal New Testament says she is the angel sent by God to receive the Lord, who enters her through the ear.

Among the saints who have had mystical visions of and encounters with Mary are Bernard of Clairvaux, Bernadine of Siena, Bridget of Sweden, Catherine Labouré, Catherine of Siena, Frances of Rome, Francis of Assisi, Gertrude, Gregory the Great, Ignatius of Loyola, John of the Cross, Mechtilde, Nicholas of Flue, Simon Stock and Teresa of Avila.

FURTHER READING

Arintero, Juan. *Mystical Evolution in the Development and Vitality of the Church*, vol. I. St. Louis: B. Herder, 1949.

Attwater, Donald. *A Dictionary of Mary.* New York: P.J. Kennedy, 1960.

St. Michael and the Angels. Rockford, Ill.: Tan Books and Publishers, 1983; first published, 1977.

Mary of Agreda, Venerable (1602–1665) *Abbess; mystic*

Also known as: Mary of Jesus

Mary of Agreda was born in Agreda, Spain, to religious parents. Her father, Francis Coronel, and her mother, Catharine de Arana, founded the Convent of the Immaculate Conception for discalced nuns in Agreda in 1619, in accordance with a revelation from God had by Catharine. Catharine, Mary and another daughter entered the convent, and Catharine and Mary were professed in February 1620. Francis entered the order of St. Francis of Assisi. After eight years, Mary was named abbess at age 25.

After entering the convent, Mary began to experience numerous ecstasies, levitations, bilocations and other mystical phenomena. During her ecstasies, her body was raised off the ground and could be moved as weightlessly as a feather. Her face was enraptured in beauty. She would remain in trances for two to three hours at a time.

Mary bilocated and traveled mystically throughout Spain and Portugal. From 1620 to 1631, she traveled to America to teach the Indians. She made more than 500 visits, sometimes as often as four times a day. The natives called her the Lady in Blue because of her blue mantle. Mary said she was commanded to travel to America by Jesus. She appeared in New Mexico and reached isolated tribes. She spoke in her native Spanish, but was understood by the Indians. She gave them Christian instruction and also directions for where to go in New Mexico and Texas to find Christian missions.

In 1665 she received divine notification of her impending death. She informed her community, and died peacefully in her sickbed while surrounded by weeping and praying people. At the moment of her death, a heavenly voice was heard repeating the words, "Come, come, come" three times.

Mary is best-known as the author of *The Mystical City of God.* From 1627 to 1637 she received many graces from the Blessed Virgin Mary, who appeared to her while she was in ecstasies and commanded her to write the Blessed Virgin's life. Mary resisted until 1637, when she began to set down what became *The Mystical City of God.* After completing it, a confessor (not her regular one), told her that women should not write in the Church and ordered her to destroy the work. Mary burned it all, not only the history that the Blessed Virgin had dictated, but also "other grave and mysterious matters." Her horrified confessor and superiors ordered her to rewrite the work under threat of censures. The Blessed Virgin also commanded her to rewrite it. Mary began the rewriting on December 8, 1655, the day of the Immaculate Conception.

Mary described how the Blessed Virgin appeared to her as she did to St. John the Divine in the Apocalypse, crowned with stars and clothed with the sun, and the moon at her feet. Mary also saw a ladder, which God told her was the ladder of Jacob and a portal to heaven, and signified the life of the most Holy Virgin and its virtues and sacraments. Mary ascended the ladder and at the top saw the Lord of Hosts and the Queen of all creation. The Blessed Virgin told her that she was unhappy with the wretched and sinful state of humankind, and would offer them a way of mercy in the mystical city of refuge.

The Mystical City of God is a four-volume, 2,676-page history of the Blessed Virgin's life, and also contains information on Jesus and his hidden life, the creation of the world, the Apocalypse, heaven and hell, and other Christian topics. It created quite a stir in Europe in ecclesiastical and academic circles. In 1686 Pope Innocent XI (r. 1676–89) declared that the book could be read by all the faithful.

FURTHER READING
Venerable Mary of Agreda. *The Mystical City of God.* Tr. Rev. George J. Blatter. Abridged version. Rockford, Ill.: TAN Books and Publishers, 1978.

Mary of Egypt (d. fifth or sixth century) *Egyptian hermit*

Much of the life of Mary of Egypt is legend. According to the *Life of St. Cyracus* by Cyril of Scythopolos, Cyracus was traveling in the Jordanian desert with companions when he found a woman who said her name was Mary, and that she was a famous singer and actress who had sinned and was atoning for her sins by living as a hermit. On their way back, they found the woman dead. From this was spun a legend that became popular during the Middle Ages.

According to a version written by St. Andrew of Crete (d. 740), who quotes St. Sophronius, patriarch of Jerusalem (ca. 560–638), an elder of a monastery in Palestine, Zosimus, went out into the Jordanian desert to fast and pray during Lent. After 20 days he came upon a naked woman with long white hair. He gave her his cloak. She addressed him by name and told him her story.

The woman said she was from Egypt. She ran away from her parents at age 12 and went to Alexandria, where she lead a life of sin and debauchery, seducing every man she could find. She rarely took money, and lived by begging and spinning flax. One day she encountered Libyans and Egyptians going to Jerusalem and decided to go with them, though she had no money to pay for her passage across the sea. She paid her way with sexual favors, even forcing youths against their will.

In Jerusalem, on the day of the Exaltation of the Cross, she experienced a conversion before an icon of the Blessed Virgin Mary. She heard a voice tell her that if she crossed the River Jordan she would find glorious rest. A stranger gave her money, with which she bought three loaves of bread. She washed in the river, crossed it and took up life as a hermit.

The three loaves of bread dried and lasted her several years. For 17 years she went through a dark night of the soul, fighting temptation and despair. She lived on herbs and whatever she could find. Another 30 went by before she was found by Zosimus.

Zosimus wanted to become her disciple, but she demurred. Instead, she asked him to bring her Communion on the next anniversary of the Last Supper. He agreed, but told his story to no one. The following year, he returned to the desert with the body and blood, and a small amount of food. He waited by the banks of the river. Mary appeared and walked across the water. She took Communion, and told him to come again the next year, and to pray for her.

Zosimus returned again as requested, but found her lying dead on the opposite shore of the river. She had written in the sand that he should bury her on the spot. He was having little success digging in the earth when a lion appeared and licked Mary's feet. It dug a hole, and Zosimus buried Mary in the cloak he had given her. Zosimus lived to age 100 and died in his monastery.

Various dates are given for Mary. Zosimus is said to have found her in 430. Her date of death also is given as 522.

Feast: April 2

FURTHER READING

"The Life of Our Holy Mother Mary of Egypt." From *The Great Canon, the Work of Saint Andrew of Crete.* URL: http://www.ofc.org/OrthodoxPage/reading/st.mary.html. Downloaded September 24, 2000.

Mary of the Incarnation (1566–1618) *Widow and founder of Discalced Carmelite convents in France*
Also known as: Barbara Acarie, Barbara Avrillot, Madame Barbé Acarie, Marie de l' Incarnation, Marie of the Incarnation

St. Mary of the Incarnation was born February 1, 1566, in Paris, France, as Barbé (Barbara) Avrillot. Her father, Sieur Nicholas Avrillot, was accountant general in the Chamber of Paris; her mother, Marie L' huillier, was a descendant of Etienne Marcel, the famous chief magistrate of the city. Her parents sent Mary to the Poor Clares at Longchamp for her early education, and in 1584 arranged for her marriage to Pierre (Peter) Acarie de Villemor, a wealthy young man of high standing.

Mary and Peter had six children together, though Peter turned out to be something of a male chauvinist. He censored Mary's reading and, being very religious, asked her confessor to recommend books for her to read. These books opened her to a new mystical reality and transformed her whole being. She found it impossible to read spiritual books without immediately falling into ecstatic trances, so had someone read them to her. While in trance, she sometimes received stigmata, the marks of Christ on the cross. As she advanced spiritually, she became better able to control her reveries, though she continued to receive stigmata.

Happily, Mary's ecstasies did not interfere with her everyday life. Indeed, she became more decisive and efficient in managing her household, skills that stood her well when Peter was forced to leave Paris in 1590. He was involved in the Catholic League, which opposed the Protestant Huguenot Henry of Navarre (Henry IV), heir to the French throne, and was one of the Committee of Sixteen, which organized the resistance in Paris after Henry had taken other French cities in the War of the Three Henrys. Peter fled as Henry's forces closed in on Paris, but the Spanish intervened on the side of the Catholics, and Paris was saved. In 1593, Henry adjured Protestantism, paving the way for his peaceful entrance into Paris in 1594. Peter returned from exile later that year.

During this time, Mary suffered a riding accident, sustaining a severe fracture that botched surgery made worse rather than better. She remained an invalid for the rest of her life. This did not prevent her from giving freely to the poor and to the hospitals, however. Mary and Peter's house became the central meeting place for French Catholics. Their regular visitors included St. Francis de Sales and a host of other religious and political dignitaries, as well as common people. Mary had a reputation for being in touch with the spirit world, and many were drawn to her because of her supernatural gifts.

In 1601, a biography of St. Teresa of Avila appeared in French translation. A few days later, Teresa's apparition appeared to Mary and informed her that God wished to make use of her to found Discalced Carmelite convents in France. When Teresa appeared a second time, Mary sought advice and help. The visions being judged genuine, an underwriter was found for the first convent, to be erected in Paris's rue St-Jacques. Letters of patent were granted by Henry IV on July 18, 1602. A meeting in which Francis de Sales, among others, took part decided on the foundation of the Reformed Carmel in France on July 27. The bishop of Geneva wrote to Rome to obtain papal authorization, and Clement VIII (r. 1592–1605) granted the bull of institution on November 23, 1603. The Discalced Carmelite order spread rapidly in France after its establishment and profoundly influenced French society of the time.

While continuing to support the Discalced Carmelites, Mary had a hand in bringing two other orders to Paris. When her Jesuit friend, Père Coton, spoke of the Oratorians as "necessary to France," Mary understood what she had to do. She urged the introduction of the Congregation of St. Philip Neri, and on November 11, 1611, had the pleasure of seeing the order formally installed in Paris.

The third order she helped bring to Paris was that of the Ursulines. The French Carmelite convents received applications from many young women believed unsuited to the order. There was at that time no place in Paris where young women could get a good Catholic education, so Mary and a friend brought the would-be Carmelites together as teachers for young girls. They appropriated the Hotel Saint-André, then near Paris, as a high school, bringing in an experienced teacher as director. Mary defrayed the expenses for the building and another benefactor funded a boarding school and a residence for the teachers. The new school was placed under the jurisdiction of Ursulines, who were already established in Marseilles, and was intended to do double duty as a convent for them. On June 13, 1612, Pope Paul V (r. 1605–21) issued a bull raising the Community of Saint-André into a cloistered convent of the Ursuline order.

Peter supported Mary in her various endeavors. When he died in 1613, Mary herself joined the Carmelites as a lay sister. Her three daughters had already become Carmelites and two sons had become priests. Mary began her novitiate at the convent of Amiens, where one of her daughters was subprioress, in 1614, taking the name Mary of the Incarnation. In 1616, by order of her superiors, she moved to Pontoise, where she died a holy death on April 18, 1618. Her relics reside in a chapel in the church there.

The cause of her beatification was introduced at Rome as early as 1627, though it was not approved for another 164 years.

Beatified: June 5, 1791, by Pope Pius VI
Feast: April 30 (in Paris and formerly April 18)
Patronage: against poverty; loss of parents; parents separated from children; widows

Mary MacKillop (1842–1909) *First native Australian to be beatified*
Also known as: Mary of the Cross

Mary Helen MacKillop was born in 1842 in Melbourne to a family of Scottish ancestry. She founded the Sisters of St. Joseph and of the Sacred Heart, dedicated to educating children. She took the name Mary of the Cross in 1873. In 1875 she was elected mother general of her congregation. She had difficulty obtaining papal approval, but finally secured it from Pope Leo XIII (r. 1878–1903) in 1888. By the time of Mary's death on August 8, 1909, there were 1,000 women in the congregation.

Beatified: January 19, 1995, by Pope John Paul II
Feast: August 8

Mary Magdalen (first century)
Also known as: Mary Magdalene, the Penitent, Apostle to the Apostles

Little is known of the life of Mary Magdalen beyond the brief mention in the Gospels of her role in the Crucifixion and its aftermath. "Magdalen" refers to the city of Magdala near Tiberius on the western shore of the Sea of Galilee, presumably Mary's home. Latin Church tradition merged the stories of Mary Magdalen with those of the woman sinner who bathed Jesus' feet with her tears and the accounts of Mary of Bethany, sister of Martha and Lazarus, turning "Mary Magdalen" into the epitome of the penitent sinner who renounced sin for a life in Christ, thereby becoming the symbol of hope for all sinners. Eastern tradition—and St. Ambrose of Milan—taught that these three women were not the same person at all, and there is no Gospel evidence that they were. Although the depictions of Mary Magdalen as a saint encompass these three personalities in one, the Church officially adopted the Eastern position in 1969.

All four Gospels mention Mary Magdalen. The first three—Matthew, Mark and Luke—tell nearly the same story. In fact, the accounts in these three Gospels (called the Synoptics after the Greek *synopikos*, meaning "from the same point of view") are so similar that scholars believe the oldest of them, Mark, tells the story of Mary Magdalen as it was passed down orally to the earliest Christians and then repeated in Matthew and Luke. In all three, Mary Magdalen is one of Jesus'

St. Mary Magdalen in prayer (Library of Congress Prints and Photographs Division)

women followers who observes the Crucifixion from afar and who watches Joseph of Arimathea place the body in the tomb. On Sunday morning, Mary Magdalen and one or more of the other women come to the sepulchre to anoint the body, but instead are met by an angel (two in Luke) who reveals that Christ has risen and that they must run and tell the disciples the good news. In both Mark and Luke the disciples do not believe Mary Magdalen (Mark 15:40–41, 16:1–11; Matthew 27:55–56, 28:1–8; Luke 23:49, 24:1–12). Both Mark and Luke identify Mary Magdalen as one from whom Jesus had cast out seven demons (Mark 16:9; Luke 8:1–3). Luke also describes Mary Magdalen as one of the women who supported Jesus.

The account in John differs in several respects. Instead of placing the women away from the Crucifixion, John states that Jesus' mother Mary, her sister Mary and Mary Magdalen stood by the cross (19:25). On Sunday, Mary Magdalen went alone to the tomb and, finding the stone rolled away and the body gone, ran for Peter and another disciple (probably John) to report this distressing news. The men returned with her and saw the burial linen left inside, but then returned home (20:1–10). Mary Magdalen, however, remained behind, weeping, eventually seeing two angels in white sitting in the tomb. When they asked why she wept, she replied that someone had taken her Lord's body, and she did not know where. Turning around, she saw another man who asked her why she wept. Thinking he might be a gardener, Mary Magdalen asked if he knew where the body had been laid so she could take it. The man said only one word, *Mary*, then she knew she was in her Lord's presence and replied, *Rabboni* (which means "teacher" in Hebrew). Jesus asked her not to embrace him, for he had not yet ascended to the Father, but to tell the disciples what she had seen. She told them she had seen the Lord, and no mention is made of any disbelief on their part (20:11–18).

So although the three earlier Gospels report that Mary Magdalen learned of the Resurrection along with other women, John is the only one to assert that Mary Magdalen was the first to see the risen Christ and tell of the miracle—the great gift that distinguished her as the "apostle to the apostles" (*apostola apostolorum*). It is in this guise that Mary Magdalen is portrayed in the Gnostic manuscript *The Gospel of Mary*, discovered in an Egyptian archaeological dig and published at the end of the 19th century. Mary Magdalen also appears in another Gnostic text, *Pistis Sophia*, owned by the British Museum and published about the same time. Her position as the imparter of *gnosis*—the secret knowledge of redemption to those capable of salvation—also appears in the *Gospel of Philip* and the *Gospel of Thomas*. She was called "Mariam, the woman who knew the All," the "inheritor of the Light," the bringer of *Sophia* or the Wisdom of God, the chief disciple, witness and herald of the New Life.

In the *Gospel of Mary*, the risen Christ appears to his disciples and exhorts them to evangelize throughout the world. But the disciples fear for their lives and do not see how they can follow the Lord's command. Mary Magdalen then becomes the leader, consoling the disciples and assuring them that the Lord is with them, making them "men." Peter acknowledges that Jesus loved Mary Magdalen more than the other women and begs to hear whatever wisdom he imparted to her alone. She tells of a vision in which Christ deems her blessed because she did not waver at the sight of him at the tomb. By stressing perception by the mind, Mary Magdalen represented the Gnostic ideal of individual experience—inner vision—which the established Church considered threatening and heretical. Peter, who had asked for her wisdom, refuses to believe her and cannot accept that Jesus would have given his knowledge to a woman rather than to the male disciples. Matthew reproves him, noting that the Savior found her worthy and loved her more than the others—man or woman.

In the *Gospel of Philip* Mary Magdalen is described as one of the "three who always walked with the Lord: Mary his mother, her sister and Magdalen . . . his companion." The Greek word for "companion," *koinonos*, translates more accurately as "partner" or "consort," a woman with whom a man has had sexual intercourse. In the same text the disciples complain jealously because Christ often kisses Mary Magdalen on the mouth, and they resent her special relationship to him. Unfortunately there is no way to prove either whether Jesus had a sexual relationship with Mary Magdalen or whether the text's author relied on erotic imagery to vividly explain the love of Christ and the Church. There is no supporting evidence for Mary's favored position in the New Testament.

By the time Paul wrote his first letter to the Corinthians, Mary Magdalen's role as the "apostle to the apostles" had changed into her more popular persona as the penitent whore. Although no Gospel identifies the sinner who washed Jesus' feet with her tears (Luke 7:37–39), dried them with her long hair and then anointed them with nard (a very expensive ointment from the Himalayas) as Mary Magdalen, the faithful associated the two. According to some Church authorities she might be the adulterous woman about to be stoned (John 8:3–11) or the Samaritan woman at the well who was living with a man not her husband

(John 4:7–26). If Jesus had cast out seven demons from her she could certainly be a sinner—although demonically inspired sin in the New Testament was not necessarily equated with carnality. Mary Magdalen might also be Mary of Bethany, another Mary who anointed Jesus' feet.

Pope St. Gregory the Great (r. 590–604) officially declared Mary Magdalen, Mary of Bethany and the unnamed sinner one and the same in the sixth century. From the "herald of the New Life" Mary had become the redeemed prostitute, a model of repentance, the embodiment of Eve and the evils of female, predatory sexuality. In an age and Church environment where celibacy and abstention were celebrated, her rejection of fornication served as encouragement for all sinners to return to God.

According to St. Gregory of Tours, after Christ's death and Ascension Mary Magdalen accompanied Mary, the mother of Jesus, and John to Ephesus. Christ had reportedly commended Mary Magdalen to John's keeping; some accounts even say that Mary and John were affianced before John answered Jesus' call. She allegedly died a martyr there, and St. Willibald saw her tomb in the eighth century. Her relics were transferred to Constantinople in 896.

Another tradition says that the Jews put Mary Magdalen, her sister St. Martha and brother St. Lazarus, her maid, SS. Maximin and Sidonius, and the body of St. Anne into a boat without sails or oars and set it adrift. After many days the ship landed at Marseilles, where the holy passengers converted all of Provence. No longer able to cope with life, Mary Magdalen retired to the desert and lived in a cave known as Sainte-Baume for 30 years. Eschewing clothing and food, she covered herself with only her long hair and subsisted on the Eucharist, administered by angels. When she was near death, at age 72, the angels transported her to the Church of St. Maximinus at Aix, thereafter known as St. Maximin, where she received the last rites. Her relics were supposedly moved to Vézelay in 745 to escape the Saracens, then moved back to La Sainte-Baume. Mary Magdalen's head supposedly lies in the grotto of the restored church.

England converted to Christianity under the pontificate of Pope St. Gregory the Great, and there were many churches and convents dedicated to Mary "Mawdleyn" in that country. Mary's common depiction in art as weeping or red-eyed from crying—along with the Old English spelling and pronunciation—led to the word "maudlin," meaning "effusively or tearfully sentimental." Both Magdalen College at Oxford and Magdalene College at Cambridge are pronounced "maudlin."

Feast: July 22

Patronage: contemplative life; contemplatives; glove makers; hairdressers; penitent sinners; penitent women; people ridiculed for their piety; perfumers; reformed prostitutes; against sexual temptation; sinners; tanners

FURTHER READING

Haskins, Susan. *Mary Magdalen: Myth and Metaphor.* New York: Harcourt Brace, 1993.

"Mary Magdalene, First Witness of the Resurrection." URL: http://elvis.rowan.edu/~kilroy/JEK/07/22.html. Downloaded July 11, 2000.

Matthew the Apostle *One of Jesus' Twelve Disciples, author of the first book of the New Testament, martyr*
Name meaning: Gift of God
Also known as: Apostle of Ethiopia; Levi; Matthias of Jerusalem

Matthew was born in Capernaum on Lake Genesareth (the Sea of Galilee), the son of Alphaeus (Alpheus). He was named Levi, or perhaps Levi Matthew, although it is more probable that Jesus conferred the name Matthew on him when he called him to join his apostolate.

At the time of his call, Matthew was working as a Roman tax collector, a job regarded by his fellow Jews as selling out to the enemy. He hosted a feast for Jesus and the other disciples to which he also invited other tax collectors. When this drew criticism from the Pharisees, Jesus replied: "I came not to call only the just, but sinners also."

Apart from his inclusion in the lists of apostles, the Bible contains little further mention of Matthew, although according to St. Peter he was with the group the entire time. He was a witness to the Resurrection, and, after the Ascension, he was selected by lot to replace Judas Iscariot.

Accounts of Matthew's later life are conflicting. Ancient sources agree that he spent some time preaching among the Hebrews, but differ in the amount of time. There is agreement that he later left Palestine, but not as to where he went. By tradition, he evangelized in Ethiopia to the south of the Caspian Sea (not the Ethiopia in Africa), hence his title as the Apostle of Ethiopia. However, he may also have preached in Persia, Macedonia and Syria.

Matthew was the author of the First Gospel of the New Testament, a work intended to convince Jewish readers that their anticipated Messiah had indeed arrived in the person of Jesus Christ. Other writings, now considered apocryphal, are also attributed to him.

There is no certainty about how, when or where Matthew died, but he is widely (though not universally) believed to have been martyred. By tradition, he was tortured before death, though there is no agree-

St. Matthew with an angel (Library of Congress Prints and Photographs Division)

ment about whether he was burned, stoned or beheaded. The places most often given for his martyrdom are Colchis and Jerusalem. The date is sometimes given as ca. 120, but this seems much too late to be accurate. Relics alleged to be his were removed from Colchis by Empress St. Helena and are now venerated at St. Matthias's abbey in Trier, Germany.

In art, Matthew is represented as an elderly apostle or winged man holding or being pierced with an axe (German images), lance (Italian images), halberd, scimitar or sword.

Feast: September 21 (in the West), November 16 (in Greece)

Patronage: accountants; bankers; bookkeepers; customs officers; financial officers; guards; money managers; security forces; security guards; stock brokers; tax collectors

Maximilian Kolbe (1894–1941) *Founder of the Knights of the Immaculata, Franciscan martyr of World War II*

Maximilian Kolbe was born Raymond Kolbe on January 7, 1894, in Zdunska–Wola, then located in Russian Poland, to a poor family. At age 10 he had a vision that changed his life. One day when he was misbehaving, his mother said, "Raymond, what is to become of you?" The boy went to church asking the same question and prayed about it. The Blessed Virgin Mary appeared in a vision and held out two crowns to him. One was white for purity, the other red for martyrdom. She asked him which would he choose, and he answered, "I choose both."

Raymond attended a trade school and entered secondary school in 1907. He had a special love for the sciences, and even designed a rocket ship and applied for a patent on it. When the Conventual Franciscans opened a minor seminary, both he and his brother, Leopoli, applied. Raymond took the habit on September 4, 1910, and adopted the name Máximilian.

He endured inner trials and was sent to Rome to study. He earned a doctorate in philosophy and later a doctorate in theology. He saw indifference as the most deadly poison, and in 1917 founded an order, the Knights of the Immaculata, to counteract it. Members dedicated themselves to Mary Immaculate and pledged to work for the salvation of souls, particularly among the enemies of the Church, through prayer and apostolic work. The order was made a Primary Union by Pope Pius XI (r. 1922–39) in 1926.

Maximilian contracted tuberculosis in 1920, and his health was severely weakened for the rest of his life. He spent two years in a sanatorium. For the remainder of the 1920s and into the 1930s, Maximilian worked to build his order, and even went to Japan. He was recalled to Poland in 1939 to head the provincial chapter, the City of the Immaculata.

World War II brought attacks by the Nazis. Maximilian was arrested by the Gestapo in 1939, then released. He was arrested again in 1941 and jailed in Warsaw. On May 28, 1941, Maximilian was among about 320 prisoners who were transported to the Auschwitz concentration camp.

His openness as a Catholic priest brought him severe treatment. He was regularly beaten, attacked by dogs, given the worst job details and made to carry corpses. Once he was beaten and left for dead; his fellow prisoners carried him back to camp, where he recovered. His chronic lung inflammation required him to spend time in the infirmary. Throughout the brutalities, Maximilian maintained a positive outlook and was a source of strength to many prisoners. He heard confessions, gave conditional absolution to the dead and counseled people. He always made himself last for any medical treatment.

In July 1941, a prisoner escaped. Camp rules were that if a missing prisoner was not caught and returned, 10 people in the cell block would be killed in reprisal. The commandant went through the ranks selecting the 10 victims at random. One was a Polish soldier, Sergeant Francis Gajowniczek, who cried out in distress, "What will happen to my family?" Immediately Maximilian stepped forward and volunteered himself as a replacement. The commandant accepted.

The 10 men were herded into a starvation cell, stripped of their clothing and left to die. They received no food or water. One by one they died; some were kicked to death by the guards. Maximilian led the survivors in prayer and hymns, reminding them that their souls could not be killed.

After two weeks four men remained, including Maximilian. The impatient commandant wanted the cell for more victims, and so he ordered the four executed by injection of lethal carbolic acid. When his turn came, Maximilian calmly raised his arm to the executioner. He died on August 14, 1941, and was cremated the following day.

The Knights of the Immaculata have spread around the world. The order is now known as the Militia of the Immaculata.

Beatified: October 17, 1971, by Pope Paul VI
Canonized: October 10, 1982, by Pope John Paul II
Feast: August 14

FURTHER READING
Mary, Francis. *The Hero of Auschwitz.* Kenosha, Wis.: Prow Books, 1970.

Maximus of Constantinople (ca. 580–662) *Abbot, mystic and Father of the Church*
Also known as: the Theologian; Maximus the Confessor

Maximus was born in Constantinople to a noble family around 580. He served as the first secretary to Emperor Heraclius, but left the post and went to the monastery at Chrysopolis near Constantinople. He studied a time with St. Sophronius. He defended Pope Honorius (r. 625–638) in a controversy over Monothelitism, but then was charged with treason at the Lateran Council convened in 649 by Pope St. Martin I (r. 649–655). Maximus was exiled for six years to Perberis (Perbera).

In 662 he was recalled to Constantinople with two companions, both named Anastasius. They were anathematized along with SS. Martin and Sophronius. They were beaten, had their tongues cut out and their right hands cut off. They were then sent into perpetual exile and imprisonment. Maximus died in 662 after having a vision foretelling his death. Tradition holds that miraculous lights appeared every night at his tomb.

Maximus is considered one of the leading theologians of the Greek Church, particularly for his work on the union of God with humanity in the Incarnation. He wrote more than 90 theological, mystical and dogmatic works. His leading mystical works are *Mystagogia,* which explains ecclesiastical symbolism; *Scholia,* an examination of the work of Pseudo-Dionysius; and *Ambigua,* on St. Gregory of Nazianzus.

Feast: August 13 (in the West); January 21 and August 12 and 13 (in the East)

Mechtilde (ca. 1240–1298) *Benedictine nun, mystic and mentor of St. Gertrude the Great*
Also known as: Mechtilde of Helfta

Little is known about Mechtilde's life. She was born in Helfta, Saxony, to a noble family; according to some accounts she was a countess and cousin of the emperor. At age seven she was placed in a Benedictine convent at Rodalsdorf. She was an excellent student and learned to write fluidly in Latin. In 1261, she took charge of the five-year-old Gertrude and became her confidante and mentor.

Gertrude recorded Mechtilde's revelations and ecstasies in the *Liber Specialis Gratiae* (Book of special grace) of St. Mechtilde, and *Legatus Divinae Pietatis* (Herald of divine love), the story of Gertrude's life.

Mechtilde received the heart of Jesus. When she asked Him how to greet Mary, He told her to hail Mary's "virginal heart." Mary appeared numerous times to the saint, including one time when she revealed her heart inscribed with letters of gold, "Hail Mary, full of grace! The Lord is with thee!"

Mechtilde died on November 19, 1298, with Gertrude in attendance. As she lay dying, she prayed earnestly to Mary for the nuns of her convent. Mary and Jesus are said to have appeared to her, and Jesus placed about her neck a necklace of sparkling gems.

Feast: November 19

Meinrad (d. 861) *Benedictine hermit and martyr*
Also known as: Meginratus

Meinrad was born in Solgen, Swabia, to the Hohenzollern nobility. He entered the Benedictine order and went to teach at a small monastery in Bollingen near Zurich. He had a special devotion to the Blessed Virgin Mary. He decided he wished to become a hermit, and received permission to do so in 828. He moved to a hut in the Dark Wood on the slopes of Mt. Etzel. According to legend, he adopted and tamed two ravens (by some accounts, crows). For seven years, he lived there and attracted many pilgrims.

The crowds became too much, and so Meinrad went deeper into the woods. He found a spring and built a hut and a chapel, in which he placed a cherished statue of Mary. He would pray there, joined by his two ravens. He was again discovered, and pilgrims made their way to him.

On January 21, 861, while Meinrad was saying Mass for the feast of St. Agnes, he received a divine revelation that this was to be his last Mass. He had no sooner finished than two strangers appeared. They had heard about the crowds of pilgrims and had come looking for jewels and valuables to steal.

Meinrad welcomed them and set out food and wine for them. When they discovered no treasures, the men clubbed Meinrad to death while the ravens attacked them in vain. They dragged his body to the bed of leaves in his hut. Two candles mysteriously lit by themselves, and a wonderful smell permeated the hut. Terrified, the murderers fled to Zurich. The ravens followed relentlessly, screeching until at last the murderers were apprehended and confessed. According to lore, the birds hovered over the scaffolding when the men were hanged.

Meinrad's remains were taken to the abbey of Reichenau near Constance, but were returned to the site of his hut in 1039.

The abbey of Einsiedeln was built at the spot where Meinrad built his hut and chapel, and remains a popular pilgrimage site. In 948, St. Conrad had a remarkable vision there.

Canonized: 1039 by Pope Benedict IX
Feast: January 21

Melito (d. ca. 180) *Bishop of Sardis, Father of the Church*

Few facts are known about the life of Melito. He was regarded in his day as one of the leading authorities in the Eastern Church. St. Eusebius praised him, Tertullian wrote favorably of him and St. Jerome noted that he was a highly respected prophet. Melito taught the dual nature of Jesus. He became bishop of Sardis, died there and was buried there.

Almost all of Melito's works have been lost. Eusebius gave accounts of most of them, along with some extracts. Best known is his *An Apology for the Christian Faith* written for Emperor Marcus Aurelius.

Feast: April 1

Methodius of Olympus (d. ca. 311) *Bishop, ecclesiastical author, martyr and Father of the Church*

Methodius's was bishop of Olympus in Lycia. Educated in philosophy, he gained stature as a theologian and writer. He was the first to mount a formidable attack on Origen. Methodius died a martyr in Tyre during the Diocletian persecution.

Methodius was a prolific author. In *On the Resurrection* he refuted Origen's argument that the resurrection body was not the same as the physical body during life. *Symposium on Virginity* is a dialogue extolling Christian virginity.

Feast: June 14

Michael the Archangel *The most prominent and greatest angel in Christian, Hebrew and Islamic lore*
Name meaning: "Who is like God" or "who is as God" in Hebrew.

Michael is warrior, protector, healer and guardian. He holds numerous offices in heaven: He is chief of the virtues and archangels, a prince of the presence, prince of the seraphim, and the angel of repentance, righteousness, mercy and salvation. Some of his roles overlap with those of the two other great archangels of Christianity—Gabriel and Raphael.

Michael is mentioned by name in Daniel, Jude and Revelation. In Daniel, he is the guardian angel of the people of God [Israel]. In 10:13, Michael is named and described as "one of the chief princes," and in 10:21, "one having the appearance of a man" tells Daniel "there is none who contends by my side except Michael, your prince." In Daniel 12:1, the prophecy of "the time of the end" states that "At that time shall arise Michael, the great prince who has charge of your people. And there shall be a time of trouble, such as never has been since there was a nation till that time; but at that time your people shall be delivered, every one whose name shall be found written in the book." (This is a reference to the Israelites' departure from Egypt, led by Moses and guided by a pillar of cloud during the day and a pillar of fire at night [Exodus 33ff]. In Exodus 23:20, God promises to send His angel before them. Though Michael is not named here, it is widely interpreted that he is that angel.)

In Jude 9, the archangel Michael contends with Satan over the body of Moses (according to Jewish lore, Satan wishes to reveal the tomb of the prophet in order to seduce the Israelites into the sin of idolatry; Michael, obeying God, concealed the tomb).

In Revelation 12:7–12, Michael and his legions battle Satan and his forces in heaven, and Satan is thrown down.

Numerous other biblical references to "the angel of Yahweh" and "the angel of the Lord" are interpreted as meaning Michael. Besides Exodus, another example is found in Zechariah 3:1–2, which tells of an angel of the Lord who confronts Satan before God and the high priest Joshua.

In Catholic devotion, there is no greater angel than Michael; the Catholic Church refers to him as "Prince of the heavenly hosts." Churches were built and dedicated to him from the fifth century on. So intense was adoration of Michael that many devotional cults sprang up all over Europe, peaking in popularity in the late Middle Ages. Devotion to Michael (as well as to Gabriel and Raphael) is still encouraged by the Catholic Church through devotional cults, prayer and Mass.

Michael wages ceaseless war against the forces of Satan. He is the special defender of Christians (and particularly Catholics) and the Church. Satan trembles at the mere mention of his name, and all the angels of heaven bow down before him in obedience. Michael inspires fidelity to God. St. Francis de Sales wrote that veneration of Michael is the greatest remedy against despising the rights of God, insubordination, skepticism and infidelity.

At Mass, Michael presides over the worship and adoration to the Most High, and sends to God the prayers of the faithful, symbolized by the smoke from incense. The prayer to St. Michael asking him to defend Christians in battle is a condensed form of the general exorcism against Satan and evil spirits composed by Pope Leo XIII (r. 1878–1903).

One of his important duties is as psychopomp to the dead, guiding the souls of the newly departed to the afterlife. In this capacity, he resembles the Greek/Roman god Hermes/Mercury and the Egyptian god Thoth. Michael weighs the souls for righteousness. He is associated with benevolent aspects of the Angel of Death and has the ability to shapeshift when he comes to take a soul away. Michael was the angel designated to appear to Mary to announce her death.

In Catholicism, Michael guards the gates of purgatory and has pity on the souls therein. Legends tell of prayers made to Michael for souls in purgatory; he appears and takes them into heaven.

Michael shares with Raphael special healing duties, a function naturally associated with him as protector of the general welfare. Catholic tradition holds that Michael caused a medicinal spring to appear at Chairotopa near Colossae; anyone who bathed there and invoked the Blessed Trinity and Michael was said to be cured. Michael also dreamed a healing spring from a rock at Colossae. Pagans attempted to destroy it by directing a stream against it, but Michael split the rock

St. Michael vanquishing the serpent (Library of Congress Prints and Photographs Division)

with lightning, giving a new bed to the stream, and sanctifying the waters forever.

Michael was considered the great heavenly physician at Constantinople, and is credited with banishing a pestilence in Rome during the days of Pope St. Gregory I (r. 590–604).

There have been numerous apparitions of Michael reported over the centuries, usually on or near mountaintops. One of the most famous sites is the Michaelion church near Constantinople, erected in the fourth century by Emperor Constantine the Great. At the command of Mary, Queen of the Angels, Michael came to the aid of Constantine in his battle against Emperor Maxentius. Constantine built the church for Michael in gratitude. After its completion, Michael appeared there to the emperor and said, "I am Michael, the chief of the angelic legions of the Lord of hosts, the protector of the Christian religion, who while you were battling against godless tyrants, placed the weapons in your hands." Miracles attributed to Michael have been reported at the Michaelion over the centuries.

Another famous apparition of Michael appeared to the bishop of Siponto on Mount Gargano in Apulia, near Naples, Italy, during the reign of Pope St. Gelasius (r. 492–496). A shrine erected in the cave of the apparition attracted hordes of pilgrims. In the seventh century, the shrine was at a peak of popularity, due in part to a Lombard victory over the Saracens in 663 that was attributed to the help of Michael. According to lore, the Lombards, who went to the shrine to pay thanks for their victory, found the imprint of Michael's foot near the south door of the temple.

In 495 in Cornwall, England, fishermen saw Michael standing on a ledge of rock atop a small mount off the coast near Mousehole. St. Michael's Mount, as it became known, was already an important trading market and port, and took on new significance with its association with Michael, and became a hallowed place. In the sixth century it was visited by St. Cadoc, one of the principal saints of Wales. According to legend, the saint needed water for his traveling party, and struck his staff into the rock, whereupon water sprang forth.

A Benedictine priory was built atop St. Michael's Mount in 1135 by Bernard Le Bec. The community was enriched by the earls of Cornwall. But on September 11, 1275, an earthquake destroyed the church. It was rebuilt in the 14th century. Between 1349 and 1362, the religious community was nearly wiped out by the Black Plague. In 1649, the property passed into private hands, the St. Aubyn family.

From the Middle Ages, St. Michael's Mount was a favorite pilgrimage. Pilgrims came to seek answers to prayer, discharge vows, do penance and seek healing. Many were spurred by the incentive that all those who came to St. Michael's Mount with alms and oblations would receive an indulgence of one-third of their penance. The indulgence was credited to Pope Gregory VII (r. 1073–85), though probably it was a tradition started by the monks and over time believed to be true.

A goal of many pilgrims was to prove their faith by sitting on "St. Michael's chair," a craggy spot with a precipitous drop to the sea. Monks built a stone lantern chair atop the church tower, to serve not only as a lighthouse but also perhaps as a more suitable substitute for the unsafe outcropping. According to lore, if a married couple visit, the first one to sit on the chair will gain mastery in their married life.

Pilgrims also were attracted to the jawbone relic of St. Apollonia, a martyr and patron against toothaches.

Many miracles of healing were reported at St. Michael's Mount and credited to the intercession of Michael.

Today the former priory is a private residence, much of it open to public tours. The church is active and is free from episcopal jurisdiction. A stone pillar marks the spot where Michael appeared. When the tide is low, St. Michael's Mount can be accessed on foot across a sandbar.

In France, a similar but grander Benedictine abbey was built on Mont St. Michel, a rock off the Normandy coast. In 708, Michael appeared three times in visions to St. Aubert, Bishop of Avranches, and instructed him to build a sanctuary there. The abbey was founded in 966 by Richard I, duke of Normandy. Construction of the church began in 1023 and was finished in 1136. By the 12th century, Mont St. Michel was called the "City of Books" and was a great center of learning. Many of the manuscripts kept by the monks were lost during the French Revolution when the monks were expelled.

Between 1155 and 1424, Mont St. Michel had jurisdiction over St. Michael's Mount in Cornwall.

In Spain, where the cult of Michael peaked in popularity in about the 13th century, one of the best-known apparitions is the 1455 appearance to a shepherd about halfway between Navagamella and Fresnedillas, in the foothills of the Sierra de Guadarrama. The sighting was investigated in 1520, when some of the witnesses were still alive, and also in 1617.

According to testimony, Michael appeared late one afternoon in 1455 on a holm-oak tree and a rockrose plant to shepherd Miguel Sanchez. Michael told the shepherd not to be frightened, but to tell others that a shrine should be erected on the site and a brotherhood founded, both in honor of angels. Sanchez protested that no one would believe him, but Michael insisted that he tell his employer. "I will make them believe you so they build a shrine here to the holy angels," he said. He then made an imprint of his hand on the tree.

However, Sanchez did not tell the story. A few days passed, and one morning he awakened crippled. His legs were folded in a bizarre manner, so that the backs of his calves touched his thighs and his heels touched his buttocks. His employer, Pedro Garcia de Ayuso, tried unsuccessfully to cure him with herbs and oils. At last Sanchez told of his vision. Garcia de Ayuso consulted with authorities, and they carried the shepherd to the site of the apparition. There they found the handprint on the tree trunk. It was considered proof, and plans were made immediately for construction of a chapel. A Mass was said there for the shepherd's health; when it was completed, he was cured and he stood up. Sanchez was named keeper of the shrine.

Today Michael is revered by millions who pray to him for intercession. He is particularly considered the champion of justice and righteousness. In Christian art, Michael is usually portrayed in warrior garb, holding a sword and scales and trampling Satan.

Feast: May 8, which commemorates the dedication of a basilica in honor of him on the Salarian Way about six miles outside of Rome, and September 29, known as Michaelmas

Patronage: Brussels, Belgium; grocers; mariners; paratroopers; police; sickness

FURTHER READING

Christian, William C., Jr. *Apparitions in Late Medieval and Renaissance Spain.* Princeton: Princeton University Press, 1981.

Guiley, Rosemary Ellen. *The Encyclopedia of Angels.* New York: Facts On File, 1996.

Steiner, Rudolph. *The Archangel Michael: His Mission and Ours.* Hudson, N.Y.: Anthroposophic Press, 1994.

Michael of Ecuador (Miguel de Ecuador) (1854–1910) *Teacher and De LaSalle Brother*

Also known as: Michael Cordero, Francisco Febles Cordero Muñoz, Miguel Febres Cordero, Miguel of Ecuador

Michael of Ecuador was born in Cuenca, Ecuador, on November 7, 1854, and baptized with the name Francisco Febles Cordero Muñoz. His was a well-to-do and influential family. His grandfather, León Febles (or Febres) Cordero, was a general who had fought in Ecuador's war of independence from Spain. His father, Francisco Febles Cordero Montoya, was a cultured man who was teaching English and French at a seminary in Cuenca at the time of Francisco's birth. His mother, Ana Muñoz, was one of 19 children, five of whom became nuns and one a Jesuit priest.

Francisco (who took the name Michael when he joined a religious order at 14) was born with a deformity of the feet that made him unable to walk until he was five. His first steps, in fact, are said to be due to a miracle. One day he happened to see a rose blooming in the garden of his house. He commented to his family on the beautiful woman above the flowers, saying that she was wearing a white dress with a blue cloak and was calling his name. The others could see nothing out of the ordinary, and they were astonished when he proceeded to get up and walk. From his childhood he had other visions of the Virgin Mary and of Jesus, with whom he conversed on a regular basis. However, he was never able to walk well, a factor contributing to his becoming a man of letters.

When the De LaSalle Brothers arrived in Ecuador in 1863 and set up a seminary, Francisco enrolled. He was attracted to the way of life and decided to join the order, though his parents objected to his plans to become a lay brother rather than a priest, since the economic status of brothers was so much lower. They placed him in the seminary where his father taught instead, but within a few months he became seriously ill and had to return home. His mother finally agreed to let him become a lay brother. On March 24, 1868, Francisco took the habit of the De LaSalle Brothers and changed his name to Michael.

Following in his father's footsteps, Brother Michael taught languages (Spanish, French and English) at the seminary in Cuenca and a year later was assigned to the Beaterio at Quito. There he specialized in preparing children for their First Communion, a job he loved and performed for the next 26 years.

Michael's talents as an educator were recognized with his appointment as a public examiner and inspector of Quito's schools. He also was a prodigious writer, producing his first book—a textbook—at the age of 17. Besides textbooks, he produced works of Christian spirituality, a catechism, poetry, and linguistic studies of Castilian Spanish. The latter were adopted as required texts for all schools in Ecuador. In 1892, Michael was elected to the National Academy of Ecuador (which included membership in the Royal Academy of Spain); in 1900, to the Académie Française; and in 1906, to the Academy of Venezuela.

In 1888 Michael traveled to Rome to attend the beatification ceremony of the founder of his order, John Baptist de la Salle. In March 1907, he was called to Europe again, this time to help translate religious documents from French into Spanish. The civil unrest in France during this period made it imperative that these works be translated in order to ensure the continuation of the order's work outside that country. He was in Spain in July 1909, when problems broke out in Barcelona. There were attacks on Church property, placing emotional stress on all the Brothers. A few months later Michael caught a cold that progressed to pneumonia, and he died on February 9, 1910.

Miracles credited to Michael's intercession began to be reported immediately after his death, and he became the center of a cult, especially strong in Spanish-speaking countries. During the Spanish Civil War, his body was returned to Ecuador, arriving there on February 4, 1937. His new tomb in Quito soon became a pilgrimage shrine. The Ecuadorian government issued postage stamps bearing his likeness and erected a bronze and marble monument to him in Quito's central park. Upon the statue's dedication in June 1965, there was a huge parade, in which 30,000 school children participated.

Beatified: October 30, 1977, by Pope Paul VI
Canonized: April 7 or October 21, 1984, by Pope John Paul II
Feast: February 9 or June 2
Patronage: Ecuador

FURTHER READING
"Beato Hermano Miguel." Santos y Beatos de America Latina: Ecuador. URL: http://www.aciprensa.com/santecua.htm. Downloaded: November 12, 1999.
"San Miguel Febres Cordero." Church Forum Santoral. URL: http://www.churchforum.org.mx/santoral. Downloaded: November 12, 1999.

Miguel Agustin Pro, Blessed (1891–1927) *Jesuit priest; martyr*

Also known as: Miguel Agustin Pro Juarez

St. Miguel Pro

Miguel Pro was born at Guadalupe, Zacatecas, Mexico, on January 13, 1891. His father was a mining engineer and Miguel retained a special affinity for the working class all his life. From childhood he had a notably cheerful personality, though he displayed little interest in religion. When two of his brothers entered the priesthood, however, Miguel began to consider such a career for himself.

In August 1911, at age 20, he entered a Jesuit seminary. However, the Mexican Revolution, which had begun the year before, turned out to be a time of persecution for the Church, and in 1914 the rector decided to evacuate all members of the community from the country. The brothers dispersed, Miguel going to study and teach in the United States, Spain and finally Belgium, where he was ordained on August 31, 1925. Soon thereafter he began to be afflicted by a severe stomach problem and when several operations failed to return him to health, his superiors allowed him to return to Mexico to recuperate.

A few days after his arrival in Mexico City in 1926, Catholicism was officially suppressed, and Miguel was forced to don disguises and to conduct his ministry in secret. It was not long before he was arrested. He was released with a warning, but far from stifling him, the experience spurred him to greater efforts. He traveled throughout Mexico City on a bicycle, conducting communions and baptisms, hearing confessions, administering last rites, performing marriages and distributing food to the poor. In November 1927, he was arrested again, along with his brothers, and accused of plotting against President Plutarco Calles. Their execution by firing squad was ordered without trial.

On November 23, Miguel was the first of the three to leave the prison. He asked to be allowed to pray one last time. He was put on his feet and extended his arms so that his body formed a cross. As he was shot, he cried out, "Long live Christ the King!" echoing the cry of earlier Mexican martyrs of this period.

Thinking that he could use the occasion to celebrate the cowardliness of Mexican Catholics, Calles had invited the press to attend. The pictures of Miguel's heroic death had the opposite effect. Although the government prohibited a public funeral, thousands of the faithful lined the streets to see his body carried to its resting place.

> *Beatified:* September 26, 1988, by Pope John Paul II in Mexico City
> *Feast:* November 23

FURTHER READING

"Beato Miguel Pro, sacerdote." website. Aci Digital website. Santos y Beatos de America Latina: Mexico. URL: http://www.aciprensa.com/Maria/migpro.htm. Downloaded: October 30, 1999.

Ball, Ann. *Blessed Miguel Pro: 20th Century Mexican Martyr.* Rockford, Ill.: TAN Books and Publishers, 1996.

Miltiades (d. 314) *Pope*
Also known as: Melchiades

The Roman see was vacant for some time after the banishment of Pope St. Eusebius, probably due to the ongoing controversy over whether Christians who had lapsed under persecutions should be allowed to return to the Church without doing penitence. Miltiades, a Roman priest of African descent, was elevated to the papacy on July 2, 311.

In October 312, Emperor Maxentius was defeated by Constantine the Great, who had experienced a vision that told him he would conquer in the sign of the Christ. Although he was not to accept baptism until his deathbed, Constantine thereafter supported the Christians in any way he could. In 313, he signed the Edict of Milan with Emperors Galerius and Licinius, putting an end to the persecution of Christians in the Roman Empire. He gave Miltiades the right to receive back all buildings and possessions that had been confiscated during the persecutions, and granted to the Church tracts of land in and around Rome on which to build new houses of worship. Either to Miltiades or to his successor, Pope St. Sylvester I, he also gave the Lateran Palace, which then became the pope's residence and the seat of the central administration of the Roman Church.

Miltiades died on January 10 or 11, 314, and was buried in the Catacomb of St. Callistus, afterward being venerated as a saint.

Feast: December 10 (January 10 in fourth century)

Monica (332–387) *Mother of St. Augustine of Hippo*
Name meaning: Advise

Monica was born in Tagaste, Africa. By her family's arrangement, she married Patricius, a violent-tempered but generous pagan official. The marriage was made even more difficult by his mother, who lived with the couple.

Monica had three children: Augustine, Navigius and Perpetua. She succeeded in converting her husband and his mother to the Catholic faith; Patricius died a year later in 370. Perpetua and Navigius entered the religious life. Augustine, however, lived a dissolute life, causing Monica to pray fervently for him for 17 years. She begged the prayers of priests, some of whom tried to avoid her because of her persistence. Her dream was realized in 387, when Augustine was baptized a Christian by St. Ambrose in Italy. Later that same year, en route back to Africa, Monica died in the Italian port of Ostia. Her relics are in the church of St. Augustine in Rome.

Monica is considered a model for Christian mothers.

Feast: August 27
Patronage: alcoholics; housewives; against infidelity; married women; mothers

Moses the Black (b. ca. 332–d. ca. 407) *Former slave and robber turned desert hermit and martyr*
Also known as: Moses the Ethiopian

Moses the Black was born around 332 in Nubia. He became enslaved to a government official in Egypt, who dismissed him for theft and suspected murder. He became the leader of a gang of outlaws that roamed around the Nile Valley, terrorizing people. Moses was large, imposing, ferocious and strong, and became notorious for his crimes. When local authorities pursued him, he hid among monks at the Petra monastery in Skete, in the western desert near Alexandria. The monks had a positive influence on him. Over the course of time, he gave up his life of crime and became a monk himself.

Moses was a zealous perfectionist and became a prophetic spiritual leader. Some credit him with establishing the paschal fast that developed in the fourth century and later became the Lenten fast. According to lore, the abbot ordered all the monks to fast during a particular week. When some brothers came to visit Moses, he cooked a meal for them. But when other monks confronted Moses about breaking the commandment, they told him that though he had not kept the commandment of men, he had kept the commandment of God.

Another story told of Moses concerns a brother who committed a fault. A council was convened to judge the brother; Moses was invited but he refused to attend. He was summoned, and so went to the meeting carrying a leaking jug filled with water (or, by other accounts, a basket of sand with a hole in it). Asked for the meaning of this, Moses said, "My sins run out behind me and I do not see them, but today I am coming to judge the errors of another." Shamed, the council forgave the brother.

Moses was ordained a priest by Theophilus of Alexandria, which was uncommon at that time for desert monks. He became the spiritual leader of a colony of hermits near Skete.

Around 407, when Moses was about 75 years old, the colony learned that a group of Bedouins planned to attack them. Moses forbade the brothers to defend themselves, telling them to retreat rather than to fight. All but seven monks and Moses left the colony. When the Bedouins arrived, they were welcomed by the hermits, but turned on them and murdered them.

Moses was buried at Dair al-Baramus, the Monastery of the Romans, in the Valley of Natron. His relics are now in the Church of Al Adra (the Virgin). He is regarded as the apostle of nonviolence. His wisdom is included in the *Sayings of the Fathers*, a collection of wisdom of the desert monks.

Feast: August 28

FURTHER READING
"Life of St. Moses the Black." URL: htt://www.premontre.org/SubPages/Loci/ZZZLocalSites/LSJackson/StMosesBio.htm. Downloaded: February 6, 2000.

Neot (d. 877) *Monk of Glastonbury, England*

Neot was revered especially in Cornwall, where his name is preserved in the town of St. Neot (pronounced Need). Several accounts of the life of Neot exist, dating from the 12th to 19th centuries. The conflicting information in them has led some historians to think that there may have been two Neots, one Cornish and another Saxon. This, however, cannot be proved from existing records.

Perhaps the most consistent and reliable accounts come from Latin versions dating to the 12th century. Even these accounts likely contain the fictions attributed to many saints, in terms of their virtues and holy deeds.

Neot was said to have been born in East England, and was a scion of the royal house of East Anglia. Drawn to religion early in life, he became a monk at Glastonbury and was a model of behavior. Visited often by angels, he was informed by them not to hide his light under a bushel but to preach God's word far and wide. Neot did as instructed, and became famous; people flocked to him. He was then instructed by a heavenly oracle (probably an angel) to go elsewhere to practice a life of virtue. He became a hermit on the Bodmin Moor, where the town of St. Neot is now. A well is dedicated to him.

The well supplied Neot with fish every day. Three fish always swam in it. God instructed Neot to take one fish a day for his food. He would express his gratitude by standing in the well waters with naked limbs reciting the Psalter.

One day Neot felt sick and could eat nothing at all. His alarmed companion and servant caught two fishes (one account says three fishes) and cooked them in different ways. Neot was so upset that he jumped up from his sickbed, threw the dishes into the well and prayed until three fishes again swam in the well.

For seven years Neot lived as a hermit, and then went to Rome, where he visited the tombs of SS. Peter and Paul. He was honored by an unnamed pope. He returned to Cornwall, where he continued his devotional life and healed many people. He was visited often by angels.

King Alfred the Great (r. 871–899) heard of Neot's fame and sought him out for his blessing. Neot rebuked him for his wickedness. In one or perhaps two dreams, Neot appeared to the king and prophesied correctly that Alfred would have much travail and would even temporarily lose his kingdom. He also said that he himself would soon die, and God would then bless the king.

Neot soon fell ill. According to legend, he died while praying and preaching to his flock. Great multitudes attended his funeral, where many were healed of sickness. His body was buried in the church, which became filled with sweet smells of flowers and spices.

Those who breathed in these odors were healed. Dust from his tomb was taken to be swallowed for the healing of humans and animals alike. His remains were removed to a shrine north of the altar.

Neot appeared to the custodian and asked for his relics to be removed to an unnamed resting place. This the custodian did, which upset the townspeople. When men tried to take Neot's body back to the church, it could not be moved. An unnamed English king ordered the relics to be left where they were. There are conflicting accounts as to whether relics remained in St. Neot, or were taken elsewhere, perhaps to St. Ives.

Neot's date of death is 877; some place it nearer to 880. One hundred years later, his relics were taken from Cornwall and sent to the monastery founded by the Saxon Leofric at Eynesbury, near St. Ives, Cambridgeshire.

Stories associated with Neot appear in the lore of other Celtic saints of the area. Similar stories of magic fishes are told about SS. Corentin and Petroc. Neot also is said to have saved a doe from hunters (a story also told about Petroc) and had his plough pulled by stags (a story told about St. Kea).

The 16th-century church of St. Neot has preserved the story of its patron saint in its stained-glass windows.

Feast: July 31; in Cornwall, the last Sunday in July
Patronage: St. Neot, Cornwall

FURTHER READING
Doble, Gilbert H. *The Saints of Cornwall:* Part Six, *Saints of North Cornwall.* Felinfach, Cornwall, England: Llanerch Publishers, 1997.

Nicholas (d. ca. 345–352) *Bishop of Myra; identified with Santa Claus*
Also known as: Nicholas of Myra, Nicholas of Bari

The only certainty about Nicholas's life is that he lived in the fourth century and was bishop of Myra in Lycia. Legends grew up around him, making him one of the most popular saints in both Western and Eastern churches. Tradition holds that he was born in Parara, Asia Minor, and went to Egypt and Palestine on pilgrimages when young. After he became bishop of Myra, he was jailed during the Diocletian persecutions, and was released after Constantine the Great became emperor in 324. Nicholas died sometime between 345 and 352 and was buried in Myra. Saracens took Myra in 1034, and several Italian cities competed for securing the saint's relics. On May 9, 1087, they were translated to Bari and enshrined. Immediately many miracles of healing were reported.

St. Nicholas of Myra (Library of Congress Prints and Photographs Division)

While still in Myra, Nicholas's bones were discovered to exude an oil or manna. According to an anonymous 13th-century account of the translation to Bari, a considerable quantity of this oil was found with the relics. The oil has been observed to exude from the pores of the bone and to collect and drip. It is collected in ampules.

The oil has stopped four times: in 887, when a legitimate successor to Nicholas was expelled from office; in 1086, the year before the relics were moved; from 1916 to 1917, during World War I; and from

1953 to 1957, when the basilica was being restored. It started again when the relics were restored to the basilica, then stopped and then resumed on April 10, 1961.

The oil has been examined scientifically, and has been determined not to come from water or humidity.

Nicholas became the progenitor of Santa Claus, perhaps from the legend about his generosity in gift-giving. Tradition holds that he secretly provided the dowries of three young women by throwing bags of gold through their father's open window (another version says that he saved three young women from prostitution by throwing bags of gold through their windows). Much later, Nicholas became identified with Father Christmas and Santa Claus. Gift-giving on his feast day, December 6, is still a tradition is some countries.

Feast: December 6
Patronage: bakers; boys; brewers; brides; children; coopers; dockworkers; mariners; merchants; pawnbrokers; spinsters; travelers; Greece; Russia; Naples; Sicily; Lorraine, France; the diocese of Liege; Campen, Netherlands; Corfu, Greece; Freiburg, Switzerland; Moscow, Russia; and many other cities in Italy, Germany, Austria and Belgium

FURTHER READING
Anonymous. *The Translation of St. Nicholas.* Tr. J. M. McGinley and H. Mursurillo. URL: http://www.fordham.edu/halsall/basis/nicholas-bari.html. Downloaded: September 10, 2000.

Nicholas I (ca. 820–867) *Pope*
Also known as: Nicholas the Great

Nicholas is one of three popes to be honored with the appellation "the Great" (the others are St. Leo I [r. 440–461] and St. Gregory I [r. 590–604]). A tireless defender of Christian morality, he insisted upon the supremacy of the Church over the state. His personal life was guided by a spirit of earnest Christian asceticism and profound piety.

Nicholas was born between 819 and 822 to Roman Defensor Theodore. He joined the priesthood of the Roman Church in his youth, was made subdeacon by Pope Sergius II (r. 844–847) and deacon by Pope St. Leo IV (r. 847–855). He was a trusted adviser of Pope Benedict III (r. 855–858).

At Benedict's death on April 7, 858, the Frankish emperor Louis II, who was then near Rome, came into the city, hoping to influence the election of a successor. On April 22, Nicholas was elected and enthroned in St. Peter's basilica, with the emperor in the audience.

Nicholas's elevation came at a time of turmoil in Western Europe, both within and without the Church. Charlemagne's Holy Roman Empire lay in ruins, and Christian lands were threatened from both the north and east. Ecclesiastical discipline, meanwhile, had largely broken down. Nicholas issued letters and decisions against bishops who were negligent in their duties. He was especially active in regard to the Church's marriage laws. When the wife of Count Boso left her husband for a lover, Nicholas commanded her bishops to excommunicate her unless she returned to her husband. When the woman ignored the summons to appear before the Synod of Milan in 860, the sentence was carried out. Nicholas also forced Charles the Bald to accept the marriage of his daughter Judith to Baldwin of Flanders, made without his consent, and compelled the Frankish bishops to withdraw the excommunication they had imposed on her.

Nicholas ran into trouble, however, when he opposed King Lothair II of Lorraine, who had left his wife Theutberga for another woman. In April 862, the bishops of Lorraine at the Synod of Aachen approved of the new union. Then in June 863, at the Synod of Metz, papal legates were bribed by Lothair to assent to the Aachen decision. This was enough for Nicholas, who brought the matter before his own council at the Lateran Palace that October. He condemned Lothair's new marriage and deposed two of the bishops who had approved it. Lothair then advanced on Rome with his army and held the city under siege, so that the pope was confined in St. Peter's for two days without food. Nicholas and Lothair eventually reconciled, and Lothair withdrew; although Nicholas never ceased trying to bring about a reconciliation between Lothair and Theutberga, he never succeeded.

Nicholas not only endeavored to enforce the Church's teachings, he sought to spread them through missionary work as well. He sent St. Anskar as a missionary to Scandinavia and when, in August 863, Prince Boris of Bulgaria—who had been converted to Christianity by Greek missionaries—sent him a delegation carrying 106 questions on the teaching and discipline of the Roman Church, Nicholas took the time to answer them exhaustively in a now-celebrated document, the "Responsa Nicolai ad consulta Bulgarorum." His return delegation was instructed to do what they could to win over Boris. Nevertheless, in the end he joined the Eastern Church.

This could not have pleased Nicholas, since he was also involved throughout his pontificate in a controversy with the Greek emperor Michael III over his illegal deposition of Patriarch Ignatius of Constantinople and the appointment of Photius in his place. In 863, Nicholas excommunicated Michael, and Photius excommunicated Nicholas. The matter was resolved only when the newly crowned emperor Basil I expelled Photius on November 13, 867, the day Nicholas died.

Feast: November 13

Nicholas II and Companions (d. 1918) *Last czar of Russia and his family*
Also known as: Imperial Martyrs of Holy Russia, Royal Russian Martyrs

Nicholas II was the last ruler of the Russian royal family of the Romanovs. He was born on May 6, 1868, in Tsarskoye Selo, near St. Petersburg, Russia. As the eldest son of Czar Alexander III, he was next in line for the throne. He received a military education from a private tutor but had little interest in ruling and was unprepared for it when his father's sudden death on November 1, 1894, thrust it upon him. At the time, he was engaged to Alix of Hesse, a minor German princess descended from the British royal family. The two were married on November 26, 1894. Alix converted to Russian Orthodoxy and changed her name to Alexandra. Nicholas was crowned czar in Moscow on May 26, 1896.

Nicholas's lack of preparation for the throne showed itself on the day of his coronation. The ceremony was a lavish affair, accompanied by a huge celebration for the Russian peasants in a field outside the city. Gift baskets and beer were given to all attendees. Suddenly, a rumor that there were not enough gifts and beer for everyone rushed through the crowd. They stampeded, and thousands were trampled to death. Nicholas's first inclination was to visit the hospital with Alexandra, but he allowed himself to be swayed by his uncles, who advised against it because Alexandra and he were expected to host a ball at the palace. His apparent callousness earned him the nickname "Bloody Nicholas."

Nicholas's reign was marred by a series of other missteps. In 1905, believing that a successful war would boost the sagging Russian morale, he went to war with Japan over a disputed piece of land in Manchuria. Unfortunately, not only did Russia lose the war, it was also dealt a humiliating blow with the loss of its entire Eastern Fleet. Also in 1905 came the Bloody Sunday massacre, so called because peasants bringing Nicholas petitions about conditions in St. Petersburg were fired upon by palace guards. Although Nicholas had not ordered the shootings, the outcry afterward forced him to concede to the formation of a parliament (duma), an important step in the decline of the Russian monarchy.

Yet another disastrous turn came in the person of Rasputin, a self-proclaimed psychic from Siberia who arrived in St. Petersburg in 1903. Rasputin's claim to be able to heal the czarevitch Alexis from hemophilia endeared him to Alexandra and he came to play a major role in running the government. Whatever his powers may have been, Rasputin was a drunkard and a womanizer and the Russian people came to distrust his influence. He finally was killed by a member of the royal family in December 1916. By this time, World War I was in progress, and so was the downfall of Nicholas. The war brought with it shortages, which led to strikes in St. Petersburg. Dissatisfaction with his leadership mounted, and Nicholas was forced to abdicate in favor of his brother Michael on March 2, 1917.

When the Bolsheviks came to power that October, they killed Grand Duke Michael. Then in 1918, Nicholas and his family, who had been exiled to Siberia, were arrested and transported to Ekaterinburg, a town in the Ural Mountains. It was there, in Ipatiev House, sometimes called the House of Special Purposes, that Nicholas and his family were murdered by firing squad on the night of July 16/17, 1918. Their bodies were dumped into a mine shaft, then, as word spread, they were burned or doused with sulfuric acid, transported into the woods outside town and buried in a shallow grave.

The burial place remained unknown until 1979, when it was discovered by two local men. Fearing official reaction, they continued to keep the secret for

Czar Nicholas II and wife, Alexandra (Library of Congress Prints and Photographs Division)

another decade, until changing political conditions made it possible for them to reveal it. The bodies were exhumed in 1991. DNA testing subsequently determined that they represented a family group, with 99 percent certainty that of Nicholas. The father was related to several Romanovs, while the mother was related to the British royal family. However, not all of Nicholas and Alexandra's children were accounted for. Their son, the czarevitch Alexei, was missing, as was one of their daughters, either Maria or Anastasia. This finding helped fuel speculation that the two children had escaped, though their fate is not known. DNA tests of a woman who claimed to be Anastasia found her more likely to have been a Polish factory worker.

In July 1998, following a three-hour farewell ceremony in the Church of the Ascension in Ekaterinburg, across the street from the former site of Ipatiev House, the bodies were transported to St. Petersburg. On July 16, they were buried in a chapel in the Cathedral of Peter and Paul, where most of the Romanov lineage were interred. The reburial was intended by the state to be an atonement for the sins of the past. The Russian Orthodox Church, however, regarded it as sacrilege, since, as sacred relics, the remains should be buried separately. The patriarch refused to participate in the reburial ceremony and held a separate service at the Church of the Holy Trinity at St. Sergius Monastery, 80 kilometers northeast of Moscow.

The reburial came just at a time when the Church was glorifying (canonizing) Nicholas and his family. The Russian Orthodox Church Abroad, which had split from the Russian Orthodox Church in Russia in 1927 and was composed of strongly anti-Soviet émigrés, held them to be martyrs, arguing that they defended the faith against communism. The Church Abroad glorified Nicholas and his family in 1981, and made their glorification by the Church in Russia a precondition of reunification. The Church in Russia took up the problem in 1992 and considered it for five years before concluding that Nicholas II was not qualified for sainthood based on the way he had lived and ruled. Nor was he strictly speaking a martyr, because a martyr is one who dies upholding his faith, and the question had never been put to him. However, he and his family could justifiably be glorified as passion bearers, a special category of Orthodox sainthood applied to those who were not strictly martyrs yet nevertheless might be revered for the humble ways in which they met their deaths. Russia's first saints, Boris and Gleb, had been glorified as passion bearers in 1015.

The Church looked upon Nicholas as a divinely anointed ruler. Anointing was a practice traced back to the time of Moses, and Nicholas was regarded as the last of an unbroken line of Russian sovereigns to have been anointed since the Russian conversion to Christianity. Nicholas himself appears to have accepted his religious position, because during his coronation, he took Communion directly from the chalice, a right reserved for the clergy. Although he abdicated, this was spiritually ineffective, it was argued, because a divinely ordained position cannot be resigned.

Whatever the position of their church, the Russian people had long regarded Nicholas as a saint. Even during the Soviet era, his photograph might be seen in homes alongside icons. Bright lights and church music were reported in the basement of Ipatiev House, before it was demolished in 1977. A cross was set up on the site on October 5, 1990. As it was erected, dark clouds moved in and snow began to fall, but then the clouds suddenly parted, allowing a ray of light to fall directly on the cross. The light then circumscribed a circle around the cross, and in this area no snow fell for the next 40 minutes, while the installation was completed.

Canonized: November 1, 1981 (by the Russian Orthodox Church Abroad); August 20, 2000 (by the Russian Orthodox Church in Russia)
Feast: July 17

FURTHER READING

Massie, Robert K. *Nicholas and Alexandra.* New York: Atheneum, 1967.

"Report of the Holy Synod Commission on the Canonization of Saints with Respect to the Martyrdom of the Royal Family." Holy Trinity Cathedral website. URL: http://www.holy-trinity.org/feasts/nicholas.html. Downloaded: September 14, 2000.

Serfes, Father Demetrios. "Recent Miracle of the Myrrh-Streaming Icon of Tsar-Martyr Nicholas II." Royal Martyrs of Russia website. URL: http://www.fr-d-serfes.org/royal/newmiracle.htm. Downloaded: September 14, 2000.

———. "The Holy Canonization of the Royal Martyrs Tsar Nicholas II and Family of Russia on August 20, 2000." Royal Martyrs of Russia website. URL: http://www.fr-d-serfes.org/royal/Holycanonization.htm. Downloaded: September 14, 2000.

Nicholas of Flüe (1417–1487) *Extraordinary hermit and civic leader in Switzerland*
Name meaning: Victory of the people
Also known as: Brother Klaus

Nicholas of Flüe was born on March 21, 1417, to a peasant farmer family near Sachseln, Canton Obwalden, Switzerland. He took his surname from the River Flueli nearby. As a boy, Nicholas was drawn to a life of self-denial and prayer, yet knew he was not destined to become a monk or priest.

He married Dorothy Wissling and had 10 children. The Flüe family prospered, and Nicholas was widely respected. He served as a soldier and was elected to public office. He was magistrate and counselor, but declined several times to serve as governor.

In 1465 he had a vision in which he was visited by Three Strangers who told him he would die at age 70 and to persevere in his devotion to God until then. Nicholas felt that the strangers were representatives of the Blessed Trinity, and he had been summoned to devote the remainder of his life to God. For two years, he spent much time in meditation on the passion of Christ.

More visions confirmed his conviction, and Nicholas informed his wife that he would leave the family, which by then was able to support itself. On October 16, 1467, Nicholas left home as a pilgrim wearing only a robe, with no hat or shoes, and carrying no money. He took only a staff and a rosary, and set out toward Alsace. A vision convinced him to remain close to home, and he went into the woods to pray and fast and live as a hermit.

Nicholas became known as Brother Klaus and "the living saint." He was revered by many and had frequent visitors. He was called upon to help settle political disputes; he played an instrumental role in preventing civil war in 1481.

According to legend Nicholas did not eat, but subsisted only on the holy Eucharist. This mystical fast lasted for 20 years. His neighbors built him a hut and a chapel, the latter of which he dedicated to the Virgin Mother of God, his special patron. Mary appeared often to him and conversed with him.

Nicholas left his hermitage only once a year, to participate in the procession of the Feast of the Annunciation in Lucerne.

Toward the end of his life, he had a glorious vision in which he was in a castle with people dressed in white robes. The Holy Trinity each personally thanked him for his love and devotion, and for teaching others to love and serve God.

Nicholas died on his 70th birthday, March 21, 1487. His beatification and canonization were championed by SS. Charles Borromeo, Peter Canisius and Robert Bellarmine.

Many credit the intercession of Nicholas with helping to keep Switzerland out of World Wars I and II. In 1917, the celebration of the 500th anniversary of his birth inspired people anew with his messages of peace and love. In 1940, when Hitler's forces threatened to invade the country, hundreds of people saw a great hand in the sky protecting the land.

Beatified: 1669 by Pope Clement IX
Canonized: 1947 by Pope Pius XII

Feast: March 21
Patronage: Switzerland

Nicholas of Tolentino (ca. 1246–1306) *Augustinian preacher, miracle-worker, Patron of the Holy Souls*

Nicholas of Tolentino was born in Sant' Angelo near Fermo, Italy, around 1246 to pious parents of small means. He entered the Augustinian order in his hometown, where he distinguished himself for his devotion and piety. He was ordained in 1271 at Cinguli and spent four years in various houses of the order. He then was assigned to the monastery at Tolentino, where he spent the rest of his life.

Nicholas preached, spent many hours in the confessional and aided the poor and sick. He quickly gained a reputation as a miracle-worker, for which he gave all credit to God. His followers believed him to have great intercessory powers for the souls in purgatory; after his death he was proclaimed "Patron of the Holy Souls."

St. Nicholas of Tolentino

Once while suffering a prolonged illness, Nicholas was urged by his superiors to eat more food. One night the Blessed Virgin Mary appeared to him in a vision and told him to take a small piece of bread, dip it in water and eat it. She promised that he would then be cured by his obedience. Nicholas did as instructed and was cured immediately. He then began the practice of blessing pieces of bread and giving them to the sick. Many miracle cures were reported. This evolved into the custom of "St. Nicholas Breads" after his death, in which blessed pieces of bread were given out at his shrine.

In 1305 Nicholas became ill and never recovered. He died on September 10, 1306, and was buried beneath the Cappellone, a chapel next to the church. Forty years later, his body was found to be incorrupt in its wooden urn and was exposed to the faithful in an exhibition. Someone—believed to be a German monk, Teodoro—attempted to sever the saint's arms and take them away. When the arms were detached, they bled profusely, and the monk was arrested.

One hundred years later, the detached arms were found to be incorrupt, but the rest of the body had decomposed. The arms were placed in silver cases and the rest of the remains were reburied. The arms were seen to bleed 20 times throughout the years; the most significant episode occurred in 1699 when the arms bled continuously from May 29 to September 1.

Nicholas's bones mysteriously disappeared in the mid-15th century and were not found until 1926, when they were discovered buried deep beneath the Cappellone.

The Chapel of the Holy Arms, built in the 16th century, contains relics of Nicholas's blood, including a silver chalice holding a quantity of blood, and a silver urn holding blood-stained linen said to be the cloth used at the amputation of the arms.

Nicholas's remains were placed in a crypt built between 1926 and 1932. An artificial figure wearing an Augustinian habit bears his silvered skull and incorrupt arms, still in their silver casings. The reliquary was personally blessed by Pope Pius XI (r. 1922–39).

In 1969 Nicholas's cult was confined to local calendars.

Canonized: 1446 by Pope Eugene IV
Feast: September 10

Nicodemus (d. first century) *Defender of Jesus*

Nicodemus is mentioned in the Gospel of John as a Pharisee and member of the ruling Sanhedrin. In John 7:50–51, he advocates giving Jesus a fair hearing while others seek to immediately condemn him. In John

St. Nicodemus, left, with Jesus

19:39 he attends to the burial of Jesus' body with Joseph of Arimathea, providing about 100 pounds of myrrh and aloes. Nicodemus is mentioned in apocryphal writings, including the *Acts of Pilate.*

Feast: August 3

Nilus (d. ca. 430) *Bishop, scholar, author and Father of the Church*
Also known as: Nilus the Elder

Nilus was among the leading ascetic writers of his day. He was married and had two sons, and worked as an officer in the court of Constantinople. He was a Praetorian prefect. Nilus was drawn to St. John Chrysostom and became one of his fervent admirers and disciples.

Around 404, Nilus left his wife and one son and took the second son, Theodolus, to Mount Sinai, where they became monks. Invading Saracens from the desert took Theodolus prisoner and sold him as a slave. He eventually was taken in by the bishop of Eleusa in Palestine. Nilus found him, and both were ordained priests by the bishop. Nilus is believed to have died around 430.

Nilus authored numerous works on virtues and vices, the monastic life and maxims for his disciples. He also wrote numerous letters, of which 1,061 survive.

Feast: November 12

Nonna (d. 374) *Wife of St. Gregory of Nazianzus*

Nonna was a Christian and converted her husband. They had three children: two sons, Caesarius and Gregory of Nazianzus the Younger, and a daughter, Gorgonia. All three became saints.

Feast: August 5

North American Martyrs (d. 1642–1649) *A group of seven French-born Jesuits who were missionaries to the Huron, Mohawk and Tobacco Indians in what is now upstate New York*
Also known as: Isaac Jogues and Companions

The Jesuits were killed by the Mohawk, bitter enemies of the Huron and Tobacco, between 1642 and 1649, making them the first Catholic martyrs in North America. The Mohawk, one of the five nations of the Iroquois (there are now six nations), all but succeeded in driving the Huron and Tobacco to extinction, and the Jesuit missions were closed shortly after the last martyr died.

There is a shrine to the North American Martyrs in Auriesville, New York, in the diocese of Albany. It is on the site of the death of the first three martyrs and the birthplace (in 1656) of the Blessed Kateri Tekakwitha, the "Lily of the Mohawks." The shrine is also a center of devotion to the Virgin Mary, for it was here that the first recorded recitation of the rosary in what is now New York State took place, on September 29, 1642. The shrine was initiated on August 15, 1885, as a wooden cross and a tiny chapel, but operated only that one day. It was re-created in 1985 as a pilgrimage center on 600 acres of land, with buildings and facilities capable of serving thousands of people.

In the order of their deaths, the martyrs are:

René Goupil (1606–1642). Also known as: Renatus Goupil. Born at Anjou, France, René was a successful surgeon when, in 1638, he went to Quebec, Canada, to work at the Jesuit mission hospital. In 1640 he became a lay assistant to the Huron mission. In 1642, while on a journey with Isaac Jogues, he was captured by a group of

Mohawk. He was tomahawked to death on September 29 at Ossernenon (now Auriesville) for making the sign of the cross on the brows of some children.

Isaac Jogues (1607–1646). Isaac was born at Orléans, France, on January 1, 1607. He studied at the Jesuit school in Orléans, joined the order at Rouen in 1624, and continued his education at La Flèche, where he was ordained in 1636. He asked to be sent as a missionary to Quebec, from where he set out to minister to the Huron. He was captured by the Mohawk along with René Goupil and endured 13 months of slavery during which he was tortured so severely that he lost the use of both hands. (He was given a special dispensation by Pope Urban VIII [r. 1623–44] to continue to say Mass despite this deformity.) Dutch Calvinists from Fort Orange (now Albany, New York) eventually helped him escape and he went back to France. However, in 1644 he returned to Quebec. In the three years since his captivity, a peace treaty had been signed with the Iroquois federation, and Isaac and John de Lalande undertook a mission to the Mohawk. On their second visit, they left behind a box of religious objects. When an epidemic of disease swept the people and crops failed shortly after their departure, the Jesuits were blamed, and on their third visit, they were killed. Isaac died on October 18, 1646.

John de Lalande (Jean de Lalande) (d. 1646). Born at Dieppe, France, John was a lay assistant to the Jesuit missionaries in Quebec. In 1646, he accompanied Isaac Jogues on his trips to the Mohawk, and was taken captive along with him in October. He was killed on October 19, the day after Isaac. Their heads were impaled on the settlement palisades and their bodies thrown into the Mohawk River.

Antony Daniel (1601–1648). Born at Dieppe, France, on March 27, 1601, Antony studied law, but gave up his career to join the Jesuits at Rouen in 1621. He was ordained in 1630, and in 1632 was sent as a missionary to Cape Breton Island, Acadia, New France (now Canada). The following year he went to Quebec, from which he launched expeditions to the Huron. In 1636, he founded a school for Native American boys in Quebec. Antony was killed by a party of Mohawk at the Huron village of Teanustaye (near Hillsdale, Ontario) on July 4, 1648.

John de Brébeuf (Jean de Brébeuf) (1593–1649). Born at Condé-sur-Vire, Normandy, France, on March

25, 1593, John attended the university in Caen and worked on his parents' farm before joining the Jesuits at Rouen in 1617. He was ordained in 1622, and in 1625 asked to be sent to Quebec as a missionary. For the next 24 years he worked with the Huron, founding schools and producing a catechism in Huron and a dictionary of the language. Responsible for some 7,000 conversions, he was captured by Mohawk warriors on March 16, 1649. Following the Iroquois practice with captives, he was cruelly tortured for hours, mutilated, burned to death and finally eaten.

Gabriel Lalement (1610–1649). Born in Paris, Gabriel joined the Jesuits in 1630. He taught at Moulins for three years, and after further study at Bourges, was ordained in 1638. After teaching at La Flèche and Moulins, he was sent to Canada at his request in 1646 as a missionary. He, too, worked among the Hurons, became assistant to John de Brébeuf at Saint Ignace in 1649, and was with him in the village when the Iroquois attacked and destroyed it on March 16, killing all the inhabitants except the two priests. After torturing them, the Iroquois tomahawked them to death the next day.

Charles Garnier (1606–1649). Charles was born in Paris in 1606, son of the treasurer of Normandy. After studying at the Jesuit Louis-le-Grand College in Clermont, he joined the order in 1624 and was ordained in 1635. He asked to go to Quebec, from which he was sent to the Hurons. When the neighboring Tobacco asked for a mission in 1646, he began to work with them, and was in one of their villages when the Mohawk attacked on December 7, 1649. Charles ran about giving absolutions and baptisms until he was killed by a hatchet blow. Some of his Indian converts buried him on the spot where the church had stood.

Noël Chabanel (1613–1649). Born near Mende, France, on February 2, 1613, Noël joined the Jesuit order in 1630. In 1643 he was sent to the Quebec mission, and from there to the Hurons. He joined Charles Garnier in establishing a mission to the Tobacco. Noel was visiting another village when Charles was killed. He himself was murdered by a Huron apostate on December 8, 1649, the day after Charles's death.

The cultus of the North American Martyrs was extended universally in 1969 as the protomartyrs of North America.

Canonized: June 29, 1930, by Pope Pius XI
Feast: October 19 (formerly March 16)
Patronage: Americas

FURTHER READING
National Shrine of the North American Martyrs website. URL: http://klink.net/~jesuit/auries.html. Downloaded: December 2, 1999.

Olaf of Norway (995–1030) *Martyred king and patron saint of Norway*
Also known as: Olaf Haraldsson; Olav

The son of King Harold Grenske, Olaf joined a band of Vikings as a youth and fought battles for Richard of Normandy and Ethelred II of England. He was baptized a Christian. At age 20, he succeeded his father on the throne, and set about converting his kingdom, more by force than persuasion.

Olaf's subjects revolted, and he was forced from the throne by Canute the Great, the king of England and Denmark. Olaf tried to regain his kingdom. On July 29, 1030, he was killed in a battle at Stiklestad, Norway. He was buried in deep sand on the spot where he fell, on a bank of the river Nid. A spring miraculously appeared there, and miracles were reported at the shrine built over his tomb. Although he was not considered much of a holy man because of his use of force against his own subjects, he nevertheless was respected for his championing of Norwegian independence and he was regarded as having died for his faith. The miracles enhanced his stature as a martyr. The cathedral of Trondheim was built over his shrine, and was a popular pilgrimage site during the Middle Ages.

Canonized: 1164 by Pope Alexander II
Patronage: Norway

Optatus of Milevis (d. 387) *Bishop of Milevis, Father of the Church*

Little is known about Optatus, though it appears he was raised a pagan and was a late convert to Christianity. He survived fourth-century persecutions and rose in the Church to become bishop of Milevis, Numidia (now Algeria), in North Africa. In a series of six treatises, he defended the orthodox doctrine of the Church in its battle with the Donatist heresy.

Optatus died about 387. Although there is no sign that he ever received a cultus, and early martyrologies and calendars do not mention him, his name was later inserted in the Roman Martyrology under June 4.

In art, Optatus is depicted as an early Christian bishop trampling heretics.

Feast: June 4

Oswald (d. 642) *Martyred king of Northumbria*

The story of Oswald is related by the Venerable Bede. He was the son of King Aethelfrith, who took the throne in 592 and was murdered in 617. Oswald was forced by his enemies to flee to Scotland, where he converted to Christianity and was baptized. In 633 he returned to Northumbria and took the throne after his uncle, King St. Edwin, was killed in battle. Oswald engaged the British king Caedwalla in battle in 635, defeating him. According to Bede, Oswald saw a vision of St. Columba prior to battle, and also carried with him a wooden cross.

Oswald strove to convert people, and enlisted the help of St. Aidan to do so, giving him the island of Lindisfarne. During his reign, he helped the poor and was popular with his subjects. He built churches and monasteries.

On August 5, 642, Oswald was killed in battle at Maserfield as he fought the forces of the pagan king Penda of Mercia. His niece, Queen Osthrida of the Mercians, had his bones taken by wagon to the monastery in Lindsey, where she wished them to be buried. But the monks there were reluctant to take them, since the king had been from another province. The bones were left out at night with a tent over them while the issue was discussed. During the night, a pillar of light was seen reaching from the wagon to the heavens. It was taken as a sign that the monks were meant to accept the relics, which they did.

Oswald's skull is preserved in St. Cuthbert's coffin in Durham. During the Middle Ages, he was widely revered as a martyr.

In art Oswald is shown with a raven holding a ring in its beak.

Feast: August 5

Pachomius (ca. 290–346) *Egyptian Copt and a founder of communal (cenobitic) monasticism*

Pachomius was the first monk to organize hermits into groups and compose a rule for them, thus preceding St. Anthony, who is regarded as the founder of monasticism.

He was born about 290 near Thebes, Egypt, and was inducted into the Roman legions at age 20. In 313 he was discharged from the military and converted to Christianity. After being baptized, he became a disciple of a famous hermit, Palemon, and took the habit. The two of them led a life of extreme austerity and total dedication to God. They combined manual labor with unceasing prayer both day and night.

Pachomius was praying alone in the desert of Tabenna when an angelic figure spoke to him and told him to found a monastery according to the rule the angel would give. In 318, Palemon helped him to build what would become the first Christian cloister on the banks of the Nile at Tabennisi. Palemon stayed himself for a while. A wall surrounded the humble structure as a symbol of the monks' separation from the world, and no stranger was allowed beyond a certain point, leaving "the inner sanctum" unsullied. Soon some 100 monks joined Pachomius, and he organized them on principles of community living.

Pachomius's "Angelic Rule," one of the major monuments of early Christian literature, was innovative in one major fact: It was a binding commandment, akin to a law. After living as a novice for a number of years, each monk accepted the rule as an unalterable canon of life.

Pachomius established 10 other monasteries for men and two nunneries for women. By the time of his death in 346, there were 7,000 monks in his houses. His order lasted in the East until the 11th century.

SS. Basil and Benedict drew from his Rule in composing their own more famous ones. Pachomius is venerated in the Western, Eastern and Coptic Churches.

Feast: May 9 or May 14

Pacianus of Barcelona (d. ca. 390) *Bishop of Barcelona, Father of the Church*
Also known as: Pacian

The date and place of birth of Pacianus are unknown. He married and had a son, Dexter, who became high chamberlain to Emperor Theodosius, and in 365 (or perhaps 373) he was elected bishop of Barcelona, Spain. He was renowned for his eloquence and learning and wrote much about ecclesiastical discipline; his *Exhortation on Penance* is considered a classic. In a letter on the Novatian heresy, he made the famous statement, "My name is Christian, my surname is Catholic."

Pacianus died in Barcelona around 390.

Feast: March 9

Padre Pio, Blessed (1887–1968) *Capuchin friar, stigmatist, miracle-worker*

Padre Pio was born Francesco Forgione on May 25, 1887, in Pietrelcina, southern Italy. He was named after St. Francis of Assisi. His father was a farmer, and from an early age the boy worked in the fields. Drawn to the priesthood, he became a Capuchin novice at age 16 in Morcone and took the habit in 1902 or 1903, becoming known as Padre Pio. Despite bad health that required him to convalesce in his hometown—he had tuberculosis—he was ordained on August 10, 1910. Due to his poor health, he was ordered to remain in Pietrelcina and spend short visits in the monastery. From 1915 to 1916 he was called into the army, but was eventually sent home because of his health. He

St. Padre Pio after receiving the stigmata

went to the monastery of San Giovanni Rotondo, where he stayed for the rest of his life.

On September 7, 1910, Padre Pio experienced bloodless, half-inch wounds appearing in the middle of his hands. They remained after several days and then disappeared after prayer. The wounds appeared intermittently for the next eight years.

On August 5, 1918, he experienced a transverberation, or mystical wounding, during a vision. He was hearing the confession of a boy when suddenly an angel appeared in his intellectual (interior) vision holding a long, sharp-pointed steel blade that spewed fire. The angel hurled the blade into his soul with all its might. So intense was the pain that Padre Pio thought he was dying. He felt as though his internal organs had ruptured. He remained in agony until morning. From then on he felt he had been mortally wounded in the depths of his soul, and the wound remained open and caused him continual agony. His experience was similar to the transverberation of St. Teresa of Avila, who perceived an angel pierce her heart with a flaming arrow.

On September 20, 1918, Padre Pio was kneeling in front of a large crucifix in the church when he received the stigmata. He was the first priest in the history of the Church to receive the five wounds of Christ. Doctors examined him but could find no natural causes. His tuberculosis disappeared at this time.

Padre Pio had the stigmata throughout his life. The wounds bled constantly and the blood was sweetly perfumed with the scent of roses and violets. He was unable to close his hands because of the wounds, and was required to wear gloves at all times except during Mass. He wore special shoes to cover the wounds on his feet. Padre Pio's stigmata lasted the longest on record. Other stigmatists experienced their wounds on certain days, or for certain durations. He accurately predicted that upon his death the wounds would completely heal.

The stigmata ignited Padre Pio's popularity and people flocked to see him. In 1923 the Church silenced him. He was forbidden to write letters and to preach, but could say Mass and hear confessions. The silencing failed to dampen public ardor, and appointments for confessions had to be made far in advance.

On January 9, 1940, he established the Home for the Relief of Suffering, which finally was dedicated on May 5, 1956. With donations he created a hospital open to anyone who appealed for assistance and love in the name of Christ.

Padre Pio died on January 23, 1968. He was considered a saint long before he died. Thousands came to pay their respects, and more than 100,000 people attended his burial on September 26. Tradition holds that he gave off a sweet fragrance as he was placed in his tomb.

Padre Pio had the gift of many miraculous abilities and acts, which attracted to him many devotees. His prophecies were accurate. He was known to bilocate on numerous occasions. The first time occurred on January 18, 1905, when he was a divinity student at San' Elia a Piansisi. Around 11 P.M. he was in the choir, when suddenly he found himself in a distant wealthy home where the father was dying while a child was being born. The Blessed Virgin Mary appeared to him and said she was entrusting the child to him. He was not to worry about how he would care for her, but he would meet her at St. Peter's in Rome. During this experience, the wife of the dying man looked up and saw Padre Pio, dressed in his Capuchin habit. He turned and left the room, and was nowhere to be found. The woman went into labor and gave birth to a daughter shortly before her husband died. Seventeen years later, Padre Pio heard the daughter's confession at St. Peter's, and then simply disappeared from the confessional. She then found him at San Giovanni Rotondo, and became a devoted disciple of his.

Many of his bilocations were to perform miraculous healing, in response to the numerous prayers made to him for his intercession. He apparently bilocated all over the world.

He often experienced supernatural fevers that could not be explained except as the product of the divine fire of love. The fevers always broke naturally and he suffered no ill effects from them.

Padre Pio had a constant and close relationship with his guardian angel. He believed that God used the angel to make it possible for him to understand foreign languages he had not learned, and to have clairvoyant knowledge of secrets within the heart (especially useful to him during confessions). Padre Pio would tell people, whenever they were in need of his prayer, to address his guardian angel through their guardian angels. Once a busload of pilgrims, en route to San Giovanni Rotondo, got caught at night in a violent lightning storm in the Apennine Mountains. They followed his advice, and weathered the storm unscathed. When they arrived the next day, and before they could tell their story, Pio announced that he had been awakened by his guardian angel during the night, and had prayed for them.

Beatified: May 2, 1999, by Pope John Paul II

FURTHER READING

Allegri, Renzo. *Padre Pio. Man of Hope.* Ann Arbor, Mich.: Servant Publications, 1999.

Carty, Rev. Charles Mortimer. *Padre Pio the Stigmatist.* Rockford, Ill.: TAN Books and Publishers, 1973.

Ruffin, C. Bernard. *Padre Pio: The True Story.* Huntington, Ind.: Our Sunday Visitor, 1995.

Pamphilus of Caesarea (d. 309) *Father of the Church, martyr*

Pamphilus was born in Berytus (now Beirut, Lebanon) to a noble family. He studied at Alexandria before selling his property and giving the proceeds to the poor. Going to Caesarea, he took over and built up the library founded by Origen. In Caesarea, also, he was ordained a priest and established a theology school. He made faithful copies of the Holy Scriptures and of the works of Origen (which had not yet been declared anathema). His home became famous as a place where domestic servants and slaves were treated as sons and brothers.

The Diocletian persecution began in 303, and the deacon and 10 other members of Pamphilus's church were martyred. Then, in November 307, Pamphilus himself was taken before the governor and when he refused to make pagan sacrifices, was cruelly tortured and imprisoned. While in prison, he continued copying and correcting manuscripts. At this time also he collaborated with Eusebius on the five-volume *Apology for Origen.* He was put to death in February 309.

In art, Pamphilus is usually dressed in a philosopher's gown and holds a book. Sometimes he is shown holding a razor, sword or knife.

Feast: June 1

Pancras (d. ca. 304) *Roman martyr popular in England*
Also known as: Pancritas, Pancratius

Church historians know little about the 14-year-old orphan boy who was martyred with SS. Nereus, Achilleus and Domitilla. His uncle brought him to Rome, where he apparently joined the Praetorian Guard, the elite soldiers who guarded the emperor, or at least was connected to a guard member, perhaps Nereus or Achilleus. When Emperor Domitian discovered that his grandniece, Flavia Domitilla, was Christian, she, her family and any servants who were Christian were banished to the island of Ponza. Nereus, Achilleus and Pancras were part of that group.

Under the reign of Emperor Trajan, Domitilla and her guards were taken to the island of Terracina. Nereus and Achilleus had been ordered to kill Domitilla, but moved by her faith they converted instead and refused to carry out the emperor's orders. All four were beheaded and their bodies placed in the Domitilla family vault in Rome. Pope St. Siricius (r. 384–399) built a church over the cemetery vault in 390.

Although Pancras was the least known of the four, Pope St. Vitalian (r. 657–672) sent the young martyr's relics to England so that England would have holy relics for the establishment of churches and be better able to promote evangelization. The relics were presented to the king of Northumberland.

Pope St. Gregory I (r. 590–604) honored Pancras along with the other three in a homily delivered at the church in St. Domitilla Cemetery when he claimed, "These saints despised the world and trampled it under their feet." More important, St. Augustine of Canterbury—Pope Gregory's emissary to England and founder of the see at Canterbury—dedicated the first church in England to Pancras. A district in London was later named after him as well.

Pope Leo III (r. 795–816) built a new church to the four saints' honor in 800, which was rebuilt by Cardinal Baronius in the 16th century. In 1874, the underground tomb at the location of Siricius's original church was discovered. It was empty.

Feast: May 12 (with Nereus, Achilleus and Domitilla)

Patronage: children; cramps; against false witness and perjury; headaches; oaths; treaties

Paschal I (d. 824) *Pope*

The date of Paschal's birth is not known. His father was a Roman named Bonosus. He entered the priesthood while still a youth and studied at the Lateran Palace. Pope St. Leo III (r. 795–816) appointed him abbot of St. Stephen's monastery, where he oversaw pilgrims to Rome.

When Pope Stephen V (r. 816–817) died on January 24 or 25, 817, Paschal was elected to succeed him. He was consecrated and enthroned the following day, an apparent attempt to bypass confirmation by the Frankish emperors of the Holy Roman Empire. Paschal justified this action to Louis I the Pious by saying that he had not sought the office but accepted it as an unwanted task. In return, Louis declared papal elections to be free of the requirement of imperial approval and in general recognized papal sovereignty.

When Lothair I, Louis's son, married, Paschal sent a special delegation bearing rich gifts. In the spring of 823, Lothair went to Rome, and on April 5 Paschal crowned him emperor. Lothair did not share his father's position on papal sovereignty, however, nor did all in the Roman Church agree with Paschal. After Lothair left Rome, two papal officers opposed to Paschal were found blinded and beheaded. Paschal was accused of ordering the murders, which had been carried out by two members of his household. Although he denied any complicity, he refused to surrender the murderers, declaring that the dead men were traitors to the Church and that secular authorities had no jurisdiction in the matter. The upshot was the Constitution of Lothair, which instituted severe restrictions on papal jurisdiction and powers.

During Paschal's pontificate, Iconoclasm—the Islamic-inspired movement that forbade the worship of images—raged in the Byzantine Empire to the east. Paschal did what he could to uphold the position of the Roman Church. He sent his aides to try to secure the release of Abbot Theodore of Studites, who had been imprisoned for defending sacred icons. He received several Greek monks fleeing the persecutions and found places for them in newly erected monasteries such as those of St. Praxedis, St. Cecilia, and SS. Sergius and Bacchus, near the Lateran Palace. He also erected new churches and chapels and had the relics of martyrs translated from the ancient catacombs to these places.

Paschal was not a popular pope. He was so unpopular, indeed, that when he died in 824, throngs prevented his funeral procession from entering St. Peter's. His relics were interred instead in the church of St. Praxedis.

Feast: February 11 (formerly May 14)

Patrick (ca. 389–461) *Archbishop of Armagh, Apostle of Ireland, one of the three patron saints of Ireland (with Brigid and Columba) and patron saint of Nigeria*
Name meaning: warlike (Succat), noble (Patricius)
Also known as: Maewyn Succat, Magonus Sucatus; Patricius

Ireland's greatest saint was not Irish at all but a Roman Briton, born ca. 389 in the little village of Bannaventa or Bannavem Taberniae and christened Patricius. His father Calpurnius was a Roman citizen, decurion and municipal official. He was also a Christian deacon. Patricius's grandfather, Potitus, was a Christian priest. By the fifth century, Rome paid scant attention to the security of Britain, at the margins of the empire, leaving the terrified citizens easy prey for Irish slavers. In 405, at age 16, Patricius was kidnapped into slavery in a raid on several western coastal villages.

Although accounts differ as to whether Patricius served a lord near the forest of Fochlat in Connaught or was enslaved to a minor king, Miliucc, in Antrim, Patricius spent the next six years tending sheep and pigs. Although he had ignored his Christian background as a youth, now he had no other companions but the Lord and began praying day and night, hoping to escape. One night he heard voices in his dreams say that his hungers would be rewarded, and that he would soon return home. Startled awake, Patricius heard the voice continue, "Behold, thy ship is ready," and he left immediately.

Such an escape seemed impossible. Patricius was about 200 miles inland from any seaport, he had no money, he risked apprehension and punishment, and he didn't really know where he was going. But he put his faith in God and reached the coast without incident, finding a trading vessel ready to sail for the continent loaded with a cargo of Irish wolfhounds. At first the captain curtly refused his request for passage, but when Patricius left, praying for deliverance, members of the ship's crew called him back, saying the captain had relented. The Irish sailors even offered to let Patricius suck their breast nipples (a sign of friendship), but he demurred.

The voyage lasted only three days, but the ship landed on a desert coast where the men and dogs wandered, starving, for nearly a month. Although there is no desert in Europe, if the ship arrived not long after the barbarian German raids, the countryside would have been devastated. The hungry crew taunted Patricius, saying that if his God were so powerful, why were they starving and alone? Patricius calmly answered that they should trust in the Lord, for whom all is possible, and He would provide. Just at that moment a herd of pigs appeared, and both men and dogs could eat their fill. Patricius eventually made it to Gaul, on the coast of Provence, where he spent about three years at the monastery on the island of Lérins, near Cannes. Finally he returned to Britain in 412–415, where his relatives welcomed him and implored him to remain.

But Patricius, no longer a carefree teenager, was restless. One night he dreamed that a man of his acquaintance, Victoricus, handed him a bundle of letters. One was addressed to *Vox Hiberionacum,* the "Voice of the Irish." As Patricius read the letters in his dream, he heard a multitude of voices, which he identified as the people of the forest of Fochlat, crying, "We pray thee, holy youth, to come and again walk amongst us as before." Patricius awoke, determined to return to Ireland and bring Christianity to a people described as living at the edge of the world. Taking the Irish form "Patrick," he left for Gaul to study and prepare for his life as a missionary.

Patrick was the first real missionary since Paul. As Christianity became synonymous with Rome, it hardly occurred to the Roman Church to expand beyond the reaches of the empire—anything outside was uneducated, threatening, even monstrous. But Patrick had no fear, just shame at his lack of education. He spent several years studying theology under St. Germanus at Auxerre, where he was ordained deacon. In 429, Pope St. Celestine I (r. 422–432) became concerned about

St. Patrick, by Currier and Ives (Library of Congress Prints and Photographs Division)

the spread of the Pelagian heresy in Ireland, and he appointed deacon Palladius—who had fought the heresy in Britain—as bishop in 431. Palladius's charge was to guide the believers, not convert the pagans. But he died within a year. Germanus consecrated Patrick as bishop, and in 432 the former slave returned to begin his mission in Ireland.

Patrick's first convert was the chieftain Dichu in Ulidia, or Ulster, who gave him a wooden barn as a place for worship. The place came to be known as Saul, derived from the Latin *stabulum,* or stable. From this base, Patrick traveled all over Ireland, converting thousands in Meath, Leinster and Connaught. He tried to win the tribal leader, knowing that the chieftain's subjects would often follow. He founded monasteries for both men and women and established the abbot-bishop form of church organization. Longing for solitude himself, Patrick spent a symbolic 40 days and nights on the promontory of Cruachan Aigli near the place of his enslavement. In 441, Patrick traveled to Rome, where Pope St. Leo I not only approved the establishment of a primatial see in Ireland, making Patrick archbishop, but also legitimized the Irish Church by giving Patrick precious relics of the apostles Peter and Paul. Patrick founded his see in 444 on the hill of Ardd Macha in Ulster, a community that became the ecclesiastical city of Armagh.

Perhaps Patrick's most formidable opponent was High King Laoghaire, a pagan who ruled over the lower kings of Ireland for 36 years from the ancestral hill of Tara in Meath. Some members of Laoghaire's family were already Christian. Legend tells that on the first Easter after he arrived in Ireland, Patrick wanted to celebrate the holiday by lighting the Easter fire on the hill of Slane not far from the high king's castle. By coincidence, this particular Easter eve was also the date of a solemn pagan festival. Custom dictated that no fires should be lit until the ritual fire in the castle had been kindled. To Laoghaire's surprise, Patrick's fire blazed from the hill of Slane. Laoghaire consulted the druid priests, who warned that unless the king quenched this fire it would never go out, referring to an old prophecy of a conqueror who seduced the people with a foreign doctrine. Laoghaire pronounced death for such impudence, and rode out to Slane with his queen, sorcerers and other nobles on horseback and in chariots. Summoning Patrick to appear some distance away from the fire, Laoghaire forbade anyone from standing in respect. But the noble Erc was overcome, stood and was converted.

Patrick began arguing with the sorcerers, matching their magic with God's. Laoghaire became angry and ordered his nobles to seize Patrick, but the bishop called upon God to lower a great darkness. The queen begged mercy for her husband's life. Laoghaire pretended to capitulate but planned to kill Patrick. Patrick supposedly read his thoughts and disappeared with his followers, not as humans but as deer.

The next day, Easter, Patrick and his companions magically appeared at Laoghaire's feast, even though the doors were shut. Again one man rose to greet Patrick: the poet Dubthach, who also converted. The Druid Lucetmael tried to poison Patrick, but Patrick blessed the cup and froze all the liquid except the poison, which he poured out. Then Patrick and the sorcerer began a magic contest, which ended in an ordeal: Patrick's pupil Benignus, wrapped in the sorcerer's cloak, was placed in a hut on the side made of dry wood, and Lucetmael stood in the half built of green wood. The hut was set ablaze, and both the sorcerer and his cloak were destroyed. Benignus was unhurt.

In another story involving Laoghaire, Patrick encountered his daughters Ethne the White and Fedelm the Red at a fountain near Rathcrochan. The girls asked Patrick whether he and his friends were fairies or earth-folk, and Patrick answered that they would be better off contemplating God. Patrick then gave the girls a brief catechism lesson, and they begged to be baptized. He baptized them in the fountain, and the girls asked to see the face of Christ. Patrick replied that they could not see Christ unless they died, and first must receive the Eucharist. He gave them the bread, and they died together. Other legends are probably apocryphal: Patrick may have used the shamrock to explain the Holy Trinity, but he didn't drive the snakes from Ireland.

Admirers credited Patrick with converting all of Ireland, but that would have been physically impossible. He accomplished three great tasks, however, with enthusiasm, wit and great energy: He organized the Christians already in Ireland; he converted pagan kingdoms; and he brought Christian Ireland into the universal Church. He worked to reform harsh Irish justice and the rule of might over law. He introduced the Roman alphabet. In an open letter, Patrick angrily denounced the Welsh king Coroticus for capturing his Irish "children" and selling them into bondage. He also railed against the slave traders and the British clerics who condoned the system.

Patrick's *Letters to the Soldiers of Coroticus* is one of three manuscripts attributed to Patrick. He also wrote the *Confessio* or *Confession,* justifying his life and work and apologizing for a sin committed in his youth. The *Lorica,* also called "Patrick's Breastplate" or "The Cry of the Deer," is a mystical poem affirming Patrick's conviction that he was chosen for his great work, and that God surrounded him always.

In 457, Patrick relinquished his post at Armagh to his friend Benignus and retired to Saul. Legend tells that when Patrick knew he was dying, he attempted to go to Armagh, but an angel sent him back. In consolation, the angel promised that the jurisdiction of the Church would remain at Armagh, and that the posterity of Dichu, who had given him the church at Saul, would not die out. The angel also predicted that Patrick's death would send light against the darkness. Patrick received the last rites at Saul from Bishop Tassach of Raholp and died in March 461. Supposedly there was no night for 12 days and less-dark nights for a year.

Although the church at Armagh wanted the body, Patrick was buried at Saul in Downpatrick. Throughout the Middle Ages, Armagh cherished two relics: a pastoral staff, or crosier, and a four-sided bell. Both the shrine at Downpatrick and the crosier were destroyed by English religious zealots in 1539 during the reign of Henry VIII.

Feast: March 17

Patronage: engineers; excluded people; fear of snakes; against snakes and snake bites; Ireland; Nigeria

FURTHER READING

Bury, J. B. *The Life of St. Patrick and His Place in History.* New York: Book-of-the-Month Club, 1999; first published, 1905.

Cahill, Thomas. *How the Irish Saved Civilization.* New York: Nan A. Talese/Doubleday, 1995.

"The Hymn of Fiacc." URL: http://www.ocf.org/Orthodox-Page/reading/St.Pachomius/Western/fiac c.html. Downloaded: September 1, 2000.

"The Confession of St. Patrick," tr. from the Latin, Ludwig Bieler. URL: http://www.ccel.org/p/patrick/confession/confession.html., Downloaded: September 1, 2000.

Paul (d. ca. 67) *Apostle to the Gentiles, mystic, martyr, theologian and missionary*
Name meaning: "Little"

One of the most influential figures in the establishment of the Christian religion.

Paul's conversion to Christianity resulted from a profound mystical experience. The Acts of the Apostles (generally ascribed to St. Luke, a close companion of Paul) and his own letters form two sources from which the facts and chronology of his life can be constructed. More is known about his life than that of any other principal leader of the early Church.

Paul, called Saul in Hebrew, was born a Jew of the tribe of Benjamin in Tarsus of Cilicia (Anatolia) between 1 and 10, and was a Roman citizen. He was schooled in Jerusalem and supported the Pharisees. At some time in his youth, he learned how to make tents, which he continued to do after his conversion and apostleship.

In his early career, Paul studied the strict observance of Jewish law. He participated in the persecution of Christians. However, while traveling on the road to Damascus to arrest Christians in about 36, Paul had a mystical encounter with the risen Christ, one of the most dramatic visionary experiences recorded in religious journals (Galatians 1:15–16; Acts 9, 22, 26). He was nearly at the end of his journey when he encountered a dazzling light and heard a voice audible only to him say, "Why do you persecute me?" Saul fell to the ground and answered, "Who art thou, Lord?" He was answered, "Jesus of Nazareth, whom thou persecutest. It is hard for thee to kick against the goad." Christ then told him to proceed to Damascus, where he would learn what was expected of him. Saul discovered when he rose up that he was blind.

In Damascus Paul went to the house of Judas. Christ appeared to a Christian, Ananais, and instructed

St. Paul (Engraving by Albrecht Dürer, 1514)

him to go to Saul and heal his blindness. This Ananais did with great trepidation, for Paul's reputation as a persecutor of Christians was well known. Ananais laid his hands on Saul and said, "Brother Saul, the Lord Jesus, who appeared to thee on thy journey, hath sent me that thou mayest receive thy sight, and be filled with the Holy Ghost." Scales fell from Saul's eyes and he could once again see. Saul was baptized as Paul and immediately began to preach that Jesus was the Son of God. He considered himself to be one of the apostles as were those who traveled with Christ before his Resurrection.

As the first leader of the early Christian movement beyond the Jewish community, Paul was soon known as the "Apostle to the Gentiles." The 14 letters (epistles) in the New Testament attributed to him are from those written during 10 years of missionary journeys to Anatolia (now the Asian part of Turkey), Cyprus and Greece. During that time, he changed his name from Saul to Paul.

Paul first evangelized his native Tarsus. He was summoned to Antioch by Barnabas. A year later, a famine occurred in Jerusalem, and the two went there with alms for the poor. Sometime after returning to Antioch, Paul and Barnabas set out on the first missionary journey, to Cyprus, Pamphylia, Pisidia and Lycaonia, establishing churches at Pisidian Antioch, Iconium, Lystra and Derbe.

A second missionary journey was undertaken after the Apostolic Council of Jerusalem. With Silas, and later Timothy and Luke, Paul returned to the churches he had helped to established and then went into Galatia. At Troas, Paul had a vision of a Macedonian, which he took as a sign from God that he was to go to Macedonia. He then went to Philippi, Thessalonica, Beroea, Athens and Corinth. He returned to Antioch via Ephesus and Jerusalem. At all the new churches, he gave advice concerning proper behavior for Christians, and preached that Jesus was the savior of all nations.

On his third missionary journey, he revisited most of the places he had been on the second journey. He stayed in Ephesus for three years. Plans for another missionary journey were hampered by persecutions from angry Jews. In Jerusalem, he was arrested and imprisoned for two years, but continued to preach. He appealed his case to Caesar and was sent to Rome to be tried as a Roman citizen. There he was jailed for two more years, but probably was acquitted and was set free. Eventually Paul was arrested again and was martyred ca. 67 when Nero had him beheaded.

At the Church of Santa Maria in Via Lata, Italy, there are remnants of an ancient building and a fountain in an underground oratory. The fountain is said to have sprung up miraculously in answer to the prayer of Paul when he baptized converts. The well was used into the Middle Ages.

In the 16th century, the Roman Church of San Paolo alle Tre Fontane was built on the spot where Paul was beheaded. The church also has a low marble column, to which Paul was said to have been bound, and a marble block upon which he was executed. According to lore, the severed head bounded down a grassy slope, touching at three places. There, fountains sprang up, which were then protected by marble buildings.

Paul was a pioneer in evolving the revolutionary concepts of Christianity. He accommodated Jewish ideas to Gentile traditions and circumstances. He was also at the heart of controversies within the Church, especially unresolved conflicts with Peter over the extent to which Gentile Christians had to observe Jew-ish law. He argued in favor of protecting Christianity from intrusion by Jewish and Hellenistic ideas and practices.

The Acts describes the pattern of his successful but often radical apostolic methods, which often resulted in the conversion of many people but also conflicted with secular authorities. He was beaten and arrested on more than one occasion.

The Epistles, preserved in Greek, were not meant to be doctrinal treatises, but reflections on situations in the particular church to which Paul was writing. The Epistles reveal Paul's syntheses of Christian belief, philosophy and practice as he himself understood it through the channel of his love of Christ and against the backdrop of his astounding conversion, hearing Jesus' voice and being struck blind. He voiced his constant sense of Christ's leading him and urged the faithful to follow his degree of faith inwardly and outwardly to "new life" in spite of the Judaic, Hellenic, Roman and other political, religious and cultural realities of the time. The Epistles quickly became canonical and appear in Christian liturgy along with the Gospels. Their complexities have proved endlessly fascinating to biblical scholars, who dispute full authorship by Paul of several sections and whole epistles. The Epistle to the Hebrews is thought not to have been written by Paul himself; several of his close followers have been suggested as authors.

The first Christology—doctrines and theories of the meaning of the belief in Christ—was developed by Paul. He conceived of Jesus as the Christ, a preexistent divine being who had descended into man to save man from the powers of law, sin and death. The resurrected Christ was raised up to sit at the right hand of God, and would return at some point in the future to judge mankind.

All of Paul's major concepts build on his analogy of the Church as the "Body of Christ." It is used throughout his teaching of the relationship between Christ and/as the Church; it is also the foundation for his theology of justification, redemption and sacraments, and his understanding of the general dynamic of the entire Christian life. Therefore, the frequent use of the phrases "in Christ" and "with Christ" by Paul is especially significant. However, modern controversies surround Paul's seemingly contradictory condemnation of the flesh while he used images of the body to praise the soul, most notably throughout his concept of the Mystical Body of Christ.

Paul's concept of justification by faith has influenced the key notions of such contrasting philosophies as Sartre's unconditioned human freedom, and psychologies such as Carl G. Jung's individuation and Abraham H. Maslow's self-actualization, since they each focus on the necessity of developing resources, creative exercise of freedom and the overcoming of self-deception in order to achieve meaningful existence.

A significant revival of interest in Paul's theology began in the 1960s with the advent of worldwide charismatic movements. Paul first introduced the word "charisma" (from the Greek meaning "grace") into theological terminology and explained the charisma as characteristic of the faithful in general, who use the special gifts of the Holy Spirit to build up the community in a special way and to get charismatic movements started. However, Paul emphasized ethics over miracles, finding the reconciliation of the different social groups within the churches as more "miraculous" than the miracles recorded in the Gospels.

Paul's symbols are a sword and a book.

Feast: June 29, with St. Peter
Feast of conversion: January 25
Patronage: public relations; against snakebites; tent-makers

FURTHER READING
Breed, James L., "The Church As the 'Body of Christ': A Pauline Analogy," *Theology Review* 2 (1985): 9–32.
Davies, W. D. *Paul & Rabbinic Judaism: Some Elements in Pauline Theology.* Minneapolis: Augsburg Fortress, 1980.
Greenspann, Frederick, Earle Hilbert, and Burton Mack, eds. *Nourished with Peace: Studies in Hellenistic Judaism,* Homage Series No. 9. Atlanta: Scholars Press, 1984.

Paul I (d. 767) *Pope*

Paul was born in Rome and along with his brother, Pope Stephen III (r. 752–757), was trained for the priesthood in the Vatican's Lateran Palace. Stephen trusted him with negotiations with the Lombards over papal lands, an experience that stood him well when he was elevated to the papacy upon Stephen's death on April 26, 757. Paul was consecrated in the Chair of St. Peter on May 29.

Paul continued Stephen's policy toward the Frankish king Pepin and thereby maintained papal supremacy over Rome and the districts of central Italy, in opposition to the Lombards, who were aligned with the Eastern Empire. In 758, when Pepin's daughter was born, he sent as a gift to the pope the cloth that was used at her baptism.

In 761, when Emperor Constantine V embraced Iconoclasm, the Islamic-inspired movement that forbade the worship of images, Paul turned his paternal home into a monastery that sheltered Greeks who fled the persecution. Nearby he built the church of San Silvestro in Capite and transferred to it and other Roman churches relics of martyrs from the ancient catacombs

that had been devastated by the Lombards five years before. Among the relics were those of St. Petronilla, whom the Franks believed was the daughter of St. Peter. Paul also built an oratory of the Blessed Virgin in St. Peter's and a church in honor of the apostles on the Via Sacra, beyond the Roman Forum.

In 767, Pepin convened a council at Gentilly, near Paris. The synod aligned itself with the Roman Church's position on the Trinity and the veneration of images, thus pitting the Franks ideologically against the Greeks.

Paul died in Rome on June 28, 767, shortly after the conclusion of the Frankish synod. His death came in the Church of San Paolo fuori le Mura, where he had gone to escape the summer's heat, and he was initially buried there. Three months later, his relics were translated to St. Peter's.

Feast: June 28

Paula (347–404) *Friend and patron of St. Jerome*

Paula was born in Rome of a noble family on May 5, 347. She married a patrician, Toxotius, and had five children: Toxotius, Blesilla, Paulina, Eustochium and Rufina. She was 32 when her husband died in 379, and Paula announced she would become an ascetic and devote herself to helping the poor. In 382 she met Jerome through St. Epiphanius and Paulinus of Antioch. She was drawn to Jerome and became his supporter and patron. They became close, causing rumors to circulate that their relationship was improper.

Eustochium took the veil from Jerome in 382. In 384 Paula's daughter Blesilla died. The following year, Paula and Eustochium left Rome with Jerome and went to the Holy Land. They settled in Bethlehem in 386 and established monastic communities for men and women. Paula worked under Jerome's direction. She and Eustochium built a hospice, a monastery and a convent, which Paula governed.

In her later years she provided great assistance to Jerome with his biblical scholarship writing. She also looked after him and assisted in the building of other churches. The churches became a financial strain. She died in Bethlehem on January 26, 404.

Feast: January 26
Patronage: widows

Paulinus of Nola (ca. 345–431) *Bishop of Nola, Father of the Church*

Pontius Meropius (or Meropius Pontius) Anicius Paulinus was born in Bordeaux, Aquitaine (now southwestern France), about 354. His father was a Roman patrician who was the Praetorian prefect in Gaul at the time of his birth. He was taught by the poet Ausonius until he was 15, then went to study Roman law, poetry, eloquence, science and Platonic philosophy at the University of Bordeaux. He became a prominent and successful lawyer, and when he was 25, Emperor Gratian nominated him to fill an unexpired term as a senator in Rome.

At age 26, he was made governor of Campania and took up residence in Nola in the mountains east of Naples. It was there that he converted to Christianity, after seeing several sick people healed at the tomb of the patron saint of Campania, St. Felix, and being cured of an eye disease by the future St. Martin of Tours. He may also have been influenced by his Spanish wife, a Christian named Teresa, and the sermons of St. Ambrose. St. Augustine's conversion two years prior may have been a factor as well. In any event, he resigned his post as governor, and he and Teresa moved to his home to Gaul. He was baptized there, together with his brother, by Delphinus, bishop of Bordeaux.

Paulinus sold his family estate in Gaul and gave much of the proceeds to his slaves and the poor. Teresa likewise sold her lands in Spain, using the money to ransom captives and free debtors from their obligations. They had a child, but it died shortly after baptism, when it was but eight days old. The couple then decided to give up living as man and wife, took vows of chastity, and spent the remainder of their lives together as brother and sister. Their decision won praise from both Ambrose and Augustine.

Three years after his baptism—about 394—at Christmas, the people of Bordeaux appealed to their bishop to ordain Paulinus a priest. Paulinus agreed to this, on the condition that he not be assigned to a parish or diocese. He received instruction in his priestly duties from Ambrose the following year, and then he and Teresa visited Rome, where they received a cold reception from Pope St. Siricius (r. 384–399). Eight years previously, Siricius had taken a strong stand against married priests, and although Paulinus and Teresa no long had conjugal relations, they were still married.

From Rome, they retired to Nola, where Paulinus spent the remainder of his family fortune on public works and charities. He built a fine avenue leading to the church holding Felix's tomb, and along the avenue raised a building whose first floor was a hospital or hospice and whose second floor was a monastery. Teresa resided on the first floor and directed the activities there, while Paulinus and his monks lived on the second floor. The monastery, devoted to an ascetic lifestyle a century before that of St. Benedict, was one of the first in Europe. Paulinus also built an aqueduct at Nola and constructed basilicas in that city and others.

In 409 or 410, he was elected bishop of Nola. Teresa died about this time, but Paulinus continued to live in his monastery and discharge his duties as bishop for another 20 years. He proved to be one of the best prelates of his time. In addition to his public works, he wrote a number of Christian poems. These included an annual poem for Felix's feast. He also composed one of the earliest Christian wedding songs.

Paulinus died on June 22, 431. He was looked upon as a saint even in his lifetime. His relics were interred in the cathedral of Nola, where they rest today, though they were translated several times in the interim. They were conveyed from Nola to Benevento, then to the Church of St. Barolomeo all'Isola, in Rome. Pope St. Pius X (r. 1903–14) ordered them returned to Nola in September 1908.

In art, Paulinus's emblem is the shovel. He is sometimes depicted with one, as he gives alms. He is also sometimes shown writing or preaching to the poor.

Feast: June 22

Pedro de San José Betancur (1626–1667) *Founder of the Hospitaller Bethlehemite (Belemite) Congregation*
Also known as: Pedro de Betancourt

Pedro Betancur may have been a descendant of Juan de Betancourt, who conquered the Canary Islands for Spain early in the 16th century. If so, the family had suffered a lowering of social and economic status by the time Pedro was born in Villaflora, on the island of Tenerife, on March 21, 1626. They were quite poor.

Pedro had a strong religious sense and zeal, which led him to want to evangelize Japan. In 1646, at the age of 20, he left his homeland for Cuba, going on to Guatemala (then the capital of New Spain) four years later. As he entered Guatemala City on February 18, 1651, the earth shook, a portent of great things to come. He enrolled in a Jesuit college, but his lessons proved too difficult for him to master and he dropped out after three years, giving up his dream of going to Japan. He turned instead to the Franciscans, joining the Secular Franciscan Order in 1655, and devoted the rest of his life to work in Guatemala.

From his arrival in Guatemala City, Pedro had been struck by the great extremes of wealth and poverty. For a while he held the position of sacristan in a church dedicated to the Blessed Virgin, where he prayed for the poor on his knees before images of the Virgin, St. Joseph and the Child Jesus. He rented a house and taught reading and catechism to poor children. In 1658, with the help of benefactors, he converted this house into a hospital. Later, benefactors provided for the purchase of other houses in the area and a proper hospital was built, Pedro himself working alongside the masons. Upon its completion, the hospital was thoroughly equipped and stocked, and placed under the patronage of Our Lady of Bethlehem.

Pedro was concerned not only with the poor but also with all social and economic classes. Every Thursday he collected alms for prisoners and visited them in their cells. Souls in purgatory also received his attention. He had two chapels built at the principal gates to the city, where he performed Masses to celebrate the souls of the deceased. At night he walked through the streets ringing a bell, asking people to pray for them as well.

About 1665 he sent one of his religious brothers to Spain to solicit the king's approbation of his congregation's work. The favor was granted, but unfortunately, Pedro had died before the messenger returned. Nor did he live to see the confirmation of the congregation and its constitution by Pope Clement X (r. 1670–76) in 1673.

Pedro is credited with originating Christmas-eve processions (called *posadas*) in which people representing Joseph and Mary seek lodgings. The practice caught on, and soon spread to Mexico and other Central American countries.

Pedro died on April 15, 1667, in Guatemala City. At the request of the Capuchin Fathers he was buried in their church where his relics are venerated to this day. Legend has it that petitioners need only tap gently on his stone tomb to have their prayers answered. Many early petitioners afterward left stone tablets scratched with thank-you notes.

Beatified: 1980 by Pope John Paul II
Feast: April 25
Patronage: Guatemala

FURTHER READING
"Beato Pedro de Betancur, apóstol de Guatemala (1626–1667)." Church Forum website. URL: http://www.churchforum.org/santoral/Abril/2504.htm#. Downloaded: January 28, 2000.

Perpetua and Felicity (d. 203) *Carthaginian martyrs, with three companions*

The martyrdom of Perpetua and Felicity (also Felicitas), which took place on March 7, 203, in Carthage, is recorded in the alleged first-person accounts of Perpetua and one of her slave companions, and by others.

Vibia Perpetua was of noble birth to a pagan father and Christian mother. She married and had an infant son. Her father tried to persuade her to renounce Christianity, but she would not. At age 22 she was a catechumen, and was arrested under the imperial edict of Septimius Severus (r. 193–211) forbidding anyone to become a Christian. She was still nursing her son at the time. Arrested with her were the slave Felicitas and her fellow slaves Revocatus, Saturninus and Secundulus. Another man named Saturus, who declared himself a Christian, also was arrested. They were all baptized before they were imprisoned.

Perpetua's father visited her in jail and begged her to renounce her faith and not disgrace her name. She refused. She was allowed to suckle her child. She had a vision in which she and Saturus went up a bronze ladder to heaven, where Perpetua was welcomed by a white-headed man in shepherd's clothing who was milking his sheep. He gave some curd to her.

At the trial of the six, her father again appeared, this time carrying her infant son, but she would not relent. Her father was forcibly removed with a whip. The six Christians were sentenced to be torn apart by wild beasts at games.

While awaiting their fate, Perpetua and Saturus had visions. In two visions, Perpetua saw her younger brother, Dinocrates, who had died at age seven. In the first vision, he was in a dark place and looking wretched; in the second he was clean and happy. In another vision, she saw herself led to the amphitheater, where she was transformed into a man and did battle with an enormous Egyptian who towered over the top of the arena. She understood that she was not fighting wild beasts, but the devil; she won.

Saturus saw himself and Perpetua transported by four angels toward the east, to a beautiful garden where they met four other North African Christians who had died in persecutions: Jocundus, Saturninus and Artaxius, who had been burned alive, and Quintus, who had died in prison. Saturus and Perpetua were taken to a building whose walls were made of light, to the presence of a white-headed man surrounded by many elders. They were blessed by the man.

Secundulus died in prison. Felicitas, who was eight months pregnant, feared she would not be martyred, for law forbade the execution of pregnant women. For three days the prisoners prayed, and two days before the games, Felicity gave birth to a daughter, who was adopted by a Christian woman.

On March 7 the five Christians were led to the arena and were scourged. A boar, bear and a leopard were set on the men as they were chained to a bridge, and a wild cow was set on the women. After they were wounded, their throats were slit by sword. The swordsman did not strike Perpetua properly, and so she set the blade on her neck herself.

They were buried at Carthage. Later a grand basilica was built over their tomb. The names of Perpetua and Felicity were entered onto the calendar of martyrs venerated in the fourth century in Rome.

Feast: March 7

FURTHER READING
The Passion of Saints Perpetua and Felicity. URL: http://www.fordham.edu/halsall/source/perpetua.html. Downloaded: September 3, 2000.

Peter (d. ca. 67)

Recognized chief of Jesus' Twelve Disciples; head of the Christian Church after the Ascension, the first pope, martyr
Name meaning: Rock
Also known as: Cephas; Prince of the Apostles; Simon Peter; Simon-Petrus

Peter's original name was Simon (Symeon). He was given the name Cephas, translated as Peter, by Jesus when the two first met, apparently to differentiate him from St. Simon, another of the apostles.

St. Peter receiving the keys to heaven from Jesus (Library of Congress Prints and Photographs Division)

From then on, Peter stayed close to Jesus, and Jesus reciprocated by granting him special recognition. When Jesus addressed the disciples collectively, it was Peter who answered for all. It was from Peter's boat on Lake Genesareth that Jesus preached to the multitude on the shore, and when he walked miraculously on the water, it was Peter whom he called to come to him across the lake. After Peter recognized him as Son of God, Jesus replied that he was blessed, since God must have revealed this to him, as no one could have told him. He added that it was upon the rock of Peter that he would found his church.

In spite of his firm faith in Jesus, and Jesus' in him, Peter had no clear knowledge of his mission and work—or of the dangers they all faced. When Jesus told Peter that he would deny him, Peter protested. However, when Jesus was arrested, Peter fled with the other disciples before turning and following the group carrying Jesus to the high priest. As Jesus had predicted, when he was asked, he denied that he knew him. Yet Jesus later unambiguously confirmed Peter's position as the head of the apostles and of the Church. The women who were the first to find Jesus' tomb empty received from an angel a special message for Peter; Jesus appeared on the first day after the Resurrection to Peter alone; and of special significance, when he appeared at Lake Genesareth, he renewed to Peter his special commission to feed and defend his flock.

Peter was thenceforth recognized as the head of the original Christian community in Jerusalem. After the descent of the Holy Ghost on the feast of Pentecost, he delivered the first public sermon to proclaim the life, death and resurrection of Jesus, winning a large number of converts. He was the first of the apostles to work a public miracle, when with John he went up into the temple and cured the lame man at the Beautiful Gate, and was the most successful of them. His reputation grew to the point that the inhabitants of Jerusalem and neighboring towns carried their sick in their beds into the streets so that his shadow might fall on them and they might be healed.

Peter preached and worked miracles not only in Jerusalem but also in other Christian communities in Palestine. In Lydda, he cured the palsied Eneas; in Joppe, he raised Tabitha (Dorcas) from the dead; and at Caesarea, instructed by a vision he had had in Joppe, he baptized and received into the Church the first non-Jewish converts, the centurion Cornelius and his kinsmen.

Peter's residence in Jerusalem and Palestine was brought to an end when Herod Agrippa I (r. 42–44) began a new persecution of the Christians in Jerusalem. Herod threw Peter and John into prison, intending to have them executed. They were freed in a miraculous manner, and, after informing the faithful and entrusting the Church of Jerusalem to St. James the Less, went into hiding.

What we know about Peter comes from the New Testament of the Bible, where his later life is described only sketchily. After (many believe) a first visit to Rome, he traveled around the Middle East. By tradition, he is the founder of the Church of Antioch, and toward the end of his life, he appointed St. Evodius as the first bishop of Antioch. He also made some return visits to Jerusalem, and was there around the year 50 when St. Paul arrived to discuss the touchy issue of circumcision for Christians. Many Jewish converts were insisting on circumcision, although it had not been the practice for non-Jewish converts, who were resisting it. Peter took the position that Jewish practices should not be impressed upon all Christians. His view was endorsed by James the Less, and the council produced an encyclical to this effect.

Peter and Paul are credited with founding the Church of Rome, although it is not known whether they lived in the city or only frequented there. It is certain that Peter died in Rome, probably in the year 67. By tradition, he was crucified, most likely in the Neronian Gardens, since it was there that the Emperor Nero carried out his executions.

Peter's body was interred in the vicinity of the Via Cornelia and at the foot of the Vatican Hills. Probably at the start of the Valerian persecution in 258 (on June 28, the feast day for Peter and Paul), his relics were translated to the Appian Way. There they lay for a time with Paul's relics, in the place where the Church of St. Sebastian now stands. Later Peter's remains were returned to their former resting place and Emperor Constantine the Great had a magnificent basilica erected over the grave. In the 16th century, this basilica was replaced by the present St. Peter's.

In art, Peter is often depicted along with Paul, the two of them flanking Jesus. Peter is also shown receiving the law—represented by a scroll or keys—from Christ. From the sixth century on, he is shown with a staff or scepter as emblem of his office.

Feast: June 29 (in the West), December 27 or 28 (in the East)

Patronage: bookbinders; bridge builders; clockmakers; fever sufferers; fishermen; against foot trouble; longevity; masons; netmakers; the papacy; shipbuilders; slavery victims; stationers; against wolves

Peter of Alcantara (Pedro de Alcántara) (1499–1562)

Penitent and mystic
Name meaning: Rock

St. Peter of Alcantara levitating

Peter was born in 1499 in Alcántara, Estremadura, Spain. His father, who was a lawyer and governor of the province of Estremadura, died in 1513. Two years later, having studied law at the university in Salamanca, Peter joined the Observant Franciscans at Manjaretes. In 1521 he was sent to Badajoz to found a friary. He was ordained in 1524, when he was 25.

Peter served as superior of missions in Spain and Portugal, and for a while was chaplain to the court of King John III of Portugal. In 1538, he was elected provincial for Saint Gabriel in Estremadura, and tried to put into play ideas he had for the reform of the Franciscan order. When his ideas were not well received by the provincial chapter at Placensia in 1540, he resigned. For the next two years he lived as a hermit with Friar Martin of Saint Mary on Arabida Mountain near Lisbon, and was named superior of the Palhaes community for novices when they found numerous other friars attracted to their ascetic way of life.

Peter became convinced of the need for an extensive Catholic reform, a Counter-Reformation to oppose the Protestant Reformation then well underway. His plan was accepted by the bishop of Coria and finally by Pope Julius III, and in about 1556 he founded the Reformed Friars Minor of Spain (usually called the Alcatrine Franciscans). Alcatrine friars lived in small groups, in great poverty, going barefoot, abstaining from meat and wine, and spending much time in solitude and contemplation. However, the Alcatrines were never really accepted by the other Franciscan orders (called the Conventuals and the Observants), and by the time Peter died in 1562, they had been placed under the Conventuals.

Peter's ideas were picked up by St. Teresa of Ávila, whom he met in 1560, and to whom he became adviser and confessor. At the time, many in the Church were suspicious of the source of Teresa's visions, but Peter had had his own, and he argued persuasively that they were sent by God rather than Satan. Peter helped Teresa gain papal approval for the Discalced Carmelites, the order she had founded on principles similar to his own.

Peter wrote several works of mysticism, including a *Treatise on Prayer and Meditation,* said by Pope Gregory XV (r. 1621–23) to be "a shining light to lead souls to heaven and a doctrine prompted by the Holy Spirit." This work was later drawn upon by St. Francis de Sales, among others. Peter was also reputed to have some unusual powers, such as levitation and the ability to walk on water as though it were dry land.

Perhaps the chief reason Peter's proposals met so much resistance was their extreme austerity, which harked back to the earliest days of Christian asceticism. Peter himself did as he preached. From the time he entered the novitiate at 16, he mortified himself so much in the little food and drink he allowed himself that he lost the sense of taste. He would regularly go three days—and at times as much as a week—without sleep, spending the time in prayer and meditation. He remained on his knees for hours, when he was tired, leaning his head against a nail in the wall. He went about barefoot and even in winter never wore a hat or hood, but only his hairshirt. For three years he never raised his eyes from the ground. For 40 years he slept only an hour and a half per night. Teresa described his penances as "incomprehensible to the human mind" and his body as so ravished that it appeared as if "he had been made of the roots of trees." He experienced "great raptures and violent impulses of love toward God," she said. Over the years Peter became less stringent in his penitence, as he realized the toll it was taking on his health. He died at Arenas, Estremadura, in 1562, while on his knees, reciting a psalm. He was 63 years old.

After his death, he appeared as an apparition to Teresa, who wrote that she "witnessed the greatness of his glory. Far from causing me the least fear, the sight of him filled me with joy. He always showed himself to me in the state of a body which was glorious and radiant with happiness; and I, seeing him, was filled with the same happiness. I remember that when he first appeared to me he said, to show me the extent of his felicity, 'Blessed be the penitence which has brought me such a reward.'"

In 1862, Peter was declared the patron of Brazil.

In art he is depicted as a Franciscan in radiance levitated before the Cross, as angels carry a girdle of nails, chain and scourge. He is also shown walking on water with a companion, a star over his head; praying before a crucifix, scourge and hair shirt; and with a dove at his ear, near a cross and scourge.

Canonized: 1669 by Pope Clement IX
Feast: October 19
Patronage: watchmen; Brazil; Estremadura, Spain

FURTHER READING
"San Pedro de Alcántara." Church Forum website. URL: http://www.churchforum.org/santoral/Octubre/2010.htm. Last updated: June 15, 1999. Downloaded: November 10, 1999.

Peter Canisius (1521–1597) *Jesuit theologian, Doctor of the Church*
Also known as: the Second Apostle of Germany

Peter Canisius was born on May 8, 1521, in Nimwegen, then under the jurisdiction of Germany and now belonging to the Netherlands. His father was a prominent man, elected nine times the burgomaster. Peter's mother died shortly after he was born. At age 15 he was sent to the University of Cologne, and studied civil law, theology and the arts. He received a master of arts degree in 1540. At the university he became friends with Nicholas van Esche, who became his spiritual adviser. In the year of his graduation, he went against his father's wishes to marry a wealthy woman and made a vow of celibacy. He met Peter Faber, one of the first companions of St. Ignatius of Loyola, and made the spiritual exercises under his direction.

In 1546 Peter was admitted to the Society of Jesus in Mainz. He founded the first German house of the order in Cologne, and lectured and taught at the university. He was a brilliant preacher and inspired many. He became known for his editing of the works of SS. Cyril of Alexandria and Leo the Great.

In 1547 Peter attended the Council of Trent as procurator for the bishop of Augsburg. He became deeply involved in the politics of the Reformation and Counter-Reformation. After a brief stint in Messina teaching at a Jesuit college at the behest of St. Ignatius, he went to Rome in 1549 for his final profession. He was appointed a professor of theology at the University of Ingolstadt, and soon became rector. He then was sent to the University of Vienna to teach theology. Peter distinguished himself with his charitable work and his attention to abandoned parishes. People flocked to hear him speak.

As part of the Counter-Reformation, Holy Roman Emperor Ferdinand I asked the University of Vienna in 1551 to compose a compendium of Christian doctrine. The job fell to Peter and a colleague, Father Lejay. Peter deferred to Lejay as the better writer of the two, but had to take over the entire project when Lejay died. The result was Peter's greatest work, his Catechism, published in 1555. In his lifetime it was translated into 200 editions in 12 languages and was a huge success. Peter wrote two shorter versions for students. By the end of the 17th century, the Catechism was available in 15 languages and was published in more than 400 editions. Despite the Catechism, Peter was at one time accused—unsuccessfully—of being Protestant.

In 1556 Peter was named provincial of southern Germany. In subsequent years, he established colleges for boys in six cities and dispatched trained priests throughout the region. He traveled and preached and responded to the needs of the papacy. For seven years he was the official pastor at Augsburg.

Peter spent the last years of his life in Fribourg, Switzerland, where he founded a school in 1580, and in 1581 founded sodalities of the Blessed Virgin for citizens and for women and students. The citizens there would not let him leave. He died on December 21, 1597, and was buried before the high altar of the Church of St. Nicolaus. In 1625 his remains were translated to St. Michael, the church of the Jesuit college.

Miracles were reported immediately after his death and his tomb was a site of pilgrimage.

Peter's Catechism became the foundation for all catechisms that followed. Other major works are *The History of John the Baptist* and *The Incomparable Virgin Mary,* which were written to refute the Protestant attack, and *Centuries of Magdeburg.* Also surviving are numerous treatises, letters and sermons on Catholic dogma and teachings.

Beatified: November 20, 1869, by Pope Pius IX
Canonized and declared Doctor of the Church: June 21, 1925, by Pope Pius XI
Feast: December 21

Peter Claver (Pedro Claver) (1581–1654) *Missionary*
Name meaning: Rock
Also known as: Slave of the Blacks

Peter Claver was born in 1581 in Verdu, Catalonia, Spain, the son of a poor farmer. After studying at the Jesuit college in Barcelona, he became a Jesuit novitiate, taking his final vows on August 8, 1604.

Under the influence of St. Alphonsus Rodriguez, Peter decided to dedicate himself to missionary work in the New World. He landed at Cartagena, in what is now Colombia, in 1610. Cartagena was then the center of the South American slave trade, and Peter was greatly disturbed by the plight of the bonded Africans he saw arriving by the hundreds. At his ordination in 1616, he vowed "to be a slave of the slaves forever," and set himself to the task with uncommon zeal.

Accompanied by African interpreters, he met every slave ship, taking them food begged in the city. Though his main concern was in saving souls, he recognized that bodily needs must be attended first. He washed and tended wounds, buried the dead and ministered to the living by use of pictures of the Trinity. During his 40-year career, he is said to have baptized over 300,000 slaves, among them many infants.

Peter was concerned not only with the slaves as they arrived but also with their continuing welfare. He fought for the enforcement of laws providing for the Christian marriage of slaves and the unity of families, and after Easter each year he journeyed into the hinterlands to preach and hear confession.

Peter also preached to the general populace in Cartagena, becoming its apostle. It is reported that his person was sometimes illuminated with rays as he passed through the hospital wards of the city. His cloak also took on a supernatural cast. He used the cloak for many purposes—as a covering for lepers and the putrescent, as a pillow for the sick, as a pall to the dead. The cloak soon became legendary. It was said that its very touch could cure, and people sought to come into contact with it, and if they could, to tear off a piece for themselves, so that before long its edge was torn ragged.

When the plague struck Cartagena in 1650, Peter was one of the first victims. For four years he was bedridden in his cell, unable to work and almost forgotten. However, when he announced that his death was near, crowds came to kiss his hands and feet and to take away from his cell whatever they could as relics. He died on September 8, 1654, and was given a public burial.

In art, Peter Claver is a Jesuit with a black person.

Canonized: 1888 by Pope Leo XIII
Feast: September 9

Patronage: African Americans; Colombia; missions to black people; missions to non-European nations; race relations

Peter Chrysologus (ca. 400–ca. 450) *Bishop of Ravena, Doctor of the Church, Father of the Church*
Name meaning: Golden-tongued

Peter was born at Imola, Emilia, in what is now Italy, around the year 400, and converted to Christianity as an adult. He was baptized, instructed and ordained deacon by Bishop Cornelius of Imola. According to legend, he was made bishop of Ravenna in 433 to replace John of Ravenna by Pope St. Sixtus III (r. 432–440) in consequence of a vision.

As bishop, John immediately set about eradicating paganism and making needed reforms to his see. He was an especially eloquent preacher, for which he was surnamed Chrysologus ("golden tongued"). It is said that at times he would get so caught up in the excitement of his own preaching that he would become momentarily speechless. Empress Galla Placida was so impressed by his first sermon that she gave generous support to his several building projects, including a baptistry and church dedicated to St. Andrew in Classis, the port of Ravenna. Imperial support continued under her son, Valentinian III.

Peter was among those who received a letter from Eutyches, leader of the Monophysite heresy, protesting his condemnation by St. Flavian of Constantinople and the Synod of Constantinople in 448. Peter referred him to the authority of the bishop of Rome and advised him to stop attempting to justify himself and dividing the Church.

In 448, Peter received St. Germanus of Auxerre in Ravenna. When Germanus died there on July 31, Peter officiated at his funeral, keeping his hood and sackcloth as relics. Soon thereafter, he had a premonition of his own death and returned to Imola for his last days. He died on July 31, 449 or 450.

In art, Peter is shown being presented to Pope Sixtus III by SS. Peter and Apollinaris of Ravenna. He is also depicted with a dish in his hand.

Declared Doctor of the Church: 1729 by Pope Benedict XIII
Feast: July 30 (formerly December 4)

Peter Damian (1007–1072) *Cardinal, reformer, Doctor of the Church*

Peter Damian was born in 1007 in Ravenna, Italy, to a large but poor, noble family. As the youngest, he was not welcomed by everyone because of the added strain on the family's meager resources. An older brother was so vehemently opposed to him that his mother stopped nursing him and he almost died. He was rescued by a family retainer.

Peter was orphaned early in life and was taken in by another brother. He was set to work as a swineherd and was treated like a slave. He remained pious and showed intellectual ability, and so another brother, Damian, archpriest at Ravenna, took him to be educated. Peter apparently later adopted this brother's name as his own in gratitude.

Peter advanced quickly in his studies and was sent to the University of Parma. By age 25 he was famous as a teacher. He did not like university life, however, and in 1035 decided to retire from the world. He met two hermits from Fonte-Avellana who invited him to join them. After a 40-day retreat in a cell, Peter agreed. At Fonte-Avellana he was made a monk immediately.

Peter's extreme austerities and mortifications impaired his health. While recuperating, he studied the Scriptures, and after recovery began lecturing the monks. He also wrote the life of St. Romuald. In 1043 he became prior, a position he held until his death.

As prior Peter established a rule of moderation and founded seven hermitages. He also introduced the regular use of discipline, and a daily siesta to make up for night offices.

Peter became deeply involved in the politics and schisms of the Church, and was summoned to help settle disputes. He was made cardinal against his objections in 1057 by Pope Stephen X (r. 1057–58). He also served Popes Nicholas II (r. 1058–61) and Alexander II (r. 1061–73).

As a reformer, Peter campaigned against simony, the buying and selling of Church offices. He reformed lax clergy who lived with women. When Ravenna was excommunicated for its support of an antipope, Peter worked to reconcile the city, succeeding in 1072. Shortly afterward, he fell ill at the monastery of Santa Maria degl'Angeli (now Santa Maria Vecchia) and deteriorated for a week. He died on February 22 and was buried immediately in the monastery. His body was translated six times, each time to a more impressive shrine, and finally in 1898 to the chapel dedicated to him in the church of Faenza.

Throughout his life, Peter was known as a vehement, strident reformer, writer and speaker, and was a forerunner of the Gregorian Revolution of the 11th century. He was a prolific writer, authoring numerous sermons, treatises and letters. He wrote the first Latin treatise devoted to omnipotence, *de Divina Omnipotencia.* In it, he argues that the traditional patristic God was unknown before Scholasticism, and God can, if he wills, annul the past. Another of his works is *Liber Gomorrhianus* (Book of Gomorrah), probably written between 1048 and 1054, in which he talks against immorality. It is the only extensive medieval treatment of sexual sins that includes homosexuality, which he termed the worst sin of all.

Peter was never formally canonized. He is portrayed in art as a cardinal holding a discipline (a copy of a system of monastic rules), and sometimes as a pilgrim holding a papal bull.

Declared Doctor of the Church: 1828 by Pope Leo XII
Feast: February 23

FURTHER READING
Resnick, Irven Michael. *Divine Power and Possibility in St. Peter Damians de Divina Omnipotencia.* Boston: Brill Academic Publishers, 1992.

Peter of Sebaste (ca. 340–391) *Bishop; brother of SS. Basil the Great, Gregory of Nyssa and Macrina the Younger*

Peter of Sebaste was born around 340 to Basil the Elder and Emmelia of Caesarea, Cappadocia (in modern Turkey). He was the youngest of 10 children. He received religious training especially from his sister, Macrina the Younger, who had been taught by her grandmother, Macrina the Elder.

After his brother Basil became bishop of Caesarea, Peter was ordained by him, and then lived the life of a solitary ascetic. When Macrina and Emmelia set up their monastery on the family estate on the River Iris, Peter assisted them and presided over the men.

Around 380–381, Peter was named bishop of Sebaste in Armenia. Like Basil and Gregory, he fought against the Arian heresy, and proved adept at administration of his duties. Peter was not a writer like his brothers, but followed their writings with great interest. He influenced Gregory to write some of his important works, including *Against Eunomius,* which defended Basil's criticism of the works of Eunomius; *Treatise on the Work of the Six Days,* also in defense of a similar treatise by Basil; and *On the Endowment of Man.*

Peter died in 391 and was venerated as a saint after his death.

Feast: January 9

Petroc (sixth century) *Welsh monastery founder and monk*

Petroc is one of the best-known Cornish saints, whose cult also extended to Devon, Wales and to Brittany in France. Accounts of his life are mostly fiction.

St. Petroc (Truro Cathedral, Truro, Cornwell)

Petroc probably was the son of a chieftain of southwestern Wales; he likely belonged to the royal house of Ghent. He became the namesake of what is now Padstow in Cornwall (Petrock-stow) and established a monastery there. He also established a community in Bodmin, which was the religious capital of Cornwall into the Middle Ages.

In 1177, a canon of St. Petroc's Priory, who had a grievance against the priory, stole the saint's body and took it to the Saint-Meen abbey in Brittany. The body was returned in an ivory shrine.

The legends of Petroc say that he renounced his royal heritage to seek the religious life and went to Ireland to study. He returned to Cornwall and founded the monasteries. Following the directions given by angels, he went on a pilgrimage to Rome and Jerusalem, and lived for seven years as a hermit on an island in the Indian Ocean, subsisting on only a single fish placed before him at intervals according to divine will. He produced numerous miracles, such as raising the dead, vanquishing a dragon, healing (including another great dragon, who had a piece of wood in its eye) and creating springs of water.

Various towns in Cornwall, Devon, Wales and Brittany take their names from Petroc.

Feast: June 4
Patronage: glovers; skinners; against storms at sea; Padstow, Cornwall

FURTHER READING
Doble, Gilbert H. *The Saints of Cornwall,* Part Four. Felinfach: Llanerch Publishers, 1998.

Pharailidis (d. 740) *Patron saint of Ghent and miracle-worker*
Also known as: Vareide, Varelde, Verrle and Verylde

Pharailidis was a Belgian laywoman. She took a secret vow of chastity, but was forced to marry against her will. She refused to consummate the marriage, and was abused by her husband. She made nightly visits to church.

According to lore, Pharailidis created a fountain of fresh springwater in the vicinity of Bruay, near Valenciennes, by striking her staff against the ground. She wished to quench the thirst of harvesters who were working for her. The fountain was said to have healing properties, especially for children's disorders.

Feast: January 4
Patronage: Ghent, Belgium; sick children

Philip (d. ca. 80) *One of Jesus' Tewlve Disciples, apostle, martyr*

Little is known about Philip, except that he was one of Jesus' disciples. Like several others, he was a native of Bethsaida, Galilee, and was a follower of St. John the Baptist. He was called to the Apostolate by Jesus the day after he called Peter and John. Philip was responsible for bringing in another of the group, St. Bartholomew.

Philip was present for the miracle of the loaves and fishes. According to tradition, he left Palestine with the other apostles during the persecutions of Herod Agrippa I (r. 41–44). He preached in Greece and was crucified head down at Hierapolis in Phrygia under Emperor Domitian, about the year 80. His relics were

St. Philip (Engraving by Albrecht Dürer, 1526)

later translated to Rome and placed in the basilica of the Twelve Apostles.

The Golden Legend says that Philip drove away a dragon to the temple of Mars with the cross. Some later traditions concerning his supposed daughters confuse him with Philip the Deacon.

The cross is an important feature in artistic representations of Philip. It represents variously his preaching on the Victory of the Cross, his weapon against the dragon and the instrument of his martyrdom. Typically he is depicted as an elderly apostle holding a long cross or a staff with a small cross on it, though sometimes he holds a basket of loaves and a cross. He is also shown crucified on a tall cross; with loaves and fishes; with a loaf and a book; with a snake or dragon; and casting a devil from the idol of Mars.

Feast (together with James the Lesser): May 3 (formerly May 1 and May 11; in Eastern church, November 14)

Patronage: hatters; pastry chefs; Luxembourg; Uruguay

Philip Neri (1515–1595) *Missionary and founder of the Congregation of the Oratory*

Also known as: the Second Apostle of Rome

Philip Romolo Neri was born on July 22, 1515, in Florence, Italy. His father, Francesco Neri, was a notary and also a friend of the Dominicans. At age eight Philip experienced a miracle later said to presage his destiny as a saint. He jumped onto a donkey laden with fruit. Startled, the donkey fell down cellar stairs, landing on top of Philip. His family feared him dead, but Philip emerged completely unharmed.

Philip exhibited spiritual interests early in life and received instruction from the Dominican friars at San Marco, but was encouraged toward a career in business. At age 16 he was sent to San Germano to assist his father's cousin in business. He performed well but preferred to spend time praying with the Benedictine monks of the nearby monastery in Monte Cassino.

In 1533 he decided to devote himself to the service of God, left his post and went to Rome without any money. He became a tutor to a family of boys in exchange for room and board. He studied philosophy and theology on his own, and wrote poetry. When he was done with his books, he sold them and gave the money to the poor.

After 17 years, Philip began his solitary apostolic work, visiting hospitals, work places and public places to assist those in need and urge others to similar service. He attracted disciples. In 1544 he befriended St. Ignatius of Loyola. Some of his followers joined Ignatius's new Society of Jesus, but most remained with Philip to form what later became known as the Brotherhood of the Little Oratory.

It was also in 1544 that Philip had his pivotal mystical experience. Though he worked in the world, privately he lived like a hermit, practicing severe austerities and spending much time in prayer and contemplation. His single daily meal consisted of bread and water with a few herbs. He disciplined himself with small chains. He successfully coped with great temptations, including those of a diabolical nature.

One day before Pentecost in 1544, Philip was keeping a vigil in the catacomb of San Sebastian, and in prayer asked the Holy Spirit to reveal his gifts. Suddenly a great globe of fire appeared and entered him through his mouth, lodging in his heart. He was consumed with an unbearable sensation of heat and fire, and took off his shirt and threw himself on the ground for some time. When he felt recovered, he arose suffused with great joy. Then his body began to shake violently. A swelling about the size of his fist arose at the side of his heart, painless, and remained there for the rest of his life. His heart would beat violently whenever he performed any spiritual action such as saying Mass, hearing confessions or distributing Communion. At such times, observers noticed the saint's entire body trembling or shaking and could hear his heart pounding like a hammer. He also was hot for the rest of his life, and went about in winter with an open shirt and was hot to the touch of others. After his death, doctors discovered that his heart had actually swelled in size, breaking two ribs, which then formed themselves outward into an arch.

In 1548 Philip co-founded, with his confessor Persiano Rosa, the Confraternity of the Most Holy Trinity, devoted to assisting pilgrims and convalescents. Though a layman, Philip preached once a month to members at the exposition of the Blessed Sacrament held in the church of San Salvatore.

In 1550 Philip began to wonder whether he should retire into solitude. He had a vision of St. John the Baptist and another vision of two souls in glory, one of whom was eating a roll of bread. He interpreted this as a sign that he should continue his work in Rome as though it were his "desert" and abstain as much as possible from meat.

In 1551 Persiano persuaded Philip to enter the priesthood. Both men entered the Confraternity of Charity at San Girolamo. There Philip spent much time in the confessional. He could read the minds and hearts of others, telling them of their secret sins without their confessions. He once told a young man there was not a word of truth in his confession, and the youth confessed to lying. He converted one nobleman by showing him a vision of hell. In his private chapel, he entered into ecstasies so long and deep that he seemed to others at the brink of death. Sometimes he was seen enraptured with his face glowing with unearthly radiance.

In 1557 Philip was inspired by the example of St. Francis Xavier to go to India, but was advised by a monk whose counsel he sought to make Rome his India, and so changed his mind. He built an oratory over the church at San Girolamo and conducted spiritual exercises. One of his admirers was Cardinal Nicolo Sfondrato, who later tried to make Philip a cardinal when he became Pope Gregory XIV (r. 1590–91). Philip successfully dissuaded him from doing so.

Philip's popularity earned him some resentment, and he was denounced as a "setter-up of new sects."

He was able to clear himself with only minor punishment.

In 1564 he reluctantly became the rector of the monastery at San Giovanni, agreeing only on the condition that he could remain at San Girolamo. The spiritual exercises were moved to St. Giovanni in 1574.

Pope Gregory XIII (r. 1572–85) formally recognized Philip's order as the Congregation of the Oratory in 1575 and gave to it the church of Santa Maria in Vallicella, which was in disrepair. Philip built it anew and went to live there in 1583.

Philip was often ill during his last years. He had severe hemorrhages in March and May of 1595 and was given last rites during the second attack, but recovered and resumed his duties. On May 15 he predicted he had 10 more days to live. On May 25, he said Mass and had a good day. But at about 1 A.M. he was heard walking about his room, and then was found lying in bed hemorrhaging again. He received his final blessing and died. He was enshrined in the motherhouse at Santa Maria. He is often portrayed in art with a lily or with an angel with a book.

About three years before his death, Philip burned most of his writings. Few of his sonnets survive.

Numerous miracles are attested about Philip. Once in 1594 when he was severely ill with fever and was feared to be dying, he suddenly cried out to the Madonna. He was found levitating about a foot above his bed, his arms appearing to embrace someone invisible. He recovered, and said that the Madonna had appeared to him and had restored his health.

Philip had the ability to smell the odor of sin on people.

Beatified: 1615 by Pope Paul V
Canonized: 1622 by Pope Gregory XV
Feast: May 26
Patronage: orators; Rome

FURTHER READING
If God Be with Us: The Maxims of St. Philip Neri. Fredeck William Faber, ed. Harrisburg, Pa.: Morehouse Publishing, 1995.
Türks, Paul of the Oratory. *Philip Neri: The Fire of Joy.* Tr. Daniel Utrecht of the Oratory. New York: Alba House, 1995.

Philomena (second or third century) *Saint whose uncertain historical authenticity led to the suppression of her popular cult in 1961*

Philomena came to public attention in May 1802 when some interesting remains were found in a sealed shelf tomb in the Catacomb of St. Priscilla in Rome. The coffin contained the remains of a girl aged 12 to 13, along with a broken ampule containing dried blood. Her skull was fractured at the base. The tomb had been sealed with terra-cotta tiles in a manner usually reserved for noble martyrs. The tiles were inscribed with the words LUMENA PAXTE CUMFI and the symbols of virginity and martyrdom: a lance, arrows, anchor and a palm or lily. The words made no sense until rearranged, and then they spelled out PAX TECUM FILUMENA, or "Peace be with you, Philomena."

The assumption was made that the remains were that of a young virgin martyr. The remains were sent to the Vatican and stored away. In 1805, a priest, Don Francesco di Lucia of Mugnano (near Naples), visited Rome and prayed for guidance. He was inspired to obtain the body of a known saint to enshrine in his chapel. He especially wanted a virgin martyr to set as an example of purity and strength for girls. In Rome he was taken to the Treasure House of Relics, where he was immediately attracted to the relics of Philomena.

Don Francesco was successful in obtaining these first-class relics, and he enshrined them in his church in Mugnano. A papier-mâché corpus was made for the bones. The arrival of Philomena stirred great interest. It was not long before signal favors, graces and miracles of healing were happening, attributed to the intercession of Philomena. Her popularity exploded, and a separate chapel was erected just for the relics. A statue of her exuded manna, a miraculous oil, from the face and neck on August 10, 1823.

Don Francesco collected stories and in 1826 published them in a book, *The Story of the Miracles of St. Philomena.* The book helped to spread her fame even more, and a case was built for her canonization. In addition, Philomena was championed by illustrious people, among them SS. John Vianney, Madeleine Sophie Barat, Peter Eymard and Peter Chanel.

John Vianney (known as the Curé d'Ars) was Philomena's greatest devotee. He learned about Philomena from Pauline Jaricot, a French aristocrat whose father had been given a piece of her relic in exchange for hospitality. When Pauline fell seriously ill, she traveled to Mugnano and was miraculously cured after praying to Philomena in her chapel. So moved was Pauline by the power of Philomena that she gained an audience with Pope Gregory XVI (r. 1831–46) to urge him to open the cause for canonization. The pope was so moved that he did so.

Calling her "the Wonder Worker of the Nineteenth Century," Gregory XVI canonized Philomena in 1837. Vianney, who had obtained a splinter of Philomena's bone from Jaricot, built a chapel to honor the saint. A miracle worker himself, he would protest, "I do not work miracles. I am but a poor ignorant man who once upon a time attended sheep. Address yourselves to St.

St. Philomena (Library of Congress Prints and Photographs Division)

Philomena; I have never asked anything through her without being answered." Vianney's own popularity helped to establish devotion to Philomena throughout Europe, and at the peak of her popularity, she became known as "Powerful with God."

Canonization had been granted solely on the strength of the intercessory miracles that were claimed. The historical authenticity of the remains was never established beyond doubt, and controversy continued into the 20th century. The argument was made that the bones and the tiles were not related, but that the tiles had been reused from another tomb. The girl buried in the Catacomb of St. Priscilla may have been merely an ordinary, unknown child.

The controversy did not dampen popular belief in Philomena, or in the miracles attributed to her intercession. Shrines devoted to her were built around the world. At Mugnano, her papier-mâché corpus is said to have miraculously shifted position several times.

On February 14, 1961, the Congregation of Sacred Rites dropped her feast day from the calendar and her cult was officially suppressed. Some, but not all, shrines closed.

Though no longer officially a saint, Philomena continues to be a popular saint and receive personal devotions. She is venerated in the external feast and Mass from the Common of the Martyrs. Her relics are still enshrined at Mugnano. In art she is often portrayed with her symbols from the tomb: a lance, arrows, lily and anchor.

Canonized: 1837 by Pope Gregory XVI
Feast: Formerly August 11
Patronage: Children of Mary; Living Rosary

FURTHER READING
Mohr, Sr. Marie Helene. *Saint Philomena: Powerful with God.* Rockford, Ill.: TAN Books, 1988.
Trochu, Abbe Francis. *The Cure d'Ars: St. Jean-Marie-Baptiste Vianney.* Rockford, Ill.: TAN Books, 1977.

Pius I (d. ca. 155) *Pope and martyr*

Little of certainty is known about Pius. He apparently was the son of Rufinas, and may have been a native of Aquileia. His brother Hermas, who claimed to be a former freedman, published a Christian journal called "The Shepard." Pius became the 10th bishop of Rome, or pope, succeeding St. Hyginus ca. 140 and reigning until ca. 155.

The Roman Church was more than ever the center of the Christian world during Pius's rule. St. Justin and other Christian evangelists visited Rome, and as did certain heretics. The Gnostics Valentinus and Cerdon continued to preach there, as did Marcion, head of the Marcionites, a group that held that Christianity should jettison all vestiges of its Jewish background. Pius presided over the council that excommunicated Marcion in 144, but it is not known whether he took any actions against the Gnostics.

Pius is sometimes said to have founded two churches in Rome. However, although these may have been built on the foundations of Christian houses dating from his day, the churches as such date from the fourth century.

Pius died ca. 155, perhaps as a martyr like many of his predecessors, although his martyrdom is not mentioned until the ninth century.

Feast: July 11

Pius V (1504–1572) *Dominican monk, Inquisitor general, pope*
Also known as: Michael Ghisleri, Michele Ghisleri, Pope of the Rosary

Pius V is remembered as one of the most important popes of the Counter-Reformation. He was born Michael Ghisleri in Bosco (near Alessandria), Italy, on January 17, 1504. His impoverished family could not afford to send him to school, and he had to assist his father as a shepherd. He was occupied with this one day when two passing Dominican friars struck up a conversation with him. Recognizing his virtuousness and intelligence, they asked for permission from his parents to take him with them. Thus, Michael left home at the age of 12.

After two years of study, in 1518, he donned the Dominican habit at the Voghera priory and, as a novice, was sent to Lombardy. He was ordained a priest in 1528, and returned home for the first time since his departure with the friars to say his first Mass, only to find that Bosco had been razed by the French. He found his parents in a nearby town, however, and after saying Mass, began his career as a lector in theology and philosophy. He also served as master of novices and was elected prior of several Dominican houses. He was a model of piety and austerity: He fasted, did penance, spent hours in meditation and prayer, and always traveled on foot and without a cloak, speaking to his companions only of religious matters.

Michael's reputation for defending the faith won him the appointment as inquisitor at Como, Italy, where many of his brethren had died as martyrs to Protestant heretics. Michael set out to quell the traffic in sacrilegious books smuggled over the Alps from Switzerland. He was ambushed on several occasions and some complicated plots were launched against him, but these only made him more determined to place the situation before the pope in Rome.

In 1556, Pope Paul IV (r. 1555–59) made Michael bishop of Nepi and Sutri and appointed him inquisitor in Milan and Lombardy; he named him inquisitor general for all of Christendom the following year. In 1559, Pope Pius IV (r. 1559–65) appointed him bishop of Mondovi. In his official capacities, Michael opposed not only the heresies of the day but also all policies he considered mistaken. Thus, he opposed Pius IV when he wanted to admit Ferdinand de' Medici to the Sacred College at age 13 and worked to defeat German emperor Maximilian II's attempt to abolish ecclesiastical celibacy. Pius IV died early in 1565 and on January 7 Michael was elected his successor and took the name Pius V.

In the Vatican, Pius continued his religious observances, meditating on his knees before the Blessed Sacrament at least twice a day. He visited hospitals and sat at the bedsides of the sick and dying. He washed the feet of the poor and embraced lepers. It is said that an English nobleman converted to Catholicism after he saw Pius kiss the feet of a beggar covered with ulcers. He forbade bull fights and relegated prostitutes to distant parts of the city. He enforced the discipline of the Council of Trent, reformed the Cistercian order and supported missions to the New World, India, China and Japan.

The signal concerns of his pontificate, however, were combating threats from Protestantism in Europe and Islam in Asia. After the Knights of St. John in Malta were defeated by the Turks in 1565, he rallied forces for what was to be the last of the Crusades. He appointed John of Austria the leader and in 1567 collected from all convents one-tenth of their revenues to help pay for the war. He ordered public prayers and increased his own supplications in support of the endeavor. When the Christian fleet finally sailed out to meet the enemy, all had received the sacraments, and all were saying the rosary. Their small fleet of 200 ships was insignificant compared to the Turkish armada. Yet when they met at the battle of Lepanto on October 6 and 7, 1571, they won, dealing the Turks a blow from which they were never to recover.

Pius was immediately aware of the victory. He was working with his cardinals when he suddenly flung open the window and, looking up at the sky, cried out: "A truce to business; our great task at present is to thank God for the victory He has just given the Christian army." In commemoration of the triumph, he instituted the Feast of the Rosary for the first Sunday of October and added the invocation, "Mary, Help of Christians," to the Litany of Loreto.

Pius was in the midst of trying to form another crusade to march against the Turks when he died on May 1, 1572. His last words were: "O Lord, increase my sufferings and my patience!" His relics are enshrined at Santa Maria Maggiore in Rome.

In art, Pius is shown reciting a rosary or kissing the feet of a crucifix. He also is depicted with a fleet in the distance.

Beatified: 1672 by Pope Clement X
Canonized: 1712 by Pope Clement XI
Feast: April 30 (formerly May 5)

Pius IX, Blessed (1792–1878) *Longest reigning pope in history, and one of the most controversial to have been beatified*

Also known as: Pio Nono

Giovanni Maria Mastai-Ferretti was born at Sinigaglia on May 13, 1792, the ninth child of a minor count. He received a classical education and went to Rome to study philosophy and theology, but political unrest caused him to leave in 1810. He returned to Rome four years later and applied for admission to the pope's Noble Guard, but was refused because he had epilepsy. Instead, he entered the Roman Seminary to study theology. By 1819 he was no longer having fits and was ordained a priest on the condition that another priest always be present when he said Mass.

Father Mastai-Ferretti was appointed spiritual director of the Roman orphanage popularly known as "Tata Giovanni" by Pope Pius VII (r. 1800–23). The same pope sent him as auditor of the Apostolic Delegation to Chile in 1823. Upon his return, Pope Leo XII (r. 1823–29) made him canon of the Church of Santa Maria in Via Lata and director of the large hospital of San Michele. In 1827, Leo XII appointed him archbishop of Spoleto. In that role in 1831 he put his diplomatic skills to work in negotiations between Italian revolutionaries and the Austrian army, bringing a peaceful end to the conflict. The following year he was transferred to the more important diocese of Imola, and in 1840 created a cardinal priest with the titular Church of Santi Pietro e Marcellino. Meanwhile, his continued friendship with some of the revolutionaries earned him the reputation of being a political liberal, liberals being those who favored some relaxation of rule in the Italian Papal States.

When Pope Gregory XVI (r. 1831–46) died at the end of May 1846, the cardinals who met to decide on a successor were divided into liberal and conservative factions. Mastai-Ferretti, the liberal candidate, won on the fourth ballot on June 16, 1846, Cardinal Archbishop Gaysruck of Milan arriving too late to make use of the right of exclusion against Mastai-Ferretti's election, given him by the Austrian government. The new pope took the name Pius IX, in memory of Pope Pius VII, his former benefactor. His coronation was held at St. Peter's Basilica on June 21.

Pius IX at once started to live up to his liberal reputation. He issued an amnesty for political prisoners and made numerous reforms in the Papal States. However, the more concessions he made, the more that were demanded. On February 8, 1848, a street riot in Rome forced him to concede to a lay ministry in the Papal States and in March he reluctantly granted a constitution—the first step to a unified and independent Italy. However, when he refused to join in war against Catholic Austria, he quickly lost popularity. The riots continued; his prime minister, Rossi, was stabbed to death; and in November, Pius himself had to flee Rome in disguise. He appealed for help from France, Austria, Spain and still-independent Naples, and in April 1850, French troops made it possible for him to return to Rome.

However, his troubles were not over. Papal forces lost control of most of the Papal States in 1860, and in

Pope St. Pius IX (Library of Congress Prints and Photographs Division)

1870, when the French pulled out of Rome, that too fell. Pius found himself confined to the Vatican, his temporal empire lost. He refused to accept the situation, and relations between the Vatican and the new Italian state were to remain strained until 1929.

Pius's experience with political liberalism turned him into a thoroughgoing conservative, in both the temporal and spiritual spheres. He had long held a personal devotion to the Virgin Mary, and in December 1854, he declared it a dogma of the Church that Mary was conceived without original sin—the dogma of the Immaculate Conception. In 1864, he issued an encyclical and a syllabus of 80 errors, which took the strongest possible stand against modernism. The Syllabus of Errors opposed not only pantheism, naturalism, rationalism, socialism, communism, freemasonry and various kinds of religious liberalism, it also pronounced against the separation of church and state and freedom of speech. Its final point rejected the idea that the pope "can and should reconcile himself with progress, liberalism, and recent civilization." Perhaps the greatest event of his reign, however, was the First Vatican Council, convened in June 1869. The council was forced to adjourn the following summer due to the outbreak of the Franco-Prussian War, but not before it had proclaimed the dogma of papal infallibility—the idea that the pope when speaking ex cathedra can make no mistake in matters of faith and morals. This proclamation prompted many dissenters to leave the Church and brought about a schism that lasted until the liberalizing decisions of the Second Vatican Council almost a century later.

Pius's conservatism showed up also in his kidnapping of a six-year-old Jewish boy, Edgardo Mortara, in 1858. The Mortara family lived in Bologna, in the Papal States, which at the time were still under the Vatican's jurisdiction. Word came that a 15-year-old Catholic housemaid had baptized Edgardo when he was seriously ill and seemed near death. Under Church law, baptism converted one to Christianity, and a Christian child should be raised in a Christian home. Thus, Vatican police stormed the house and grabbed the boy from his father's arms. Although the action was not unprecedented, it met with international outrage. The *New York Times* ran 20 articles on it in one month. However, Pius formally adopted Edgardo, who grew up in the Vatican and eventually became a priest, lecturing on the miracle of conversion to Christianity. The kidnapping became a major issue in 2000, as the Vatican prepared to beatify Pius.

Pius died on February 7, 1878, at the age of 86, after a reign of 33 years. Italian liberals tried to throw his body into the Tiber River, but it was saved and interred instead in the Church of San Lorenzo fuori le Mura, now named after him. When his tomb was opened in 2000 to verify his remains in the Rite of Recognition, an important step in the process of beatification, his body was found to be almost perfectly preserved.

Pius's cultus today is largely confined to the Vatican and certain conservative bishops there. Nevertheless, he was put forward as an 11th-hour substitute for his even more controversial successor, Pope Pius XII (r. 1939–58)—who came under fire for not having done enough to oppose the Holocaust—and was beatified along with the much-beloved liberal, Pope John XXIII (r. 1958–63).

Beatified: September 3, 2000, by Pope John Paul II
Feast: February 7

FURTHER READING
Van Biema, David, "Not So Saintly?" *Time,* September 4, 2000, pp. 60–64.
Kertzer, David. *The Kidnapping of Edgardo Mortara.* New York: Random House, 1998.

Pius X (1835–1914) *Pope*

Also known as: Joseph Sarto, Pope of the Blessed Sacrament

Pope St. Pius X (Library of Congress Prints and Photographs Division)

Giuseppe Mechiorre Sarto, who was to become Pope Pius X, was born on June 2, 1835, at Riesi (Riese), Treviso, in Austrian-controlled Venice. His was a poor family, but Giuseppe took Latin lessons from the archpriest of Riesi, then studied for four years at the gymnasium of Castelfranco Veneto. In 1850, he received a scholarship to the seminary in Padua, where he completed his studies in classics, philosophy and theology with distinction.

After his ordination in 1858, he spent nine years as a chaplain at Tombolo; but the parish priest was old and an invalid, and Giuseppe had to assume most of his duties. He studied canon law assiduously, established a night school for adult students and in 1867 he was named archpriest of Salzano, a large borough of the diocese of Treviso. In 1875, he became a canon of the cathedral there. In 1878, upon the death of Bishop Zanelli, he was elected vicar-capitular. An even more prestigious position followed in November 1884, when he was elected bishop of Mantua. Then in June 1893, at a secret consistory, Leo XIII (r. 1878–1903) created him cardinal under the title San Bernardo alle Terme; in the public consistory three days later, he named him patriarch of Venice. However, Giuseppe had to wait 19 months before taking possession of his new diocese because the Italian government refused to recognize his appointment.

Leo XIII died at the end of July 1903, and on August 4, Giuseppe was elected his successor. At his coronation on August 8, he assumed the name Pius X. As pope, Pius continued to promote the doctrine and method of St. Thomas and to battle against what he considered the Modernist heresy.

Pius gave particular attention to the Eucharist, recommending that the First Communion of children not be delayed after they reached the age of discretion, advising all healthy Catholics to take Communion frequently—daily, if possible—and lifting the injunction on the sick to fast so that they, too, could participate. He embraced the Immaculate Conception and enjoined Marian devotion. He promoted sacred music, published a new catechism for the diocese of Rome and, most important, produced a new codification of Canon Law that separated the juridical from the administrative.

Pius died on August 20, 1914, of natural causes aggravated by worries over the beginning of World War I. In his will we find the words: "I was born poor; I lived poor; I wish to die poor."

Canonized: May 31, 1954, by Pope Pius XII
Feast: August 21
Patronage: Pilgrims

Polycarp of Smyrna (d. ca. 155?) *Martyred bishop of Smyrna and Greek Father of the Church whose body refused to burn in fire*

Little is known about the life of Polycarp of Smyrna, who was born about 70, but the details of his martyrdom are preserved in a written account.

At about age 10 Polycarp was converted by St. John the Evangelist and became his disciple. At about age 26 he was consecrated bishop of Smyrna by John before the apostle's banishment to the isle of Patmos.

According to accounts, Polycarp was a wise and prudent bishop, one of the foremost in Asia; St. Irenaeus of Lyons wrote that he was privileged to receive instruction from him when Irenaeus was a young man. St. Ignatius of Antioch (another martyr) called him one of the most important figures bridging the apostolic and patristic eras of the Church. Polycarp was a vigorous opponent of the Marcionite heresy.

When bloody persecutions began against Christians, Polycarp was targeted for arrest. He was persuaded by friends to take refuge in a house outside Smyrna, where he prayed day and night. He moved to a second farmhouse. He was betrayed by a servant who was threatened with torture. Polycarp was not caught offguard. Three days prior to his arrest he had a trance vision in which his pillow was in flames, and knew he would be martyred by fire. He surrendered himself willingly when the soldiers arrived, and invited them to dinner. Upon his request, they granted him two hours to pray.

During the journey by chariot to Smyrna, the soldiers urged Polycarp to obey the imperial edict to sacrifice to the pagan gods in order to save his life. When he refused, they pushed him from the chariot, and he bruised (or broke) his leg in the fall.

Polycarp was taken before the proconsul, Statius Quadratus, who ordered him to blaspheme Jesus Christ. Polycarp refused and was threatened with wild beasts. This did not daunt him, so the proconsul decreed that he should be burned alive.

Polycarp asked not to be nailed to the stake, promising that he would not move. According to an account of his execution, "the fire making the appearance of a vault, like the sail of a vessel filled by the wind, made a wall round the body of the martyr; and it was there in the midst, not like flesh burning, but like [a loaf in the oven or like] gold and silver refined in a furnace. For we perceived such a fragrant smell, as if it were the wafted odor of frankincense or some other precious spice."

Exasperated, the pagans stabbed him to death. Out of the wound came a dove and so much blood that the fire eventually was extinguished. Christians asked for the body but were refused; the body was burned in another fire. Polycarp's supporters stole his bones for burial.

According to Irenaeus, a "voice like a trumpet" announced in Rome, "Polycarp is martyred" at the exact time the deed was committed in Smyrna.

Different dates of his martyrdom have been given, from 155–156 to 160 to 167–168. His age at death is given as 86, which, depending on the year of death, would affect the date of his birth.

Extant is a letter from Polycarp to the Philippians, an inspiring message that the Philippians solicited and that quotes from the Gospels of Matthew and Luke, the Acts of the Apostles and the first letters of Peter and John.

Feast: February 23
Patronage: earache sufferers

FURTHER READING
St. Alphonsus Liguori. *Victories of the Martyrs.* Brooklyn: Redemptorist Fathers, 1954.

"The Epistle of Polycarp." URL: http://www.ccat.sas.upenn.
    edu:333/00/Religious/ChurchWriters/Apostolic
    Fathers/Polycarp. Downloaded on February 13, 2000.

"The Letter of the Smyrnaeans or the Martyrdom of Poly-
    carp." URL: http://www.ccat.sas.upenn.edu:3333/00/Reli-
    gious/ChurchWriters/Apostoli/Martyrdom_Polycar. Down-
    loaded on February 13, 2000.

Pontian (d. ca. 236) *Pope and martyr*

Pontian was from Rome, the son of Calpurnius. He succeeded St. Pope Urban I as bishop of Rome on July 21, 230.

Pontian presided over the synod at Alexandria, which condemned Origen. In 235, Emperor Maximinus the Thracian began a persecution of Christians aimed chiefly at the heads of the Church. One of its first victims was Pontian, who was banished to the mines on the island of Sardinia. In order to make possible the election of a new pope, Pontian resigned on September 28, 235.

St. Hippolytus was banished to Sardinia along with Pontian. Up until this time Hippolytus had persisted in his claim to be bishop of Rome, in other words, had stood as an antipope. However, while in exile he became reconciled with the recognized Church, and his schism ended.

Pontian and Hippolytus died in Sardinia, though it is not known when. Pope St. Fabian (r. 236–50) had their relics brought to Rome. Pontian was buried in the papal crypt of the Catacomb of Callistus on August 13, 354.

Feast: November 19

Proclus (d. 446 or 447) *Patriarch of Constantinople, Father of the Church*

Proclus was born in Constantinople. A good student, he became a lector at an early age and was especially skilled in rhetoric. He studied under St. John Chrysostom, and then became secretary to one of John's opponents, Atticus, who became patriarch of Constantinople after the deposition of John. Atticus ordained Proclus a priest. But when Atticus died, Proclus was passed over for patriarch in favor of Sissinus. When Sissinus died in 427, Proclus was passed over again in favor of Nestorius. Nestorius was deposed for heresy by the Council of Ephesus in 431, and Proclus lost out still again to Maximian. Finally he was made patriarch upon the death of Maximian ca. 434. In 438 Proclus translated the body of John Chrysostom to the Church of the Apostles in Constantinople.

Proclus died in Constantinople in 446 or 447. He wrote important treatises and homilies and argued against heresies. Most notable among his works is *Tome of St. Proclus,* about the two natures of Christ, aimed at the unorthodox teachings of Theodore of Mopsuestia.

Feast: October 24 in the West; November 20 in the East

Quentin (d. 287) *Roman missionary and martyr*
Also known as: Quintin, Quintinus

Quentin went to Gaul as a missionary with St. Lucian of Beauvais. He settled at Amiens in Picardy, where he enjoyed great success as a preacher. The prefect Rictiovarus had him imprisoned and tortured. Quentin was taken to Augusta Veromanduorum (which became Saint-Quentin), where he was again tortured and then was beheaded. He is often depicted in art as a soldier or bishop holding two spits.

Feast: October 31

Quiricus (d. 304) *Three-year-old martyr with his mother, St. Julitta*
Also known as: Cyr, in France

During Christian persecutions, Julitta attempted to find safety with her son in Seleucia, Tarsus, but was arrested. Quiricus was made to watch her be tortured. Struggling, he declared himself a Christian as well, and then was either dashed to death on stone steps or beaten to death before his mother's eyes. Julitta was beheaded.

The story may be all or part fiction. In the fourth century, the relics of Quiricus and his mother reportedly were taken to France and distributed to several churches and monasteries.

Feast: June 16

Quirinus (d. ca. 117) *Roman tribune and martyr*

According to tradition, he was the jailer of Pope St. Alexander I (r. 105–115), and was converted with his daughter, Balbina. He is buried with her in the Praetextatus catacomb on the Via Appia. In 1050, Pope Leo IX (r. 1049–54) gave his relics to his sister, Gepa, abbess of Neuss, who placed them in the Church of St. Quirinus there.

Feast: March 30

R

Raphael the Archangel *One of the principal angels in Judeo-Christian angelologies, accorded the rank of archangel*

Name meaning: "The shining one who heals," "God heals," or "the medicine of God" in Hebrew

Raphael's name originates from the Hebrew "rapha," which means healer or doctor. He is entrusted with the physical well-being of the earth and its human inhabitants, and is said to be the friendliest of the angels.

Raphael has numerous titles and duties. He is counted among the seven angels who stand before God as mentioned in Revelation. He is the angel of the evening winds, guardian of the Tree of Life, and the angel of prayer, peace, joy, light and love.

Raphael is credited with being the angel who stirs the waters of the healing pool by the sheep gate in Bethesda. According to lore, when the angel comes down from heaven and stirs the waters, all those who bathe there are healed. John 5:22 refers to this pool in the story of Jesus and the paralyzed man. The man had been ill for 38 years. When Jesus found him lying by the pool, he asked the man if he wanted to be healed. The man replied he had no one to lift him into the waters when they were troubled. Jesus told him to rise up and walk, and the man was immediately healed.

The apocryphal *Book of Enoch* terms Raphael one of the "watchers" and a guide to the underworld. In Enoch, he heals the earth when it is defiled by the sins of the fallen angels.

Raphael is not mentioned by name in the Protestant Bible, but he does play a prominent role in the book of Tobit, part of the Catholic canon, which establishes the healing ministry of angels and their role as emissaries of God. In it, Raphael teaches the arts of both healing and exorcism. He acts as a guide and companion on a journey, thus making him the angel of travelers and safety.

The book of Tobit was originally written in Hebrew or Aramaic, probably in the second century B.C. The story concerns a pious man named Tobit and his son, Tobias. It takes place in the late eighth century B.C. in the Assyrian capital of Nineveh, where the people of northern Israel have been taken captive. The storyteller is Tobit himself, who is instructed by Raphael to write an account of the events that happen to him, his son and others.

Tobit was a model of piety, giving money, food and clothing to the poor. He defied Sennacherib the king by burying his fellow Israeli dead, whose bodies were left in the open by their captors. One evening, the 50-year-old man was defiled by handling a corpse and so did not return home, but slept by the wall of a courtyard. He left his face uncovered. Sparrow droppings fell into his eyes, rendering him blind. He sought help of various physicians, to no avail. His wife was forced to work to earn money.

After eight years in despair, Tobit begged God to let him die. In preparation for death, he called in his only son, Tobias, and told him to journey to Media, where he had left some money in trust with another man. He instructed Tobias to find a man to accompany him on the journey, and he would pay the man's wages.

In Media, a young woman named Sarah was possessed by the demon Asmodeus, "the destroyer." Sarah had been given to seven men in wedlock, but the demon had killed them all on their wedding night, before the marriages could be consummated. Sarah's parents feared they would never marry off their only daughter.

God heard the prayers of both Tobit and Sarah's parents, and dispatched Raphael to heal Tobit's blindness and exorcize the demons from Sarah.

Raphael appeared to Tobit in the form of a man and introduced himself as Azarius, the son of one of Tobit's relatives. Tobit hired him.

Along the way, Raphael taught Tobias healing lore. He instructed him to use the heart and liver of a fish for exorcizing demons, and the gall of a fish for curing blindness. He also instructed Tobias to wed Sarah and drive Asmodeus away with smoke from the burning fish parts and incense.

Tobias did so, and the demon fled to "the remotest parts of Egypt" (the traditional home of magic and witchcraft), where Raphael bound him up.

Upon Tobias's return home, he cured his father's blindness. Raphael declined a generous payment and revealed his true self to the men. "I am Raphael, one of the seven holy angels who present the prayers of the saints and enter in the presence of the glory of the Holy One," he said. He told Tobit that he had been ever present with him, and had taken his prayers for healing to God. He urged the men to praise and thank God, and to lead righteous lives.

Tobit and Tobias were alarmed to be in the presence of an archangel, and fell to the ground in fear. But Raphael assured them no harm would befall them. "For I did not come as a favor on my part, but by the will of our God," he said. "Therefore praise him forever. All these days I merely appeared to you and did not eat or drink, but you were seeing a vision. And now give thanks to God, for I am ascending to him who sent me. Write in a book everything that has happened." Raphael vanished. Tobit wrote the story.

Catholic devotional lore contains numerous stories about the deeds of Raphael. The Roman widow Cyriaca (also called Dominica), who was martyred in the fourth century, was addressed by Raphael during her tortures. The archangel, identifying himself by name, said he had heard her prayers and congratulated her on her courage. Because of her suffering, she would glorify the Lord. Sister Mary Francis of the Third Order of St. Francis, who lived during the late 18th century, was frequently ill and was told on one occasion by the archangel that he would heal her—and he did. She and others were witness to a smell of sweet perfume, which she attributed to the presence of Raphael. The archangel also is credited with healing other afflictions, including epilepsy, and of providing protection during journeys.

Feast: September 29
Patronage: the blind; happy meetings; nurses; physicians; travelers

FURTHER READING

Guiley, Rosemary Ellen. *The Encyclopedia of Angels.* New York: Facts On File, 1996.

O'Sullivan, Fr. Paul. *All about the Angels.* Rockford, Ill.: Tan Books and Publishers, 1990; first published, 1945.

Rita of Cascia (1381–1457) *Augustinian nun*
Also known as: Margarita

Rita was born in Roccaporena, near Spoleto, Italy, in 1381, to elderly parents. At an early age, she begged her parents to allow her to enter a convent. Instead they arranged a marriage for her at age 12 to a man known for his harsh temper and cruel treatment of others. Rita bore two sons. After nearly 18 years of marital misery, Rita was released from her marriage when her husband was stabbed in a fight. According to lore, before he died, Rita prayed for him and he repented.

Archangel Raphael with Tobias (Library of Congress Prints and Photographs Division)

Her sons sought to avenge his death, but Rita prayed that they might die rather than commit murder. Soon thereafter, Rita's two sons contracted a fatal illness and died. She turned to her original desire to be a nun, but the Augustinian convent at Cascia, Umbria, refused to admit her because they required novitiates to be virgins, and she had been married and was a widow. Three times she applied and three times she was rejected. Finally the order admitted her in 1413. She distinguished herself with her piety, devotion and charity. She filled her days with prayer, fasting, good works and penances. She undertook the most severe austerities.

To test her obedience, the mother abbess instructed her to plant a dry stick and water it every day until it bloomed. Rita did so dutifully for an entire year, to the amusement of her sister nuns. Then the stick miraculously bloomed and grew grapes, and reportedly continues to do so today. The leaves are ground to powder and given to the sick.

Rita had a great devotion to the Passion of Christ. In 1441 she heard a sermon on the suffering of Christ from his crown of thorns, and prayed for a thorn to experience this suffering. Immediately she felt as though a thorn from the crucifix detached and penetrated her forehead. It left a deep, ugly and open wound that so revolted the nuns that Rita spent most of her time in her cell as a recluse for the last 15 years of her life. The wound caused her great pain. In 1450, it healed long enough for her to accompany her sister on a pilgrimage to Rome, but returned after she was back at her convent.

Rita died on May 22, 1457. In death her thin and frail body took on a radiant splendor and the ugly wound became like a beautiful jewel. The body gave off a sweet smell that filled first her cell and then the entire convent. Her body was still incorrupt in contemporary times.

For centuries after her death, her body was reported to move and levitate inside its glass reliquary. These events had numerous witnesses. One incident was recorded on May 21, 1628. A large crowd had gathered in Cascia for Rita's feast. A dispute arose between the Augustinians and the secular clergy concerning who had the right to conduct the Vespers of the Office of the Saint. The nuns prayed to Rita for a solution. To their amazement, her eyes opened and her body levitated to the top of the reliquary. Others were summoned to witness the miracle. The secular clergy was allowed to conduct vespers. The eyes remained open for years.

Rita's body levitated again in 1730, when earthquakes forced people to come to the church of St.

St. Rita of Cascia

Rita in Cascia for protection. Cascia was spared damage.

On numerous occasions, witnesses reported seeing Rita's body move: it changed position inside the reliquary to turn from one side to the other, and the head would turn toward people.

Miraculous manifestations have been reported as the result of prayer to Rita after her death. On one occasion the superior at Cascia urgently needed money to pay a debt; after prayer the superior found exactly the sum needed in the alms box. On another occasion, the nuns needed wine for their meals but had none. Shortly after prayer, a man appeared at the door with a barrel of wine. As soon as it was placed in the cellar, the man and his donkey and cart vanished.

A relic—a scrap of woolen cloth that had touched the veil of Rita—was credited for extinguishing a fire in Narni on April 27, 1652. A fire broke out in a house, and there was not enough water available to extinguish it. The relic was thrown into the flames, which immediately were extinguished.

Canonized: 1900 by Pope Leo XIII

Feast: May 22

Patronage: bleeding; desperate, impossible and hopeless causes; infertility; against marital problems; parenthood

FURTHER READING

Sicardo, Joseph A. *St. Rita of Cascia.* Tr. Dan J. Murphy. Rockford, Ill.: TAN Books and Publishers, 1993.

Robert Bellarmine (1542–1621) *Cardinal, theologian, Doctor of the Church*

Robert Bellarmine was born on October 4, 1542, in Montepulciano, Tuscany, to a noble family. His mother, Cinzia Cervini, a niece of Pope Marcellus II (r. 1555), was a devout woman. In 1560 Robert joined the Jesuits and was sent to Rome to study at the Jesuit Roman College. In 1563 he taught classics at the Jesuit colleges of Florence and then Mondavì in Piedmont. In 1567 he went to the University of Padua to study Thomistic theology. Upon graduation he became the first Jesuit professor at the University of Louvain. He was ordained in 1570. For the next five years, he taught Thomistic theology, Greek and Hebrew at Louvain. He studied the Scriptures and began writing.

In 1576 Pope Gregory XIII (r. 1572–85) brought him to Rome to be chair of controversial theology at the Roman College. The lectures that Robert gave at the college became the foundation for one of his most significant works, *Controversies of the Christian Faith against the Heretics of This Time,* a defense of Catholic theology against Protestantism. Three volumes of *Controversies* were published between 1586 and 1593. But Pope Sixtus V (r. 1585–90) thought Robert went too far in limiting the pope's temporal jurisdiction, and he intended to include *Controversies* on his revised Index, a list of forbidden books. Sixtus died before the list was published, thus sparing Robert official censure.

Despite his disapproval of *Controversies,* Sixtus, prior to his death in 1590, sent Robert to Paris to serve as theological adviser to Cardinal Enrico Gaetani during a bitter civil war. Robert was there during a siege of the city by Henry of Navarre, who claimed the throne as Henry IV, and his health, delicate from childhood, suffered.

Upon his return to Rome Robert served as spiritual director of the Roman College, where he met Aloysius Gonzaga, destined for sainthood himself.

In 1592 Robert was named superior of the college, and in 1594 or 1595 was named provincial of Naples. He was recalled to Rome in 1597 by Pope Clement VIII (r. 1592–1605), who appointed him his own theologian and also examiner of bishops and consul-

St. Robert Bellarmine (Library of Congress Prints and Photographs Division)

tor of the Holy Office. In 1599 Clement made him a cardinal.

When Clement died in 1605, Robert was put forward as a successor, but the electors did not care for the fact that he was a Jesuit. Pope Leo XI reigned only 26 days, and Robert was again advanced as a successor, but he lost to Pope Paul V (r. 1605–21).

Robert remained as a member of the Holy Office and became involved in Church disputes and campaigns against heresies. He became head of the Vatican Library in 1605. In 1615, he warned that the heliocentric theory of the universe was "a very dangerous thing" because it contradicted the Scriptures, and urged Galileo to drop his defense of it. When the Holy Office condemned the theory, it fell to Robert to convey the decision to Galileo and receive his submission. He opposed severe action against Galileo.

Robert lived long enough to see Pope Gregory XV (r. 1621–23) elected in 1621. His health failing, he died on September 17 of that year in Rome. His relics are in the church of St. Ignatius there.

Robert's career was propelled by his brilliant and prolific writings. At Louvain he authored a Hebrew grammar and a work on the Fathers of the Church. Besides *controversies*, he wrote two catechisms, one for children and one for teachers, both of which have had continual popularity. He also wrote numerous catechetical and spiritual treatises, commentaries on the Scriptures and other works. *The Mind's Ascent to God* and *The Art of Dying Well* remain popular in present times.

Throughout his life, even after his appointment as cardinal, Robert lived simply, practicing an ascetic life and giving most of his money to the poor. He once ripped the tapestries off his walls so that clothing could be made for the poor, saying, "The walls will not catch cold."

Beatified: 1923 by Pope Pius XI
Canonized: 1930 by Pope Pius XI
Declared Doctor of the Church: 1931 by Pope Pius XI

Feast: September 17
Patronage: canonists; catechists; catechumens

FURTHER READING

Godman, Peter. *The Saint As Censor: Robert Bellarmine between Inquisition and Index.* Harrisburg, Pa.: Brill Academic Publishers, 2000.

Robert Bellarmine: Spiritual Writings. Tr. John Patrick Donnelly and Roland J. Teske. Mahwah, N.J.: Paulist Press, 1994.

St. Robert Bellarmine. *Live Well, Die Holy: The Art of Being a Saint, Now and Forever.* Manchester, N.H.: Sophia Institute Press, 1998.

Roch (ca. 1295–1378) *Miracle healer, especially of plague victims*
Also known as: Rock, Rocco (Italy), Roque (Spain), Rollock and Seemie-Rookie

Roch's birthplace is said to be Montpellier, France; his father was the governor there. At birth he had a red cross on his chest. Roch's parents died when he was 20. He went on pilgrimage to Rome and in the town of Aquapendente found many people ill of the plague. He

St. Roch giving away his clothes to the poor (Library of Congress Prints and Photographs Division)

healed them (as well as animals) through prayer and making the sign of the cross. He performed similar miracles of healing in Parma, Modena and Mantua. He visited other countries.

In Piacenza, Italy, he fell ill himself, but rather than go to a hospital, he went off into the woods, prepared to die. According to lore, he was sustained by a dog who brought scraps from his master's table. Curious as to where the dog went every day with the scraps, the master followed it and discovered Roch. He nursed the saint back to health, and gained faith from him.

Once recovered, Roch returned to Montpellier, but not even his own family recognized him. He was suspected of being a spy in pilgrim's disguise. His uncle, the governor, ordered him imprisoned. Roch would not identify himself, and spent the last five years of his life in miserable conditions in jail. He died there, and his true identity was discovered after his death when the cross-shaped birthmark on his chest was seen.

After his death, miracles were reported at his intercession. He was invoked in 1414 during the Council of Constance when plague threatened the city.

Roch's relics were translated to Venice. The Franciscans accept him as one of their tertiaries. In art he is shown dressed as a pilgrim wearing a hat, cloak and boots and carrying a staff, with a dog by his side.

Feast: August 17
Patronage: against cholera; the falsely accused; invalids; against plagues

Romuald (952–1027) *Abbot, hermit, founder of the Camadolese Order*
Also known as: Romuald of Ravenna

Romuald of Ravenna was an important figure in the medieval revival of eremitic monasticism. An account of his life was written by St. Peter Damian, a Father of the Church.

Romuald was born around 952 in Ravenna, Italy, to a noble family. He was a young man when he saw his father kill a relative. To atone for his father's sin, he entered the monastery of San Apollinare-in-Classe. He saw Apollinaris in a vision and became a monk.

After three years Romuald departed to find a more austere way of life. In Venice he became a disciple of the hermit Marinus, who exacted harsh discipline. He went to the monastery at Cuxa, where he lived for 10 years. Meanwhile, his father had become a monk in an effort to atone for his own sins. Romuald returned to Ravenna to encourage him.

Romuald's reputation as a holy man attracted the attention of Emperor Otto III. The emperor appointed him abbot at San Apollinare-in-Classe. But after about

a year Romuald resigned in order to establish hermitages and reform monasteries throughout northern Italy and the Pyrenees. He founded the monastery of Camadoli near Arezzo, which later became the mother-house of the Camaldolese Order. The order merged the cenobitical, or monastic, life of the West with the eremitical, or hermit, life of the East.

Romuald tried several times to journey to Hungary to evangelize, but his health prevented him from doing so. He died on June 19, 1027, at Val di Castro near Camadoli. Miracles were reported after his death. His hair shirt reportedly expelled a demon from the church, and was kept as a relic.

Five years after his death, the remains of Romuald were exhumed in order to be placed in a new coffin beneath an altar. The monks expected to move bones and dust and so built a small coffin. One of them was warned in a dream by a venerable old man that the coffin would be too small. When the saint was uncovered, his body was found to be incorrupt, with a sheen of liquid on some of the parts. A new coffin was constructed, and the saint was reburied beneath the new altar.

His body was exhumed again in 1466 and 1481 and was found to be still incorrupt. The remains are now in the crypt of St. Romuald at the monastery of SS. Biagio and Romuald, in Fabriano (Ancona), Italy.

Canonized: 1595 by Pope Clement VIII
Feast: February 7

FURTHER READING
"The Relics of St. Romuald of Ravenna from Peter Damian's *Life of St. Romuald*." URL: http://www.urban.hunter. cuny.edu/~thead/romuald.htm. Downloaded: October 9, 2000.

Rose of Lima (Rosa de Lima) (1586–1617) *First person from the Americas to be canonized*

Born in Lima, Peru, on April 20, 1586, a half-century after the Spanish conquest of the Incas, Rose of Lima's parents were Gaspar de Flores, a Spaniard, and Maria de Oliva, who was part-Inca. She was baptized Isabel, but had such a beautiful face that after a few years her mother took to calling her Rose instead.

Rose began to show her religious devotion at a very early age. She spent hours each day in prayer. Once when she was praying before an image of the Virgin Mary, she imagined that the Infant Jesus appeared to her and said, "Rose, consecrate all of your love to me." From that point on she decided to live only for the love of Jesus Christ.

One day, her mother put a wreath of flowers on her head to show off her beauty to friends. Rose, though, had no desire to be admired, since she was committed to Christ. She drove a long pin through the wreath, piercing her head so deeply that afterward she had a hard time getting the wreath off. Except when they clashed over her religious devotion, Rose was obedient to her parents and worked hard, especially at sewing, at which she excelled.

She received confirmation from St. Turibius Mogoroveio, then the archbishop of Lima, in 1597, when she was 11. At this time she formally took the name Rose. But she continued to be troubled by her beauty and the implications her name carried, so on one occasion she rubbed her face with pepper until it was red and blistered. On another occasion she rubbed her hands with quicklime, causing herself great suffering.

When her brother told her that men were drawn to her for her long hair and fair skin, she cut her hair short and took to wearing a veil. Nevertheless, she attracted particularly one young man who wanted to marry her. Her father was delighted, because this man came from a good family, and he foresaw a brilliant future for her. Rose, however, declared that she would never marry.

She decided to enter an Augustinian convent, but the day that she was to go she knelt before her image of the Virgin to ask for guidance, and found she could not get up. She called her brother to help, but even with his assistance she could not rise. It came to her then that God must have other plans for her, and she said to Mary, "If you don't want me to enter the convent, I will drop the idea." As soon as she had said this she found herself able to stand without difficulty. She asked for a sign of which religious denomination she should join, and soon thereafter a black and white butterfly began to visit her daily, flitting about her eyes. She realized that she must look for an order that was associated with black and white, and soon discovered the Third Order of Dominic, whose nuns wear white tunics covered by black cloaks. She applied to the order in Lima and was admitted. She was then 20 years old.

Third Order Dominican nuns lived at home rather than in a convent, and with her brother's help Rose built a hut in her family's garden and there became a virtual recluse, going out only to Mass and to help those in need. Inspired by St. Catherine of Siena, she also began to subject herself to severe mortification. She wore a spiked silver crown covered by roses, a hair shirt, gloves filled with nettles, and an iron chain around her waist. She flogged herself three times a day, gouged out chunks of her skin with broken glass, and dragged a heavy wooden cross around the garden. She never ate meat and fasted three times a week. On the hottest days, she refused to drink, reminding herself of the thirst suffered by Jesus on the cross. She slept on a hard board with a stick for a pillow, a pile of bricks, or a bed that she constructed of broken glass, stone, potsherds and thorns.

Not surprisingly, Rose suffered from frequent ill health and went through periods of self-doubt, during which she felt revulsion toward all prayer, meditation and penance. She was also rewarded with many ecstasies and visions. One day she announced to the citizens of Lima that, through her prayers, she had prevented an earthquake from devastating the city. She was examined by priests and physicians, who decided that her experiences were in fact supernatural.

Rose was often ridiculed for the extreme forms of her devotion. She was not entirely detached from the world about her, however. When her father's business failed, she sold her splendid embroidery and took up gardening, producing beautiful flowers that were sold at the market. Rose also spoke out against the excesses of the colonial regime of the time and for the Indians and other common people. Sometimes she brought sick and hungry persons into her home so that she could care for them more easily.

Rose spent her last years in the home of a government official, Gonzalo de Massa. She was living then in an almost continuous mystical ecstasy. During an illness toward the end of her life, she prayed, "Lord, increase my sufferings, and with them increase Thy love in my heart." From 1614 onward, as the August 24 feast day of St. Bartholomew approached, Rose became very happy. She explained her great happiness by saying that she would die on a St. Bartholomew feast day. Indeed, she did die on August 24, 1617, at the age of 31.

Rose's sacrifices and penitence attracted many converts and increased the fervor of many priests, but not until after her death was it known how deeply she had affected the common people of Lima. Crowds of mourners lined the streets to watch the procession carrying her body to the cathedral, where it was to be displayed, and so many people came to view it that her burial had to be delayed. She was buried first in the Dominican convent, but after a few days moved to a special chapel in the Church of San Domingo. A great number of miracles and cures were at that time, and have since been, attributed to her intervention.

Rose's patronage extends beyond the Americas to the West Indies, the Philippines and India. The emblems associated with her are an anchor, a crown of roses and a city. She continues to be a popular saint in her native Peru, where her feast day is a national holiday. Her family home is now a shrine with a well where the faithful go to drop appeals for her help. The house where she died is now a convent (the Monasterio de Santa Rosa) named in her honor.

Beatified: 1667 by Pope Clement IX
Canonized: April 2, 1671, by Pope Clement X
Feast: August 30 (Peru); August 23 (elsewhere)
Patronage: florists; gardeners; needle workers; people ridiculed for their piety; Americas; India; Peru; Philippines; West Indies

FURTHER READING

Alphonsus, Mary. *St. Rose of Lima.* Rockford, Ill.: TAN Books, and Publishers, 1993.

"Santa Rosa de Lima." *Santos Peruanos.* Available online. URL: http://ekeko.rcp.net.pe/IAL/cep/santpapa/santos-los.htm. Downloaded: November 17, 1999.

"Saint Rose of Lima." *Stories of the Saints.* Available online. URL: http://members.tripod.com/~dymphna/saints/stbio.html. Downloaded: November 17, 1999.

Rose of Viterbo (1235–1252) *Franciscan tertiary*

Rose of Viterbo was born in 1235 in Viterbo, Italy, to a poor but pious family. Tradition holds that she was a miracle-worker from an early age and loved to spend time in churches praying. She was three years old when her aunt died. Rose is said to have prayed, touched the corpse and called her aunt by name, thus restoring the woman to life.

By age seven, Rose lived like a recluse and gave herself penances. These practices damaged her health. During a serious illness at age eight, the Blessed Virgin Mary appeared and miraculously healed her, and instructed her to join the Third Order of St. Francis of Assisi and preach penance in Viterbo. The city at that time was under the control of the anti-papal, Holy Roman Emperor Frederick II of Germany, and was influenced by the Ghibellines, an anti-papal party. Rose did as instructed, inspired further by a vision of a wounded and bloody Christ. For two years she went about Viterbo preaching penance and denouncing the enemies of the pope. Her father threatened her, but she would not stop. A plot to murder her was hatched by the Ghibellines, and Rose and her parents were banished from the city, perhaps for her own protection. In 1250 Rose went to Sorbiano and accurately prophesied the imminent and unexpected death of the emperor.

In Sorbiano, she campaigned against pagan heresy. One of her miracles consisted of standing for three hours in the flames of a burning pyre.

When papal power was restored in 1251, Rose returned to Viterbo. She tried several times to enter the convent of St. Mary of the Roses, but was refused because she had no dowry. She told them, "You will not have me now, but perhaps you will be more willing when I am dead." She returned to her father's house, where she died on March 6, 1252, at the age of 17.

Rose was buried in the Church of Santa Maria in Podio, but six years later Pope Alexander IX (r. 1254–61) ordered her remains translated to St. Mary of the Roses in return for her support of the papacy. In 1357 the church was destroyed by fire, but her incorrupt body remained unharmed. It was enshrined in the Monasterio Clarisse S. Rosa in Viterbo.

In 1921, her incorrupt heart was placed in a reliquary and was afterward paraded through the city every September 4, her feast day. Her incorrupt body, now dark but still flexible, is exposed in a reliquary.

Numerous miracles were attested to Rose. She communicated with animals, especially birds. Once while preaching in Viterbo, she and the stone platform on which she stood levitated into the air before spectators. Rose remained suspended in the air while she spoke to the crowd.

Canonized: 1457 by Pope Callistus III
Feast: September 4
Patronage: exiles; people in exile; people rejected by religious orders; tertiaries

Scholastica (ca. 480–543) *Benedictine sister, abbess and twin sister of St. Benedict of Nursia, considered to be the first Benedictine nun*

Very little is known about Scholastica, save for a few comments by Pope St. Gregory I (Gregory the Great, r. 590–604) in *Dialogues,* in which he records events of St. Benedict's life. In early youth, she consecrated her life to God. After Benedict established his monastery at Monte Cassino, Italy, she moved to nearby Plombariola, where she founded and governed a monastery of nuns. Benedict directed his sister and her nuns.

Scholastica visited her brother once a year, and stayed in a house separate from the monastery, which she was not allowed to enter. Benedict and several of his brothers would meet her there and spend the day discussing spiritual matters.

The best-known story about Scholastica took place in 543 on one of these visits. Toward evening, Benedict prepared for his return to the monastery. Scholastica begged him to stay the night, but Benedict replied, "By no means can I stay out of my monastery." Scholastica bowed her head and prayed. When she raised her head, there was a sudden and dramatic shift in the weather. The sky had been clear and serene; now lightning flashed and thunder boomed. A heavy rainfall commenced.

Benedict was not pleased, and said, "God Almighty forgive you, sister. What is this you have done?"

Scholastica said, "I prayed you to stay and you would not hear me. I prayed to Almighty God and he heard me. Now, therefore, if you can, go forth to the monastery and leave me."

Benedict and his brothers were forced to spend the night. They continued their discussions.

Benedict and his party left in the morning, never to see Scholastica again. She died three days later. Benedict beheld her soul in a vision as it ascended into heaven. He had her body brought to his monastery and laid it in the tomb he had prepared for himself. He died within the year and, as requested, was laid to rest with his sister.

Feast: February 10
Patronage: convulsive children; against storms

Sebastian (d. ca. 288–304) *Roman martyr famed for the manner in which he died*

Little is known about Sebastian prior to his martyrdom during the reign of Emperor Diocletian (284–305). St. Ambrose speaks of him, and other accounts tell of his martyrdom: the *Depositio Martyrum* and the *Hieronymian Martyrology.*

The Martyrdom of St. Sebastian (Engraving by Albrecht Dürer, n.d.)

free, freed his slaves and resigned as prefect. Sebastian also is credited with healing others of the plague.

Sebastian was named captain in the Praetorian guards by Emperor Diocletian, and again by Emperor Maximian when Diocletian went to the East. Neither knew that Sebastian was a Christian. When it was discovered during Maximian's persecution of the Christians that Sebastian was a Christian, he was sentenced to be executed. He was shot with arrows by archers from Mauretania and left for dead. Irene, the widow of the martyr St. Castulus, went to collect his body and discovered him still alive. She nursed him back to health. Recovered, he went before Diocletian and denounced him for his cruelty to Christians. The astonished emperor ordered him to be clubbed to death. This time the sentence was carried out successfully.

His remains were buried on the Via Appia with other martyrs. The basilica San Sebastiano is named after him. He was venerated in the times of Ambrose.

Sebastian is often portrayed in art—he was especially popular with Renaissance painters and sculptors—tied to a column and shot full of arrows. His symbol is the arrow.

Feast: January 20
Patronage: archers, athletes; plague sufferers; soldiers

Serapion the Scholastic (d. ca. 370) *Bishop, scholar and head of the famed Catechetical School of Alexandria, Egypt; Greek Father of the Church*
Also known as: Serapion of Arsinoc

Serapion was a monk in the Egyptian desert and a companion to St. Anthony, who left in his will the gift of two sheepskin cloaks, one for Serapion and the other for the patriarch St. Athanasius of Alexandria. Serapion was a close friend of Athanasius, and gave support to him against the heretic Arians in Egypt. His appointment as bishop of Thmuis, on the Nile Delta in Lower Egypt, enabled him to increase his efforts against the heretics. These efforts, however, led to his exile for a time by the ardent Arian emperor Constantius II. A brilliant scholar and theologian, he was also the author of a series of writings on the doctrine of the divinity of the Holy Spirit (addressed to the emperor), the *Euchologium* (a sacramentary) and a treatise against Manichaeanism.

Feast: March 21

Sergius I (d. 701) *Pope*

Sergius, son of the Syrian merchant Tiberius, was born at Palermo, Italy. He was educated in Rome at the

According to legend, Sebastian was born at Narbonne, Gaul; other sources place him from Milan. He became a soldier in the Roman army at Rome in about 283 in order to defend confessors and martyrs without drawing attention to himself. He encouraged Marcellian and Marcus, under sentence of death, to remain firm in their faith. Sebastian made numerous converts, including the master of the rolls, Nicostratus, who was in charge of prisoners, and his wife, Zoe, a deaf mute whom he cured; the jailer, Claudius; Chromatius, prefect of Rome, whom he cured of gout; and Chromatius's son, Tiburtius. Chromatius set the prisoners

schola cantorum (church choir school). He was ordained a priest by Pope St. Leo II (r. 682–683) and served as the titular priest of Sta. Susanna before being elected the successor of Pope Conon (r. 686–687) on December 15, 687.

His elevation to the Chair of St. Peter came not without controversy, however. As Pope Conon lay on his deathbed, his archdeacon, Pascal, promised the exarch John of Ravenna a considerable sum of money to bring about his election. Upon Conon's death, Pascal was duly elected by one faction of the Roman Church, while another elected the archpriest Theodosius, and the majority of the clerics and laity went for Sergius. Theodosius quickly bowed to Sergius, and his supporters stormed the Lateran Palace and had him consecrated. Pascal appealed to John of Ravenna, who came to Rome, but approved Sergius's election only when he had been paid the bribe he had been promised by Pascal.

Sergius was active in promoting the interests of the Church in England. In 689, he baptized St. Caedwalla, king of the West Saxons. In 695, he consecrated St. Willibroard bishop and sent him as a missionary to the Frisians (Germans).

Sergius is also remembered for his refusal to endorse the Quintisext (Trullanum) Council of 692, at which the Greek Church decreed that priests and deacons who had married before their ordinations could keep their wives, and that also sought to place the patriarch of Constantinople on equal footing with the bishop of Rome. Sergius's rejection of the council's acts led Emperor Justinian II to dispatch an officer to bring him to Constantinople. The Roman people protected the pope, but the crisis came to an end only when Justinian II was deposed in 695.

Sergius repaired and adorned several Roman basilicas, added the Agnus Dei to the Mass, inaugurated the Feast of the Exaltation of the Cross, and instituted processions in feasts associated with the Theotokos. He died in Rome on the seventh or eighth of September 701.

In art, Sergius is shown sleeping as an angel brings him the episcopal insignia for Bishop Saint Hubert of Liège.

Feast: September 8

Seven Holy Helpers (13th century) *Seven Florenctine businessmen led by the Blessed Virgin Mary to establish the Servants of Mary, known as the Servite Friars or Servite Fathers*

Also known as: Seven Servites

The businessmen were members of the Confraternity of Our Lady in Florence, Italy. They were: Bonfilio Monaldo; Alexis Falconieri; (Benedict) Manettus dell' Antello; Bartholomew Amidei (or Rocovero); Uguccio Uguccione (or Gherardino); Sostenes Sostegno; and (John) Buonagiunta Monetti.

In 1233, the businessmen, all well-to-do, were between the ages of 27 and 35, and had been members of the confraternity for five years. They were quite concerned about the lifestyles they saw around them: excessive immorality, humanism and materialism. At their meetings, they prayed and sang songs to Mary.

After receiving Communion at the Feast of the Assumption, the seven shared a mutual mystical experience that changed their lives. A supernaturally bright light appeared, and in the center was Mary surrounded by a host of angels. She said to them: "Leave the world and retire together in solitude in order to fight yourselves. Live wholly for God. You will thus experience heavenly consolations. My protection and assistance will never fail you."

Thus fired, the men received the blessings of the confraternity and the bishop of Florence. They sold their possessions, gave the money to the poor and left their families to live in a dilapidated farmhouse outside of town. They intended only to live in extreme mortification and penance. They begged for food. Many townspeople considered them cranks. They were unofficially dubbed "the Servants of Mary."

In May 1234, Mary appeared in another vision and directed them to go farther away, to Mt. Senario, and live even more austerely. They did as instructed. Some lived in caves on the mountainside; some subsisted solely on herbs. They maintained silence for prolonged periods of time. So severe was their lifestyle that once a visiting cardinal, shocked, ordered them to be kinder to themselves.

Despite their austerity, other young men asked to join them. They were given a sign on February 27, 1239—the third Sunday of Lent—when they discovered that a grapevine they had planted was blooming and had ripe fruit, while other vines remained frostbitten. The bishop told them that this meant others would join the order.

On Good Friday, April 13, 1239, Mary appeared to the seven after they had finished their night prayers. She said, "beloved and elect Servants, I have come to grant your prayers. Here is the habit which I wish you to wear henceforth. It is black that it may always remind you of the keen sorrow which I experienced through my son's crucifixion and death. This scroll bearing the words 'Servants of Mary' indicates the name by which you are to be known. This book contains the Rule of St. Augustine. By following it you will gain these palms in heaven, if you serve me faithfully on earth!"

Mary gave the same message to the bishop, who approved the new Order of Servants of Mary. Six of the original seven entered the priesthood; one remained a lay brother. Within a few years, there were more than 100 houses. Women became Servite nuns.

The order gave the Church the Feast of the Seven Sorrows of the Blessed Virgin Mary, and greatly increased the popularity of the Sorrowful Mother Novena.

Canonized: 1888 by Pope Leo XIII
Feast: February 17

Seven Sleepers of Ephesus (third century) *Martyrs*

This curious medieval legend exists in different versions in several languages. Probably it was first recorded in Greek, by Symeon Metaphrastes, and later translated into Latin (by St. Gregory of Tours) and Syriac and other Middle Eastern languages. It is also told in an Anglo-Norman poem and in Old Norse. An Arabic version appears in the Koran.

The story is simple, though powerful. When Emperor Decius (r. 249–251) came to Ephesus to enforce his persecutory decrees against Christians, he found there seven young men—their names vary in different versions—who were believers. He had them put on trial and gave them a short time to decide whether they would abrogate their faith and live or persist in it and die. Deciding on the latter course, the seven gave their property to the poor and, keeping only a few coins, went into a cave on Mt. Anchilos to pray and prepare for death. They were warned of Decius's return, said a final payer, then fell asleep. Meanwhile, Decius had ordered his soldiers to find them, and when they were discovered sleeping in the cave, had it walled up.

A Christian came along and on the outer wall wrote the story and the names of the martyrs. Years passed and times changed. The Roman Empire became Christian. Then sometime during the reign of either Theodosius the Great (r. 379–395) or Theodosius the Younger (r. 408–450), at a time when the doctrine of bodily resurrection was much debated, a rich landowner decided to have the cave opened in order to use it as a cattle stall. The seven young men then awoke, and, thinking they had slept only one night, sent one of their number, Diomedes, into town to buy food, so that they might have one last meal together. Diomedes found Ephesus much altered, and the people could not understand where he got the coins minted under Decius. At length the truth came out, and Diomedes lead the bishop and the prefect to the cave, where his companions were found. Theodosius

was sent for, and this proof of resurrection was much celebrated.

At this point, the seven died for good. Theodosius wished to build golden tombs for them, but they appeared to him in a dream and asked to be buried in the earth in their cave. Their bodies were duly returned to the cave and interred there, and a great church was built over it. Every year, the feast of the Seven Sleepers is kept.

In the Roman Martyrology, the Seven Sleepers are commemorated individually under the names Dionysius, Maximianus, Malchus, Martinianus, Joannes, Serapion and Constantinus.

Feast: July 27 (in the West); August 4 and October 22 (in the East)

FURTHER READING
"Seven Sleepers." Encyclopedia Mythica website. URL: http://wwwntheon.org/mythica/articles/s/seven_sleepers.html. Downloaded: September 10, 2000.

Silverius (d. ca. 537) *Pope and martyr*

Silverius was the son of Pope St. Hormisdas, who had been married before becoming one of the higher clergy in the Roman Church. Silverius followed his father into the Church and was subdeacon at Rome when Pope St. Agapetus (r. 535–536) died at Constantinople on April 22, 536. Silverius was ordained his successor on June 1 or 8, 536.

From the beginning, he was caught up in the political intrigues of the day, as the Byzantine Empire and the Ostrogoths struggled for control of Italy. He is thought to have died on December 2, around the year 537, while in captivity on the island of Palmaria. Another source says that he was buried there on June 20. By the 11th century, he was venerated as a saint.

In art, Silverius is usually portrayed as a pilgrim pope with a small piece of bread on a plate. He is also shown with a paten or as he sits by a table on which there is a scroll while armed men approach.

Feast: June 20

Simeon Stylites (390–459) *Ascetic; first of the stylitae, hermits who lived on top of pillars*

Simeon Stylites is worthy of note for the extremes of his asceticism and mortification, and for establishing the practice of pillar-living for those who found ordinary asceticism insufficient.

Simeon was born in northern Syria and entered a monastery at Eusebona near Antioch. His practices were too extreme for the monks, so they persuaded him to leave. He spent three years living in a hut. He became renowned for fasting during Lent and his feat of standing for as long as his body could endure.

Simeon seemed always to look for even more extreme ways to practice asceticism, and struck upon the idea of confining himself to a platform atop a nine-foot pillar. Understandably, this attracted crowds, who came not only to see the human oddity but to ask his advice as well. Simeon remedied this by increasing the height of the pillar to 50 (some accounts say 60) feet. On these pillars he spent the last 37 years of his life.

Simeon ate one small meal per week and fasted throughout the entire season of Lent. His disciples gave him food and removed his waste with buckets and ropes. Even this deprivation was not enough for him, so he had himself bound to the platform so tightly that the ropes cut into his flesh. He had maggots brought to the platform and set upon the wounds, so that they began eating his flesh. He wore a heavy iron chain. People came from Persia, Ethiopia, Spain and even Britain to see him and hear him preach. He inspired other ascetics to live atop pillars.

According to lore, Simeon was often and visibly visited by his guardian angel, who devoted many hours to teaching him the mysteries of God. The angel also foretold his death. When he developed an ulcer on his right leg, he stood for the remaining year of his life upon his good leg.

In 459, his disciple Anthony was unable to get a response from him and so climbed up to the platform. There he found the saint dead, his body exuding a perfume that seemed made from many spices.

His remains were taken to Antioch and his body remained well preserved until nearly the seventh century. Some teeth were removed for relics. The head was considered to have protective powers against invasion from Eastern armies.

Feast: January 5

FURTHER READING

Evagrius. "St. Simeon Stylites," from *Ecclesiastical History*, I.13. Medieval Sourcebook website. URL: http://www.fordham.edu/halsall/source/evagrius-simeon.html. Downloaded: February 13, 2000.

Gordon, Anne. *A Book of Saints*. New York: Bantam Books, 1994.

Simon Stock (ca. 1185–1265) *Carmelite mystic who helped the Carmelites become a mendicant order*

Simon Stock's was born in Aylesford, Kent, England. According to legend, the name Stock, meaning "tree trunk," derives from the fact that, beginning at age 12,

he lived as a hermit in the hollow trunk of an oak tree until he became an itinerant preacher. However, Stock probably was added postmortem to his first name because of his tree-living.

Legend has it that while he lived in the tree, Simon was visited daily by a small dog who brought him crusts of bread. He was especially devoted to Mary, and composed poems in her honor and carved her names on trees. He had many visions of the Blessed Virgin Mary, who foretold that holy hermits would come from Mt. Carmel, and he would join them.

As a young man, Simon reputedly went on a pilgrimage to the Holy Land where he joined up with a group of Carmelites and later returned to Europe with them. He was one of the first Englishmen to enter the Carmelite order. In 1245 he was elected sixth master-general and became well-known. He founded many Carmelite communities, especially in university towns such as Cambridge, Oxford, Paris and Bologna. He received papal approval for changing the Carmelites from a hermit order to one of mendicant friars, a move that enabled them to spread rapidly throughout Europe. In 1254 he was elected superior-general of his Order at London.

Simon is best-known for a vision of Mary he had in Cambridge, England, on July 16, 1251, during a time of oppression of the Carmelites. Simon, in despair over the trouble in the order, had withdrawn to his cell to pray. He recited one of his youthful poems to Mary. Suddenly his cell filled with radiant light, and he saw Mary holding the infant Jesus, surrounded by angels.

Mary held a brown scapular in one hand and presented it to him, saying, *"Hoc erit tibi et cunctis Carmelitis privilegium, in hoc habitu moriens salvabitur."* ("Receive, my beloved son, this scapular of thy Order; it is the special sign of my favor, which I have obtained for thee and for thy children of Mount Carmel. He who dies clothed with this habit shall be preserved from eternal fire.")

The following January, Pope Innocent IV (r. 1243–54) and the king of England issued an order of protection for the Carmelites.

Simon died on May 16, 1265, in Bordeaux, France. His relics are enshrined in Aylesford. He is said to be the composer of the *Ave Stella Matutina* and *Flos Carmeli*. He was never formally canonized, but is venerated as a saint by the Carmelites and is recognized in some dioceses.

Mary's scapular became adopted as the regular habit of the White Friars, and the scapular devotion spread through Europe. The Carmelites established Scapular Confraternities, which gave small woolen scapulars to lay members. In 1276, Pope Gregory X (r. 1271–76) died and was buried in a such a scapular, which was found incorrupt in his tomb when it was opened in 1830.

Mary's brown scapular has become a popular Catholic devotion.

Feast: May 16
Patronage: tanners

Simon the Zealot *One of the Twelve Disciples of Jesus; martyr*
Also known as: Simeon, Simon the Canaanaean, Simon the Canaanite

Simon was probably born in Galilee, although nothing is known about his parentage. He was called by Jesus to be one of his 12 disciples; since St. Peter's given name also was Simon, in order to distinguish them, Simon was surnamed Kananaios, Kananites, or Zelotes—all translations of the Hebrew *qana* ("the Zealous"). This referred to the zeal for Jewish law he possessed before his conversion to Christianity, not, as sometimes has been assumed, his membership in the party of Zealots, Jewish patriots opposed to the Roman occupation of Israel. Similarly, the assumption that he was a Canaanite is based on a mistranslation; had be been from Cana, his surname would have been "Kanaios." Nevertheless, in the Greek Church he is identified with Nathanael of Cana, the bridegroom recipient of Jesus' first public miracle, when at his mother's request he turned water into wine, and in English he is sometimes called Simon the Canaanean or Canaanite.

Simon's later life is as confused as his name, with the various Christian churches having different traditions about his career. He certainly left Palestine when the apostles fanned out to evangelize the world, but where is uncertain. The Abyssinians hold that he preached in Samaria; the Greeks that he went to the Black Sea, Egypt, North Africa and Britain; the Georgians that he was in Colchis. According to the apocryphal *Passion of Simon and Jude*, he served with St. Jude in Persia.

Eastern traditions hold that Simon died peacefully at Edessa (Mesopotamia), although in the West he is believed to have been martyred. This may have occurred in Jerusalem, to which Simon may have returned from the field to succeed St. James the Less as bishop. However, at least since the sixth century, there have been legends about his martyrdom with Jude in Persia, although with variations. Some hold that their bodies were cut to pieces with a saw or falchion (a short sickle-shaped sword), others that they were beaten to death with a club, then beheaded. According

St. Simon (Engraving by Albrecht Dürer, 1523)

to *The Golden Legend*, Simon died when his body was sawed in half by pagan priests.

Simon's original burial place is unknown, and there are widely discrepant accounts of what became of his relics. At least some of them are believed to rest under the altar of the Crucifixion in St. Peter's in Rome. Reims and Toulouse in France claim to have others.

In art, Simon is symbolized by the saw or, more rarely, the lance, in commemoration of his death; or fish, boats or oars, in commemoration of his putative profession as a fisherman. Typically he is depicted as a middle-aged man holding one of his symbolic items. He may also be shown being sawn in two longitudinally. When he and Jude appear together, one holds a saw and the other a sword, though they are often confused.

Feast: October 28 (in the West, celebrated with St. Jude), May 10 (among Greeks and Copts), July 1 (elsewhere in the East)

Patronage: curriers; sawyers; tanners

Simplicius (d. 483) *Pope*

Simplicius, son of Castinus, was born in Tivoli (Italy). He succeeded St. Hilarus as bishop of Rome on March 3, 468.

During his pontificate, the Roman Empire came to an end. In 476, Odoacer of the Heruli, a Germanic tribe, deposed the last emperor of the West, Romulus Augustulus, occupied Rome and proclaimed himself king of Italy. Since Christianity had for some time been the official religion of the empire, this could have spelled trouble for the Church, but fortunately Odoacer was favorably disposed toward the Vatican.

In the East, however, the Church was in greater danger, threatened by the Monophysite heresy. Monophysitism was popular in the Eastern Church and in Africa and had support among the secular authorities as well. The controversy, concerning the true nature of Jesus, was a longstanding one. Simplicius struggled to uphold the authority of the Roman Church, not always successfully.

He died on March 10, 483, after a long illness, and was buried in St. Peter's on Vatican Hill. Afterward he was venerated as a saint.

Simplicius was the first pope to be depicted with a square nimbus in a contemporary mosaic.

Feast: March 10 (formerly March 2 or 3)

Siricius (ca. 334–399) *Pope and martyr*

Siricius, son of Tiburtius, was born in Rome about 334. He entered the Roman Church at an early age and served as lector and later deacon under Pope Liberius (r. 352–366) and Pope St. Damasus (r. 366–383). Damasus died on December 11, 384, and although the antipope Ursinus (who had been excommunicated by Damasus) claimed the see, Siricius was consecrated bishop on December 17.

His pontificate was marked by his denunciation and excommunication in 392 of the monk Jovinian, who averred that Mary had lost her virginity with the birth of Jesus and that she and Joseph had had other children after Jesus. Siricius is known also for a papal decree sent to Bishop Himerius of Tarragona (Spain) requiring married priests to desist from cohabitation with their wives and threatening sanctions against those who did not obey. This was the earliest insistence on clerical celibacy and also the earliest decretal that has survived in its entirety.

Siricius died on November 26, 399, and was buried in the Catacombs of St. Priscilla on the Via Salaria. His tomb became a popular site in seventh-century pilgrimages. His name was inserted in the Roman Martyrology by Pope Benedict XIV (r. 1740–58).

Feast: November 26

Sixtus I (d. ca. 125) *Pope and martyr*
Also known as: Xystus

Sixtus was born in Rome, the son of Pastor; his name suggests that he may have been of Greek origin. He was the seventh pope, reigning for about 10 years, from the death of Alexander I ca. 115 to ca. 125.

According to the *Liber Pontificalis,* Sixtus passed three ordinances, decreeing that: only sacred ministers were allowed to touch the sacred vessels; bishops who had been summoned to the Holy See could not be received by their dioceses without presenting Apostolic letters; and after the Preface in the Mass the priest should recite the Sanctus with the people. However, this last decree is wrongly attributed to him, raising doubts about whether he was responsible for the former two decrees.

Like his predecessors, Sixtus is thought to have died a martyr. He was buried in the Vatican, near St. Peter, but his relics may have been moved later. Some sources say that they were translated to Alatri in 1132; in his *Lives of Saints,* Butler contends that Pope Clement X (r. 1670–76) gave some of them to Cardinal de Retz, who placed them in the abbey of St. Michael in Lorraine. However, it is possible that they still rest in the Vatican basilica.

Feast: April 6

Sixtus II (d. 258) *Pope and martyr*
Also known as: Xystus II

Sixtus II may have been a Greek philosopher, though more probably this impression arose from a confusion of names. He served as a deacon in the Church of Rome and succeeded St. Stephen I as bishop on August 30, 257.

Sixtus repaired the rift between the sees of Rome and Carthage that had developed under Stephen over the issues of baptism and rebaptism. Like Stephen, Sixtus believed that a single baptism was sufficient to bring persons into the Church but, unlike him, was tolerant of those who disagreed.

He is probably best remembered, however, for the way in which he met his death. Early in his reign, Emperor Valerian had shown compassion toward Christians, but later he issued an edict requiring Christians to participate in the national cult of the pagan gods and forbade them to assemble in the cemeteries (or catacombs), at the penalty of death. He followed this up at the beginning of August 258, with an order that all bishops, priests and deacons were to be killed.

Flaunting death, Sixtus assembled his followers in the Catacomb of Prætextatus (on the Appian Way across from the Catacomb of St. Callistus) on August 6. He was seated in his chair addressing his flock when a band of soldiers appeared and cut off his head. (He may have been taken before a tribunal, which pronounced sentence on him, then returned to the cemetery and decapitated.) Several other church officers with him suffered the same fate. Followers carried his relics to the papal crypt in the St. Callistus catacomb, placing the blood-stained chair on which he died behind his tomb. Later an oratory (the Oratorium Xysti) was erected over the St. Prætextatus catacomb, becoming a pilgrimage site in the seventh and eighth centuries.

There is a legend that on the way to his execution Sixtus met his deacon St. Lawrence, who was to be martyred three days later.

Sixtus was one of the most highly esteemed martyrs of the early Church. His name is mentioned in the canon of the Roman Mass.

In art, he is shown with Lawrence and St. John the Baptist, holding a money-bag. He may also be shown ordaining Lawrence, giving him a bag of money to distribute to the poor, or with Lawrence on the way to his death.

Feast: August 7 (formerly August 6)

Sixtus III (d. 440) *Pope*
Also known as: Xystus III

Not much is known about Sixtus III. He was prominent in the Roman Church when he was elevated to the Chair of St. Peter, succeeding St. Celestine I (r. 422–432) on July 31, 432.

Sixtus III was falsely accused of sympathy toward Nestorianism and Pelagianism, against both of which heresies he acted. He also defended the pope's right of supremacy over the ecclesiastical province of Illyricum against Proclus of Constantinople.

In Rome, he restored the basilica of Liberius (now St. Mary Major) and enlarged the basilica of St. Lawrence-Outside-the-Walls. He received precious gifts from Emperor Valentinian III for St. Peter's and the Lateran basilica.

Sixtus III died in 440.

Feast: March 28

Sophia (Sofia)
Name meaning: Wisdom
Also known as: Sapientia

Sophia is a legendary saint in the cult of Divine Wisdom. She is said to be the mother of Faith, Hope and Charity. The origins of her legend can be traced to the *Pistis Sophia,* a fourth-century Coptic manuscript.

The *Pistis Sophia* is a Gnostic gospel professing to contain the esoteric teachings of the risen Christ to his disciples in response to their questions and in the form of dialogue. It was purchased from a London bookshop in 1733 and was given to the British Museum in 1785. The codex is divided into four books, the first three of which are considered the true *Pistis Sophia,* and probably were written between 250 and 350.

The title, *Pistis Sophia,* has been translated as "Faithful Wisdom." According to the *Epistle of Eugnostos,* a Nag Hammadi codex, Sophia is both the consort of the Savior and the female designation of the sixth of the emanations manifested by him.

According to the text, after Jesus rose from the dead he taught among his disciples for 11 years. In the 12th and final year of his sojourn, prior to his final Ascension, Jesus revealed the "supreme mystery" to his followers on the 15th of January. The disciples gathered around Jesus at the Mount of Olives. As the sun came up, a light beyond measure, coming from "the Light of lights," descended and enveloped Jesus. It extended from below the earth to the heavens. Before his trembling disciples, Jesus ascended into heaven. Angels and archangels and the "powers of the heights" praised the "Inmost of the Inmost" for all the world to hear.

The following day, Jesus descended from heaven in a cloud of brilliant light. He told his disciples that he had journeyed through the aeons (Gnostic levels of heaven) and had met Pistis Sophia alone and in mourning. At the request of Mary, he told of her lamentations at having fallen from the 13th aeon into the realm of matter. He restored her to her heavenly place. He went on to discuss the mysteries of light, the Ineffable, the origin of sin and evil, and the after-death punishments of the wicked.

In Christian lore, Sophia's daughters suffered martyrdom during Emperor Hadrian's (r. 117–138) persecution of Christians. Faith, 12, was scourged and went unharmed when boiling pitch was poured on her; she was beheaded. Hope, 10, and Charity, nine, were

St. Sophia with the symbols of faith, hope and charity
(copyright © Robert Michael Place. Used with permission.)

tossed into a furnace and emerged unscathed; they also were beheaded. Sophia died three days later while praying at their graves.

In the Roman Martyrology, Sophia is a Roman widow, and her feast is September 30.

Feast: August 1

FURTHER READING
Schneemelcher, Wilhelm, ed. *New Testament Apocrypha,* Volume One: *Gospels and Related Writings,* rev. ed. Tr./ed. R. McL. Wilson. Westminster, Ky.: John Knox Press, 1991.

Sophronius (560–638) *Patriarch of Jerusalem, writer and Father of the Church*

Sophronius was born in Damascus around 560. In his late teens or early twenties, he became an ascetic and went to either Jordan or Egypt. In 605, invading Persians forced him to go to Alexandria, and when the invaders arrived there in 616 he went to Rome. In 619, he returned to Palestine and lived in the Theodosius monastery in Jerusalem.

Sophronius was an opponent of Monothelitism, and went to Alexandria to argue unsuccessfully against Patriarch Cyrus of Alexandria. He went to Constantinople in 633 to argue against Patriarch Sergius of Constantinople, again unsuccessfully.

Sophronius was elected patriarch of Jerusalem in 634. Muslims captured the city in 637, and Sophronius died the following year.

Many of Sophronius's works no longer exist. He wrote on the life of St. John the Almsgiver, homilies, treatises, sermons and poems. He wrote about the martyrs John and Cyrus, and also an account of St. Mary of Egypt.

Feast: March 11

Soter (d. ca. 175) *Pope and martyr*

Soter was an Italian from the Campagna. He succeeded St. Anicetus as pope around 166 and reigned until about 175. During his rule, Easter became an annual celebration.

Soter's influence was widespread, thanks partly to his charity, his personal kindness, and his support for those who were persecuted for their faith by being deported from Rome to the mines and prisons. Like SS. Paul and Clement, he wrote a pastoral letter to the troubled Church of Corinth, even sending gifts to the congregation.

Soter also was called upon to discipline the Montanists, a Christian sect that preached that the heavenly Jerusalem would soon descend near Pepuza, a town in Phrygia. They criticized other Christians for not fasting enough and not prophesying enough, for want of the gift of the Holy Spirit. Moreover, said the Montanists, Christians should not marry again if one partner had died. The movement was dividing the Roman Church. Soter condemned the leaders, issuing an encyclical outlining their errors.

No records of Soter's death survive, though he is listed in early martyrologies.

Feast: April 22

Stanislaus (1030–1079) *Bishop of Cracow*
Also known as: Stanislaus Szcepanowski

Stanislaus was the long-awaited son of Belislaus and Bogna Szcepanowsky, noble and devout parents, born on July 26, 1030, at Szczepanow, Poland. His parents dedicated the boy to God's service. He was educated at Gnesen (also known as Gniezno) and perhaps Paris, then ordained a priest by Lampert Zula, bishop of Cracow. Bishop Lampert appointed the young man his preacher and archdeacon and awarded him a canonry benefit in the cathedral. Stanislaus's eloquent preaching and holy example drew converts and reformed the morals of many who had strayed, both clergy and laity. Bishop Lampert offered to resign the see in Stanislaus's favor, but Stanislaus would not accept the offer. Upon Lampert's death, however, Stanislaus was consecrated bishop in 1072 under the direct orders of Pope Alexander II.

The king of Poland at this time was Boleslaus II, called "the Cruel" for his rapacious lust and savage tyranny. He little resembled Boleslaus I, named "the Brave," who was crowned the first Christian king of Poland in the year 1000 by Holy Roman Emperor Otto III. Boleslaus II continually antagonized the clergy and nobility, and Bishop Stanislaus often remonstrated with the king for his scandalous behavior. At first Boleslaus tried to vindicate himself, then he appeared to seek repentance, then to relapse into his old ways. The final straw was the abduction of a noble's beautiful wife and her forced imprisonment because she refused his adulterous proposals.

Outraged, the Polish nobility called upon the archbishop of Gnesen and other court prelates to confront Boleslaus, but fear of reprisals kept them silent, leading the nobles to accuse the officials of conspiracy to commit the crime. But Stanislaus, upon hearing the nobles' appeal, had no reservations about rebuking the king and reminded the monarch that if he persisted he would bring upon himself the censure of the Church and a sentence of excommunication. Furious, the king threw Stanislaus out, declaring that any man who addressed his sovereign with such effrontery was more fit to be a swineherd. The king next tried slander and harassment against Stanislaus, accusing the bishop of never paying for a piece of land that had been bought years before and suggesting to the seller's surviving nephews that they should sue for claim to the property. According to one biographer, the dead seller, a man named Peter, appeared in his grave clothes in court and vindicated Stanislaus. Boleslaus also accused Stanislaus of treason when the bishop sided with a group of nobles who were unjustly treated after being forced from their homes. Seeing no signs of a change of heart, Stanislaus excommunicated the king.

Boleslaus coldly ignored the ban, but when he attempted to enter the cathedral at Cracow and the priests suspended the services at Stanislaus's order,

Boleslaus became enraged. He and some of his men pursued Stanislaus to the little chapel of St. Michael outside Cracow where the bishop was performing Mass. Boleslaus ordered his guards to kill Stanislaus, but the guards could not, claiming that the bishop was surrounded by a heavenly light. Disgusted by the guards' weakness, Boleslaus entered the chapel and murdered Stanislaus himself. The guards then hacked the body to pieces and scattered them to be eaten by animals of prey. The Lord protected the body parts, however, and they were collected by the cathedral canons three days later and buried at the door of St. Michael's chapel where the bishop had died.

Later historians have alleged that Stanislaus's motives were more political than spiritual, and that Boleslaus may have had cause to kill the bishop for treason. But this is a position hotly denied by the Polish faithful. The murder of Stanislaus did not directly force the overthrow of Boleslaus II, but that act certainly added to the people's discontent, especially after Pope St. Gregory VII placed Poland under an interdict. Bishop Lampert II moved Stanislaus's relics to Cracow Cathedral in 1088.

Canonized: 1253 by Pope Innocent IV
Feast: April 11
Patronage: Cracow, Poland; Poland

FURTHER READING
Reston, James, Jr. *The Last Apocalypse: Europe at the Year 1000 A.D.* New York: Doubleday, 1998.

Stephen (d. ca. 35) *Revered as the first martyr, and the most famous deacon in the early Christian Church*
Name meaning: "Crown"
Also known as: Stephen the Deacon

Little is known of Stephen's early life and conversion. His name is Greek, but he is believed to have been of Jewish origin. Kelil, the Aramaic equivalent of Stephen, is inscribed upon his tomb, found in 415. He is mentioned in Acts 6:5 as one of seven deacons chosen by the apostles to help look after widows and the poor. He is described as "a man full of faith and of the Holy Ghost." He spent his time among the Hellenists, preaching bold sermons and performing miracles. He attracted many followers.

Acts 6-8:2 tells of his martyrdom. His popularity earned him many enemies among the Jews, who plotted his downfall. He was accused of blasphemy against Moses and God and was brought before the Sanhedrin in Jerusalem. Acts 7:2–53 tells how eloquently he defended himself, radiant as an angel. He spoke about Jesus as the Savior that God had promised to send. It was to no avail. He certainly earned no quarter by

The martyrdom of St. Stephen (Engraving by Gustave Doré, c. 1875)

chastising his attackers for not believing in Jesus, and calling them "stiff-necked people, uncircumcised in heart and ears," and betrayers and murderers. His opponents only rose up in great anger and shouted at him. Stephen looked up to heaven and said that he saw the heavens opening and Jesus standing at the right hand of God.

Stephen was condemned under Mosaic law and was dragged outside of Jerusalem and stoned to death. Saul—later to become St. Paul—approved of the execution, and witnesses and executioners surrendered their garments to him for safekeeping. Stephen's last words were "Lord, Jesus, receive my spirit," and a request that his killers be forgiven.

Stephen was buried in a tomb and was for the most part forgotten until the fourth century, when St. Gregory of Nyssa composed two homilies to him. Gregory saw him as a key figure in a struggle against demonic forces, and one who caused great awe and wonder among the angels. Stephen imitated Christ by being sweet and compliant and bearing no hatred toward his murderers. Gregory made a play on words, comparing Stephen's name to the word for crown in Greek, *stephanos.*

Stephen's tomb was discovered by Lucian. Empress Eudoxia (r. 455–460) built a church in his honor outside the Damascus Gate.

Stephen's blood is a relic in the Church of San Guadioso in Naples, Italy. As late as 1624, the blood was said to liquefy whenever the hymn *Deus tuorum militum* was sung.

Feast: December 26
Patronage: bricklayers; deacons; stonemasons

Stephen I (d. 257) *Pope*

Stephen was born in Rome, the son of Jovius, progeny of the clan Julia. He was an archdeacon in the Roman Church under Popes SS. Cornelius and Lucius, and was nominated as his successor by the latter. Stephen was elected bishop of Rome on May 3 and consecrated on May 12, 254.

Stephen was the first bishop of Rome to assert the primacy of Rome over affairs of the universal Christian Church, based on its link to the apostle St. Peter. He also ordained that vestments worn for ecclesiastical purposes were not to be used in daily wear, thus setting the clergy apart from the hoi polloi in their dress.

His pontificate was largely concerned with the Novatian controversy that had been raging since the days of Cornelius. Cornelius had excommunicated Novatus, whereupon Novatus had himself consecrated bishop of Rome by some dissident deacons, bringing about a schism in the Church. Novatus and his followers held that Christian baptisms performed by sinners such as heretics, apostates and murderers were invalid because one could not receive the Holy Spirit at the hands of one who did not possess Him. Stephen replied that baptism by heretics was a practice that went back to the apostles of Jesus, and since it was Christ who actually bestowed the sacraments, their validity and efficacy did not depend on the grace of the human minister. On the same grounds, he argued that it was not necessary to rebaptize apostates and heretics who had lapsed, but that a simple laying-on of hands was sufficient to bring them back into the Church. His positions alienated many, including St. Cyprian, who had supported Cornelius and Lucius.

Stephen died on August 2, 257, after a reign of a little more than three years. He is sometimes said to have died a martyr, beheaded while saying Mass in the catacombs, but this idea seems to have arisen from confusion with his successor, St. Sixtus II (r. 257–258). The earliest liturgical documents describe Stephen as bishop and confessor, not as martyr. He was buried in the Catacombs of St. Callistus. Pope St. Paul I (757–767) had his relics moved to a monastery that he founded in Stephen's honor. In 1682, his relics were again translated, this time to Pisa, where they are venerated in a church named after him. His head is enshrined in Cologne, Germany.

In art, Stephen is depicted as beheaded in his chair at Mass. He may also be shown stabbed at the altar or with a sword in his breast.

Feast: August 2 (Western Church); September 7 (Eastern Church)

Stephen of Hungary (ca. 970–1038) *King and patron of Hungary*
Name meaning: Vajk: rich or master
Also known as: Vajk, Vaik, Stephen the Great

Vajk was born in 970 to the Magyar leader Geza and his wife Charlotte. That year also marked an end to the threat of terror from the great barbarian hordes when they suffered a crushing defeat by the Byzantines at Arcadiopolis (located in what is now northwestern Turkey). By 972, Otto II had married the Byzantine princess Theophano, uniting the Holy Roman and Eastern Empires and leaving Hungary squeezed in the middle. In order to survive, Geza determined that his people's aggressive tribal and heathen culture had to be destroyed and replaced by Christianity so that paganism could not be used as an excuse for invasion.

So in 972, Geza announced the conversion of his people: an act of political expediency. Bishop Pilgrim of Passau established the first episcopal see near the royal residence at Esztergom on the Danube River. About 980, Bishop Pilgrim returned and baptized Geza and about 5,000 Hungarian nobles at Pannonholma (an event described as resembling a cattle round-up). Although Geza ruthlessly imposed Christianity on his people, he and Charlotte continued to worship their pagan gods.

Young Vajk was baptized along with the rest, receiving the name Stephen (Istvan), but legend tells that he had been destined for Christian greatness. During her pregnancy, his mother Charlotte supposedly saw St. Stephen the Protomartyr in a dream. He told her that she would bear a son who would be the greatest leader Pannonia (which became Hungary) had ever seen, and that the boy should be named after him. Young Stephen received Christian instruction from the martyred St. Adalbert of Prague.

By 995, Geza was old and ill, exhausted from 10 years of battle with Bavaria's Prince Henry the Quarrelsome. He named Stephen the future king, ignoring the practice of "seniorate," in which the next member of the ruling family ascends the throne—in this case Geza's brother Koppany. In the old traditions, Koppany also had the right to Geza's widow, a practice called "levirate." To protect her son's interests, Charlotte arranged Stephen's marriage to Gisela, daughter of Prince Henry and sister of Emperor St. Henry II. Geza died in 997, and Stephen became king after defeating and killing his uncle. Koppany's lands were given to the abbey of Pannonholma for the establishment of the great church of St. Martin, still the mother church of the Hungarian Benedictines.

In 999, still uncrowned officially, Stephen decided to cast Hungary's lot with Rome and the German princes. He also desired official recognition by the new pope, Sylvester II, formerly the learned French cleric Gerbert of Aurillac. So in 1000 Stephen sent St. Astrik to Rome to ask that the pope name him King of Hungary by the Grace of God, a designation that would make Stephen an apostolic king and canon of the Church. Sylvester II eagerly agreed, sending Astrik back to Hungary with the official papers and a crown originally made for Duke Boleslaus the Brave of Poland. When Astrik arrived at Esztergom, Stephen rode out to meet his envoy and stood at attention to hear the pope's message. On August 15, 1000, Stephen received the papal crown in a coronation ceremony based on the Mainz Sacramentary, including his anointing with holy oil and reception of the ring, sword and scepter of the Church.

The young king concentrated on the organization of the Church and the just administration of his nation. He established the Church's primatial see at Esztergom, the royal residence, and used the spoils of a war with the Bulgarians to build the cathedral at Szekesfehervar. Next the king divided his country into dioceses, decreeing that every 10 villages join together and build a church and support the local priest. Tithing was mandatory. Any family fortunate enough to have 10 children must dedicate the tenth as a monk at the abbey at Pannonholma. All people except churchmen and members of religious orders were required to marry. To establish control, Stephen built an extensive system of castles and royal residences that employed about a third of the population on their maintenance and subverted traditional clan loyalties in favor of the king. Stephen introduced private land ownership, wrote laws and established royal courts, repressed murder, theft, blasphemy and adultery, and established a security force in the Alps and along the Danube to protect travelers.

In 1014, Stephen allied Hungary with his former enemies, the Byzantines, against the Bulgarians, and his success yielded not only the booty, which became Szekesfehervar Cathedral, but a Greek princess for his second son, Emeric. Stephen's first son, Otto, had died in childhood, and the king placed all his dreams for a Christian monarchy on the young prince. Emeric's early spiritual adviser was St. Gellert (who was martyred by pagans, like his predecessor St. Adalbert), and Stephen himself trained and educated his son in the responsibilities of a Christian king and servant. In 1030, Prince Emeric successfully led an army against the ambitious German emperor Conrad II, and Stephen, convinced his son was ready for kingship, prepared to name him regent.

But a wild boar killed Emeric in a hunting accident in 1031, and the devastated Stephen faced the prospect of succession by his cousin Vazul, described as stupid and half-pagan. Often sick and delirious, Stephen began seeing parallels between his life at the millennium and that of Christ. Fears of the apocalypse abounded, and Queen Gisela set craftsmen and seamstresses to work making crosses and sacred vestments, particularly a red and gold silk mantle for the king that portrayed St. Stephen and King Stephen together with God. In an act establishing the cult of the Virgin in Hungary, Szekesfehervar Cathedral was dedicated to the Virgin Mary—a move that appealed to the still-pagan worshipers of the goddess whose gown was the blue sky.

Shocking even his closest followers, the dying Stephen named his nephew Peter Orseolo as his successor, cutting out Vazul. Such a move also curtailed Hungarian independence since Orseolo was the son of the Venetian doge. Vazul sent assassins to kill the king in his bedchamber, but they were apprehended. He was convicted and punished by being blinded and having hot lead poured in his ears.

King Stephen I died on August 15, 1038, exactly 38 years after his coronation. Orseolo ascended the throne, but Vazul's sons soon overthrew him, establishing a 200-year dynasty. Stephen was buried next to his son, now Blessed, in Szekesfehervar, but his relics were eventually enshrined in a chapel of the Church of Our Lady of Buda. Reports of miracles at his tomb circulated almost immediately, and Hungarians—even during the years of communist rule—still appeal to their patron for aid in time of crisis.

Canonized: 1083 by Pope Gregory VII
Feast: August 16
Patronage: bricklayers; against death of children; kings; masons; stonecutters; stonemasons; Hungary

FURTHER READING

Reston, James, Jr. *The Last Apocalypse: Europe at the Year 1000 A.D.* New York: Doubleday, 1998.

Sylvester I (d. 335) *Pope*
Also known as: Silvester I

Sylvester was born in Rome, the son of Rufinus and Justa. He became a priest in the Church of Rome, serving in the parish of Equitius, and succeeded St. Miltiades (also Melchiades) in the Chair of St. Peter on January 31, 314.

Sylvester became counselor and spiritual adviser to Emperor Constantine the Great, a visionary sympathetic to Christianity. According to legend, Constantine, a leper, had been told that the best way to cure his disease was to bathe in children's blood. However, he had a vision in which SS. Peter and Paul appeared to him and advised him to seek baptism from Sylvester, which he did. He was healed, and in thanks ceded to the Church the islands of Sicily, Sardinia and Corsica (sites of work camps to which many Christians had been banished in the past). This dispensation is historic fact; it became known as the Donation of Constantine, and formed the basis of the Papal States. Nevertheless, whatever the truth about the miraculous cure, it is certain that Sylvester did not baptize the emperor, for that came only on his deathbed.

Constantine continued the support for the Church he had shown Miltiades. It is probable that it is to Sylvester rather than to Miltiades that he gave the Lateran Palace, and that Sylvester had its famous basilica built. Sylvester also either founded or restored the churches of St. Peter, on Vatican Hill, St. Lawrence-Outside-the-Walls and Santa Croce. His episcopal chair and his mitre, the oldest to have survived, are on display in the church of San Martino ai Monti, which he had built over a house used for worship during the persecutions of previous decades. Sylvester also had a church raised over the Catacombs of St. Priscilla on the Salerian Way.

He was concerned not only with building churches but also with constructing the authority of the universal Church. His pontificate lasted 21 years and eleven months—the longest of any up until his time—during which 300 laws concerned with justice, equity and an evangelical purity were passed. In this work, also, he enjoyed Constantine's support.

Sylvester died before Constantine and was buried on December 31, 335, in the church on the Salerian Way. Unfortunately, his tomb was destroyed by the Arian Lombards. In 761 the major part of his relics were translated to the Church of San Silvestro in Capito, today the national church of English Catholics in Rome, where they now rest.

Although he did not die a martyr, Sylvester is honored as a saint. His cultus did not arise for 150 years after his death, however. Pope St. Symmachus (r. 498–514) had a mosaic honoring him placed behind the episcopal throne in the titular church of Equitius. Sylvester is especially venerated in Pisa. In the Eastern Church, he is celebrated with the title *isapostole,* "equal to the apostles."

In art, Sylvester is depicted in various scenes with Constantine. Generally he is represented by a chained dragon or bull and a tiara, and the principal scene is that of the baptism of Constantine. He is also shown trampling a dragon or with an angel holding a cross and olive branch.

Feast: December 31 (Western Church); January 2 and May 21 (Eastern Church)

Symmachus (d. 514) *Pope*

Symmachus, son of Fortunatus, was born in Sardinia. He was baptized in Rome and joined the Roman clergy, rising to the post of archdeacon under Pope Anastasius II (the successor of St. Gelasius I). On November 22, 498, he was elected to the Chair of St. Peter in the Vatican's Lateran palace.

That same day a dissident faction of the clergy, with Byzantine leanings, elected the archpriest of St. Praxedes, Laurentius, bishop (and thus antipope), in the basilica of Santa Maria Maggiore. When King Theodoric of the Ostrogoths ruled in favor of Symmachus on the grounds that he had been elected first and by a majority of the clergy, Laurentius capitulated, and subsequently was made bishop of Nocera in Campagna (also Campania).

His Byzantine supporters were not so easily mollified. They brought trumped-up charges against Symmachus and occupied the Lateran palace, obliging him to move to the Church of St. Peter outside the walls of the city. They then reinstalled Laurentius and asked Theodoric to consider their charges. They were not above using violence. On his way to speak at a synod considering the charges against him, Symmachus and his entourage were ambushed; although Symmachus himself escaped, several priests were killed or severely wounded. However, thanks to support from clergy outside Rome, the matter was finally decided in favor of Symmachus at a synod on November 6, 502.

In his remaining years as pontiff, Symmachus was concerned with more typical matters: fighting heresies, shoring up Church discipline and undertaking new construction. In addition to building or repairing ecclesiastical buildings, he built three asylums for the poor. He also sent money to Catholic bishops in Africa to ransom Christians from their Vandal persecutors. His generosity to the poor led to the bestowal of the well-deserved title, "father of the poor."

Symmachus died on July 19, 514, and was buried in St. Peter's the following day. He is venerated in the Roman Church as a saint.

Feast: July 19

Tarsilla See EMILIANA AND TARSILLA.

Telesphorus **(d. ca. 136)** *Pope and martyr*

Telesphorus was Greek, probably from Calabria. The eighth pope, he succeeded Sixtus I as bishop of Rome ca. 125 and reigned until ca. 136. He regularly celebrated Easter on Sunday, without abandoning fellowship with those communities that did not follow this custom. It is sometimes said that he instituted Lent, but this is doubtful, as is the legend that he was a hermit.

Most of the early popes are listed in ancient martyrologies, although historical circumstances make this suspect in some cases. Not so with Telesphorus, who is known from an independent source to have been martyred. The details of his death, however, are not known. He is commemorated in both the Greek and Roman churches.

In art, Telesphorus is shown as a pope with a chalice, over which three Hosts hover, sometimes with a club nearby.

Feast: January 5 (Western Church); February 22 (Eastern Church)

Teresa of Avila **(1515–1582)** *Mystic and authority on mystical prayer, founder of the Discalced Carmelite Order, the first woman declared a Doctor of the Church*

Name meaning: "Reaper"
Also known as: Teresa de Jesus; Spouse of Christ

Teresa of Avila was born Teresa de Cepeda y Ahumada to a noble family on March 28, 1515, in or near Avila in Castile. As a child she exhibited an interest in saints and martyrs, and in the monastic life. Her mother died when she was 14, which upset her so much that her father sent her at age 15 to an Augustinian convent in Avila. She decided she wanted to become a nun, but her father forbade it as long as he was living. At about age 20 or 21, she left home secretly and entered the Incarnation of the Carmelite nuns in Avila. Her father dropped his opposition.

In 1538, soon after taking the habit, Teresa began to suffer from ill health, which she attributed to the change in her life and diet. It was through her chronic and severe afflictions that Teresa discovered the power of prayer, which enabled her to heal herself, and which then became the focus of her spiritual life and her writings.

During her first year in the convent, she suffered increasingly frequent fainting fits and heart pains so severe that others became alarmed. She was often semi-conscious or unconscious altogether. She opined that these problems were sent by God, who was offended at her innate "wickedness." It is thought she may have suffered from malaria.

317

Her father sent her to Becedas, a town that had a great healing reputation. There she stayed for nearly a year, but failed to improve. She was given experimental cures by a woman healer that only worsened her condition and reduced her to misery.

The trip to this healing center was fortuitous, however, because en route Teresa visited an uncle, who gave her a book entitled the *Third Spiritual Alphabet,* which contained lessons in the prayer of recollection (introspection). Teresa began to use it as her guide in prayer, and it served as her primary guide for the next 20 years.

When she failed to improve at Becedas, her father brought her home. There she deteriorated badly over several months, and finally she fell into a death-like coma for three days. The sacrament of Extreme Unction was given to her in expectation of her imminent death. For a day and a half, a grave was left open for her at her convent, and rites for the dead were performed at a Carmelite friary nearby. Teresa made a complete confession, but instead of dying, she began to recover.

For eight months Teresa lay paralyzed in great pain. Gradually, the paralysis improved—she began to crawl around on her hands and knees—but it continued in some form for three years. Teresa said that her sole anxiety was to get well so that she could pray in solitude. Through daily mental prayers, she healed herself over a long and slow recovery.

She attributed her return to health to St. Joseph, who became her patron saint. It took her three years to recover the ability to walk. She was 40 when the principal symptoms of her illness finally disappeared.

During the early years of slow recovery, Teresa struggled with her spiritual life and described her prayer life as unpleasant. She neglected her prayer because she felt unworthy to talk to God, but after her father died, she returned to regular prayer practice, and stayed with it for the rest of her life.

Teresa felt a kinship with two other great penitents, SS. Mary Magdalen and Augustine. She resigned herself to God's will. Her prayer life became punctuated with mystical experiences. She spent long periods alone in the prayer of quiet and the prayer of union, during which she often fell into a trance, and at times entered into mystical flights in which she felt as though her soul were lifted out of her body. She likened ecstasy to a "delectable death," saying that the soul becomes awake to God as never before when the faculties and senses are "dead."

Once she complained to God in prayer about her sufferings. His answer came to her: "Teresa, so do I treat my friends!" She understood it to mean that there was purification in her suffering, but she nonetheless had the pluck to retort, "That's why you have so few [friends]!"

Teresa exhorted others to prayer, and especially to passive, mental prayer, though she continued to do both vocal and mental prayer throughout the rest of her life. She believed that vocal prayer required mental prayer in order to be effective.

Prayer, she said, was the door to "those very great favors" that God then conferred on her, in the form of intellectual visions (formless, neither external or internal), raptures, ecstasies, levitation, being engulfed in the presence of God, and—most important—union.

Teresa likened prayer to the cultivation of a garden. She outlined four steps for the watering of the garden so that it would produce fruits and flowers, which are the measure of the progress in love of the one who prays.

The first, and simplest, step is meditation, which is like drawing water from a deep well by hand, in that it is slow and laborious.

The second step is through quiet, in which the senses are stilled and the soul can then receive some guidance; thus, the one who prays gets more water for the energy expended. The soul begins to lose its desire for earthly things.

The third step is through the prayer of union, in which there is contact between the praying one and God, and there is no stress. The garden seems to be self-watered as though from a spring or a little stream running through it. Teresa confessed that she had little understanding herself of this step. The senses and mental faculties, she said, could occupy themselves only and wholly with God.

The fourth step is done by God himself, raining water upon the garden drop by drop. The one who prays is in a state of perfect receptivity, loving trust and passive contemplation. Physically, he or she faints away into a kind of swoon, Teresa said; her description resembles the trance states described by many mystics of many faiths.

Teresa often came out of deep prayer states to find herself drenched in tears. These were tears of joy, she attested.

She made such rapid progress in her prayer that she was concerned that she was being deceived by the devil, because she could not resist the favors when they came, nor could she summon them—they came spontaneously. Also, she considered herself to be a weak and wicked person. Nonetheless, she was granted many prayers of silence and union, some of which lasted for long periods of time.

To allay her fears, Teresa sought out spiritual counsel. Some of her advisers, including a respected priest named Dr. Daza, could not believe that such favors could be experienced by a weak woman, and fueled her fears of devilish interference. One more objective adviser told her to put the matter before God by reciting the *Veni Creator Spiritus* hymn as a prayer. This she did for the better part of a day, at which point a rapture came over her that was so strong it nearly carried her away. She said, "This was the first time that the Lord had granted me this grace of ecstasy, and I heard these words: 'I want you to converse now not with men but with angels.' This absolutely amazed me, for my soul was greatly moved and these words were spoken to me in the depths of the spirit. They made me afraid therefore, though on the other hand they brought me much comfort, after the fear—which seems to have been caused by the novelty of the experience—had departed."

In 1559 Teresa had her most remarkable experience involving an angel who pierced her heart with an arrow of love. Swept into a rapture, she beheld a short, beautiful angel whose face was aflame. The sight of the angel was unusual in itself, for she usually perceived angels through intellectual vision. She was given to understand that the angel was of the highest rank, closest to God, a cherub. She said in her autobiography:

> In his hands I saw a great golden spear, and at the iron point there appeared to be a point of fire. This he plunged into my heart several times so that it penetrated to my entrails. When he pulled it out, I felt that he took them with it, and left me utterly consumed with the great love of God. The pain was so severe that it made me utter several moans. The sweetness caused by this intense pain is so extreme that one cannot possibly wish it to cease, nor is one's soul then content with anything but God. This is not a physical, but a spiritual pain, though the body has some share in it—even a considerable share. So gentle is this wooing which takes place

St. Teresa of Avila in a state of enraptured inspiration (Library of Congress Prints and Photographs Division)

between God and the soul that if anyone thinks I am lying, I pray God, in His goodness, to grant him some experience of it.

Teresa thus was inspired to do everything in a manner that would be perfect and pleasing to God.

The sculptor Giovanni Bernini immortalized this experience in his statue, "The Transverberation of St. Teresa of Avila," housed in the Church of Santa Maria della Vittoria. Transverberation is the spiritual wounding of the heart.

In 1562, despite tremendous opposition, Teresa received permission from Rome to found an unendowed convent in Avila with stricter rules than those that prevailed at Carmelite convents, many of which had become little more than relaxed social havens. She established a small community that would follow the Carmelite contemplative life, in particular unceasing prayer. Her rules were strict. The nuns wore coarse habits, sandals instead of shoes (hence their name "Discalced Carmelites"), and lived in near-perpetual silence and committed to perpetual abstinence. The extreme poverty and austerity found favor, however, and by 1567 Teresa was permitted to establish other convents. She went on to found 16 others, and dedicated herself to reforming the Carmelite order.

Her discipline impressed others, and she was named prioress of the convent of the Incarnation in Avila in order to correct its laxity. There she was greeted with insults and hatred. She won over the nuns by placing an image of Our Lady of Mercy in the prioress's seat, and sitting at the feet of it. She credited Mary with her eventual acceptance at the convent. One evening during choir, Teresa had a vision in which Mary, with a multitude of angels, descended to the prioress's seat and sat in it herself. She told Teresa she had done well.

At age 53, she met the 25-year-old John de Yepes y Alvarez (later known as St. John of the Cross), who worked to reform the male Carmelite monasteries. After a period of turbulence within the Carmelites from 1575 to 1580, the Discalced Reform was recognized as separate from the original Carmelite order. During this period, Teresa suffered much opposition and persecution, and was on occasion comforted by Mary.

By 1582, Teresa had founded her 17th monastery, at Burgos. Her health was broken and she decided to return to Avila. The rough journey proved to be too much; food was scarce and at one point Teresa fainted on the road. Upon arriving at the convent, Teresa went straight to her deathbed. Three days later, on the feast day of St. Francis of Assisi, October 4, 1582, she died. The next day, the Gregorian calendar went into effect,

dropping 10 days and changing her death date to October 14. She was buried in Alba de Tormes and later was moved to Avila.

During Teresa's travels throughout Spain on her reform mission, she wrote a number of books, some of which have become spiritual classics. The first of those was *Life,* her autobiography, written in 1565. On November 18, 1572, Teresa experienced a spiritual marriage with Christ as bridegroom to the soul. One of the fruits of that marriage was *The Way of Perfection* (1573), about the life of prayer, and *The Interior Castle* (1577), her best-known work, in which she presents a spiritual doctrine using a castle as the symbol of the interior life. The latter book was revealed to her in a vision on the eve of Trinity Sunday, 1577, in which she saw a crystal globe like a castle, which had seven rooms; the seventh, in the center, held the King of Glory. One approached the center, which represents the Union with God, by going through the other rooms of Humility, Practice of Prayer, Meditation, Quiet, Illumination and Dark Night. She often referred to Christ as the "heavenly bridegroom," but her later visions became less erotic and more religious in character.

There is a timelessness to Teresa's writings, and elements of feminist spirituality. Her words continue to inspire modern audiences. As she once said to her followers, "I will give you a living book."

Besides her raptures, levitations and mystical experiences, Teresa also is credited with other saintly miracles. For workmen repairing one of her nunneries on a hot day, she multiplied wine for them, and gave God the credit. Like many saints, she seemed to give off a sweet fragrance. Her face often radiated a glow of light, which on at least one occasion was quite brilliant: The saint sat bathed in rays of brilliant gold while writing at her desk in her cell.

Once while holding the cross of her rosary, Teresa had a vision of God taking it from her and replacing it with a bejewelled cross of exquisite workmanship, bearing four large stones, which she described as "much more precious than diamonds." The cross showed the five wounds of Christ. God told her that only she would be able to see these things. She did see, every time she looked at the rosary for the remainder of her life, but no one else ever saw the jewels or the wounds. The crucifix was preserved by the Carmelites, but was lost during religious persecutions in 1835.

Teresa banished lice from her convent of San Jose. The lice infested the horsecloth garments of the nuns. One night Teresa performed a ritual for the extermination of the lice, which then vanished.

After her death, her body gave off a heavenly perfume that permeated her tomb. Nine months later, her body was exhumed and found to be incorrupt, though the coffin lid was smashed, rotted and full of mildew. Pieces of her body were amputated for relics. Her left hand strangely exuded oil, and was sealed in a casket at Avila. Her left arm was given to a convent at Alba de Tormes. Three years later, her body was examined again and was still incorrupt and sweet-smelling, despite having never been embalmed. Her left shoulder socket exuded an odd moisture and gave off a perfume.

Teresa's symbols are a heart, arrow and book.

Canonized: 1662 by Pope Gregory XV
Declared Doctor of the Church: 1970 by Pope Paul VI for her teaching on prayer
Patronage: against headaches; heart attack sufferers

FURTHER READING

Brown, Raphael. *Saints Who Saw Mary.* Rockford, Ill.: TAN Books, 1955.

Teresa of Avila, St. *The Life of Saint Teresa of Avila by Herself.* London: Penguin Books, 1957.

——. *The Interior Castle.* New York: Paulist Press, 1979.

——. *The Way of Perfection.* New York: Doubleday/Image Books, 1964.

Teresa Benedicta of the Cross (1891–1942) *Martyr.*

Also known as: Edith Stein, Teresia Benedicta

Edith Stein, who was to convert to Christianity and take the religious name Teresa Benedicta of the Cross, was born on October 12, 1891, in Breslau, Germany (now Wroclaw, Poland), as her Jewish family was celebrating Yom Kippur, the Day of Atonement.

Her father died when she was two, and by the time she was 13, Edith had lost faith in God and trust in Judaism. She entered the University of Breslau in 1911, when matriculation was opened to women. Although she studied German and history there, she was more interested in philosophy and women's issues. She became a member of the Prussian Society for Women's Suffrage, and in 1913 transferred to the University of Göttingen to study under philosopher Edmund Husserl, the father of phenomenology. She graduated with distinction in January 1915.

After training as a nurse, she volunteered for work in a field hospital during World War I, receiving the medal of valor when she completed her term of service. In 1916, she went with Husserl to the University of Freiburg, where she worked as his teaching assistant while studying for her doctoral degree. She graduated summa cum laude in 1917, and the following year left her position with Husserl. She hoped to obtain a professorship, a career not then generally open to women in Germany, but was unable to find a job. Returning to Breslau, she began writing articles about the philosophical foundation of psychology. She also read the

New Testament, Kierkegaard, the *Spiritual Exercises* of St. Ignatius of Loyola and an autobiography of St. Teresa of Avila. Of the last she later wrote, "When I had finished the book, I said to myself: this is the truth."

Edith had gradually been drawn to Catholicism, and reading Teresa of Avila was the final push she needed. She was baptized on January 1, 1922, and confirmed by the bishop of Speyer in his private chapel. She wanted to join a Carmelite convent immediately, but was persuaded not to do so. However, she took vows of poverty, chastity and obedience and found a position teaching German and history at the Dominican Sisters' school and teacher-training college in Speyer. In 1932, she accepted a position at the University of Münster, but a year later anti-Semitic legislation forced her out. On October 14, 1933, she joined the Discalced Carmelite cloister in Cologne, taking the name Teresa Benedicta of the Cross. She donned the habit in April 1934, took her temporary vows a year later, and her perpetual vows on April 21, 1938.

As the anti-Semitic rhetoric and actions of the Nazis became more strident, Edith (now Teresa) requested transfer to a convent outside Germany. On New Year's Eve of 1938, the prioress of the Cologne convent helped her get to the Discalced Carmelite convent of Echt in the Netherlands. She and her sister Rosa, also a convert to Christianity, remained there until they were arrested by the Gestapo on August 2, 1942—among 200 Catholic Jews arrested in the Netherlands in reprisal for a pastoral letter written by Dutch Catholic bishops against the Nazi pogroms and deportations of Jews. In a holding camp on the way to Auschwitz, Teresa is said to have given support and solace to many. On August 7, she and Rosa were carried to Auschwitz; they died in the gas chambers there on August 9.

Teresa authored several books, both before and during her Carmelite period. These include *Potency and Act,* a study of the central concepts developed by Thomas Aquinas, and *Finite and Being,* considered her magnum opus. When she was removed from Echt, she had almost completed *The Science of the Cross,* a study of St. John of the Cross. She is also remembered for her activism on behalf of women's rights.

As a martyr, under new Church rules, Teresa was automatically beatified, which meant that she needed only one certified miracle to become a saint. In 1997, the Vatican recognized the cure of an American girl as a miracle via Teresa's intercession, and the way for her canonization was cleared.

Beatified: May 1, 1987, by Pope John Paul II in Cologne
Canonized: October 11, 1998, by Pope John Paul II
Feast: August 9

FURTHER READING

Thavis, John, "Edith Stein Becomes a Saint on Sunday: Declared Miracle Cure of U.S. Girl Cleared Way for Her Canonization," *Baltimore Catholic Review,* October 8, 1998. Available online. URL: http://www.geocities.com/ Wellesley/1561/esrev2.html. Downloaded: January 28, 2000.

"Saint Edith Stein." Holy Cross Hiatt Holocaust Collection website. Available online. URL: http://www.holycross. edu/departments/library/website/hiatt/estein.htm. Downloaded: November 10, 1999.

Teresa Maria of the Cross (1846–1910) *Discalced Carmelite nun*

Also known as: Teresa Maria de la Cruz

Teresa Maria de la Cruz was born March 2, 1846, in Florence, Italy, and baptized with the name Teresa Adelaida Cesina Manetti. Her father died when she was a child. The loss stayed with her all her life and led her to devote her life to helping the poor and disadvantaged, especially orphans, whom she called her greatest treasure.

In 1872, she and some girlfriends formed a small circle to educate young people in the Christian doctrine. On July 16, 1876, at the age of 30, she was admitted to the third order of the Carmelites and changed her name to Teresa Maria of the Cross. On July 12, 1888, she was among the first 27 nuns to take the habit of the Discalced Carmelites. The order was approved by Pope Pius X on February 27, 1904, with the name Carmelite Tertiaries of Santa Teresa.

Teresa Maria was always in poor health, physically and spiritually, deserving of the name "of the Cross." She often prayed to God to make her suffer more, to squeeze her to the last drop. Meanwhile, her caring knew no bounds—she would give anything to anyone, never thinking of herself.

Teresa Maria died in Florence on April 3, 1910, while repeating: "Oh, my Jesus, if you want, make me suffer more. . . ." Then she cried ecstatically: "It's open . . . I'm going!"

Beatified: October 19, 1986, by Pope John Paul II
Feast: April 23
Patronage: people ridiculed for their piety

FURTHER READING

López-Melús, P. Rafael María. "Beata Teresa María de la Cruz." Carmelite website. Available online. URL: http://www. carmelnet.org/chas/santos/teresa5.htm. Downloaded: November 16, 1999.

Terese of the Andes (1900–1920)

Also known as: Juanita Fernandez Solar, Teresa de Los Andes, Teresa of the Andes, Teresa of Jesus of the Andes, Teresa of Jesus "de Los Andes." Teresita de Los Andes

The saint who has come to be known as Terese of the Andes was born to Miguel Fernández Jara and Lucia Solar Armstrong in Santiago, Chile, on July 13, 1900. Two days later, on the eve of the feast day of Our Lady of Mt. Carmel, she was baptized Juana Enriqueta Josefina de los Sagrados Corazones. Her parents were well-to-do and very religious, and she grew up in a Christian home, receiving a good education in one of the finest schools in Santiago. From a very young age she developed a profound faith in the Eucharist. She received her First Communion in October 1909, when she was only nine, and her Confirmation in September (or perhaps November) 1910.

During her adolescence she suffered from numerous illnesses that weakened her health but helped her to discover her religious vocation. On April 3, 1919, she wrote a letter to her parents asking permission to join the Carmelites, and on May 7 entered the convent of the Discalced Carmelite Nuns of Los Andes for a trial period. She donned the habit on October 14, taking the name Teresa de Jesús (Teresa of Jesus), and from that moment on submerged herself in the religious life. According to her sisters, she always wanted to be the last in everything.

Terese's health gradually deteriorated, and at the beginning of the following March she wrote that she would soon die, but would go without fear. On Good Friday, April 2, she contracted typhus. She received the last sacrament on April 5 and after making her religious profession *in articulo mortis* on April 6, she died on April 12, 1920, at the age of 19. She had been with the Carmelites only about 11 months, as a postulant and as a novice.

Since her death many have gone to pray at her grave and to request her intervention in miracles. On March 4, 1987, before a million people in Santiago, Pope John Paul II (r. 1978–) declared her Blessed. She was canonized by the same pope on March 21, 1993.

Terese of the Andes is the first Chilean saint and is considered a role model for youth in the Catholic Church.

Beatified: April 3, 1987, by Pope John Paul II
Canonized: March 21, 1993, by Pope John Paul II in Santiago, Chile
Feast: July 13
Patronage: bodily ills; illness; sick people; sickness; young people

FURTHER READING

"Beata Teresa de Los Andes." Los Santos Carmelitas. Available online. URL: http://www.carmelnet.org/shas/santos/ santos.htm. Downloaded: November 18, 1999.

"Santa Teresa de los Andes" Santos y Biatos de America Latina: Chile. Available online. URL: http://www.aciprensa.com/santchil.htm. Downloaded: November 18, 1999.

"Teresa of Jesus 'de Los Andes'" O.Carm. Available online. URL: http://www.ocarm.org. Downloaded: November 18, 1999.

"Teresita de Los Andes." Red Informática de la Iglesia Católica en Chile: Testigos de Christo. Available online. URL: http://www.iglesia.cl. Downloaded: November 18, 1999.

Thecla (d. first century) *Virgin and martyr*

The story of Thecla is told in the apocryphal *Acts of Paul and Thecla*, written in the second century. Thecla probably was a real person, a maiden of Iconium (now in Turkey) who was so impressed by the preaching of St. Paul that she converted, took a vow of virginity and gave up her betrothal in marriage. *Acts* records her sufferings, adventures, tortures, miraculous cures and interactions with Paul. In Antioch she was condemned to be thrown to wild beasts, but the lioness that was supposed to kill her merely licked her feet. She was then stripped naked and thrown to two lions, but the beasts killed each other instead of her. Released, she went to Seleucia, where she became a hermit. She died at age 90.

Thecla's story probably is mostly fiction. Tertullian said that *Acts* had been forged by an Asian priest. Thecla's story was popular during the early centuries of the Church and was considered to be genuine history. It was cited by many Church fathers and eminent theologians, among them Eusebius, Epiphanius, Gregory of Nazianzus, John Chrysostom and Severus Sulpitius.

The description of Paul in *Acts* matches iconographic tradition: He was "of a small stature with meeting eyebrows, bald [or shaved] head, bow-legged, strongly built, hollow-eyed, with a large crooked nose; he was full of grace, for sometimes he appeared as a man, sometimes he had the countenance of an angel."

Because of doubts about the historical validity of the account of her life, however, her cult was suppressed in 1969.

Feast: September 23

FURTHER READING
The Life of the Great Martyr Thecla of Iconium, Equal to the Apostles, As recorded in the Acts of Paul. URL: http://www.ocf.org/OrthodoxPage/reading/St.Pachomius/Saints/thecl a.html. Downloaded: September 24, 2000.

Theophilus (d. second century) *Bishop of Antioch and Father of the Church*
Also known as: Theophilus of Antioch

Theophilus was a pagan philosopher and converted to Christianity after studying the Scriptures. He was active during the reign of Pope Soter (169–177) and was alive after the death of Emperor Marcus Aurelius in 180.

Theophilus was an eloquent Christian apologist. His only surviving work is *Autolycus,* which champions Christianity over paganism and develops the doctrine of the Word as found in the Gospel of John.

Feast: October 13

Thérèse of Lisieux (1873–1897) *Discalced Carmelite nun, mystic, Doctor of the Church*
Also known as: Sister Teresa of the Child Jesus, the Little Flower, the Saint of the Little Way

Thérèse of Lisieux was born on January 2, 1873, in Alcon, Normandy, the ninth child of a middle-class, devout French family. Her father, Louis Martin, was a watchmaker. The parents, who had desired cloistered lives themselves, encouraged religious interests in their children. Thérèse was four when her mother died of cancer, and she was placed in the care of her sisters Marie and Pauline. She was especially close to Pauline, and when her sister announced her intention to become a nun, Thérèse expressed not only the same desire but also the desire to become a saint. Later, she wrote her autobiography as though it were a letter to Pauline.

From an early age Thérèse exhibited a delicate constitution, a strong desire for the religious life, and an intense desire to suffer for God. She called herself "the Little Flower." She was concerned about the poor and gave alms to them as a child. After Pauline entered the Discalced Carmelite convent at Lisieux, nine-year-old Thérèse went to the mother superior and expressed her desire to join as well. She was told she would have to wait until age 16 to become a postulate.

At age 10, Thérèse fell seriously ill. In her autobiography she blamed the illness on the devil, who was angry at Pauline for entering the convent and so punished the family for the harm that would come to him as a result. Her illness brought fits of delirium and strange behavior, as well as great suffering. One day she was cured when she had a vision in which a statue of the Blessed Virgin Mary came to life and smiled at her.

The entrance of Marie into the Carmelite convent intensified Thérèse's desire to become a nun herself. Her father refused to give her his permission to do so until she was 17. She appealed to her uncle, who gave his consent, but Pauline told her that the superior of Carmel would not allow her to enter until she was 21.

At 15 she accompanied her father on a pilgrimage to Rome to celebrate the jubilee of Pope Leo XIII (r. 1878–1903). In an audience before the pope, Thérèse begged him to allow her to join the Carmelites at her young age. He told her to follow the guidance of the appropriate authorities, and that it would happen if God willed it so. Upon their return, Thérèse was admitted on April 9, 1888. She chose the name Thérèse of the Child Jesus to distinguish herself from another nun whose name was Thérèse. She took the veil on September 24; her ailing father was too ill to attend. Her spiritual marriage took place on September 8, 1890.

Thérèse suffered through an initial spiritual dryness after entering the convent, and then seemed to go back and forth from great happiness to great sadness. She gave instruction to novices and devoted herself to her spiritual work. She constantly sought suffering to purify herself, and wished to die young. Once toward the end of her life she had a dream in which she was walking in the convent corridor with the mother superior, when three veiled Carmelite nuns suddenly appeared. She knew they were from heaven. One was the Venerable Mother Anne of Jesus, the founder of Carmel in France. Her face was lit by an unearthly radiance. Thérèse asked her if God would come for her soon. She said yes, and that God was very pleased with her.

In 1895 Thérèse, in prayer, offered herself as a victim to "God's merciful love." She had begun the stations of the cross when she felt herself wounded by a flaming dart, and thought she would die from the intensity of the fire of divine love. The experience was similar to the transverberation, or the piercing of the heart, with fiery arrows and blades, as experienced by St. Teresa of Avila and Padre Pio.

In 1895, her sister Pauline, then prioress, and whose religious name was Mother Agnes of Jesus, instructed her to write an account of her early life. She did so in the small amount of spare time she had in the evenings. In April 1896 Thérèse showed the first symptoms of tuberculosis. Initially her illness was not seen as serious, but by wintertime it was evident that she was fatally ill. She was relieved of all her duties in May 1897, and was instructed to continue her story with her experiences at Carmel. She began that work in June 1897. During her final illness, Mother Agnes recorded all of her conversations, spiritual experiences and counsels, which later were published in a small book, *Novissima Verba*.

Thérèse died on September 30, 1897, at the convent, with the cry of "My God, I love thee!" on her lips and a radiant look upon her face. She was buried at the cemetery of Lisieux.

Many miracles were reported through her intercession, among them a manifestation of much-needed money at a Discalced Carmelite convent in Gallipoli, Italy, in 1910. The prioress, Mother Mary Carmela, dreamed one night that Thérèse appeared to her in heavenly raiment, bilocated the two of them to the parlor and placed 500 francs inside a box. The money was found there the following morning.

Thérèse's autobiography was published in 1898 on the anniversary of her death. Interspersed with accounts of her life are Thérèse's spiritual insights, profound for such a young and relatively inexperienced person. She called her doctrine "the little way of spiritual childhood," which involves an infallible trust in, and love of, God. Its simplicity and purity have had an enduring appeal. *The Story of a Soul* remains one of the most popular of Catholic books. It has been published in 38 languages. Mother Agnes of Jesus devoted much time to answering the letters that poured in from Thérèse's devotees around the world.

Her body was exhumed on September 6, 1910. A strong scent of violets permeated some of the boards of the coffin that had been removed, as well as the saint's clothing and a palm that was still fresh in her hand. The palm was considered a sign of her martyrdom of self, of which she had said, "I desire at all costs to win the palm of Agnes; if not by the shedding of blood, it must be by Love." The palm was kept at the convent.

Throughout her monastic life Thérèse experienced many graces and mystical experiences in addition to the spiritual wounding. During her novitiate, she had transports of love, or raptures in which she felt far removed from the earth. During her final illness, she exhibited an unusual rapport with birds, who came to the window of the infirmary and sang until she died.

On her deathbed, Thérèse made many prophesies, and said she would be the instrument of much good to many souls after her death. She had cleared clouds from the sky, and decreed that at the moment of her passing the sky would be cloudless. The sky was cloudy on the day of her death, but cleared rapidly at the time she passed, at about 7 P.M.

Pope Pius X (r. 1903–14) called her "the greatest saint of modern times." Pope Pius XI (r. 1922–39) called her "the star of my pontificate."

Canonized: May 17, 1925, by Pope Pius XI
Declared Doctor of the Church: 1997 by Pope John Paul II
Feast: October 1
Patronage: African missions; AIDS sufferers; air crews; aircraft pilots; aviators; Belgian air crews; black missions; bodily ills; florists; flower growers; foreign missions; against illness; loss of par-

ents; missionaries; parish missions; restoration of religious freedom in Russia; against sick people; against sickness; Spanish air crews; tuberculosis; France; Russia

FURTHER READING

"Homily of Pope Pius XI at the Canonization of St. Thérèse on 17 May 1925." URL: http://www.ewtn.com/thérèse/readings/readng2.htm. Downloaded: August 24, 2000.

Saint Thérèse of Lisieux. *The Story of a Soul.* Tr. John Beevers. New York: Image Books/Doubleday, 1957.

Thomas the Apostle (d. ca. 72) *One of the Twelve Disciples of Jesus*

Name meaning: Twin (Didymus)
Also known as: Apostle of India; Didymus; Doubting Thomas; Judas Thomas; Jumeau; the Twin

Thomas was most likely born into a humble Jewish family in Galilee, though nothing is known for certain about his early life, or how he was called to the Apostolate. An apocryphal tradition asserts that he was the twin brother of Jesus.

Thomas's skepticism about Christ's Resurrection gave rise to the phrase, "a doubting Thomas." "Except I see in his hands the print of the nails, and put my finger into the print of the nails, and thrust my hand into his side, I will not believe," he is reported to have told the other disciples (John 20:25). Eight days later, Christ appeared to him and said, "Reach hither thy finger, and behold my hands; and reach hither thy hand, and thrust it into my side: and be not faithless, but believing" (John 20:27). This not only satisfied Thomas, it is also considered one of the proofs of Christ's Resurrection.

Thomas is widely believed to have carried the Gospel to India. According to the apocryphal *Acts of Thomas,* when this lot fell to him, he protested that he was too ill to go; not even a vision of Jesus could change his mind. Christ then appeared to a merchant named Abban and sold Thomas into slavery to become

St. Thomas touching the wounds of Christ (Engraving, 19th century)

a carpenter for the Indian king Gundafor (or Guduphara). When he learned of this, Thomas at last submitted, and sailed for India with Abban. He is said to have preached the Gospel, founding parishes and churches, along the way. When he reached India, Gundafor gave him 20 pieces of silver to finance the construction of a castle for him, but Thomas gave the money to the poor. When he discovered this, Gundafor had him imprisoned, intending to have him flayed alive. However, Gundafor's brother died, and having been shown the place in heaven Thomas's good deeds had reserved for Gundafor, the brother asked for and received permission to return to earth to purchase the spot for himself. Gundafor, however, not only refused to sell it, he also released Thomas, and was at once converted to Christianity.

How much of this story is true is impossible to ascertain. However, it does not seem unlikely that Thomas reached southern India and preached there. Christians along the Malabar Coast in Kerala maintain that they were converted by Thomas. Their tradition holds that after building seven churches, Thomas was speared to death on the "Big Hill" near Madras, then was buried in nearby Mylapore. According to one account, this occurred about the year 72 after he made converts in the city of King Misdai. He was led out of the city to the hill where four soldiers ran him through with spears.

According to the *Acts of Thomas,* Thomas was initially buried in the tomb of ancient Indian kings but some of his relics were translated to Edessa (in Mesopotamia), in the fourth century. In 1522, Portuguese sailors found the tomb, and carried other relics back with them; these were eventually taken to Ortona in the Abruzzi, where they are honored even today. Other of the relics remain in India, where they are venerated at the Cathedral of Saint Thomas in Mylapore. Thomas's July 3 feast day commemorates the translation of his relics to Edessa.

In art, Thomas typically is depicted as a young or middle-aged man with a carpenter's rule or builder's square, or as an elderly man holding a lance or pierced by one. He is also shown touching Christ's side, catching the girdle dropped by the Virgin at her Assumption, or casting out the devil from an Indian king's daughter.

Declared Apostle of India: 1972 by Pope Paul VI
Feast: July 3 (formerly December 21), July 1 (India)
Patronage: architects; blind people; builders; carpenters; construction workers; against doubt; geometricians; masons; stone cutters; theologians; India; Pakistan; Sri Lanka

Thomas Aquinas (1225 or 1227–1274) *Dominican, scholar, Doctor of the Church*
Also known as: Doctor Angelicus; Doctor Communas

Thomas Aquinas is called Doctor Angelicus and Doctor Communas for his great teachings. The 1917 Code of Canon Law lists only Thomas Aquinas as required for the training of priests, "according to his method, doctrine and principles," and the 1983 Code states that Thomas is to be taken "in particular as their teacher." Catholic children are taught to invoke St. Thomas at the beginning of study. At a phenomenal rate, Thomas synthesized in the light of *sacra doctrina* (God's truths revealed in Scripture): Plato, Aristotle and their interpreters; the other classical Greek and Roman thinkers; all preceding Fathers of the Church and contemporary theologians; Arab and Jewish philosophers and texts. He is regarded as the chief synthesizer of philosophy and theology for the Catholic Church, and his early death may have been caused by overwork. About a thousand years following St. Augustine's *City of God,* Thomas provided the Church a second grand synthesis: a system of *sacra doctrina* in the context of all knowledge available in the West at the time, coupled with a strong method of ordering, reason and argument. Also, Thomistic angelology became that of the Catholic Church and remains so.

Thomas Aquinas was born Tomasso Aquino into the local, central Italian gentry in Roccasecca near Aquino. At the age of six he was sent to study at the famous Benedictine monastery at Monte Cassino. When he was 14 he entered the University of Naples, a school known for being innovative and for being one of the first conduits of Aristotle's complete works, which had only recently entered the Western world via Arabic translations. At 18 Thomas decided to join the Dominicans, a new order of mendicant monks especially committed to study, teaching and preaching. His family attempted to foil this decision by detaining him for almost two years, but they failed to deter him.

He rejoined his Dominican brethren and soon was sent to Paris, where he transcribed the lectures of the Dominican scholar Albert (St. Albert the Great) on Dionysius the Areopagite, a strong influence on Thomas's angelology. From 1248 to 1252 Thomas lived at the priory of the Holy Cross in Cologne, studying with Albert especially the works of Aristotle, impressing his teachers and superiors. Tradition says he was called "the dumb ox" because he was physically heavy and had a silent, reserved manner. Albert reportedly told his classmates: "we call this lad a dumb ox, but I tell you that the whole world is going to hear his bellowing!"

Thomas was then sent back to Paris to prepare to teach Dominicans. He received a license to teach in

1256 and first worked as an apprentice professor lecturing on Scripture. Next he was promoted to teach from the official university textbook for theological instruction, the *Sentences* of Peter Lombard. Throughout his years of official teaching and writing, Thomas carried on a "moonlighting" project: his line by line commentary on Aristotle's texts.

In 1257 he was made a professor of theology and for the next few years lectured on the Bible and worked on a series of discussions based on classroom debates. These became some of his earliest written works, the so-called Disputed Questions, and *On Spiritual Creatures,* his earliest comment on angels. From 1258 to 1269 Thomas taught in various cities in Italy: Naples, as Dominican preacher general; Orvieto in the curia of Pope Urban IV (r. 1261–64); and in 1267–68 at Viterbo with Pope Clement IV (r. 1265–68). In 1269 he returned to Paris to resume his teaching post; and he wrote volumes. In addition to his incessant work, he was devoted to prayer and to the life of his religious order.

Thomas's complete writings include biblical commentaries, his series on Aristotle and polemical tracts. His most famous works are two enormous treatises covering the whole range of Christian doctrine and its philosophical background: the *Summa Contra Gentiles* ("on the truth of the Catholic faith against the unbelievers," supposedly commissioned as an aid to Dominican missionaries among Muslims and Jews); and the *Summa Theologica,* ranging over God, creation, angels, human nature and happiness, grace, virtues, Christ and sacraments. Begun in 1266, it remained unfinished at his death. He intended it to be a simple manual for students; it turned into the greatest theological document ever written in the Church. Organized into three parts, it contains 38 treatises, 612 questions, 3,120 articles and about 10,000 objections. The *Summa Theologica* amazed Thomas's own and subsequent generations with its orderly system, unflagging intellectual eagerness and sustained clarity. He acquired a reputation for supernormal mental capacity. One report said he dictated to more than one secretary on different subjects at the same time; another insists that he composed even in his sleep.

In December 1273 he suddenly abandoned his usual routine and neither wrote nor dictated anything else. When urged by his serving companion to return to work, he reportedly replied: "No, Reginald, I cannot, because all that I have written seems like straw to me." This remark has often been blown out of proportion. Most probably, he had suffered a stroke or breakdown from nervous exhaustion caused by overwork. Soon he was called to attend the Second Council of Lyons as a Dominican theologian. He set out in late December,

and became ill on the way. He lodged with his niece in Maenza, but after two months it is said he told her "if the Lord is coming for me, I had better be found in a religious house than a castle." He was taken to a nearby Cistercian monastery, where he died in a guest room on March 7.

When it was protested at the canonization proceedings for Thomas Aquinas that few miracles were attributed to him, Pope John XXII (r. 1316–34) declared that every proposition he wrote was a miracle.

It struck Thomas in his early study of Aristotle that philosophers had arrived at truths about God that are equivalent to some revealed truths. The first question that Thomas takes up in *Summa Theologica* is: What need is there for any science other than those that make up philosophy? The question makes sense only if one knows those philosophical sciences. The answer is: We cannot arrive at the revealed content of Christian faith merely by philosophical argument. Philosophical argument, however, is the most convincing way to present all truths. Thomas's reasoning and communication method was firmly grounded in Aristotle's, and his major teacher Albert was an Aristotelian thinker as well. He approaches theological issues like a philosopher.

Other writings include *De Ente et Essentia* (On being and essence); *De Regimine Principium* (On kingship); *Contra Impugnantes Religionem,* defending Mendicant Orders; *De Perfectae Vitae Spiritualis,* on the spiritual life; *De Unitate Intellectus Contra Averroistas,* against the Averroists; *Quaestiones Disputatae* and *Quaestiones Quodlibetales,* debated questions for lecture halls; and commentaries on Aristotle.

Thomas's treatment of angels fits into the schematic typical of all his thinking and writing: a synthesis of *sacra doctrina,* what can be assumed true from Scripture as revealed by God (theology), and what can be assumed true on the basis of common experience of the world (philosophy). He applies to angels the same grid he applies to God, creation, the soul, etc., involving language and distinctions common to philosophic discourse: cause and effect, general and principle causes, matter and form, essence and being. Thomas organized angels into a hierarchy of triads: seraphi, cherubim and thrones in the first order; dominations, virtues and powers in the second order; and principalities, archangels and angels in the third order.

Thomas had a major impact on the importance of dreams. Siding with Aristotle, Thomas considered our knowledge of the world to come through our senses. Because of biblical tradition, he had to acknowledge that some dreams could come from God. For the most part, he said, dreams came from demons, false opinions and natural causes such as conditions of the body.

It was not unlawful to divine from dreams as long as you were certain that the dreams were from a divine source and not from demons.

Like St. Jerome, Thomas is said to have had life-changing dreams or visionary experiences that altered the course of his work. During his composition of *Summa Theologica,* he struggled with completing a theological passage. One morning he suddenly dictated it with ease. He told his scribe that he had had a dream in which he dialogued with the apostles SS. Peter and Paul, and they told him what to say.

Thomas Aquinas's symbols are the chalice, dove, monstrance and ox. In art he is often depicted as a Dominican, holding a book or a church, with rays of light streaming from his chest.

Canonized: 1323 by Pope John XXII
Declared Doctor of the Church and *Doctor Angelicus:* 1567 by Pope Pius X
Named Patron Saint of Catholic Schools: 1880 by Pope Leo XIII
Feast: January 28
Patronage: academics; Catholic schools, colleges and universities; chastity; pencil makers; students

FURTHER READING
Clark, Mary T. *An Aquinas Reader.* New York: Fordham University Press, 1988.
Davies, Brian. *The Thought of Thomas Aquinas.* Oxford: Clarendon Press, 1992.
Kelsey, Morton. *God, Dreams and Revelation: A Christian Interpretation of Dreams.* Minneapolis: Augsburg Publishing House, 1968, 1974, 1991.
St. Thomas Aquinas. *Summa Theologiæ.* Timothy McDermott, ed. Allen, Tex.: Christian Classics, 1989.

Thomas Becket (1118–1170) *Archbishop of Canterbury, martyr*
Also known as: Thomas Becket; Thomas of Canterbury

Thomas Becket, the most revered English saint, was born in London to middle-class Norman parents. As a young boy he studied with the canons regular at Merton priory in Surrey. At age 24, he accepted a post in the household of Theobald, archbishop of Canterbury, who was quite taken with the young man. Thomas received minor orders under the archbishop's tutelage, and the archbishop sent him to study law in Bologna and Auxerre. Theobald also provided Thomas with several church benefices for his support. In 1154, Thomas was ordained a deacon, then appointed archdeacon of Canterbury, the highest ecclesiastical position in England after the bishops and abbots.

On Theobald's urging, King Henry II Plantagenet named Thomas as chancellor in 1155, a post equaled only by the justiciar and ranking second only to the king. Thomas was 36 years old; Henry was 22, married for three years and king for one. They became great friends and fellow carousers; one account described their merrymaking as "frolicsome." Thomas lived more grandly than his liege, owning palaces, giving banquets, wearing fine clothing and employing hundreds. In 1159, Thomas served as one of Henry's generals on a campaign to Toulouse to recover Queen Eleanor of Aquitaine's property, engaging in hand-to-hand combat. Henry and Thomas were inseparable.

Archbishop Theobald died in 1161 while Thomas and Henry were at court in Normandy. Henry, eager to assert his secular authority, proposed that his friend Thomas assume the see. But Thomas, realizing the potential for church-state conflict, declined, remarking that if he were archbishop many of the king's policies would put them at odds, jeopardizing their friendship. Henry scoffed at Thomas's objections and pressed his chancellor to accept, but Thomas refused. Finally Cardinal Henry of Pisa, papal legate, convinced Thomas to accept the post, and the election was made in May 1162. As Thomas was not even a priest, he was first ordained by Walter, bishop of Rochester, and consecrated by Henry of Blois, bishop of Winchester, before receiving the official pallium from Pope Alexander III.

Relations between Thomas and Henry remained good for a few months, but by the end of 1162 Thomas was a changed man. He took his responsibilities on behalf of the Church as seriously as he had those of the king. Thomas no longer wore fine robes but instead donned a hair shirt crawling with vermin under a simple black cassock. He read Scripture continuously and performed self-flagellation. He ate sparingly, took a personal interest in the household, gave away much of his fortune, and frequently celebrated Mass at the cathedral.

Tensions mounted, and in October 1163 Henry convened a meeting of the bishops at Westminster to demand that the "criminous clerks"—clergy convicted of civil crimes—be handed over to the king's authorities and not judged solely by the Church. Henry had long believed Church courts were far too lenient. The bishops were prepared to acquiesce, but Thomas saw such efforts as an affront to Church jurisdiction. Then King Henry demanded the bishops promise to observe unspecified royal customs. Thomas agreed conditionally as long as the customs didn't infringe on the Church. Insulted, King Henry demanded Thomas renounce certain castles and honors he had held since his chancellorship. Thomas refused, and the conflict came to a head at the Council of Clarendon, near Salisbury, in early 1164.

Although Thomas initially tried to be conciliatory and accept some of the so-called Constitutions of Clarendon, he angrily rejected the entire document when he read the king's proposed customs: No prelate could leave the kingdom without royal permission nor appeal to Rome without the king's consent; no tenant-in-chief could be excommunicated against royal will; custody of empty Church benefices—and, most important, their revenues—were to be held by the king; and most critical, clerics convicted and sentenced in ecclesiastical courts could be at the disposition of royal authorities, leading to double punishment. Thomas was filled with remorse at the thought that he considered accepting such an attack on church jurisdiction and refused to perform Mass for over 40 days.

Henry saw Thomas's intransigence as disloyalty and betrayal. Henry sued Thomas for 30,000 marks then refused to speak to him. In October 1164 Henry summoned the bishops and barons to a council at Northampton, which deteriorated into antagonism toward the archbishop. On October 13, without wearing his mitre or pallium, but carrying his metropolitan's cross of office, Thomas went to the council hall after celebrating a Mass for St. Stephen. He was kept waiting for quite a while; finally, the earl of Leicester came out and demanded that Thomas render his accounts or suffer the king's judgment. Thomas indignantly replied that he had received the see of Canterbury without temporal obligation and was not liable for any judgment from the king. He, the archbishop, would answer only to the pope and God. Thomas fled Northampton that night and arrived in Flanders three weeks later.

King Louis VII of France welcomed Thomas in exile. Meeting Pope Alexander III at Sens, Thomas tried to resign his office, but the pope refused, instead sending him to the Cistercian monastery at Pontigny. Thomas lived there as a simple monk; Henry, meanwhile, confiscated the goods of anyone connected to Thomas and suggested they travel to Pontigny to plead their case. Negotiations among King Henry, Pope Alexander and Thomas dragged on for six years. King Louis VII tried to arrange a reconciliation at least 10 times. By 1169 Thomas had excommunicated some of his adversaries and was preparing a sentence of interdict on England. Still, in July 1170, Henry and Thomas unexpectedly met in Normandy and briefly reconciled without settling anything.

On December 1, 1170, Thomas landed in England and made a triumphal return to Canterbury. But the archbishop did not come in peace. Thomas was furious that during his exile King Henry's oldest son, Henry, had been crowned the heir-apparent by the archbishop of York, Roger de Pont-l' Eveque, assisted by the bishops of London and Salisbury. By Church tradition, coronations could be performed only by the archbishop of Canterbury. So before returning to Canterbury, Thomas had already excommunicated the bishops and suspended the archbishop. The three clerics went to Normandy to plead their case at court, and someone said there would be no peace as long as Becket lived. In a rage, King Henry reportedly asked if no one could rid his kingdom of the "pestilent clerk," and four knights left for England to answer the king's "order": Reginald Fitzurse, William de Tracy, Hugh de Morville and Richard le Breton.

The knights arrived during the afternoon of December 29 and demanded that Thomas remove the bishops' censures. Thomas refused, and the four left while threatening his life. Shouting and breaking of doors was heard moments later as Thomas slowly walked to the church, holding his cross before him. As Thomas entered the cloister of the church, armed men were seen in the dim light. The frightened monks bolted the doors in confusion, but Thomas opened them. Only three clerics accompanied Thomas as he walked toward the front, and finally only Edward Grim remained. According to Grim's first-person account, the knights were joined by a subdeacon, Hugh of Horsea. The five angrily called for the traitor Thomas. Thomas identified himself and came down to stand between the altars of Our Lady and St. Benedict. After again demanding the removal of the bishops' censures, Fitzurse grabbed the archbishop's robe and tried to pull him from the altars, threatening him with an axe. Thomas wrenched free and courageously demanded submission from the knights. Fitzurse dropped the axe and struck Thomas with his sword. Then Tracy swung his sword, nearly severing Grim's arm. Tracy struck again, knocking Thomas to his knees, and Thomas commended his soul to God. Le Breton sliced off Thomas' scalp, coming down so hard on the stones that he broke his sword, and then the subdeacon Hugh of Horsea stepped on Thomas' neck and scattered his brains on the floor. The knights fled while Thomas's body remained on the floor.

Although King Henry may not have been legally responsible for Thomas's death, outrage throughout Christendom required that the most powerful king in Europe humble himself. King Henry performed a public penance in July 1174 and received absolution. Pope Alexander III canonized Thomas in 1173, and reports of miracles at his tomb appeared almost immediately. In July 1220, Thomas's body was transferred to a shrine behind the high altar in Canterbury Cathedral, where it became one of the most popular medieval pilgrimage sites. Geoffrey Chaucer's pilgrims were going there in *The Canterbury Tales*. The shrine was destroyed in September 1538 by King Henry VIII, who appropriated the jewels, exhumed Becket's bones and allegedly burned them, condemning the saint for daring to oppose his king.

Canonized: 1173 by Pope Alexander III
Feast: December 29
Patronage: Secular clergy in England; officials; Portsmouth, England

FURTHER READING
Barlow, Frank. *Thomas Becket.* Berkeley: University of California Press, 1990.
Butler, John. *The Quest for Becket's Bones: The Mystery of the Relics of St. Thomas Becket of Canterbury.* New Haven, Conn.: Yale University Press, 1996.

Thomas More (1478–1535) *Lord chancellor of England; scholar; martyr*

Thomas More was born in London in 1478. His father, John More, was a lawyer and a judge, and Thomas followed in his footsteps. After working as a page for John Morton, archbishop of Canterbury, he entered Oxford University and studied law in Lincoln's Inn. He was admitted to the bar in 1501 and joined Parliament in 1504.

In 1505 he married Jane Colt; they had three daughters and a son. Jane died in 1511, and Thomas married a widow, Alice Middleton, to care for his children. In 1510, he was elected undersheriff, the first of various posts that led him to the top of royal government. In 1520 he accompanied King Henry VIII on a trip to the Continent. Henry was taken by his keen intellect and wit, and in 1521 had him knighted. Thomas became speaker of the House of Commons in 1523, high steward for the University of Cambridge in 1525 and chancellor of the duchy of Lancaster the same year. After Cardinal Thomas Wolsey failed to get Henry a divorce from his wife, Catherine of Aragon, Wolsey was removed as chancellor of England in 1529 and Thomas succeeded him.

But More could not reconcile himself with Henry's insistence on divorce, and on May 16, 1532, he resigned his post. He retired in exile to his estate in Chelsea and wrote in defense of the Church. Henry split from the Church and set himself up as head of the Church of England. In 1534, Thomas and a close friend, John Fisher, refused to take the Oath of Succession acknowledging Henry as the head of both church and state. Thomas was arrested and sent to the Tower

Sr. Thomas More (Library of Congress Prints and Photographs Division)

of London on April 17, 1534. He languished there for over a year. In July 1535 he was tried for treason and was convicted on the perjury of Richard Rich, who succeeded him as chancellor.

Thomas was beheaded on July 6, 1535 (John Fisher was beheaded the same year). Prior to his execution, the king had ordered him to keep his final words short. He asked the crowd to pray for him and the Church, and said he was dying as "the King's good servant—but God's first." His head was spiked on Tower Bridge and then buried in the Roper Vault at St. Dunstan's Church in Canterbury. His body was buried at St. Peter ad Vincula in the Tower of London. An account of his life was written by his son-in-law, William Roper.

Thomas's best-known work is *Utopia*, written in 1515–16, a criticism of English society that may have been inspired by his lectures on St. Augustine's *City of God*. Other notable works are *The Four Last Things*, published in 1520, *Dialogue of Comfort against Tribulation* (1553) and *Dialogue concerning Heresies and Confutation of Tyndale's Answer,* which refuted the Protestant writings of Matthew Tyndale.

In art Thomas is portrayed in his chancellor's robes, carrying a book and an ax.

Beatified: 1886 by Pope Leo XIII
Canonized: 1935 by Pope Pius XI
Feast: June 22

Patronage: adopted children; civil servants; court workers; lawyers

FURTHER READING

Ackroyd, Peter. *The Life of Thomas More.* New York: Double-day and Co., 1999.

The Last Letters of Thomas More. Alvaro da Silva, ed. Grand Rapids, Mich.: William B. Eerdmans Publishing Co., 2000.

Maruis, Richard. *Thomas More: A Biography.* Cambridge, Mass.: Harvard University Press, 1999.

Roper, William. *The Life of Sir Thomas More.* URL: http://www.fordham/edu/halsall/mod/16Croper-more.html. Downloaded: August 17, 2000.

Timothy (d. 97) *Disciple of St. Paul; Evangelist; by tradition, the first bishop of Ephesus; martyr*
Also known as: Timotheus

Timothy was born in Lystra, Lycaonia; his father was Greek, his mother Jewish. His mother, Eunice, her mother, Lois, and Timothy converted to Christianity during St. Paul's visit to Lycaonia. Because Timothy's mother was Jewish by birth, St. Paul allowed him to be circumcised to satisfy the Jews.

When Paul returned to Lystra seven years later, Timothy replaced St. Barnabas at the evangelist's side. When Jewish opposition forced Paul to leave Beroea, Timothy remained behind to baptize, organize and

St. Timothy reading the sacred writings with his mother and grandmother (Engraving, 19th century)

confirm new Christian converts. Later he was sent to Thessalonica to report on the status of Christianity there, and to support believers faced with persecution from Rome. His report served as the basis for Paul's First Letter to the Thessalonians, believed to be the earliest writing in the New Testament.

In A.D. 58, Timothy went with St. Erastus to Corinth. They then accompanied Paul into Ephesus and Asia Minor. It is likely that Timothy was with Paul when the latter was imprisoned in Caesarea and in Rome. Timothy himself was imprisoned in Rome for a while.

Paul sent Timothy two epistles, one from Macedonia around A.D. 65, the other from Rome, during his third and last imprisonment, while he was awaiting his death. These letters instructed Timothy to correct false doctrine and to appoint bishops and deacons.

According to tradition, Timothy went to preach in Ephesus and established the Church there. After denouncing the Dionysian festival of Katagogia, the tradition continues, he was stoned and clubbed to death about the year 97. His relics are said to have been translated to Constantinople in 356, and cures at his shrine there were later mentioned by St. Jerome and St. John Chrysostom.

In art, Timothy often is portrayed as a bishop with a club and stone, or being stoned to death. He is also shown receiving an epistle from Paul.

Feast: January 26 (formerly 24 in the West); January 22 (in the East)
Patronage: against intestinal disorders; against stomach diseases

Turibius Mogroveio (1538–1606) *Bishop; missionary; founder*

Also known as: Toribio or Turibius of Lima, Turibius of Mongrovejo, Toribio de Mongrovejo

Turibius Mogroveio was born in Mayorga, León, Spain, on November 16, 1538, the son of Luis Alfonso de Mogroveio (or Mongrovejo) and Ana de Robles y Moran. Although he was religious from an early age, he did not enter the Church, but instead studied law and was a professor of law at the University of Salamanca when King Philip II appointed him chief judge of the Court of the Inquisition at Granada in 1571. In 1580, the king called on him again, this time to become the new archbishop of Lima. Although the Vatican supported the nomination, Turibius protested, presenting canons forbidding the promotion of laymen to high Church offices. He continued to resist for three months before finally assenting. He was duly ordained a priest, consecrated bishop, named to the office by Pope Gregory XIII (r. 1572–85) and sailed for Peru. He was 42 years old.

Turibius landed in Piura in March 1581, and walked the 285 miles from there to Lima, arriving at the end of May. This was the first of many long walks he was to take over the remaining 25 years of his life. His archdiocese covered some 18,000 square miles, encompassing the present countries of Venezuela, Colombia, Ecuador, Peru, Chile, Bolivia and a portion of Argentina. Turibius traveled through this vast territory three times, the first time spending seven years in the process. He found a region much in need of aid, not only because of the many unsaved souls but also because of the cruelties of the colonial regime. This was less than a half-century after the subjugation of the Inca Empire, and many of the scars were still bare.

Turibius came into immediate conflict with secular authorities over the treatment of the Andean Quechua, whose rights he defended and whose dialects he learned to speak. He fought injustice and vice, among the clergy as well as laymen, and succeeded in eliminating many of the worst abuses. At the end of his life he sent a message to the king saying that he had administered the sacrament to and confirmed more than 800,000 persons.

His legacy is larger than this, however. He put considerable effort into organizing the Church in Peru, building churches and hospitals and almost doubling the number of parishes in the archdiocese—when he arrived there were 150 and when he died there were 250. He also founded the first seminary in the Americas (1591) and established a biannual diocesan synod. He convened and presided over the Third Council of Lima (1582–83), attended by prelates from throughout Hispanic America. This historic assembly established important pastoral norms relating to the evangelization of the Indians and produced texts of the catechism in Spanish, Quechua and Aymara, the first books published in South America.

Turibius confirmed three others who have become saints—Rose of Lima, Martin de Porres and Francis Solanus—and worked with a fourth, John Massias.

In his 78th year, Toribius was taken ill in the town of Pacasmayo, on the northern coast of present-day Peru. He continued traveling and working, however, and died a short while later, on May 23, 1606, in Saña (Zaña). It took almost a year for his body to be carried back to Lima, but it arrived there in a remarkable state of preservation, as if he had only recently died.

After his death many miracles were received at his intercession.

In 1983 Pope John Paul II (r. 1978–) proclaimed him Patron of Latin American bishops and set his feast day on the universal calendar as March 23. In Peru, however, it is still celebrated on its former date of April 27.

Beatified: 1679 by Pope Innocent XI
Canonized: 1726 by Pope Benedict XIII
Feast: April 27 (Peru), March 23 (elsewhere)
Patronage: Latin American bishops; native rights; Peru

FURTHER READING

"Santo Toribio de Mogrovejo," Santos Peruanos. Available online. URL: http://ekeko.rcp.net.pe/IAL/cep/santpapa/santoslos.htm. Downloaded: November 14, 1999.

"Santo Toribio de Mogrovejo." Santos y Biatos de America Latina: Perú. Available online. URL: http://www.aciprensa.com/santperu.htm. Downloaded: November 14, 1999.

Ulric (890–973) *Bishop of Augsburg, Germany; first saint to be canonized by a pope*
Also known as: Ulrich

Ulric was born in 890 at Kyburg in the Swiss canton of Zurich, to Count Hucpald and Thetbirga. His parents were connected to the dukes of Alamannia and the imperial family of the Ottos. Ulric was sent to the monastic school of St. Gall. Though sickly, he excelled in his studies.

Ulric was attracted to the priesthood and was sent to Augsburg, where he became the chamberlain of Bishop Adalbero. Upon Adalbero's death on April 28, 910, Ulric returned home, where he remained until 923, when Adalbero's successor, Bishop Hiltine, died.

His influential relatives, especially his uncle, Duke Burchard of Alamannia, succeeded in getting him appointed to the post of bishop of Augsburg. He was consecrated on December 28, 923.

Ulric set high moral standards and sought to improve the low moral and social conditions of the clergy, and to enforce a rigid adherence to the laws of the Church. He made his presence known by visiting as many churches as possible, and by playing an active role in the politics and judicial proceedings of the Ottonian empire. He traveled to Rome to obtain relics for his churches in either 952 or 953 (he had also gone to Rome for the same purpose in 910). In 955 the Magyars besieged Augsburg, and Ulric was instrumental in leading the city to hold out until Holy Roman Emperor Otto I's troops could arrive and defeat the invaders.

Ulric's unbending adherence to Church laws is illustrated in the lore surrounding him. According to the most popular story, one Thursday night he dined late with a colleague. The meal went on past midnight. An aide deferentially observed that it was now Friday, and the two were still eating meat. The meat then miraculously turned to fish.

On July 4, 973, the ailing Ulric anticipated and arranged the setting for his death. At dawn he had ashes strewn on the ground in the shape of a cross and sprinkled with holy water. Ulric was placed upon it. His nephew Richwin came with a message and greeting from Emperor Otto II. Ulric died beneath the rising sun while the clergy sang the litany. His body was interred in the Church of St. Afra, which had been rebuilt by him. Many miracles were reported at his grave.

In art he is often shown with a fish.

Canonized: 993 by Pope John XV
Feast: July 4

Ulrich (d. 1093) *Benedictine monk and monastery founder*

Ulrich was born in Ratisbon, Germany. He served as a page at the court of Empress Agnes, but left to enter

335

St. Ulrich, left, *with saints at the foot of the cross* (Library of Congress Prints and Photographs Division)

the religious life. He became archdeacon of the cathedral in Ratisbon. But while on a pilgrimage to Rome and Jerusalem, another man was appointed to his position. In 1052, Ulrich went to Cluny and became a Benedictine monk. After ordination, he was named chaplain to the nuns at Marcigny. Loss of sight in one eye caused him to resign and return to Cluny.

Ulrich then was prior at Peterlingen, was founding friar of the Ruggersberg Priory, and was founding abbot of the monastery at Zell in the Black Forest and of a convent at nearby Bollschweil. In 1091 he became totally blind. He died on July 10, 1093, at Augsburg.

Ulrich is known for his authorship of *Consuetudines cluniacences,* on the liturgy and the direction of monasteries and novices.

Feast: July 14

Urban I (d. 230) *Pope*

Urban was born in Rome, the son of Pontianus. About the year 222 he was elected bishop of Rome to succeed the martyred St. Callistus, and ruled for eight years during a relatively peaceful period of the early Church. St. Hippolytus, as antipope, persisted with his schism, but seems to have had no direct confrontations with Urban.

An increase in the extent of the Roman catacombs at this time suggests that the Christian community was growing, not surprising since it had the support of Emperor Alexander Severus. Severus went so far as to grant the Church the right to build a new church on land that was also claimed by tavern-keepers, declaring that it would be better for God to be worshiped there.

Urban died, most likely of a natural death, on May 23, 230, and two days later was laid to rest in the Catacomb of Prætextatus on the Via Appia. Although he is sometimes said to have been buried in the San Callistus cemetery, that was almost certainly a different bishop Urban.

Feast: May 25

Urban II (ca. 1042–1099) *Benedictine monk, pope*
Also known as: Otho; Otto or Odo of Lagery

Urban was born to a noble family at Châtillons-sur-Marne, Champagne, France, and christened Odo (sometimes written Otho or Otto). Odo studied under St. Bruno (later founder of the Carthusian order) at Reims. He became archdeacon there, and, about 1070, joined the Benedictine monastery at Cluny, of which he was named prior by the abbot, St. Hugh.

After a few years, Odo was sent to Rome to assist Pope St. Gregory VII (r. 1073–85) in his Church reforms. In 1078, Gregory created him cardinal-bishop of Ostia. From 1082 to 1085 he was the papal legate to France and Germany, and was briefly imprisoned by the Holy Roman Emperor Henry IV in 1083. He returned to Rome upon Gregory's death in 1085, and served in the Vatican under the following pope, Bl. Victor III (r. 1086–87). Both Gregory and Victor having proposed him as their successor, Odo was unanimously elected to the Chair of St. Peter on March 12, 1088, whereupon he assumed the name Urban II.

The reigns of Gregory and Victor had been troubled by the antipope Clement III (Archbishop Guibert of Ravenna), who had been seated under the influence of Henry IV in 1084. Clement was in control of Rome at the time of Urban's succession, and Urban was able to enter the city (with Norman assistance) for the first time only in November 1088. Because of the support Guibert enjoyed, however, Urban had to take refuge on the island of St. Bartholomew. He was not able to enter St. Peter's until after a three-day battle that drove Guibert from Rome.

Urban left Rome again in the fall of 1089 to attend a council of bishops at Melfi, in southern Italy, but when he tried to return to the city in December, he found Guibert there again. Guibert celebrated Christmas Mass in St. Peter's while Urban anathematized him from outside the walls. Unable to enter the city, Urban then began a three-year tour of southern Italy, holding councils that promulgated decrees against simony, clerical marriage, and the royal investiture of bishops and monasteries without prior church approval.

By 1093, Urban was in desperate straits, deeply in debt and dependent on charity. A French abbot, Gregory of Vendôme, came to his assistance, and when the governor of the Lateran Palace offered to surrender it to Urban for a fee, Gregory raised the ransom by selling possessions of his monastery. Urban was able to return to St. Peter's in time for the Easter solemnities.

Once again, he did not stay long in Rome, but left, this time traveling north into France. He convened councils that took strong stands in favor of ecclesiastical discipline and other matters of consequence to the Church. The most important council of this period was held at Clermont (Claremont) in Auvergne in November 1095. In response to a request from Emperor Alexis I in Constantinople, Urban declared the Truce of God and proposed a crusade to retake Jerusalem from the Muslims. The call met a sound response, and Urban began traveling around France to drum up further support. Although he was urged repeatedly to lead the crusade, he appointed Ademar, Bishop of Le Puy, in his place. The First Crusade was launched in 1097 and on July 15, 1099, reclaimed Jerusalem.

Victory came before Urban died, but he did not live to hear the news. He passed away in Rome on July 29, 1099. Guibert's followers prevented his burial in the Lateran and his relics were conveyed instead to the crypt of St. Peter, where they were interred close to the tomb of Pope Adrian I (r. 772–795).

Urban is listed as a saint in many medieval martyrologies. According to Guibert of Nogent, miracles attended his tomb, and his cultus seems to have formed at the time of his death. His feast day, however, was never extended to the Universal Church.

Urban appears in a painting in the apse of the Lateran Palace oratory built by Pope Callistus II (r. 1119–124). He is depicted at the feet of Our Lady, his head is crowned by a square nimbus, the words *sanctus Urbanus secundus* beneath him.

> *Beatified:* July 14, 1881, by Pope Leo XIII
> *Feast:* July 29

Pope St. Urban II recruiting knights for the Crusades (Library of Congress Prints and Photographs Division)

Urban V (1310–1370) *Benedictine monk, pope*
Also known as: Guillaume de Grimoard; William of Grimoard

The pope who was to take the name Urban V was born to a knightly family in Grisac, in the Languedoc of southern France, in 1310, as William (Guillaume) de Grimoard. He joined the Benedictines at the priory of Chirac, near Grisac, but also was ordained a priest, and pursued an academic career. He studied law, letters and philosophy at universities in Toulouse, Montpellier and Paris, receiving his doctorate in 1342. He became one of the greatest canonists of his day, and taught canon law as a professor at Montpellier as well as in other places.

William served as vicar general at Clermont and Uzès and as prior of Notre-Dame du Pré (a priory dependent on St. Germain d'Auxerre). In 1352, Pope Clement VI (r. 1342–52) appointed him abbot of St. Germain d'Auxerre. He was a papal legate in Italy in 1354 and 1360, then in 1361 Pope Innocent VI (r. 1352–62) sent him to the abbey of St. Victor at Marseilles.

William was on a papal mission to Naples when, on September 28, 1362, he learned that Innocent had died and that he had been elected his successor. He returned to Avignon, where the papacy was then based, on October 31, and was consecrated on November 6.

He took the name Urban V because, he said, all the popes of that name had been saints.

Urban devoted much attention to education, reforming or creating universities (including ones at Cracow in 1364 and Vienna in 1365) and student scholarships. He implemented needed Church reforms, strengthened ecclesiastical discipline, and restored churches and monasteries. He supported the last of the Crusades against the Turks, in which Peter de Lusignan, king of Cyprus, succeeded in taking and temporarily occupying Alexandria in October 1365, but the initiative failed.

William was closely involved with affairs of state, but probably the most momentous event of his pontificate was his decision to move the Holy See from Avignon (where it had been based for 50 years) back to Rome. The decision met universal acclaim from all but the French, who rightly feared a diminution of their influence. Urban nevertheless left Avignon on April 30 and entered Rome on October 16, 1367, after a stay of some months in the citadel at Viterbo.

In Rome, he set about restoring the city, reviving religion and tightening clerical discipline. The unemployed were put to work in the neglected gardens of the Vatican, and the papal treasure, which had been preserved at Assisi since the days of Pope Boniface VIII (r. 1294–1303), was distributed among city churches. Urban negotiated a new treaty with German emperor Charles IV and crowned his empress. He also attempted to bridge the schism with the Eastern Church, which seemed to him a permanent injury to Jesus Christ. However, although he reconciled with the Greek emperor, John V Palaeologus, the latter was unable to bring his people along, and the schism persisted.

As important a political and religious event as the return to Rome was, political realities made it impossible to sustain. Urban decided to move his court back to Avignon, even though St. Bridget had come to warn him of her premonition that if he did, he would shortly die. He left Rome on September 5, and was back in Avignon on September 24, 1370.

Less than three months later, he had his own premonition of impending death, and, not wanting to die in fine sheets, had himself moved from the Papal Palace to his brother's house at the foot of the hill. He had all the doors to the street opened, so that he could receive farewell visitors, and expired on December 19. His relics were interred in Notre-Dame des Doms at Avignon, but in accordance with his own wishes, were translated two years later to the abbey church of St. Victor at Marseilles.

The many miracles reported at his tomb led to demands for his canonization by King Waldemar of Denmark. Though promised by Gregory XI (r. 1370–78) in 1375, this did not occur, owing to the disorders of the time.

Beatified: March 10, 1870, by Pope Pius IX
Feast: December 19

Ursula (fourth or fifth century?) *Legendary martyred virgin whose cult has been suppressed*

Ursula was one of the most popular saints in the Middle Ages. Ursula seems to have been associated with several martyred virgins; accounts of her story have been embellished. The basis for the legend is a true account of a senator, Clematius, who rebuilt a basilica in Cologne, dated to perhaps the fourth century, that honored a group of virgins who had been martyred there. The identities and circumstances of their martyrdom are not known.

According to a 10th-century legend, Ursula was the daughter of a Christian king in Britain, who planned to marry her to a pagan prince. As she did not want this marriage, she asked for and was granted a three-year postponement. With 10 ladies in waiting, each attended by 1,000 maidens, Ursula embarked on a voyage across the North Sea, sailed up the Rhine to Basel, Switzerland, and then went to Rome. On their way back in about 451, they went to Cologne, where Ursula refused to marry the chieftain of the Huns. All the women were massacred.

According to another even more embellished legend, Ursula and an army of women met their demise after a battle. Armorica was settled by British colonizers and soldiers after Emperor Magnus Clemens Maximus conquered Britain and Gaul in 383. The ruler of the settlers, Cynan Meiriadog, called on King Dionotus of Cornwall for wives for the settlers. Dionotus promised his daughter Ursula for Cynan, and sent her off by ship with 11,000 maidens and 60,000 common women. The fleet was wrecked and all the women were enslaved or murdered.

Pope Benedict XIV (r. 1740–58) allegedly planned to remove Ursula from the Roman martyrology. Her cult was suppressed in 1969.

Feast: formerly October 21
Patronage: drapes; schoolgirls; young women

Ursus (sixth century) *Archdeacon of Aosta, Italy, and miracle-worker*

A native of Ireland, Ursus traveled to Europe and was made archdeacon of Aosta in northern Italy, where he spent many years preaching against the Arian heresy.

Middle level: *Ursula with the 11,000 virgins.* Top level: *Mary with Jesus.* Bottom level: *Young boys being boiled in oil.*
(Library of Congress Prints and Photographs Division)

Ursus is credited with miraculously manifesting a stream of water in time of need. On a hot summer day in rural Burseia, he listened to people complaining about the lack of a fountain. Calling up his faith that all things are possible for those who believe, he struck the rock with his staff and a fountain bubbled forth. It was named St. Bear's Fountain, and was still bearing water in the 13th century.

His story is similar to stories of other saints who struck rocks with staffs to find water.

St. Ursus is depicted in art as striking a rock with his staff.

Feast: February 1

Valentine (d. ca. 269–270)

Name Meaning: Valor
Also known as: Valentine of Terni, Valentine of Rome

Little is known about the real Valentine. In fact, many early martyrologies listed two and sometimes three Valentines: a priest in Rome, a bishop in Interamna (now Terni) and a third in Africa. Most scholars now presume that all three Valentines are the same man.

Most probably, Valentine either lived in Rome or was called from Terni to Rome as a consequence of his giving comfort to the martyrs under Emperor Claudius II, known as the Cruel. Imprisoned, Valentine, also a physician, reportedly converted his jailer to Christianity by restoring the eyesight of the jailer's daughter. Brought before the Roman prefect, Valentine refused to renounce his faith and was beaten and beheaded on February 14. On the morning of his execution, he supposedly sent a farewell message to the jailer's daughter, signed "from your Valentine." His body was buried on the Flaminian Way in Rome, and his relics were taken to the church of St. Praxedes.

Another legend about Valentine has the priest surreptitiously marrying Roman couples when Claudius II, frustrated at his difficulty in taking men from their homes to be soldiers, outlawed marriage. In this version, Valentine languishes and dies in prison on the emperor's orders but is not executed.

Such stories—that Valentine helped lovers and that he sent loving messages—have connected the saint with romance. Other sources of the connection between Valentine's date of martyrdom and love stem from early Roman festivals, such as the *Lupercalia,* that involved young noblemen running through the streets with thongs made from the skins of sacrificed goats. They lashed young women, which was believed to improve their chances at childbearing. The thongs were called *februa,* and the lashing *februatio,* from a Latin word meaning "to purify," the same root as February. In other celebrations, Roman men drew names of available young ladies out of a box and promised to love them—at least until the festival next year.

In England, both men and young women put their names into the box and were drawn in pairs. Each couple exchanged gifts, and the man wore his love's name on his sleeve. Perhaps more significant to love and February is that birds choose mates around February 14, a fact noted by Chaucer. The custom of giving flowers for Valentine's Day supposedly began with a daughter of King Henry IV of France, who threw a party to honor the saint and gave every lady present a bouquet.

Feast: February 14
Patronage: beekeepers; betrothed couples; epilepsy; fainting; greetings; happy marriages; love and lovers; plague; travelers; young people

Victor I (d. ca. 199) *Pope*

Victor was a native of North Africa. He became the 14th bishop of Rome, succeeding St. Eleutherius around the year 175.

During Victor's rule, the Christians of the Roman Empire enjoyed a peace they had not known before. Emperor Commodus (r. 180–192) had once been cured by a Christian named Proculus, whom he kept with him in his palace. He employed other Christians as officials at his court and pardoned those who had been sent to do forced labor in the Sardinian mines, after his mistress Marcia obtained a list of names from Victor. One of those freed was St. Callistus, a later pope, who chose to live at Antium with the support of a monthly pension from Victor.

The external peace was, however, marred by internal dissent. For some time there had been conflict between the Church of Rome and the Quartodeciman churches of Asia Minor over the scheduling of Easter. Rome celebrated Easter on Sunday, whereas the Quartodecimans had always followed the Hebrew calendar and celebrated it instead on the first day of Passover— on whatever day of the week that might fall. The conflict came to a head when the growing number of Asian immigrants in Rome tried to celebrate Easter on the day to which they were accustomed. Victor instructed the Quartodecimans to change their celebration to Sunday, threatening their bishops with excommunication if they did not. When they defied him, he made good his threat, though this seems not to have been enforced. In Rome, his attempt to enforce the decree was met by the Asian Blastus, who brought about a short-lived schism.

Victor also had to contend with Gnostics and other heretics, such as the Monarchians. Monarchians denied the Trinity, holding that God was supreme, and that Jesus was merely a man endowed at baptism with supernatural power. Victor convened several synods to deal with the sect and excommunicated its head, Theodotus the Tanner. Theodotus responded by forming his own schismatic church, which persisted in Rome for some time thereafter.

Victor, the first Latin writer in the Church, declared Latin the official language of the Church of Rome. Also under Victor, the Roman Church became the proprietor of a cemetery on the Appian Way.

Feast: Formerly July 28

Victor III (ca. 1026–1087) *Pope*
Also known as: Desiderius

A sickly and reluctant pope, Victor is remembered for sending the military force to North Africa that in 1087 defeated the Muslim Saracens, prefiguring the Crusades.

He was born in 1026 or 1027 to a family of Lombard nobles. From his youth he yearned to become a monk, but since he was an only son, his parents opposed this plan, and arranged a marriage for him instead. After his father died fighting the Normans in 1047, he fled his marriage and went to Cava, only to be captured and brought back home by force. Again he escaped to Cava, where he received permission to enter the monastery of Santa Sophia at Benevento, and took the name Desiderius.

Finding the life at Santa Sofia less strict than he wished, Desiderius soon moved to the island monastery of Trimite in the Adriatic Sea, then, in 1053, went to live with some hermits at Majella in the Abruzzi. His austerity brought him to the attention of Pope St. Leo IX (r. 1049–54) and his successor, Pope Victor II (r. 1055–57). He attached himself to Victor's court at Florence, where he met two monks from Monte Cassino, and in 1055 he returned with these monks to their monastery. Joining the community shortly thereafter, he was appointed superior of the dependent house at Capua.

In 1058, Desiderius succeeded Pope Stephen X (r. 1057–58)—who had retained the abbacy even while he held the papacy—as abbot of Monte Cassino. He proved to be a great abbot, who rebuilt the church and established schools of art, while he reinstated monastic discipline. His reputation brought the abbey many gifts and exemptions. Pope Alexander II (r. 1061–73) gave him the power to reform other monasteries in his region as well. He was well positioned to act as a go-between for Rome and the Normans in Italy, a role he performed under Pope St. Gregory VII (r. 1073–1085).

In May 1085, as he lay dying, Gregory named Desiderius as one of the fittest to succeed him. After Gregory's death, Desiderius went to Rome to consult on the succession, but when he discovered that he was the leading candidate, returned to Monte Cassino. There he involved himself in political affairs, trying to get the Normans and Lombards to support the Holy See. In the autumn, he marched on Rome with the Norman army, but when he discovered that the Norman princes were conspiring with the Vatican's cardinals to seat him, he refused to enter the city unless they desisted. Since neither side would give in, the election was postponed.

In 1086, Desiderius was importuned to return to Rome and was once again pressed to accept the Chair of St. Peter. When he continued to resist, the cardinals lost patience with him. On May 24, they seized him and carried him to the Church of St. Lucy, where they dressed him in the pope's red cape and gave him the name Victor. Four days later he abandoned the papal insignia, and again returned to Monte Cassino. He spent about a year there before finally accepting the throne during Lent in 1087. After the Normans had driven the soldiers of the antipope Clement III (Guibert of Ravenna) out of St. Peter's, he was consecrated there on May 9, and gave the Easter Mass. However, he remained in Rome only eight days before returning once more to Monte Cassino.

Victor's short papacy was much concerned with struggles with Clement and his supporters. In August 1087, at a synod in Benevento, Victor renewed Gregory VII's excommunication of Clement, who was once again ensconced in the Lateran Palace. While the council was under way—on August 5—the army he had sent to North Africa under the Banner of St. Peter captured the town of El Mahadia and forced the Islamic ruler of Tunis to free all Christian slaves and to pledge tribute to the Holy See. The Benevento council had lasted only three days, however, when Victor entered his final illness. He retired to Monte Cassino, where he had himself carried to the chapter house, which he had built. He died there on September 16, 1087, and was interred in a tomb he had prepared for himself. Four hundred years after, his relics were translated to the church, then later were moved again.

Victor's only known literary work is his *Dialogues* on the miracles of St. Benedict and others at Monte Cassino.

His cultus seems to have begun no later than the reign of Pope Anastasius IV (r. 1153–54), only decades after his death, though it was largely confined to the region of Monte Cassino. In 1727, the monastery's abbot obtained permission to keep his feast.

Cultus approved: 1727 by Benedict III
Feast: September 16

Vincent Ferrer (1350–1419) *Dominican friar and missionary*

Vincent Ferrer was born on January 23, 1350, in Valencia, Spain, to a noble family. At age 17 he entered the Dominican order and was sent to Barcelona to complete his studies. In 1370 he began teaching at Lerida, and had for a pupil Pierre Fouloup, who later became the grand inquisitor of Aragon.

Vincent returned to Barcelona in 1373 and aided famine sufferers. While preaching one day he accurately predicted that ships bearing grain were approaching. In 1377 he continued his studies in Toulouse. In 1379, he was employed by Cardinal Pedro de Luna, the papal legate to the court of Aragon, and from 1385 to 1390 taught at the cathedral of Valencia.

St. Vincent Ferrer

Pedro de Luna became the antipope Benedict XIII, and appointed Vincent as his confessor and apostolic penitentiary. Vincent declined appointment as cardinal.

Vincent fell seriously ill during a French siege of Avignon in 1398. He had a miraculous recovery after having a vision of Christ and SS. Dominic and Francis of Assisi, who told him to go out and preach. Benedict opposed this but allowed him to do so in 1399. For 20 years, Vincent traveled throughout western Europe preaching penance for sin and preparation for judgment. Huge numbers came to hear him preach. Though he spoke only his native dialect, Vincent made himself understood to foreign audiences, apparently through the gift of tongues. St. Bernadine of Siena was among those who heard him speak.

In 1408 Vincent went to Genoa to try to help plague victims and to try to heal the schism between Benedict and Pope Gregory XII (r. 1406–15). Though he supported Benedict, he was unsuccessful in getting Benedict to resign for the good of the Church.

He returned to Spain, and spent the next eight years preaching and working miracles throughout the southern part of the country. He converted thousands of Moors. In 1416, he announced in his preaching that Benedict was the legitimate pope, but due to the fact that he would not resign, King Ferdinand of Aragon was withdrawing his states from obedience to Avignon. The same year Gregory XII resigned, paving the way for the schism to be healed. Pope Martin V was elected in 1417, and reigned until 1431.

Throughout his life, Vincent lived simply, dressing poorly, observing austerities and fasting perpetually. He usually tended to sick children every day. In his last years, Vincent traveled throughout northern France. He died in Vannes, Brittany, on April 5, 1419.

In art Vincent often is portrayed as a Dominican holding an open book while preaching, and as a Dominican preacher with a flame on top of his head.

Canonized: 1455 by Pope Callistus III
Feast: April 5
Patronage: brick makers; builders; construction workers; pavement workers; plumbers; tile makers

FURTHER READING
Pradel, Andrew. *St. Vincent Ferrer: Angel of the Judgment.* Rockford, Ill.: TAN Books and Publishers, 2001.

Vincent of Lérins (d. ca. 445) *Father of the Church*

Vincent of Lérins was born into a noble family of Gaul (now France); he is believed by some to have been the brother of St. Lupus of Troyes. After serving as a soldier, he gave up the military life and entered a monastery on the island of Lérins (today Isle St. Honorat). He was ordained there and in about 434 wrote his best-known work, the *Commonitorium,* under the pseudonym Peregrinus.

The *Commonitorium* offered a guide to orthodox Christian teaching and included the famous Vincentian Canon, by which he sought to differentiate between true and false tradition: *quad ubique, quad semper, quad ab omnibus credituni est* ("what has been believed everywhere, always, and by all"). Vincent held that the ultimate source of Christian truth lay in the Holy Scriptures and that the authority of the Church was to be invoked to guarantee their correct interpretation. Ironically, he was a strong proponent of Semi-Pelagianism and opposed the Augustinian model of Grace. However, since he wrote before Semi-Pelagianism had been declared heretical by the Church, this is not now held against him.

The date of Vincent's death is not known, but it was certainly before 450 and probably around 445.

Feast: May 24

Vincent de Paul (ca. 1581–1660) *Founder of the Congregation of the Mission and the Sisters of Charity, Patron of all Charities*
Also known as: Apostle of Charity; Friend of the Poor

Vincent was born on April 24, 1581, at Pouy (now called St.-Vincent-de-Paul) near the village of Dax in Gascony, the third of six children. His parents, Jean de Paul and Bertrande de Moras, were poor peasants, but they managed to send Vincent to study with the Cordeliers, a strict sect of Franciscans. In 1597 he began theological studies at the University of Toulouse, with a short stay at the University of Saragossa in Spain, receiving his degree in 1604. In 1600, at age 19, Vincent entered the priesthood, ordained by Francois de Bourdeille, bishop of Perigueux.

In 1605, Vincent returned to Toulouse from his home to recover a small legacy left him by a parishioner. Returning by boat from Marseilles to Narbonne, Vincent and the other travelers were attacked by Turkish pirates from the Barbary Coast of North Africa. Three were killed, and the survivors were chained and sold into slavery in Tunis. Vincent was bought by a fisherman, who sold him to an old Muslim alchemist. When the man died, his nephew sold Vincent to a former monk that had renounced Christianity for Islam and had taken three wives. According to legend, one of the wives—a Turkish Muslim—took an interest in Vincent and his faithfulness. She pestered her husband to return to Christianity, and he and Vincent safely escaped from Africa to Marseilles in 1607. The next year the man supposedly accompanied Vincent to Rome, where the former monk entered the order of the Brothers of St. John of God and spent the rest of his life in hospital service.

Vincent came to Paris in 1609. He became almoner to the former wife of King Henry IV, Marguerite of Valois—a post that earned him the income from a small abbey. He also attracted the attention of Pierre de Berulle, who eventually became a cardinal. In 1612, Father Berulle found Vincent a curacy at Clichy, just north of Paris. The next year Vincent entered service as tutor and chaplain to the family of Philip de Gondi, count of Joigny and general of the galleys. It was customary for French convicts to serve their sentences as slaves, manning the oars in French warships. Vincent also listened to the confessions of the peasants on the de Gondi properties, and in 1617 was called to hear the confession of a dying man in Folleville who admitted that all his previous confessions had been lies. Appalled, Mme. de Gondi arranged for Vincent to preach in the Folleville parish church and teach the country people the sanctity of the sacraments and liturgy. Vincent was so successful that he had to call for help from the Jesuits in Amiens.

In July of that year, Vincent left the de Gondi family to become pastor of the parish church at Châtillon-les-Dombes in eastern France. He restored the building and inspired the congregation, even converting the apparently notorious count of Rougemont and other dissolute aristocrats. He also founded the first Confraternity of Charity to encourage wealthy ladies—who had little or no experience with charity—to raise funds and to minister to the sick and poor as if they were caring for their own sons. Returning to the de Gondis in December, Vincent was soon ministering to the galley slaves held in the Conciergerie in Paris, showing these wretched prisoners that they, too, were beloved. In 1619 Vincent was named chaplain-general of the galleys and their royal almoner.

About 1623, Mme. de Gondi offered Vincent a large endowment to found a perpetual mission for whatever purpose he saw fit. Vincent humbly averred, not believing himself worthy. Meanwhile, Mme. de Gondi prevailed upon her husband to organize a group of missionaries to work among the peasants and discussed their plans with M. de Gondi's brother, Jean Francois de Gondi, archbishop of Paris. The archbishop gave the mission the Collège des Bons Enfants as a home for their new community. Vincent took possession of the house and became director of its mission in April 1625, although he continued to serve Mme. de Gondi until her death later that year.

Members of this new Congregation of the Mission were secular priests who were devoted to ministry in the towns and villages, vowing to live in poverty, chastity, obedience and stability. They tended the poor and sick and provided seminaries for those considering the priesthood. In 1632, Pope Urban VIII (r. 1623–44) approved the rules of the community, and in 1633 the archbishop gave Vincent the priory of St. Lazare, which became the motherhouse. Henceforth the fathers often were called Lazarists but are also known as Vincentians. Besides the mission, Vincent also held retreats, conferences and seminaries at St. Lazare and at Bon Enfants to adequately educate clerics and those in religious orders about the spiritual and practical aspects of their vocation.

In 1633, Vincent and St. Louise de Marillac cofounded the Sisters (also called the Daughters) of Charity. The Sisters undertook more direct service and hospital work than the original Confraternities of Charity, renamed the Ladies of Charity, could handle. Through generous contributions from wealthy families, the Ladies of Charity and even Cardinal Richelieu, Vincent was able to establish asylums and hospitals for the old, the sick, the insane, foundling infants, orphans, beggars, the poor, galley convicts—all who suffered, whether physically, emotionally or spiritually.

Vincent was active in the politics of his day and at court as well, always seeking opportunities to serve. When Cardinal Richelieu brought France into the fighting against Germany in 1635, during the Thirty Years' War, Vincent organized relief for the war-torn province of Lorraine. He attended King Louis XIII on his deathbed in 1643 and remained a valued adviser to the king's widow, Anne of Austria, who became regent on behalf of the five-year-old dauphin Louis XIV. Remembering his own enslavement, Vincent raised enough funds to free 1,200 slaves in North Africa and acted as agent for the families. During the Fronde, a period of rebellion by the nobility against the monarchy in 1649–53, Vincent worked tirelessly to petition Anne for clemency for the nobles and the establishment of peace. He implored her to dismiss her minister, Cardinal Mazarin, for the good of France, but she declined (giving credence to rumors that Jules Mazarin, born Giulio Mazarini, was secretly married to Anne after Louis XIII's death).

Not long after assuming the regency, Anne had named Vincent the head of the Council of Conscience, a panel charged with reforming ecclesiastical abuse, particularly the bestowing of wealthy religious benefices to aristocrats who were often too young or spiritually untrained for the posts. At one meeting, the Comtesse de Chavigny took great offense at Vincent's refusal to approve an abbacy for her five-year-old son. Supposedly she threw a stool at Vincent, hitting him in the head. Walking calmly from the room, bleeding, Vincent commented, "What a wonderful thing is mother love!" Vincent's efforts at reform annoyed Cardinal Mazarin, who had ascended to his position as cardinal without ever being ordained a priest. Finally, Mazarin quit informing Vincent of the council's meetings and removed him in 1652.

A staunch defender of the faith, Vincent fought vigorously against the Jansenist heresy. Cornelius Jansen was a Dutch Catholic theologian and bishop of Ypres who attempted to reform the faith by returning to the principles of St. Augustine. His treatise "Augustinus" and emphasis on personal holiness received wide acceptance in France. Vincent took issue with the bishop's belief in predestination, denying man's free will and ability to contribute to his salvation—in other words, some few are chosen but most are not—and campaigned for the pope to condemn these ideas.

At the end of his life Vincent suffered ill health and became unable to visit his many ministries. He died peacefully in his chair on September 27, 1660, and was buried in the motherhouse at St. Lazare. St. Louise de Marillac died later that year. In Vincent's spirit,

Frédéric Ozanam founded the St. Vincent de Paul Society in Paris in 1833. Pope Leo XIII declared Vincent the patron of all charitable societies in 1885.

During the French Revolution, enraged citizens ransacked St. Lazare on July 13, 1789, the day before the crowds stormed the Bastille. All of the community's buildings were confiscated in 1792; the current motherhouse in Paris was given to the congregation in 1817 as compensation. But when the mob broke into the Pantheon and destroyed the religious statues, supposedly they spared the statue of Vincent de Paul, for even the most angry and desperate realized that he was the friend of all.

Beatified: August 13, 1729, by Pope Benedict XIII
Canonized: June 16, 1737, by Pope Clement XII
Feast: September 27
Patronage: charities and charitable societies; horses; hospitals; hospital workers; lepers and leprosy; lost articles; prisoners; spiritual help; St. Vincent de Paul Societies; Vincentian Service Corps; volunteers; Madagascar

FURTHER READING

Freund, John C.M. "Saint Vincent de Paul: Following Christ" and "Chronology of Important Dates." URL: http://www.cptryon.org. Downloaded: October 10, 2000.
"Vincent de Paul." St. Vincent de Paul Society (England and Wales), 1998. URL: http://home.btconnect.com. Downloaded: August 15, 2000.
Vincent de Paul and Louise de Marillac: Rules, Conferences and Writings. Frances Ryan and John E. Rybolt, eds. Mahwah, N.J.: Paulist Press, 1995.
"Vincent de Paul, Helper of the Poor." URL: http://elvis.rowan.edu. Downloaded: October 10, 2000.

Vitalian (d. 672) *Pope*

Vitalian was born in Segni, Campagna (Italy), the son of Anastasius. He entered the priesthood and was active in the Church of Rome, being consecrated bishop to replace Pope St. Eugene I on July 30, 657.

Vitalian continued the Roman Church's battle against Monothelitism that had so occupied his immediate predecessors. He was on better terms than they with Byzantine emperor Constans II, and after Constans was assassinated in 688, supported his son, Constantine IV, in his political struggles. However, he was unable to get Byzantium to abrogate the heresy.

He was more successful in promoting Catholicism in the West. In 664, at the Synod of Streaneshalch (Whitby), King Oswy of Northumberland decided to observe Easter according to the Roman Church and to follow it in the shape of the tonsure. He dispatched a candidate for archbishop to be consecrated by the pope, but the man died in Rome. Vitalian then decided to send St. Theodore of Tarsus in his stead. Theodore was consecrated by Vitalian on March 26, 688, and went to England, where he was recognized as archbishop of Canterbury and head of the Church in England by all the clergy.

Vitalian died on January 27, 672, and was buried in St. Peter's at the Vatican.

Feast: January 27

Vladimir I of Kiev (ca. 956–1015) *Patron saint of Russia*

Also known as: Vladimir Svyatoslavich, Vladimir the Great, Svyatoy Vladimir, Vladimir Veliky

Grand Duke Vladimir I was the illegitimate third son of Svyatoslav by his favorite court mistress Olga Malushka. His great-grandfather, the Varangian adventurer Oleg, had ousted the Viking invaders from the Slavic city-state of Novgorod in the ninth century and eventually expanded his kingdom to include the principality of Kiev, forming Kievan Rus. By the early 10th century, Kievan Rus was economically stable enough to challenge the nearby Byzantine Empire and establish trade routes. Oleg's son Igor, Vladimir's grandfather, was killed in 945 during a trading expedition.

Vladimir's grandmother, St. Olga, could not convert her son Svyatoslav to Christianity, and his three sons—Yaropolk, Oleg and Vladimir—lived as pagan chieftains. Before Svyatoslav's murder in 970 at the hands of his own barbarian tribes (legend tells that the men were so angry at their defeat by the Byzantines at Arcadiopolis that they used Svyatoslav's empty skull as a drinking vessel), he had divided his kingdom, giving the grand duchy of Kiev to Yaropolk and the Drevlani (now part of Poland and Hungary) to Oleg. Vladimir received the rebellious Russian capital of Novgorod. War broke out between Yaropolk and Oleg, with Yaropolk conquering Drevlani and ousting his brother. Vladimir feared a similar fate and fled to his Varangian uncle in Scandinavia, leaving Novgorod vulnerable to attack. Yaropolk conquered the city and united all the principalities of Russia under his reign. But by 980 Vladimir had not only retaken Novgorod but had also conquered the city of Polotzk and slain its prince, Ragvald, and had married Ragvald's daughter Ragnilda, who was supposed to marry Yaropolk. Vladimir then took Kiev and Rodno, where he killed Yaropolk, and declared himself grand duke of Kiev and all Russia.

Russia now extended from the Ukraine to the Baltic Sea. Vladimir lived like an Eastern pasha, with at least four, and possibly six, other wives besides Ragnilda and many concubines. He built pagan temples and was rumored to practice strange rites. Before becoming grand duke, Vladimir had nominally converted to Islam, but he reverted to his pagan upbringing. Realizing, however, what a unifying force religion could be, Vladimir reportedly invited representatives of Latin Christianity, Eastern Christianity, Judaism and Islam to make presentations for his consideration. He liked the Muslim practice of having many women to enjoy but disliked the rules against drink. The German Christians were no better since they emphasized fasting and celibacy (the Germans also represented a political threat to Russian sovereignty). And Vladimir could not believe the Khazarian Jews had any real religious authority if God had scattered them throughout the world as punishment for their unfaithfulness.

Finally a representative from the Orthodox patriarch made his appeal, and Vladimir supposedly chose the Eastern Church because of its beautiful liturgy and art. A more likely consideration was Vladimir's desire to maintain independence from the Germans. He remembered that his grandmother, St. Olga, had been Orthodox.

About 987, Byzantine emperor Basil II appealed to Vladimir for help in putting down an insurrection, and Vladimir requested marriage to Basil's sister Anne in return. Basil II replied that his sister, a devout Christian, could not marry a heathen, but that he would consider the union if Vladimir converted. Vladimir acquiesced, and a pact was reached. In 988 Vladimir was baptized by the Orthodox metropolitan Michael and took the baptismal name Basil, then married Princess Anne. Marriage to Anne was quite a coup, as she was born in the Porphyra, the purple marble bedroom of the Byzantine empress, and was thereby considered the most desirable consort in Christendom. It is from this that the phrase "to the purple born" originates. Emperor Otto I had already sought Anne's hand for his son Otto II, as had the French king Hugh Capet for his son Robert. Vladimir was the first foreigner to marry a "purple" princess.

Vladimir may have chosen Christianity because of political reasons, but once he accepted the faith he embraced it wholeheartedly. Upon his marriage to Anne he put away all other wives and concubines. He built churches and monasteries, ordered the conversion of Kiev and Novgorod with penalties for resistance, and threw pagan idols into the Dnieper River. Although Vladimir adopted the Byzantine rites in the Old Church Slavonic language, he maintained ties with Rome, introduced tithing in the East, and exchanged papal legates. He expanded schools and the justice system, even questioning the use of capital punishment. In 989 he built the large Church of St. Mary Ever Virgin in Kiev, usually called the *Desyatinnya Sobor*, or Cathedral of the Tithes.

Anne and Vladimir, now called the Fair Sun, had two sons, Boris and Gleb, martyrs also known as SS. Romanus and David. When Anne died in 1011, Vladimir remarried, and their daughter became the consort of Casimir I, Restorer of Poland.

Vladimir's later years were spent in dealings with his children from the earlier marriages. In keeping with ancestral custom, Vladimir had divided his kingdom among his children. One son, Vsevolod, prince of Volhynia, met an untimely death in a fire when his pursuit of the widowed queen Sigrid of Sweden displeased her. Vladimir's son Yaroslav became prince of Novgorod, but he rebelled against homage to his father and refused service and tribute. In 1014 Vladimir prepared to march on Novgorod, but Yaroslav called in Varangian forces, just as his father had done 34 years earlier.

Vladimir died while on campaign in Berestova, near Kiev, on July 15, 1015. His death ignited a brutal civil war, with Yaroslav the eventual victor over his brother Mstislav. Yaroslav came to be called "the Wise" as he ruled over a united Russia; supported trade, education and the arts; built the Great Gate of Kiev; and helped draft the *Ruskais Pravda*, the first law code in Russia.

Feast: July 15
Patronage: converts; kings; murderers; parents of large families; Russia

FURTHER READING
Reston, James, Jr. *The Last Apocalypse: Europe at the Year 1000 A.D.* New York: Doubleday, 1998.

Walburga (710–779) *Abbess*

Walburga was born in Devonshire, England, around 710. She was the daughter of a West Saxon chieftain and the sister of SS. Willibald and Winebald (also given as Winnebald and Wunebald). She was educated at Wimborne Monastery in Dorset, where she became a nun. In 748, she was sent with St. Lioba to Germany to help St. Boniface in his missionary work. She spent two years at Bishofsheim. Her brother Winebald, bishop of Eichstadt, appointed her abbess of the Benedictine double monastery at Heidenheim, which he had founded. Walburga served as superior of both men and women until her death in 779.

She was buried first at Heidenheim. Between 870 and 879 her body was interred next to that of her brother Winebald in the Holy Cross Church at Eichstadt. The Church of St. Walburga is there today.

After the remains were moved, Walburga's bones began to secrete a manna called "pearls," a clear, tasteless and odorless liquid described as resembling fresh water and said to have great healing power. For more than 10 centuries, this manna—also called an oil— has been collected by Benedictine nuns, bottled and given out to the faithful. It is consumed and used as an ointment.

The bones are housed in a reliquary that has two compartments separated by a shelf. The bones rest in a silver bowl in the top compartment. A silver shell is in the bottom compartment. Oil from the bones drips through silver pipes into the shell. It is collected and placed into ampules.

The oil flow begins every year between October 12, the date her remains were moved, and stops on February 25, the date of the anniversary of her death.

In the Roman Martyrology, Walburga's feast day was observed on May 1, which became known as Walburga's night, or Walpurgisnacht. May 1 was a major pagan festival, Beltane, which became demonized as a night of witches' revelries. Rites were performed on this night for protection against witches and witchcraft.

Feast: February 25
Patronage: crops; against famine; against plagues

Wenceslaus (d. 929) *Duke of Bohemia, patron saint of Bohemia and of other parts of the present Czech Republic, martyr*
Also known as: Wenceslas

Wenceslaus was born near Prague, the older of two sons of Ratislav, king of Bohemia, and his wife, Drahomira. He was raised by his grandmother, Ludmila, a convert. He was still a boy when his father was killed fighting the Magyars. Drahomira assumed control of

St. Walburga

the government and pursued a vigorous anti-Christian policy and a cruel reign. Fearing the influence of Ludmila, Drahomira had her strangled in her castle. Wenceslaus overthrew his mother in about 924 or 925 and banished her to Budech.

After Wenceslaus restored a more moderate reign that encouraged Christianity, he recalled his mother, who evidently posed no further problem. But when the duke married and had a son, his brother Boleslaus (also Boleslav) lost his succession to the throne, and began plotting against him. Wenceslaus also lost popularity as a result of his capitulation to the invading German king, Henry I the Fowler.

In September 929 Boleslaus invited Wenceslaus to celebrate the feast of its patron saints, Cosmas and Damian. As Wenceslaus went to Mass on the morning after the festival, Boleslaus and his companion knights attacked him. The two brothers fought, and then the friends of Boleslaus killed the duke.

Wenceslaus immediately was proclaimed a martyr, and miracles were reported at his tomb. Fearful of the growing cult, Boleslaus three years later had the body translated to the Church of St. Vitus in Prague, which then became a site of pilgrimage.

Wenceslaus is featured in the Christmas carol, "Good King Wenceslaus."

Feast: September 28
Patronage: Czech Republic

William of Norwich (d. 144) *Alleged martyr*

William of Norwich supposedly was a boy apprenticed to a tanner in Norwich, England. When he was 12 years old, the Jews in the town plotted to mock the Crucifixion at Passover by kidnaping him, torturing him and murdering him. They bound him up, pierced him with nails to mimic the wounds of Christ and then poured boiling water over him.

No historical basis for the story has been found, and it probably was written to appeal to medieval Christian beliefs that, during Passover, Jews would steal children and put them to death. The story served to stir up anti-Jewish sentiments.

The complete story, *The Life and Miracles of St. William of Norwich*, was written in 1173 by Thomas of Monmouth, a monk in the Norwich Benedictine abbey. The cult is now suppressed.

Feast: formerly March 26

FURTHER READING
Thomas of Monmouth. *The Life and Miracles of St. William of Norwich.* URL: http://www.fordham.edu/halsall/source/1173williamnorwich.html. Downloaded: August 20, 2000.

Z

Zachary (first century) *Father of St. John the Baptist*
Name meaning: Jehovah hath remembered
Also known as: Zacharius; Zechariah

Little is known about Zachary. He is mentioned in
Luke 1 in connection with the birth of John. He
belonged to the tribe of Abia (Abijah) and was married
to Elizabeth, kinswoman of Mary (destined to become
the Blessed Virgin Mary). He was a priest in the temple
at Jerusalem.

Zachary and Elizabeth were childless and well
advanced in years when they were informed by Gabriel
the Archangel that Elizabeth would bear a child.
Zachary received this news one day while he was performing his assigned rites in the temple and was alone
at the altar. Gabriel appeared on his right and said that
the couple's prayers would be answered with the birth
of a son, who was to be named John. Zachary doubted
this because of their ages and so asked for a sign.
Gabriel said he would be stricken dumb and would
regain his speech when the prophecy was fulfilled. The
angel departed and Zachary could not speak.

Elizabeth did conceive and she bore a son. After
eight days, the parents took him to the temple to be
circumcised. Elizabeth said the child's name was John,
but the priests did not believe her, saying no one in her
family was named thus. Zachary, still dumb, wrote on a
tablet for the priest, "His name is John." At that

Zachary and the angel

moment his speech was restored and he began to praise the Lord.

According to ex-canonical sources, Zachary was killed when he refused to tell King Herod the location of his son.

Feast: November 5 (with Elizabeth)

Zachary I (d. 752) *Pope*
Also known as: Zacharias I

Zachary was born at San Severino, Calabria, Italy, of Greek parents. He joined the priesthood and was made a deacon in the Roman Church by Pope St. Gregory III (r. 731–741). Immediately after Gregory's burial on November 29, 741, Zachary was unanimously elected his successor. He was consecrated and enthroned on December 5.

Zachary was soon called upon to intervene with King Liutprand of the Lombards, who was about to invade Roman lands. Legend has it that the Lombards were moved to tears at the devotion with which they heard Zachary say Mass. He presented Liutprand (St. Ratchis) with a Benedictine habit. More important, he succeeded not only in dissuading Liutprand from his campaign but also in getting him to return lands he had seized and occupied for 30 years, and in winning the liberty of all Roman prisoners of war—concessions that led to a lasting peace between the Lombards and the Eastern Empire.

At the same time, Zachary sowed the seeds for the Papal-Frankish alliance, which also was to have lasting implications for the Roman Church. Relations between Rome and the Eastern churches, led by Constantinople, had been strained for some time over Iconoclasm, the Muslim-influenced movement that banned the worship of images. Meanwhile, St. Boniface in Germany was shoring up the Roman Church's influence with the Franks. Zachary instructed Boniface to recognize baptisms of persons whose Latin was imperfect, on the grounds that it was the intention that was important. He also told him to suspend polygamous and murderous priests and to abolish superstitious practices, even those that were then current in Rome.

Zachary is remembered also for translating the *Dialogues* of Gregory the Great (Gregory I, r. 590–604) from Latin into Greek, for providing refuge to nuns driven from Constantinople by the Iconoclasts, and for opposing the Mediterranean slave trade. He ransomed slaves from the Venetians and forbade the selling of Christian slaves to the Muslim Moors. He also aided the poor of Rome. So great was his popularity that he began to be venerated as a saint immediately after his death in 752.

In art, Zachary is shown making peace with King Liutprand. Sometimes he has a dove and olive branch over him.

Feast: March 15 (formerly March 22; in the East, September 5)

Zephyrinus (d. 217) *Pope and martyr*

Zephyrinus was born in Rome. He succeeded St. Victor I as bishop of Rome about the year 199. He was apparently a simple man, without higher learning, who devoted himself more to practical matters than to theological pronouncements. Immediately upon his election, he called St. Callistus to Rome from Antium, ordained him deacon, and put him charge of the Church's coemeterium (cemetery) on the Appian Way. Callistus also became Zephyrinus's counselor and succeeded him in 217.

The pontificate of Zephyrinus was marked by the ongoing challenge to the Church from heretical sects. Victor had excommunicated Theodotus the Tanner and members of his group, the Monarchians. Monarchians denied the Trinity, declaring that it was God who died on the cross and that Jesus was merely a man who had received supernatural powers at baptism. The sect continued in Rome after its excommunication and persuaded a confessor named Natalis to be ordained bishop for a fee. Natalis accepted, but began to experience dreams in which he received warnings. He paid little attention to these until he dreamt that he had been severely tortured by angels. He then put on a penitential garment, covered himself with ashes and presented himself to Zephyrinus. Confessing his wrongdoing, he begged to be received again into the Church, which in the end Zephyrinus granted. However, he took no action against the Monarchians or other rival schools of the day; critics charged that he himself was Monarchian.

The imperial attitude toward Christianity, which had been exceptionally tolerant for a decade, took a turn for the worse in 202 or 203 when Emperor Septimius Severus (r. 193–211) issued an edict that forbade conversion to Christianity under any circumstance. Zephyrinus died a few years later, probably in 217. He is listed in the Roman Martyrology, though it is not certain that he was killed, because his body—placed originally in its own tomb over the Appian Way cemetery and now interred in the San Sisto Vecchio Church in Rome—is intact. He may have been considered a martyr for his faith because of the trials he underwent.

In art, Zephyrinus is shown as a pope with a sword.

Feast: August 26

Zita (1218–1272) *Servant renowned for her charity and miracles*

Zita was born at Monte Sagrati, Italy, into a poor but holy Christian family. Her older sister became a Cistercian nun and her uncle Graziano was a hermit whom the local people regarded as a saint. Zita herself always tried to do God's will obediently whenever it was pointed out to her by her mother. At the age of 12 Zita became a housekeeper in the home of the wealthy Fatinelli family in Lucca, eight miles from her home at Monte Sagrati. The other servants took an immediate dislike to her because she worked hard, prayed and went to Mass daily, and gave away food and clothing—including those of her employers—to the poor. In time, she won over the members of the household.

Zita's generosity with her employer's goods once nearly got her into trouble. She gave away a lot of the household stock of beans. When Signor Fatinelli decided to inspect the stock, intending to sell it, Zita worried. The supply, however, had been miraculously replenished.

St. Zita

According to tradition, she had extra help that enabled her to do an extraordinary amount of work. Zita went to Mass and prayed every day. One day she stayed in church too long and was late starting her baking. When she arrived home, she found loaves of bread prepared and neatly laid out in rows in the kitchen, ready to be baked. Another story tells that the other servants found an angel taking Zita's place in baking and cleaning.

Because of her efficiency, she was given a free reign over her working schedule. She visited the sick and those in prison. She was sought out by many important people.

Zita stayed with the Fatinelli family for the last 48 years of her life. She died in 1278 and was buried in the Church of St. Frediano in Lucca. Her casket was opened in 1446 and 1581 and her body was found to be dark and dry, but incorrupt. She is now enshrined in a glass-sided reliquary in the church.

In art Zita is depicted with a bag and keys, or loaves of bread and a rosary.

Canonized: 1696 by Pope Innocent XII
Feast: April 27
Patronage: domestic workers and servants

Zosimus (d. 418) *Pope*
Also known as: Zozimus

Nothing is known about the life of the Greek Zosimus, son of the priest Abram, before he was consecrated bishop of Rome to succeed Pope St. Innocent I on March 18, 417.

Like his recent predecessors, Zosimus acted decisively as head of the universal church. However, he ran into trouble when he attempted to overrule certain African bishops in their efforts to discipline their own priests. There was in Africa a well-prescribed system of appeal of ecclesiastical decisions, but the defrocked priests appealed directly to Rome, and Zosimus made the mistake of backing the priests without first allowing the appeals process to run its course. He also caused confusion by referring to a decision of the Council of Nicaea when in reality it had come from the Council of Sardica, and was unknown in Africa. The resulting crisis was but the latest tension in eastern-western Church relations that was eventually to lead to a parting of ways between them.

Zosimus issued decrees instructing deacons in the country parishes of the Roman Church to wear the maniple on the dedication of the Easter candles and forbidding clerics to visit taverns.

He died on December 27, 418, after a reign of 21 months, and was buried in the sepulchral Church of St. Laurence in Agro Verano.

Feast: December 26

APPENDICES

APPENDIX 1
PATRON SAINTS BY TOPIC

Saints can be petitioned for their intercession in any matter, but many of them have areas of specialty, or patronage. Patronages are related to the saints' interests and activities during life, or perhaps events that happened to them. Patronages are designated by venerable tradition and sometimes by papal decree. Many early saints and martyrs are patrons, but under present practices only canonized saints can become patrons.

A

Abandoned children: Jerome Emiliani
Abuse victims: Adelaide; Agostina Pietrantoni; Joaquina de Vedruna
Academics: Thomas Aquinas
Accidents (against): Christopher
Accommodations: Gertrude of Nivelles
Accountants: Matthew the Apostle
Actors: Genesius; Vitus
Actresses: Pelagia
Adopted children: Clotilde; Thomas More
Adultery victims: Elizabeth of Portugal; Marguerite d'Youville
Advertising: Bernardino of Siena
African Americans: Benedict the Black; Peter Claver
African missions: Thérèse of Lisieux
Agricultural workers: Phocas
AIDS caregivers: Aloysius Gonzaga
AIDS sufferers: Aloysius Gonzaga; Thérèse of Lisieux
Aircraft pilots: Thérèse of Lisieux
Air crews: Thérèse of Lisieux
Air travelers: Joseph of Cupertino
Alcoholics: John of God; Monica
Alpine guides: Agatha
Alpinists: Bernard of Montjoix
Altar boys and girls: John Berchmans
Altar servers: John Berchmans
Ammunition workers: Barbara

Amputees: Anthony of Padua; Anthony
Anesthetists: Rene Goupil
Anglers: Andrew the Apostle
Animals: Anthony of Padua; Francis of Assisi
Animals, domestic: Ambrose
Apologists: Justin Martyr
Apoplexy (against): Andrew Avellino
Apostleship of prayer: Francis Xavier
Apothecaries: James the Greater, Apostle; James the Lesser, Apostle; Raphael the Archangel
Apple orchards: Charles Borromeo
Apprentices: John Bosco
Archaeologists: Damasus I; Helen
Archers: Sebastian
Architects: Barbara; Thomas the Apostle
Armorers: Dunstan; Sebastian
Art: Catherine of Bologna
Art dealers: John the Divine
Art guilds: Luke the Evangelist
Arthritis (against): James the Greater, Apostle
Artillery: Barbara
Artists: Catherine of Bologna; Luke the Evangelist
Art schools: Luke the Evangelist
Astronauts: John the Divine; Joseph of Cupertino
Astronomers: Dominic
Athletes: Sebastian
Attorneys: Francis de Sales; Mark the Evangelist
Authors: Lucy; Francis de Sales; Paul
Aviators: Joseph of Cupertino; Thérèse of Lisieux; Our Lady of Loretto

B

Babies: Holy Innocents; Zeno
Bachelors: Theobald; Christopher
Bad luck (against): Agricola of Avignon
Bad weather (against): Eurosia

Bakers: Elizabeth of Hungary; Honoratus; Nicholas; Meingold
Bakers of honeybread: Ambrose
Bankers: Matthew the Apostle
Baptism: John the Baptist
Barbers: Louis IX; Cosmas and Damian; Martin de Porres
Barrelmakers: Abdon; Senen
Barren women: Anthony of Padua; Felicitas
Barristers: Mark the Evangelist
Basketweavers: Anthony
Battle: Michael the Archangel
Beekeepers: Ambrose; Valentine
Bees: Ambrose; Bernard of Clairvaux
Beggars: Alexis; Giles; Benedict Joseph Labre
Belgian air crews: Thérèse of Lisieux
Bell founders: Agatha
Beltmakers: Alexis
Betrothed couples: Ambrose Sansedoni; Valentine
Birds: Gall; Francis of Assisi
Birth: Margaret of Antioch
Bishops: Ambrose
Black Catholic missions: Peter Claver
Black missions: Thérèse of Lisieux
Blacks: Martin de Porres
Blacksmiths: Brigid of Ireland; Dunstan; James the Greater, Apostle
Bleeding (against): Bernadine of Siena; Rita of Cascio
Blind people: Lucy of Syracuse; Clare of Assisi; Lawrence the Illuminator; Odilia; Raphael the Archangel; Thomas the Apostle
Blood banks: Januarius
Boarding schools: Charles Borromeo
Boatmen: Anthony of Padua; Brendan of Clonfort; Brigid of Ireland; Julian the Hospitaller
Bodily ills: Angela Merici; Terese of the Andes; Thérèse of Lisieux
Bookbinders: Bartholomew the Apostle; Luke the Evangelist; Celestine V; Columba; John the Divine; Peter; Sebastian
Bookkeepers: Matthew the Apostle
Booksellers: John of God; John the Divine
Bowel disorders (against): Bonaventure
Boys: Nicholas
Boy Scouts: George
Brass workers: Barbara
Breast disease (against): Agatha
Breast Feeding: Giles
Brewers: Arnulf of Metz; Augustine of Hippo; Luke the Evangelist; Nicholas
Bricklayers: Stephen; Stephen of Hungary
Brick makers: Vincent Ferrer
Brides: Adelaide; Clotilde; Elizabeth of Portugal; John Nepomucene; Nicholas; Dorothy; Tugal

Bridge builders: Peter
Bridges: John Nepomucene
Broadcasters: Gabriel the Archangel
Broken bones (against): Stanislaus Kostka
Broommakers: Anne, Matron
Bruises (against): Amalburga
Brushmakers: Anthony
Builders: Barbara; Blaise; Louis IX; Thomas the Apostle; Vincent Ferrer
Burglary (against): Leonard
Burns (against): John the Divine
Bus drivers: Christopher
Businessmen: Homobonus
Businesswomen: Margaret Clitherow
Butchers: Adrian; Anthony; Luke the Evangelist
Butlers: Luke the Evangelist
Buttonmakers: Louis IX

C

Cab drivers: Fiacre
Cabinetmakers: Anne
Cancer victims: Ezequial Moreno; Peregrine Laziosi; Bernard of Clairvaux
Candlemakers: Ambrose
Canonists: Raymond of Penafort
Captives: Mark the Evangelist
Carpenters: Anne; Joseph; Thomas the Apostle
Carvers: King Olaf II
Casket makers: Stephen
Catechists: Charles Borromeo; Robert Bellarmine
Catholic action: Francis of Assisi
Catholic press: Francis de Sales
Catholic universities: Thomas Aquinas
Catholic youth: Aloysius Gonzaga
Cats: Gertrude of Nivelles
Cattle: Blaise; Brigid of Ireland
Cattle diseases: Sebastian
Cavalry: George
Cemetery workers: Anthony
Champions: Drausin
Chandlers: Ambrose; Bernard of Clairvaux
Chaplains: John of Capistrano
Charitable societies: Elizabeth of Portugal; Vincent de Paul
Charitable workers: Elizabeth of Portugal
Chastity: Agnes of Rome; Thomas Aquinas
Chemical industries: Cosmas and Damian
Chest problems (against): Bernadine of Siena
Child abuse victims: Alodia
Childbirth: Gerard Majella; Raymond Nonnatus
Childbirth complications (against): Ulric
Childhood illnesses (against): Aldegund; Pharailidis
Childless people: Anne, Matron; Anne Line

Children: Nicholas; Maria Goretti; Pancras

Children, death of: Alphonsa Hawthorne; Isidore the Farmer; Joaquina de Vedruna; Louis IX; Marguerite d'Youville

Children, disappointing: Clotilde

Children, sick: Alphonsa Hawthorne; Beuno; Pharailidis

Children of Mary: Philomena

Children receiving their first communion: Pancras

Children whose parents are not married: Brigid of Ireland

Chills (against): Placid

Chivalry: Demetrius

Choirboys: Dominic Savio; Holy Innocents

Cholera (against): Roch

Choristers: Leo I

Church, The: Joseph

Circus people: Julian the Hospitaller

Civil servants: Thomas More

Clairvoyance: Agabus Clergy, secular: Charles Borromeo; Thomas Becket

Clerics: Gabriel the Archangel; Gabriel Francis of Our Lady of Sorrows

Clerks, courtroom: Cassian

Climbers: Bernard of Clairvaux

Clockmakers: Peter

Cloth dyers: Lydia

Cloth workers: Homobonus; Paul the Hermit

Cobblers: Bartholomew the Apostle; Crispin and Crispinian

Coffeehouse keepers: Drogo

Coin collectors: Stephen the Younger

Colds (against): Maurus

Cold weather (against): Sebald

Colic: Charles Borromeo

Collectors: Benedict Biscop

Colleges: Thomas Aquinas

Comedians: Genesius; Vitus

Communications: Bernardino of Siena; Gabriel the Archangel

Composers: Cecilia

Compositors: John the Divine

Computer hackers: Columba

Computer technicians: Isidore of Seville

Computer users: Isidore of Seville

Confessors: Alphonsus Marie Liguori; Francis de Sales; John Nepomucene

Construction workers: Louis IX; Thomas the Apostle; Vincent Ferrer

Conversion and baptism: John the Baptist

Converts: Anne Line; Helena; Flora; Vladimir I of Kiev

Convulsive children: Scholastica

Cooks: Lawrence; Martha

Coopers: Nicholas

Coppersmiths: Maurus

Corn chandlers: Bartholomew the Apostle

Coughs (against): Quentin

Court workers: Thomas More

Cowherds: Gummarus

Cows: Perpetua

Cramps (against): Maurice; Pancras

Cripples: Giles

Crops: Ansovinus; Walburga

Crusades and Crusaders: Louis IX

Curriers: Simon the Zealot

Customs officials: Matthew the Apostle

Cutlers: Lawrence; Lucy of Syracuse

D

Dairyworkers: Brigid of Ireland

Dancers: Genesius; Vitus

Deacons: Stephen

Dead, recently: Gertrude of Nivelles

Deaf: Francis de Sales

Death, sudden (against): Andrew Avellino

Death of children (against): Marguerite d'Youville; Stephen of Hungary

Death row inmates: Dismas

Dentists: Apollonia

Desperate situations: Jude; Gregory of Neocaesare; Rita of Cascia

Detraction: John Nepomucene

Devil possession (against): Quirinus; Bruno; Dymphna

Dieticians (in hospitals): Martha

Difficult marriages: Alphonsa Hawthorne; Elizabeth of Portugal; Louis IX; Marguerite d'Youville

Dioceses of Lugano and Basel, Switzerland: Charles Borromeo

Diplomats: Gabriel the Archangel

Disabled people: Angela Merici

Disasters (against): Genevieve

Displaced persons: Frances Xavier Cabrini

Distillers: Louis IX

Divine intervention: Margaret

Divorce (against): Fabiola; Helena

Divorced people: Alphonsa Hawthorne

Dizziness (against): Avertinus

Dockworkers: Nicholas

Doctors: Blaise; Luke the Evangelist; Cosmas and Damian; Pantaleon

Dog fanciers: Roque

Dogs: Hubert

Dog bites (against): Hubert

Domestic animals: Anthony

Domestic help: Martha; Zita

Donkeys: Anthony of Padua

Doubt (against): Joseph; Thomas the Apostle

Doves: David
Drapes: Ursula
Drivers: Fiacre
Drought (against): Swithin; Godberta
Drowning (against): Adjutor
Drug addiction: Maximilian Kolbe
Druggists: Cosmas and Damian; James the Greater, Apostle; Raphael the Archangel
Dyers: Bartholomew the Apostle; Maurice
Dying: Barbara; Catherine of Siena; Joseph
Dying people: James the Less, Apostle; John of God
Dysentery sufferers: Matrona

E

Earache sufferers: Polycarp of Smyrna
Earthquakes (against): Agatha; Alexis
Ecologists: Francis of Assisi
Ecology: Kateri Tekakwitha
Ecumenists: Cyril and Methodius
Eczema sufferers: Anthony
Editors: John Bosco; John the Divine
Elderly people: Anthony of Padua
Embroiderers: Clare of Assisi; Louis IX; Rose of Lima
Emergencies: Expeditus
Emigrants: Frances Xavier Cabrini
Empresses: Adelaide; Helena
Endurance: Pantaleon
Enemies of religion: Sebastian
Engaged couples: Valentine
Engineers: Ferdinand III; Joseph; Patrick
Engravers: John the Divine
Enlightenment: Our Lady of Good Counsel
Environment: Kateri Tekakwitha
Epidemics (against): Godberta
Epileptics: Anthony; Dymphna; Genesius; Valentine; Vitus
Ergotism sufferers: Anthony
Eruptions of Mt. Etna (against): Agatha
Evil spirits (against): Agrippina
Excluded people: Patrick
Exiles: Adelaide; Clotilde; Joaquina de Vedruna
Expectant mothers: Anthony of Padua; Elizabeth; Gerard Majella
Exposure (against): Valerian
Eyes: Lucy of Syracuse
Eye trouble (against): Aloysius Gonzaga; Clare of Assisi; Herve; Lucy of Syracuse; Raphael the Archangel

F

Fainting (against): Valentine
Falsely accused: Elizabeth of Portugal; Gerard; Raymond Nonnatus; Roch

False witness (against): Pancras
Families: Joseph
Family harmony: Dymphna
Famine (against): Domitian; Walburga
Farmers: George; Isidore the Farmer
Farm workers: Isidore the Farmer
Farriers: Eligius; John the Baptist
Fathers: Joseph
Fear of the Lord: Holy Spirit
Ferrymen: Julian the Hospitaller
Fever sufferers: Albert of Trapani; Antoninus; Peter
Fieldworkers: Notburga
Financial officers: Matthew the Apostle
Finding lost objects: Arnulf of Metz
Fire: Agatha; Francis of Assisi
Firefighters: Florian
Fire prevention: Agatha; Barbara; Catherine of Siena
Fireworks: Barbara
First communicants: Imelda; Pius X; Tarsicius
Fishermen: Andrew the Apostle; Anthony of Padua; Peter
Fishmongers: Andrew the Apostle; Magnus of Scotland
Flight attendants: Bona
Floods (against): Florian
Florentine salt and cheesemakers: Bartholomew the Apostle
Florists: Dorothy; Thérèse of Lisieux; Rose of Lima
Flour industry workers: Arnulph of Metz
Flower growers: Thérèse of Lisieux
Flyers: Joseph of Cupertino; Our Lady of Loretto
Foot trouble (against): Peter; Victor of Marseilles
Foreign missions: Francis Xavier; Thérèse of Lisieux
Foresters: John Gualbert
Forgotten causes: Jude
Fortifications: Barbara
Fortitude: Holy Spirit
Foundations: Anthony Mary Claret
Founders: Barbara
Foundlings: Holy Innocents
Freemasons: Four Crowned Martyrs
Freezing victims: Sebald; Valerian
French monarchs: Louis IX Friendship: John the Divine
Fugitives: Brigid of Ireland
Fullers: Anastasius; James the Less, Apostle
Funeral directors: Dismas; James the Greater, Apostle; Joseph of Arimathea
Furriers: Bartholomew the Apostle; James the Greater, Apostle

G

Gallstones (against): Albinus; Liberius
Gambling, uncontrolled: Bernardino of Siena; Cajetan

Garage mechanics: Eligius
Gardeners: Adelard; Dorothy; Fiacre; Phocas; Rose of Lima; Sebastian
Geese: Ambrose
Geometricians: Thomas the Apostle
Gilders: Clare of Assisi
Gingerbread makers: Ambrose
Girdlers: Agatha
Girls: Agnes of Rome
Girl Scouts: Agnes of Rome
Glandular disorders: Cadoc
Glass painters: Clare of Assisi; James Grissinger
Glassworkers: Lucy of Syracuse; Luke the Evangelist
Glaziers: Lucy of Syracuse; Clare of Assisi; Lawrence; Mark the Evangelist
Glovers: Bartholomew the Apostle; Petroc
Goldsmiths: Anastasius; Dunstan; Luke the Evangelist
Good weather: Agricola of Avignon
Gout (against): Andrew the Apostle; Maurice
Governors: Ferdinand III of Castile
Grandmothers and grandparents: Anne, Matron
Gravediggers: Anthony
Greeting card industry: Valentine
Grocers: Michael the Archangel
Grooms: Hormisdas; Louis IX
Guardians: Mamas
Guards: Matthew the Apostle
Guild, Fraternity, and Brotherhood of the Most Glorious and Undivided Trinity of London: Clement I
Gunners: Barbara

H

Haberdashers: Louis IX
Hail (against): Ansovinus
Hairdressers: Louis IX
Hairstylists (men): Martin de Porres
Hairstylists (women): Mary Magdalen
Handicapped people: Angela Merici
Hangings (against): Colman
Hangovers (against): Bibliana
Happy death: Joseph
Happy marriage: Valentine
Hardware: Sebastian
Harvests: Anthony of Padua
Harvests, corn: Medard
Hatters: Blaise; James the Less, Apostle; Philip; Severus
Haymakers: Gervase and Protase
Headaches (against): Avertinus; Denis; Pancras; Teresa of Avila
Healers: Brigid of Ireland
Healing of wounds: Rita of Cascia
Health workers: Martin de Porres
Heart attack sufferers: Teresa of Avila

Heart patients: John of God
Heirs: Felicity
Hemorrhaging (against): Lucy of Syracuse
Hemorrhoids (against): Fiacre
Hermits: Giles; Anthony
Hernia sufferers: Conrad; Drogo
Hesitation: Joseph
Hoarseness (against): Bernadine of Siena
Holy death (for): Andrew Avellino
Home builders: Our Lady of Loretto
Homeless: Benedict Joseph Labre; Margaret of Cortona
Hopeless cases: Jude
Horned cattle: Colman
Horsemen: Anne, Matron; Martin of Tours
Horses: Anthony of Padua; Hippolytus; Giles
Hosiery workers: Blaise
Hospital administrators: Basil the Great; Frances Xavier Cabrini
Hospitals: Camillus de Lellis; John of God; Jude; Vincent de Paul
Hospital workers: Jude; Vincent de Paul
Hotel employees: Amand; Julian the Hospitaller
Housekeepers: Anne, Matron; Martha; Zita
Housewives: Anne, Matron; Monica
Hunters: Eustachius; Hubert
Husbandmen: Isidore the Farmer

I

Illegitimate children: John-Francis Regis
Illness (against): Terese of the Andes; Thérèse of Lisieux
Immigrants: Francis Xavier Cabrini
Impenitence (against): Barbara; Mark the Evangelist
Impossible causes: Jude
Impotence (against): Winwaloe; Gummarus
Impoverished: Marguerite Bourgeoys; Martin of Tours
Infantrymen: Maurice
Infants: Wite; Nicholas of Tolentino
Infertility (against): Rita of Cascia
Infidelity (against): Monica; Fabiola; Gengulphus
Infidelity victims: Elizabeth of Portugal; Marguerite d'Youville
Infirmarians: Camillus de Lellis
Injuries (against): Aldegonda
In-law problems: Adelaide; Marguerite d'Youville
Innkeepers: Armand; Julian the Hospitaller; Martin de Porres
Innocence: Hallvard
Insanity (against): Dymphna; Fillan
Insect bites (against): Mark the Evangelist
Internet: Isidore of Seville
Intestinal diseases (against): Elmo; Bonaventure
Invalids: Roch

Irish nuns: Brigid of Ireland
Ironmongers: Sebastian

J

Janitors: Theobald
Jaundice sufferers: Albert of Trapani
Jealousy (against): Elizabeth of Portugal; Hedwig
Jealousy victims: Elizabeth of Portugal
Jesuit Order: Ignatius Loyola
Jewelers: Agatha; Dunstan; Eligius
Journalists: Francis de Sales; Paul
Jurists: Catherine of Alexandria; John of Capistrano; Ivo Kermartin

K

Kidnapping victims: Arthefius
Kidney disease (against): Albinus
Kings: Louis IX; Olaf Il of Norway; Stephen of Hungary; Vladimir I of Kiev
Knife sharpeners: Maurice
Knights: Gengulphus; James the Greater, Apostle; Michael
Knights of Columbus: Columba
Knowledge: Holy Spirit
Korean clergy: Andrew Kim Taegon

L

Laborers: Isidore the Farmer; James the Greater, Apostle; John Bosco; Lucy of Syracuse
Lacemakers: Anne, Matron; Francis of Assisi; John-Francis Regis; Luke the Evangelist
Lame people: Clotilde
Lampmakers: Our Lady of Loretto
Last sacraments: Stanislaus
Laundresses: Clare of Assisi; Hunna; Veronica
Lawsuits: Agia
Lawyers: Ivo Kermartin; Genesius; Thomas More
Lay apostolate: Alphonsus Marie Liguori
Lead-founders: Fabian
Lead workers: Sebastian
Learning: Ambrose; Margaret of Scotland
Learning and the arts: Charles Borromeo
Leatherworkers: Bartholomew the Apostle; Crispin and Crispinian
Lectors: Pollio; Sabas
Leg disorders (against): Servatius
Lepers: Vincent de Paul
Liberal arts: Catherine of Bologna
Librarians: Jerome
Libraries: Jerome
Libraries, public: Charles Borromeo
Lies (against): Felix

Lighthouse keepers: Dunstan; Venerius
Lightning (against): Alexis; Barbara
Linguists: Gotteschalk
Lions: Mark the Evangelist
Lithographers: John the Divine
Livestock: Isidore the Farmer
Living Rosary: Philomena
Locksmiths: Dunstan
Loneliness: Rita of Cascia
Longevity: Peter
Loss of parents: Marguerite Bourgeoys; Marguerite d'Youville; Thérèse of Lisieux
Lost articles (against): Anne, Matron; Anthony of Padua; Arnulf of Metz
Lost causes: Jude
Lost souls: Nicholas of Tolentino
Love: Valentine
Lovers: Raphael; Valentine
Lumbago: Lawrence
Lunatics: Christina; Dymphna
Lungs and chest: Bernadine of Siena

M

Machinists: Hubert
Madmen: Romanus
Magistrates: Ferdinand III of Castile
Maidens: Andrew the Apostle; Catherine of Alexandria
Maids: Zita
Manual laborers: James the Greater, Apostle
Marble workers: Clement I
Mariners: Anthony of Padua; Brendan of Clonfort; Brigid of Ireland; Cuthbert; Michael the Archangel; Nicholas of Myra; Nicholas of Tolentino
Marital problems (against): Elizabeth of Portugal; Rita of Cascio; Pharailidis; Hedwig
Married couples: Joseph
Married women: Monica
Martyrs: Agatha; Agostina Petrantoni
Masons: Louis IX; Peter; Stephen of Hungary; Thomas the Apostle
Mass media: Gabriel the Archangel
Mathematicians: Hubert
Medical social workers: John-Francis Regis
Medical technicians: Albert the Great
Mental disorders (against): Dymphna
Merchants: Armand; Francis of Assisi; Nicholas of Myra
Messengers: Gabriel the Archangel
Metal workers: Hubert
Midwives: Brigid of Ireland; Margaret of Cortona; Raymond Nonnatus
Migraine sufferers: Gerson
Military: Theodore Tiro

Military chaplains: John of Capistrano
Millers: Arnulf of Metz; Victor of Marseilles
Milliners: James the Less, Apostle
Miners: Albert the Great; Anne, Matron; Barbara; Piron
Miscarriages (against): Dorothy; Bridget of Sweden
Misfortune (against): Agricola of Avignon
Missionaries: Thérèse of Lisieux
Missionary labors: Barnabas
Missions, foreign: Francis Xavier; Leonard of Port
    Maurice; Thérèse of Lisieux; Teresa of Avila
Monastic life: John the Baptist
Monastics: Benedict
Money managers: Matthew the Apostle
Monks: Anthony; Benedict
Moral theologians: Alphonsus Marie Liguori
Mortal dangers (against): Christopher
Morticians: Joseph of Arimathea
Mothers: Anne, Matron; Blessed Virgin Mary; Gerard
    Majella; Monica
Motorcyclists: Our Lady of Grace
Motorists: Christopher
Mountaineers: Bernard of Montjoix
Murderers: Vladimir I of Kiev
Music: Arnulf of Metz; Cecilia
Musicians: Benedict Biscop; Cecilia; Dunstan;
    Gregory I; Leo I; Odo of Cluny
Mystics: John of the Cross

N

Nailmakers: Claud
Natural disasters (against): Agatha
Naturalists: Albert the Great
Natural sciences students: Albert the Great
Naval officers: Francis of Paola
Navigators: Our Lady, Star of the Sea
Nearsightedness: Clarus
Neck disorders (against): Blaise
Needleworkers: Francis of Assisi; Louis IX; Rose of
    Lima
Nerves: Dymphna
Nervous diseases (against): Bartholomew the Apostle
Netmakers: Peter
Newborn babies: Brigid of Ireland
Nightmares (against): Christopher
Notaries: Ives; Luke the Evangelist; Mark the
    Evangelist
Nuns: Brigid of Ireland
Nurses: Agatha; Alexis; Camillus de Lellis; John of
    God; Raphael the Archangel
Nursing homes: Catherine of Siena; Elizabeth of Hungary
Nursing mothers: Concordia
Nursing service: Elizabeth of Hungary

O

Oaths: Pancras
Obsession (against): Quirinus
Obstetricians: Raymond Nonnatus
Officials: Thomas Becket
Old clothes dealers: Anne, Matron
Old maids: Andrew the Apostle
Opposition of Church authorities: Marguerite
    d'Youville
Oppressed people: Anthony of Padua
Orators: John Chrysostom; Philip Neri
Organ builders: Cecilia
Orphans: Jerome Emiliani; Louise

P

Pain (against): Madron
Painters: Benedict Biscop; John the Divine; Luke the
    Evangelist
Papacy: Peter
Paper makers: John the Divine
Paralyzed: Osmund
Paratroopers: Michael the Archangel
Parents (loss of): Alphonsa Hawthorne; Angela Merici;
    Marguerite Bourgeoys; Marguerite d'Youville; Mary
    of the Incarnation
Parenthood: Adelaide; Clotilde; Ferdinand III of
    Castile; Louis IX; Rita of Cascia
Parents of large families: Adalbald of Ostrevant;
    Adelaide; Louis IX; Vladimir I of Kiev
Parents separated from their children: Mary of the
    Incarnation Parish missions: Thérèse of Lisieux
Parish priests: John Baptiste Marie Vianney
Park services: John Gualbert
Pastry chefs: Philip
Pavement workers: Vincent Ferrer
Pawnbrokers: Nicholas of Myra
Peace: Irene
Peasants: Lucy of Syracuse
Pencil makers: Thomas Aquinas
People of mixed race: Martin de Porres
People rejected by religious orders: Marguerite
    Bourgeoys
People ridiculed for their piety: Agostina Petrantoni;
    Marguerite d'Youville; Rose of Lima; Teresa Maria
    of the Cross
People who have suffered the death of children:
    Clotilde
Perfumers: Mary Magdalen
Perjury (against): Pancras
Pestilence (relief from): Aloysius Gonzaga
Pestilence sufferers: Anthony
Pets: Blaise Cecilia; Caedmon

Pharmacists: Gemma Galgani; Cosmas and Damian; James the Greater, Apostle; James the Less, Apostle

Philosophers: Catherine of Alexandria; Justin Martyr

Physical abuse (against): Pharailidis; Louise de Marillac; Fabiola

Physically disabled: Giles

Physicians: Cosmas and Damian; Luke the Evangelist; Raphael the Archangel

Pilgrims: Alexis; James the Greater, Apostle; Pius X

Pilots: Joseph of Cupertino

Plagiarists: Columba

Plagues (against): Agricola of Avignon; Aloysius Gonzaga; Christopher; Genevieve; Roch; Sebastian; Walburga

Plasterers: Bartholomew the Apostle; Blaise

Plumbers: Vincent Ferrer

Poets: Brigid of Ireland; Columba; David

Poison (against): Benedict; John the Divine

Police officers: Michael the Archangel

Polio: Margaret Mary Alacoque

Political prisoners: Maximilian Kolbe

Poor: Anthony of Padua; Lawrence

Popes: Gregory I

Porters: Christopher

Possession (against): Dymphna

Postal workers: Gabriel the Archangel

Potters: Fabian; Justta and Rufina

Poverty (against): Agostina Petrantoni; Anne, Matron; Mary of the Incarnation; Regina

Preachers: Catherine of Alexandria; John Chrysostom

Pregnant women: Anne, Matron; Gerard Majella; Margaret of Antioch; Raymond Nonnatus

Press: Edmund Campion

Priests: John Baptiste Marie Vianney

Princes: Gottschalk; Casimir

Princesses: Adelaide

Printers: Augustine of Hippo; Genesius; John of God; John the Divine

Printing press: Brigid of Ireland Prisoners: Adelaide; Barbara; Beatrix da Silva; Dismas; Louis IX; Vincent de Paul

Prisoners of war: Leonard

Prisons: Joseph Cafasso

Procrastination (against): Expiditus Professors; Alphonsus Marie Liguori

Psychics: Agabus

Public education: Martin de Porres

Public health: Martin de Porres

Public libraries: Charles Borromeo

Public relations: Bernardine of Siena; Paul

Publishers: John the Divine; Paul

Q

Queens: Elizabeth of Portugal; Clotilde; Hedwig

R

Rabies (against): Hubert

Race relations: Martin de Porres

Racquet makers: Sebastian

Radiologists: Michael the Archangel

Radio workers: Gabriel the Archangel

Rain (for): Agricola; Isidore the Farmer; Scholastica; Swithun

Ranchers: Isidore the Farmer

Rape victims: Agatha; Maria Goretti

Rats (against): Gertrude the Great

Reconciliation: Theodore

Refugees: Alban

Religious orders: Benedict Joseph Labre

Repentant prostitutes: Mary Magdalen

Restaurateurs: Laurence

Restoration of religious freedom in Russia: Thérèse of Lisieux

Retarded children: Hilary of Poitiers

Retreats: Ignatius of Loyola

Rheumatism (against): James the Greater, Apostle

Rheumatoid sufferers: James the Greater, Apostle

Rulers: Ferdinand III of Castile

Runaways: Alodia; Dymphna

S

Saddlers: Crispin and Crispinian; Lucy

Safe journey: Raphael the Archangel

Sailors: Brendan of Clonfort; Christopher; Cuthbert; Elmo; Erasmus; Michael the Archangel; Our Lady Star of the Sea

Sales people: Lucy of Syracuse

Savants: Isidore of Seville

Sawyers: Simon the Zealot

Scholars: Bede the Venerable; Brigid of Ireland; Thomas Aquinas

Schoolchildren: Albert the Great; Ambrose

Schoolgirls: Ursula

Schools: Joseph Calasanz; Thomas Aquinas

Scientists: Albert the Great

Scrofulous diseases (against): Balbina; Mark the Evangelist

Sculptors: Claude; Four Crowned Martyrs; John the Divine; Louis IX; Luke the Evangelist

Seafarers: Francis of Paola; Michael the Archangel

Seafood: Corentin

Seamstresses: Anne, Matron

Seasickness (against): Elmo

Second marriages: Adelaide

Second parents: Adelaide

Secretaries: Genesius; Mark the Evangelist

Security guards: Matthew the Apostle

Seminarians: Charles Borromeo

Separation from a spouse: Gummarus; Nicholas of Flüe; Gengulphus

Servants: Martha; Zita

Service women: Joan of Arc

Sheep raisers: Raphael the Archangel

Shepherdesses: Agatha; Bernadette Soubirous; Regina

Shepherds: Drogo

Shipbuilders: Peter

Shipwrecks (against): Anthony of Padua

Shoemakers: Bartholomew the Apostle; Blaise; Crispin and Crispinian

Sick children: Pharailidis

Sickness (against): Angela Merici; Thérèse of Lisieux

Sick people: Camillus de Lellis; John of God; Louis IX; Raphael the Archangel; Terese of the Andes; Thérèse of Lisieux

Silence: John Nepomucene

Silversmiths: Andronicus; Dunstan

Singers: Andrew the Apostle; Cecilia; Gregory I

Single lay women: Agatha; Andrew the Apostle

Single mothers: Margaret of Cortona

Single women: Catherine of Alexandria

Skaters: Lidwina

Skiers: Bernard of Montjoix

Skin diseases (against): Anthony; Marculf; Peregrine Laziosi; Roch

Skinners: Petroc

Slander (Against): John Nepomucene

Slavery victims: Peter Claver

Sleep disorders (against): Seven Sleepers of Ephesus

Sleepwalking (against): Dymphna

Smelters: Stephen the Younger

Snakebites (against): Hilary of Poitiers; Patrick; Paul

Snakes: Patrick

Snakes, fear of (against): Patrick

Social justice: Joseph; Martin de Porres

Social workers: Joseph; Louise de Marillac

Soldiers: Joan of Arc; George; Hadrian; Ignatius of Loyola; Louis IX; Martin of Tours; Sebastian; Demetrius

Solitary death: Francis of Assisi

Solutions: Expeditus

Songwriters: Caedmon

Sore throats (against): Andrew the Apostle

Spanish air crews: Thérèse of Lisieux

Spanish cattle breeders: Mark the Evangelist

Spanish conquistadors: James the Greater, Apostle

Speleologists: Benedict

Spinsters: Andrew the Apostle; Nicholas of Myra; Catherine of Siena

Spiritual directors: Charles Borromeo

Spiritual help: Vincent de Paul

Spiritual retreats and exercises: Ignatius of Loyola

Stable workers: Anne, Matron; Hormisdas

Stained-glass workers: Luke the Evangelist; Mark the Evangelist Stamp collectors: Gabriel the Archangel

Starvation (against): Anthony of Padua

State schools: Martin de Porres

Stationers: Peter

Steelworkers: Eligius

Stenographers: Cassian; Genesius

Step-parents: Adelaide

Sterility (against): Agatha; Anne, Matron; Anthony of Padua; Emperor Henry II

Stiff neck (against): Andrew the Apostle

Stockbrokers: Matthew the Apostle

Stomachaches (against): Wolfgang

Stomach diseases (against): Brice; Charles Borromeo

Stonecutters: Blaise; Clement I; Stephen of Hungary; Thomas the Apostle

Stonemasons: Ambrose; Barbara; Louis IX; Reinhold; Sebastian; Stephen; Stephen of Hungary

Storms (against): Alexis; Barbara; Scholastica; Theodore

Storms at sea (against): Petroc

Stress: Walter of Portnoise

Strokes (against): Andrew Avellino

Stroke victims: Andrew Avellino

Struma (against): Balbina; Mark the Evangelist

Students: Albert the Great; Catherine of Alexandria; Isidore of Seville; Thomas Aquinas

Successful enterprises: Servatius

Sudden death (against): Andrew Avellino; Barbara; Christopher

Surgeons: Cosmas and Damian; Luke the Evangelist

Swimmers: Adjuto

Swordsmiths: Dunstan; Maurice

Syphilis (against): Fiacre

T

Tailors: Bartholomew the Apostle; Homobonus; John the Baptist; Martin of Tours

Tanners: Bartholomew the Apostle; Blaise; Crispin and Crispinian; John the Divine; Simon Stock; Simon the Zealot

Tax collectors: Matthew the Apostle

Teachers: Catherine of Alexandria; Francis de Sales; John Baptist de la Salle; Gregory I

Teenagers: Aloysius Gonzaga

Telecommunications workers: Gabriel the Archangel

Telegraph: Gabriel the Archangel

Telephone workers: Gabriel the Archangel

Television: Clare of Assisi; Martin de Porres

Television workers: Gabriel the Archangel
Temptation: Michael
Tentmakers: Paul
Tertiaries: Elizabeth of Hungary; Elizabeth of Portugal;
    Louis IX; Margaret of Cortona
Theologians: Alphonsus Marie Liguori; Augustine of
    Hippo; John the Divine; Thomas the Apostle;
    Thomas Aquinas
Theology students: Albert the Great
Therapists: Christina
Thieves: Dismas
Throat diseases (against): Blaise; Lucy of Syracuse
    Thunderstorms (against): Agrippina
Tile makers: Vincent Ferrer
Tinworkers: Joseph of Arimathea
Toddlers: Vaast
Toothache sufferers: Apollonia
Torture victims: Agatha; Alban; Eustachius; Regina
Toymakers: Claude; Benedict Joseph Labre
Trappers: Bartholomew the Apostle
Travelers: Alexis; Anthony of Padua; Brendan of Clon-
    fort; Brigid of Ireland; Christopher; Julian the Hos-
    pitaller; Nicholas of Myra; Paul; Raphael the
    Archangel; Three Wise Men; Valentine
Treaties: Pancras
Truck drivers: Christopher
Tuberculosis sufferers: Pantaleon; Gemma Galgani;
    Thérèse of Lisieux
Tumors: Rita of Cascia
Tuners: Claud
Turners: Anne, Matron
Twitching (against): Bartholomew the Apostle

U

Ulcers (against): Charles Borromeo
Understanding: Holy Spirit
Undertakers: Dismas; Joseph of Arimathea; Sebastian
Unfaithfulness victims: Marguerite d'Youville
Universal church: Joseph
Universities: Contardo Ferrini
Unmarried women: Andrew the Apostle

V

Vanity (against): Rose of Lima
Venetian gondoliers: Lucy of Syracuse
Veterinarians: Blaise; James
Vinegrowers: Bartholomew the Apostle; Tychon
Vintages: Medard
Vintners: Amand; Francis Xavier; Morand; Vincent
Virgins: Agnes of Rome; Blessed Virgin Mary; Joan of
    Arc
Vocalists: Cecilia

Vocations: Alphonsus Marie Liguori
Volcanic eruptions (against): Agatha

W

Waitpersons: Martha
War: Elizabeth of Portugal
Warehouses: Barbara
Watchmen: Peter of Alcantara
Watermen: Brigid of Ireland
Wax melters and refiners: Ambrose
Weavers: Anastasia; Anastasius; Barnabas; Blaise; Paul
    the Hermit; Maurice
Wet nurses: Agatha
Whales: Brendan of Clonfort
Wheelwrights: Catherine of Alexandria
Whiteners: Bartholomew the Apostle
Widowers: King Edgar the Peaceful
Widows: Adelaide; Anne Line; Clotilde; Elizabeth of
    Portugal; Fabiola; Joaquina de Vedruna; Louise;
    Marguerite d'Youville; Mary of the Incarnation;
    Paula
Wild animals: Blaise Wind musicians: Blaise
Wine merchants: Amand; Walter of Portnoise
Wineries and winegrowers: Amand; Francis Xavier;
    Morand; Vincent
Witchcraft (against): Benedict
Wolves (against): Herve; Peter
Women in the air and naval service: Joan of Arc
Women in army corps: Genevieve
Women in labor: Anne, Matron; Leonard
Women who wish to become mothers: Andrew the
    Apostle
Women with unfaithful husbands: Clotilde
Woods: Giles
Woodsmen: Wolfgang
Wool dealers: Blaise
Wool workers: Bernadine of Siena
Working men: Joseph
Working women: Flora
Writers: Francis de Sales; John the Divine; Lucy of
    Syracuse; Paul

Y

Yachtsmen: Adjutor; Our Lady of the Star of the Sea
Young women: Ursula
Youths: Aloysius Gonzaga; Dominic Savio; Gabriel of
    the Sorrowful Mother; John Berchmans; Laura Vi-
    cuña; Maria Goretti; Terese of the Andes; Valentine

Z

Zoos: Francis of Assisi

APPENDIX 2
PATRON SAINTS OF COUNTRIES, CITIES, TOWNS, REGIONS, PLACES AND PEOPLES

Many saints become patrons of the places where they lived and worked. They are adopted as patrons of places and peoples as well, especially if their activities and accomplishments resonate with others. Saints may also be named patrons of organizations and places of learning.

Achaia: Andrew the Apostle
Africa: Our Lady Queen of Africa; Moses the Black
Algeria: Cyprian of Carthage
Alsace: Odilia
Amalfi, Italy: Andrew the Apostle
America: Christopher
America North: Our Lady of Guadalupe
Americas: North American Martyrs
Americas Central and South: Our Lady of Guadalupe; Rose of Lima
Angola: Immaculate Heart of Mary
Argentina: Our Lady of Luzon; Laura Vicuña
Armenia: Bartholomew the Apostle; Gregory the Illuminator
Asia Minor: John the Divine
Assisi, Italy: Clare of Assisi
Australia: Our Lady Help of Christians; Francis Xavier
Austria: Our Lady of Mariazell; Colman; Stephen
Avranches: Andrew the Apostle
Bavaria: Hedwig
Belgium: Joseph
Blacks: Martin de Porres
Bohemia: Adalbert of Prague; John Nepomucene; Wenceslaus
Bologna, Italy: Ambrose Borneo: Francis Xavier
Brabant, Germany: Andrew the Apostle
Brazil: Nossa Senhora de Aparecida; Immaculate Conception; Peter of Alcantara
Brittany: Anne, Matron

Brunswick: Andrew the Apostle
Brussels: Michael the Archangel
Burgundy, France: Andrew the Apostle; Bernard of Clairvaux
Camden, Netherlands: Nicholas of Myra
Canada: Anne, Matron; Joseph
Carthage: Augustine of Hippo
Catania, Sicily: Agatha
Chile: James the Greater, Apostle; Our Lady of Mt. Carmel
China: Joseph; Francis Xavier
Cologne University: Albert the Great
Colombia: Peter Claver; Luis Beltrán
Corfu, Greece: Nicholas
Corsica: Immaculate Conception; Devota
Cracow, Poland: Stanislaus
Cuba: Our Lady of Charity
Czech Republic: Adalbert of Prague; John Nepomucene; Wenceslaus
Denmark: Anskar; Canute
Dominican Republic: Our Lady of High Grace; Dominic
East Indies: Thomas the Apostle
Ecuador: Michael of Ecuador; Sacred Heart
Egypt: Mark the Evangelist
El Salvador: Our Lady of Peace
England: Augustine of Canterbury; George
Estremadura, Spain: Peter of Alcantara
Ethiopia: Frumentius
Europe: Benedict
Finland: Henry of Uppsala
Florence, Italy: Barnabas
France: Our Lady of the Assumption; Joan of Arc; Thérèse of Lisieux
Freiburg, Switzerland: Nicholas
French Army Commissariat: Ambrose

Germany: Boniface; Michael

Ghent: Pharailidis

Gibraltar: Bernard of Clairvaux

Goa, India: Francis Xavier

Greece: Andrew the Apostle; Nicholas

Guatemala: James the Greater, Apostle; Pedro de San José Betancur

Hebrew Nation: Michael the Archangel

Holland: Willibrord

Holstein: Andrew the Apostle

Hungary: Blessed Virgin, Great Lady of Hungary; Stephen of Hungary

Iceland: Thorlac

India: Our Lady of the Assumption; Thomas the Apostle

Ireland: Brigid of Ireland; Columba; Patrick

Italy: Catherine of Siena; Francis of Assisi

Japan: Peter Baptist; Francis Xavier

Knights of St. John: Casimir

Krakow, Poland: Faustina Kowalska

Latin America: Rose of Lima

Liège diocese: Nicholas

Liguria, Italy: Bernard of Clairvaux

Lithuania: Casimir; Blessed Cunegunda

Lorraine, France: Nicholas

Lyons, France: Bonaventure

Luxembourg: Andrew the Apostle; Philip the Apostle

Madrid, Spain: Isidore the Farmer

Malta: Agatha; Paul; Our Lady of the Assumption

Massa Marittima, Italy: Bernadine of Siena

Mexico: Our Lady of Guadalupe

Milan, Italy: Ambrose; Barnabas

Monaco: Devota

Moravia: Cyril; Methodius

Moscow: Boris; Nicholas

Naples: Andrew Avellino

Naples kingdom: Nicholas

Native Americans: Anthony of Padua

New Zealand: Francis Xavier; Our Lady Help of Christians

Nigeria: Patrick

Norway: Olaf of Norway

Padstow, Cornwall: Petroc

Pakistan: Thomas the Apostle

Paraguay: Martyrs of Paraguay (Roque Gonzalez, Alphonsus Rodriguez, John of Castillo); Our Lady of the Assumption

Patras, Greece: Andrew the Apostle

Peru: Joseph; Rose of Lima

Pesaro: Andrew the Apostle

Philippines: Sacred Heart of Mary; Rose of Lima

Plock, Poland: Faustina Kowalska

Poland: Adalbert of Prague; Casimir; Bl. Cunegunda; Stanislaus; Our Lady of Czestochowa

Portsmouth, England: Thomas Becket

Portugal: Immaculate Conception; Francis Borgia; Anthony of Padua; Vincent; George

Prussia: Adalbert of Prague

Quebec, Canada: Anne, Matron

Queen's College, Cambridge, England: Margaret of Antioch

Rome: Catherine of Siena; Philip Neri

Russia: Andrew the Apostle; Boris; Nicholas; Thérèse of Lisieux; Vladimir I of Kiev

Salzburg University: Charles Borromeo

Santa Ana Pueblo: Anne, Matron

Scandinavia: Anskar

Scotland: Andrew the Apostle; Columba

Sicily: Nicholas

Siena, Italy: Ambrose Sansedoni, Blessed

Silesia: Hedwig

Slovakia: Our Lady of Sorrows

South Africa: Our Lady of the Assumption

South America: Rose of Lima

Spain: James; Teresa of Avila

Speyer Cathedral, Germany: Bernard of Clairvaux

Sri Lanka (Ceylon): Lawrence; Thomas the Apostle

St. Neot, Cornwall, England: Neot

Sweden: Bridget of Sweden; Gall; Eric

Switzerland: Antiochus; Gall; Nicholas of Flüe

Syria: Addai; Mari

Taos, New Mexico: Anne, Matron; John the Divine

Tigua Indians: Anthony of Padua

Turkey: John the Divine

Ukraine: Josaphat

United States: Immaculate Conception

United States National Rural Life Conference: Isidore the Farmer

University of Patras: Andrew the Apostle

Uruguay: James the Less, Apostle; Our Lady of Lujan; Philip

Venezuela: Our Lady of Coromoto

Venice, Italy: Mark the Evangelist

Vilnius, Lithuania: Faustina Kowalska

Wales: David

West Indies: Gertrude the Great; Rose of Lima

Women Appointed for Voluntary Emergency services (WAVES): Joan of Arc

Women's Army Corps (WACs): Joan of Arc

Zamarramala, Spain: Agatha

Appendix 3
Calendar of Feast Days

JANUARY

1   Mary, Mother of God
    Fulgentius of Ruspe
    Gregory of Nazianzus the Elder
2   Basil the Great
    Gregory of Nazianzus
    Sylvester I (Western Church)
3   Anterus
4   Elizabeth Ann Seton
    Pharailidis
5   John Nepomucene Neumann (in United States)
    Simeon Stylites
    Telesphorus
    Emiliana and Tarsilla
6   Brother André Bessette; Blessed Epiphany of Our Lord (Sunday after) Charles of Sezze
7   Raymond of Penafort
    Lucian of Antioch
8   The Baptism of Our Lord
    Apollinaris of Hierapolis
9   Marciana
    Peter of Sebaste
10   Marcian
    Laura Vicuña
    Agatho
    Gregory X
11   Theodosius the Cenobiarch
    Hyginus
12   Marguerite Bourgeoys (Canada)
    Arcadius
    Benedict Biscop
13   Hilary of Poitiers
    Berno
14   Felix of Nola
    Macrina the Elder
15   Paul the First Hermit
    Macarius the Elder
16   Marcellus I
    Fursey

17   Anthony the Abbot
18   Prisca
19   Canute
    Henry of Uppsala
    Marguerite Bourgeoys
20   Fabian
    Sebastian
21   Agnes of Rome
    Meinrad
    Maximus of Constantinople (in the East)
22   Vincent
    Laura Vicuña
23   Emerentiana
24   Francis de Sales
25   Conversion of Paul
26   Timothy
    Titus
    Paula
27   Angela Merici
    Vitalian
28   Thomas Aquinas
29   Sabinian
30   Martina
    Felix IV
31   John Bosco

FEBRUARY

1   John of the Grating
    Brigid of Ireland
    Ursus
2   The Presentation of Our Lord
    Adalbald of Ostrevant
    Lawrence of Canterbury
3   Blaise
    Ansgar
    Blessing of Throats
4   Andrew Corsini
    Isidore of Pelusium

5   Agatha
6   Paul Miki and Companions
7   Theodore of Heraclea
    Piux IX, Blessed
    Romuald
8   Jerome Emiliani
9   Apollonia
    Michael of Ecuador
10 Scholastica
11 Our Lady of Lourdes
    Paschal I
12 Marina
    Julian the Hospitaller
13 Catherine de' Ricci
14 Cyril
    Methodius
    Valentine
15 Agape
16 Gilbert of Sempringham
    Juliana of Cumae
17 Seven Holy Helpers
18 Simeon
    Colman of Lindisfarne
    Leo I (Eastern Church)
19 Mesrop
20 Tyrannio
21 Peter Damian
22 The Chair of Peter the Apostle
23 Polycarp of Smyrna
    Peter Damian
24 Praetextatus
25 Victorinus
    Walburga
    Caesarius of Nazianzus
    Jacinta and Francisco Marto
26 Nestor
27 Gabriel Francis of Our Lady of Sorrows
    Anne Line
    Forty Martyrs of England and Wales
28 Romanus and Lupicinus I

MARCH

1   David
    Felix III
2   Chad
3   Aelred of Rievaulx
    Katharine Drexel
4   Casimir
    Pope Lucius I
5   Phocas of Antioch
6   Chrodegang of Metz
    Colette
7   Perpetua and Felicity
8   John of God

9   Frances of Rome
    Dominic Savio
    Catherine of Bologna
    Pacianus of Barcelona
    Gregory of Nyssa
10 Macarius of Jerusalem
    Simplicius
11 Constantine
    Gregory II
    Sophronius
12 Alphege
13 Euphrasia
14 Matilda
15 Longinus
    Zachary I
16 Julian of Antioch
17 Patrick
    Alexis (Eastern Church)
    Joseph of Arimathea
18 Cyril of Jerusalem (Eastern Church)
19 Joseph (Husband of Mary)
20 Martin of Braga
    Andrew Sansedoni of Siena
    Cyril of Jerusalem (Western Church)
    Cuthbert
21 Serapion the Scholastic
    Nicholas of Flüe
22 Basil of Ancyra
23 Turibius Mogroveio
24 Irenaeus of Sirmium
    Catherine of Sweden
25 Annunciation of the Lord
    Urban I
    Dismas
26 Basil the Younger
    Mariana of Quito
27 John of Egypt
28 Tutilo
    Sixtus III
29 Cyril of Heliopolis
30 John Climacus
    Quirinus
31 Balbina

APRIL

1   Melito
2   Francis of Paola
3   Mary of Egypt
4   Isidore of Seville
5   Vincent Ferrer
6   Martyrs of Persia
    Sixtus I
    Celestine I (Western Church)
7   The Annunciation of Our Lord

8   Dionysius of Corinth
    Celestine I (Eastern Church)
9   Mary Cleophas
10 Fulbert
11 Stanislaus
    Marguerite d'Youville
12 Julius I
13 Martin I
14 Tiburtius, Valerius, and Maximi
15 Basilissa and Anastasia
16 Bernadette Soubirous
    Optatus and Companions
    Stephen of Hungary
    Benedict Joseph Labre
17 Stephen Harding
    Anicetus
18 Apollonius the Apologist
19 Leo IX
20 Hildegund
21 Anselm
    Anastasius the Sinaite
22 Agapetus I
    Soter
    Caius
23 George
    Adalbert of Prague
24 Fidelis of Sigmaringen
    Gregory of Elvira
25 Mark the Evangelist (in the West)
    Pedro de San José Betancur
26 Peter of Braga
    Anencletus
    Marcellinus
27 Zita
28 Peter Mary Chanel
    Vitalis
29 Catherine of Siena
    Peter of Verona
30 Pius V
    Mary of the Incarnation

MAY

1   Joseph the Worker
2   Athanasius
3   Philip and James the Less, Apostles
    Juvenal
    Alexander, Eventius, and Theodolus
4   Cyriacus
5   Hilary of Arles
6   Evodius
    Petronax
7   Domitian
    John of Beverly

8   The Ascension of Our Lord
    Peter of Tarantaise
    Boniface IV
    Benedict II
    John the Divine (Greek Orthodox)
9   Pachomius
    Beatus
    Gregory Nazianzen
10 Antoninus
    Simon the Zealot (Greek Orthodox and Coptic
    Churches)
11 Mamertus
    Asaph
12 Nereus and Achilleus
    Pancras
    Epiphanius of Salamis
    Germanus I
13 John the Silent
14 Matthew the Apostle
15 Isidore the Farmer
    Dymphna
    John Baptist de la Salle
16 Ubaldus
    Brendan of Clonfort
    John Nepomucene
    John Nepomucene Neumann (outside
    United States)
    Simon Stock
17 Paschal Baylon
18 Pentecost Sunday
    John I
19 Celestine V
    Pudentiana and Pudens
    Dunstan
20 Bernardino of Siena
21 Andrew Bobola
    Sylvester I (Eastern Church)
    Constantine the Great
22 Rita of Cascio
    Joaquina de Vedruna
23 Ivo of Chartres
24 Donatian and Rogatian
    Vincent of Lérins
25 Bede the Venerable
    Gregory VII
    Mary Magdalene de Pazzi
    Martyrs of Mexico
    Madeleine Sophie Barat
26 Philip Neri
    Mariana of Quito
    Eleutherius
27 Augustine of Canterbury
28 Senator
    Justus of Urgel
29 Cyril of Caesarea

30 Joan of Arc
   Rose of Lima (in Peru)
   Felix I
31 The Visitation of Our Lady to Elizabeth

JUNE

1 Justin Martyr
2 Marcellinus and Peter
   Eugene I
3 Charles Lwanga and Companions
   Michael of Ecuador
   Clotilde
   John XXIII
4 Francis Caracciolo
   Morand
   Optatus of Milevis
   Petroc
5 Boniface
6 Norbert
7 Paul of Constantinople
   Médard
9 Ephraem
   Columba
10 Getulius
   Margaret of Scotland
11 Barnabas
   Bartholomew the Apostle (in the East)
12 John of Sahagun
   Leo III
13 Anthony of Padua
   Bartholomew the Apostle (in Persia)
14 The Sacred Heart of Jesus
   Methodius I of Constantinople
   Methodius of Olympus
15 The Immaculate Heart of Mary
   Vitus
16 John Francis Regis Clet
   Julitta and Quiricus
17 Avitus
18 Mark and Marcellian
   Elizabeth of Schonau
19 Romuald
   Juliana of Falconieri
   Gervase and Protase
20 Silverius
   Aloysius Gonzaga
   Lawrence of Brindisi
   Paulinus of Nola
   John Fisher
   Alban
22 Innocent V
   Paulinus of Nola
   Thomas More
23 Alban

24 The Birth of John the Baptist
25 William of Vercelli
26 John and Paul
   Anthelm
27 Cyril of Alexandria
28 Irenaeus of Lyons (Latin Church)
   Leo II
   Paul I
29 Peter and Paul
30 Protomartyrs of Rome

JULY

1 Junipero Serra
   Oliver Plunkett

2 Processus and Martinian
3 Thomas the Apostle
   Jude and Simon the Zealot (in the East)
4 Elizabeth of Portugal
   Ulrich
   Andrew of Crete
5 Anthony Mary Zaccaria
6 Maria Goretti
7 Ethelburga
   Benedict XI
8 Adrian III
   Eugene III
   Raymond of Toulouse
9 The Martyrs of Gorkurn
10 Rufma and Secunda
11 Benedict
   Pius I
12 John Gualbert
   Nabor and Felix
13 Henry II
   Terese of the Andes
   Margaret of Antioch (in the East)
14 Camillus de Lellis
   Francis Solanus
   Kateri Tekakwitha
   Ulrich
15 Bonaventure
   Vladimir I of Kiev
16 Our Lady of Mt. Carmel
   Beatrix da Silva
   Eustathius
17 The Scillitan Martyrs
   Alexis (in the West)
   Leo IV
   Ennodius of Pavia
   Nicholas II and Companions
18 Bruno of Segni
   Arnulf of Metz
19 Macrina the Younger
   Symmachus

20 Ansegisus
    Margaret of Antioch (in the West)
21   Lawrence of Brindisi
22 Mary Magdalen
23 Bridget of Sweden
    John Cassian
24 Christina
    Boris and Gleb
25 James the Greater, Apostle
    Christopher
26 Joachim and Anne—Parents of Our Lady
27 Pantaleon
    Seven Sleepers of Ephesus (West)
28 SS. Nazarius and Celsus
    Innocent I
    Botwid
29 Martha
    Lazarus
    Urban II
    Olaf of Norway
30 Peter Chrysologus
31 Ignatius of Loyola

AUGUST

1   Alphonsus Marie Liguori
2   Eusebius of Vercelli
    Stephen I (Western church)
3   Finding of the Body of Stephen Protomartyr
4   John Baptiste Marie Vianney
    Nicodemus
    Seven Sleepers of Ephesus (East)
5   Dedication of Mary Basilica in Rome
    Oswald
    Nonna
6   Transfiguration of Our Lord
    Justus and Pastor
    Hormisdas
7   Sixtus II and Companions
    Cajetan
8   Dominic
    Mary MacKillop
9   Romanus
    Teresa Benedicta of the Cross
10 Lawrence
11 Clare of Assisi
    Philomena (former feast date)
12 Euplius
    Maximus of Constantinople (in the East)
13 Pontian
    Maximus of Constantinople (in the West)
    Hippolytus
    John Berchmans
14 Maximilian Kolbe
15 The Assumption of Our Lady

16 Stephen (Hungary)
17 Hyacinth
    Clare of Montefalco
    Roch
18 Jane Frances de Chantal
    Helena
19 John Eudes
    Ezequial Moreno
20 Bernard of Clairvaux
21 Pius X
22 The Queenship of Mary
23 Rose of Lima (outside of Peru)
    Irenaeus of Lyons (Greek Church)
24 Bartholomew the Apostle (in Rome)
25 Louis IX, King of France
    Joseph Calasanz
    Bartholomew the Apostle (in Eternach and
    Cambrai)
26 Teresa of Jesus de Ibars
    Zephyrinus
27 Monica
    Caesarius of Arles
28 Augustine of Hippo
    Moses the Black
29 The Martyrdom of John the Baptist
30 Felix and Adauctus
31 Raymond of Nonnatus
    Aidan of Lindisfarne
    Cyprian of Carthage (in the East)

SEPTEMBER

1   Giles
    Fiacre
2   Antoninus of Apamea
3   Gregory I
4   Boniface I
    Marcellus and Valerian
    Rose of Viterbo
5   Lawrence
    Justinian
6   Donatian, Laetus, and Companions
7   Anastasius the Fuller
    Stephen I (Eastern church)
8   Birth of Mary
    Sergius I
9   Peter Claver
10 Nicholas of Tolentino
    Finian
11 Protus and Hyacinth
12 Ailbhe
13 John Chrysostom (in the West)
14 The Triumph of the Holy Cross
15 Our Lady of Sorrows
    Catherine of Genoa

16 Cornelius
    Cyprian of Carthage (in the West)
    Victor III
17 Robert Bellarmine
    Hildegard of Bingen
18 Joseph of Cupertino
    John Massias
19 Januarius
    Peter of Alcantara
20 Andrew Kim Taegon,
    Paul Chong Hasang and Companions
21 Matthew the Apostle (West)
22 Thomas of Villanova
    Maurice and Companions
    Phocas the Gardener
23 Adamnan
    Mark the Evangelist (in the East)
24 Our Lady of Ransom
25 Cadoc
    Sergius of Raonezh
    Finbar
26 Eusebius I
    John the Divine (in the East)
27 Vincent de Paul
    Cosmas and Damian
28 Wenceslaus
    Lawrence Ruiz and Companions
29 Michael, Gabriel, and Raphael—Archangels
30 Jerome

OCTOBER

1   Thérèse of Lisieux
    Gregory the Illuminator
2   Holy Guardian Angels
3   Hesychius
4   Francis of Assisi
5   Apollinaris of Valence
    Faustina Kowalska
6   Bruno
    Marie-Rose Durocher
    Faith
7   Our Lady of the Rosary
    Marcus
8   Marcellus
9   Denis and Companions
    John Leonardi
    Luis Beltrán
10 Francis Borgia
11 Bruno the Great
12 Maximilian
    Ethelburga of Barking
13 Edward the Confessor
    Theophilus
14 Callistus I

15 Teresa of Avila
16 Hedwig
    Margaret Mary Alacoque
    Gerard Majella
    Gall
17 Ignatius of Antioch
18 Luke the Evangelist
    Alexander I
19 Paul of the Cross
    North American Martyrs
20 Andrew of Crete
22 Philip of Heraclea
    Seven Sleepers of Ephesus (East)
23 John Capistrano
24 Anthony Mary Claret
    Proclus (in the West)
25 Chrysanthus and Daria
    Marcellinus
    Crispin and Crispinian
26 Lucian and Marcian
    Evaristus
    Alfred the Great
27 Frumentius
28 Simon the Zealot and Jude—the Apostles (in the West);
    Anastasia
29 Abraham of Rostov
30 Serapion of Antioch
    Alphonsus Rodriguez
31 Quentin
    Foillan

NOVEMBER

1   All Saints' Day
2   All Souls' Day
3   Martin de Porres
4   Charles Borromeo
5   Elizabeth and Zachary
6   Leonard of Noblac
7   Willibrord
8   Four Crowned Martyrs
9   Dedication of John Lateran Basilica in Rome
    Martyrs of Paraguay (Roque Gonzalez, Alphonsus Rodriguez, John of Castillo)
10 Leo I
    Andrew Avellino
11 Martin of Tours
12 Josaphat
    Nilus
13 Frances Xavier Cabrini
    John Chrysostom (in the East)
    Pope Nicholas II
14 Laurence O'Toole
15 Albert the Great

16 Margaret of Scotland
   Gertrude the Great
   Clare of Assisi
   Matthew the Apostle (Greece)
   Cornelius
   Eucherius of Lyons
   Hugh of Lincoln
17 Elizabeth of Hungary
   Dionyius of Alexandria
18 The Dedication of Peter and Paul Basilica
   Rose Philippine Duchesne
19 Barlaarn
   Mechtilde
   Pontian
20 Felix of Valois
   Edmund the Martyr
   Proclus (in the East)
21 The Presentation of Our Lady
   Gelasius I
22 Cecilia
23 Clement I
   Columban
   Miguel Agustin Pro
24 Christ the King
25 Mercurius
26 Peter of Alexandria
   Conrad
   Siricius
27 Barlaarn and Josaphat
   Maximus of Riez
28 Simeon Metaphrastes
   Catherine Labouré
29 Saturninus
30 Andrew the Apostle

DECEMBER

1 Edmund Campion
2 Bibiana
3 Francis Xavier

4 John Damascene
   Barbara (former feast day)
   Clement of Alexandria (former feast day)
5 Sabas
   Crispina
6 Nicholas
7 Ambrose
8 Immaculate Conception of Mary
   Eutychianus
9 Seven Martyrs of Samosata
   Gorgonia
   Juan Diego
10 Miltiades
   Gregory III
11 Damasus I
12 Our Lady of Guadalupe
   Finian of Clonard
13 Lucy of Syracuse
14 John of the Cross
15 Paul of Latros
16 Adelaide
17 Lazarus
18 Rufus
19 Anastasius I
   Urban V
20 Ursicinus
21 Peter Canisius
22 Chaeremon and Ischyion
23 John Kanty
24 Christmas Vigil
   Anastasia of Sirmium
25 Christmas, The Birth of Our Lord
26 Stephen
   Dionysius
   Zosimus
27 John the Divine (in the West)
28 The Holy Innocents
   Peter (Apostle) (in the East; also December 29)
29 Thomas Becket
30 Sabinus
31 Sylvester I (Eastern Church)

APPENDIX 4
FATHERS OF THE CHURCH

The title Father of the Church is bestowed upon the great early teachers of the Church who handed down the tradition taught by the apostles of Jesus. The first age of the Church has no definite dates but generally is thought to extend to the Council of Chalcedon in 451. Some of the Fathers lived much later than that, into the eighth century.

Criteria for the title of Father of the Church include orthodox doctrine and learning, holiness of life, and antiquity. Their work must be cited by a general council, in public acts of popes addressed to the Church or concerning the faith, in public readings in churches in early centuries, or by other illustrious Fathers. Those who do not meet the criteria are known simply as ecclesiastical writers.

GREEK FATHERS

St. Anastasius the Sinaite (d. 700)
St. Andrew of Crete (d. 740)
Aphraates (fourth century)
St. Archelaus (d. ca. 278)
St. Athanasius (d. 373)
Athenagoras (second century)
St. Basil the Great (d. 379)
St. Caesarius of Nazianzus (d. 369)
St. Clement of Alexandria (d. ca. 215)
St. Clement I of Rome, Pope (r. 88–97)
St. Cyril of Alexandria (d. 444)
St. Cyril of Jerusalem (d. ca. 386)
Didymus the Blind (d. ca. 398)
Diodore of Tarsus (d. 392)

St. Dionysius the Great (d. ca. 265)
St. Epiphanius (d. 403)
Eusebius of Caesarea (d. 340)
St. Eustathius (fourth century)
St. Firmillian (d. 268)
Gennadius I of Constantinople (fifth century)
St. Germanus I (d. 733 or 740)
St. Gregory of Nazianzus (d. 390)
St. Gregory of Nyssa (d. after 385 or 386)
St. Gregory Thaumaturgus (d. 270 or 275)
Hermas (second century)
St. Hippolytus (d. 236)
St. Ignatius of Antioch (d. ca. 107)
St. Isidore of Pelusium (d. ca. 450)
St. John Chrysostom (d. 407)
St. John Climacus (d. 649)
St. John Damascene (d. 787), last Father of the East
St. Julius 1, Pope (r. 337–352)
St. Justin Martyr (d. 167 or 168)
St. Leontius Byzantinus (sixth century)
St. Macarius (d. ca. 390)
St. Maximus of Constantinople (d. 662)
St. Melito (d. ca. 180)
St. Methodius of Olympus (d. ca. 311)
St. Nilus (d. ca. 430)
Origen (d. 254)
St. Polycarp of Smyrna (d. ca. 155)
St. Proclus (d. ca. 446)
Pseudo-Dionysius the Areopagite (sixth century)
St. Serapion the Scholastic (d. ca. 370)
St. Sophronius (d. 638)
Tatian (second century)
Theodore of Mopsuestia (d. 428)

Theodoret of Cyrrhus (d. ca. 458)
St. Theophilus (second century)

LATIN FATHERS

St. Ambrose (d. 397)
Arnobius (d. 330)
St. Augustine of Hippo (d. 430)
St. Benedict (d. ca. 547)
St. Caesarius of Arles (d. 543)
St. Celestine 1, Pope (r. 422–432)
St. Cornelius, Pope (r. 251–253)
St. Cyprian of Carthage (d. 258)
St. Damasus I, Pope (r. 366–384)
St. Dionysius of Alexandria (d. 265)
St. Ennodius of Pavia (d. 521)
St. Eucherius of Lyons (d. ca. 450)
St. Fulgentius of Ruspe (d. 533)
St. Gregory of Elvira (d. ca. 392)
St. Gregory I, Pope (r. 590–604)

St. Hilary of Poitiers (d. 368)
St. Innocent I, Pope (r. 401–417)
St. Irenaeus of Lyons (d. 202)
St. Isidore of Seville (d. 636), last Father of the West
St. John Cassian (d. 433)
St. Lactantius (d. 323)
St. Leo I (r. 440–461)
Marius Mercator (d. 451)
Marius Victorinus (fourth century)
Minucius Felix (second century)
Novatian (d. ca. 257)
St. Optatus of Milevis (fourth century)
St. Pacian (d. ca. 390)
St. Pamphilus of Caesarea (d. 309)
St. Paulinus of Nola (d. 431)
St. Peter Chrysologus (d. 450)
St. Phoebadius of Agen (4th century)
Rufinus of Aquileia (d. 410)
Salvian (fifth century)

APPENDIX 5
DOCTORS OF THE CHURCH

The title of Doctor of the Church, one of the Church's highest honors, is conferred upon great ecclesiastical theologians and preachers of great sanctity whose work has made a lasting contribution to the Church as a whole. In the Western Church, four Fathers of the Church were given this honor in the early Middle Ages: Ambrose, Augustine, Gregory the Great and Jerome. The Eastern Church recognized three great Doctors: John Chrysostom, Basil the Great and Gregory of Nazianzus. To these, others have been added. There are no martyrs on the list; only confessors may be considered. Only three women have been given the title, all since 1970: Teresa of Avila, Catherine of Siena and Thérèse of Lisieux.

A careful examination of a saint's life and writings is made to establish the saint's eminent learning and a high degree of sanctity. The decree naming a Doctor of the Church is issued by the Congregation of Sacred Rites and approved by the pope.

St. Albert the Great (d. 1280); declared 1931

St. Alphonsus Marie Liguori (1696–1787); declared 1871

St. Ambrose (d. 397); Father of the Church

St. Anselm (1033–1109); declared 1720

St. Anthony of Padua (1195–1231); declared 1946

St. Athanasius (d. 373); Father of the Church

St. Augustine of Hippo (354–430); Father of the Church

St. Basil the Great (d. 379); Father of the Church

St. Bede the Venerable (673–735); declared (n.d.)

St. Bernard of Clairvaux (ca. 1090–1153); declared 1830

St. Bonaventure (ca. 1217–74); declared 1588

St. Catherine of Siena (ca. 1347–80); declared 1970

St. Cyril of Alexandria (ca. 376–444); declared 1882

St. Cyril of Jerusalem (ca. 315–386); declared 1882

St. Ephraem (ca. 306–373); declared 1920

St. Francis de Sales (1567–1622); declared 1877

St. Gregory I, Pope (d. 604); Father of the Church

St. Gregory of Nazianzus (d. ca. 390); Father of the Church

St. Hilary of Poitiers (d. 368); declared 1851

St. Isidore of Seville (d. 636); declared 1722

St. Jerome (d. 419); Father of the Church

St. John Chrysostom, Greek Father (d. 407); declared 451

St. John Damascene (ca. 676–754 to 787); declared 1890

St. John of the Cross (1542–91); declared 1926

St. Lawrence of Brindisi (1559–1619); declared 1959

St. Leo I (d. 461); declared 1574

St. Peter Canisius (1521–97); declared 1925

St. Peter Chrysologus (d. ca. 450); declared 1729

St. Peter Damian (1007–72); declared 1828

St. Robert Bellarmine (1542–1621); declared 1931

St. Siricius, Pope (r. 384–399)

St. Teresa of Avila (1515–82); declared 1970

Tertullian (d. ca. 222)

St. Thérèse of Lisieux (1873–97); declared 1997

St. Thomas Aquinas (1225–74); declared 1567

St. Vincent of Lérins (d. ca. 445)

APPENDIX 6
BEATIFIED AND CANONIZED POPES

Reign dates are given.

Peter (d. 64 or 67)
Linus (67–76)
Anacletus (76–88)
Clement I (88–97)
Evaristus (97–105)
Alexander I (105–115)
Sixtus I (115–125)
Telesphorus (125–136)
Hyginus (136–140)
Pius I (140–155)
Anicetus (155–166)
Soter (166–175)
Eleutherius (175–189)
Victor I (189–199)
Zephyrinus (199–217)
Callistus I (217–222)
Urban I (222–230)
Pontian (230–235)
Anterus (235–236)
Fabian (236–250)
Cornelius (251–253)
Lucius I (253–254)
Stephen I (254–257)
Sixtus II (257–258)
Dionysius (259–268)
Felix I (269–274)
Eutychian (275–283)
Caius (283–296)
Marcellinus (296–304)
Marcellus I (308–309)
Eusebius (309 or 310)
Miltiades (311–314)
Sylvester I (314–335)

Marcus (336)
Julius I (337–352)
Damasus (366–384)
Siricius (384–399)
Anastasius I (399–401)
Innocent I (401–417)
Zosimus (417–418)
Boniface I (418–422)
Celestine I (422–432)
Sixtus III (432–440)
Leo I the Great (440–461)
Hilary (461–468)
Simplicius (468–483)
Felix III (II) (483–492)
Gelasius I (492–496)
Symmachus (498–514)
Hormisdas (514–523)
John I (523–526)
Felix IV (III) (526–530)
Agapitus I (535–536)
Silverius (536–537)
Gregory I the Great (590–604)
Boniface IV (608–615)
Adeodatus I (615–618)
Martin I (649–655)
Eugene I (654–657)
Vitalian (657–672)
Agatho (678–681)
Leo II (682–683)
Benedict II (684–685)
Sergius I (687–701)
Gregory II (715–731)
Gregory III (731–741)
Zachary (741–752)
Paul I (757–767)

Leo III (795–816)
Paschal I (817–824)
Leo IV (847–855)
Nicholas I (858–867)
Adrian III (884–885)
Leo IX (1049–1054)
Gregory VII (1073–1085)
Urban II, Blessed (1088–1099)
Eugene III, Blessed (1145–1153)
Gregory X, Blessed (1271–1276)

Innocent V, Blessed (1276)
Celestine V (1294)
Benedict XI, Blessed (1303–1304)
Urban V, Blessed (1362–1370)
Pius V (1566–1572)
Innocent XI, Blessed (1676–1689)
Pius IX, Blessed (1846–1878)
Pius X (1903–1914)
John XXIII, Blessed (1958–1963)

APPENDIX 7
BEATIFICATION AND CANONIZATION

In the Roman Catholic Church a holy person is officially recognized as a saint through a formal process of
investigation. The process begins after a candidate's
death and can go on for many years before it is completed. The Church considers saints to be the servants
of God and does not "make" saints, but rather recog-
nizes the holiness in them, and that they are in heaven
and can intercede on behalf of those who petition
them.

Canonization is a decree regarding the public ecclesiastical veneration of an individual. If the veneration
is universal, that is, if it involves the entire Church, it
is a decree of canonization. If the veneration is not to
be universal, but may be exercised locally or by individuals, it is a decree of beatification. There are two
ways to canonize. Formal canonization results from
judicial process. Equivalent canonization can be
decreed by a pope for persons who have long been venerated and whose miracles and virtues—or martyrdom—can be historically established, and whose
miraculous intercessions have continued uninter-
rupted. In all cases, the recognition is extended
posthumously; there are no "living saints."

In the days of early Christianity, sainthood was
established by popular acclaim. The early martyrs, for
example, were proclaimed saints, as were the Fathers
of the Church and confessors, people who lived lives of
heroic virtue and died peacefully. Such people were
accorded ecclesiastical honors by local authorities. By
the 11th century, it became increasingly apparent that a
system of regulation was needed in order to prevent
abuses, and to ensure that those venerated were done
so with good cause. Popes Urban II (r. 1088–99), Callistus II (r. 1119–24) and Eugenius III (r. 1145–53)
decreed that the examination of the virtues and mira-

cles of proposed saints be done by general councils. In
the 12th century, Pope Alexander III (r. 1159–81) prohibited veneration as a saint without the authority of
the Roman Church. In 1234, Pope Gregory IX (r.
1227–41) declared that the right to canonize belonged
exclusively to the papacy. In 1634 Pope Urban VIII (r.
1623–44) issued a bull extending the Church's exclu-
sive authority to beatification as well as canonization.
Formal review procedures were developed.

In 1983 significant changes were made in the process of canonization by Pope John Paul II (r. 1978–   ).
The cause of beatification, the first step, is initiated
after the death of a candidate. Often the followers of
the candidate want the process to begin immediately,
but years may elapse first. This waiting period is bene-
ficial, in that it allows for a more objective perspective.
The life, writings and works (or martyrdom) of the
candidate are investigated locally by the bishop for
heroic virtue and orthodoxy of doctrine. The investigation is evaluated by a panel of theologians at the Vatican. If the candidate has lived a life of faith and morals
and is approved by the panel and by the Congregation
for the Causes of Saints (see Glossary), the pope proclaims the candidate "Venerable."

In order to be beatified, there must be proof of at
least one posthumous miracle that results from a petition (martyrs are excepted from this requirement). The
miracle establishes that the candidate is in heaven and
has the ability to intercede on behalf of the living, and
to mediate a divine intervention that cannot be
explained according to the laws of science. First all the
evidence for the miracle is gathered, including historical and clinical data and depositions of witnesses. The
evidence is critically studied. A postulation is written
of the "Positio" that proves the miracle took place. If

the miracle involved a physical event such as a healing, the Positio is reviewed by a board of medical specialists. The case is assessed by a board of theologians, and evaluated at a meeting of cardinals and bishops who are members of the Congregation for the Causes of Saints.

If the miracle can be proved and the cause goes forward, the pope proclaims the candidate "Blessed" (*Beatus*), which means he or she can be venerated in localities or by groups of people to whom they have an importance.

For canonization, in which the candidate is proclaimed "Saint," a second miracle is required. This requirement applies to martyrs, too. The same process as for beatification is followed. Saints are "raised to the altars," that is, they are venerated by the entire Church and given feast days observed throughout the entire Church.

Saintly figures are venerated in all religions, but only the Roman Catholic Church has a formal procedure for establishing sainthood. The Russian Orthodox Church venerates the early church fathers and martyrs, and occasionally adds new saints to the list of the venerated. Several hundred persons have been canonized. There are about 10,000 saints who have cults, and historians believe that thousands more have been lost to history due to lack, or destruction, of records. Pope John Paul II has beatified more than 900 persons and canonized more than 300 persons—more than any other pope.

GLOSSARY OF TERMS

All Saints A feast honoring all saints of the Church, those declared, those not in the calendar and those unknown. The All Saints feast is one of the highest-ranking. Formal observances for All Saints began in the early eight century and have evolved throughout the centuries.

All Souls A feast honoring the faithful dead, celebrated on November 2, or on November 3 if November 2 falls on a Sunday. The origins of the feast can be traced to prayers for the dead performed in the early Church. The feast is especially for those departed who did not atone for their venial sins while living.

audition An experience of hearing a direct voice, which may be attributed to God or another divine or holy figure. Audition can occur in dreams, as part of visions, or alone during waking consciousness.

bilocation Being in two distant places simultaneously. Bilocation of saints has been especially reported when saints are called to minister to others in different locales. They appear real to all witnesses. Bilocation becomes apparent only when testimonies are compared. Alphonsus Marie Liguori would attend confession and preach sermons simultaneously. Once he went into a trance-like state for two days, after which he said he had gone to assist the pope, who was dying. Venerable Mary of Agreda reportedly bilocated from Spain to America more than 500 times (up to four times a day) from 1620 to 1631, in order to teach the natives. Padre Pio reportedly bilocated around the world in response to prayers for his intercession in healing.

communion of the saints The tradition of the spiritual union among the saints, the faithful on Earth and the souls in purgatory. According to St. Thomas Aquinas, angels participate in it as well, under the grace of Christ. The origins of the communion of saints are expressed in St. Paul's concept of the Mystical Body of Christ; the communion of saints is held to be much larger, because it does not require membership in the true Church, but is a union of Christ through charity and in association with his Church. Practices of this communion include prayers for the dead and the invocation, intercession and veneration of the saints in heaven.

Congregation for the Causes of Saints The administrative agency of the Church responsible for overseeing all things related to the causes of the saints, such as beatification, canonization and preservation of relics. The Congregation was established in 1588 by Pope Sixtus V (r. 1585–90) and was initially called the Congregation of Rites.

cults of the saints Devotions, honors and veneration paid to saints.

ecstasy A state of heightened consciousness in which one is infused with joy, awe, wonder, rapture and love. Long periods of time in intense prayer, coupled with deprivations and mortifications, can facilitate the onset of an ecstasy.

graces Gifts of the Spirit. Saints are bestowed with the favors of working miracles, healing, discernment of spirits, prophecy, visions and so forth as part of their spiritual advancement.

hagiography A writing of the lives and works of a saint. "Hagiography" is an ancient term derived from the Greek terms *hagios* (holy) and *graphein* (to write). The earliest collections were of the martyrs and church fathers, and date to St. Eusebius of Caesarea in the third and fourth centuries. Hagiographies contain mythology and legends in addition to historical fact; many were written expressly to inspire wonder and awe.

incorruptibility Unusual preservation of saints' bodies after death, without embalming. Incorruptibility is taken as evidence of sanctity. Some bodies have remained incorrupt for hundreds of years, though the tissue dries and darkens. Many incorrupt saints are on display in glass reliquaries. Persons who are candidates for sainthood are periodically exhumed and examined.

intercession The act of intervention by a saint in heaven in the lives of the living. Through prayer and invocation, saints are invited to help the living in all manner of needs, such as healing, financial distress, decision-making, protection and so on. Many intercessions are described as miraculous events.

levitation The rising up from the ground and into the air. Numerous saints reportedly have levitated while in ecstasy or in prayer, sometimes for extended periods and sometimes in a kneeling position. Often the bodies of the saints glow with a supernatural light. The levitation comes spontaneously, an uprushing force that lifts and sustains the saint.

lights and luminosities The emanation of, or being surrounded by, brilliant, unearthly light, such as during intense prayer or in ecstasy. This phenomenon is reported in intense spiritual practices around the world. Such lights may be accompanied by other phenomena, such as levitation, heat and the perception of spiritual presences. Faces may be transfigured.

manna A mysterious oil or powder that forms on or flows from the incorrupt bodies of saints or the bones of saints. Manna usually is an oil or liquid that is colorless, odorless and tasteless. If a powder, it can be granular or like flour. Manna, which manifests in small quantities, sometimes appears regularly on feast days or other significant anniversaries. It is collected and often distributed to ranking ecclesiastical persons or to the sick; it may be believed to have miraculous powers for healing.

martyrology A list of martyrs, either for cities, countries or regions, or for the entire Church. The earliest martyrologies, notably of Rome and Carthage, were calendars noting death dates. Other martyrologies may have brief descriptions of saints' lives.

miracle A witnessed event that contradicts the laws of nature. The Church considers miracles signs of God's intervention in the world. Many saints who worked miracles served as conduits for the glory of God to be witnessed by others. Two validated miracles are required for canonization. The Church investigates claims of miracles in the course of the causes for beatification and canonization.

miraculous protection Many saints are credited with performing miraculous acts that saved and protected themselves and others from danger and death.

miraculous transport The ability to suddenly be in a distant location. Saints have transported themselves and others in situations of need. Miraculous transport is not the same as bilocation, which is being in two locations simultaneously. An old term used in psychical research to describe this phenomenon is teleportation.

mortification The deprivation of physical comfort in order to purify the body. Many saints undertook varying degrees of mortification, such as wearing hair shirts, sleeping on uncomfortable beds, wearing chains, scourging themselves and fasting. Some also practiced mortification of the senses by keeping their eyes cast downward so as not to see the beauty of the world, by not engaging in mirth, and by lacing their meager diets with unpleasant-tasting additives. Many damaged and ruined their health in the process.

multiplication The miraculous increase of any substance. Many saints were said to increase food and money in accordance with the needs of others. Jesus multiplied fishes and loaves to feed the multitudes.

mystical fasting The ability to exist on food and water that normally could not sustain life. As part of their lives, saints were in prolonged or perpetual fasts, and often credited their ability to thrive on the inspiration of God and the sustenance provided by the Eucharist. St. Nicholas of Flüe was said to have lived for 20 years on Communion wafers.

mystical jewelry A ring of precious metals and jewels or a bejeweled crucifix given in mystical marriage or in ecstasy. The ring may or may not be visible to others, but the recipient always sees it. Sometimes the finger on which it is worn is indented, marked or reddened. Saints usually kept their mystical crucifixes hidden away, but bequeathed them to others upon death.

mystical knowledge The ability to see into the minds and hearts of others, to know their thoughts, desires and sins; also the direct knowledge of profound spiritual truths. In the language of parapsychology, the ability to know the thoughts and desires of others would be called clairvoyance.

mystical marriage   The union of the soul with God. Saints experienced the mystical marriage in an enraptured vision in which they were spiritually united with the Lord of Hosts or the Blessed Virgin Mary. Departed saints may also participate in the ceremony. Records exist of nearly 100 saints experiencing mystical marriage, with 55 of them receiving a mystical ring.

odor of sanctity   A sweet perfume emitted by the bodies of saints; evidence of their holiness. The odor of sanctity might be detected during prayer or ecstasies; some saints reportedly smelled sweet all the time. Many exuded heavenly fragrances upon and after death. Scents have been described as sweet, floral, spicy and like incense.

odor of sin   The presence of evil in a person, which some saints can detect as an overwhelming stench. The odor of sin—not detectable to others—is so repulsive as to cause some saints to become ill and even faint.

oil of the saints   See manna.

prophecy   The accurate knowing of the future. Many saints have prophesied important historical events and also the date of their own death.

relic   An object that serves as a memorial of a saint. The most important relics are bodies and body parts, including limbs, organs, bones and bone fragments. A saint's clothing can become a relic, as well as his or her personal belongings (such as a crucifix) and casket.

Objects that touch relics become relics of lesser status. The veneration of relics was widespread in Christianity by the fourth century. Miracles are associated with them. In the recognition of the holiness of a saint, his or her relics are translated, or elevated, to a shrine above ground.

stigmata   Physical wounds corresponding to the wounds suffered by Jesus during his Passion and Crucifixion. The wounds, which vary in number, spontaneously appear and bleed. Most stigmatists have five wounds, in the hands, feet and side. Some are marked according to the scourging that Christ received, and also according to the wounds produced by his crown of thorns. St. Francis of Assisi received the stigmata from an angel. Other saints received the wounds while in intense prayer or during an ecstasy. For some, the wounds are temporary, and may reappear on Fridays or at Easter, and then close and disappear. Padre Pio was a young man when he received the stigmata, and the wounds on his hands and feet remained open and bleeding for the rest of his life.

transverberation   Spiritual wounding of the heart; literally, "striking through of." The most famous example is Theresa of Avila, whom an angel pierced with a flaming arrow of love while she was in ecstasy. Thérèse of Lisieux was wounded by a dart of love, and Blessed Padre Pio was visited by an angel who hurled a fiery weapon like a sharp-pointed steel blade into the depths of his soul.

veneration   Devotion. The Church distinguishes between veneration paid to saints and the worship of God.

APPENDIX 9
CALENDAR OF FEASTS OF THE BLESSED VIRGIN MARY

January 1	Solemnity of Mary, Mother of God
February 2	Presentation of Our Lord
February 11	Our Lady of Lourdes (optional)
March 25	Annunciation of the Lord
May 31	Visitation to Elizabeth
July 16	Our Lady of Mt. Carmel (optional)
August 5	Dedication of the basilica in honor of St. Mary Major (optional)
August 15	Assumption
August 22	Queenship of Mary
September 8	Birth of Mary
September 15	Our Lady of Sorrows
September 24	Our Lady of Ransom
October 7	Our Lady of the Rosary
November 21	Presentation of Mary (optional)
December 8	Immaculate Conception
December 12	Our Lady of Guadalupe (optional) Saturday after the Second Sunday after Pentecost Immaculate Heart of Mary (optional)

APPENDIX 10
AUTHENTICATED APPARITIONS OF THE BLESSED VIRGIN MARY

The Catholic Church holds that religious apparitions are mystical phenomena permitted by God. Both corporeal and incorporeal apparitions are recognized, and are mentioned in both Old and New Testaments of the Bible. Marian apparitions are not accepted as articles of faith, but those that are deemed authentic are celebrated. The Church is painstaking in its investigation of Marian apparitions.

Visions of the Blessed Virgin Mary are accompanied by a host of glorious phenomena, such as visions of angels, heavenly music and singing, miraculous healing, luminosities, trance states, extrasensory perception and prophesying. The apparitions tend to be apocalyptic in nature, with Mary exhorting people to prayer and righteous living, and to build churches in her honor. She also warns of dire consequences if people continue their sinful ways. She bestows secret prophecies on a select few who perceive her (frequently children). In this respect, Mary has taken over the primary functions of the prophets of old, who were transported to heaven to receive the same admonitions and prophecies from God. But Mary, out of her love for humanity and her loyalty to those devoted to her, is able to intercede with an angry God on humanity's behalf.

Authentic sightings approved by the Church are:

Guadalupe, Mexico, 1531 Mary's appearances were accompanied by heavenly singing, and one of her miraculous signs involved an angel. She appeared five times to Juan Diego, a middle-aged Aztec convert to Catholicism. The first episode occurred in the pre-dawn one morning as Juan was on his way to attend Mass. He suddenly heard a heavenly choir, and then a lady's voice calling out to him by name. Diego then saw a woman standing in a luminous cloud of mist iridescent with rainbow hues. She identified herself immediately as Mary.

On another occasion, Mary appeared and told Diego to pick flowers, despite the fact that it was too cold a time of the year. Miraculously, he found a garden of roses at a site where no flowers had grown before. He followed her instructions to wrap the flowers in his cape and take them to the bishop.

When Diego revealed the flowers and cape to the bishop and others who were present, a beautiful image of the Immaculate Conception was found to be imprinted on the cape—a woman with the sun and stars, standing on a new moon, with an angel at her feet. The style of the "painting" is not in the Maya-Toltec-Aztec tradition of the time, which resembled primitive hieroglyphics. The cape was made of ayate, a coarse fabric made of cactus fiber, and had a maximum life span of about 30 years. It and the "painting" have lasted to the present day, and are on display in the church shrine that was built at Mary's request.

Specialists have examined the figure's eyes in the "painting" and confirm what appear to be images of a man, perhaps Juan Diego, in each eye.

Pope Pius XII (1939–58) said that "on the *tilma* (cape) of humble Juan Diego—as tradition relates—brushes not of this earth left painted an Image more tender which the corrosive work of the centuries was marvelously to respect."

Paris, 1830   Mary appeared to Catherine Labouré, a nun with the Sisters of Charity in the Rue du Bac. Catherine had entered the convent in 1830, shortly before the sighting. Within a few days of her arrival, she had a vision of the heart of St. Vincent, glowing above a case containing some of his relics. She prayed to St. Vincent and to her guardian angel to be granted a vision of Mary, her greatest ambition.

On July 18, Catherine was awakened at 11:30 P.M. by the sound of her name being called. She saw a child of about four or five years of age with golden hair, whom she took to be her guardian angel. The angel told her to go to the convent chapel; upon arrival, she found it brilliantly lit. Mary appeared at midnight and delivered her customary messages of exhortation to prayer. She asked Catherine to undertake a mission that would require her suffering, and also gave her prophecies.

Mary appeared to Catherine again on November 27 in a glorious vision while Catherine was praying in the chapel at about 5:30 P.M. She told Catherine to have a medal struck of her vision, and that all who wore it would receive graces. Catherine was not able to do this until six months before her death in 1876. The medal, called "the Miraculous Medal," is now worn by millions worldwide.

La Salette, France, 1846   Mary appeared once on September 19, 1846, to two children, a boy and a girl—who had known each other for only two days—who were herding cows in the French Alps. Awakening from a nap, 14-year-old Melanie Mathieu and 11-year-old Maximim Giraud discovered that their cows had wandered off. In rounding them up, Melanie looked into a ravine and saw a brilliant light that transformed into a weeping woman sitting on a rock. She wore a headdress capped by a crown ringed with roses. Her long white dress and slippers were decorated with pearls, and her slippers also had gold buckles and roses.

The woman rose and approached the children. She spoke in French, which they did not understand well (they spoke a local dialect). She made a long complaint about the social and political turmoil in France and the neglect of religion. If people did not convert, if people did not pray and observe the Sabbath, she would be compelled to set loose her Son's arm is punishment, she said.

As she spoke, only one child could hear her at a time. She gave each child a secret and warned of coming famine. She admonished them to pray.

The woman was identified as Mary after they told their story to others. The children were interrogated. A spring was said to have miraculously appeared at the spot where Mary had appeared, and people who drank the water reported being healed.

The Church authenticated La Salette in 1851; a church and statue of Mary were consecrated in 1879 by the cardinal archbishop of Paris.

Lourdes, France, 1858   On 18 occasions, from February 11 to July 16, 1858, 14-year-old Bernadette Soubirous reportedly saw Mary in a grotto along the Gave du Pau River near Lourdes. Bernadette said she saw "a girl in white, no taller than I, who greeted me with a little bow of her head." On one occasion, the Lady spoke, in the Lourdes dialect, and said, "Will you please come here every day for a fortnight. I do not promise to make you happy in this world but in the next." In the last apparition, the woman identified herself as, "I am the Immaculate Conception."

As a result of the apparitions, Bernadette reportedly experienced trances or ecstasies, some lasting an hour. After her series of visions ceased, a spring near the site became credited with miraculous healing powers. The spring has no known natural therapeutic properties; believers attribute its curative powers to the patronage of Mary. Numerous other claims of visions and miracles proved to be spurious. The Catholic Church authenticated Bernadette's apparitions four years later, and canonized Bernadette as a saint on December 8, 1933.

The identification of the apparition as the Immaculate Conception is important to Catholicism, and has been taken by many Catholics to be heavenly confirmation of the doctrine of the Immaculate Conception, which had been defined as a Catholic dogma in 1854, (see MARY). The "immaculateness" of Mary is a theme of the apparitions at Guadalupe and Fatima.

At Mary's request, a chapel was built in 1871 at the Lourdes site; it has grown to be one of the great churches of southern France.

Up to six million pilgrims visit Lourdes each year. Supervision and examination of people who claim to be healed is done by a Medical Bureau established in 1883 as an independent group of doctors, which also is open to qualified visiting physicians. There are documented cases of cures associated with both the waters and the site.

Knock, Ireland, 1879   Mary, other figures and perhaps angels were seen on August 21, 1879, by 15 people at the village chapel at dusk. Besides Mary, there were figures of St. Joseph and a bishop or St. John the Evangelist (accounts differ). There also was an altar, above which was a lamb with a halo of gold stars; behind the lamb was a cross. Mary had her hands raised in prayer. Although it was raining, no rain fell where the apparition appeared. One witness, Patrick Hill, was 11 years old. Interviewed again in 1897, he embellished his account with visions of winged angels who fluttered in the air for some 90 minutes.

Fatima, Portugal, 1917   In the most dramatic of all authenticated sightings, three children were paid three visits by an angel who identified itself as the Angel of Portugal, who acted as an annunciating figure. Mary then appeared to the children: Lucia dos Santos, 10, and her two cousins, Jacinta and Francisco Marto, seven and nine, respectively. The two girls saw a "young lady" and heard her speak; the boy saw her but did not hear her speak. The children said the lady was dressed in white and stood above a small tree. She asked them to return to the same place at the same hour of the same day for six consecutive months. Tens of thousands of spectators showed up at the appointed time and place to witness the six apparitions.

At the final sighting on October 13, a crowd of 50,000 or more gathered in the rain. Mary appeared to the children and told them to build a chapel in her honor. She said she was the "Lady of the Rosary," and that people must say the rosary daily. Then the rain stopped, and a phenomenon now known as the "miracle of the sun" occurred. The sun appeared suddenly through a rift in the clouds and seemed to spin, throwing off multicolored light. It appeared to plunge to earth, giving off heat, and then returned to normal in the sky.

A cult devoted to the Angel of Portugal, the guardian angel of the state, was sanctioned by the Catholic Church.

Lucia wrote four memoirs between 1935 and 1941. In her *Second Memoir,* she made the new claim that she and her cousins had been visited by an angel in 1916. This "Angel of Peace," as he identified himself, taught the children a special prayer, and said that the hearts of Jesus and Mary were attentive to them. Lucia described him as looking about 14 or 15 years of age, whiter than snow, transparent as crystal, and quite beautiful when the sun shone through him. She warned the other two that the visit must be kept secret (secret visits, messages and prophecies are an integral part of Marian apparitions, and conform with apocalyptic experiences).

On a second visit, the angel urged them to pray constantly to God, and said that the hearts of Jesus and Mary had "designs of mercy" on them. He instructed them to make everything possible a sacrifice offered to God, which would be reparation for the sins that offend God, and supplication for the conversion of sinners. The angel said that if they did this, their country would have peace. He then identified himself as the Angel of Portugal. He ended his visit by telling them to bear the suffering that God would send them.

On a third visit, the angel gave them Communion. Lucia received the consecrated host, and Jacinta and Francisco were allowed to share the chalice.

Beauraing, Belgium, 1932–33   Mary made numerous appearances to children between November 29, 1932, and January 3, 1933, in the farming town of Beauraing in southern Belgium. On the evening of November 29, with her feet covered in small clouds, she appeared to five children near the Sisters of Christian Doctrine Academy, where one of them was a student. No one believed the children because they had a reputation for pranks.

The children saw the apparition again on the next two days. Attempts to find a prankster failed. Mary emerged from shrubs and ascended to heaven. Later on the evening of December 1, the children went to school and recited the rosary outside the gate. Mary, wearing a white gown and radiating a blue light, appeared beneath a hawthorn tree.

In subsequent appearances, Mary exhorted the children to be good. She ignored requests to produce miracles to convince the growing crowd of spectators accompanying the children. She asked them to come to the school garden on December 8, the Feast of the Immaculate Conception. Expecting a miraculous cure of two invalid children, 15,000 people showed up. Though the children saw Mary, they were not healed.

Mary requested that a chapel be built where the hawthorn tree stood. She spoke to each child individually and exhorted them all to pray.

She made her last appearance on January 3, revealing to some children her heart of gold. Fernande Voisin witnessed a blaze of flame in the hawthorn tree and a vision of Mary. She asked the child to sacrifice herself for Mary.

The church authenticated the apparitions in 1949.

Banneux, Belgium, 1933   Eight apparitions of Mary appeared to 11-year-old Mariette Beco between January 15 and March 2. In the first apparition, Mary appeared as a glorious lady in white outside the window of the Beco home. The figure beckoned Mariette to come outside. The girl's mother, who could see a shadowy white form in less detail, feared it was a witch and kept the child indoors. Mariette insisted it was Mary.

In subsequent visions, Mary uncovered a spring that she said had healing waters. She asked for a chapel to be built on the spot, and told Mariette to pray and believe in her. She gave Mariette two secrets. On at least two occasions, Mariette witnessed Mary floating or gliding in the sky. Mariette sometimes fainted after the apparitions ended. One apparition lasted 37 minutes.

Though her priest considered her an unlikely visionary due to her lack of education and piety, others felt differently. Miracles of healing were reported at the spring. Banneux became one of the great healing shrines of Europe.

APPENDIX 11
UNAUTHENTICATED APPARITIONS OF THE BLESSED VIRGIN MARY

Alleged sightings of Marian apparitions have a powerful effect on witnesses, even if the apparitions are not authenticated by the Church. Investigations can take years before a decision on authenticity is made; meanwhile, sites of apparitions continue to draw new pilgrims who hope to have miraculous experiences. The Catholic Church remains very cautious about investigating reported Marian apparitions. The overwhelming majority of them fade away over time. Major unauthenticated sightings are:

Garabandal, Spain, 1961–63 Apparitions occurred at San Sebastian de Garabandal in northern Spain; they are unauthenticated. The sightings involved the archangel Michael, who, like the Angel of Portugal at Fatima, gave witnesses Communion. The case began on June 18, 1961, when four girls reported that they had seen an angel. Over the next two weeks, the angel made nine appearances. In the two years following, there were more than 2,000 reports of Marian apparitions by the girls.

One of the chief documents is the *Diary* of one of the witnesses, Conchita Gonzalez, who was 12 at the time. She began to write the account in September of 1962 and finished it in 1963.

According to Gonzalez, she and the other viewers were stealing apples on June 18—and arguing over whether it was right—when a beautiful figure appeared, brilliant in light. The girls told others about this angel, and were ridiculed by some. The girls returned to the spot the next day to pray, but the angel did not reappear. Gonzalez was consoled by a voice that night that assured her she would see the angel

again. The angel did appear the following day, causing some disbelievers to recant.

Others joined them in prayer at the site, and over the next 11 days, the girls had various ecstasies and eight more sightings of the angel, in front of numerous witnesses (who could not see the phenomena themselves). On six of the eight appearances, the angel only smiled at the girls. On June 24, he appeared with a sign beneath him; they could remember only that the first line began with "Hay" and the second line contained roman numerals.

On July 1, the angel appeared with the sign again and spoke for the first time, telling the girls that he had come to announce the arrival of Mary on the following day. Mary appeared on July 2, accompanied by two angels who looked like twins. One was Michael, the angel who had been appearing to them; the other was not recognized (Gonzalez never said how she was able to identify the angel as Michael). On Mary's right side was a large eye of God.

During these and other visions, the girls were subjected to crude experiments by researchers to test their ecstatic states by measuring their sensitivity to pain. During the June 25 appearance of the angel, Gonzalez was dropped on her knees, pricked and scratched with needles and subjected to strong electric light, none of which broke her trance or made her feel any pain.

On May 18, 1962, the girls began announcing that they had been receiving Communion from Michael. Mari Loli was first to make the claim. She said Michael told her he would give her Communion while the local priest was absent. The four girls said that from then on, they received frequent Communions from the angel.

Gonzalez said that Michael used unconsecrated hosts in order to teach them how the host should be received. One day, the angel told them to fast and to bring another child along as a witness. He then gave them consecrated hosts. These reports generated much controversy. Priests said that angels did not have the ability to consecrate a host. Gonzalez took this objection to Michael, who then told her he had taken consecrated hosts from tabernacles on Earth. Nonetheless, some people doubted the story.

Gonzalez's father verified that, prior to their public admission of Communion from Michael, he had witnessed the girls going through gestures of putting their hands together, sticking out their tongues and swallowing, all of which now made sense. After the admission, numerous photos were taken of them receiving invisible Communion.

On June 22, 1962, the angel told Gonzalez—who had been asking for a miracle as a sign of proof—that during the next Communion God would perform a miracle through the angel's intercession by making a host visible on her tongue. (Until then, Gonzalez had no idea that no one else could see the hosts given them by the angel.) She told the angel that this would be a tiny miracle, and he laughed. On July 18, a host appeared on her tongue.

Though the girls later retracted some of their statements about their experiences, believers were not dissuaded. Even the retractions seemed part of the overall experience, with Gonzalez's diary claiming that Mary predicted that retractions would be made. Supporters of the apparitions at Garabandal have worked to try to convince the Catholic Church to authenticate the sightings.

Zeitoun, Egypt, 1968–69 More than 70 Marian apparitions and other unusual phenomena were reported in the vicinity of St. Mary's Coptic Church in Zeitoun, a suburb of Cairo. The first eyewitnesses were three Muslim mechanics, who reported seeing a woman dressed in dazzling white, standing on top of the central dome of the church in the late night hours. The light was so brilliant that they could not make out facial features. Others saw it, and a crowd gathered within minutes; someone recognized the apparition as Mary. The crowd shouted and the figure acknowledged by bowing. After a few minutes, it ascended rapidly into the night sky and disappeared.

The first sighting on April 2 was followed by hundreds of alleged spontaneous cures of all manner of diseases and illnesses. One of the mechanics, who suffered a gangrenous finger and was due for surgery the next day, completely recovered.

From April 2 until August 1969, Marian apparitions occurred two to three times a week, then were sporadic for the remainder of 1969. They were most frequent on early Sunday mornings and on the 32 Marian feast days of the Coptic Church. Total eyewitnesses were estimated at 250,000 to 500,000.

The apparitions included full and partial figures in at least 10 different shapes, which bowed and waved to the witnesses; reddish clouds of sweet incense, which appeared and disappeared with great rapidity; unusual lights shooting across the sky; and luminous doves or dove-like objects of silver and other brilliant colors, some of which appeared in the shape of a Christian cross. None of the apparitions was accompanied by sound. The shortest lasted about one minute, while the longest, on June 8, 1968, lasted for more than seven hours. The General Information and Complaints Department of the Egyptian government investigated and declared it "an undeniable fact" that Mary had appeared to both Christians and Muslims.

Medjugorje, Bosnia-Herzegovina, 1981– A remote village tucked into the mountains, Medjugorje (formerly in Yugoslavia) has attracted millions of pilgrims and tourists since Mary first appeared on a hill to six adolescent villagers on June 24, 1981. Four were girls and two were boys; they ranged in age from 10 to 17. For the next 18 months, there were daily apparitions to one or more of the adolescents, who came to be called the "seers" or "visionaries." Apparitions have continued, and thousands of them have been recorded. Many have occurred in the "chapel of apparitions," the rectory behind St. James Roman Catholic Church in Medjugorje. Most last a few minutes, but some have lasted 20 to 45 minutes.

In addition to the apparitions, miraculous healings have been reported of a range of physical and psychological conditions, from eye diseases and vascular problems to substance addictions. Other miracles occurred nearly daily. In August 1981, the Croatian word for peace, Mir, was seen written in the sky at night above the cross on the hill where Mary first appeared, now known as the Hill of Apparitions. Her silhouette has also been seen on the hill. Like the "miracle of the sun" at Fatima, the sun has been reported to either pulsate, spin hypnotically, change into a white disc, or shine in a rainbow of brilliant colors. The cross behind the church has been seen to spin or disappear. On October 28, 1981, a bush spontaneously ignited on the hill. People rushed to extinguish it, but by the time they reached it, it had burned itself out, leaving no charring or burned evidence.

According to the visionaries, the purpose of the apparitions is to bring a message from Christ, which the seers would then communicate to the world. Essentially, the message is that atheists must convert and return to the ways of God, to change their lives to peace with God and with their fellow humankind. Returning to God can be achieved through peace, conversion, fasting, penance and prayer. Peace is the most important, for it makes everything else possible. Prayer is vital because faith cannot be maintained without it. Prayer must be directed to Jesus, and Mary will intercede with him. The purpose of the supernatural events, according to Mary, is to give credence to the apparitions and underscore the importance of the message.

Mary further communicated that Medjugorje was selected because the village of about 400 families included many good believers who were capable of restoring their faith, and serving as an example, to other people in the world regarding the need to convert.

After their first vision, the visionaries spent at least six hours in prayer, and fasted up to three times a week. They said they conversed with Mary in normal conversation tones, and in their native Croatian. They learned that each of them would be given 10 secrets, after which time Mary would cease to appear to them, except on special occasions. The children did not receive their secrets at the same time; four messages were to concern mankind as a whole, while the rest would be directed to individuals or the village of Medjugorje.

As a result of the apparitions, the villagers, with few exceptions, converted and began attending daily church services.

Pilgrims who visit the church and rectory say Mary appears to them during prayer. Others report unusual experiences, such as the changing of silver rosary chains to gold. Photographs appear to show images of the figure of Jesus on the cross on the Hill, Mary in prayer against the cross, Mary and child in the sky, and unnaturally originating rays of light striking across the cross. In some cases, the images are evident only after the film is developed.

By the fall of 1987, Mary was appearing on the 25th day of each month, giving messages to visionaries to spread throughout the world about the need for prayer and the need to dedicate time to Jesus.

The messages support Catholic teachings; most fall into five themes: peace, faith, conversion, prayer and fasting. In 1984, Mary began giving "special messages."

By 1999, three visionaries had received all 10 secrets, and three had received nine. The ninth and tenth secrets were supposed to be "very grave, having to do with the sins of the world." Prayer and penance will help to ward off evil and war.

Only one secret was revealed to the public: that Mary would leave a visible sign on the mountain where she first appeared.

After all the secrets are given, three warnings will be given to the world. Ten days before each warning, a priest will be notified so that he can fast and pray for seven days, and then announce the warning that will take place in three days. The three warnings will occur in rapid succession. Those who have not converted will have little time to do so.

The Catholic Church's position on Medjugorje is that supernatural apparitions and revelations have not been affirmed. Private pilgrimages are permitted as long as they are not taken as authentification of events.

In 1998, a scientific study was done on the visionaries at the request of the Parish Office of Medjugorje. It was concluded that none of the visionaries demonstrated any pathological symptoms such as trance interference, dissociative interference or loss of reality interference, and that their states of ecstasy were not hypnotically induced.

APPENDIX 12
GLOSSARY OF HERESIES AND SCHISMS

From its beginnings, Christianity was beset by heresies, schisms and competing religions. Some of these were confined to small areas and lasted but a few decades or a century or so. Others became powerful and well established, threatening the growth of the Church.

A heretic is one who accepts only part of the doctrine of the Church. Apostasy, on the other hand, rejects the entire faith of Christ. All heresies are schisms but not all schisms are heresies. A schism may uphold the entire doctrine of the Church but attempt to assert some independence. Heresy is considered a sin. Heretics once were subject to excommunication, and perhaps also to fines, seizure of estates and banishment. During the Inquisition, heretics were arrested, severely tortured and turned over to the secular courts for punishment, usually execution by burning or hanging. Today heresy is punishable by excommunication, public humiliation and—for clerics—a stripping of all clerical orders.

The establishment of Christian doctrine was a long process studded with great controversies. It was not uncommon for defenders of orthodoxy to find themselves condemned as heretics because their views and writings fell into error.

The following are brief summaries of some of the notable heresies and schisms referred to in entries in this encyclopedia. *The Catholic Encyclopedia* provides detailed entries on these and other heresies and schisms.

Adoptionism A heresy that held that Christ was a man and was the Son of God only by adoption. The heresy arose toward the end of the eighth century in Spain, where Islam and the Nestorian heresy had

found support. Its chief proponent was Elipandus, the archbishop of Toledo. Adoptionism was condemned by Pope Adrian I in 785 and 794. Also in 794 the Council of Frankfort rejected it as heresy. Adoptionism was largely gone by the Middle Ages. In 1177 Pope Alexander III anathematized anyone who did not recognize Christ as the natural Son of God.

Apollinarianism A heresy that Christ had a human body and soul, but no human intellect; that is, his rational side, or human spirit, was replaced by the Divine Logos.

The heresy was conceived by Apollinaris the Younger, Bishop of Laodicea (d. 392), and gained popularity during the latter part of the fourth century. Apollinaris held that humanity's rational mind is capable of sinning, and thus Christ, as the perfect union of humanity and God, had to possess the Divine Logos in its stead.

Apollinaris wrote numerous works, including treatises on the Scriptures and apologies for Christianity against other heresies. His views about the Divine Logos in Christ initially were highly regarded by major Fathers of the Church such as SS. Athanasius, Basil and Jerome. The Apollinarists fabricated supporting writings supposedly authored by SS. Athanasius, Gregory Thaumaturgus and others in order to gain adherents. This worked for a time, and Apollinarianism was especially strong in the Eastern Church.

Church councils in Rome in 377 and Constantinople in 381 denounced the theory as heresy. Athanasius, Gregory of Nazianzus, Gregory of Nyssa and others wrote against it. The defenders of orthodoxy held that Christ experienced joy and sadness, which are properties of the human soul, and that without a rational spirit he was not a man, nor was he God-man, and therefore he could not serve as the model for Christian life.

Apollinaris died a heretic in 392. Many of his followers returned to orthodoxy, and some became supporters of another heresy, Monophysitism.

Arianism A heresy that denied the divinity of Christ. Arianism was the first major heresy to arise after Emperor Constantine recognized Christianity in 313, and it created a significant struggle of doctrine that engaged some of the leading figures of the Church, including SS. Athanasius, Basil the Great, Gregory of Nyssa and Gregory of Nazianzus.

Arius, the namesake of the heresy, was a Libyan who grew up in Antioch and went to school with Eusebius, who became bishop of Nicomedia. Despite Jesus' statement in the Gospels that "I and the Father are one," Arius held that God was without beginning and therefore could not create himself as Son. Christ, who had an origin, was a second, inferior God. A huge controversy over this raged in the Church, but Emperor Constantine treated it as a minor matter.

The response to Arianism was the Nicene Creed, which affirmed that Father and Son were "consubstantial." This was affirmed by a council, and Arius and his supporters were exiled. But the Nicene term itself then came under controversy. Thanks to schemes and intrigues, Constantine was persuaded to accept Arius back, and ordered Athanasius, the patriarch of Constantinople, to do so. Athanasius refused, and was deposed and banished. In 336 Arius made a triumphant return to the city, but his triumph was short-lived—he died suddenly, to the satisfaction of his opponents. This, however, did not end Arianism, for Constantine favored it until his own death in 337.

Athanasius fought Arianism to his death in 373. There were constant intrigues and various new sects that arose. Constantinople remained an Arian stronghold; the battle against it was continued by Basil, the two Gregorys and others. In 381 the Council of Constantinople approved the Nicene Creed, which affirmed the unity of Father, Son and Holy Ghost, and set forth the fundamentals of the Christian faith. Arianism was condemned and quickly lost power. It lingered in patches throughout Europe and among barbarians, but was essentially dead by the eighth century.

Docetism A heresy that arose from Gnosticism during the first century of Christianity. The *Docetae*, or Illusionists, held that Christ only "seemed" to be human. Some Docetae denied the entirety of Christ's human nature, while others denied only his human birth and death, or only his human body. St. Clement of Alexandria credited a Julius Cassianus as the founder of Docetism, but the ideas were in existence long before him. The Apostles and early Church fathers campaigned against Docetism and Gnosticism.

Docetism was absorbed by Manichaeanism.

Donatism A schism in Africa that lasted from about 311 to 411. The Donatists were not heretics. However, St. Augustine, who vigorously and successfully opposed them, said that schismatics were just as bad as heretics, if not worse.

The schism arose in the wake of the terrible Christian persecutions in North Africa in the early fourth century. Christians were giving themselves up, but Mensurius, bishop of Carthage, decreed that those who surrendered voluntarily could not be glorified as martyrs. Mensurius died in 311 after the persecutions abated. The schism arose during the controversy over selecting a new bishop, and was led by Donatus of Casae Nigrae, a forceful and eloquent figure. Much of the polarization of sides concerned the treatment of the martyrs. A bishop was chosen who had been antagonistic toward the martyrs. Dissenting bishops declared the bishop's ordination invalid, and elected their own replacement. Soon there were many cities having two bishops.

The Donatists gained power and were tolerated by Emperor Constantine. The Arian heretics tried to gain the support of the Donatists, but failed.

After Augustine was ordained a priest in 391, he began a strong campaign against the schism. He prevailed at a conference in Carthage in 411, at which Donatist assemblies were forbidden, and other measures were taken against them. In 412, Pope Honorius outlawed them, and by 430 they had disappeared.

Eastern Schism Numerous schisms plagued the Eastern Church, culminating in a great schism that completely separated Eastern and Western churches in the 15th century. The Eastern Schism was not the product of a single controversy, but the result of a long and gradual process.

From the beginning of Christianity, differences appeared in the Eastern and Western churches. They had different capitals of activity (Rome and Constantinople), different philosophies and their own loyalties and politics. There was constant friction between Rome and Constantinople. The East had its own troubled history, spending 203 years of the 544-year period between 323 and 867 dealing with a series of schisms and heresies.

The Eastern Schism took shape in 1053, when Michael Caerularius, patriarch of Constantinople, declared war on the West and closed down the Latin churches in the city. He and his followers were excommunicated by Rome in 1054. Attempts were made to heal the breach on into the 15th century, but reunions never lasted. In 1472 the East formally broke away from the West.

Eutychianism A heresy in the fifth century that rejected the orthodox, two united natures of Christ in favor of one nature. The heresy was a response against another heresy, Nestorianism, and is often identified with the Monophysite heresy. It was named after Eutyches, though he contributed little to it.

At the time the heresy arose, Eutyches was 70 years old and for 30 years had served as archimandrite of a monastery of 300 monks outside of Constantinople. Eutyches opposed Nestorianism, but could not accept the concept, expressed by St. Cyril of Alexandria, that Christ was of two natures united after the Incarnation, consubstantial with God and with the flesh of humanity. Eutyches held that nothing could be imposed by faith that was not found in the Scriptures.

Eutyches was tried for heresy and was excommunicated and deposed. He appealed to Pope St. Leo, who decided that Eutyches was a foolish old man and could be restored if he repented. In 449 a council held in Ephesus absolved him, but another council in Chalcedon in 451 exiled him. He is believed to have died soon thereafter.

Gnosticism An intellectual religion espousing salvation through *gnosis*, or knowledge. Gnosticism was in existence several centuries before Christianity. It borrowed from Christianity and lasted into the fifth century. The exact origins of Gnosticism are not known, but it appears to have drawn from Babylonian, Persian, Judaic and Hellenistic thought. The Gnostic cosmology drew upon Chaldean astrology.

The Gnostics viewed the cosmos as a series of concentric spheres. They called them aeons, each with its own ruler or aeon (comparable to a very high angel). The highest, 365th circle was ruled by Abraxas, the chief of the heavens. At the summit, or the center, was the good God, otherwise called the Father, essentially unknowable to humans. Aeons could combine and subdivide and multiply themselves in a process called syzygy. Descending in tiers down to the terrestrial world were 30 circles, which constituted the Pleroma.

Sophia was the aeon of the 30th circle. According to one version of her story, she desired to contemplate on her own the splendor of the Pleroma. This was an ill-fated wish, for when she crossed the last circle, she was dazzled by light and fell down to our world. Sophia was made pregnant by the Pleroma and gave birth to a creature, the Demiurge, who, after modifications by the Aeons of the Pleroma, created humankind. Gnostics associated their many versions of this "accursed god" with the God of the Old Testament.

Gnostics considered the world of matter evil and polluted, deteriorated from the Godhead. Through knowledge, which included the use of magical spells, the *pneuma,* or spirit, struggled to ascend to the Pleroma.

Numerous Gnostic systems and schools proliferated. Christianity refuted it from its beginnings. Many of the early Church fathers wrote strongly against it, especially St. Irenaeus and Tertullian. Beginning in the fourth century, Gnosticism fell into rapid decline and was no longer a force by the fifth to sixth centuries.

Iconoclasm A heresy of the eighth and ninth centuries in the Eastern Church, before the final break between East and West. The heresy centered around the veneration of images, or icons. In the eighth century, Emperor Leo III (the Isaurian) instigated persecutions against icon worship on the grounds that images were idols that fostered superstition and hindered the conversion of the Jews and Muslims. The Iconoclasts, as the opponents of icons were called, burned monasteries in the East and tortured, killed and banished monks. They then turned on relics, and vandalized shrines and burned the bodies of saints. The papacy's defense of holy images only intensified the persecutions.

In 731 Pope Gregory III held a synod in Rome that declared that anyone who broke or defiled holy images would be excommunicated. The response of Leo III was to send a fleet to Rome to punish the pope, but it was wrecked by storms. When Leo III died in 741, his persecutions were carried on by his son Constantine V. In 754 a synod in Constantinople declared that the only lawful image of Christ was the Eucharist; all others were either Monophysite or Nestorian, since they confounded or divorced his two natures. The destruction of images and relics continued. When Constantine V died in 775, his son Leo V maintained the persecutions, though less vigorously than his father.

Leo V died in 780 and the throne went to his nine-year-old son, Constantine VI. The boy's mother, Empress Irene, served as regent. She began a campaign to reverse Iconoclasm and reopen and restore the monasteries. Pope Adrian I demanded restitution of the property confiscated by Leo III.

The lawfulness of venerating holy images was reestablished at a synod at Nicaea in 787. But peace did not last, for the Iconoclast party still existed, especially in the army. Twenty-seven years later, a second Iconoclastic persecution erupted. There were countering synods that rejected and upheld icons, and much fighting. The Iconoclasts regained the upper hand. The persecutions became so great that many monks fled to the West.

The situation did not change until 842, when another empress regent, Theodora, gained control and restored icon worship. The Iconoclasts were excommunicated. The Feast of Orthodoxy was established to commemorate the defeat of Iconoclasm, and became symbolic of the defeat of all heresies. The Iconoclast party gradually died out.

Twenty years later, the Eastern and Western Churches separated.

Manichaeanism An intellectual and dualistic religion founded in Persia by Mani in the last half of the third century. Presenting itself as a synthesis of all religions, Manichaeanism spread rapidly from Asia Minor to Europe, Africa, India, China and Tibet, lasting about 700 years.

Mani (the name is more a title than a personal name) was born ca. 215–216 in Babylonia to a religious family. He became a pagan priest. In 242 he proclaimed himself "Apostle of the true God," evoking Buddha, Zoroaster and Jesus. He began evangelizing abroad in Turkestan and India. Returning to Persia, he was imprisoned by King Sapor I, and either was released or escaped after the king's death in 274. Sapor's successor, Ormuzd I, favored Mani, but lived only one year on the throne. The next king, Bahram I, had Mani crucified in 276–277, his corpse flayed and the skin stuffed and hung up at the city gate. Manichaeans were persecuted viciously.

Like Gnosticism, Manichaeanism promised salvation through knowledge. It had an elaborate cosmology of light and dark; the world of matter was polluting and had to be overcome. Mani proclaimed himself the Paraclete promised by Jesus, although he claimed no divinity. He repudiated the historical Jesus as an ordinary man, a "devil" who was fittingly punished. Jesus Christ was only an aeon, or personification of Light. He accepted portions of the New Testament but rejected all of the Old Testament.

Manichaeanism was especially popular in the Arab world and the East; it also gained a strong following in Egypt. It was at its peak around 400, and its followers suffered persecution as heretics. It lasted until about 1000, becoming absorbed into other sects such as the Paulicians, Cathars and Bogomils, which were eradicated by the Inquisition.

Marcionism A heresy that survived for about 300 years in early Christianity and that rejected the God of the Old Testament as the Father of Christ.

The heresy was conceived by Marcion, born to wealthy parents in Pontus ca. 110, and who became a bishop. He went to Rome ca. 140, announcing that he would divide the Church forever. His final breach with the Church occurred in 144.

Marcion could not reconcile the cruel God of the Old Testament with God the Father of Christ. He said the Old Testament God was really a lesser God, a Demiurge who created the world and was given to anger. Christ was the son of a great God, the good God who was nothing but love. He created his own New Testament that included a chopped up version of the Gospel of St. Luke and 10 letters of St. Paul.

Marcion attracted many followers who further developed his ideas toward Gnosticism. By 154 Marcionism was widespread. Opponents included some of the most prominent fathers of the Church, such as SS. Irenaeus, Justin the Martyr, Epiphanius and Hippolytus of Rome, as well as Tertullian.

Marcion was thrown out of the Church. At some point he is said to have professed penitence and promised to bring back to the fold those whom he had led astray, but he died—the date is not known—before he could do so. Marcionism eventually was absorbed into Manichaeanism.

Monophysitism One of the most important early heresies of the Church, which had strength in the fifth and sixth centuries. It denied the united two natures of Christ in favor of one nature.

The most famous of all Monophysite proponents was Severus, who served as bishop of Antioch from 512 to 518. After his baptism, Severus renounced bathing and took to fasting and holding vigils. He died in 538, having retired to Egypt. He refused to bathe even to save his life, although at the end he did allow himself to be bathed with his clothes on. After his death, miracles were worked by his relics.

Severus was considered a great enemy of orthodoxy, which held that Christ was one person, one hypostasis (basis or foundation) and two natures, divine and human. Severus and the Monophysites held that he was one person, one hypostastis and one nature. The Nestorians divided Christ into two.

Monophysitism thus denied that Christ had any human acts of cognition and will. This position led inevitably to the idea that either the whole of God had incarnated, suffered and died, or that each of the three persons in God—Father, Son and Holy Ghost—had a divine nature of its own. Monophysitists split on this question, and a schism of Tritheists supported the idea of a threefold divine nature. The Tritheist in turn split into factions, and were excommunicated.

Monophysitism was condemned as a heresy and eventually lost force. During its heyday, it attracted numerous prolific supporters who produced a large body of writings, more than on any other heresy of the early Church.

Monothelitism   A heresy of the seventh century that was a modification of Monophysitism. The original intent of Monothelitism was to reconcile Monophysitism with orthodoxy, but it fell into heresy itself. Catholic doctrine holds that Christ had two wills, one human and one divine. Monothelites held that this was contrary, and that Christ could have had only one divine will. Parallel to the will is the operation, or energy, for action. Monothelites held that Christ could have only one operation.

The Monothelite heresy arose almost accidentally around 622. Emperor Heraclius heard an argument from a Monophysite, and refuted him with theological arguments. Heraclius incidentally referred to the "one operation" of Christ. At the time the Church was badly fractured by a long history of heresies, and Heraclius badly wanted to reunite the factions. Previous efforts by other emperors had met with dismal failure. Heraclius was heartened when the Monophysites accepted the idea of one operation.

Monothelitism was condemned by the Sixth General Council in Constantinople in 680.

Montanists   A schism founded in the second century by the prophet Montanus and two women prophets, Maximilla and Priscilla (also known as Prisca). The Mantanists first were known as the Phrygians, then the Montanists, Pepuzians and Cataphrygians.

Montanus and his prophetesses were based in the village of Pepuza. They would fall into ecstatic trances and speak in the name of the Father, the Word, the Paraclete and Jesus. Entranced, they issued instructions to their followers for the spiritual life; Maximilla especially predicted continual wars and fighting that didn't happen. They advocated fasts and abstinence; chastity was a way to ecstasy. Martyrdom was valued. Second marriages were forbidden.

It is likely that the Montanists drew from, and appealed to, followers of the orgiastic cult of Cybele, which was popular in Phrygia. Christians were among those drawn to the trance spectacles that would take place.

Incredible stories about the Montanists circulated. One tale held that on a certain feast they stuck an infant with brazen pins and used the blood to make cakes for sacrifices. If the infant died it was a martyr; if it lived, it became a high priest. This sort of story was similar to the stories that were rampant during the Inquisition about witches and other heretics assembling for orgiastic feasting and the sacrificing and eating of babies. Another story was that the Montanists baptized the dead. Such accounts were repudiated as fiction even as they circulated, but nonetheless they found credulous ears.

The schism was short-lived. Maximilla died in 179 and Montanus and Priscilla died some time before that (according to one anonymous account, the latter two hanged themselves). Montanism was at its peak around 177. The prophecies were condemned as profane heresy and followers were excommunicated. This did not end the sect, which gained much popularity in both East and West into the third century. Christian emperors beginning with Constantine I outlawed the Montanists, but the laws were seldom enforced. The sect became increasingly secretive and dwindled.

Nestorianism   A heresy whose main points held that Christ had two natures, not one, and condemned the term *Theotokos* ("God-bearer") as applied to the Blessed Virgin Mary.

The heresy's proponent, Nestorius (d. ca. 451), was an eloquent Syrian priest and monk who was chosen by Emperor Theodosius to become patriarch of Constantinople in 428. He came from a school of thought that held that Christ had two natures, divine and human, which were unified in him. Although Nestorius did not admit to the existence of two Christs, such was the inevitable outcome of this theory. The denial of *Theotokos* as a title to Mary implied that she was not the mother of the Son of God.

After becoming bishop, Nestorius made a vigorous campaign against heretics, especially the Arians. But in 428 or 429 he preached the first of his sermons against the *Theotokos*, a title he held would turn Mary into a goddess. His views excited opposition, first among his own clergy and then by powerful persons such as St. Cyril of Alexandria. In 430 Nestorius assembled a council, which, led by his rival Cyril, then condemned him.

Nestorius refused to submit, but bishops who supported him were deposed, and his friends deserted him. He retired to his monastery at Antioch in 435. Emperor Theodosius II condemned his writings to be burnt. A few years later, Nestorius was banished.

A Nestorian Church was founded in Persia, but was cut off from the Catholic Church. The Nestorians established themselves in India, China and Mongolia. Much later, the last remnants of the Nestorian Church reunited with the Catholic Church.

Novatianism   A schism of the third century created by Novatian, a Roman priest who made himself antipope. In 250 Pope St. Fabian was martyred in the persecutions launched by Emperor Decius. Novatian reportedly escaped persecution by denying he was a priest. In 251 St. Cornelius was elected pope, but Novatian also laid claim to the honor, and the two began attacking each other with charges. The legitimacy of Novatian's ordination was questioned. He had been given baptism while thought to be on his deathbed from a demonic possession, and he had never been confirmed by a bishop.

A serious division in the Church resulted. Before the end of 251, Cornelius assembled a council of 60 bishops that excommunicated Novatian. Later, Novatian was called a heretic for his strict views that idolatry was an unpardonable sin, and that the Church had no right to restore to Communion anyone who had committed such a sin. His followers extended this view to all mortal sins. Novatian also separated God the Father from Christ the Son of God, identifying the Son with the angels who appeared to Abraham in the Old Testament.

Novatianism spread throughout Christendom. In Phrygia, its followers combined with the Montanists. The schism ran out of steam by the end of the third century, but Novatians were still in existence in Alexandria in 600.

Origenism   Theology and philosophy expressed in the work of Origen (185–253 or 254), an early Church father.

Born in Alexandria, Origen was a brilliant and precocious student. He became the head of a catechetical school. On a trip to Greece, Origen was ordained a priest by the bishop of Caesarea, which did not sit well with the bishop of Alexandria, who may also have been jealous of Origen's popularity and influence. He succeeded in having Origen deposed and banished.

In 232 Origen went to Caesarea and founded a new school and attracted many pupils, among them St. Gregory Thaumaturgus. During the persecution of Emperor Decius in 250, Origen was severely tortured and imprisoned. While in prison, he wrote numerous letters to help the martyrs maintain their faith. Decius died in 251, and Origen retired to Tyr, where he died around 253–254. He was buried with honor as a confessor of the faith, and pilgrims visited his tomb in the cathedral at Tyr. The cathedral has long been in ruins and the location of Origen's tomb is not known.

Origen was extremely prolific, leaving a body of work numbering about 6,000 pieces. His theology and teachings influenced many of the great figures of the early Church. Some of his points of doctrine were refuted by orthodox writers, in controversies that continued long after his death.

Refutations of the errors of Origenist thought broke out around the turn of the fifth century, especially in Egypt, and in the mid-sixth century. Origen's writings were condemned and anathematized.

Pelagianism   A heresy that denied original sin and Christian grace. Pelagianism flourished in the fifth to mid-sixth centuries. One of its chief opponents was St. Augustine.

Little is known about the originator of the heresy, Pelagius. His home has been placed in England, Scotland and Ireland. He went to Rome and became a monk, and authored treatises that formed the core of his heresy. He was aided by a eunuch lawyer, Caelestius, whom he met in Rome.

The principle ideas of Pelagianism, as expressed by Caelestius, were that: Adam died not from his sin but from natural causes; Adam's sin harmed only himself; newborn children are in the same state as Adam before the fall; humanity does not die through Adam's sin or death and does not rise through the resurrection of Christ; Mosaic Law is as effective a guide to heaven as the Gospels; before Christ there were men without sin; and men have the natural ability to conquer sin and gain eternal life without the aid of grace.

Pelagius and Caelestius went to North Africa, where they excited the opposition of Augustine. Pelagius went to the East. A synod condemned Caelestius's theses, and he went to Ephesus. In 415 a synod was convened against Pelagius in Diospolis (the ancient Lydda) in Asia Minor, but his chief accusers failed to appear. Pelagius declared that the doctrines in question came from Caelestius, and so no action was taken against him. Two subsequent synods in North Africa rejected the doctrines. In 417 Pope Innocent I sided with the North Africans, developed the orthodox teachings on original sin and grace, and excommunicated Pelagius and Caelestius.

Pelagius modified his stance and Caelestius affirmed his belief in all doctrines of the Church. Innocent I died, and his successor, Zosimus, considered rescinding the sentence against the two. He was persuaded against that by another synod convened in Carthage.

In 418 Emperor Honorius banned all Pelagians from all cities in Italy. Zosimus made all bishops refute Pelagianism in writing, or be deposed and banished; 18 suffered this fate. Pelagius and Caelestius ended their days in Asia Minor.

Pelagianism gained a foothold in Gaul and Britain, but finally died out in the middle of the sixth century.

Tritheism   See Monophysitism.

Western Schism   A 40-year dispute in the Latin Church that ended in 1417 with the election of an undisputed pope. It was a disagreement more than a schism, for it involved no revolt against papal authority itself.

From the beginning of the 14th century, the pope had lived in Avignon, France. Pope Gregory XI returned the Holy See to Rome, and died there in 1378. His successor was Urban VI, who quickly proved himself unpopular with the cardinals. His opponents left Rome and elected their own pope, Clement VII, who had friends and relatives in the major royal families of Europe. He established himself at Avignon.

Loyalties quickly divided. SS. Catherine of Siena and Catherine of Sweden were among those who supported Urban VI, while SS. Vincent Ferrer and Colette were among those who supported Clement VII. Most of the Italian and German states, plus England and Flanders, supported Urban VI, and France, Spain, Scotland and their allies supported Clement VII. The rival popes excommunicated each other.

The controversy extended beyond the deaths of both popes. Boniface IX succeeded Urban VI and Benedict XIII succeeded Clement VII. Boniface IX in turn was succeeded by Innocent VII and then Gregory XII. In 1409, there was a third claimant to the papacy, John XXIII.

In 1414 the Council of Constance deposed John XXIII, forced Gregory XII to abdicate and dismissed Benedict XIII. In 1417 Martin V was elected pope and was accepted by both factions. The papacy remained in Rome.

Sources and Further Reading Recommendations

Many of the entries in this book include suggestions for further reading. In addition, the following books were consulted and are sources of biographical and anecdotal information on saints:

Ball, Ann. *Modern Saints: Their Lives and Faces, Book One* and *Book Two.* Rockford, Ill.: TAN Books and Publishers, 1983 and 1990.

Bunson, Matthew, and Margaret Bunson and Stephen Bunson. *Our Sunday Visitor's Encyclopedia of Saints.* Huntington, Ind.: Our Sunday Visitor, 1998.

Butler, Alban. *Lives of the Saints.* Michael Walsh, ed. San Francisco: HarperSanFrancisco, 1991.

Cantor, Norman F., gen. ed.. *The Encyclopedia of the Middle Ages.* New York: Reference Works/Viking, 1999.

Cruz, Joan Carroll. *Mysteries, Marvels, Miracles in the Lives of the Saints.* Rockford, Ill.: TAN Books, 1997.

Cruz, Joan Carroll. *Secular Saints.* Rockford, Ill.: TAN Books and Publishers, 1989.

Cruz, Joan Carroll. *The Incorruptibles.* Rockford, Ill.: TAN Books, 1977.

de Voragine, Jacobus. *The Golden Legend.* Vols. I and II. Tr. William Granger Ryan. Princeton, N.J.: Princeton University Press, 1993.

Dunn-Mascetti, Manuela. *Saints: The Chosen Few.* New York: Ballantine Books, 1994.

Kelly, J. N. D. *The Oxford Dictionary of Popes.* Oxford: Oxford University Press, 1986.

Newland, Mary Reed. *The Saint Book.* New York: Seabury Press, 1979.

One Hundred Saints. Boston: Little, Brown and Co., 1993.

Stevens, Rev. Clifford. *The One Year Book of Saints.* Huntington, Ind.: Our Sunday Visitor, 1989.

The following websites also were among sources consulted.

The Catholic Encyclopedia, which can be found at Eternal World Television Network, http://www.ewtn.com and New Advent, http://www.newadvent.org/cathen

Internet Medieval Sourcebook, at http://www.fordham.edu/halsall/search.html

Catholic Community Forum, at http://www.catholic-forum.com/saints

St Patrick's Church, at http://www.users.erols.com.saintpat/ss

Church Forum, at http://www.churchforum.org.

INDEX

Note: Page numbers followed by the letter *f* indicate figures. **Boldface** page numbers indicate the primary discussion of a topic.